PERCEPTION and PRODUCTION of FLUENT SPEECH

Edited by
RONALD A. COLE
Carnegie-Mellon University

LEA LAWRENCE ERLBAUM ASSOCIATES, PUBLISHERS
1980   Hillsdale, New Jersey

Lawrence Erlbaum Associates, Inc., Publishers
365 Broadway
Hillsdale, New Jersey 07642

Library of Congress Cataloging in Publication Data

Main entry under title:

Perception and production of fluent speech.

  Bibliography: p.
  Includes indexes.
  1. Speech perception. 2. Speech. I. Cole,
Ronald Allen, 1944-
BF455.P388   153.6   78-25481
ISBN 0-89859-019-1

Contents

PART IV: PRODUCTION OF FLUENT SPEECH

Preface

Perception and Production of Fluent Speech looks at the mental processes involved in producing and understanding spoken language. Although there have been several edited volumes on speech in the past ten years, this volume is unique in that it deals exclusively with perception and production of *fluent* speech. A little reflection reveals what a curious state of affairs this is. Why should a volume on speech be unique because it deals with natural continuous speech? The answer is that, in the past 25 years, the study of speech perception has dealt mainly with "low-level" processes—processes involved in recognizing individual speech sounds. These experiments have provided important information about how we categorize and discriminate among speech sounds, but have left unanswered the question of how people communicate using natural continuous speech.

Fortunately, the past few years have seen an increase in research and theory by psychologists, linguists, and computer scientists on perception and production of fluent speech. The chapters in this volume, contributed by distinguished scientists from each of these fields, deal with such questions as: How are ideas encoded into sound? How does a speaker plan an utterance? How are words recognized? What is the role of knowledge in speech perception? In short, how do people communicate with each other using speech?

I have arranged the chapters within the book into four sections. The chapters in Section 1, *The Patterns of Speech,* provide three opinions on the best way to look at speech. When reviewing these chapters, I was reminded of the parable of the three blind men who attempt to discover the nature of an elephant by examining its individual parts. One blind man examines the elephant's ear, another its leg, and another its trunk, and each arrives at a vastly different conception of the structure and function of an elephant. So it is with speech. In order to examine its structure, it is necessary to *look* at the energy in sound, and any visual transformation of the energy in speech emphasizes some important features and leaves us blind to others. If we look at the energy in speech as it is displayed on an oscilloscope, we appreciate its rhythmic and temporal structure, but are blind to most of its spectral detail. If we look at a speech spectrogram, we see a detailed layout of spectral information, but are blind to its prosodic structure. Thus, the way we choose to look at speech turns out to be critically important in structuring our hypotheses about what information is important to its perception.

In Chapter 1, Cole, Rudnicky, Zue, and Reddy ask the question: How much of the phonemic information in natural continuous speech is displayed on a speech spectrogram? Their answer is that at least 90% of the phonemes in a spoken sentence can be identified from a spectrogram. They report the performance of an expert spectrogram reader who is able to identify between 85 and 90% of the phonemes in an unknown utterance from a spectrogram. Cole et al. conclude that there is a direct and learnable relationship between the visual patterns displayed on a spectrogram and the phonemes of a language, and discuss the implications of their research to theories of speech percpetion, machine recognition of speech, and speech therapy.

In Chapter 2, Scott argues that "the almost exclusive use of the spectrograph for speech analysis has confined our concept of the speech signal to a spatio-temporal display that is quite unlike the signal as it exists in space." As an alternative, Scott offers a Gestalt theory of speech perception that views speech as integrated patterns in time rather than spectral patterns laid out in space, and emphasizes the importance of relations among elements rather than individual spectral cues. The theory receives empirical support in studies that demonstrate the importance of relational cues in vowel perception. The theory has also led to two inventions: a tactile aid to speech reception that conveys relational information about time and frequency (and has been shown to produce immediate and substantial improvement in lip reading) and a speaker-independent pitch meter that follows the intonation contour of a speaker's voice.

In Chapter 3, Searle, Jacobson, and Kimberly provide us with a new look at speech. They argue that, if we want to understand how humans perceive speech, we should be looking at a visual display that models the human ear. That is, the speech scientist should look at the same information that is presented to the auditory cortex. A speech spectrogram does not provide this information. It acts as a constant bandwidth filter system, and therefore provides the same frequency–time resolution at all frequencies. Experiments in auditory psychophysics and physiology demonstrate that the human ear provides excellent frequency resolution at low frequencies, and excellent temporal resolution at high frequencies. Based on this research, Searle et al. conclude that a visual display of the output of a one-third octave filter system accurately reflects the tradeoff between time and frequency found in the peripheral auditory system. A computer analysis of the parameters of their display produced excellent recognition of the stop consonants of English.

In his discussion of Chapters 1–3, Stevens raises specific problems with each approach, and offers a theoretical framework for considering the three rather disparate views of speech provided in the first three chapters. Because the comments offered by the discussants require a thorough reading of the chapters, I will not attempt to summarize them here. But I urge you to read them carefully—they are uniformly insightful and entertaining.

The chapters in Section 2, *Understanding Spoken Language,* examine the information-processing strategies that humans use to transform sound into meaning. In Chapter 5, Bond and Garnes provide both experimental and observational evidence that various sources of knowledge are used during speech perception. Their experiments show that the interpretation of an ambiguous stimulus—such as a word that can be heard as either "date" or "gate"—is consistent with the semantic structure of the sentence in which it occurs. At the observational level, Garnes and Bond have collected over 900 cases of misperceptions of conversational speech—"slips of the ear." Their sophisticated analysis of these errors provides convincing evidence that listeners interpret conversational speech in terms of their knowledge of the phonological, syntactic, and semantic structure of their language.

In Chapter 6, Cole and Jakimik offer a model of speech perception that describes the information-processing strategies that transform speech into an ordered series of words. The model consists of four assumptions about the way in which sound and knowledge are used to recognize words. The results of a series of experiments in which listeners monitor fluent speech for mispronounced words provide support for each of the assumptions of the model.

Foss, Harwood, and Blank in Chapter 7, argue that two independent codes are activated during word recognition—a phonetic code that is computed directly from the acoustic input, and a more abstract phonological code that is stored with each lexical item in memory and emerges as the item is retrieved. Foss et al. use the dual code hypothesis to explain why listeners are able to detect target phonemes faster in predictable words than unpredictable words, while no such difference exists between frequent and infrequent words. In Chapter 8, Posner and Hanson discuss the three chapters in Section 2 in terms of the similarities and differences between speech perception and reading.

The chapters in Section 3, *Machine-Motivated Models,* present models of speech recognition based on recent advances in computer science in the development of speech understanding systems. In Chapter 9, Reddy describes two of the speech understanding systems developed at Carnegie-Mellon

University—HEARSAY II and Harpy. These systems are able to recognize over 1,000 words in connected speech from a large (but finite) number of sentences. Although the two systems are similar in their performance statistics, they provide very different solutions to the problems involved in recognizing natural continuous speech. HEARSAY consists of independent knowledge sources that interact with each other to arrive at the best interpretation of a sentence. Harpy consists of a single precompiled network of sound sequences, and a sentence is recognized by finding the "best" path through this network. Reddy describes the architecture and design principles of the two systems, and illustrates the operation of each system by working through an example sentence. The chapter concludes with a discussion of the strengths and limitations of the two approaches to automatic speech recognition.

The HEARSAY system is a psychologist's dream. It provides a complete information-processing model of speech perception in which independent sources of knowledge dynamically interact to understand a spoken sentence. The Harpy system, on the other hand, is (at least at first glance) a brute force, engineering solution to the problem of connected speech recognition. It is somewhat surprising then, that both Klatt, in Chapter 10, and Newell, in Chapter 11, present models of speech perception that incorporate the basic features of Harpy, rather than HEARSAY. In Chapter 10, Klatt identifies eight problems that any speech recognition system must overcome in order to recognize words from fluent speech. The solution to these problems is offered in two new computer systems—SCRIBER and LAFS. Taken together, these systems provide a model of lexical access from acoustic data. Although the model is presented as an engineering solution to the problem of word recognition, it is intended to be taken seriously as a model of human speech perception.

In Chapter 11, Newell combines two artificial intelligence models to produce a theory of human speech perception. Newell first describes a production system architecture called HPSA77, "a proposed structure of the architecture within which human cognition occurs." The principles of the Harpy speech understanding system are then incorporated into the production system architecture. The result is PS.Harpy, "a theory of speech perception embedded in a theory of general cognition." After constructing the theory, Newell considers the way in which PS.Harpy handles various phenomena in speech perception, such as the predictive use of knowledge, categorical perception, and phonemic restorations. Newell's chapter is a fine example of *sufficiency analysis,* in which a system that is sufficient to perform a complex congnitive task is evaluated as a model of human cognition.

After Norman's discussion of the models by Klatt and Newell in Chapter 12 (in which he offers timely advice on "copycat science" to cognitive psychologists), we turn to the final section of the book, *Production of Fluent Speech.*

In Chapter 13, Sorensen and Cooper examine the relationship between the syntactic structure of a sentence and its physical realization. They find that reliable changes in fundamental frequency occur at those points in a sentence at which transformational rules have been applied. For example, in the sentence "The seamstress wove your hat and the maid your scarf," the verb "wove" has been deleted from the underlying structure "the maid wove your scarf." Sorensen and Cooper find a reliable change in fundamental frequency between "maid" and "your." This same change is not observed in the control sentence "The seamstress wove your hat and then made your scarf." The experiments provide impressive support for the operation of abstract grammatical operations during speech production.

In Chapter 14, Fay considers the best way to represent the grammar of a language in a model of speech production. His proposal is as intriguing as it is bold. Fay argues for a *direct realization* of transformational rules in models of speech production. He argues that the processing operations that map ideas into words preserve both the substance and the form of transformational rules. After describing the difference between direct and indirect realization models of speech production, Fay offers support for a direct realization model from errors observed in spontaneous speech.

In Chapters 15 and 16, Sternberg, Monsell, Knoll, and Wright report an extensive series of studies of rapid speech, which show how a motor program for an entire utterance, prepared in advance, controls the execution of its elements. In Chapter 15, they report their initial experiments on the latency and duration of rapid utterances, show how the phenomena generalize to typewriting (another domain of motor control), develop a model for the control of rapid movement sequences, and reject various competing explanations. In Chapter 16 they extend their findings in several directions that should be of special interest to students of speech, elaborate their model, defend it against a new contender, and test it further. Although Chapter 15 has been published elsewhere, it was included here because it serves as a necessary prelude to Chapter 16.

The book concludes—most appropriately, I believe—with Herb Simon's discussion of the chapters on speech production. Simon's chapter includes advice on how experimental psychologists can win at twenty questions with nature—a question that has bothered many of us in recent years.

I would like to thank a number of friends for their help in making this book a reality. Karen Locitzer provided invaluable editorial assistance on each chapter in this volume. Without her help, it is doubtful that this book would have appeared during my lifetime. Ed Seiger and Betty Boal typed many of the chapters, and did so extremely well. I am indebted to the staff of the Psychology Department at Carnegie-Mellon University—Janet Mazefsky, Lou Beckstrom, Lois Iannacchione, and Muriel Fleishman—for taking care of the numerous arrangements and details before, during, and after the Carnegie Symposium, from which this book emerged. Most of all, I thank my wife, Loretta, and my children, David and Debbie, for their love, patience and encouragement while I was editing this book, and for allowing me to smoke large aromatic cigars in the house during this project.

Finally, I thank the participants in the Carnegie Symposium—the authors of this volume—for their excellent contributions. I forgive Al Newell, John Sorensen, and Bill Cooper for causing me to spend a week of my summer vacation reading their chapters rather than sunbathing on the Jersey shore. It was worth it.

RONALD A. COLE

THE PATTERNS
OF SPEECH

1 Speech as Patterns on Paper

Ronald A. Cole

Alexander I. Rudnicky
Carnegie-Mellon University

Victor W. Zue
Massachusetts Institute of Technology

D. Raj Reddy
Carnegie-Mellon University

INTRODUCTION

Ever since the invention of the sound spectrograph some thirty years ago (Koenig, Dunn, & Lacey, 1946), the spectrogram has been the single most widely used form of display for speech. The popularity of the spectrogram is at least partly due to the fact that it is relatively easy to produce, and that it provides a visual display of the relevant temporal and spectral characteristics of speech sounds. To be sure, a speech spectrogram sometimes introduces distortions to the acoustic structure of speech and often does not provide adequate information on certain linguistically relevant cues, such as stress and intonation. Nevertheless, a speech spectrogram gives a good description of the segmental acoustic cues of speech, and it has been an invaluable tool in the development of our understanding of speech production and perception.

A speech spectrogram of the utterance, "The boy was there when the sun rose," is shown in Fig. 1.1. As Fig. 1.1 reveals, the speech spectrogram provides a display of the energy in the speech wave in terms of frequency—along the vertical axis; time—along the horizontal axis; and intensity—by the darkness of the markings.

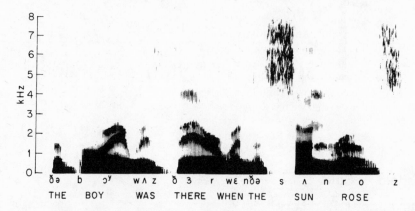

FIG. 1.1.   Speech spectrogram of "the boy was there when the sun rose."

Is it possible to read a spectrogram? Can one (who is familiar with such a visual representation) examine a speech spectrogram of an unknown utterance and determine what was said? The common view is that speech spectrograms cannot be read (e.g., Fant, 1962; Liberman, 1970; Lindblom & Svensson, 1973). Fant (1962), for example, states that "I have not met one single researcher who has claimed he could read speech spectrograms fluently, and I am no exception myself [p. 4]."

It is obvious that Fant never met Lev Rubin, an inmate of a prison camp for scientists in Solzhenitsyn's *The First Circle* (1968). We are introduced to Lev Rubin as "the only person in the Soviet Union who can read visible speech." As part of a secret project suggested by Stalin, Rubin learned to read the output of

A visible speech device—known as VIR—which turns out what is called a 'voice print'.... In these voice prints speech is measured three ways at once: frequency—across the tape; time—along the tape; and amplitude—by the density of the picture. Therefore each sound is depicted so uniquely that it can be recognized easily, and everything that has been said can be read on the tape [pp. 186–187].

A description is even provided of Rubin reading a voiceprint:

"You see, certain sounds can be deciphered without the least difficulty, the accented or sonorous vowels, for example. In the second word the 'r' sound is distinctly visible twice. In the first word the accented sound of 'e' and in front of it a soft 'v'—for there can't be a hard sound there. Before that is the formant 'a,' but we mustn't forget that in the first, the secondary accented syllable 'o' is also pronounced like 'a'. But the vowel 'oo' or 'u' retains its individuality even when it's far from the accent—right here it has the characteristic low-frequency streak. The third sound of the first word is unquestionably 'u.' And after it follows a palatal explosive consonant, most likely 'k'—and so we have 'ukovi' or 'ukavi.' And here is a hard 'v'—it is clearly distinguished from the soft 'v' for it has no streak higher than 2,300 cycles. 'Vukovi'—and then there is a resounding hard stop and at the very end an attenuated vowel, and these together I can interpret as 'dy.' So we get 'vukovidy'—and we have to guess at the first sound, which is smeared. I could take it for an 's' if it weren't that the sense tells me it's a 'z.' And so the first word is—'' and Rubin pronounced the word for ''voice prints''— '' 'zvukovidy' '' [p. 189].

Solzhenitsyn's report of an expert spectrogram reader has had little impact on the field of speech perception. It is widely believed that it is *not* possible to determine the content of an unknown utterance from a speech spectrogram. One reason for this belief is that research with synthetic speech has led various investigators to conclude that each sound of speech is *not,* in Solshenitsyn's words, ''depicted so uniquely that it can be recognized easily.'' In an article entitled ''Why are speech spectrograms hard to read?'', Liberman, Cooper, Shankweiler, and Studdert-Kennedy (1968) describe the problem:

Visible speech is hard to read largely because speech is not a simple alphabet. Speech is, rather, a complex code in the sense that the phonemic message is quite drastically restructured at the level of sound. As a consequence, the acoustic signal corresponding to a particular phoneme is typically different in different phonetic environments. Worse yet, from the standpoint of one who is trying to read spectrograms, definable segments of sound do not correspond to segments at the phoneme level [p. 128]. Moreover, there are, in general, no acoustic segments corresponding to the phoneme segments. As a consequence, looking at a spectrogram does not readily reveal how a stretch of speech might be divided into segments corresponding to phonemes, or even how many phonemes it might contain [p. 130].

It is clearly the case that the consonant and vowel sounds that one hears when listening to speech do not exist as discrete non-overlapping acoustic segments in the speech wave. It is not possible, for example, to insert silent periods between segments of a naturally recorded utterance and still perceive all of the phonemes. But is the relationship between sound and phoneme so complex that it cannot be learned?

On theoretical grounds, Liberman and his colleagues have argued that spectrogram reading cannot be learned. In their view, the speech signal is such a complex code that phonemes can only be perceived through the working of a special decoder. Liberman et al. (1968) argue that:

Encoded sounds can be efficient vehicles only if there is a decoder—a special device that processes the complex signal so as to recover the string of phonemes. There is such a device in human beings, but, unfortunately for those of us who would send speech through the eye, that decoder can be made to work only from an auditory input. It does not process speech signals (in spectrographic form, for example) that come in through the eye, and it cannot be made to do so by training [p. 128].

In this chapter, we offer an alternative view. We suggest, following Cole and Scott (1974), that there may be sufficient invariant information in the speech wave for humans to be able to perceive phonemes without recourse to a special decoder. Moreover, enough of this information is present in a spectrographic display so that phonemes can often be recognized reliably from a speech spectrogram. The experiment reported in this chapter demonstrates that given sufficient experience, it is possible to identify the phonetic content of an unknown utterance from a speech spectrogram and thereby determine what was said. In addition, protocols provided by the expert spectrogram reader demonstrate that spectrogram reading is a skill that is based on *explicit* knowledge—the identification of specifiable visual features and visual patterns and the application of well-defined rules.

PAST ATTEMPTS AT SPECTROGRAM READING

In order to understand why spectrograms have been considered difficult, if not impossible, to read, we must consider some of the past attempts at learning spectrogram reading and the reasons for their failure.

Potter, Kopp, and Green (1947)

The first attempt at teaching spectrogram reading was reported by Potter et al. in their classic book, *Visible Speech* (1947). The original purpose of the Potter et al. study was to develop a speech understanding aid for the deaf based on the newly constructed Direct Translator, a real-time spectrograph. The Direct Translator was a device based on the original spectrograph except that it produced a continuous dynamic spectrographic display instead of a static display on paper. The dynamic display was produced by having a phosphor belt move past a row of lights activated by a bank of 12 filters into which the speech signal was fed. The device functioned as a 12-channel vocoder, transmitting speech through a telephone-like bandwidth (300–3,000 Hz).

In order to assess the feasibility of such a device as an aid to the deaf, an evaluation program was undertaken at Bell Laboratories using normal hearing subjects. It was reasoned that if normal hearing subjects could not master the task, there would be little point in attempting to train deaf subjects. Accordingly, an initial group of two women began a training program with the Direct Translator which included the following: speaking into the machine and becoming familiar with their own speech patterns, reading the voice of an instructor, and finally, carrying on conversations mediated by the Translator. The material taught to the subjects consisted of word patterns and short phrase patterns chosen from a basic vocabulary that was oriented towards simple conversation. In addition, the trainees learned phonetic principles and studied the acoustic correlates of phonemes from speech spectrograms produced on paper.

As the study progressed, two more women joined the original group, and these in turn were joined by a congenitally deaf Bell employee who became interested in the project. The experiment with the original group of normal-hearing subjects was terminated after 90 hours of training (30 hours for the late joiners). The deaf subject went on to train for a total of over 200 hours and acquired a vocabulary of about 800 words, a rather impressive achievement. Vocabulary acquisition appeared to be a steady linear function of training; a word took about 15–20 minutes of practice to acquire. In theory, the training procedure could have been extended indefinitely to provide a trainee with as large a vocabulary as needed.

During the experiment, pairs of subjects attempted to communicate with each other without sound by means of the Direct Translator. Subjects were seated in separate sound proof booths from which they could view the Direct Translator. Each booth was equipped with a telephone with a mouthpiece but no receiver. As each subject spoke, his or her speech was displayed in real time on the Direct Translator. Subjects attempted to communicate by reading each other's speech on the Direct Translator.

According to Potter et al.,

> The visible speech class members were able to converse satisfactorily among themselves by talking clearly and at a fairly slow rate. Within the limits of their vocabularies, they were able to carry on conversations with about the same facility as a similarly advanced class in some foreign language. When new and entirely unfamiliar words were displayed on the translator screen, the more experienced students usually were able to read the words after a few repetitions [p. 26].

Unfortunately, a number of factors temper a positive evaluation of the Potter et al. effort. There were no methodological details provided about the training procedures used in the study. It is therefore impossible to determine whether the linear function of training on word acquisition reflects the participants' ability to learn spectrographic patterns, or reflects the fact that words were presented at a set pace. Another unfortunate omission is any mention of the test procedures used to determine learning. What were the criteria used? How often were items tested and how?

In addition to these problems in the evaluation of the program, there were a number of constraints, some noted by the authors, that limit the generality of the results. For example, the speech to which the trainees were exposed was of a particularly simple kind both in its content and in its form—spoken slowly and clearly. This is very much unlike the speech, rapid and distorted, to which one is exposed in normal conversation (Klatt & Stevens, 1973; Reddy, 1976). Also, as the authors point out, the particular representation chosen (which we described as a 12-channel vocoder) was in all probability not the optimal one, emphasizing irrelevant and hiding relevant features of the speech signal.

Even with all of these potential problems and qualifications, the Potter et al. study represents a substantial achievement. After all, the participants in the study did learn to read speech from a visual display. Moreover, they were able to do this in real time and with vocabularies as large as 800 words. The achievement is even more impressive when it is considered that it was not until a decade later that comprehensive accounts of the acoustics of speech became available (Fant, 1960; Stevens & House, 1961). The Bell Labs project represents a substantial achievement, even by our contemporary standards. It was a demonstration that, in principle, speech could be understood in an other-than-auditory modality.

Despite the potential shown by the Potter et al. study, the Direct Translator did not find much use outside speech therapy, most likely because of its impractical size and large cost. Since the Potter et al. study, there have been no further published attempts to teach real-time spectrogram reading.

Svensson (1974)

As part of a study of prosodic and grammatical influences on speech perception, Svensson (1974) had a group of subjects read spectrograms. Svensson's subjects consisted of workers at the Speech Transmission Laboratory of the Royal Institute of Technology in Stockholm and of students at the University of Stockholm who had participated in a spectrogram reading course. Thus, these subjects had a relatively high degree of sophisitcation in spectrogram interpretation. In the first part of the study, the subjects were all presented with spectrograms of nonsense utterances, consisting of phonologically permissible nonsense words spoken with sentence intonation. The subjects were given written instructions on spectrogram interpretation, which included relevant acoustic data and a decision procedure for segment identification. A total of nine spectrograms were presented, an hour being allotted for reading each one. The results, according to Svensson, were disappointing, with performance ranging from a low of 22% segments identified to a high of 51%. The average level was 38%. In the second part of the study, spectrograms of meaningful utterances were used. Performance on this material was almost identical to that in the first part of the study, despite the fact that the subjects knew that they were dealing with meaningful utterances generated from a restricted grammar and a limited lexicon.

Klatt and Stevens (1973)

In the Klatt and Stevens study, the authors attempted to label phonetically a set of 19 spectrograms of unknown utterances spoken by five unfamiliar talkers. In order to minimize the possibility of recognizing words in the spectrogram, a mask was placed on each spectrogram, allowing only 300 msec of speech to be visible at one time. In addition, the reading was done in a single pass. Despite these constraints, 33% of all segments were correctly transcribed, with a further 40% given a correct partial specification. Given the limited opportunity to scan the spectrogram, this performance is quite good.

The Klatt and Stevens study is unfortunately limited, for our present purposes, in that the readers gave themselves only a single opportunity to scan the spectrogram. It is not clear whether they could have realized a substantial improvement in reading accuracy if they had used a less restricted procedure.

Summary of Past Attempts

Taken together, the results of these studies do not make one overly optimistic about the potential of spectrogram reading. While the Potter et al. study demonstrated that it is possible to learn to read spectrograms of carefully articulated speech in real time, its generality is limited, since the task did not reflect the complexity of conversational speech. On the other hand, the contemporary studies, despite the fact that they could benefit from over twenty years of intensive research into the acoustics of speech, revealed surprisingly low accuracies in attempts to identify phonetic segments from speech spectrograms.

What has been lacking is an approach that combines the better aspects of the previous work: the detailed knowledge gained from contemporary acoustic phonetics and the systematic training used in the Potter et al. study. The expert spectrogram reader (whom we shall call VZ) described in this chapter has managed to combine these aspects successfully.

THE EXPERIMENT

The purpose of the experiment was to arrive at a better understanding of the process of spectrogram reading by examining in detail the methods used by VZ. While it was evident from casual observation that VZ was a highly skilled spectrogram reader, we did not have a clear idea of the extent of this skill. Thus, one of the goals of the study was to form a quantitative description of VZ's performance, both in terms of the accuracy of his transcriptions and in terms of the type of material he is able to interpret.

In addition to establishing the level of VZ's skill, we were also interested in learning something about the methods VZ uses to interpret spectrograms. For example, it has been suggested that high-level sources of knowledge, such as syntax and semantics, play an important role in speech understanding (Lindblom & Svensson, 1973; Miller & Isard, 1963). To what extent does VZ make use of such knowledge in interpreting the phonetic content of a spectrogram? Finally, a detailed examination of VZ's methods was undertaken to provide information that could be of use in the design of speech understanding systems.

The Subject

The expert reader VZ began his systematic study of spectrograms in 1971. At that time, he was taking part in the Advanced Research Projects Agency (ARPA) speech understanding project at Massachusetts Institute of Technology Lincoln Laboratories while completing his graduate studies at MIT. As an initial attempt to learn about the acoustic cues of speech sounds in continuous speech, VZ began to study the material in *Visible Speech*. He soon decided that this approach was inadequate for the study of real speech, since, among other things, the carefully articulated material in *Visible Speech* lacked many of the characteristics of continuous speech. He then began to collect his own data by preparing spectrograms from recordings made for him by various talkers, using such materials as nonsense consonant–vowel (CV) utterances and the Harvard Phonetically Balanced List of Sentences (Egan, 1944). During this time, he concentrated on trying to identify the relationships between the segmental features of individual speech sounds and their acoustic correlates. After two years of attention to segmental features, VZ became interested in the transformations that an individual speech sound undergoes when it appears in the context of other sounds, and began to systematically study the acoustic–phonetic and phonological rules of American English. Since that time, VZ has made extensive use of spectrograms in his research and has maintained a consistent interest in spectrogram reading. Between 1971 and the present, VZ has devoted, on the average, between one-half and a full hour per day on spectrogram reading. He estimates that over the years he has spent between 2,000 and 2,500 hours reading spectrograms. It is this extensive amount of practice that enables him to perform at his present level of skill.

General Procedure

All formal spectrogram reading sessions took place at the Department of Psychology at Carnegie-Mellon University on two separate occasions, the first in October, 1977, the second in February, 1978. On both occasions, VZ came to Carnegie-Mellon for a period of two days, during which he participated in four experimental sessions. During each of these sessions, which lasted from two to three hours, VZ read the equivalent of about four to six spectrograms of full utterances. In order to preserve all details of the sessions for later analysis, all sessions were recorded on video-tape.[1]

The spectrogram reading sessions were organized as follows. VZ sat at a table, together with a prompter who handed him spectrograms for reading. These spectrograms were chosen randomly from one of the sets available to the prompter (the spectrogram sets are described later in this text). Thus, the prompter, except under a few circumstances, was not aware of the correct identity of a spectrogram being read by VZ. The spectrogram was placed in a work area in view of the video camera. VZ then proceeded to interpret the spectrogram in his customary manner. VZ was asked to make his notations directly on the spectrogram in order to preserve a permanent record of his transcription.

Since one of the main purposes of this study was to analyze the methods used by VZ, he was instructed to verbalize the decisions he was making and to describe those features of the spectrogram he was attending to at any one time. The main task of the prompter was to ask VZ to elaborate interesting or unclear points. For example, if VZ said "This looks like an [l]," the prompter would say, "Why does that look like an

---

[1]A short film (15 min) based on the October, 1977 visit has been made and is available from any of the authors, or from the Computer Science Library at Carnegie-Mellon University. The film shows how a typical spectrogram is read, and describes in some detail the procedures used by VZ.

[l]?''. If VZ replied "Because of the relationship of the second and third formants," the prompter would say, "What is the relationship?''. By the end of our experiment, VZ was an extremely verbal and informative spectrogram reader.

Selection and Preparation of Spectrograms

Several sets of spectrograms were prepared for this study. The largest set consisted of normal English utterances; the other sets consisted of altered utterances, described in detail later in this text. One of our concerns in producing the spectrograms was the fact that VZ was accustomed to working with spectrograms made with a "Voice-Print" (Model 4691A) spectrograph, while the machine used to generate the spectrograms at C-MU was a "Kay Sona-Graph" (Model 6061B). While both spectrographs produce basically similar displays, a number of differences exist, most notably an expanded frequency display in the Voice-Print (a 7 kHz frequency range, compared to 8 kHz for the Kay Sona-Graph) and a low-frequency attenuation feature of the Voice-Print. In order to determine that VZ's performance was not due to the exact form of the representation, we asked William Cooper, then at MIT, to prepare a set of spectrograms of normal English sentences using the Voice-Print with which VZ was most familiar. All remaining spectrograms used in the experiment were produced on the Kay Sona-Graph at Carnegie-Mellon University.

Examples of spectrograms produced on each machine are shown in Fig. 1.2. These spectrograms show the utterances, "The soldiers knew the battle was won," produced on the Sona-Graph, and "Yesterday Bill saw the Goodyear blimp," produced on the Voice-Print. The transcriptions produced by VZ, including segmentation marks, are shown directly below each spectrogram. (For presentation purposes, we had the transcription copied professionally.) The transcription of the utterance "The soldiers knew the battle was won" represents VZ's first attempt to read a spectrogram made on a Kay Sona-Graph, from an utterance produced by an unfamiliar speaker. The transcription was accurate enough to enable a linguist to identify the sentence without hesitation.

The talker for the Carnegie-Mellon spectrograms was one of the authors, RC. The talker for the MIT spectrograms was John Sorensen. VZ had had no previous opportunity to read spectrograms made from utterances spoken by these talkers.

Table 1.1 displays the 23 normal and anomalous sentences that were presented to VZ on speech spectrograms during the experiment. Fifteen of the spectrograms—11 from the C-MU set and four from the MIT set—displayed normal English sentences. In addition to the normal

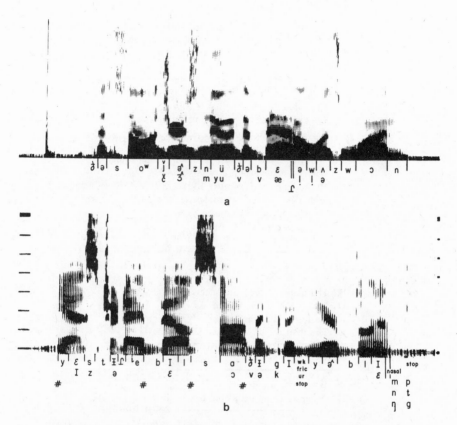

FIG. 1.2.   Spectrograms: (a) "The soldiers knew the battle was won," produced on a Kay Sona-Graph. (b) "Yesterday Bill saw the Goodyear blimp," produced on a Voiceprint.

sentences, eight spectrograms were presented in an effort to determine what sources of knowledge VZ used to read spectrograms. If VZ is in the habit of using higher-level information to guide the interpretation of phonetic information, then giving him a spectrogram of some familiar utterance, such as a proverb, should make this apparent by producing an increase in the accuracy of his performance relative to less familiar utterances. In addition, we tried to assess the salience of the nonphonetic information by deliberately introducing mispronunciations into proverbs. If nonphonetic information carries a great deal of weight for VZ, then the mispronunciations should go undetected.

A set of phonetically anomalous sentences was used to see whether VZ made use of lexical information, i.e., whether he was able to detect word patterns in the spectrograms. Phonetically anomalous sentences were produced by including nonsense words along with normal words in En-

TABLE 1.1
Utterances Read by VZ from Spectograms

English Sentences

C-MU Set
1. The soldiers knew the battle was won.
2. Smoking is bad for your mind and body.
3. Basketball is fun to play.
4. Folk dancing makes me dizzy.
5. The cross-eyed seamstress couldn't mend straight.
6. Winning is never a pretty thing for him.
7. The baby gave its mother a kiss.
8. A shark may be dangerous when hurt.
9. Go paddle your own canoe.
10. After the sixth story, Alice fell asleep.
11. Bill knew his aardvark was smaller.

MIT Set

12. The plants in the office needed more light.
13. I left my house at nine o'clock.
14. Yesterday Bill saw the Goodyear blimp.
15. Tim read the novel last week.

Proverbs

16. Waste not want not.
17. An apple a *t*ay keeps the *b*octor away.

Phonetically Anomalous Utterances

18. What teelings are we day with?
19. Give mine yadiya of his hate raret.
20. Our young people leh nose today.
21. Good tar hand zaim to come by.

Syntactically Anomalous Utterance

22. Bears shoot work on the country.

Nonsense Utterance

23. Wake jungles gasoline sudden bright.

glish sentences. This manipulation should make it impossible to use word-level knowledge to interpret the phonetic content.

There were at least two other potential sources of knowledge available to VZ: syntactic constraints and semantic content. Knowledge of syntactic structure can be used to predict the class of an unknown word and thus

TABLE 1.2
Words Used as Stimuli in the Carrier Phrase "Say _____again"

baby	hatch	elephant	slow	yoyo
tribe	paper	breath	snowshoe	whorehouse
feather	toothache	clover	pleasure	move
smooth	rocket	spinner	stitches	drum
zebra	swinger	thread	garage	fuzzy
shallow	florist	this	wagon	thing
fresh	tower	dog	soap	vest
change	criminal	bladder	letter	school
jade	knife	glasses	cages	prize

facilitate its identification. Similarly, once several words of an utterance are known it becomes possible to guess the remainder on the basis of the semantic context, the "meaning" of the utterance. Two utterances taken from Miller and Isard (1963), one semantically anomalous and one both syntactically and semantically anomalous, were presented to VZ in order to assess the role of syntactic and semantic knowledge during spectrogram reading.

In addition to the spectrograms of normal and altered sentences, spectrograms of 45 words in the carrier phrase "Say _____ again" were prepared. The purpose of this set was to evaluate VZ's ability to interpret a phone string (i.e., a word) in connected speech when the word boundaries were known. The words in this set were balanced for phonetic content by having all consonants appear in all permissible positions within words: initially, medially, and finally. Table 1.2 shows the words included in this set.

The results are presented in two parts. The first part examines the subject's ability to segment and label speech spectrograms, and the second part examines the nature of the segmentation and labeling process.

PART I: PERFORMANCE

How Performance Was Measured

VZ's ability to label phonetic segments in spectrograms was measured against phonetic transcriptions produced by three phoneticians. Each phonetician (a) had received formal training in transcription phonetics; (b) was currently teaching (or had recently taught) a course in phonetic transcription or English phonology; and (c) used phonetic transcription as part of his or her research.

Transcribers were provided with a high-fidelity cassette recording (produced on a Dolby system) of the 23 utterances and the 45 words in the carrier phrase "Say _____ again." Transcribers were warned that utterances might contain nonsense words or mispronunciations.

Each transcriber was provided with a copy of the ARPAbet symbol system shown in Table 1.3. As the table reveals, the ARPAbet contains a set of phonetic symbols, a corresponding set of orthographic symbols, and an example of a word containing the sound corresponding to each symbol. Transcribers were instructed to use only the phonetic symbols listed in the ARPAbet in their transcription. We explained that in order to minimize scoring problems based on differences in phonetic notation, it was essential that all transcribers use the same symbol system.

The ARPAbet system provides a broad, *phonetic* transcription that is nearly phonemic. For example, the same symbol—/t/—is used to indicate aspirated [tʰ] (in a stressed CV syllable), unaspirated [t] (in an /st/ cluster) and unreleased (word-final) [t˺]. For the purposes of this study, the loss of phonetic detail was more than compensated for by the convenience of having a standardized transcription system.

TABLE 1.3
Phonetic Symbols[a] Used by VZ and the Three Transcribers

Phoneme	ARPAbet	Example	Phoneme	ARPAbet	Example
/i/	IY	b*eat*	/ŋ/	NX	si*ng*
/ɪ/	IH	b*i*t	/p/	P	*p*et
/e/ (eʸ)	EY	b*ai*t	/t/	T	*t*en
/ɛ/	EH	b*e*t	/k/	K	*k*it
/æ/	AE	b*a*t	/b/	B	*b*et
/ɑ/	AA	B*o*b	/d/	D	*d*ebt
/ʌ/	AH	b*u*t	/g/	G	*g*et
/ɔ/	AO	b*ou*ght	/h/	HH	*h*at
/o/ (oʷ)	OW	b*oa*t	/f/	F	*f*at
/ʊ/	UH	b*oo*k	/θ/	TH	*th*ing
/u/	UW	b*oo*t	/s/	S	*s*at
/ə/	AX	*a*bout	/ʃ/	SH	*sh*ut
/ɨ/	IX	ros*e*s	/v/	V	*v*at
/ɝ/	ER	b*ir*d	/ð/	DH	*th*at
/ɚ/	AXR	butt*er*	/z/	Z	*z*oo
/aʷ/	AW	d*ow*n	/ʒ/	ZH	a*z*ure
/aʸ/	AY	b*uy*	/č/	CH	*ch*urch
/ɔʸ/	OY	b*oy*	/ǰ/	JH	*j*udge
/y/	Y	*y*ou	/ʍ/	WH	*wh*ich
/w/	W	*w*it	/l̩/	EL	batt*le*
/r/	R	*r*ent	/m̩/	EM	bott*om*
/l/	L	*l*et	/n̩/	EN	butt*on*
/m/	M	*m*et	/ɾ/	DX	ba*tt*er
/n/	N	*n*et	/ʔ/	Q	(glottal stop)

[a]From Bolt, Beranek and Newman, Inc. Report No. 3438, Vol. II, p. 72.

Definition of a Segment

Fig. 1.3 displays the phonetic transcription produced by each transcriber for the utterance "The soldiers knew the battle was won," and the transcription produced by VZ while reading this spectrogram (shown in Fig. 1.1). As this figure suggests, transcribers almost never disagreed on the number of segments in an utterance. Moreover, there was unanimous agreement on 85% of all segment labels, so there was little difficulty in aligning the three transcriptions for each utterance.

We adopted a majority-vote criterion for the definition of a segment:

A segment was assumed to exist when two transcribers produced a segment label—even if they did not produce the same label.

The utterance depicted in Fig. 1.3, for example, contains 22 segments according to such a criterion.

In the 23 utterances shown in Table 1.1, there were only four cases where one transcriber produced a segment label and the other two did not. Two of these involved insertion of [ə] by a single transcriber, once before [r] and once before [n] (the other two transcribers indicated syllabic [n̩]). In a third case, one transcriber produced [ur], while the other two produced [ɚ]. In the fourth case, one transcriber inserted an [m] in "apple", producing "ample." In these four cases, we assumed that no segment existed.

In an additional six cases, two transcribers produced a segment label while the third did not; in these six cases a segment was assumed to exist. Finally, there were 493 cases where all three transcribers produced a segment label. There was thus a total of 499 phonetic segments, defined by the agreement of two or more transcribers on the existence of a phonetic segment. VZ's ability to segment and label speech spectrograms was based on these 499 segments.

By the same token, the 45 words shown in Table 1.2 contain 201 seg-

VZ: ð ə soʷ ǰ ɚ z nü ð ə bɛ ɾə wʌz wɔn
          č ʒ   yu v væ ! lə

T1: ð ə sol ǰ ɚ z nu ð ə bæɾ! wɨz wʌn

T2: ð ʌ sol ǰ ɚ z nu ð ə bæɾ! wʌz wɔn

T3: ð ə sol ǰ ɚ z nu ð ə bæɾ! wəz wʌn

FIG. 1.3. Transcriptions produced by VZ from a speech spectrogram, and by three transcribers (Ts) who listened to the speech.

ments. There was only one case where all three transcribers did not provide a segment label: Two of them decided that the word "criminal" contained a final reduced vowel followed by [l], while the third indicated a syllabic [l̩].

Definition of a Label

As a working hypothesis, speech scientists typically assume that speech is composed of an ordered sequence of phonetic segments. But it is important to remember that a phonetic transcription is an *interpretation* imposed upon a continuously varying acoustic signal. In a typical utterance, the identity of one or more phonetic segments may be ambiguous due to imprecise articulation or masking caused by environmental noise (although the latter presumably was not a factor in the present experiment). In such cases, listeners are known to generate a phonetic interpretation of the input that is consistent with their expectations about what the speaker is likely to be saying (Garnes & Bond, 1977; Miller, 1956; Schubert & Parker, 1955; Warren, 1970).

The point of this discussion is that, because the acoustic signal is sometimes ambiguous and therefore open to interpretation, there is no single "correct" phonetic transcription of a spoken utterance. As we shall see, even under the most ideal conditions (unlimited time, high-fidelity recording, broad transcription, native language, familiar speaker) transcribers disagreed on about 15% of all segment labels. Therefore, in order to produce a fair picture of VZ's labeling ability, we used three different scoring measures.

Measure 1: VZ and All Ts.   The first measure (M1) asks: When all three transcribers agree on the same segment label, how often does VZ produce the same label? M1 examines all cases where, according to the transcribers (Ts), segments are perceptually unambiguous. This measure has the advantage that we can be fairly confident about the identity of each segment, since all Ts provided the same label. The measure will inflate performance somewhat, since it examines only those segments that are perceptually unambiguous, and these segments may also be acoustically less ambiguous than the remaining segments.

For purposes of analysis, we divided segments into three broad classes: consonants, vowels, and a third class consisting of the liquids [r] and [l], the semivowels [w] and [y], the syllabic consonants [l̩] and [n̩], and the retroflexed vowels [ɝ] and [ɚ]. For convenience, we will call this class "others." There were no instances where the transcribers did not agree on the class of a segment, according to our rather broad classification.

According to the transcribers, the 499 segments consisted of 245 consonants, 171 vowels, and 83 others. In order to examine how well the transcribers agreed on the specific segment labels in each class, we counted the number of instances in which all three transcribers produced the same segment label. For consonants, all Ts agreed on 235 of the 245 segments, or 96% agreement. It is interesting that six of the 10 cases where agreement was not unanimous involved a word-final stop. For vowels, the three transcribers agreed on 121 of the 171 segments, or 71% agreement (specific vowel disagreements are described below). Finally, for liquids, semivowels, and syllabic consonants, transcribers agreed on 68 of 83 segments, or 81% agreement. To summarize, the transcribers agreed unanimously on 85% (424 out of 499) of the segment labels. They were much more likely to agree on consonant labels than vowel labels, although a few acoustically (and perceptually) similar vowels accounted for most of the vowel disagreements.

Measure 2: VZ and Any T. M2 asks: How often does VZ produce the same segment label as *any* transcriber? This measure considers all 499 segments. At first glance, this measure may seem liberal, since VZ is given credit for a correct label if he agrees with *any* transcriber. However, the 75 segments on which the Ts disagree are probably acoustically more ambiguous than the segments on which agreement is unanimous. We favor this measure because it captures the variability inherent in phonetic transcription.

Measure 3: VZ and Each T. The third measure asks: How well does VZ agree with the transcription produced by each transcriber? This is the most severe measure, because VZ is penalized for each disagreement with each transcriber. For this analysis we computed, for each utterance, the proportion of segments on which VZ agreed with each transcriber, and then calculated the average agreement.

Performance on Utterances

Segmentation

In this subsection we examine VZ's ability to parse a speech spectrogram into units corresponding to phonetic segments. VZ indicates segments in two ways: (a) by the placement of "segment markers" directly under the spectrogram; and (b) by the placement of segment labels side by side between two markers. Such cases almost always involved sonorant–vowel or vowel–sonorant combinations. For example, the phrase "for your" was represented by VZ as [f|ɔ˞yɔ˞], with three labels sharing the same segment markers.

VZ produced both optional segments (indicated by longer segment markers or by an annulus around a segment label) and alternate segmentations. When scoring the data, credit was given for correct optional segments and correct alternate segmentations. We felt that in these cases, VZ provided information that could be used by a perceiver (or a computer) during the recognition process, and that no penalty was deserved. Finally, in measuring segmentation, we were concerned only with VZ's ability to identify the existence of phonetic segments; accurate segmentation did not necessarily correspond to accurate labeling.

VZ identified 485 of the 499 segments defined by the transcribers. Thus, slightly more than 97% of all segments were identified from the speech spectrogram. The 14 missed segments were: [d] in "land," "read," and "couldn't," [t] in "plants," [n] in "want," [ð] in "the" (twice), [h] in "his" (twice), [l] in "Bill" and "soldiers," [ə] in "gasoline," and both [y]s in "yadiya." Examination of the speech spectrograms revealed that the visual cues for these segments were either very weak or completely absent. For example, in Fig. 1.2, we can find no visual cues for the [l] in "soldiers," whereas all transcribers indicated the presence of this segment. We expect that for some of these segments, the transcribers' perception may have been influenced by their use of context. For example, the nonsense word "leh" in the phrase "leh nose today", was transcribed as "land" by all Ts. Similarly, "gasoline" was probably produced as "gas'line," since no formants were visible for the vowel [ə], although all Ts agreed on its existence.

VZ produced 20 alternate segmentations. An alternate segmentation was written below the original segmentation and was sometimes produced after the initial segmentation, during the labeling process, upon closer examination of the spectrogram. In 16 of the 20 cases, the alternate segmentation indicated two segments where a single segment had been originally proposed. In one case, three segments were proposed instead of two, and in three cases, a single segment was postulated where two were originally proposed. When an alternate segmentation was proposed, it was correct 13 of 20 times.

Labeling

VZ used a single label to identify a segment 52% of the time (254 out of 485 cases), two labels 35% of the time, and three labels 6% of the time (30 cases). On the remaining 33 segments, VZ produced 17 partial transcriptions, 13 optional segments, and provided no label in three cases. If we exclude optional labels from consideration, and count each partial transcription as three labels, then VZ produced an average of 1.53 labels to each segment. When more than one label was given, they were almost always rank ordered so that it was possible to score VZ's performance for first, second, and third choices. We arbitrarily decided to score all partial transcriptions as equivalent to a third choice.

TABLE 1.4
Agreement among VZ and all Ts on Segment Labels

	Consonants	Vowels	Other	Total
All Ts	235	121	68	424
VZ				
1st choice	165	78	48	291
2nd choice	26	18	10	54
3rd choice and partial	19		2	21
VZ/Ts	210/235	96/121	60/68	366/424
Percent agreement	89	79	88	86

Measure 1. Table 1.4 reveals the number of cases where VZ's segment label agreed with the label produced by all three transcribers. It can be seen that 210 of 235 (89%) consonants were correctly labeled, 96 of 121 (79%) vowels were correctly labeled, and 60 of 68 (88%) others were

TABLE 1.5
VZ's Agreement with all Ts for Each Consonant Segment
in Word-Initial, Medial, and Final Position

	Initial		Medial		Final	
	Ts	VZ	Ts	VZ	Ts	VZ
/b/	13	12	2	1	0	0
/d/	4	4	8	5	5	4
/g/	6	5	1	1	0	0
/p/	5	5	3	2	2	2
/t/	7	6	10	8	14	12
/k/	7	6	6	6	5	4
/m/	9	7	4	4	4	4
/n/	9	9	10	9	10	8
/y/	0	0	2	2	5	5
/r/	0	0	2	2	0	0
/ə/	1	1	0	0	1	1
/ð/	11	8	1	0	0	0
/f/	5	5	3	3	0	0
/v/	0	0	3	3	3	3
/s/	1	1	9	8	11	10
/z/	1	1	1	1	11	10
/š/	2	2	0	0	0	0
/j/	1	1	2	2	0	0
/h/	7	5	0	0	0	0
Total	97	89	67	57	71	63
Percent Correct		92%		85%		89%

correctly labeled. Across the three categories, about 80% of all agreements occurred on the first (or only) choice, while most of the remaining agreement involved a second choice. For consonants, 17 of the 19
third-choice agreements were partial transcriptions. All but one partial
transcription indicated an unreleased stop, a weak fricative (or weak
voiced fricative), or both. Only one partial transcription (out of 20) was
incorrect. To summarize, when transcribers provide the same label, VZ
produced the same label, usually as a first chioce, 86% of the time.
Agreement was better on consonants and others (88.5%) than on vowels
(79%).

Table 1.5 displays the number of times that all transcribers produced
each consonant label in word-initial, word-medial, and word-final position, and the number of times that VZ produced the same label, on any
choice, as the three transcribers. Note that agreement between VZ and
the three transcribers was slightly better in word-initial and word-final
position (92% and 89% respectively) than in word-medial position (85%).
It should be remembered, however, that agreement for the word-final
stops (22 out of 26) includes credit for the partial transcription "unreleased stop" which was used by VZ most of the time.

Table 1.6 displays, for individual vowel segments and for [r], [l], [w],

TABLE 1.6
VZ's Agreement with All Ts for Each Vowel Segment and for /r/, /l/, /w/,
/y/, /l/, /n/, /ɚ/, and /ɝ/ in Word-Initial, Medial, and Final Position

Vowels				Other					
					Initial		Medial		Final	
	Ts	VZ		Ts	VZ	Ts	VZ	Ts	VZ
/i/	16	13	/r/	2	1	13	12	5	4
/ɪ/	15	10	/l/	2	2	10	9	4	3
/e/	15	14	/w/	12	11	1	1	0	0
/ɛ/	9	6	/y/	5	4	2	2	0	0
/æ/	8	6	/l/	0	0	1	1	5	4
/ə/	15	13	/n/	0	0	1	1	0	0
/ʌ/	6	4	/ɚ/	0	0	1	1	4	4
/aʸ/	9	9							
/aʷ/	2	2							
/a/	13	11							
/ /	1	1							
/o/	6	5							
/u/	4	2							
/u/	2	0							
Total	121	96		21	18	29	27	18	15
Percent									
Correct		79%			86%		93%		83%

TABLE 1.7

All Cases where VZ Disagreed, on any Choice, with the Labels Produced by All Three Transcribers

	Consonants			Vowels			Others	
All Ts	VZ[a]	Word	All Ts	VZ[a]	Word	All Ts	VZ[a]	Word
/b/	/n/	Bill	/i/	/ɪ/	dancing	/r/	/ɚ/	goodyear
/d/	missed	couldn't	/i/	/ɪ/	keeps	/r/	/w, l/	read
/d/	missed	read	/ɪ/	/i/	be	/r/	/ɜ, ɚ/	bears
/d/	/r/	body	/ɪ/	/i/	Tim	/l/	missed	soldiers
/d/	wk. vcd. fric.	sudden	/ɪ/	/ə, ɚ/	pretty	/l/	missed	Bill
/d/	/k, g/	aardvark	/i/	/iu/	give	/w/	/f, b/	when
/g/	/y/	give	/i/	/ə/	Alice	/y/	missed	yadiya
/p/	/b/	keeps	/e/	/ɑʸ/	play	/l/	/l, m/	apple
/t/	/s/	left	/ɛ/	/ʌ, ə/	fell			
/t/	/s/	feelings	/ɛ/	/ɪ/	bears			
/t/	/m, n/	Basketball	/æ/	/ɛ, ɪə/	after			
/t/	/k/	want	/æ/	/ɛə/	Alice			
/t/	missed	Plants	/ə/	/ɪ, ʌ/	a			
/k/	/g/	work	/ə/	/ɚ/	mother			
/n/	missed	want	/ʌ/	/ɛ/	jungles			
/n/	missed	in	/ʌ/	/ɑ, ɑʷ/	mother			
/n/	/m/	fun	/ɑ/	/ɔ/	o'clock			
/ð/	missed	the	/ɑ/	/ɔ/	novel			
/ð/	missed	the	/o/	missed	gasoline			
/ð/	/f, θ/	the	/u/	/ɛ, o/	knew			
/ð/	/r/	mother	/u/	/æ, ɛ/	canoe			
/s/	/z/	its	/u/	/ɪ, ɨ, ɛ/	couldn't			
/s/	/z/	basketball	/u/	/ɪ/	goodyear			
/z/	/s/	is						
/h/	missed	his						
/h/	missed	his						

[a] When VZ made more than one choice, all are listed: /first, second, ... /.

[y], [ḷ], [n̩], [ɜ˞], and [ɚ], the number of times the three transcribers produced the same segment label, and the number of times that VZ agreed with the label produced by the transcribers. Since vowels occurred in medial position a vast majority of the time, data are combined for vowels in word-initial, word-medial, and word-final position.

To summarize, Tables 1.5 and 1.6 present, *for each segment*, (a) the number of times the three transcribers produced the same segment label, and (b) the number of times that VZ, on any choice, agreed with the transcribers. Table 1.7 presents all cases where VZ *disagreed*, on any choice, with the label produced by the three transcribers and displays the word or nonsense word in which the segment occurred. Taken together, these three tables present an exhaustive description of VZ's performance for cases in which the segment label is unambiguous.

Measure 2.   Segment labels produced by VZ agreed with at least one transcriber on 424 of 499 segments, or 85% agreement. Table 1.8 summarizes VZ's agreement with at least one transcriber for segments in each sound class. As before, there was more agreement on consonants (87%) and others (86%) than vowels (81%).

Table 1.9 displays all cases where the three Ts disagreed on a vowel label, the word in which the vowel occurred, and the label(s) produced by VZ. This table reveals that half of all disagreements among the Ts involved [i]–[ɪ]–[ɨ], with the remainder involving mainly confusions among [ɛ]–[æ], [ʌ]–[ə], and [ɑ]–[ɔ]–]o]. On cases where the three transcribers did not agree, VZ agreed with at least one transcriber over 85% of the time.

There were only 10 cases in which the three transcribers disagreed on a consonant label, and these are shown in Table 1.10. Five of the ten disagreements occurred on a word-final stop consonant, and two occurred on a word-final fricative. On the remaining three disagreements, two transcribers indicated a medial /d/ in "paddle," "needed," and "yester-

TABLE 1.8
Agreement among VZ and any Ts on Segment Labels

	Consonants	Vowels	Other	Total
All Ts	245	171	83	499
VZ				
1st choice	169	109	57	335
2nd choice	26	27	11	64
3rd choice	19	3	4	26
VZ/Ts	214/245	139/171	72/83	425/499
Percent agreement	87	81	86	85

TABLE 1.9
Labels Provided by VZ and Each T for All Cases in Which the Three Transcribers Disagreed on a Vowel Label

Word	VZ[a]	T1	T2	T3
pretty	/e, i/	/i/	/i/	/ɪ/
thing	/ɪ/	/i/	/i/	/ɪ/
teelings	/ɪ/	/i/	/i/	/ɪ/
yadiya	/i/	/i/	/y/	/ɪ/
the	/i/	/i/	/ə/	/ɪ/
dangerous	/e, i/	/æ/	/e/	/e/
dancing	/ɛ, æ/	/æ/	/æ/	/ɛ/
apple	/æ, ɛ, ɪ/	/æ/	/æ/	/ɛ/
paddle	/æ, ɛᵊ, ə/	/æ/	/æ/	/ɛ/
plants	/ɛ, æ/	/æ/	/æ/	/ɛ/
is	/ɪ, i/	/ɨ/	/ɪ/	/ɪ/
basketball	/ɨ, ə/	/ɨ/	/ɪ/	/ɪ/
its	/ə, ɨ/	/ɨ/	/ɪ/	/ɪ/
in	/ə/	/ɨ/	/ɪ/	/ɪ/
his	/ʌ/	/ɨ/	/ɪ/	/ɪ/
body	/i, e/	/i/	/ɪ/	/ɪ/
winning	/ɪ/	/ɪ/	/ɪ/	/ɪ/
baby	/ɪ, i/	/i/	/ɪ/	/ɪ/
Goodyear	/ə/	/i/	/ɪ/	/ɪ/
office	/ʌ/	/ɨ/	/ɪ/	/i/
is	/ʌ, ə/	/ɨ/	/ɪ/	/i/
seamstress	/ɨ/	/ɨ/	/ə/	/ɨ/
needed	/ɪ, ɨ/	/ɪ/	/ə/	/ɨ/
dangerous	/ʌ/	/ɪ/	/ə/	/ɨ/
a	/ə, ɨ/	/ə/	/ʌ/	/ə/
at	/ə, ɨ/	/ɨ/	/ə/	/ə/
was	/ə, ʌ/	/ə/	/ʌ/	/ɨ/
today	/ɨ, ə/	/u/	/ə/	/ə/
the	/ə/	/ɪ/	/ə/	/ə/
the	/ə/	/ə/	/ʌ/	/ə/
the	/ə/	/ə/	/ʌ/	/ə/
the	/ə, ʌ/	/ɨ/	/ə/	/ə/
was	/ʌ, ə/	/ɨ/	/ʌ/	/ə/
sudden	/ə/	/ə/	/ʌ/	/ʌ/
of	/ə, ɔ, ʌ/	/ə/	/ʌ/	/ʌ/
won	/ɔ/	/ʌ/	/ɔ/	/ʌ/
office	/ɔ/	/ɑ/	/ɑ/	/ɔ/
smaller	/ɔ/	/ɔ/	/ɑ/	/ɔ/
saw	/ɑ, ɔ/	/ɑ/	/ɑ/	/ɔ/
cross	/ɑ/	/ɔ/	/ɑ/	/ɔ/
on	/ɛ, æ, ɑ/	/ɔ/	/ɑ/	/ɑ/
want	/ɑ, ɑʸ, æ/	/ɔ/	/ɑ/	/ɑ/
yadiya	/ɛ, ɑ/	/ɑ/	/ə/	/ɑ/
what	/ɛ, ɪ, ɑ/	/ɑ/	/ɔ/	/ɑ/
more	/ɔ/	/o/	/o/	/ɔ/
story	/ɔ/	/o/	/o/	/ɔ/
folk	[+back, −high]	/o/	/u/	/o/
to	/ə, ɨ/	/u/	/u/	/ə/
your	/u/	/ɚ/	/ʊ/	/ɔ/

[a]When VZ made more than one choice, all are listed: /first, second, ... /.

25

TABLE 1.10
Labels Produced by VZ and Each T for All Cases in Which the Three
Transcribers Disagreed on a Consonant Label

Utterance	Word(s)	T1	T2	T3	VZ
4	fol*k* dancing	/k/	/ʔ/	/k/	no label
8	shar*k* may	/k/	/k/	/p/	/k/
9	pa*dd*le	/ɾ/	/d/	/d/	/ɾ/
12	nee*d*ed	/ɾ/	/d/	/d/	/ɾ, v, ð/
14	yester*d*ay	/ɾ/	/d/	/d/	/ɾ/
18	wi*th*	/f/	/ə/	/ə/	/ə/
20	lan*d* nose	no label	/d/	/d/	no label
21	han*d* zaim	/t/	/d/	/d/	/n, m/
22	bear*s* shoot	/ž/	/z/	no label	no label
23	wa*k*e jungles	/k/	/t/	/k/	/k/

day," while the third transcriber indicated a flap. It is interesting to note that VZ indicated a flap in each case. It is also of interest to note that five of the ten disagreements occurred in the anomalous utterances.

Measure 3. The average agreement between VZ and each transcriber for all segments was 81%. The average agreement among the three transcribers for all segments was 90%.

Use of Higher-Level Knowledge

All of the evidence suggests that labeling was performed without the use of syntactic or semantic knowledge. Labelling performance was *better* on the four utterances consisting of nonsense words interspersed with normal words. For the three measures just considered (agreement with all Ts, with any T, and with individual Ts), VZ averaged 93%, 92%, and 88%, respectively, on utterances containing nonsense words. This compares to 86%, 85%, and 81% agreement for the three measures on the entire set of utterances. VZ was therefore slightly more accurate labeling segments in nonsense syllables.

A number of tests were originally designed to determine the extent to which higher-order contextual information was used during labeling. Observation of the labeling process soon revealed, however, that syntactic and semantic information was rarely used during labeling (although certain common words, such as "the," were probably recognized on sight). The labeling process was typically not left-to-right, and labels were not consistently placed first at beginnings of words. Moreover, when labeling was completed on a particular utterance and we asked VZ to identify the sentence, it was obvious that even in utterances where all segments were correctly identified, VZ had not yet identified the words.

But Were They Read?

So far, we have only considered the identification of phonetic segments. The more interesting question is whether VZ's transcriptions are sufficiently accurate to determine what was actually said. To answer this question, we presented a linguist with the 15 transcriptions produced by VZ from spectrograms of the normal English utterances. If we exclude three confusions of "a" and "the," 10 of the transcriptions were read perfectly. Of these 10, four were read from left to right without hesitation. The remaining six were interpreted by first identifying individual words, and then "solving" the sentence like a puzzle. Of the five utterances in which all words were not identified, four involved an error on a single word: "Ella's" for "Alice," "leave" for "left," "square" for "folk" (a guess, which followed identification of "dancing") and "lack" for "want" (another guess, in "waste not, want not"). In the remaining utterance, the linguist identified "New knowledge aardvark was smaller" from the transcription of "Bill knew his aardvark was smaller." The linguist was extremely clever at interpreting the sentences from VZ's transcriptions and performed slightly better than VZ did when attempting to identify the utterances he had transcribed. Altogether, the linguist identified 92% of the words.

Performance on Words in a Carrier Phrase

Segmentation

The 45 words in carrier phrases contained 201 segments. VZ identified all 201 segments. Moreover, VZ did not propose any optional segments or alternate segmentations. VZ was apparently quite confident in his segmentation of words in the carrier phrase, a confidence justified by perfect performance.

Labeling

Measure 1. The 201 segments consisted of 102 consonants, 64 vowels, and 35 others. The three Ts produced the same segment label on 187 of the 201 segments. All but one of the 14 disagreements (the final [l] in "criminal") occurred on vowels, and eight of the 13 vowels involved confusion of [ɪ] or [ɨ], either with each other or with other vowels. To summarize, all Ts produced the same segment label on all 102 consonants, on 51 of 64 vowels, and 34 of 35 others.

For the 187 cases in which all Ts produced the same segment label, VZ produced the same label, on any choice, on 173 segments, or 92.5%. VZ agreed with all Ts on 99 of 102 consonants (97%), 42 of 51 vowels (82%), and 32 of 34 others (94%). The specific disagreements are shown in Table 1.11.

Measure 2.   Of the 14 cases where the three transcribers did not produce the same segment label, VZ agreed with at least one of them on all 14 segments. By this measure, the number of VZ's disagreements stays the same (14), but the total number of segments increases (from 187 to 201), so the proportion of agreements increases slightly, to 93% of all segments. Agreement was again 97% on consonants (99 of 102), rose to 86% for vowels (55 of 64), and stayed at 94% for others (33 of 35).

Why does VZ identify phonetic segments more accurately when a word is in a carrier phrase, rather than an unknown utterance? The major advantage provided by the carrier phrase was that it defined the beginning of the unknown word. VZ was able to use his knowledge of English phonotactics (permissible phoneme sequences) to identify segments. In natural continuous speech, virtually any sequence of segments can occur at a word boundary. Since VZ did not attempt to label spectrograms of unknown sentences word by word (or even left to right), word boundary information, and therefore phonotactic knowledge, was typically not used to identify segments from spectrograms of unknown sentences. The use of

TABLE 1.11
All Cases Where the Label Produced by VZ
Disagreed with the Label Produced by all Three
Ts, for Word in a Carrier Phrase

	Ts	*VZ* [a]	*Word*
Consonants	/ð/	/g/	smoo*th*
	/b/	/f/	*f*resh
	/ǰ/	/č/	ca*g*es
Vowels	/e/	/i/	c*a*ges
	/ɛ/	/ʌ/	fr*e*sh
	/æ/	/i, ɪ, e/	w*a*gon
	/æ/	/ɪ, ɛ/	h*a*tch
	/æ/	/oʷ/	sh*a*llow
	/ʌ/	/ɑ/	dr*u*m
	/ɑ/	/ɛ, æ/	r*o*cket
	/o/	/w, ɪ/	shall*ow*
	/u/	/ʌ/	sm*oo*th
Other	/l/	/l/	sha*l*low
	/r/	/ɚ/	who*re*house

[a] When VZ made more than one choice, all are listed: /first, second, . . . /.

phonotactic knowledge for words in a known carrier phrase probably accounts for the better performance on these words.

Summary

To summarize, VZ correcly identified the existence of 485 of 499, or 97%, of all segments from speech spectrograms of normal and anomalous sentences. Depending upon the scoring method used, VZ agreed with a panel of phoneticians who listened to the sentences on between 81% and 86% of the segment labels. Performance on words in a known carrier phrase was substantially better. VZ identified the existence of all 201 segments identified by the panel of phoneticians, and agreed with the phoneticians on 93% of the segment labels.

PART II: PROCESS

The Segmentation Process

The initial step taken by VZ in reading a spectrogram was to segment the continuous speech wave into units that corresponded roughly to phones. Segmentation is often the necessary prerequisite for labeling, although in some cases a partial hypothesis of segment identity will aid the segmentation process. In this section, we will discuss the criteria that VZ used to locate segment boundaries and the strategies used for segmentation.

Boundary Placement Criteria

Conceptually, the criteria for boundary placement are quite simple, and VZ appeared to make use of only a few simple principles, as shown in the following protocol excerpt:

I am marking at various places
where it shows, you know,
maximal spectral difference...
I'm basically using the spectral change
as a parameter for marking the boundaries...
There is an intensity,
a sharp intensity difference....

Spectral changes accompany changes in manner of articulation. Each phone has a characteristic acoustic form that is a function of the manner in which it is articulated. A succession of phones will produce successive changes in the form of the speech wave. VZ places boundaries at these points of change.

Spectral Discontinuities.   The most striking change in the speech wave occurs in the transition between sonorants (vowels, nasals, and liquids) and obstruents (stops, fricatives, and affricates). Sonorants are often characterized by the presence of low-frequency energy, formant structure,and glottal striations. In contrast, obstruents usually have an aperiodic structure, and little or no energy in the low frequencies. Because of these differences, a boundary between a sonorant and an obstruent is usually easy to detect.

Within the sonorant category, there is a major acoustic difference between nasal and nonnasal segments similar in its distinctiveness to the difference between sonorants and obstruents. A transition from a nonnasal to a nasal is marked by a sharp amplitude drop and an abrupt change in the formant structure, while transitions between nonnasal sonorants are usually marked by smooth formant movements. Again, this usually allows a boundary to be easily detected.

Note, however, that a spectral discontinuity in itself does not constitute a segment boundary, since abrupt spectral changes can occur within single phonetic segments. For example, when a prestressed syllable-initial plosive follows a vowel, as in "the *c*ake," spectral discontinuities occur at the onset of the closure interval, the onset of the stop burst, and the onset of voicing of the following vowel. The discontinuity at the burst onset is (correctly) ignored and the closure and release are considered to be part of a single segment—[k]. Thus, a sharp discontinuity in the spectrograms is not *by itself* a sufficient cue to segmentation; the cue must be interpreted in light of acoustic–phonetic knowledge.

Together, sonorant/obstruent and nasal/nonnasal boundaries account for over 75% of all boundary types. Thus, 75% of all segment boundaries can be easily detected and are accurately marked by VZ. The remaining 25% of the boundaries involve transitions between acoustically similar segments—for example, between vowels and liquids, or between two nasals or two stops—and consequently are more difficult to detect.

Duration.   Some portions of the speech wave can be segmented on the basis of duration cues. For example, two adjacent stops, as in "Fol*k* *d*ancing..." (sentence 4) can be identified as such by noting the duration of the closure interval between the two words. When compared to other (single stop) closure durations in the utterance, it is unusually long. Similarly, two adjacent nasals can be identified by the presence of an uncharacteristically long nasal segment. Duration also serves to indicate the presence of adjacent sonorant segments, although additional information is needed for accurate boundary placement.

Formant Movements.   Boundary placement within sonorant sequences is difficult, since there are no discrete cues such as spectral discontinuity to guide interpretation. Nevertheless, there is sufficient information in such cases to allow fairly accurate segmentation. Intervocalic glides and liquids can be identified by the dip they induce in the first formant frequency. Some examples of this phenomenon are shown in Fig. 1.4a. More generally, the presence of multiple sonorant segments can be identified by nonmonotonic formant movement within a sonorant stretch (excluding, of course, the transition movements that occur at boundaries between obstruent and nasal segments).

An additional cue is provided for glides in the drop in formant amplitude due to the close articulation of these sounds. Figure 1.4b shows a good example of this cue.

When dealing with adjacent sonorants, VZ usually found it easier not to place boundary markers at all, and instead marked off an aggregate segment. Quite often VZ would not place boundaries between liquids and

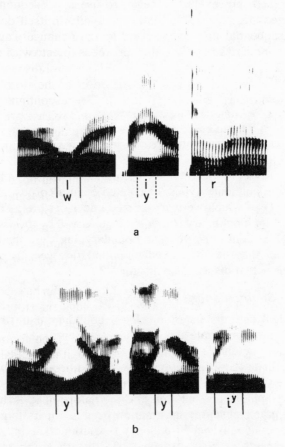

FIG. 1.4. Cues for segmentation. (a) First formant movement within sonorant stretches. (b) Drop in formant amplitude.

vowels and would consider the resulting segment as a single unit, although eventually two labels were placed between the segment markers. In the case of liquid–vowel sequences, this is probably the preferred solution, since liquids have a marked influence on adjacent segments and the two segments are difficult to consider in isolation.

Boundary Placement Strategies

We can define two basic segmentation strategies, left-to-right and nonsequential. VZ is apparently able to use either strategy. Some utterances were segmented in a single left-to-right pass, while others were segmented in an apparently random order. Some of the variation in segmentation can apparently be attributed to the task demands: At the beginning of the experiment, VZ confined himself to a strict left-to-right strategy, apparently believing that this was expected of him. As the session progressed, however, VZ began to use a nonsequential strategy, which seemed more natural to him.

The nonsequential strategy is not random. VZ typically marks the most distinctive boundaries first, and then proceeds to deal with more difficult boundaries:

> Um, I'm segmenting again
> where I consider sonorant stretches are . . .
> and then . . . I'll try to break it down
> primarily using spectral changes. . . .

Table 1.12 shows the mean rank order of VZ's boundary placements for representative boundary types, calculated from a corpus containing 244 boundaries (17 of which were considered unclassifiable). The rank order of placement for a boundary is predicted quite well by the visual clarity of the spectral discontinuity at that boundary, as described previously. Thus, it seems that the order in which boundaries were marked probably reflects their actual discriminability for VZ.

Optional Segmentation

Under ideal circumstances, placing a boundary is a straightforward procedure: The appropriate acoustic cues are identified and a boundary is marked. Under actual circumstances, however, various factors will conspire to eliminate the information necessary to detect a boundary.

There are two sources of difficulty in segmentation: the limitations of the spectrographic representation and the nature of speech production. The spectrograph obscures information because of its limited dynamic range and occasionally poor frequency resolution. The information content of the spectrogram is also degraded by processes intrinsic to the

TABLE 1.12
Mean Rank Order of Boundary Placement for All
Boundary Types of Frequency Greater Than 1[a]

Boundary Type	Mean Rank	Category Frequency
fricative–vowel	7.8	39
stop–glide	8.3	3
stop–vowel	8.5	82
stop–liquid	9.4	5
nasal–stop	9.8	10
nasal–fricative	10.2	6
nasal–vowel	13.3	32
fricative–stop	13.5	13
glide–vowel	15.4	11
fricative–fricative	16	3
liquid–vowel	18.6	7
nasal–nasal	19.5	4
stop–stop	20.3	6
vowel–vowel	21	4

[a] Segment sequence is not considered separately,
i.e., a stop–vowel boundary and a vowel–stop are
considered to be the same for the purpose of this
analysis.

nature of speech production. A good example of this is the drop in pitch
and amplitude that normally occurs at the end of an utterance. This makes
the detection of utterance-final segments difficult, or it can produce spurious cues (e.g., an amplitude drop could be natural, or it may be due to an
utterance-final nasal segment).

Unambiguous interpretation of the spectrographic trace may also be
difficult because of speaker characteristics. For example, a high-pitched
voice will produce a choppy formant pattern that mimics certain boundary
cues and makes boundary placement difficult.

In cases where insufficient information was available to unambiguously
establish boundaries, optional segments were sometimes proposed. If we
examine the identity of the optional segments proposed by VZ, we find
that, with a few exceptions, they are either utterance-initial stops and
weak fricatives or postvocalic liquids. Spectrographically, these segments
are difficult to identify, either because of their weak energy, (e.g., [ð]) or
because they produce only subtle changes in the signal (e.g., the [l] in
"soldiers" in Fig. 1.2).

Optional segments were also postulated when duration alone was a
potential cue to segmentation. In the utterance "Bears shoot...", the
boundary between the first two words consisted of a long fricative seg-

ment which was initially marked as a single segment. Subsequently, this decision was reconsidered: "It is quite long ... it could in fact be two segments." Since duration, in most instances, is only a partial cue, segmentation must remain optional.

Summary

The first step in interpreting a spectrogram was to segment the speech wave into units corresponding to phones. This process was seen to be relatively straightforward, once relevant acoustic dimensions were identified: (a) spectral discontinuities; (b) duration; and (c) formant movement. An analysis of the segmentation strategy revealed that segmentation was essentially context-free and could be performed in a serial left-to-right manner. More commonly, easily distinguished boundaries were marked first, then the more ambiguous ones. Factors such as deficiencies in the spectrographic representation and the nature of speech production introduced difficulties, but despite these, segmentation was carried out with a high degree of accuracy; over 97% of all segment boundaries were identified.

The Labeling Process

One of the main goals of this study was to describe the nature of the methods that VZ used to identify the phonetic content of an utterance. To achieve this goal, we analyzed in great detail a set of twelve protocols chosen from those recorded during the first (October 1977) session. Table 1.13 shows the distribution of segments in this corpus by representative category. The categories were chosen to reflect similarities in the way their members were dealt with by VZ during labeling. Note that the categories represent sets of acoustically (or rather, visually) similar phones.

TABLE 1.13
Distributions of Segments in
Corpus Used for Analysis

Segment	Number
Stops	60
Strong fricatives	30
Weak fricatives	11
Nasals	32
Liquids	14
Glides	10
Back vowels	12
Front vowels	43
Central vowels	17
Reduced vowels	19

Labeling Sequence

The first question we asked was whether it was possible to identify an order in which phone categories were labeled, perhaps similar to the order based on acoustic distinctiveness found for segmentation. The sequence in which labels were assigned was tabulated for each utterance and the mean rank for each category was calculated. Unlike the results obtained from the analysis of segmentation, no clear-cut pattern emerged. Closer examination of the results, however, suggested that there is some tendency for easily identifiable segments (such as strong fricatives) to be labeled first. Ease of identification depends on such factors as the acoustic distinctiveness of a pattern, its freedom from contextual influences and its clarity of realization. In this exchange, VZ elaborated a part of his strategy:

> [AR: Why do you move around?
> How do you select the spots you move to?]
> ah, for example,
> I'm going to ignore this one
> because in order to make that decision . . .
> I have to make a few decisions
> before I can label it a vowel . . .
> I'm trying to do the segmental labeling
> independent of . . . phonetic context . . .
> ah, then I try to do the other places . . .

Segment Identification

In this section, we consider in greater detail the methods that VZ used to label individual phones. These methods are of particular interest as they can provide useful insights into human perception and can serve as a guide for improving automatic speech-understanding systems.

For any one segment, VZ would verbalize only a small portion of the information he was using to come to a decision (despite our prompting). Since this meant that the information used to identify a particular phone was present only in a fragmented form, the labeling information was analyzed in two stages. First, VZ's remarks about each individual segment were recorded and summarized. Second, all remarks made about a given phone in the entire corpus were collected together. This allowed us to specify both the core of the procedure and also the variations induced by particular contexts.

The analysis of the protocols revealed that VZ approached the labeling task in one of three ways:

1. By far the greatest number of labeling decisions were based on the identification of *unique spectral patterns* characteristic of individual phones.

2. Pattern detection is augmented by an extensive *knowledge of coarticulatory effects* that distort spectral patterns.
3. In addition, VZ is able to make use of the *constraints imposed by English phonology and phonotactics* to narrow down possible interpretations.

Note that none of these procedures make use of the types of information thought necessary for speech perception. For example, VZ labeled individual segments without reference to the syntactic structure of the utterance or to its semantic content. The error analysis supports this interpretation of VZ's behavior.

Acoustic Patterns.   Acoustic patterns, as we define them, consist of easily identified spectral configurations that are unique to a particular phone. Nasals provide one such pattern. Because of the manner in which nasals are articulated, a marked change occurs between a nasal and, say, an adjoining nonnasal sonorant. The regular formant structure is replaced by a steady-state pattern composed of several nasal formants; the overall amplitude drops markedly from adjoining segments. Information about place of articulation is usually available from adjacent sonorant segments or from other sources of knowledge (for example, phonological constraints, as discussed below). Once learned, the basic nasal pattern is almost always recognized correctly. The only difficulties that arise involve unusual circumstances, such as a very rapid speech rate or deficiencies in the representation. The identifying characteristics for a number of phones are listed in Table 1.14.

Apart from vowels, the most common segments in our corpus and in spoken language (Carterette & Jones, 1974; Fletcher, 1953) are the stop consonants. Stop consonants have been perhaps the most thoroughly studied consonants in speech perception, and this research has played an important role in theoretical approaches to speech perception (Cole & Scott, 1974; Liberman, Cooper, Shankweiler, and Studdert-Kennedy, 1967; Stevens & Blumstein, 1977). It is therefore of interest to examine the methods used by VZ to detect and label stop consonant segments.

A stop is easily detected by the presence of a closure interval. A somewhat more difficult problem is to specify the place of articulation and the voicing value for a stop. Previous work (see Liberman et al., 1967) has indicated that this may be a formidable task, because of the diversity of the acoustic realizations of stops. However, an analysis of VZ's protocols indicates that, at least in the case of spectrogram reading, the discriminations can be made with a high degree of accuracy. The reason for this is that it is possible to define a unique and distinctive pattern for each stop.

Bilabial stops have a characteristic short rising formant pattern which

TABLE 1.14
Some Descriptors Used by VZ in Reference to Phones

Vowels	height	varies inversely with F1
	frontness	varies directly with F1–F2 spread
		duration: /ɪ/ shorter than /i/
		offglides: /ɪ ᵊ/, /æ ᵊ/
	/ɑ/	F1 highest of all vowels
	reduced	short duration
		neutral formant pattern
	diphthongs	spreading formants (e.g., /ɑʸ/)
		lowering F1 (e.g., /ɑʷ/)
Strong fricatives	voicing	duration (voiced are shorter)
	/s/	aperiodic energy > 4kHz
	/š/	aperiodic energy < 4kHz
Nasals		energy below 300 Hz
		abrupt amplitude onset
		lower amplitude than vowels
		nasalization of adjacent vowels
Place of articulation		labial: all formants move down to closure
		velar: F2 and F3 merge at point of closure
Retroflex sounds		F3 dips below 2 kHz
		/ɚ/: F3 follows F2
		/r/: F3 touches F2
Flaps		short duration < 20, 25 msec
Stops	closure	lack of energy
	burst	labial: little or none
		alveolar: high frequency
		velar: strong, occasionally double bursts
	voicing	voice-onset time (VOT) duration (longer for voiceless)
	transitions	labial: point down
		alveolar: F2 locus at 1800 Hz
		velar: F2 and F3 merge

is markedly different from the patterns observed for alveolar and velar stops. Bilabial stops also have weak release bursts, in contrast to the alveolar and velar stops which both have strong bursts with identifiable energy concentrations. Alveolar stops always have burst frequencies above 3.0 kHz (except when followed by liquids, which tend to lower the burst frequencies) and can be distinguished from velar bursts on the basis of frequency (which, in the case of the velars, is a function of the following vowel). The form of the burst also serves to distinguish the two stops—the velar burst is usually longer, more intense, and is sometimes doubled. Additional information is obtained from the associated transitions, either from their implied "loci" or from special characteristics. (For example, front and central vowels will show a distinctive joining of the second and third formants at the point of velar articulation.)

If we examine labeling errors for stops, we find that most of them involve incomplete specifications due to missing acoustic information. Thus, for word-final stops produced without a release burst, the place judgment is unreliable and in many cases was not attempted. The remaining errors show that stops were misidentified because of missing major class cues (e.g., the stop closure) or because of inadequacies in the spectrographic representation.

VZ's labeling of vowels presents an interesting case, since proportionately the largest number of segment label errors were due to vowel misidentifications. The possible source of these errors will be considered in a later section. At present, we would like to examine the cues used by VZ to classify vowels.

The easiest distinction was between reduced and unreduced vowels. Reduced vowels are characterized by their short length, often as short as two glottal pulses, which sets them off from all other vowels in an utterance. Once a reduced vowel was identified, the high variant ([ɨ]) was distinguished from the low one ([ə)] by comparing the distance between the first and second formants and the distance between the second and third (F2 and F3 are closer for [ɨ]). Often, VZ did not distinguish between the two, as indeed it is unnecessary to do in natural speech.

To identify the remaining vowels, a variety of cues was used. Surprisingly, VZ rarely took advantage of his ability to directly measure formant frequencies with a template, and appeared to work directly from the formant patterns. In describing vowels, VZ often appeared to make use of the Jakobson, Fant, and Halle (1963) features of compact–diffuse and grave–acute. (This is not surprising, as the Jakobson et al. system was derived mainly from acoustic characteristics.) Front vowels were distinguished by their diffuseness (essentially the separation between F1 and F2), with different degrees of diffuseness indicating vowel height. Within the front series, finer discriminations were made on the basis of other cues. For example, duration was used to distinguish between [i] and [ɪ], which have similar formant patterns ([ɪ] is usually shorter). Offglides were also used to distinguish vowels. Thus, [e] will have a pronounced [y] offglide, in contrast to [ɪ] and [ɛ], while [æ] will often exhibit a schwa offglide, being realized as [æə]. Similar statements can be made about the remaining vowels and indeed about all other speech sounds. That is, all segments can be classified into general categories, and then distinctive cues can be used to identify the phones within each category.

As the examples discussed thus far show, patterns can be composed of either steady-state distributions of energy, as in the case of the fricatives, or of dynamic patterns, such as formant movements. The pattern for a given phone is not always confined to a single segment, but quite often extends to adjoining segments, most notably in the case of stops. That each phone has associated with it a characteristic set of acoustic features is not a novel proposal (see, for example, Fant, 1968). VZ's achievement is in having developed the ability to recognize the characteristic pattern for each phone, as it occurs under a large variety of conditions. Extensive exposure to spectrogram representations has allowed VZ to develop the appropriate prototypes for each English phone.

Phonetic Context.   While many segments can be readily identified on the basis of their acoustic characteristics, there are cases in which coarticulatory effects disguise the identity of a segment. This is less of a problem with consonants, which, as we have seen, have essentially invariant cues, than with vowels, which tend to be highly influenced by surrounding segments. This is quite evident from the error scores for the two classes: Vowels were mislabeled more often than consonants. Figure 1.5 shows some examples of highly coarticulated vowels. In most cases, these are short vowels, surrounded by consonant segments that have very different places of articulation. In such cases, VZ is usually able to make a fairly accurate guess. The basis for these identifications is not always clear, but it appears that VZ is able to *compensate* for the coarticulation by computing appropriate formant displacements, arriving at a "noiseless" vowel.

Knowledge of coarticulation is an essential part of VZ's skill, as the following excerpt shows:

Given that it's a /w/
rather than an /l/
Compensation of the second formant
probably is not as much

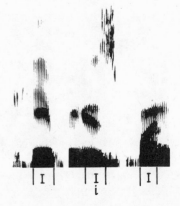

FIG. 1.5.   Differences in formant structure of /ɪ/ in different phonetic environments.

because /w/ articulation involves
just releasing the lips
whereas /l/ involves the tongue
which is also used in the vowel.

In a sense, every phone in connected speech is dependent on context, due to the effects of coarticulation. However, in most cases, the original acoustic pattern is still visible in the spectrogram. The context effects that we consider now are those that produce major changes in the acoustic pattern of a phone.

By far the largest contextual effect observed in our corpus is exerted by retroflexed sounds. The nature of their articulation is such that they substantially influence both preceding and following segments. For example, in a stop–[r] cluster such as [tr], the burst frequency of the [t] will drop about 600 Hz from its usual position due to its proximity to the [r] (Zue, 1976). This can be seen clearly in Fig. 1.6. A retroflex consonant affects vowels in a similar fashion by lowering their formant frequencies. VZ apparently finds it easier to deal with liquid–vowel clusters as single units. Such clusters are treated as allophones of the vowel, perhaps the most efficient solution under the circumstances.

Speech rate is also an important factor in a number of decisions, most commonly in the assignment of the voicing feature for stops and fricatives. The distinctions between [s] and [z], and [š] and [ž] depend primarily on the duration of frication, the voiced fricatives being shorter than the voiceless. VZ often tried to compare the duration of a fricative segment to the duration of other segments in an utterance before selecting a value for voicing. In some cases, he was able to compare two fricatives directly. A transcription error made by VZ reveals another implicit use of rate information. When the [w] in "... dangerous when..." was incorrectly labeled as a [b], and we asked VZ to comment on the error, he remarked that

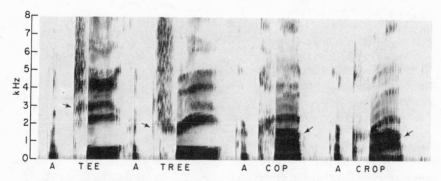

FIG. 1.6. Lowering of burst frequency in /tr/cluster (left), lowering of vowel formats (right).

the [w] seemed to be a [b] because of the rapid formant motion, resembling transitions for a stop more than for a glide.

The explicit use of contextual information was relatively uncommon in our corpus; approximately 18% of segment decisions made use of context. There were probably other instances of the use of context that were not mentioned by VZ. Certainly some generaly types of information, such as speech rate, are used when reading every utterance.

Phonological Knowledge. The English language, as indeed all languages, is a highly constrained system. It is constrained, for example, by its phonetic inventory, which is only a small sample of all possible speech sounds. Thus, in English we find the labiodental and alveolar fricatives /f/ and /s/, but not the velar fricative /χ/. It is also constrained in the possible combinations of these sounds through phonotactic rules. For example, in English we find the word-initial clusters /bl/ and /gl/ but not /dl/. The presence of these constraints act to reduce the amount of uncertainty in the spectrogram-reading task and no doubt contributes to VZ's high degree of accuracy.

On the other hand, fluent speech quite often alters the phonetic information in an utterance through additions, deletions, and transformations. Although these transformations are often complex, their occurrence is systematic and can be captured by the appropriate phonological rules. In this section we will examine some of the structural information that was used by VZ.

A well known example of a phonotactic constraint in English is the fact that [ŋ] is never allowed to occur in word–initial position, while [h] is never allowed to occur in word-final position. VZ is able to make use of such knowledge to eliminate label possibilities that would lead to impossible combinations in English. Knowledge of the sound pattern also allows VZ to detect the presence of non-English sounds and to interpret them correctly:

This is a front rounded vowel, look
I should mark it like this, [ü]
but this is not English,
so I would say it's probably
coarticulatory effect,
and this is really . . . [yu]
something like that.

Another example is the interpretation of a glottal stop ([ʔ]), which is not considered a phoneme in American English, but can occur as a possible transition between two vowels that are word-final and word-initial. The utterance, "Go paddle your own canoe," shows an example of this process, [yɚɔn] is realized as [yɚʔɔn], with the [ʔ] inserted between the two syllabic segments.

Phonological rules also allow a systematic approach to the recognition of segmental variation in different contexts. For example, a [t] will be unaspirated in an [st] cluster, but will be aspirated in word-initial position, even though in both cases it is preceded by an [s] segment.

Several other examples of rule usage turned up in our study. For example, a [ð] may be deleted in the phrase "on the," [ɔnðə] becoming [ɔnə]. By recognizing the deletion, VZ is able to restore the original form of the utterance. This particular example is also interesting in that although the spectrographic record quite clearly showed a [... ɔnə...] sequence, and was labelled as such by VZ, *all* transcribers inserted a fricative, marking the sequence as [... ɔnðə...], and thus demonstrating the compelling nature of phonological compensation.

A similar example, also in our corpus, involves the interpretation of the word "nine." Most listeners would agree that the first vowel in this word is [aʸ]; however, examination of a spectrogram and perhaps closer listening will reveal that the correct transcription is [na:n] and *not* [naʸn]. Again, all transcribers interpreted a segment according to phonological constraints and not according to the acoustic signal.

Knowledge of the phonetic and phonological structure of English allows VZ to correctly interpret acoustic phenomena that cannot be dealt with as simple patterns. This in turn allows VZ's transcription to approach what is actually perceived by the listener.

This is perhaps a good place to point out that VZ is a skilled reader of *English* spectrograms, and not of "speech" spectrograms as such. As mentioned earlier, each language has its own individual phonetics and phonology, different from all other languages. Experience with the structure of one language is probably not transferable to other languages, and if VZ wanted to be able to read spectrograms of, say, French utterances, he would have to go through much of the same procedure he went through in learning English. However, someone wishing to learn to speak a new language is faced with this same laborious task.

IMPLICATIONS

The performance of VZ reported in the previous section should be viewed with two facts in mind. First, the transcriptions produced by VZ and by the phoneticians are derived from different modalities (aural versus visual), and different sources of knowledge are brought to bear during the different transcription tasks. In the visual transcription task, VZ determines the presence and the identity of a given segment almost exclusively from acoustic cues, or at least their visual representation. Any context-dependent knowledge that he utilizes is represented at the segmental level. This is necessarily the case since at no time during the segmentation and labeling process was he aware of the linguistic content of the utterance. In the aural transcription task, however, the transcribers know exactly what the utterance is *before* actually transcribing it, and thus have at their disposal higher level sources of knowledge (such as syntax and semantics) that will enable them to "fill in" the segments when the acoustic cues are inadequate or even missing (Warren, 1970). The resulting transcription, therefore, is a composite of the acoustic as well as other linguistic and extralinguistic knowledge of the utterance, and it is impossible to separate the relative contribution of each knowledge source. As a consequence, some of the segmentation and labeling "errors," as we defined them, might not have been errors at all.

One should also bear in mind that our spectrogram-reading experiment is performed under ideal conditions. The sound recordings were made in quiet environments by cooperative male speakers, resulting in a spectrographic representation that is rich in acoustic information. It is not clear, and we are in no position to speculate, what VZ's performance might be if the signal-to-noise ratio or the bandwidth of the acoustic signal were decreased, as is often the case in conversational speech. We are certainly not making the categorical claim that all (or even most) spectrograms can be read.

Nevertheless, VZ has demonstrated that phonemes are accompanied by acoustic features that are recognizable on a speech spectrogram, and that with sufficient training it is possible to learn enough about these features and the modifications they undergo in fluent speech to read a speech spectrogram of an unknown utterance. In this section, we discuss the implications of VZ's achievement for: (a) theories of speech perception; (b) computer recognition of speech; and (c) speech training for the speech and hearing impaired.

Implications for Theories of Speech Perception

VZ's ability to identify about 85% of all phonetic segments from spectrograms of fluent speech has two strong implications for theories of speech perception. The first implication is based on the fact that phonemes are accompanied by specifiable acoustic features. The implication of this fact is that phonemes can be perceived *directly* from the information in the acoustic signal. This is exactly the argument offered by Cole and Scott (1974) and Cole (1977) as an alternative to the motor theory of speech perception (Liberman et al., 1967). The motor theory suggests that the conversion from sound to phoneme must be mediated through a special decoder, since individual phonemes are not accompanied by discrete acoustic features. According to Liberman et al. (1967):

> The acoustic cues for successive phonemes are intermixed in the sound stream to such an extent that definable segments of sound do not correspond to segments at the phoneme level. Moreover, the same phoneme is most commonly represented in different phonemic environments by sounds that are vastly different. There is, in short, a marked lack of correspondence between sound and perceived phoneme. This is a central fact of speech perception [p. 432].

Based on a consideration of the acoustic structure of *natural* speech, Cole and Scott (1974) argued that many of the acoustic cues for phonemes are invariant across different syllable environments, and that these invariant cues provide the major source of information about phonemes. To be sure, the main point made by Cole and Scott was that speech perception requires the interaction of three different types of cues (invariant spectral cues, transitional cues, and envelope cues), but "the major source of information is provided by invariant acoustic features."

How can Cole and Scott (1974) and Liberman et al. (1967) view the same stimulus and arrive at such vastly different conclusions? We suggest that it is a case of the glass being half full or half empty. In natural continuous speech, a given phoneme is usually characterized by a number of different features; Liberman et al. have chosen to emphasize those features which differ for phonemes across different environments, while Cole and Scott have chosen to emphasize those features that remain the same.

When reading speech spectrograms, VZ is refreshingly atheoretical. The various features of speech—bursts, closure intervals, frication, formants and formant transitions (to name but a few)—are all regarded as *information*. By regarding all features as sources of information, VZ has made them functionally equivalent. VZ does not regard formant transitions as "special"; they are simply regarded as another source of usable information. In some cases, formant transitions provide direct and reliable information about the place of articulation of a segment. For example, converging second and third formant transitions before a closure interval are a reliable cue that the upcoming stop is a velar. When all formant transitions are relatively short and point to a low frequency, they reliably signal a labial stop. But when these features are not present, VZ is able to utilize other information, such as burst frequency, amplitude, duration, or the telltale presence of a double burst to identify the individual stop consonant. Perhaps the major contribution that VZ has made to our conception of speech perception is the following insight: There is nothing to be gained by dichotomizing the sounds of speech as context-dependent versus context-independent. Rather, all cues—from the frication noise of [s] to the transitions of [d]—should be viewed as information. When all relevant acoustic events are viewed as pieces of information, it becomes possible to learn the relationship between phonemes and their acoustic cues.

A second implication of VZ's ability to read speech spectrograms is that speech can be interpreted in a modality other than audition. Liberman et al. (1967) have argued that speech perception requires a special decoder that is biologically tied to the auditory system. As Liberman (1970) explains:

> However much the speech processor may stand on its own linguistic feet, it is nonetheless firmly attached to the ear. Consider that, in 20 years of trying, no one has really learned to read speech spectrograms (Fant, 1962, p. 4). This is not because the spectrogram fails to extract the right parameters of the signal. The spectrographic transform is quite appropriate for showing the formants, where almost all of the linguistic information is to be found. Spectrograms cannot be read because the eye cannot cope with the code-like complexities of the signal. The fact that we cannot learn to read spectrograms means that we cannot, by training alone, develop an appropriate decoder and make it work in cooperation with the eye [p. 319].

One might argue that VZ has developed a special decoder for visible speech. But this is not the case. According to Liberman et al., the function of the special decoder is to cause different sounds to be perceived as the same phoneme. They argue (1968) that the development of a special encoder for vision (through practice reading speech spectrograms) would cause visual patterns to *look* alike:

> But will training in reading spectrograms ever cause the different patterns to look alike? Those of us who have been studying speech spectrograms these many years would testify, I think that training will not produce that happy result. The patterns (for the same phoneme) that looked very different to me when I first saw a spectrogram twenty years ago look just as different today. We believe that no amount of training will cause an appropriate decoder to develop for visual input [p. 131].

We are in complete agreement. No amount of training is likely to cause the visual system to process speech in the same way as the auditory system. We do not suggest that the process by which VZ reads speech spectrograms mimics the normal process of speech perception. But the implication is that, if the eye can perceive speech without the working of a special decoder, perhaps the ear can too. This suggestion is supported by the fact that the visual features that VZ uses to identify phonemes are *specifiable*, and the knowledge about contextual variation is *explicit*. In explaining VZ's performance, we do not need to postulate an abstract grammar that mediates the conversion from sound to phoneme.

Implication for Machine Recognition of Speech

The design philosophy of most speech recognition (or understanding) systems in the past decade has been based on the belief that the acoustic signal does not provide sufficient information to identify the linguistic content of an utterance. In fact, the change in terminology from "speech recognition" to "speech understanding" reflects a departure from the view that speech can actually be "recognized" by machine, and the acceptance of the view that prosodic, syntactic, semantic and pragmatic knowledge must be used to recognize an utterance (Reddy, 1976).

In contrast, our research demonstrates that the acoustic signal is the primary information-bearer. The results of our spectrogram-reading experiment suggest that there exists a great deal more phonetic information in the speech signal than was previously believed, and that such information is often explicit and can be captured by rules.

It is obvious that improving the segmentation and labeling performance of current speech recognition systems will increase the accuracy and speed of system performance. Our results suggest that efforts at improving the "front end" of current speech understanding systems are probably worthwhile. The presently published labeling performance of the C-MU, BBN and IBM systems range from 49% to 67% first-choice accuracy (Klatt, 1977) over a somewhat larger set of labels than those used by VZ. VZ's performance of high labeling accuracy and significantly better rank-order statistics (and fewer alternatives) suggests that search-time can be significantly reduced and that substantially lower error rates can be achieved in present speech understanding systems.

While the most significant implication of our work for the design of speech understanding systems is the fact that front-end performance can in principle be improved to high levels of accuracy, there are a number of other implications. First, it is interesting to note that VZ's performance is based on the recognition of acoustic patterns that are apparently speaker-independent and are not degraded by the use of a spectrographic representation. A spectrogram-like representation of the speech signal would thus appear to be adequate, at least for high-quality speech systems. Second, our data indicate that VZ does not make use of suprasegmental cues, except for occasional references to duration and speech rate. (This is no doubt due to the fact that such information is not readily extracted from a normal spectrogram.) Finding effective techniques for using suprasegmental information might lead to additional improvement in performance. Third, our research addresses one of the questions often raised by researchers in speech recognition: What is the most appropriate basic unit for recognition? There have been serious attempts to use the transeme (Tappert, Dixon, & Rabinowitz, 1973) and the syllable (Fujimura, 1974; Mermelstein, 1975; Smith, 1977) as the basic unit of representation. In our experiment, VZ appears to use a mixture of phonemes, diphones, and sub-phonemic units. While this does not invalidate the use of the syllable as a unit, it seems to suggest that greater flexibility in the choice of units may be beneficial.

Implications for Training the Speech and Hearing Impaired

The fact that acoustic features for phonemes are identifiable in a speech spectrogram has important implications for training the speech and hearing impaired. The present experiment has demonstrated a direct and perceptible relationship between what one says and what one sees on a spectrogram. It is therefore possible to learn the relationship between the articulatory movements used to produce a particular speech sound and the visual patterns observed on the spectrogram. With some explanation of the visual features to be attended, immediate feedback of spectrographic information should be an effective way to teach correct production of any phoneme in any environment.

A spectrographic display that presents speech on a videoscreen as it is spoken has recently been developed, and is now commercially available. Stewart, Larkin, and Houde (1976) have described this device and report the results of some preliminary attempts to use the real-time sound spectrogram for speech training of the deaf. Two evaluation studies have been performed. In one study, an adult male deaf student tried to produce the front vowels [i] and [ɪ] in one syllable words. Using a split screen, a spectrogram of the target vowel was displayed on the top of the screen, and the student tried to match the target by comparing the spectrographic representation of his own utterance (shown on the bottom of the screen) to this display. In three sessions of about one half hour each, the student improved from "one successful production in twenty attempts at the beginning of training to more than half at the end of the third session [p. 593]." It is interesting that, in the final sessions, the student worked independently, without a teacher in attendance.

In a second study using the real-time spectrograph, performed by Maki (reported in Stewart et al., 1976), three students received training in a single phoneme, either [b], [z], or [i], during three one-hour sessions.

"Two of the three students showed considerable improvement in the production of the target phoneme and the third (/b/) showed essentially no improvement [p. 593]."

Based on our experiences with VZ, we are very enthusiastic about the potential for using the real-time speech spectrograph for training the deaf to speak. We expect that even the profoundly deaf can eventually be taught to speak. But truly intelligible speech by the deaf will require a great deal of training, patience, and perseverance by teachers and students. VZ spent over 2,000 hours learning to read speech spectrograms. Although the skill can certainly be taught much more quickly, we must still remember that children require many months (perhaps years) of practice before their speech can be understood. We cannot expect better from the deaf, even with the best training aids. It is therefore essential that evaluation of the real-time speech spectrograph involve extensive training over a long period of time.

A question that immediately comes to mind is whether spectrogram reading can be performed in real time, the question originally asked in the Bell Laboratories study 30 years ago. We can only speculate, but our initial feeling is that spectrogram reading in real time (i.e., in synchrony with the speech input) *is* possible. Spectrogram reading in real time may in fact prove to be too difficult to learn or require too much practice to be practical. But we do not doubt that the skill might be attainable. After all, by the time a child is five, when he has just about mastered the phonological system of his language, he has been exposed to at least 5,000 hours of speech. With that much training with an improved version of a direct translator, on-line spectrogram reading may be learnable.

However, even if one could teach a hearing-impaired person to read speech spectrograms in synchrony with the incoming speech, and even if a portable display could be developed, it would be impractical. In order to perceive the incoming speech, the individual would have to attend visually, so speech would be traded for sight. But even with these problems in mind, we prefer to take an optimistic view about the possibility of real-time reception of visible speech; after all, not long ago it was thought that no amount of training would allow one to identify the phonetic content of a speech spectrogram.

ACKNOWLEDGMENTS

The research reported in this paper has been supported in part by National Institute of Mental Health Grant MH-07722-15 to the Department of Psychology at Carnegie-Mellon University. We would like to acknowledge the critical comments offered by Dr. Jared Wolf of Bolt, Beranek and Newman, Inc., who read several versions of the manuscript.

REFERENCES

Carterette, E. C., & Jones, M. H. *Informal speech: Phonemic and alphabetic texts with statistical analysis.* Berkeley: Univeristy of California Press, 1974.

Cole, R. A. Invariant features and feature detectors: Some developmental implications. In S. J. Segalowitz & F. A. Gruber (Eds.), *Language development and neurological theory.* New York: Academic, 1977.

Cole, R. A., & Scott, B. Towards a theory of speech perception. *Psychological Review,* 1974, *81,* 348–374.

Egan, J. Articulation testing methods, II. Office of Scientific Research and Development, Report No. 3802, 1944.

Fant, G. *Acoustic theory of speech production.* The Hague: Mouton, 1960.

Fant, G. Descriptive analysis of the acoustic aspects of speech. *Logos,* 1962, *5,* 3–17.

Fant, G. Analysis and synthesis of speech processes. In B. Malmberg (Ed.), *Manual of phonetics.* Amsterdam: North-Holland, 1968.

Fletcher, H. *Speech and hearing in communication.* New York: Van Nostrand, 1953.

Fujimura, O. Syllable as a unit of speech recognition. *Proceedings of the IEEE Symposium on Speech Recognition,* 1974, 148–153.

Garnes, S., & Bond, Z. S. The influence of semantics on speech perception. *Journal of the Acoustical Society of America,* 1977, *61,* 565(A).

Jakobson, R., Fant, G., & Halle, M. *Preliminaries to speech analysis.* Cambridge, MA: MIT Press, 1963.

Klatt, D. H. Review of the ARPA speech understanding project. *Journal of the Acoustical Society of America,* 1977, *62,* 1345–1366.

Klatt, D. H., & Stevens, K. N. On the automatic recognition of continuous speech: Implications from a spectrogram-reading experiment. *IEEE Transactions on Audio and Electroacoustics,* 1973, *AU-21,* 210–217.

Koenig, W., Dunn, H. K., & Lacey, L. Y. The sound spectrograph. *Journal of the Acoustical Society of America,* 1946, *18,* 19–49.

Liberman, A. M. The grammars of speech and language. *Cognitive-Psychology,* 1970, *1,* 301–323.

Liberman, A. M., Cooper, F. S., Shankweiler, D. P., & Studdert-Kennedy, M. Perception of the speech code. *Psychological Review,* 1967, *74,* 431–461.

Liberman, A. M., Cooper, F. S., Shankweiler, D. P., & Studdert-Kennedy, M. Why are speech spectrograms hard to read? *American Annals of the Deaf,* 1968, *113,* 127–133.

Lindblom, B. E. F., & Svensson, S. G. Interaction between segmental and nonsegmental factors in speech recognition. *IEEE Transactions on Audio and Electroacoustics,* 1973, *AU-21,* 536–545.

Mermelstein, P. Automatic segmentation of speech into syllabic units. *Journal of the Acoustical Society of America,* 1975, *58,* 880–883.

Miller, G. A. The perception of speech. In M. Halle (Ed.), *For Roman Jakobson, Essays on the occasion of his sixtieth birthday.* The Hague: Mouton, 1956.

Miller, G. A., & Isard, S. Some perceptual consequences of linguistic roles. *Journal of Verbal Learning and Verbal Behavior,* 1963, *2,* 217–228.

Potter, R., Kopp, G., & Green, H. *Visible speech.* New York: Van Nostrand, 1947.

Reddy, D. R. Speech recognition by machine: A review. *Proceedings of the IEEE,* 1976, *64,* 501–531.

Schubert, E. D., & Parker, G. P. Addition to Cherry's findings on switching speech between the two ears. *Journal of the Acoustical Society of America,* 1955, *27,* 792–794.

Smith, A. R. *Word hypothesization for large-vocabulary speech understanding systems.* Unpublished doctoral dissertation, Carnegie-Mellon University, Pittsburgh, 1977.

Solzhenitsyn, A. I. *The First Circle*. Translated from the Russian by T. P. Whitney. New York: Harper & Row, 1968.

Stevens, K. N., & Blumstein, S. E. Onset spectra as cues for consonantal place of articulation. *Journal of the Acoustical Society of America*, 1977, *61*, 548(A).

Stevens, K. N., & House, A. S. An acoustical theory of vowel production and some of its implications. *Journal of Speech and Hearing Research*, 1961, *4*, 303–320.

Stewart, L. G., Larkin, W. D., & Houde, R. A. A real-time sound spectrograph with implications for speech training for the deaf. *IEEE International Conference on Acoustics, Speech and Signal Processing*. New York: Institute of Electrical and Electronic Engineers, 1976.

Svensson, S. G. Prosody and grammar in speech perception. *Monographs from the Institute of Linguistics*, University of Stockholm (MILOS), 1974, *2*.

Tappert, C. C., Dixon, W. R., & Rabinowitz, A. S. Application of sequential decoding for converting phonetic to graphic representation in automatic recognition of continuous speech (ARCS). *IEEE Transactions on Audio and Electroacoustics*, 1973, *AU-21*, 225–228.

Warren, R. M. Perceptual restoration of missing speech sounds. *Science*, 1970, *167*, 393–395.

Zue, V. W. *Acoustic characteristics of stop consonants: A controlled study*. Unpublished doctoral dissertation, Massachusetts Institute of Technology, 1976.

2 Speech as Patterns in Time

Brian L. Scott
Scott Instruments
Denton, Texas

In this chapter, I discuss an approach to speech perception borrowing much from the Gestalt psychologists. The approach stresses the importance of the *relations* among acoustic components of the speech signal as a source of information for perception. It emphasizes viewing the speech signal as integrated acoustic patterns in time rather than as the segregated frequency patterns in space seen in speech spectrograms. It is the oscilloscope, not the spectrograph, which provides the analog most appropriate for this approach.

The spectrograph is a time-honored tool for the study of speech perception. However, it cannot be denied that there are many differences between a spectrogram and the neural output of a cochlea. For example, the output of the cochlea is linear up to about 1000 Hz and logarithmic above that, whereas the spectrograph is either logarithmic or linear. The role of temporal processing by the ear cannot be demonstrated by a spectrogram. This is not a trivial matter given that the fundamental frequency and first formant information of speech are coded, at least to some extent, by temporal information. These inadequacies do not represent the basic problem with the spectrograph. The primary problem, I believe, is that the almost exclusive use of the spectrograph for speech analysis has confined our concept of the speech signal to a spatio-temporal display which is quite unlike the signal as it exists in space. The acoustic signal does have spatial properties, but they are unrelated to the spatial separation of frequencies manifested in the spectrogram. The acoustic signal is a frequency-integrated, complex waveform whose actual spatial properties are dictated by radiation and reflection, not by frequency. If we could see the acoustic world we live in, it would not look like a spectrogram.

We are dealing with a problem of perception. Specifically, how does the auditory system selectively extract and relate aspects of its environment? The study of the principles of perceptual organization—that is, the why and how of the relational aspects of perception—was the approach taken by the Gestalt psychologists toward understanding the complexities of perception. Figure 2.1 illustrates the kind of phenomenon they studied. One perceives this figure to be a diamond even though its components are dots, circles, and squares. It is of course the relations among the dots, circles, and squares that give rise to this percept. Gestalt psychologists derived their organizational principles by relating the physical structure of such stimuli to an individual's description of his percept. I share the Gestalt psychologists' emphasis on "physical reality": the way that objects exist in space and time. Any transformation of Fig. 2.1, such as that shown in Fig. 2.2, will not provide the same relational qualities which give rise to the diamond percept. We can more easily count the dots, circles, and squares in Fig. 2.2 than in Fig. 2.1; however, we shall never understand why subjects would persist in describing Fig. 2.1 as a diamond by studying Fig. 2.2.

The point illustrated in Figs. 2.1 and 2.2 applies to the use of the speech spectrograph. The spectrogram is analogous to Fig. 2.2, in that the frequency components of the speech waveform are laid out in space by the

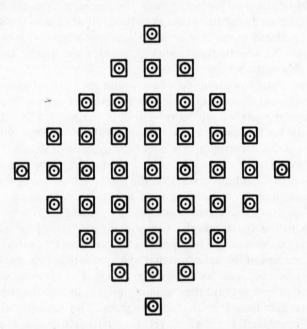

FIG. 2.1.   Visual pattern of the type studied by the Gestalt psychologists.

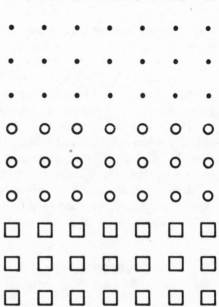

FIG. 2.2.   Reorganization by size
of elements comprising Fig. 2.1.

spectrograph for scientific analysis. Through this reorganization, however, certain relations among components are obscured: relations which
may be important for perception. This hypothesis—that *relations* among
the physical attributes of the speech waveform are important for
perception—is based on the premise that the auditory system has evolved
to accurately represent internally the external acoustic environment. Our
external acoustic environment consists of soundwaves emanating from
various points in space. The soundwaves are seldom pure tones, but are
almost always complex waveforms consisting of combinations of many
sinusoids. We perceive these complex waveforms *as* complex
waveforms; that is, we perceive the Gestalt resulting from the specific
combination of a set of discrete frequency components. To return to our
analogy, we not only perceive the dots, circles, and squares in Fig. 2.1,
we also perceive the relations among them.

   Although I am arguing that the *percept* of an acoustic event bears a
greater similarity to the waveform than to the spectrum, I am not denying
the spectrum-analyzing function of the inner ear. Indeed, it is the
spectrum-analyzing capacity which enables us to perceive signals of much
higher frequency than would be possible by directly driving our relatively
slow neurons. However, the perceptual system must re-integrate the
spectral components derived from cochlear analysis in order to retain an
accurate internal representation of the acoustic signal. Reliance on the
speech spectrograph as the source of information about the speech signal

has restricted us to observing merely an analog of the neural output of the cochlea and has caused us to miss the hypothesized higher order re-integration stage of perceptual analysis. To put it more succinctly, we sould be looking at the speech waveform *in addition to* the spectrogram. The spectrogram provides the components of the signal and the waveform shows how those components are integrated.

In the following paragraphs we examine the speech waveform for kinds of information not readily observable from the spectrogram and determine how these kinds of information can be applied to practical problems in speech science. Specifically, this theory has been applied to the development of a tactile speech reception aid for the deaf, to the problem of vowel-sound categorization, and to the problem of developing a real-time speaker-independent pitch extractor.

DEVELOPMENT OF A TACTILE AID TO SPEECH RECEPTION

A tactile aid to speech reception is a device which presents information about the speech signal to the observer through the skin. Our approach toward developing a tactile aid began with a study of the waveform envelope of speech (Cole & Scott, 1974). In brief, the hypothesized perceptual role of the waveform envelope is to provide a single, slowly varying reference for the many rapid spectral changes in speech. This slowly varying reference provides the perceptual system with a means of both integrating information over relatively long periods of time (across syllables) and maintaining the temporal order of the speech elements.

This concept has direct implications for the use of vocoder-type aids for the conveyance of tactile speech cues. Vocoder-type aids separate spectral information into spatially arrayed areas on the skin. If the perceptual system requires a single time-envelope for the integration of spectral information, then subjects using a vocoder-type aid should encounter difficulties ordering spectral information in time, since the vocoder-type aid will have as many separate time-envelopes as it has spectral channels.

We can demonstrate the importance of the envelope as an integrator by comparing a single-unit vibrator, which provides an intact speech envelope, with a vocoder-type aid, which does not. This was done in a study by Scott (1974), in which discriminability of speech sounds with each device was compared using a same–different task. The single-unit vibrator and a five-channel vocoder-type aid were compared on same–different tasks with both syllable-length and sentence-length materials. The hypothesis was that the vocoder aid would help subjects discriminate syllables better, while the single-unit vibrator would produce better performance on sentences. The data supported the hypothesis. The subjects performed better when responding "same" or "different" to pairs of syllables when using the five-channel vocoder aid but demonstrated better performance responding "same" or "different" to sentence pairs when using the single-unit vibrator. The conclusion was that a tactile aid to speech reception should retain an integrated amplitude envelope as part of the display. This led to a series of experiments in which the goal was to develop an aid which conveyed as much spectral information to the skin as possible without sacrificing the waveform envelope.

The last of three generations of the aid are discussed in this chapter. (For a complete summary of this work see Scott & DeFilippo, unpublished.) The aid is shown schematically in Fig. 2.3. The device divides the signal into three spectral channels: (1) a high-pass channel at 8 kHz; (2) a mid-frequency channel at 2.4 kHz; and (3) a low-frequency channel from 250 Hz to 900 Hz. A noise source (bandpass-filtered at 250 Hz) is peak-clipped, then modulated by the amplitude envelope of the high-pass channel and fed to a single vibrator. The same noise source is also amplitude-modulated by the envelope from the mid-frequency channel and fed to two additional vibrators. The vibrator conveying the high-frequency channel is placed between these vibrators. Finally, the low-frequency channel serves to detect the first formant of vowel sounds and convert it to a low frequency signal (15–200 Hz) which the skin can appreciate

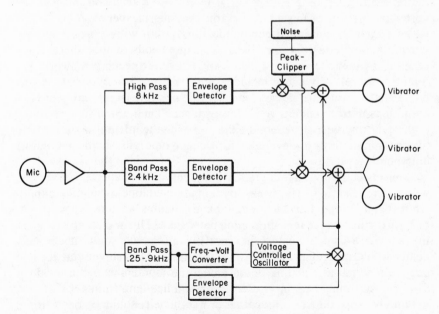

FIG. 2.3.   Schematic of tactile aid to speech reception.

(Rothenberg, Verrillo, Zahorian, Brachman, & Bolanowski, 1977). The low-frequency first formant information is fed to all three vibrators which are secured in a rubber mold. The center vibrator serves as a transducer for the high-frequency channel as well as the low-frequency vowel channel. The vibrators on either side carry both mid-frequency and vowel information.

The sensations produced by the device are: (1) periodic, low-frequency vibrations spread over a large surface; (2) aperiodic, high-frequency stimulation (high frequency for the vibro-tactile sense) spread over a large surface; and (3) aperiodic, high-frequency stimulation over a small surface area (the center vibrator). The transducers are placed on the abdomen just below the rib cage. Thus, a high frequency fricative, such as /s/, is conveyed as a high-frequency, aperiodic sensation at the center of the chest. A fricative with lower frequency, such as /sh/, is felt as an aperiodic sensation spread over a larger area. Vowels are felt as a periodic signal spread over a large area. Since all signals are felt in the center of the chest, the display preserves the time-integrated envelope of the original speech signal. The speech waveform emanates from a single point in space, the speaker, and is perceived through the auditory system as such. The user of the aid also perceives the speech sound as coming from a single point.

The aid was evaluated using ongoing speech. The procedure, termed the "tracking procedure" (DeFilippo & Scott, 1978), involves an individual reading ongoing text material to a "receiver" who must repeat verbatim what has been said. Any errors that the receiver makes may only be corrected by continued communication between the speaker and receiver. Ten-minute trials are used. The number of words successfully repeated by the receiver are counted and converted to a mean "words per minute" score. This score includes *only* the number of words of *text* completed. Errors are not included in this score, nor are any words or definitions used to elicit a verbatim response. Thus, the faster and more accurately the receiver responds, the higher the words per minute score. Six ten-minute trials are averaged for a single one-hour words per minute data point.

Subjects consisted of four graduate students at Washington University, with normal hearing, who were functionally deafened during the experiment. None had had any lipreading experience prior to the experiment. Subjects worked in teams alternating between reader and receiver. When the subject was serving as the receiver he or she was functionally deafened with earplugs and noise. In addition, the receiver was located outside a sound-attenuating booth facing the reader through a window. The receiver could see the reader's face and lips at all times.

Our goal was to discover whether or not the aid could help one learn to lipread. We therefore used two main conditions: (1) lipreading alone, and

(2) lipreading with the tactile aid. Half the subjects began lipreading alone for four hours, then switched to aided lipreading for four more hours. The other half began in the aided condition and switched to the unaided condition. Results are shown in Fig. 2.4. The left panel shows the results for the subjects who began lipreading alone, then switched to aided lipreading. The slopes of the lines defined by the first four data points for subjects 1 and 2 are 3.94 and .16 respectively. These slopes define the learning curves for subjects 1 and 2 in the lipreading alone condition. Hours 5 through 8 are data points collected while the subjects were using the aid. The slopes of these lines are 8.35 and 4.07 for subjects 1 and 2 respectively. Thus, the slope of the learning curve for subject 1 increased by a factor of 2 when the aid was turned on and the slope of the learning curve for subject 2 was increased by a factor of 25 when the aid was turned on. In order to relate lipreading scores to normal hearing performance, consider that normal hearing persons were able to "track" the text that was used at a little over 100 words per minute (DeFilippo & Scott, 1978). Thus, subject 1 is lipreading (using the aid) at over half the rate of a normal hearing person. Subject 2 is performing at about a third the rate.

Subjects 3 and 4 began the experiment in the aided condition, then switched to unaided. The slopes from these data points are 9.26 and 1.48 for subjects 3 and 4 respectively in the aided condition. The slopes in the unaided condition are 1.59 and 2.66, respectively. Thus, the slope of the

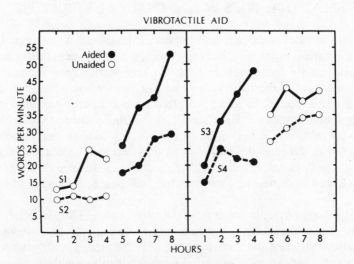

FIG. 2.4.   Results from tactile aid research. Left panel shows data from subjects who lipread without the aid for four hours, then switched to aided lipreading. Right panel shows data from subjects doing aided lipreading followed by lipreading alone.

learning curve is about six times as steep for subject 3 when the aid is on while subject 4 demonstrated a steeper slope in the unaided condition.

For three of the four subjects there was a marked improvement in performance using the aid. The fourth subject complained of nausea when using the aid, which possibly explains her poor performance. This should have been remedied by changing the location of the transducers. In the present context these scores are significant, not because of the overall improvement in performance when using the aid, but because of the rate of improvement. These subjects had had *no* previous experience or training with the aid, yet three of the four benefited immediately from its use. An explanation for the immediate improvement is that subjects perceive the signal presented to the skin to be similar to that presented to the ear. Subjects therefore do not have to learn a special code to benefit from the tactile speech.

In this section we have considered some of the results from a project on the development of a tactile aid for speech reception. The aid serves as an illustration of how a temporally based theory of speech perception can be applied. The major premise behind the design of the aid has been that speech is perceived as a temporal pattern, not as a spatial or spatiotemporal pattern. Therefore, the signal presented to the skin is a facsimile of the speech waveform, not the speech spectrum.

RELATIONAL CUES IN TEMPORAL FINE-STRUCTURE

In the last section, the integrative aspect of the theory was stressed. The major theoretical point was that the speech signal is processed as a signal integrated across frequency in time. In this section, we focus on the relational aspect of the theory. In brief, the theory holds that the speech signal is being treated by the perceptual system as an integrated signal; therefore, important cues should exist as relations between spectral components. Again, this is very much a Gestalt approach to perception. Returning to Fig. 2.1, it is the *relations* among the circles, dots, and squares that give rise to perceiving the figure as a diamond. In speech, the components we are concerned with are spectral and their relations are of importance.

Relevant experiments were published by Scott (1976). In brief, there were five experiments on vowel perception dealing with the cue value of the relation between the first formant (F1) frequency and fundamental frequency (F_o) of a vowel sound. Figure 2.5 shows single fundamental frequency periods taken from seven synthetic vowels. The vowels represent points along a continuum from /i/ to /ɪ/. The formant values and fundamental frequency for the /i/ and /ɪ/ endpoints were taken from Peter-

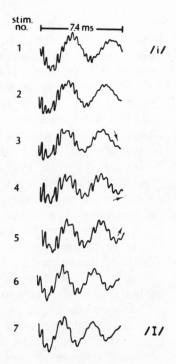

FIG. 2.5. Single pitch periods from a synthesized seven-vowel series from /i/ to /ɪ/.

son and Barney (1952). Thus, the first vowel sound, /i/, has a first formant center frequency of 270 Hz and a second formant center frequency of 2290 Hz. The final vowel sound, /ɪ/, has a first formant value of 390 Hz and a second formant value of 1990 Hz. The formant values for the five sounds between the endpoints are linearly related. The fundamental frequency for all seven vowels was 135 Hz; therefore, the fundamental frequency period for all vowels was 7.4 msec. As we descend the series, note the change in the number of cycles of the first formant within the 7.4 msec fundamental frequency period. This change is manifested in the waveform's slope at the end of the period. Note that this occurs at stimulus number four; stimuli 1–3 all end with a negative slope and stimuli 5–7 with a positive slope. This difference is viewed as an acoustic "pattern" change inherent in the relation between the first formant and the fundamental frequency. The argument is that perceptual judgments will be based on a change in the slope of the waveform at the end of each pitch period.

Is there reason to believe that such a change is too subtle for the ear to detect? Research by Greenberg, Smith, Marsh, and Brown (1978) would suggest not. These authors examined the Frequency Following Response (FFR) in humans to vowel sounds. The FFR is a neurogenic potential representing the phase-locked activity of a population of auditory neurons. Results showed that first formant information and fundamental frequency can be seen in the temporal patterns of neural firings recorded from the scalp. This result indicates that information about the waveform temporal fine-structure is preserved at levels at least as high as the inferior colliculus. For the vowel waveforms shown in Fig. 2.5, this could mean that the change in slope of the waveform elicits an additional firing every pitch period for the entire duration of the vowel. The subtle waveform change at stimulus 4 could therefore mean a 50% increase in the total number of neural firings to the first formant (a change from two cycles of F1 per period to three cycles).

A subtle relationship of this kind cannot be seen on a speech spectrogram since the spectral components are separated. A relational pattern of this type can only be viewed from the waveform. If the perceptual system views the speech signal as a waveform rather than as a spectrum, the kind of pattern change like that found at stimulus 4 in Fig. 2.5 may have perceptual significance.

Figure 2.6 shows how these seven vowel sounds were perceived. The top of the figure shows the formant structures of the seven vowels and the bottom shows the percent of /i/ responses made by four subjects listening to a randomized series of these vowel sounds. The first three sounds were perceived as /i/ and the last three as /ɪ/. The fourth sound was ambiguous. Obviously these results are far from conclusive, but note that there is *nothing* in the spectral continuum shown at the top of this figure to explain

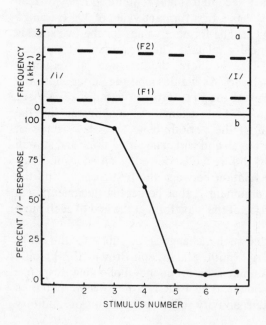

FIG. 2.6. Panel (a) shows formant center frequency values for each of the seven stimuli designated by "stimulus number." Panel (b) shows the perceptual boundary for this series in terms of percent of /i/ responses.

the abrupt change in perception from /i/ to /ɪ/. As was seen in Fig. 2.5, there *is* such a change in the waveform pattern.

The fact that the pattern change shown in Fig. 2.5 is a function of the relation between the first formant and the fundamental frequency means that altering either F1 or F_0 will cause the pattern to vary. If the pattern change is a perceptual cue for indicating a shift in phonetic category, then altering the fundamental frequency should also have an effect on phonetic boundaries. The following experiment was done to illustrate the effect of F_0 on the phoneme boundary between /i/ and /ɪ/.

Figure 2.7 shows single fundamental frequency periods from three vowel series. The formant frequency steps from stimulus 1 to 7 were equal for all three series. The endpoint values were again taken from Peterson and Barney (1952), and the steps between the endpoints were linear. The fundamental frequency was the only acoustic factor altered from one series to the next. The choice of F_0 was made to provide an abrupt change in the number of cycles of F1 per fundamental period. In series 1, the change occurs between stimulus 3 and 4. The fundamental increases from stimulus 1 to 3 to compensate for the increase in the first formant. At stimulus 4 the F_0 is dropped in order to vary the number of cycles of F1 per period from three to four. After stimulus 4, the F_0 is increased to compensate for further increases in F1. In series 2, the increase from three cycles of F1 per fundamental period to four cycles occurs between

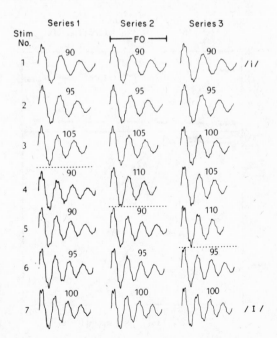

FIG. 2.7. Single pitch periods from three seven-vowel series. Stimuli were chosen for the three series to give a waveform change from three cycles of F1 per pitch period to four cycles at different points along the seven-step series.

stimuli 4 and 5. Finally, in series three, the pattern change occurs between stimuli 5 and 6. If the relational pattern between F1 and F_0 does have an effect on phonetic categorization, then the phoneme boundaries for these series should follow the variations in pattern illustrated in Fig. 2.7.

Figure 2.8 shows the results of the identification tests run on these three series. Note that boundary shifts occur at the predicted points, that is, where the patterns changed from three cycles of F1 per fundamental period to four cycles of F1 per fundamental period.

This effect was not unlimited, and it could only be shown to affect stimuli 4 and 5. That is, stimuli 4 and 5 appeared to be the only ambiguous stimuli along these continua and were therefore the only ones which could belong to either phoneme category. The tentative conclusion formulated from these data was that a clearly articulated vowel is probably perceived in terms of its formant frequency ratios, but given an ambiguous vowel lying between vowel categories, the perceptual system will search for some "pattern change" to indicate that the speaker intended a phonetic change. This hypothesis is of obvious interest to anyone concerned with the "fuzziness" of the boundaries between vowel categories. The ambiguity may well be accounted for by a continuous comparison of vowels in running speech with surrounding vowels. It is well known that target formant values are not always reached in running speech. This research indicates that a missed target value may be compensated for by adjusting

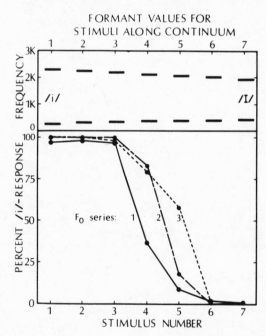

FIG. 2.8. Data showing the perceptual boundary shift as a result of the fundamental frequency selection for each series shown in Fig. 2.7.

the fundamental frequency to assure an appropriate pattern change in the waveform.

The pattern change hypothesis was further tested in two speech synthesis experiments. The object in these experiments was to produce maximally ambiguous vowels in the spectral domain and to attempt to disambiguate them in the temporal domain. Figure 2.9 illustrates the stimuli. Recall from the previous experiment that changing the first formant in the /i/ to /ɪ/ series produced an increase in the number of cycles of F1 per fundamental period. In this figure we can see how the number of cycles of F1 per fundamental period can be varied without affecting formant center frequency. The four stimuli shown all consist of a two-tone complex (500

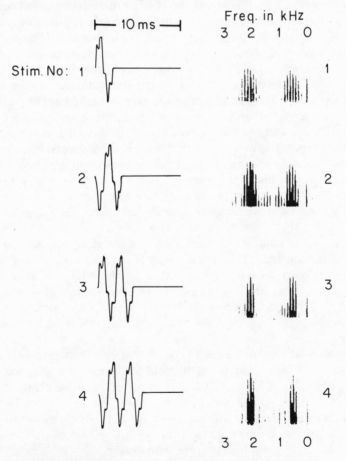

FIG. 2.9.   Single pitch period waveforms and spectral sections of the four pseudo-vowels. Descending the figure, the waveforms increase in the number of cycles per period and the formant bandwidths narrow.

and 2200 Hz) gated on and off at a repetition rate of 10 ms. The ten millisecond repetition rate gave all sounds a periodicity pitch of 100 Hz. The two tones produced formants at 2200 Hz and 500 Hz. The effect on the spectrum of changing the number of cycles per fundamental frequency period is shown on the right. Note that although the center frequencies are all identical, the bandwidths are different. The fewer cycles per period, the broader the bandwidth. These sounds were not vowel sounds, but they were vowel-like in quality.

Initially, it was thought that these pseudo-vowel sounds should approximate the vowel series: /i/, /ɪ/, /æ/, /ɒ/. These four vowels have first formants which increase in the number of cycles per fundamental period, from /i/ to /æ/. In fact, this vowel series was precisely what was perceived by the author when first hearing the pseudo-vowels. Despite this, the first two experiments using these sounds failed to demonstrate the perceptual similarities between them and the real vowel series. These initial failures are of some interest. The pseudo-vowels were first presented to subjects as single, isolated vowels. Subjects responded randomly to the sounds; that is, even with a closed response set, subjects could not identify these sounds as specific vowels. In a second experiment, subjects were presented with pairs of the pseudo-vowels. With this kind of presentation, responses began to correlate with predictions. Subjects still could not agree that a given stimulus was a specific vowel-sound; however, they did agree on the ordering of the pseudo-vowels. If stimuli 1 and 2 were presented, subjects might respond /i/ and /ɪ/, or /ɪ/ and /ɛ/, or /ɛ/ and /æ/. They did not agree on which exact vowels were heard, but there was agreement on which vowel was the more front vowel.

In order to get subjects to identify a given vowel, all four sounds had to be presented together. This was done by presenting several sequences of the pseudo-vowels which subjects had to match to different sequences of real vowel sounds. Thus, a subject might have a series of stimuli in the order: 1, 2, 3, 4. A correct response would be to match this series with the real vowel series: /i/, /ɪ/, /ɛ/, /æ/. Subjects made the matches with 80% accuracy.

In the second synthesis experiment, two more parameters were added. They were: (1) the second formant could be turned on or off; and (2) the number of cycles of F1 per fundamental period could be changed within the sound. This allowed for more vowels to be modeled. The vowel sounds that were modeled are shown in Fig. 2.10. The waveforms on the left are individual periods taken from the first 80 ms of the designated vowels, while those on the right are individual periods obtained from the final 80 ms of the vowels. Note that for /ei/, the only obvious change is in the number of cycles of F1 from the onset to the offset of the vowel. There

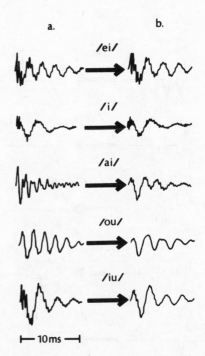

FIG. 2.10. Single pitch periods taken from the indicated vowels. Column (a) waveforms were taken from initial portions of the vowels and column (b) waveforms from final portions.

is no observable change in /i/. The diphthong /ai/ changes in number of cycles per period and shows a noticeable increase in the second formant frequency. The glide /ou/ changes in the number of cycles of F1. Finally, the glide /iu/ shows less second formant energy toward the end. Figure 2.11 shows how these changes were modeled. Note that for /ei/, there is a decrease in the number of cycles of F1 per period. The sound modeled after /i/ does not change at all. The sound modeled after /ai/ goes down in the number of cycles per period. In addition, the second formant is turned on. The vowel /ou/ decreases in the number of cycles per period, while /iu/ loses the second formant. The sounds were recorded in different random orders and played to subjects. Subjects heard these vowels to be /ei/, /i/, /ai/, /ou/, and /iu/.

These experiments suggest that an important cue for vowel categorization lies in the *relation* between the first formant frequency and the fundamental frequency, and that the relation is temporal, not spectral. This suggestion fits the premise of the present chapter in that it implies a degree of cycle-by-cycle waveform encoding rather than spectrum coding. In other words, the auditory system appears to be processing the speech signal as a complex waveform rather than as a frequency-separated spectrum.

a.   b.

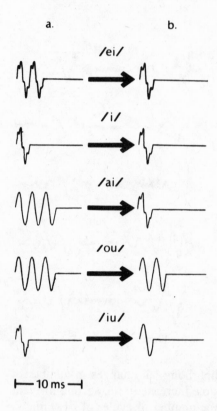

/ei/

/i/

/ai/

/ou/

/iu/

├── 10 ms ──┤

FIG. 2.11. Waveforms of pitch periods of synthetic vowels modeled after the normal vowels shown in Fig. 2.10.

DEVELOPMENT OF A PITCH METER

In the first section, we saw that a frequency-integrated speech stimulus is perceived more easily than a frequency-segregated one. In the second section, we saw that important relational information is available from a frequency-integrated signal. In both cases, the cues apparently used by perceivers to make linguistic judgements were obtained by relating different kinds of information in time. In this section, we are also concerned with the integrative aspect of the theory, but here we focus on the integration of *redundant* information in time. We are concerned with how the perceptual system might integrate the periodicities of several spectral channels to aid in the perception of pitch.

The design of the pitch detector described next is based on the fact that no matter how the speech signal is filtered, it will always have the periodicity of the fundamental frequency. Obviously enough, this is because all resonances of the vocal tract are excited by the same source function and therefore must have the same periodicity. Due to the more rapid decay times at high frequencies, these periodicities are actually more apparent in the high frequencies than in the low frequencies.

A premise here is that the common periodicities seen across spectral channels in response to a vowel sound are reflected in neural responses. This is not unreasonable considering that the amplitudes of the signals across the basilar membrane will be greatest at the beginning of each fundamental period. If this assumption is correct, it would seem likely that the perceptual system would take advantage of this redundancy about the pitch of the sound. In fact, Smith, Marsh, Greenberg, and Brown (1978) found that they could observe the "missing fundamental" from the Frequency Following Response in humans. Their results provide considerable evidence in support of the above view.

An analog hardware pitch meter was constructed using the above principles (Scott, 1978). Figure 2.12 shows a schematic of the device. The signal is first amplified, then fed to eight bandpass filters. The center frequencies for the bandpass filters are spaced equidistantly on a log scale, the lowest center frequency being 550 Hz and the highest being 3.5 kHz. The eight filtered signals are amplified so that all eight channels are approximately equal in output amplitude. Each channel is passed through an envelope detector consisting of a full-wave rectifier and low-pass filter. The eight channels are then reduced to four by adding a low-frequency bandpass channel with a high-frequency bandpass channel. Channel 1 is added to 5, channel 2 to 6, channel 3 to 7, and channel 4 to 8. This is done

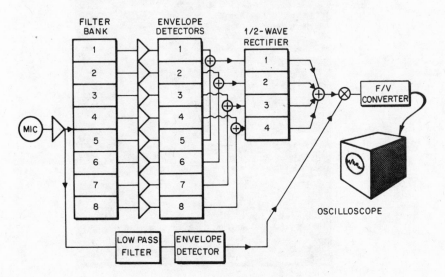

FIG. 2.12.   Schematic of pitch extractor.

to balance the four channels so that vowels with very different formant values are still represented in all four channels. After this, the four channels are sent through half wave rectifiers and low-pass filters for smoothing, then added together to produce a signal relatively free of vocal tract resonances. The signal is passed through a one-shot circuit which yields a one-millisecond by fifteen-volt pulse at every positive x-axis crossing. The pulses are then integrated by passing the signal through a 20 Hz low-pass filter, and the resultant DC voltage is displayed on the screen of an oscilloscope.

Preliminary observations with the device demonstrated a need for an additional high-pass filter on the front end. A high-pass filter at 1200 Hz

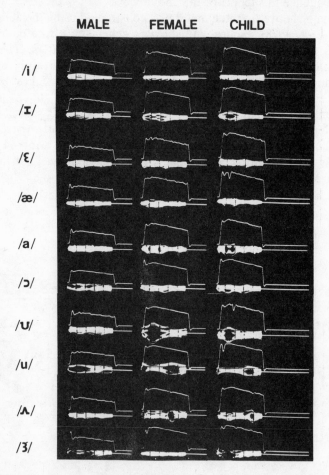

FIG. 2.13.   Response of pitch extractor to the synthesized vowels indicated on the left in male, female, and child voices.

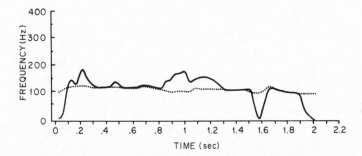

FIG. 2.14. Response of pitch extractor to male voice saying "we were away a year ago." Dotted line is pitch contour extracted pitch period by pitch period, and solid line is pitch contour extracted by machine.

was added just in front of the eight bandpass channels and the gains on the first three filters were adjusted to compensate. The initial evaluation was done with synthetic vowels with a known F_0 contour. Three sets of ten vowels approximately 450 msec long were used. One set was spoken by a male voice, another by a female voice, and the third by a child's voice. The F_0 contours were the same for all three sets of vowels but differed in absolute values. Maximum F_0 for the male voice was 135 Hz, for the female voice, 220 Hz, and for the child's voice, 265 Hz. Figure 2.13 shows the response of the device to these synthesized vowels. There are errors, but note that the device does an adequate job of tracking the pitch contours of these vowels.

A somewhat more stringent evaluation was performed on the device using natural continuous speech. The sentence "we were away a year ago" was recorded in a male voice, a female voice, and a child's voice. The output of the instrument in response to the male voice is shown in Fig. 2.14. The dotted line is the true pitch contour, as calculated by

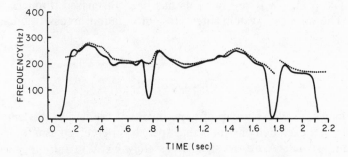

FIG. 2.15. Response of pitch extractor to female voice saying "we were away a year ago." Dotted line is pitch contour extracted pitch period by pitch period, and solid line is pitch contour extracted by machine.

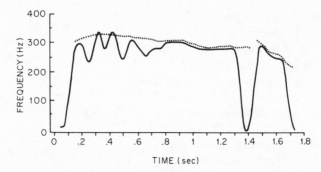

FIG. 2.16. Response of pitch extractor to child's voice saying "we were away a year ago." Dotted line is pitch contour extracted pitch period by pitch period, and solid line is pitch contour extracted by machine.

measuring each pitch period, while the solid line is the output of the pitch meter. Although there are several errors, particularly at the onset and near the middle, the fit appears to be fairly good. Figure 2.15 shows the output of the device when the female voice says the same sentence. Here, the fit is somewhat better, with only one major error occurring about one third of the way through the sentence. In Fig. 2.16, we see the response of the device to the child's voice. There are several errors at the onset of the utterance, followed by a good fit for the remainder of the sentence.

The device is obviously not yet perfected. However, the extraction of these three pitch contours did not require any adjustment of the pitch meter. In addition, these pitch contours were extracted in real time. We are currently involved in improving the circuitry to eliminate many of the errors the device makes and in improving the method of displaying pitch contours.

The intent in developing this pitch meter was not to show how a pitch meter should work, but to demonstrate how the auditory system might work. The principle is the same as has been discussed throughout this paper: The auditory system integrates information across frequency in time.

DISCUSSION

The somewhat diverse group of experiments presented in this paper are united in that each demonstrates that speech is perceived as a frequency-integrated signal. Acoustic signals, as they exist in our physical environment, are frequency-integrated, complex waveforms. The auditory system, like all perceptual systems, strives to maintain as accurate a representation of the physical environment as possible.

The speech signal is perceived through the auditory system as emanating from a single locus in space. This aspect of auditory processing was the basis for the design of the tactile aid. The success of the aid with ongoing speech implies the importance of viewing the speech signal as having a single temporal structure regardless of spectral content. The studies on vowel perception presented in this paper indicate the presence of *relational* cues resulting from the integration of spectral components. These relations can best be observed from the *waveforms* of speech. Finally, the pitch meter illustrates how the auditory system may be integrating *temporal* information across spectral channels for perceiving pitch (under certain conditions, such as over the telephone).

Together, these studies illustrate an *approach* to the study of speech perception. This "approach" differs from traditional "approaches" in only one respect: that the speech signal be viewed as an *integrated* signal in order that the importance of the relations between components might be better understood. Thus, the first step in searching for a given speech cue is to break the signal down into its components. Traditionally, this is as far as we go. We look at the components for the cues. However, the second step in this approach is to return to the *waveform* and search for cues that may exist as *relations* among the spectral components. This may well be how the auditory system works.

REFERENCES

Cole, R. A., & Scott, B. L. Toward a theory of speech perception. *Psychological Review,* 1974, *81,* 348–374.

DeFilippo, C. L., & Scott, B. L. A method for training and evaluating the reception of ongoing speech. *Journal of the Acoustical Society of America,* 1978, *63,* 1186–1192.

Greenberg, S., Smith, J. C., Marsh, J. T., & Brown, W. S. *Human frequency following response to synthetic vowels.* Paper presented at 95th meeting of the Acoustical Society of America, Providence, R.I., 1978.

Peterson, G. E., & Barney, H. L. Control methods used in the study of vowels. *Journal of the Acoustical Society of America,* 1952, *24,* 175–184.

Rothenberg, M., Verrillo, R. T., Zahorian, S. A., Brachman, M. L., & Bolanowski, S. J. Vibrotactile frequency for encoding a speech parameter. *Journal of the Acoustical Society of America,* 1977, *62,* 1003–1012.

Scott, B. L. *Speech perception: A theory and application.* Unpublished doctoral dissertation, University at Waterloo, 1974.

Scott, B. L. Temporal factors in vowel perception. *Journal of the Acoustical Society of America,* 1976, *60,* 1354–1365.

Scott, B. L. *Development of a real-time voice pitch extractor.* Paper presented at 95th meeting of the Acoustical Society of America, Providence, R.I., 1978.

Scott, B. L., & DeFilippo, C. L. *Development of a tactile aid for the reception of speech.* Manuscript submitted for publication.

Smith, J. C., Marsh, J. T., Greenberg, S., & Brown, W. S. Human auditory frequency following responses to a missing fundamental. *Science,* 1978, *201,* 639–641.

3 Speech as Patterns in the 3-Space of Time and Frequency

Campbell L. Searle

J. Zachary Jacobson

Barry P. Kimberley
Departments of Psychology and Electrical Engineering
Queen's University, Kingston, Ontario

INTRODUCTION

Understanding human auditory perception—how we perceive speech, music, tones, noise, etc.—has been a goal of scientists since before the time of Helmholtz. Advances in auditory research within the last ten years now permit us to model with some certainty the first processing step in the perception chain, and at the same time provide us with important constraints on any model of subsequent higher-level processing in the system.

The aforementioned auditory research concerns the nature of the filtering performed by the basilar membrane. After forty years of conflicting results, several quite different types of experiments attempting to measure the tuning characteristics of the peripheral auditory system now yield convergent results. Measurements of basilar membrane motion using the Mössbauer Effect (Johnstone & Boyle, 1967; Rhode, 1971) and measurement of tuning curves of primary auditory nerve fibres in the eighth nerve of cats (Kiang, Watanabe, & Clark, 1965; Kiang & Moxon, 1974) show frequency selectivity much sharper than previously assumed. Typical tuning curves for nerve fibers maximally sensitive in the 500 to 2000 Hz range are shown in Fig. 3.1a. Note that the 650 Hz curve matches in detail the masking data of Egan and Hake (1950), shown in Fig. 3.1b, if these data are replotted as in Fig. 3.1c to represent an assumed filter shape which could produce the masking. Kiang's tuning curves are also consistent with the critical band measurements summarized in Fig. 3.2 (from Tobias, 1970), both Johnstone's and Rhode's basilar membrane data (see Allen,

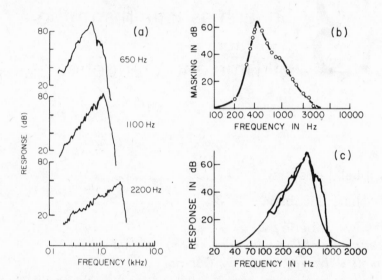

FIG. 3.1.   a. Response of three auditory nerve fibers (after Kiang & Moxon, 1974). b. Masking curve (Egan & Hake, 1950). c. Filter response deduced from (b) superimposed on auditory nerve fiber response from (a).

1977), and the just noticeable difference (JND) in frequency of 5 Hz at 1 kHz (Zwicker, Flottorp, & Stevens, 1957), if one assumes we use the steep skirt above resonance as a frequency discriminator.

The tuning curves shown in Fig. 3.1 are also consistent with the known monaural temporal resolution of the ear. Psychophysical experiments indicate that the ear cannot resolve pairs of pulses presented monaurally if the pulses are closer together than about 2 msec. Using the fact that, for a bandpass filter, the product of bandwidth in Hertz and rise time in seconds is approximately 0.7, we find that 2 msec temporal resolution corresponds to 350 Hz bandwidth, a value consistent with bandwidths´ measured on auditory nerve fibers for characteristic frequencies above 2 or 3 kHz. We conclude that a consistent explanation of masking experiments, critical band measurements, and monaural frequency and time resolution of the ear is that the basilar membrane and hair cells split up the incoming sound wave into a large number of separate channels. Above 400 Hz, these channels have a frequency resolution of roughly one third of an octave, and skirt response slopes of 20 dB per octave below resonance and 60 dB per octave above resonance.[1]

---

[1]There are several observed effects which complicate this simple view of neural response, such as two-tone inhibition (Sachs & Kiang, 1968), the broad-band tails of single nerve responses for high signal levels (Kiang & Moxon, 1974), and the increase in filter bandwidth with increasing signal level (Møller, 1977; Rhode, 1971). We hope to examine these effects at a later date.

The general agreement about the gross characteristics of the peripheral auditory system suggests that, if we want to build an automatic speech recognition system that models man, the first step in the recognition system should be some form of filtering with ⅓-octave frequency resolution. As noted in the preceding paragraph, bandwidth (or spectral resolution) is inversely related to rise-time. Hence, with a *constant bandwidth* system—such as that used in a speech spectrograph or linear predictive coding system—it is not possible to obtain both narrow bandwidth (good frequency resolution) and fast rise time. In a ⅓-octave filter system, bandwidth is by definition proportional to frequency, so it is possible to have good *spectral* resolution at low frequencies and good *temporal* resolution at high frequencies (as in the human ear). For speech, this is a very appropriate choice of parameters, because the low-frequency spectral resolution allows us to track separately the first and second formants with ease, while maintaining enough temporal resolution to measure the relatively slow low-frequency events such as voice onset time (VOT). The good temporal resolution at high frequencies allows us to pinpoint bursts of plosives to within a few milliseconds, without suffering unduly from the

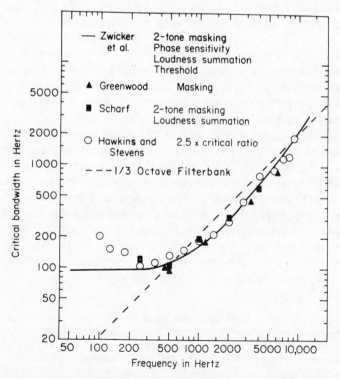

FIG. 3.2.   Critical bandwidth as a function of frequency (from Tobias, 1970).

loss of spectral resolution, because fine spectral detail in this range is much less important than at low frequencies. There is little point, for example, in analysing the high-frequency frication noise of /s/ and /f/ with a resolution of 40 Hz. This important issue of the trade-off between spectral resolution and temporal resolution will be discussed in detail in a later section.

We have indicated that certain physiological and psychophysical experiments impose strong constraints on the design of our acoustic analyser. In like manner (but unfortunately not as strongly), other psychophysical experiments constrain the design of the remainder of our speech recognition system. Specifically, experiments involving cutting and splicing of tape-recorded consonant–vowel (CV) pairs (Cole & Scott, 1974; Fischer-Jorgensen, 1972; Schatz, 1954) demonstrate a substantial invariance of initial stop consonants across vowel context, especially /b/, /d/, /p/, and /t/. This suggests that reasonable (but certainly not perfect) recognition scores should be possible by acoustic analysis alone, without the help of semantics, syntax, context, etc. Cole's experiments also indicate an appropriate time interval following the release of the stop burst over which the acoustic wave should be analysed for each stop consonant. Further, psychophysical experiments on identification of consonants under conditions of artificial variation of voice onset time (Cole and Cooper, 1977; Cooper, 1974; Eimas and Corbit, 1973; Miller, 1975) indicate that voice features are often perceived in a categorical fashion, suggesting that $1/3$-octave filters should be followed by feature detectors measuring such things as voice onset time, rate of change of filter outputs, etc. The outputs from the feature detectors should then pass to a discriminant analysis program for classification.[2]

The specifics of the system design which has evolved from the cited physiological and psychophysical experiments are discussed in the next section, along with details of the detector output displays and system performance in a phoneme discrimination task. In the third section, we present an approach to the design of acoustic analysers which is based not on auditory psychophysics as presented above, but on the characteristics of the speech signal. It is not surprising that the $1/3$-octave design turns out to be the best match to the constraints imposed by the speech signal, because evolutionary pressures must also certainly have forced the speech and hearing systems to be appropriately matched.

---

[2]Others who are following this approach to phoneme perception via auditory physiology and psychophysics are Chistovich, Grostrem, Kozhevnikov, Lesogor, Shupljakov, Taljasin, and Tjulkov (1974); Dolmazon, Bastet, and Shupljakov (1977); Klein, Plomp, and Pols (1970); Mariani and Lienard (1977); Miller, Engebretson, Spenner, and Cox (1977); Mundie (in Steer, 1975); Schouten and Pols (1977); and Zwicker, Terhardt, and Paulus (1979).

SYSTEM DESIGN AND PERFORMANCE

The phoneme recognition system which we have modeled on human audition is shown in block diagram form in Fig. 3.3. The filters in the model
have $1/3$-octave spacing of center frequencies, and $1/3$-octave bandwidth.
The three-pole-pair Butterworth response we chose matches the above-
resonance skirt of some of Kiang's curves quite closely, as shown in
Fig. 3.4. Unfortunately, the below-resonance skirt falls off too quickly, but
we feel that the overall response shape is a reasonable first approximation
to human tuning curves. These filters are followed by envelope detectors
which sense the energy in each filter, and thus represent the gross function of the hair cells. A logarithmic amplifier is included after the multi-
plex switch to match the logarithmic nature of perceived loudness.

Display

The response of each of the 16 filter-detector channels to the words *beer*
and *peer* are shown in Fig. 3.5. Several temporal details are immediately
visible. Note first the abrupt onsets at the bursts of both stops. The signal
amplitude rises 40 dB in less than 3 msec in many of the high-frequency
channels: an obvious cue for an initial stop consonant. Second, the VOT
is clearly visible, especially for /p/, from the delay of signal onset in the
low frequency channels following the burst, or from the delay in starting
of glottal pulses, which appear as roughly 100 Hz oscillations visible in the
high-frequency channels.

There is also a wealth of spectral information in Fig. 3.5, but unfortunately this particular method of presentation of the data does not permit
ready visual interpretation of this information, primarily because it is
difficult with this display to visually compare the relative amplitudes of
the various filter outputs at a given instant of time. To enhance the spectral information, we plot the *same* amplitude data as in Fig. 3.5, but in this
case with time as a parameter rather than frequency, thereby producing
the "running spectra" plots in Fig. 3.6.

Figure 3.6a shows the first 100 msec of the word *beer*. Each line in the
figure is a plot of the 16 filter output amplitudes as a function of frequency
over a particular 1.6 msec sampling interval. The first eight lines thus
represent a 13 msec interval of relative silence. Then an abrupt cliff looms
up as a result of the burst explosion (imagine the figure to be a three-
dimensional display of terrain, with amplitude plotted "up"). For the /b/,
the spectrum of this explosion is typically concentrated in the region
between 1.5 and 3 kHz. Note that around 2 kHz the signal amplitudes go
from threshold to roughly full amplitude of 60 dB within 2 lines, or 3 msec.
For /bi/, there is a 10 msec transition interval, during which the peak

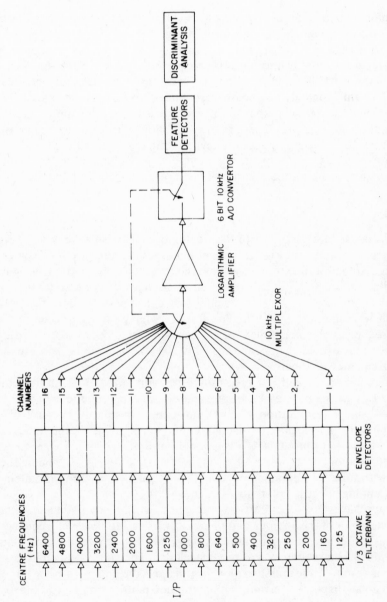

FIG. 3.3. Block diagram of analysis system.

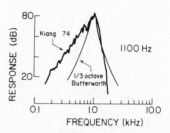

FIG. 3.4. Comparison of response of an auditory nerve fiber (Kiang & Moxon, 1974) with the response of a ⅓-octave Butterworth filter.

spectral energy shifts up from 1.8 kHz to 2 kHz. From then on, the spectral pattern remains unchanged, indicating a steady-state vowel. At the same time, periodic bunching and spreading of the spectra as a function of time suddenly appears, with a period in this case of roughly 10 msec. This periodicity is an indication of glottal pulsing, and occurs in the outputs of filters above 1 kHz, which are too broad in bandwidth to resolve the individual harmonics of the glottal pulses. (See the later discussion of filter bandwidths for more details.) The onset of banding, together with an increase in energy in the low-frequency channels, are indications of voice onset. In Fig. 3.6a, the VOT for /bi/ occurs about seven lines after the burst, indicating a VOT of about 11 msec.

These same features of burst onset, VOT, and periodic bunching are also visible in Figs. 3.6b and 3.6c. For /d/ in Fig. 3.6b, the energy distribution in the burst spectrum is clearly broader than for /b/, and centered about 1 kHz higher. Also the VOT is longer—roughly 20 msec. For /g/ in Fig. 3.6c, the burst spectrum is obviously vowel-dependent. For front

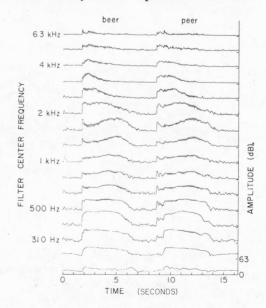

FIG. 3.5. Filter-detector outputs versus time.

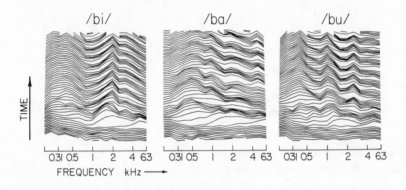

a

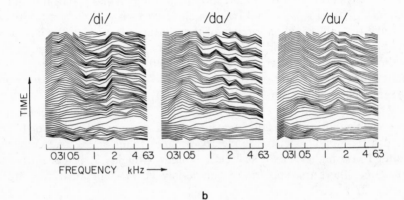

b

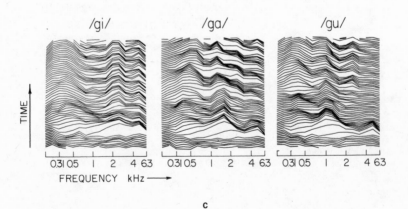

c

FIG.3.6. Running spectra for stop consonants. A three-dimensional representation of the acoustical event showing amplitude (in dB) as a function of frequency (in kHz) and time (100 msec full scale).

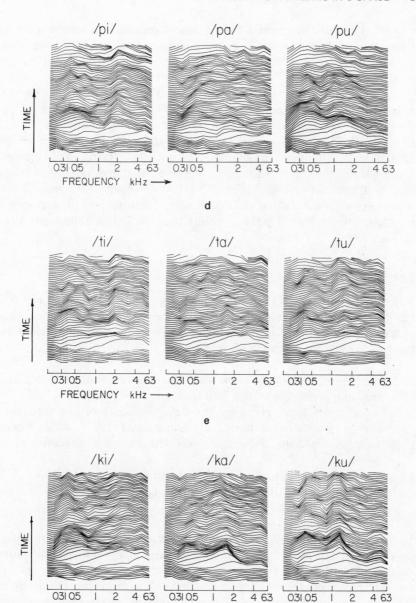

FIG. 3.6. (con't)

vowels, the burst resembles the /d/ burst spectrum, whereas for back vowels the spectrum is sharply peaked between 1 and 1.5 kHz, even lower than the /b/ burst. The VOT for /g/ in this figure varies from about 20 msec to about 40 msec.

The burst spectra for the voiceless stops (Figs. 3.6d, 3.6e, and 3.6f) are very similar to their voiced counterparts. Further, the transition regions for the voiceless stops are seen to be noisy copies (with no voicing bands, of course) of the corresponding regions in the voiced consonants, Figs. 3.6a, b, and c. Compare, for example, /pi/ with /bi/. The onset of voicing is just visible at the top of the diagrams in Figs. 3.6d and 3.6e, whereas for the /k/ utterances in Fig. 3.6f, the VOT is too long to be seen. These results are all in substantial agreement with measurements of corresponding parameters reported in the literature (e.g. Stevens & Blumstein, 1977, or Zue, 1976).

Feature Analysis

Examination of many tokens of stop consonants displayed as in Fig. 3.6, together with the psychophysical evidence cited in the introduction, suggests that the following characteristics of the filter outputs should form the basis of the feature analysis program:

1. the abrupt onset (at least 20–30 dB in 1.6 msec), measured by taking the time derivative of the high-frequency filter outputs;
2. voice onset time, given by the delay in onset of low frequency energy relative to the burst, or voicing onset relative to the burst;
3. location and shape of spectral peaks within a few milliseconds of the burst;
4. location and shape of spectral peaks in the transition region;
5. average formant track slopes (in Hz per msec) during the first 100 msec after the burst.

As indicated in Fig. 3.3, the numbers derived from the feature detectors listed above are subjected to discriminant analysis for classification (see Klecka, 1975). The program performs the discrimination among stops on the basis of the minimum Mahalanobis distance. Discriminant functions are first formed which separate as much as possible the groups in a set of "known" utterances. The grouping is done in a multidimensional space in which the variance of each feature has been normalized. "Unknown" utterances are then located in this space, and assigned to the "known" group whose centroid is nearest to this location. We typically used 10 or 12 features for discrimination.

Results

Our initial runs on all six stop consonants produced nearly 100% separation of voiced from voiceless stops, as reported by other studies, so in our present program there is an initial sort for voicing, then a final sort for place of articulation. Results for /b/, /d/, and /g/ are summarized in Table 3.1a. For the "within-dataset" classification of 77 "known" utterances involving 10 different speakers, 90% were correctly classified, using the best 12 of the features described above. A much more significant test is summarized in Table 3.1b. Here the same classification system derived for the 77 "known" utterances was applied to 92 "unknown" utterances not included in the original classification. This prediction run yielded 78% overall accuracy, with 83% correct classification for /b/, 91% for /d/, and 59% for /g/. The corresponding results for /p/, /t/, and /k/ are shown in Table 3.2. Here prediction on 56 unknown utterances yielded 80% correct overall, with 74% correct /p/, 80% correct /t/, and 89% /k/.

Analysis of Fluent Speech

In our view, the same analysis methods discussed above can be used for phoneme recognition in fluent speech. We show in Fig. 3.7 the running

TABLE 3.1
Discrimination Among Voiced Stops

a. Within-dataset classification of known utterances.
   Overall percentage correct = 90%.

Actual Phoneme	Number of Cases	Computer Grouping		
		/b/	/d/	/g/
/b/	27	25	1	1
/d/	28	3	25	0
/g/	22	1	2	19

b. Predictive classification of unknown utterances.
   Overall percentage correct = 78%.

Actual Phoneme	Number of Cases	Computer Grouping		
		/b/	/d/	/g/
/b/	29	24	4	1
/d/	34	1	31	2
/g/	29	3	9	17

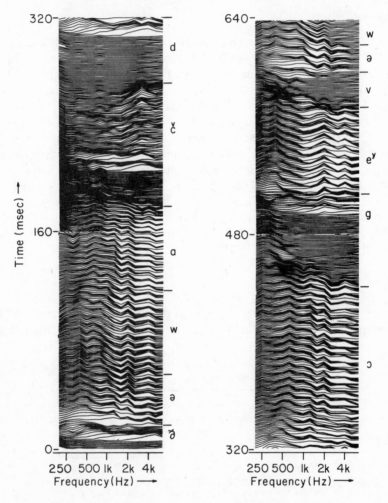

FIG. 3.7.   Running spectra of the sentence, "The watchdog gave a warning growl."

spectrum of the sentence, "The watchdog gave a warning growl." Figure 3.8 shows a conventional sound spectrograph analysis of the same utterance. Comparison of the two presentations shows the expected improvement in spectral resolution below 1 kHz in Fig. 3.7, as well as the improved temporal resolution above 2 kHz (compare the initial stop in *dog* in the two presentations) as discussed in the introduction. Also note the much improved dynamic range of amplitude (compare the aspiration following the /g/ stop in *growl*).

Of particular interest is the similarity between certain parts of the

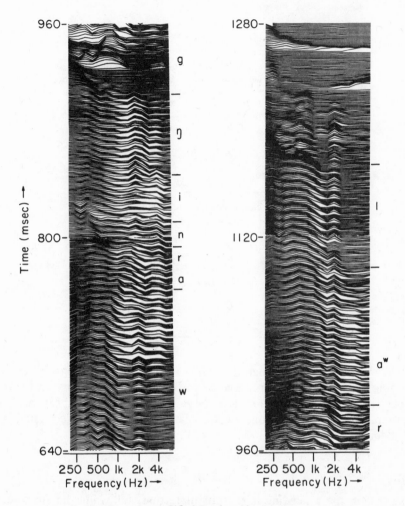

FIG. 3.7.   (con't)

fluent speech plot and the plots in Fig. 3.6 of isolated words. Compare, for example, the /d/ in *dog* in Fig. 3.7 with the /d/ in /da/ in Fig. 3.6b. In both utterances there is a high-frequency burst, centered around 3 to 4 kHz. Then a low-frequency formant develops around 400 to 500 Hz, drifting up to 630 Hz as the vowel develops. Two other formants, one at 1.25 kHz and one at 2kHz, are also seen in both figures.

We are now attempting to "read" these running spectra using the approach suggested by VZ (Chap. 1). Limited observations to date indicate that substantial invariance at the phoneme level remains in our displays of fluent speech. This is no surprise in view of VZ's results. In fact, VZ's

TABLE 3.2
Discrimination Among Voiceless Stops

a. Within-dataset classification of known utterances.
Overall percentage correct = 94%.

Actual Phoneme	Number of Cases	Computer Grouping		
		/p/	/t/	/k/
/p/	24	24	0	0
/t/	24	0	22	2
/k/	23	1	1	21

b. Predictive classification of unknown utterances.
Overall percentage correct = 80%.

Actual Phoneme	Number of Cases	Computer Grouping		
		/p/	/t/	/k/
/p/	23	17	0	6
/t/	15	2	12	1
/k/	18	2	0	16

success in reading spectrograms, when viewed in the context of the preceding discussion on the relative merits of $^1/_3$-octave displays and sound spectrograms, encourages us to believe that substantial improvement in automatic acoustic-to-phonemic translation can be achieved using our system.

Short-Term Storage

Implicit in the preceding is the postulate that, following the short-term spectral analysis of the speech wave, the human auditory system requires some form of short-term storage capable of storing up to about 100 msec of spectral data so that invariant features of phonemes can be recognized. We showed in our introduction that the spectral analysis takes place in the peripheral auditory system, in the cochlea. Hence the short-term storage could very well be done at the first levels of processing above the cochlea, possibly in the auditory cortex, an area known to be essential for speech processing. Some physiological examination of this area has already been done (see, for example, Abeles & Goldstein, 1970; Kay, 1974) and shows tonotopic mapping in a more or less orderly way from low to high frequencies in the horizontal dimension along the surface of the cortex. In

FIG. 3.8.   Sound spectrogram of "The watchdog gave a warning growl."

addition, columnar organization is noted: As the cortex is probed roughly at right angles to the surface, the tuning of the cells stays within a tenth of an octave of the tuning at the surface. Both of these findings are consistent with the idea that this area of the cortex is used for short-term storage, but physiological evidence of a distribution of response delays is needed to verify this speculation.

One particularly attractive feature of this form of short-term auditory storage, wherever it is located, is the ease with which all of the feature extraction discussed in this paper could be performed physiologically. Short-term storage constitutes the basic element in a finite-impulse response (FIR) filter (see, for example, Oppenheim & Schafer, 1975, p. 237). All that is needed in addition to the storage is a means of forming the weighted sum of signals present at various places in the store. Both the storage and the summing network are simple to realize with neurons. Constructing the FIR filter by summing together appropriately weighted samples of the stored image along the time dimension would produce a "third filter" for detecting individual spectral components of vowels or musical tones. Alternatively, a different weighting of samples in the time dimension would detect specific temporal events such as rapid onsets. Constructing the FIR filter in the frequency dimension could serve to detect the spectral shapes. And constructing the filter diagonally across the stored image would serve to detect glides or frequency sweeps. The existence of single cells in the auditory cortex sensitive to particular frequency sweeps has already been reported (Whitfield and Evans, 1965), and the summing node (i.e., neuron) of the FIR filter postulated above would be just such a cell. The material in this section is pure speculation at this point, but it is sufficiently well anchored in known physiology and psychophysics to be worthy of further investigation.

FILTER BANDWIDTHS TO MATCH THE PROPERTIES OF
SPEECH

We presented in our introduction a rationale for the design of an acoustic analyser based on the physiology and psychophysics of the human ear. In this section we present a quite different approach to the same design problem—an approach based on the properties of human speech.

Acoustic processors presently employed in speech recognition systems (for example, LPC, fast Fourier transform, filter bank, spectrograph, or the human ear) have one property in common: They all perform some transformation on the incoming speech wave to generate a new representation which is essentially *two-dimensional*, showing both the *spectral* and *temporal* aspects of the speech wave. There is, of course, an essential trade-off between the spectral resolution and temporal resolution of any such system, namely that the product of bandwidth and rise time must be approximately 0.7 (this is a minimum figure, but most systems come close to this value). A tabulation of design parameters in present acoustic processors (Searle, Jacobson, and Rayment, 1979) indicates that there is a twenty-to-one spread in the temporal resolution (or spectral resolution) parameter chosen for these processors. Hence, it is useful to discuss the effects of this parameter choice on system performance, and derive criteria for choosing appropriate temporal resolution or spectral resolution (i.e., filter bandwidth) for speech analysis.

A cursory examination of Figs. 3.5 and 3.6 indicates that there are many important events in speech, such as bursts, which are rather brief in duration—even as short as 3 msec. Thus it is immediately clear that systems which choose poor temporal resolution (long sampling windows) to achieve good spectral resolution will hopelessly smear these brief temporal events. Unfortunately, the converse is also true. Systems with good temporal resolution will tend to smear spectral details. There is a way out of this dilemma: Follow the design of the human ear and use narrow bandwidths at low frequencies to achieve good spectral resolution there, and wide bandwidths at high frequencies to achieve good temporal resolution in that frequency range. Systems employing ¹/₃-octave filter banks follow this design philosophy.

Constraints on Bandwidth

It is possible, however, to be more explicit than this. The speech production model of Flanagan (1972) postulates that voiced speech can be described as the convolution of a glottal pulse wave with the vocal cavity impulse response. In other words, voiced speech has encoded in it two independent components: the voice pitch as transmitted by the glottal pulses, and the place of articulation as transmitted by the vocal cavity shape. These two components are muddled together (by convolution) in such a way that separating them is a difficult task in signal processing. But we have already seen evidence of such signal separation in Fig. 3.6, so it is reasonable to ask whether we can choose filter bandwidths (or in other systems, the equivalent rise time or sampling-window size) in such a way that the analyser performs this separation without requiring further processing (such as cepstral analysis). The answer is a qualified *yes*: We have two signals we wish to separate, and two orthogonal dimensions— frequency and time—in the system output, so we can choose the filter parameters in such a way that the glottal pulses appear mostly in the temporal dimension of the output and the cavity shape appears mostly in the spectral dimension. The formal proof of this assertion is given in the Appendix. But in simple terms, we must choose the filter bandwidth to be narrower than the vocal cavity spectral shape, yet wide enough to include at least two of the harmonic components of the glottal pulse spectrum (that is, the filter must *not* resolve the individual spectral components of the glottal pulses). Under these conditions, when voiced speech is presented to the analyser, the only variation in the spectral dimension of the analyser output comes from variations in vocal cavity shape, and the only variation in the temporal dimension comes from the glottal-pulse time waveform, as desired.

We now must determine whether it is possible to design a filter-bank system to simultaneously meet the two conditions on filter bandwidth stated above: (1) filter bandwidth narrower than vocal cavity bandwidths at resonances; and (2) filter bandwidth greater than voice pitch. It is also necessary to impose a third basic restriction on bandwidth to ensure that the filter bank analysis is a good approximation to the short-term Fourier transform (Flanagan, 1972, p. 146: (3) the low-pass equivalent response of the filter should not overlap the center frequency of the filter.

To quantify condition 1, we plot as a dashed line in Fig. 3.9 the vocal cavity bandwidths for vowels as a function of frequency (Dunn, 1961, from Flanagan, 1972, p. 182). A literal interpretation of condition 1 requires that the filter bandwidth fall below this dashed line. But this seems overly restrictive. Work of Peterson and Barney (1952) suggests that formant frequencies of female speakers are about 15% higher than the corresponding formants produced by males. Thus it serves no purpose to measure accurately the narrow resonances of an individual voice as dictated by Fig. 3.9 if there is an underlying 15% uncertainty in formant frequency. Hence a more realistic statement of condition 1 is that the filter bandwidth Δf should be less than 15% of the filter center frequency f_c:

$$\Delta f < 0.15 f_c \qquad (1)$$

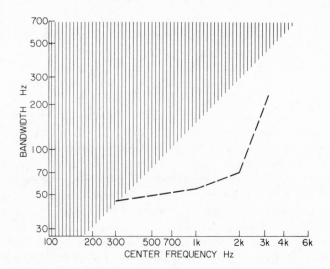

FIG. 3.9. Bandwidth constraint imposed by condition 1. Dashed line: estimate of vocal cavity bandwidths for vowels spoken by adult males (Dunn,
1961). Shaded area: region disallowed by the less stringent constraint of
Equation 1.

This constraint is shown in Fig. 3.9. The shaded area represents the region
excluded by the constraint.

To quantify condition 2, we note that voice pitch ranges from about 100
Hz for male speakers to 300 Hz for female. Hence condition 2 dictates
that

$$\Delta f > f_c \qquad \text{(100 to 300 Hz)} \tag{2}$$

$$\Delta f > 300 \text{ Hz} \qquad \text{(300 Hz to 6 kHz)} \tag{3}$$

where Δf is the filter bandwidth, and f_c is the filter center frequency. This
constraint is plotted in Fig. 3.10.

To quantify condition 3, for the three-pole-pair filters we are using, the
low-pass equivalent response of such filters will be down 42 dB at five
times its cutoff frequency. So if we translate "does not overlap" as
"down 42 dB at," then the center frequency of the bandpass filter must be
at least five times the low-pass cutoff, or 2.5 times the bandpass filter
bandwidth:

$$\Delta f \leq 0.4 f_c \tag{4}$$

as shown in Fig. 3.11.

Figure 3.12a shows a superposition of the unacceptable areas corresponding to each of the above three conditions. The only region in which

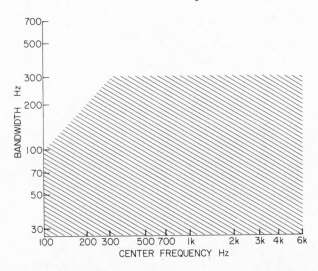

FIG. 3.10. Bandwidth constraint imposed by condition 2. Shading represents the region disallowed by Equation 2.

all conditions are satisfied is above 2 kHz, marked as region 1 in the figure. Obviously the upper edge of region 1 is preferable, because it gives us the broadest permissible bandwidth, hence fastest allowable rise time to follow fast transients such as stop consonant onsets. Below 2 kHz, we must compromise somewhat on conditions 1 and 2 to obtain a workable design (we assume condition 3 is inviolate, to prevent aliasing). On this

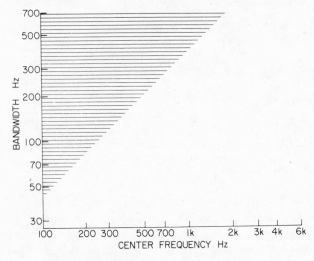

FIG. 3.11. Bandwidth constraint imposed by condition 3. The region disallowed by Equation 3 is shaded.

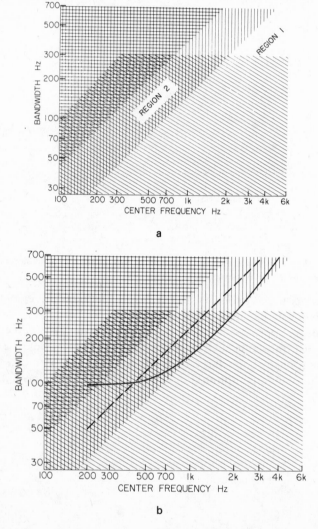

FIG. 3.12. a. Superposition of the three bandwidth constraints. b. The critical band function (solid line) and ⅓-octave function (dashed line) added to the constraint plot.

basis, region 2 represents a reluctantly acceptable design, in that both conditions have been compromised equally and minimally. In Fig. 3.12b we have added the curves of bandwidth as a function of center frequency derived from critical band data and for a ¹/₃-octave filter-bank system. Both are seen to follow the above-stated design criteria reasonably well. By contrast, any constant-bandwidth analysis system clearly does not follow these design criteria.

The preceding discussion should not be construed to argue that the ear evolved to match the characteristics of speech. There is ample phylogenetic evidence to indicate the converse. But our argument would remain substantially unaltered if presented from the point of view that speech evolved to match the characteristics of the ear rather than from the approach chosen above.

Let us now restate these conclusions in temporal terms for those systems which are specified in terms of sampling windows. Clearly systems with fixed window widths cannot meet the above conditions. Rather, we require that the window width change when analysing different parts of the spectrum. The basic requirement of at least 300 Hz bandwidth above 1.5 kHz translates to a Hanning window of 6.7 msec or less total width. To follow the 1/3-octave pattern, this window width should vary inversely with frequency, e.g. 1.7 msec at 6 kHz, and 17 msec at 600 Hz. Algorithms for variable-window-width digital analysis are not conceptually any more difficult than the present fixed-window algorithms, except that one can no longer take advantage of the computational efficiency of the fast Fourier transform (Oppenheim, Johnson, & Steiglitz, 1977).

Evidence of Signal Separation

As indicated above, the running spectra in Fig. 3.6 provide considerable support for the concept of orthogonal display of vocal cavity spectra and glottal pulses. To emphasize the point, we show in Fig. 3.13a and b the first 100 msec of the word *beer*, abstracted from Fig. 3.5, shown as a time plot with frequency as the parameter in Fig. 3.13a, and as a running spectral plot with time as the parameter in Fig. 3.13b. Note in Fig. 3.13a that all filters above 1 kHz show a strong periodic component, which is the fundamental pitch of the voice. If we average the filter outputs across *frequency*, then the spectral shapes should average out, but a strong pitch component should appear. Figure 13c was obtained by summing together all channel outputs above 1 kHz, and shows just this effect. Similarly, averaging across *time* should suppress the temporal information, and enhance the cavity spectral shape. Figure 13d shows an average of 20 spectra from Fig. 3.13b taken in the vowel part of /bi/, and again shows the predicted effect.

It is possible that the ear and brain uses a system like the one described above to extract one of several cues for the determination of voice pitch. (See, for example, Scott, Chap. 2.) It is also possible that the system would make a useful pitch extractor for such applications as vocoders. Both of these possibilities will be investigated.

Evidence supporting Equation 1 as a realistic constraint relating to vocal cavity bandwidth (condition 1) can be obtained by analysing a sen-

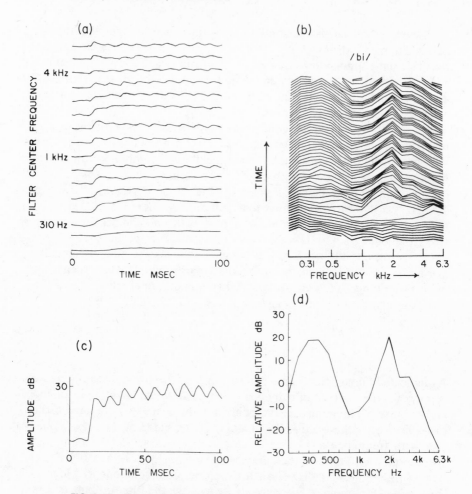

FIG. 3.13. Spectral and temporal details of /bi/. a. Time plot of filter outputs. b. Corresponding running spectra (100 msec). c. Average of top 9 channels in (a). d. Average of top 20 spectra in (b).

tence with both a wide-band and a narrow-band spectrum analyser, and looking for regions where the narrow filter shows more spectral detail of the vocal cavity shape than the wide filter. Figure 3.14a, a wide-band spectrogram obtained using a fixed 300 Hz bandwidth in the analyser (Gold, 1977) shows the familiar vertical banding resulting from resolving the glottal pulses in the *time* dimension, as would be expected from the discussion above. Figure 3.14b is a narrow-band spectrogram with a constant 45 Hz bandwidth and shows no time banding, but instead shows frequency banding, resulting from resolution of the glottal pulses in the *frequency* dimension. If we now focus attention on the spectral details of the vocal cavity, by ignoring both the vertical and horizontal banding, we note that below about 1.5 kHz there are many areas in the narrow-band plot that have much finer detail on vocal cavity spectral shape (the vertical dimension) than seen in the wide-band plot, whereas above 2 kHz, there is minimal improvement in resolution of cavity shape from narrow-band analysis, and above 4 kHz there is *no* improvement. Thus a 45 Hz analysis bandwidth can be justified below 1.5 kHz, but bandwidths of at least 300 Hz are more appropriate above a few kilohertz. This result is broadly consistent with the constraints discussed above and summarized in Fig. 3.12.

It is also clear that the spectrograph, either in wide-band or narrow-band configuration, does not adequately meet the constraints of Fig. 3.12. The two possible spectrograph bandwidths would plot as horizontal lines on the figure, one at 45 Hz and the other at 300. The 45 Hz spectrograph meets the design criteria only at low frequencies, and the 300 Hz machine only between 700 Hz and 2 kHz. What is needed is a combination of the two instruments, or, better still, a spectrograph whose bandwidth increases linearly with frequency.

CONCLUSIONS

All phoneme recognition systems, including the human ear, employ some sort of acoustic analyser to measure the *spectral* properties of the speech signal, while at the same time retaining some of the *temporal* properties of the original wave. We have cited physiological and psychophysical experiments which indicate that the human peripheral auditory system is performing this analysis with roughly $1/3$-octave frequency resolution, and hence 1 or 2 msec temporal resolution at high frequencies. We have constructed a phoneme recogniser with these properties, and have obtained roughly 80% correct discrimination on stop consonants in initial position. We attribute this score, and the 93% correct identification of vowels achieved by Klein, Plomp, and Pols (1970) with a similarly designed system, to the correct choice of temporal and spectral resolution in the acoustic analyser. One-third-octave analysers not only conform to the design of the human peripheral auditory system, they also match the properties of human speech: good *spectral* resolution at low frequencies assures separation of the important first and second formants, and good *temporal* resolution at high frequencies assures accurate timing information for rapid acoustic events such as stop consonant attacks. Acoustic analysers with constant bandwidth (for example, the spectrograph) cannot simultaneously achieve both of these desirable properties. Preliminary examination of fluent speech on our analyser indicates that the es-

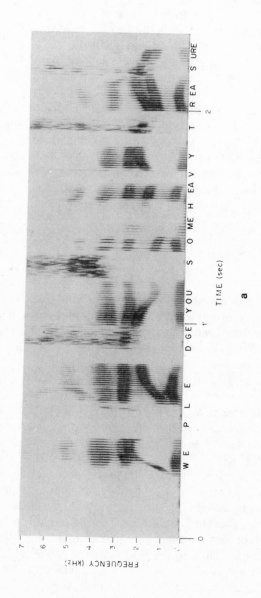

a

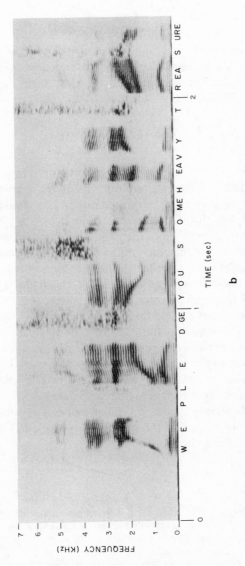

FIG. 3.14.   Conventional spectrogram (from Gold, 1977, diagrams reversed in original publication). a. 300 Hz bandwidth. b. 45 Hz bandwidth.

sential features of most phonemes are still retained, even in this more complicated environment, so we are encouraged to believe that substantial improvement in automatic acoustic-to-phonemic translation of continuous speech can be achieved with our system.

APPENDIX

Filter-envelope detector systems can be characterized mathematically as systems which calculate the magnitude of the short term Fourier transform, as defined by Flanagan (1972):

$$F(\omega,t) = \int_{-\infty}^{t} v(\tau) h (t - \tau) e^{-j\omega\tau} d\tau \qquad (4)$$

where ω is a frequency variable equal to 2π times the frequency in Hz, τ is a dummy time variable of integration, and $v(\tau)$ is the incoming speech wave. The term $h(t - \tau)$ can be interpreted either as a window function applied to the time waveform $v(t)$, or, for filter banks, the impulse response of the low-pass equivalent of the band-pass filter (Flanagan, 1972, pp. 143–146).[3] In contrast to the conventional Fourier transform, which is a function of frequency only, the short-term transform in Equation 4 is a function of both frequency and time, to model both the spectral and temporal aspects of the filter-detector outputs. The specific compromise struck between time resolution and frequency resolution in the transform is determined by $h(t)$, which is the only free design parameter in the equation. We wish to explore the possibility of selecting $h(t)$ so that the two important aspects of the speech wave, the glottal pulse wave and the vocal cavity shape, are separated directly into the two dimensions of the transform, without requiring further signal processing.

Flanagan's (1972) simple model of voiced speech assumes that the speech wave is a convolution of the glottal pulse wave $i(t)$ and the impulse response $c(t)$ of the vocal cavity:

$$v_1(t) = i(t) \otimes c(t) \qquad (5)$$

---

[3]To represent the constant-Q filter bank in Fig. 3.3 (and hence, to a first approximation, the ear) Youngberg and Ball (1978) have recently shown that Equation 4 can be generalized by scaling $h(t)$ linearly with frequency:

$$F_1(\omega,t) = \int_{-\infty}^{t} v(\tau) h(\omega t - \omega\tau) e^{-j\omega\tau} d\tau$$

Youngberg and Ball also derived the corresponding inverse transform, proving that a Fourier transform pair exists even in this case of a frequency-dependent impulse response.

The functions $i(t)$ and $c(t)$ actually change with time, as the voice pitch and vocal cavity shape change, but we assume that these changes take place slowly enough that the speech wave can be analysed as a succession of steady states. In phoneme recognition, we wish to separate the two important sources of information in Equation 5 which are unfortunately entwined (by convolution) in the speech wave. One method of effecting this separation is cepstral analysis (Bogert, Healy, & Tukey, 1963; Oppenheim, Schafer, & Stockham, 1968; Oppenheim & Schafer, 1975). We outline here a second method of separation, in which the two implicit functions in Equation 5 are displayed separately in the two orthogonal dimensions of the short-term Fourier transform of Equation 4. For simplicity, we assume that the glottal pulses in Equation 5 are impulses. If a more accurate description is desired, we can redefine $c(t)$ to be the convolution of the vocal cavity impulse response and the true shape of the glottal pulse.

The filter-bank representation of the short-term Fourier transform is shown in Fig. 3.15. If we apply the speech signal $v_1(t)$ at the input of the analyser, then the signal $v_2(t)$ at the output of the nth band-pass filter is

$$v_2(t) = i(t) \otimes c(t) \otimes p_n(t) \qquad (6)$$

or, in the frequency domain,

$$V_2(\omega) = I(\omega) \times C(\omega) \times P_n(\omega) \qquad (7)$$

If we choose the filter characteristic $P_n(\omega)$ to be much narrower than the resonances in the vocal tract response $C(\omega)$, then the filter output can be approximated as

$$V_2(\omega) \simeq I(\omega) \times C(\omega_n) \times P_n(\omega) \qquad (8)$$

where $C(\omega_n)$ is the value of $C(\omega)$ at the center frequency of the nth filter. Hence

$$V_2(\omega) = [|C(\omega_n)|e^{j\theta_n}] [I(\omega) \times P_n(\omega)] \qquad (9)$$

where $C(\omega_n)$ has become a scalar multiplier, different for each filter channel, but independent of ω for any given channel. Because the filter is followed in Fig. 3.15 by an envelope detector (here shown as a full wave

FIG. 3.15.   Filter-bank representation of the short-term Fourier transform of Equation 4, showing a block diagram of the channel with center frequency ω_n.

rectifier followed by a low-pass filter), the phase angle $e^{j\theta_n}$ does not contribute to $|F(\omega, t)|$, so that we can neglect its effect on the time waveform $v_2(t)$, which thus becomes

$$v_2(t) \simeq |C(\omega_n)|[i(t) \otimes p_n(t)] \tag{10}$$

Equation 10 indicates that because of the constraint imposed above on filter bandwidth, the cavity frequency characteristic $|C(\omega_n)|$ has become a series of scalar multipliers on the entire filter bank, and except for these scalar multipliers the effective input to the system in Fig. 3.15 is the glottal pulse waveform $i(t)$.

We now place additional constraints on the filter to ensure that information on the glottal pulse wave $i(t)$ appears only in the time dimension of $|F(\omega, t)|$, and not in the frequency dimension. To ensure that the individual components in $I(\omega)$ are not resolved by the filter bank, we require that the bandwidth of the filter is greater than the pitch of the glottal pulse train, so that at least two components of $I(\omega)$ will be in each filter. To ensure that some of the temporal details of $i(t)$ appear in $|F|$, we require that the convolution $i(t) \otimes p_n(t)$ in Equation 10 still show the periodicity of $i(t)$. Periodicity is assured if there are at least two components of $I(\omega)$ in the filter passband, the same condition as above. These last two conditions are not in general identical, as can be seen by examining the corresponding conditions for pulsed white noise.

REFERENCES

Abeles, M., & Goldstein, M. H. Functional architecture in cat primary auditory cortex: Columnar organization and organization according to depth. *Journal of Neurophysiology*, 1970, *33*, 172–187.

Allen, J. B. Cochlear micromechanics—A mechanism for transforming mechanical neural tuning within the cochlea. *Journal of the Acoustical Society of America*, 1977, *62*, 930–939.

Bogert, B., Healy, M., Tukey, J. The quefrency alanysis of time series for echoes. In M. Rosenblatt (Ed.), *Proceedings of the Symposium on Time Series Analysis*. New York: Wiley, 1963.

Chistovich, J. A., Grostrem, M. P., Kozhevnikov, V. A., Lesogor, L. W., Shupljakov, V. A., Taljasin, P. A., & Tjulkov, W. A. A functional model of signal processing in the peripheral auditory system, *Acustica*, 1974, *31*, 349–353.

Cole, R. A., & Cooper, W. E. Properties of frication analyzers for /j/. *Journal of the Acoustical Society of America*, 1977, *62*, 177–182.

Cole, R. A., & Scott, B. Toward a theory of speech perception. *Psychological Review*, 1974, *81*, 348–374.

Cooper, W. E. Adaptation of phonemic feature analyzers for place of articulation. *Journal of the Acoustical Society of America*, 1974, *56*, 617–627.

Dolmazon, J. M., Bastet, L., & Shupljakov, V. S. A functional model of peripheral auditory system in speech processing. *Conference Record: 1977 IEEE International Conference on Acoustics, Speech and Signal Processing, (76CH1067-8 ASSP), Rome, N.Y.: Canterbury Press, 1977, 261–264.

Dunn, H. K. Methods of measuring vowel formant bandwidths. Journal of the Acoustical Society of America, 1961, 33, 1737–1746.

Egan, J. P., & Hake, H. W. On the masking patterns of a simple auditory stimulus. Journal of the Acoustical Society of America, 1950, 22, 622–630.

Eimas, P. D., & Corbit, J. D. Selective adaptation of linguistic feature detectors. Cognitive Psychology, 1973, 4, 99–109.

Fischer-Jorgensen, E. Tape cutting experiments with Danish stop consonants in initial position. Annual Report VII, Institute of Phonetics, University of Copenhagen, 1972.

Flanagan, J. L. Speech analysis, synthesis, and perception. New York: Springer-Verlag, 1972.

Gold, B. Digital speech networks. Proceedings of IEEE, 1977, 65, 1636–1658.

Johnstone, B. M., & Boyle, A. J. F. Basilar membrane vibration examined with the Mössbauer effect. Science, 1967, 158, 389–390.

Kay, R. H. The physiology of auditory frequency analysis. In J. A. V. Butler & H. E. Huxley (Eds.), Progress in biophysics and molecular biology (Vol. 14). New York: Pergamon Press, 1974.

Kiang, N. Y. S., Watanabe, T. E. C., & Clark, L. F. Discharge patterns of single nerve fibers in a cat's auditory nerve. Cambridge, Mass.: M.I.T. Press, 1965.

Kiang, N. Y. S., & Moxon, E. C. Tails of tuning curves of auditory-nerve fibers. Journal of the Acoustical Society of America, 1974, 55, 620–630.

Klecka, W. R. Discriminant analysis. In N. H. Nie, C. H. Hull., J. G. Jenkins, K. Steinbrenner, & D. H. Bent (Eds.), Statistical package for the social sciences. New York: McGraw-Hill, 1975.

Klein, W., Plomp, R., & Pols, L. C. W. Vowel spectra, vowel spaces, and vowel identification. Journal of the Acoustical Society of America, 1970, 48, 999–1009.

Mariani, J. J., & Lienard, J. S. Acoustic–phonemic recognition of connected speech using transient information Conference Record, IEEE Acoustical Speech and Signal Processing 1977, 667–670.

Miller, J. D., Engebretson, A. M., Spenner, B. F., & Cox, J. R. Preliminary analyses of speech sounds with a digital model of the ear. Journal of the Acoustical Society of America, 1977, 62 (Supp. 1), 13 (abstract).

Miller, J. L. Properties of feature detectors for speech. Perception & Psychophysics, 1975, 18, 389–397.

Møller, A. R. Frequency selectivity of single auditory-nerve fibers to broadband noise stimuli. Journal of the Acoustical Society of America, 1977, 62, 135–142.

Oppenheim, A. V., Johnson, D., & Steiglitz, K. Computation of spectra with unequal resolution using the fast Fourier transform. Proceedings of the IEEE, 1971, 59, 299–301.

Oppenheim, A. V., & Schafer, R. W. Digital signal processing. Englewood Cliffs, N.J.: Prentice-Hall, 1975.

Oppenheim, A. V., Schafer, R. W., & Stockham, T. G., Jr. Nonlinear filtering of multiplied and convolved signals. Proceedings of the IEEE, 1968, 56, 1264–1291.

Peterson, G. E., & Barney, H. L. Control methods used in a study of vowels. Journal of the Acoustical Society of America, 1952, 24, 175–184.

Rhode, W. S. Observations of the basilar membrane in squirrel monkeys using the Mössbauer Technique. Journal of the Acoustical Society of America, 1971, 49, 1218–1231.

Sachs, M. B., & Kiang, N. Y. S. Two-tone inhibition in auditory-nerve fibers. Journal of the Acoustical Society of America, 1968, 43, 1120–1128.

Schatz, C. The role of context in perception of stops. Language, 1954, 30, 47–56.

Schouten, M. E. H., & Pols, L. C. W. Vowel segments in consonantal contexts: A spectral study of coarticulation. *Report IZF 1977–14*. Soesterberg, The Netherlands: Institute for Perception, 1977.

Searle, C. L., Jacobson, J. Z., & Rayment, S. G. Stop consonant discrimination based on human audition. *Journal of the Acoustical Society of America*, 1979, *65*, 799–809.

Steer, R. W., Jr. Design of an active COC filter for audio frequency signal processing. AMRL TR 75–78, 1975, Wright-Patterson AFB, Ohio, Aerospace Medical Division.

Stevens, K. N., & Blumstein, S. E. Onset spectra as cues for consonantal place of articulation. *Journal of the Acoustical Society of America*, 1977, *61* (Supp. 1).

Tobias, J. V. *Foundations of Modern Auditory Theory* (Vol. 1) Academic Press. 1970.

Whitfield, I. C., & Evans, E. F. Response of auditory cortical neurons to stimuli of changing frequency. *Journal of Neurophysiology*, 1965, *28*, 655–672.

Youngberg, J. E., & Ball, S. F. Constant-Q signal analysis and synthesis. *Conference Record 1978, IEEE International Conference on Acoustics, Speech and Signal Processing*. Rome, N.Y.: Canterbury Press, 1978, 675–678.

Zue, V. W. *Acoustic characteristics of stop consonants: A controlled study*. Unpublished Sc. D. thesis, Massachusetts Institute of Technology and TR523, Lincoln Laboratory, M.I.T., Cambridge, Mass., 1976.

Zwicker, E., Flottorp, G., & Stevens, S. S. Critical bandwidth and loudness summation. *Journal of the Acoustical Society of America*, 1957, *29*, 548–557.

Zwicker, E., Terhardt, E., & Paulus, E. Automatic speech recognition using psychoacoustic models. *Journal of the Acoustical Society of America*, 1979, *65*, 487–498.

4 Property-Detecting Mechanisms and Eclectic Processors

Kenneth N. Stevens
Massachusetts Institute of Technology

The three papers I have been asked to review are all concerned with the operations performed on the speech signal to extract information about its phonetic content, that is, the string of phonetic segments contained in the sound. In all three papers it is assumed that some transformation of the signal needs to be made initially in order to provide a representation or a display from which appropriate attributes or cues can be extracted. The three approaches each use a different display, and therefore differ in terms of the attributes that are extracted to derive a sequence of phonetic segments, but each approach contributes some insights into how these operations might be performed in the auditory and speech-perception system of the human listener.

In the paper by Cole, Rudnicky, Zue, and Reddy, the display is the conventional three-dimensional intensity–frequency–time representation, or spectrogram, and the relevant attributes or cues are extracted visually. The cues that are used by the observer to identify particular phonetic segments are quite varied and are often context-dependent; that is, the acoustic evidence for a particular segment is interpreted with reference to its phonetic context. In spite of the large variety of acoustic cues that are used by the observer, and in spite of the fact that the spectrographic display is not intended to bear a direct relation to the way the signal is represented in the auditory system, the performance of VZ is quite re-markable. Apparently the information is present in the spectrogram in a form that an experienced observer can learn to utilize in order to identify the phonetic segments.

Scott takes a somewhat different approach toward the extraction of phonetic information, particularly in his work on the development of a tactile aid. He encodes the signal into certain envelope characteristics and gross spectral characteristics and, through a series of experiments, evaluates the performance of a receiver using ongoing speech. The receiver extracts whatever information he can from the vibrator concerning the prosodic and segmental attributes of the signal.

The approach taken by Searle, Jakobson, and Kimberly toward the problem of extracting phonetic segments differs from that of Cole and his colleagues in that a careful attempt is made to provide an auditory display that is consistent with what we know about the temporal and spectral resolution of the human auditory system. But their point of view regarding the extraction of appropriate properties from this display in order to identify the phonetic segments is similar to that of Cole et al. Searle et al. are willing to accept any combination of attributes that leads to correct phonetic identification, and no predisposition toward particular acoustic properties is assumed. Searle et al. do, however, attempt to derive a combination of properties that is independent of context for each of the stop consonants.

I have some specific comments on these three papers relating to models, segmentation, and speech training for the deaf, and also some more general comments relating to theoretical issues. I will consider the more detailed items first, and follow with a discussion of theoretical issues.

Speech as Patterns on Paper

In the Cole et al. paper, there is an implication, in fact a belief, that what VZ is doing when he reads spectrograms is dividing up the speech signal into stretches of sound separated by boundaries. Between two adjacent boundaries there lies a speech sound—a phonetic segment. To be sure, it is recognized that there is a blurring at the edges, resulting from the influence of one sound on an adjacent one, but these effects are regarded as perturbations that somehow have to be dealt with—bothersome effects that modify the otherwise ideal signal. This may be an overstatement, but it is an impression I get from the use of the term *segmentation*.

An alternative view is that the speech stream is regarded as a series of *events*—points in the signal where there are abrupt onsets and offsets and where there are rapid spectrum changes (as in a consonantal region of the syllable), or points in time where there is a peak in energy (as in the middle of a vowel). What VZ tends to mark on the spectrogram are the abrupt onsets or offsets, but it is not necessary to think of these points as boundaries of segments. He classifies these events, and he classifies the vowel nuclei, thus identifying the consonants and the vowels respectively. The acoustic material between these two classes of events acts as joining material. This way of looking at the speech stream as sequences of *events* rather than as sequences of short stretches of signal marked by boundaries may be more in accord with how the auditory system processes sound.

Use of Spectrographic Displays for Speech Training.   Cole et al. conclude that there is a "direct and perceptible relationship between what one says and what one sees on a spectrogram [p.]." From this observation, they infer that "immediate feedback of spectrographic information should be an effective way to teach correct production of any phoneme in any environment [p.]."

It has been a common mistake in the past to assume that if the right kind of visual feedback can be provided to the deaf speaker, then this feedback will almost automatically assist the speaker in developing good speech or in correcting improper speech patterns. The following few comments may introduce some caution in interpreting this assumption.

1. The visual feedback that one can obtain from a display cannot be used on-line by a speaker to correct articulatory patterns during the production of continuous speech. At best, a speaker can observe an incorrect pattern and then, on a subsequent utterance, attempt to make some modification to the articulation in order to produce a pattern that is closer to being correct.

2. One of the greatest problems in speech training to the deaf is *not* to get the student to produce a correct pattern in a training session but to produce carry-over into the student's spontaneous speech away from the training situation. (See, for example, Ling, 1976.) While a visual display may indeed be useful in helping the student to acquire a particular skill during a training session, this represents only one part of the overall speech training strategy.

3. Many speech teachers of the deaf have assumed that the basic goal of speech therapy is to get the student to correctly produce speech sounds. Speech therapy consists, then, of going systematically through an inventory of speech sounds, and training the student to correctly produce each one in turn, often in the context of single-syllable utterances. There are several problems with this approach. One is that, underlying the production of speech, there is a basic posture or state of the articulatory, laryngeal, and respiratory systems that is different from the state assumed during quiet breathing and resting. This speech posture is assumed independently of the particular sequence of sounds to be generated, and forms a sort of starting point for the production of specific speech gestures. To try to train a student to produce individual speech gestures when this

basic posture is incorrect would be a mistake, and could not result in fluent speech, any more than a student could be expected to learn to play the piano starting from an incorrect positioning of the arms and hands. Furthermore, concentration on the production of individual speech sounds may tend to draw attention away from the fact that speech is more than a sequence of sounds. The sounds are concatenated to form phrases and sentences. Teaching strategies should be organized and sequenced so as to take account of these larger units.

From these remarks it should not be concluded that a spectrographic display will not be useful as an aid for speech training of the deaf. The introduction of such a display must, however, be coupled with carefully designed training sequences and training procedures.

Speech as Patterns in Time

In his introductory remarks, Scott argues that the units of speech perception are not separate spectral elements or patches of energy in the frequency–time plane, but integrated properties that may span a broad range of frequencies. The implication is that several attributes that are individually visible on the spectrogram may together contribute to some integrated property. This point of view is consistent with the early ideas of Jakobson, Fant, and Halle (1963) and of Fant (1960), who suggested that certain phonetic features are based on concepts of compactness–diffuseness and gravity–acuteness. These terms are derived from integrated properties of the gross shape of the spectrum. Thus, for example, an alveolar stop consonant is characterized by a diffuse spread of spectral energy over a wide frequency range, with the spectrum weighted toward higher frequencies, rather than by a burst of energy at a particular frequency or a particular starting frequency for the second-formant transition. (See also Stevens & Blumstein, 1978.)

The tactile aid described by Scott exploits these principles by providing a display of the gross spectral shape in terms of a compact–diffuse dimension without varying the locus of sensation. This approach is in contrast to the vocoder-like approach which lays out the tactile stimulation in space much like a spectrogram. (See, for example, Pickett & Pickett, 1963; Sparks, Kuhl, Edmonds, & Gray, 1978.) Scott's device represents, however, only a partial application of the principles he sets forth, and further work will be necessary to incorporate additional "integrated" properties into such a device. A tactile device based on the Tadoma method (Norton, Schultz, Reed, Braida, Durlach, Rabinowitz, & Chomsky, 1977) is an example of an approach that codes the speech signal into a variety of parameters or properties. This device has been used successfully by experienced subjects.

The vowel studies of Scott attempt to show that the temporal fine structure of the vowel waveform can be utilized by listeners in categorizing vowels. The argument is not entirely convincing, because, at least in some of the examples given, it is possible to interpret his results in terms of spectral patterns, rather than temporal fine structure. While temporal fine structure of the waveform may play a role in vowel perception, a theory of vowel perception which combines spectral analysis with detection of temporal structure within broad frequency bands probably comes closer to explaining the experimental data from various sources (Carlson, Fant, & Grandstrom, 1975; Scott, 1976), as well as being consistent with what is known about auditory physiology (Kiang, Watanabe, Thomas, & Clark, 1965).

Speech as Patterns in Space

In developing on overall model of speech perception, Searle et al. have emphasized the importance of incorporating within this model the constraints that are known to be imposed by the peripheral auditory system (see also Chistovich, Granstrem, Kozhevnikov, Lesogor, Shupljakov, Taljasin, & Tjulkov, 1974). The filter characteristics utilized by Searle and his colleagues provide the necessary constraints on the frequency and time resolution of the human auditory system in different parts of the frequency range. As we learn more about the auditory system, still further constraints can be built into the model. For example, data on the response of auditory neurons to various kinds of acoustic signals have demonstrated several properties beyond those used in the system of Searle (see, for example, Kiang et al., 1965; and Kiang & Moxon, 1972). Among those properties are:

1. Responses of neurons with low characteristic frequencies are time-locked to the stimulus waveform (giving some support to the notions concerning vowel perception presented by Scott).
2. The responses at onsets and offsets of a stimulus show large transient effects that cannot be accounted for simply on the basis of the transient response of the filters.
3. Special inhibitory effects occur in the responses of the auditory nerve when two tones are presented simultaneously.

Auditory psychophysics is leading to new insights into the nature of the auditory processing of complex signals of the type that occur in speech

(Cutting & Rosner, 1974; Leshowitz & Cudahy, 1975; Pisoni, 1977). As cooperation develops between those who are studying auditory physiology and auditory psychophysics and those who are investigating the properties of speech, it is to be hoped that improved models of the auditory periphery can be used as the first stage of a more general speech-processing model.

SOME THEORETICAL ISSUES

What can the experiments reported in these papers tell us about how the human listener processes speech? The papers under review share a common view about the process by which a string of phonetic segments is extracted from the signal. In this view, the decoding system utilizes a variety of pieces of acoustic information to identify phonetic segments—burst spectra, formant frequencies and formant spacing, directions of formant motions, durations of acoustic events, relative amplitudes of different parts of the display, abrupt discontinuities, etc. In the terms used by Cole et al., the speech perception system, like VZ, takes an "eclectic" view of the information in the speech signal.

This approach, if viewed as a general model of the speech perception system, is unsatisfactory and incomplete for two reasons. One is that it gives no indication of how the system can get started. How is the infant, when faced with this complex acoustic signal, able to organize and categorize the events within the signal? It seems unlikely that an infant is predisposed toward utilizing the combination of cues employed by VZ or proposed by Searle et al. A more reasonable hypothesis is that the infant responds to simpler, integrated properties in order to classify the sounds he hears (Stevens & Blumstein, 1978). The model of an eclectic processor may have some plausibility for how an adult listener processes the signal, but it cannot explain how the adult was able to reach that state.

A second reason why this kind of model is unsatisfactory is that it does not try to take into account the basic capabilities and constraints that the auditory system imposes on the speech perception process. The model holds the point of view that the speech perception system is flexible; it can make use of any piece of acoustic information that can contribute to identification of the phonetic features. It does not specify how the constraints imposed by the auditory system help to delineate the kinds of acoustic events that are used in language for signalling phonetic information. It is necessary, in the long run, to explain why the sounds in all languages can be classified in terms of a relatively small number of categories based on their acoustic properties (Chomsky & Halle, 1968; Jakobson et al., 1963). Presumably these regularities in speech-sound categories are due in part to propensities of the auditory system for selecting particular acoustic properties in the signal and using these properties for classifying speech sounds. This property-detecting view of speech processing is rather different from the eclectic view described in the papers under review.

The model that I find implicit in the papers by Cole et al., and by Searle et al. seems to downgrade the importance of phonetic features and of property-detecting mechanisms in the speech perception process. Evidence from a variety of sources and from a variety of disciplines indicates that we cannot dismiss them lightly (Abbs & Sussman, 1971; Cole & Scott, 1974; Jakobson et al., 1963; Stevens, 1975).

It is possible to propose a point of view that can encompass both concepts—the concept of property-detecting mechanisms to which the attributes of the speech signal are matched, and the concept of an open-ended strategy for adult perception of continuous speech in which a variety of cues are utilized by listeners. A recent version of this point of view is elaborated in Stevens and Blumstein (1978).

They suggest that the infant auditory system is endowed with property-detecting mechanisms that facilitate the classification of the incoming speech sounds into categories. Thus, for example, if an abrupt onset of sound energy occurs, preceded by a sufficiently long interval of silence or of relatively low acoustic energy, then this event marks the occurrence of a particular phonetic feature—call it the feature *stop*. It is postulated that the auditory system responds in a special way to such an abrupt onset, but fails to respond in this way when the abruptness of the onset is reduced (cf. Cutting & Rosner, 1974).

Or, if the short-time spectrum sampled at an onset shows a relatively compact spectral prominence in the midfrequency range, it may be that the auditory system responds in a special or distinctive way, whereas such a response is not obtained if the spectral energy is spread diffusely over a wide frequency range (Fant, 1960; Jakobson et al., 1963; Stevens & Blumstein, 1978). Velar consonants are characterized by a compact spectral prominence, and it is suggested, therefore, that the auditory system is endowed with detecting mechanisms that respond selectively to these types of consonants.

Another class of acoustic events which may be categorized by the workings of a special detector are those distinguishing voiced from voiceless stop consonants. There is evidence that the auditory system responds differently when consonantal release and voice onset occur within 20–25 msec of each other than when the separation between these two events is more than 25 msec (Miller, Wier, Pastore, Kelly, & Dooling, 1977; Pisoni, 1977). This basic property of the auditory system to interpret acoustic onsets as either simultaneous (if the time separation is less than 25-odd msec) or successive (if their time separation is greater than 25 msec) is apparently exploited in languages that distinguish aspirated from unaspirated consonants (Lisker & Abramson, 1964).

In searching for a minimal inventory of primary acoustic properties that enable the listener to classify phonetic events, it is probably not appropriate to look for detailed attributes such as individual formant frequencies, spectra of bursts, or directions of formant motions. Rather, these properties are, perhaps, more appropriately specified in terms of gross spectrum shapes or integrated attributes that may, for example, include both burst and transitions. I am in agreement with Scott's comments that "the acoustic signal is not perceived as separate, spectral elements," but rather is perceived as a "frequency-integrated signal."

It is postulated, then, that the auditory system is endowed with detecting mechanisms that aid the young listener in classifying the sounds he hears—in putting these sounds into bins, as it were. The acoustic properties to which these detectors respond bear a close relationship to the phonetic features. In fact, the existence of these property-detecting mechanisms, which are presumably employed for nonspeech as well as for speech sounds, almost certainly plays a role in shaping the kinds of sounds that are used in speech.

As we have seen, however, not all manifestations of a given phonetic feature show invariant, context-independent, acoustic attributes. And the effects of noise, stress reduction, sloppy articulation, etc., serve to further modify the acoustic attributes associated with certain features, so that these occurrences may be classified incorrectly by the young receiver of speech. Nevertheless, a sufficient number of tokens have the requisite invariant properties that the listener is able to classify correctly a substantial majority of phonetic features.

At the same time that the listener is exposed to tokens that are classified correctly on the basis of their primary acoustic attributes, he also hears secondary context-dependent attributes that accompany the primary properties. By some learning mechanism that is not understood at present, these secondary attributes come to be used by the listener as cues for the features, particularly in situations where the primary attributes are distorted or missing or obscured by noise. In time, the listener develops strategies that utilize a variety of cues, much as VZ develops such strategies, and much as the analysis procedures of Searle et al. find such strategies.

The hypothesis, then, is that primary property-detecting mechanisms, combined with the property-generating propensities of the speech production system, serve to set up the system of phonetic categories that play a basic role in language (Stevens, 1972). By developing strategies to bypass these primary property-detecting mechanisms, the experienced listener can utilize secondary cues or shortcuts to speech perception when the primary attributes are distorted or missing.

ACKNOWLEDGMENT

The preparation of this paper was supported in part by Grant NS 04332 from the National Institutes of Health.

REFERENCES

Abbs, J. H. & Sussman, H. M. Neurophysiological features and speech perception: A discussion of theoretical implications. *Journal of Speech and Hearing Research*, 1971, *14*, 23–36.

Carlson, R., Fant, G., & Grandstrom, B. Two-formant models, pitch, and vowel perception. In G. Fant & M. A. A. Tatham (Eds.), *Auditory analysis and perception of speech*. London: Academic, 1975, pp. 55–82.

Chistovich, L. A., Granstrem, M. P., Kozhevnikov, V. A., Lesogor, L. W., Shupljakov, V. W., Taljasin, P. A., & Tjulkov, W. A. A functional model of signal processing in the peripheral auditory system. *Acustica*, 1974, *31*, 349–353.

Chomsky, N., & Halle, M. *The sound pattern of English*. New York: Harper & Row, 1968.

Cole, R. A., & Scott, B. Toward a theory of speech perception. *Psychological Review*, 1974, *81*, 348–374.

Cutting, J. E., & Rosner, B. S. Categories and boundaries in speech and music. *Perception and Psychophysics*, 1974, *16*, 564–570.

Fant, G. *Acoustic theory of speech production*. The Hague: Mouton, 1960.

Jakobson, R., Fant, G., & Halle, M. *Preliminary to speech analysis*. Cambridge, Mass.: MIT Press, 1963.

Kiang, N. Y-S. & Moxon, E. C. Physiological considerations in artificial stimulation of the inner ear. *Annals of Otology, Rhinology, and Laryngology*, 1972, *81*, 714–730.

Kiang, N. Y-S., Watanabe, T., Thomas, E. C., & Clark, L. F. *Discharge patterns of single fibers in the cat's auditory nerve*. Cambridge, Mass.: MIT Press, 1965.

Leshowitz, B., & Cudahy, E. Masking patterns for continuous and gated sinusoids. *Journal of the Acoustical Society of America*, 1975, *58*, 235–242.

Ling, D. *Speech and the hearing-impaired child: Theory and practice*. Washington, D.C.: A. G. Bell Association for the Deaf, 1976.

Lisker, L., & Abramson, A. A cross-language study of voicing in initial stops: Acoustical measurements. *Word*, 1964, *20*, 384–422.

Miller, J. D., Wier, C. C., Pastore, R. E., Kelly, W. J., & Dooling, R. J. Discrimination and labeling of noise–buzz sequences with varying noise-lead times: An example of categorical perception. *Journal of the Acoustical Society of America*, 1977, *60*, 410–417.

Norton, S. J., Schultz, M. C., Reed, C. M., Braida, L. D., Durlach, N. I., Rabinowitz, W. M., & Chomsky, C. Analytic study of the Tadoma method: Background and preliminary results. *Journal of Speech and Hearing Research*, 1977, *20*, 574–595.

Pickett, J. M., & Pickett, B. H. Communication of speech sounds by a tactual vocoder. *Journal of Speech and Hearing Research*, 1963, *6*, 207–222.

Pisoni, D. Identification and discrimination of the relative onset time of two-component tones: Implications for voicing perception in stops. *Journal of the Acoustical Society of America*, 1977, *61*, 1352–1361.

Scott, B. L. Temporal factors in vowel perception. *Journal of the Acoustical Society of America*, 1976, *60*, 1354–1365.

Sparks, D. W., Kuhl, P. K., Edmonds, A. A., & Gray, G. P. Investigating the MESA: The transmission of segmental features of speech. *Journal of the Acoustical Society of America*, 1978, *63*, 246–357.

Stevens, K. N. The quantal nature of speech. In E. E. David & P. B. Denes (Eds.), *Human communication: A unified view*. New York: McGraw-Hill, 1972, 51–66.

Stevens, K. N. The potential role of property detectors in the perception of consonants. In G. Fant & M. A. A. Tatham (Eds.), *Auditory analysis and perception of speech*. London: Academic, 1975, 303–330.

Stevens, K. N., & Blumstein, S. E. Invariant cues for place of articulation in stop consonants. *Journal of the Acoustical Society of America*, 1978, *64*, 1358–1368.

UNDERSTANDING
SPOKEN LANGUAGE

5 Misperceptions of Fluent Speech

Z. S. Bond
Ohio Univeristy

Sara Garnes
Ohio State University

INTRODUCTION

During the past few decades, research concerning the perception of speech has focused on discovering the acoustic cues for phonemes. This research has usually employed synthetic speech-like stimuli to examine the perceptual effect that is produced by manipulating a particular acoustic feature, such as the second formant transition in providing place of articulation information (Liberman, Harris, Hoffman, & Griffith, 1957) or the rate of formant change in providing information about manner of articulation (Liberman, Delattre, Gerstman, & Cooper, 1956). Typically, these studies have employed isolated words or syllables as stimuli.

Such experiments have been invaluable in determining which acoustic cues are adequate to cause subjects to label various syllables appropriately and consistently. But we believe that these studies contain a hidden assumption: that the essential problems of speech perception can be solved by understanding the mechanisms underlying phoneme perception, and that perception of fluent speech does not involve, at least in terms of processing the acoustic signal, any more than making use of acoustic cues whenever they are available. In other words, the perception of fluent speech may be thought to be identical to the perception of isolated words or syllables, with the only difference being that the listener simply has more syllables to perceive.

Whether or not this assumption was ever really held by any researcher is irrelevant; the important consideration is that this assumption is most certainly false. Both the acoustic structure of continuous speech and the data obtained in experiments involving continuous speech suggest that a listener uses not only acoustic information but also employs strategies of various sorts in order to understand conversation.

It is quite well known by now that the acoustic realization of continuous speech is severely degraded when compared to the maximally distinct isolated utterances often used in laboratory situations. The acoustic cues that accompany words spoken in isolation are often simply not present in fluent speech; segments and syllables are omitted, vowel color is significantly changed by consonantal environment, and so forth (see Bond, 1976a, 1976b; Klatt & Stevens, 1973; Oshika, Zue, Weeks, Nue, & Aurbach, 1975; Shockey, 1974; Stampe, 1973). This variability of the acoustic realization of words has been underlined by the difficulties encountered in attempts to develop automatic speech recognition systems; it appears that the acoustic cues for a given lexical item may differ radically from production to production (see Klatt, 1977). Reddy's discussion (Chap. 9) illustrates the highly constrained nature of a successful speech recognition system.

With regard to experiments involving the perception of continuous speech, the early studies of Miller, Heise, and Lichten (1951) and Miller and Isard (1963) clearly suggest that the syntax and semantics of an utterance contribute to its recognition when presented in noise. Research by Pickett and Pollack (1963) and Pollack and Pickett (1963) on the intelligibility of excerpts from conversation also shows that acoustic information must be supplemented by other sources of information during the perception of conversational speech. Cole and Jakimik (Chap. 6) and Foss (Chap. 7) have shown that listeners respond to predictable words faster than to unpredictable words in fluent speech.

We have tested the hypothesis that listeners advert to nonacoustic sources for word identification (Garnes & Bond, 1976, 1977a). Our experiments show that the perception of an acoustically ambiguous word (e.g., "date" or "gate") is determined by the semantic content of the sentence in which it occurs. In one experiment, we used the synthesized carrier sentences:

1. Here's the fishing gear and the _____.
2. Check the time and the _____.
3. Paint the fence and the _____.

Each of 16 different stimuli representing an acoustic continuum from *bait* to *date* to *gate* was spliced in as the last word in each of the three carrier sentences. The continuum was produced by varying the starting frequency of the second formant transition from 1050 Hz to 2850 Hz in 120 Hz steps, thereby crossing through the range from *bait* to *date* to *gate*.

Subjects were asked to indicate which of the three words they thought they heard at the end of each sentence.

The results of the experiment show that subjects do report hearing unexpected semantic combinations such as "Check the time and the bait," and "Check the time and the gate," when the acoustical information in the target word is unambiguous. However, when the second formant transition falls in the crossover range between the phonetic categories of [b], [d], and [g] so that the acoustic information is ambiguous, the subjects' judgments are shifted to the semantically appropriate word, compared to the identification pattern for the same stimuli obtained in isolation. The results indicate that the semantic content of a carrier sentence can affect the categorization of phonetic information.

In a second study (Garnes & Bond, 1977a), we investigated a related hypothesis, that misperceived sentences preserve semantic integrity, i.e., perception is guided by the listener's attempt to understand. Twenty subjects listened to natural recordings of 17 semantically anomalous and semantically well-formed sentences under two different listening conditions, and were instructed to repeat exactly each sentence which they heard. When the listening conditions were excellent, subjects made few errors. However, when listening conditions were poor ($S/N = -3$dB), subjects tended to "correct" semantically strange sentences by imposing upon them a semantically appropriate interpretation; for example, sentences such as "Check the time and bait" or "Check the dime and the date" were repeated as "Check the time and the date."

The results of the two experiments are quite consistent. Under ideal listening conditions, listeners do report hearing anomalous sentences. However, if the phonetic signal is unclear, listeners use semantic information to aid in their final decoding of the message. Since most normal speech perception undoubtedly takes place under less than ideal circumstances, the final decoding of ambiguous phonetic input in normal everyday speech must utilize considerable semantic information.

MISPERCEPTIONS OF FLUENT SPEECH

Our experiments were designed to test hypotheses that were suggested to us while analyzing misperceptions. We expected that errors in listening to conversational speech—or misperceptions—would provide information about the speech perception process in general, as well as about the heuristic and pragmatic strategies which listeners employ in conversational situations.

In this endeavor, we are following a long tradition which attempts to explicate the functions of a system by examining the nature of its failures.

Thus, errors in speech production, commonly known as "slips of the tongue," have been analyzed to show the systematic characteristics of anomalous utterances (Fromkin, 1971). The study of errors in reading, known as miscue analysis, has been used to indicate the components of the reading process which have not yet been fully mastered (Goodman, 1973), while errors in the writing of young adults elucidate the composing process (Shaughnessy, 1977). Slips of the ear—or misperceptions—provide insight into the speech perception process.

The Data

We have collected approximately 1,000 examples of errors in the perception of fluent conversational speech. In collecting errors, we simply noted, whenever a misperception occurred, the actual spoken utterance and the (mis)perceived utterance. The nature of these errors is best clarified by the following example, in which a speaker is explaining the subdivisions of geology:

> Another area is seismology.
> What?
> Seismology.
> Oh, I thought you said, "Psychology."

The listener hears, clearly and distinctly, something that does not correspond to what the speaker has said. This, then, is a misperception, a slip of the ear.

In the ideal data gathering situation, one of us is a third party observer of a face-to-face conversation in which the speaker is misunderstood by the listener, and the listener immediately reports what she thinks she has heard, as in the following example:

> I teach speech science.
> Speech signs?
> Speech science!
> Speech sinus?
> Speech science!!
> Oh. . . .

In this conversation, one of us was present as a third party observer and was able to both confirm that the speaker's intended utterance was correctly produced and to record the listener's attempts to verify her perception—or misperception—of the utterance. However, optimal data gathering conditions do not always obtain. At times, we have observed misperceptions in our own conversations when no third party observer was present. In this situation, of course, we cannot *prove* that the speaker said what she thinks she said—that is, we cannot distinguish between a slip of the ear and a slip of the tongue.[1]

Even though some of our data have been obtained under less than optimal conditions, we believe that the consistency we have found in the types of perceptual errors that occur is such that we can, on the whole, rely on our observations. Furthermore, when there is evidence obtained in controlled experimental conditions that bears on our observations, the laboratory evidence confirms our naturalistic observations.

Our data presentation employs a classification scheme in which errors are described in terms of the linguistic category to which the error is sensitive, whether it be phonology, morphology, or semantics. Obviously, errors sensitive to syntax or semantics may also involve a radical phonological restructuring of an utterance.

Segmental Substitutions

Errors which involve only the misperception of one or more segments in an utterance are quite common, accounting for 26.6% of all the misperceptions we have collected.[2] The first type of error involving segmental misperception is exemplified by the following:

Let's look for the *cape→cake*

In this example, the labial plosive /p/ is misidentified as the velar plosive /k/; the error involves only one feature—the place of articulation of the word-final consonant. It is also possible for an error to result in a greater

---

[1]Some of the examples of misperceptions have occurred in unnatural conversational settings, such as telephone conversations. It is well known that under such conditions the acoustic signal is degraded. We note in this paper whatever unusual factors may have occasioned perceptual errors.

[2]The percentages presented here are based on the tabulation in Garnes and Bond (1977b). There we sorted the misperceptions into four main categories: (1) errors involving one segment within one word, e.g., *since→sense* (26.6%); (2) errors involving more than one segment within one word, e.g., *raised→glazed* (32.4%); (3) errors involving more than one word, e.g., *we got our Task Force Grant→tennis court grant* (25.4%); and (4) a category of miscellaneous errors including examples from languages other than English and examples gleaned from the media (which, we assume are not as spontaneous as the rest of the errors are) (15.6%). All percentages given in this paper are in relationship to the total corpus. A more sophisticated analysis which tabulates each kind of segmental or multisegmental error in examples involving more than one word awaits a more sophisticated system of analysis than is presently available.

mismatch between the perceived and the spoken utterance, yet still reside in one segment:

All of the members of the group *grew* up in Philadelphia→*threw* up

In this case, not only is the point of articulation misidentified but also the manner of articulation and voicing—a voiced plosive /g/ is heard as a voiceless fricative /θ/.

In general, the misperceptions affecting consonants are readily explicable in terms of the traditional consonant classification of manner, place, and voicing. In this sense, our data correspond reasonably well with analyses of perceptual confusions among consonants obtained under laboratory conditions (cf. Miller & Nicely, 1955; Singh, Woods, & Becker, 1973). The distribution of segmental errors in our corpus is in close agreement with Miller and Nicely's data on misperceptions of consonants presented in noise. For example, the most common segmental substitution that we have observed in conversational speech involves the misperception of the place of articulation of a consonant (7.0%), as in the following examples:

*p*orpoise lady→what's a *c*orpus lady
Councilman *P*ortman for Democratic candidate for mayor→*C*ortman
It's hard to hear the difference between f and th over a *ph*one→what's a *th*one?[3]
Dea*th* in Venice→dea*f*

Other common errors in our corpus include substitution of voicing in stops and fricatives (cu*p*id→Cu*b*an, maple lea*f*→make-belie*ve*) (1.7%); and substitution of manner of articulation (*m*arried→*b*uried, *v*iable→*b*uyable, F*r*y's→f*l*ies) (4.0%).

Errors involving the misperception of stressed vowels are also present in our data, but, unlike errors involving single consonants, which account for 22.5% of the total corpus, stressed vowel errors are quite rare, accounting for only 4.1% of the corpus. Most commonly, errors involving stressed vowels only are made when a vowel is in the environment of /l/, /r/, /m/, /n/, or /ŋ/ (2.8%). These are consonants which are known to affect significantly both the spectral composition and the identification patterns of vowels (Bond, 1976a, 1976b; Lehiste, 1964). For example:

The *bell* isn't working→the *bill*
Bill has now found his favorite kind of *shirts*→*shorts*
Wendy will come→*windy*

---

[3]This confusion between *thone* and *phone* occurred in a telephone conversation.

In some sense, it is not surprising that stressed vowel errors are rare (only 1.3% when not in liquid or nasal environments), since vowels are characterized by greater intensity and duration than consonants. Thus, it would be expected that listeners would take advantage of the relative clarity and distinctness with which the phonetic information concerning vowel identity is made available in the speech signal.

Preliminary results from an experiment designed to test the hypothesis that listeners are most sensitive to stressed vowels are encouraging. We produced a series of paragraphs by applying various systematic phonological distortions; for example, all voiced obstruents were replaced by voiceless obstruents and vice versa; all nasal consonants were replaced by voiced oral plosives, and vice versa, and so forth. Obviously, all of the phonological distortions led to difficulty in understanding the spoken paragraphs; however, the most serious decrement in comprehension occurred when stressed back vowels were substituted for front vowels, and vice versa. The error rate, in terms of words correctly reported, was twice as great under this condition as under any of the other conditions (Bond, 1978).

We have collected only one example which involves *only* an unstressed vowel error:

He's going to write a paper on tonology→tenology?

In this instance, the unstressed, first vowel in *tonology* is undoubtedly reduced to a schwa [ə] by the speaker, but is not recovered by the listener. All other examples in which unstressed vowels are misperceived contain multiple errors:

I think I see a place→I think I see his face.

The unstressed indefinite article, *a*, is misperceived, but so is the following noun. Another complex example (a more detailed discussion is presented in Word Boundaries, to follow) is:

descriptive→the script of

which involves an unstressed [ɪ] (in *-ive*) being misperceived as [ə] (*of*). The fact that so few examples involve unstressed vowels alone suggests that unstressed vowels are correctly perceived most of the time, not because their phonetic realization is clear, but rather because of the redundancy of language—their correct identity is usually implied by context.

To summarize, errors involving segmental substitutions are among the most common in conversational speech (26.6%). The substitution patterns typically involve acoustically similar consonants which differ by a single feature. However, substitutions involving acoustically dissimilar segments do occur. Simple vowel substitutions almost always involve unstressed syllables; substitution of stressed vowels is very rare when compared to consonantal errors.

Phonological Errors

A second type of perceptual error seems to involve the application of phonological rules. In casual, fluent speech, various systematic simplifications take place (Klatt & Stevens, 1973; Oshika et al., 1975; Shockey, 1974; Stampe, 1973; Zwicky, 1972), and numerous perceptual errors apparently hinge on these simplifications. Errors involving phonological rules are of two general types: A listener either fails to realize that a particular simplification rule has been applied in production and does not "recover" a reduced segment or syllable, or alternatively supposes that a rule has applied in production and reports hearing a spurious segment or syllable.

In production, it is quite possible to reduce a consonant cluster to one member, producing /tɛs/ for /tɛst/ (test), for example. In perception, listeners' errors may result from not compensating for this sort of possible consonant cluster reduction. Consonant deletion errors constitute 3.6% of the total corpus. Examples are:

> The no*des* of the moon→the no*se*
> I have a de*nt*al appointment→di*nn*er appointment
> In harmony with the te*xt*→te*st*

The reverse process, the perceptual insertion of consonants, apparently results from the listener's assumption that the speaker has simplified a consonant cluster in production, when in fact he has not. The listener attempts to compensate for the supposed reduction and reports hearing a consonant which was never spoken in the first place. Perceptual insertion of consonants, therefore, is evidence for the active use of phonological knowledge in speech perception. The fact that the listener reports hearing a possible, though not produced, sequence provides evidence that speech perception is a creative, generative process. Consonant insertion errors account for 3.8% of the total errors in our corpus. Examples are:

> gra*ss* roots→gras*p* roots
> i*nn*er tube→i*nt*er tube
> a basket of a*pp*les→a*mp*les
> What kind of pa*ns* did you use?→pa*nt*s

On occasion, the perception of spurious consonants seems to result from regional dialect differences. These errors involve two participants in a conversation who speak different regional dialects. The listener's errors show an attempt to compensate for reductions possible to the speaker, though not to himself:

It's Lawson [New York]→Larson
Kama Sutra [Massachusetts]→Kama? Did you say Kama or Karma?

Just as segments may be deleted or inserted in perceptual errors, so may syllables. Typically, syllables which are deleted in perception are unstressed; thus, these syllables are often either quite weakly articulated or deleted in production (e.g., go away→go 'way). Perceptual deletion of syllables involves, therefore, either simply not noticing a very short segment or not compensating for a deleted syllable. Some examples of syllable deletion, which account for 5.4% of the total corpus, are:

A phonetic explanation of phonology by *Ohala→Halle?* Morris Halle?
This report is *tolerable→horrible*
Two *models* of speech perception→two *miles*

Syllable insertion also demonstrates the generative use of phonological information during speech perception, since the process typically occurs in environments in which an unstressed syllable could have been deleted, but in fact was not. The listener assumes that the deletion did occur, and supplies the missing syllable. Typically, when syllable insertion is observed, we find additional changes in the misperception which allow the misperception to fit into the conversation in the most meaningful manner possible. Examples of syllable insertion (which accounts for 2.8% of the total corpus) are:

I bought a slide *hammer→slide camera*
Isn't it nice not to have all these *deadlines?→dandelions*[4]

On occasion, an error involving the insertion of syllables is probably attributable to lack of compensation for dialect differences on the part of the listener. For example:

Does he have any *hair?* [Tennessee]→*higher*

---

[4]The listener is an eleven-year-old child sitting with her mother in the front seat of a moving car driving past their house.

The diphthongized, drawled vowel of the speaker is given a value of two syllables, which it may well have phonetically, rather than being recovered as the intended vowel.

In summary, perceptual errors may simply result from a listener's not compensating for a phonological reduction which has occurred in production. Alternatively, a listener may supply a spurious segment or syllable on the assumption that a phonological rule has applied in production when it has not; this latter type of perceptual error clearly indicates that knowledge of possible phonological reductions is actively employed in the perception of fluent speech.

Another common perceptual error involves metathesis—a change in the order of segments or syllables. Errors involving metathesis account for 4.3% of the total corpus; the occurrence of this type of error gives support to the theories of speech perception which claim that perception does not proceed linearly, segment by segment, but rather that a chunk of speech is processed before order is imposed on segments. It is quite possible for a metathesized pattern to be more complex than the mere reversal of two segments. Perceptual metatheses can affect segments separated from each other for a considerable distance in a particular word and even across word boundaries. Consider this perceptual error:

Do you *own* a gray Cortina→*know*

It changes the consonant–vowel order of the syllable, from a VC to CV pattern. The error:

hockey pucks→*coffee* pots

involves misordering the fricative /h/ with the plosive /k/ in the first word of the utterance; then, probably because initial /h/ is inadmissible in an unstressed syllable, the frication is reinterpreted as /f/.

In the misperception:

*Fr*iar *Tuck* pizza→Ken*tucky Fr*ied pizza

The syllable /tʌk/ and the syllable-initial sequence /fraɪ/ are metathesized, and numerous other compensatory adjustments are made.

It is interesting to note that the metatheses we have observed seldom cross phrase boundaries marked by an intonation contour. The domain of metathesis appears to be a part of one "breath group," suggesting that phrases marked by an intonation contour form perceptual units at some level of processing (see Bond, 1976c; Garnes, 1976).

Word Boundary Errors

As Cole and Jakimik (Chap. 6) have pointed out, word boundary cues are often absent in conversational speech, and the acoustic signal can be parsed into words in more than one way (also see Lehiste, 1960). In conversational speech, errors involving juncture are common, accounting for 17.9% of the total corpus. In some cases, the spoken phonetic string and the perceived mis-segmented string are identical. The listener has recovered the phonological representation of the utterance properly; he has merely deleted the word boundary. Consider these:

They had a *ten-year* party for Marlene→*tenure*
Do you know anything about four-*term analogy?*→four *terminology*
... *to missions*→*temissions?* What are they?

In other examples the listener reports having heard a sequence which is somewhat different from the spoken phonetic sequence, with an error in the assignment of the word boundary:

Get a *pill out*→pillow
It's made with *ham bone*→handbone
I need to *talk to him*→to calculate
I told him to go *n' find* a store→*infine?* What does infine mean?

Deletions of word boundaries account for 8.3% of the misperception in our corpus.

Shifts in word boundary assignments also occur (4.4%). As in the case of the examples discussed above, the misperceived string can be phonologically identical to the produced string with the exception of the placement of the word boundary, or it can incorporate other perceptual errors as well.

Maybe we could give them *an ice* bucket→*a nice* bucket
I'm in a hopeles*s q*uagmire→hopeles*s sq*uagmire
There*'s some ice tea* made→There*'s a nice team ma*te
If you enjoyed V*iet N*am, you'll love Angola→What does *meat 'n' ham* have to do with Angola?

Finally, the perceptual error can involve the insertion of a word boundary (5.2%), creating more word boundaries than existed in the original utterance. The error can merely reside in the boundary insertion or it can involve other subsidiary changes as well:

> I was looking at this *photograph→soda graph*
> *assorted→a sordid*
> Oh, he's Snoopy in *disguise→the skies*

Lexical Errors

The misperceptions discussed so far, although sometimes semantically and pragmatically odd, typically result in perceived utterances which are grammatical and are composed of existing lexical items. On occasion, however, a listener hears a nonword, a lexical item which fits the phonotactic structure of English, but does not occur. For example:

> I wanted to go to a *party→a burly* [bɜˑli]
> Her *obituary* was in the paper→her *habituary*
> The *anechoic* chamber→*ambionic* chamber
> She wrote a fancy, *seductive* letter to Boston→*structive* letter
> male *fur seal*→male *phariseal*
> I told him to go *n' find* a store→What does *infine* mean?

Although nonwords occur with some frequency in our data, we have observed only one instance of a violation of the phonotactic rules of English—when a ten-year-old child misperceived 'tlumbering' from the phrase 'out lumbering.'

Typically, a misperception is a transitory phenomenon which is readily rectified in the ensuing conversation. However, we have some evidence that misperceptions can result in a permanent erroneous representation of a word in the mind of the subject. Several people have reported that "for years I thought the word was...." Examples of relatively permanent misperceptions or "mislexicalizations" are:

> *frothing* at the mouth→*throffing*
> *never* mind→*lever*
> *next door* neighbor→*next store*

Such errors account for 8.3% of the total corpus.

Editing: Preserving Grammatical Structure

Misperceptions almost always preserve the grammatical structure of the language; we term this phenomenon "editing." Editing refers to the fact that unstressed function words and grammatical morphemes are most often perceived as required by the sense of the sentence. In other words, a listener "edits" the perceived utterance and reports the function words and grammatical morphemes which are appropriate to his interpretation of what he has heard. For example, in the two misperceptions:

hypnotic age regression→hypnotic aid *to* regression
you swallowed a watermelon→you smiled *at* a watermelon

the listener supplies prepositions which are required to make the utterances grammatical and meaningful, probably because he has misperceived the lexical item "age" in the first example and "swallowed" in the second example. The grammar of English requires prepositions in the two perceived contexts, so they are supplied by the listener.

Just as function words can be added in perception as required for grammatical purposes, so function words can be reported as not heard. For example, the two errors:

Where are your jeans?→Wear your jeans?
I've never cooked anybody's goose→. . . never cooked anybody mousse

both involve reporting a perception that is missing a function word or morpheme. The function word or morpheme has to be omitted for the utterance to be grammatical in English. It is likely that in conversational speech, unstressed function words and morphemes are often perceived from partial acoustic information. As Umeda (1977) has shown, segmental cues are dramatically reduced in duration in function words, compared to content words, so that recognition of these words no doubt requires contextually guided interpretation of partial acoustic information. Thus, in an utterance like "Where are your jeans?" the grammatical morpheme "are" is likely to be articulated with a single /r/-like sound from the end of "where" to the beginning of "your." The listener interprets the utterance as the semantically appropriate "wear your jeans." Essentially, then, editing is a process which adds or deletes morphological material so that the perceiver can interpret the sentence in a semantically and grammatically appropriate manner. Insertions, deletions, and changes of function words and/or morphemes account for 2.0% of the corpus.

Semantic Errors

We have already shown that misperceptions preserve the phonological and syntactic structure of the language. It is less likely, however, that misperceptions will be semantically appropriate, since a misperception will probably not be noticed (or at least reported) unless the listener thinks that the speaker said something rather odd or unusual. We have found several examples of misperceptions that are semantically bizarre:

After the rubber boat had been wrecked in the squall
→After the rubber boot had been erected in the squirrel
I seem to be thirsty→I sing through my green Thursday
That's the mother in me→that's the multi-runway
A linguini is a noodle→A lean Wheatie is a noodle

The occurrence of such errors casts some doubt on the universal applicability of the hypothesis that listeners take advantage of the contingencies of the environment, the history of the discourse, or selectional restrictions to interpret speech. Certainly, all of these factors are operative and function to point out the occurrence of a misperception; however, they do not completely constrain possible perceptions.

IMPLICATIONS OF THE DATA FOR FLUENT SPEECH PERCEPTION

The nature of perceptual errors in fluent speech provides a unique insight into the speech perception process which people employ in listening to conversational speech. We believe that the following inferences can be drawn from an examination of our data:

1. Speech perception is an active rather than a passive process. It is possible of course that "feature detectors," as suggested by Abbs and Sussman (1971), are employed for some of the analysis of the acoustic signal. However, active hypothesizing concerning the intended message is clearly a part of the speech perception process.

2. Listeners actively employ grammatical information in speech perception—on phonological, lexical, and sentence levels. Listeners are aware of "fast speech" rules and compensate for either real or supposed phonological reductions which have affected lexical representations. Listeners are also aware of the segments and sequences possible in a language, and "hear" only those that are possible.

Syntactic and morphological knowledge appears to be employed in two different ways. First, the appropriate morphological markers, such as the plural morpheme -s, the third person present tense verb morpheme -s, and so forth, are reported to have been heard, even when not uttered, and are not perceived when inappropriate to the reconstructed sentence. The implication is that listeners know what is appropriate grammatically and edit what they hear, supplying the required markers automatically.

Listeners seem also to be aware of surface syntactic organization, such as the basic noun phrase and verb phrase structure of utterances, which is probably linked to the suprasegmental pattern. Thus, even when some of the lexical items are misperceived, the basic syntactic organization is maintained. This fact suggests that the surface syntactic structure of sentences, independent of particular lexical items, is employed as a basic schema into which the lexical items are hypothesized to fit by the listener. For example, NP's remain NP's (this is Bear country→this is Erica), and VP's remain VP's (I need to talk to him→I need to calculate). However, misperceptions such as Where are your jeans?→ Wear your jeans, in which an interrogation (with both an NP and VP) is misperceived as an imperative (lacking a surface structure NP), show that the relationship between perception of syntactic and phonological structure can be complex.

3. Speech perception employs heuristic strategies, as opposed to formal grammatical operations. Four possible strategies are suggested by our data:

Pay Attention to Stress and Intonation Patterns. In our data, we have observed only a handful of examples in which the stress or intonation pattern is inaccurately reported:

    kétchup→a chíp
    róll up→patról

Typically, the perceived suprasegmental pattern matches the spoken pattern.

Find a Phrase. This strategy undoubtedly involves the use of the first strategy. The listener segments the spoken sequence into phrases which can be at least partially identified on the basis of stress and intonation patterns. These phrases must then be given some semantic analysis and "edited" for appropriate morphological markers. We find support for this strategy in the paucity of word-boundary or metathesis errors crossing phrase boundaries.[5]

Find a Word. Listeners employ knowledge of the existing lexicon, typically reporting that they "hear" real words rather than possible but nonexistent words. The use of lexical information is probabilistic rather than absolute, however, since listeners do report hearing (phonologically permissible) nonsense words. This is not surprising when we consider that adding a word to the lexicon is a common enough occurrence for adults. Some perceptual errors suggest that a listener is scanning the speech

---

[5]David Fay has suggested to us that the absence of errors occurring across phrase boundaries may simply result from a gap in our data.

signal for the occurrence of possible lexical items. For example, the speaker says,

"I had this appointment..." The listener interrupts, asking, "Disappointment?" The listener reacts appropriately to a message which he believes is going to convey something rather serious. He does this on the basis of a hypothesized lexical match; however, this hypothesis is erroneous. The impression is quite irresistible that the lexical item arrived as a "best match" as soon as the speaker's phrase "this appointment" was available.

Pay Attention to Stressed Vowels. The scarcity of stressed vowel misperceptions suggests that listeners make use of their relatively clear acoustic structure. A salient property of the speech signal is probably salient in perception as well.

SUMMARY

In this paper we have attempted to characterize the properties of misperceptions of fluent speech which we feel have implications for models of speech perception. In addition, we have briefly reported the results of several experiments which bear on the hypotheses suggested by our data. Finally, we have suggested several properties which speech perception mechanisms seem to exhibit.

We would like to emphasize two points: First, speech perception is an active process; second, listeners employ grammatical information as well as heuristic strategies in order to understand fluent speech.

Though the hypotheses suggested by our data obviously require experimental testing, we believe that the data are of value as a source of hypotheses about the perception of fluent speech and as a measure for the adequacy of proposed speech perception models.

ACKNOWLEDGMENT

We want to thank Donald Fucci, Director of the School of Hearing and Speech Sciences at Ohio University, for his support of this project.

REFERENCES

Abbs, J. H., & Sussman, H. M. Neurophysiological feature detectors and speech perception: A discussion of theoretical implications. *Journal of Speech and Hearing Research*, 1971, *14*, 23–36.

Bond, Z. S. Identification of vowels excerpted from neutral and nasal contexts. *Journal of the Acoustical Society of America*, 1976, *59*, 1229–1232. (a)

Bond, Z. S. Identification of vowels excerpted from /l/ and /r/ contexts. *Journal of the Acoustical Society of America*, 1976, *60*, 906–910. (b)

Bond, Z. S. On the specification of input units in speech perception. *Brain and Language*, 1976, *3*, 72–87. (c)

Bond, Z. S. Listening to elliptical speech: pay attention to stressed vowels. Linguistic Society of America, Boston, December, 1978.

Fromkin, V. A. The non-anomalous nature of anomalous utterences. *Language*, 1971, *47*, 27–53.

Garnes, S. *Quantity in Icelandic: Production and perception*. Hamburg: Helmut Buske Verlag, 1976.

Garnes, S., & Bond, Z. S. The relationship between semantic expectation and acoustic information. *Phonologica*, 1976, 285–293.

Garnes, S., & Bond, Z. S. *Influence of semantics on speech perception*. Presented at 93rd Meeting of the Acoustical Society of America, University Park, PA, 1977 (a).

Garnes, S., & Bond, Z. S. A slip of the ear: A snip of the ear?, A slip of the year? Paper presented at the Working Group on "Slips of the Tongue and Ear," Twelfth International Congress of Linguistics, Vienna, 1977 (b).

Goodman, K. S. (Ed.) *Miscue analysis: Applications to reading instruction*. Urbana, Ill.: National Council of Teachers of English, 1973.

Klatt, D. H. Review of the ARPA speech understanding project. *Journal of the Acoustical Society of America*, 1977, *62*, 1345–1366.

Klatt, D. H., & Stevens, K. N. On the automatic recognition of continuous speech: Implications of a spectrogram-reading experiment. *IEEE Transactions: Audio and Electroacoustics*, 1973, *AU-21*, 210–217.

Lehiste, I. An acoustic–phonetic study on internal open juncture. *Phonetica*, 1960, *5*, 1–54.

Lehiste, I. *Acoustical characteristics of selected English consonants*. Bloomington: Indiana University Press, 1961.

Liberman, A. M., Delattre, P. C., Gerstman, L. J., & Cooper, F. S. Tempo of frequency change as a cue for distinguishing classes of speech sounds. *Journal of Experimental Psychology*, 1956, *52*, 127–137.

Liberman, A. M., Harris, K. S., Hoffman, H. S., & Griffith, B. C. The discrimination of speech sounds within and across phoneme boundaries. *Journal of Experimental Psychology*, 1957, *54*, 358–367.

Miller, G. A., Heise, G. A., & Lichten, W. The intelligibility of speech as a function of the context of the test materials. *Journal of Experimental Psychology*, 1951, *41*, 329–335.

Miller, G. A., & Isard, S. Some perceptual consequences of linguistic rules. *Journal of Verbal Learning and Verbal Behavior*, 1963, *2*, 217–228.

Miller, G. A., & Nicely, P. E. An analysis of perceptual confusions among some English consonants. *Journal of the Acoustical Society of America*, 1955, *27*, 338–352.

Oshika, B. T., Zue, V. W., Weeks, R. V., Nue, H., & Aurbach, I. The role of phonological rules in speech understanding research. *IEEE Transactions: Acoustics, Speech, Signal Processing*, 1975, *23*, 104–112.

Pickett, J. M., & Pollack, I. Intelligibility of excerpts from fluent speech: Effects of rate of utterance and duration of excerpt. *Language and Speech*, 1963, *6*, 151–164.

Pollack, I., & Pickett, J. M. The intelligibility of excerpts from conversation. *Language and Speech*, 1963, *6*, 165–171.

Shaughnessy, M. *Errors and expectations*. New York: Oxford, 1977.

Shockey, L. Phonetic and phonological properties of connected speech. In *Working papers in linguistics* (No. 17). Department of Linguistics, The Ohio State University: Columbus, Ohio, 1974.

Singh, S., Woods, D. R., & Becker, G. M. Perceptual structure of 22 prevolic English consonants. *Journal of the Acoustical Society of America*, 1973, *62*, 1698–1713.

Stampe, D. *A dissertation on natural phonology*. Unpublished doctoral dissertation, University of Chicago, 1973.

Umeda, N. Consonant duration in American English. *Journal of the Acoustical Society of America*, 1977, *61*, 846–858.

Zwicky, A. Note on a phonological hierarchy in English. In R. P. Stockwell & R. K. S. Macauley (Eds.), *Linguistic change and generative theory*. Bloomington: Indiana University Press, 1972.

6

A Model of Speech Perception

Ronald A. Cole

Jola Jakimik
Carnegie-Mellon University

If a tree falls in a forest and no one hears it, does it make a sound? This question is fun to contemplate, but since it has no answer, let us consider a similar question, which does have an answer. If Lincoln's Gettysburg address is broadcast in a forest, and no one hears it, do the words exist? The answer to this trick question is "no": Words do not exist as discrete physical events in fluent speech. This can be shown by a simple experiment. If we remove the sounds which accompany a word from their fluent speech context and listen to them in isolation, we often cannot recognize the word. The sounds which accompany a word may be insufficient by themselves to produce its recognition. Words, then, are the product of speech perception. They exist in the mind of a perceiver, and not in the physical stimulus.

How do listeners recognize words from fluent speech, often on the basis of partial acoustic information? In this chapter, we will attempt to answer this question within the framework of a model of speech perception. We describe, and attempt to substantiate, four assumptions about the way in which words are recognized. The assumptions are:

1. Words are recognized through the interaction of sound and knowledge.
2. Speech is processed sequentially, word by word. Each word's recognition:
   a. locates the onset of the immediately following word; and
   b. provides syntactic and semantic constraints that are used to recognize the immediately following word.

3. Words are accessed from the sounds which begin them.
4. A word is recognized when the sequential analysis of its acoustic structure eliminates all candidates but one.

Taken together these four assumptions outline a model of word recognition that is consistent with the results of a number of recent experiments, and with the experience of listening to fluent speech: the experience of hearing a series of words, one after another, as they are being spoken.

The model was originally proposed to account for two problems in word recognition from fluent speech: *segmentation* and *variation*. Segmentation refers to the problem of locating word boundaries in a continuous signal, in which physical cues to word boundaries are rarely present. As we will see, locating word boundaries is an important part of word recognition, because a given stretch of speech can often be parsed into words in more than one way. Variation refers to the fact that fluent speech is characterized by "sloppy" articulation, so that words must often be recognized from partial acoustic information.

The problem of segmentation is addressed by assuming that speech is processed sequentially, word by word. That is, the words in an utterance are recognized one after another. Each word's recognition locates the onset of the following word, and (along with all preceding words) provides syntactic and semantic constraints on its identity. Thus, listeners know where words begin and end by recognizing them in order. The problem of variation is handled by assuming that a word's recognition is constrained both by the context in which it occurs, and by its acoustic structure. Recognition occurs through the interaction of these two sources of constraint.

Perhaps the most attractive feature of the model is that it provides a straightforward description of the moment by moment processing of any sentence. In order to describe these information processing strategies in some detail, it is helpful to work through an example. Consider the sentence "Tell the gardener to plant some more tulips," spoken with the following phonetic structure:

/tɛlðəgɑrdnɚtəplænsʌmɔrtulɪps/

The spoken version of the sentence contains several alternative word-level segmentations. "Plant some" can be perceived as "plan some" (due to stop deletion of the word-final /t/ in "plant"), "some more" may be perceived as "some ore," and "tulips" may be parsed as "two lips." As we will see, the intended segmentation is provided by the listener's use of context, and not by acoustic information.

We assume that, when a listener hears the beginning of this sentence, all possible words beginning with /tɛl/ are immediately activated as word candidates. For convenience (and for lack of data) we will describe the recognition process syllable by syllable, rather than phoneme by phoneme. Since almost any word can begin an English sentence, all words beginning with /tɛl/ will be activated, including "tell," "television," "telephone," etc. The next syllable, /ðə/ eliminates all candidates but "tell," since there are no English words beginning /tɛlð/, and no alternate word-level segmentations of /tɛlðə/. Recognizing "tell" causes /ðə/ to be considered as the beginning of a new word. There are only a few English words beginning with /ðə/, but "the" is the only syntactically appropriate word following "tell," so "the" is immediately recognized, probably before the stop burst of /g/ has been analyzed. Recognizing "the" defines /gɑr/ or /gɑrd/ as the beginning of a new word, and this syllable will be used to activate a set of candidates including "guard," "gardener," "garment," etc. The syllable /nɚ/ eliminates all word candidates but "gardener." The listener has now recognized "Tell the gardener." Recognition of "gardener" defines /tə/ as the first syllable of a new word. Since /tə/ contains a reduced vowel, it is perceived as an unstressed syllable and is used to access "to," "today," "tomorrow," etc., all of which occur in fluent speech with a reduced first syllable. The phonetic sequence /pl/ eliminates all words but "to" and is used to access all words beginning with this common cluster. The next sequence of syllables, /plænsʌm/, is ambiguous; it could be parsed as "plant some" or "plan some." [1] In the present example, we will assume that the listener recognizes "plant," because planting is an activity that gardeners often enjoy. The syllable /sʌm/ is then used to activate "some," "summer," etc. The syllable /ɔr/ eliminates all candidates but "some." The sequence /sʌmɔr/ is again ambiguous—"some more" or "some ore"—but semantic and syntactic constraints will cause "more" to be recognized rather than "ore." Given recognition of "Tell the gardener to plant some more... ," the syllable /tu/ will be perceived as the first stressed syllable of a multisyllabic word (since the vowel is not reduced). Since "tulips" will have been partially activated by prior syntactic and semantic constraints, it will probably be recognized during or possibly before a complete phonetic analysis of its second syllable.

The model can be similarly applied to any sentence. The basic pattern

---

[1]The listener may consciously recognize the ambiguity, but we assume that typically only one word is recognized. If it is not the intended word, the listener will have to change his interpretation of the sentence when subsequent context provides conflicting information. If the listener perceives the nonintended word "plan" and subsequent context does not provide conflicting evidence, a misunderstanding has occurred. The gardener will be planning to plant tulips rather than planting them.

that emerges from working through numerous examples is that word choice is constrained both by prior context and by the number of words that can begin with a particular first syllable. When word choice is highly constrained by either of these factors, the intended word can be recognized without waiting for information from subsequent syllables. When many words can occur in a given context, or begin with a particular syllable (or both), it is necessary to consider additional syllables before it is possible to recognize the word under analysis. Thus, the time to recognize a particular word depends both upon the constraint provided by prior context, and the number of words that begin with the same sounds as the intended word.

In the remainder of this chapter, we consider each of the assumptions of the model, and describe the experimental support for each assumption. Then we will integrate the four assumptions to explain the results of some recent experiments.

ASSUMPTION 1:
WORDS ARE RECOGNIZED
THROUGH THE INTERACTION
OF SOUND AND KNOWLEDGE

Fluent speech is an extremely complex stimulus. Consider that despite years of intensive research (and millions of dollars) spent in trying to program computers to recognize fluent speech, man is still orders of magnitude better at understanding speech than the most successful speech understanding system (see Norman, Chap. 11, for a discussion of this point).

Why has it proved to be so difficult to program computers to recognize words from fluent speech? The answer is that natural continuous speech is a highly ambiguous stimulus. According to Reddy (1976):

> In connected speech it is difficult to determine where one word ends and another begins. In addition, acoustic characteristics of sounds and words exhibit much greater variability in connected speech, depending on the context, compared with words spoken in isolation [p. 509].

The two problems identified by Reddy—*variation* (the lack of stable patterns for words) and *segmentation* (the lack of cues to word boundaries)—will be considered in turn.

Variation

The structure of words in fluent speech can be compared to their structure when spoken in isolation. Words spoken in isolation display relatively stable auditory patterns. If we ask an informant to read a list of isolated words, we note that each is articulated in a fairly precise manner. Because of this careful articulation, words spoken in isolation can be regarded as stable patterns. Reddy (1976) notes that words spoken in isolation can be recognized by computer using classical pattern matching techniques with accuracies around 99%.

By contrast, words in fluent speech are not usually observed as stable patterns of sound. Fluent speech is characterized by phonological variation, so the acoustic structure of a word may vary substantially from one utterance to the next. Consider, for example, the different realizations of "what" in "What are you doing?"; "Whacha doing?"; "Whadaya doing?"; and "Whaya doin?" The phonetic segments that are clearly present when a word is spoken in isolation may be reduced, altered, deleted, or combined with other segments when the same word is produced during conversation (Klatt & Stevens, 1973). Recent attempts to recognize speech by computer have confirmed that words do not exist as stable patterns in fluent speech, and cannot be recognized using classical pattern matching techniques (Reddy, 1976; Klatt, 1977).

Pollack and Pickett (1963) were the first to demonstrate that the acoustic information which accompanies a word is sometimes insufficient to specify its identity. They surreptitiously recorded the conversations of students, and then examined the intelligibility of "words" excised from the conversations. When excised words were presented in isolation to a separate group of subjects, only about half of the words were correctly identified. Recognition was only 70% when portions of speech containing two or three words were presented to subjects.

Because we typically perceive words clearly and automatically, it is difficult to appreciate the fact that words are recognized from an ambiguous signal. But by depriving the listener of the use of context (by constructing unusual utterances) it is possible to illustrate the problem. For example, it is virtually impossible to identify all the words in the spoken sentence "In mud eels are, in clay none are" or the utterance "In pine tar is, in oak none is." The response of four subjects who listened to these sentences, taken from Reddy (1976, p. 504) are given below:

in mud eels are	*in clay none are*
in muddies sar	in clay nanar
in my deals are	en clainanar
in my ders	en clain
in model sar	in claynanar

in pine tar is	*in oak none is*
in pine tarrar	in oak ? es
in pyntar es	in oak nonus

in pine tar is   in ocnonin
en pine tar is   in oak is

The errors subjects make on these sentences are instructive. According to Reddy (1976, p. 504):

> The responses show that the listener forces his own interpretation of what he hears, and not necessarily what may have been intended by the speaker. Because the subjects do not have the contextual framework to expect the words 'mud eels' together, they write more likely sounding combinations such as 'my deals' or 'models.' We find the same problem with words such as 'oak none is.' Notice that they failed to detect where one word ends and another begins. It is not uncommon for machine recognition systems to have similar problems with word segmentation.

Segmentation

A pervasive and equally serious problem is *segmentation*—finding word boundaries. In fluent speech there are no physical cues that consistently and reliably indicate where one word ends and the next begins. To be sure, there are some physical events that signal word boundaries. For example, the occurrence of a glottal stop almost always signals the presence of a word boundary in American English. Similarly, intonation contours at major constituent boundaries are reliable cues to word juncture (Sorensen & Cooper, Chap. 12). But cues to word juncture are the exception rather than the rule. At a conservative estimate, less than 40% of all word boundaries are marked by some physical event, and most of these coincide with a constituent boundary.

The impression that words in fluent speech are separated in time is an illusion. Words exist in the mind of the perceiver—not in the stimulus. The continuous nature of conversational speech is apparent when we listen to an unfamiliar language—we hear a rapidly changing, rhythmic stream of sound. Because speech is continuous across word boundaries (and because fluent speech is characterized by phonological variation), a given stretch of speech can usually be parsed into words in more than one way. For example, "more rice" can also be heard as "more ice," "some more" as "some ore," "fresh shout" as "fresh out," "real love" as "reel of," and "grew wise" as "grew eyes." One of the best examples of this sort was produced by B. F. Skinner, who created the following sequence of words: "Anna Mary candy lights since imp pulp lay things." If these words are spoken rapidly and without hesitation, they provide a passable version of the sentence "An American delights in simple play things." This example shows that a given utterance may contain many words that *could* be heard, but are not.

The fact that speech can often be parsed into words in alternate ways is the basis of many popular ditties. Examples are "I scream, you scream, we all scream for ice cream"; "Mares eat oats and does eat oats and little lambs eat ivy"; and "Fuzzy wuzzy was a bear, Fuzzy wuzzy had no hair, Fuzzy wuzzy wasn't fuzzy, was he?" The ambiguous nature of fluent speech is also the basis of many puns (e.g., They fed the catatonic [cat a tonic]). The presence of a prolific punster can make us painfully aware of the extent to which fluent speech can be variously parsed.

To summarize, fluent speech is an ambiguous stimulus. A given stretch of speech can often be parsed into words in more than one way, and because of phonological variation, the acoustic information that accompanies an intended word may be insufficient, by itself, to uniquely specify its identity. The first assumption of the model, that words are recognized through the interaction of sound and knowledge, is an attempt to come to grips with the fact that words are often recognized from partial acoustic information. The assumption is that words are constrained both by their acoustic structure and the context in which they occur, and that listeners use both sources of information to recognize words from fluent speech.

The Use of Knowledge in Speech Perception

We have considered the structure of words in fluent speech in some detail in order to emphasize the critical role of knowledge in word recognition. It is obvious that linguistic and real-world knowledge must be used to recognize words when speech is partially masked by noise; when we are confronted with an unfamiliar dialect or accent; or when a speaker's articulation is unusually imprecise. But we are saying more than this: Our claim is that knowledge is used to recognize words even when the acoustic input is crystal clear. The use of knowledge during word recognition is needed to explain the fact that we hear only the words we are *intended* to hear. Remember, a spoken sentence often contains many words that were not intended to be heard. The last sentence, for example, contains "Ream ember, us poke can cent tense off in contains men knee words that were knot in ten did tube bee herd." We recognize the words we are intended to hear by using knowledge both to locate word boundaries and to interpret the acoustic input.

Spoken language is a highly structured system, and structural organization can be identified at various linguistic levels. At the phonological level, the order of phonemes within words is highly constrained. There are, for example, only 27 word-initial clusters in English consisting of two consonants or a consonant followed by /r/, /l/, or /w/, out of 210 possible clusters. Speakers are extremely sensitive to the phonotactic structure of their language. We know that "blit," "shrat," or "fren" *could* be English words, but that "dlit," "srat," or "vren" could not, since English words cannot begin with /dl/, /sr/, or /vr/. Marslen-Wilson (1978) has recently shown that spoken words like "dlit," which violate English phoneme sequence constraints, can be judged as nonsense words more quickly than words like "blit," which do not violate these constraints.

It is likely that listeners use their knowledge of phoneme sequence constraints to segment speech into words. For example, the spoken utterance "This lip" can be misinterpreted as "The slip" or "This slip," but the utterance "This rip" cannot be parsed in more than one way, since /sr/ is not a permissible word-initial cluster in English. Knowledge of phoneme sequence constraints may be particularly useful in the beginning of a sentence, where prior context is least likely to constrain word choice. A sentence which begins "I'm a..." (as in "I'm aching...") can be segmented as "I'm a... ," "I may... ," or "I'm ma..." (as in "I'm making..."). The intended segmentation cannot be determined until additional phonetic information is available. But a sentence beginning "I'm g..." (as in "I'm going...") can only be interpreted as beginning with the word "I'm," since /mg/ does not occur in word-initial position in English.

Experimental Evidence

Speech in Noise.   It is an axiom of speech perception that listeners use context to understand speech. Some of the earliest studies of speech perception (e.g., Miller, Heise, & Lichten, 1951) showed that words presented in noise are recognized more accurately in a sentence context than in isolation (even though words spoken in isolation are acoustically better defined than words in fluent speech). One of the most impressive demonstrations of the importance of syntactic and semantic structure in speech perception was provided by Miller and Isard (1963), who compared the intelligibility of words presented in noise in normal sentences like "Gadgets simplify work around the house," in syntactically correct but meaningless sentences like "Gadgets kill passengers from the eyes," and in ungrammatical strings like "Between gadgets highways passengers the steal." Subjects correctly recognized 89% of the normal sentences, 79% of the semantically anomalous sentences, and 56% of the ungrammatical strings. The results show that both syntactic and semantic structures are used to perceive speech in noise.

Phonemic Restorations.   Perhaps the most dramatic effect of context on speech perception is the "phonemic restoration" effect investigated by Richard Warren. Warren (1970) replaced a phoneme—such as the first /s/ in legislatures—with a coughing sound of about the same intensity as the speech. He then presented the word with the missing phoneme in a sentence context to subjects, and asked them to indicate where in the sentence the cough occurred. The subjects were unable to accurately locate the cough. More important, the missing phoneme was completely "restored"; that is, it was not perceived as missing. The subjects heard the /s/ in "legislatures," and the cough was heard as background noise. Warren's demonstration of phonemic restorations suggests that under the right circumstances, a listener can use contextual information to generate phonemes that do not exist in the sound stream.

Phoneme Monitoring. When words are only partially specified by their acoustic structure, the use of prior context is crucial to their recognition. We wish to emphasize, however, that contextual information is used during word recognition *whenever* it is available, and not only when the acoustic input is ambiguous. Even carefully articulated words, presented under ideal listening conditions, are recognized more quickly when they are predictable from prior context. This point was first made by Morton and Long (1976), who measured reaction times to word-initial target phonemes in words with high or low transitional probability. A word's transitional probability was defined as its probability of occurrence given the preceding words in the sentence. For example, in the sentences "The sparrow sat on the *branch* singing a few shrill notes to welcome the dawn," and "The sparrow sat on the *bed* singing a few shrill notes to welcome the dawn," the word "branch" has a higher transitional probability than "bed." Morton and Long found that subjects responded about 80 msec faster to target phonemes in high transitional probability words. This result, which has been replicated several times (see Foss, Harwood, & Blank Chap. 7, for a review), demonstrates that listeners combine semantic information from a sentence (a sparrow sat) with real-world knowledge (sparrows sit on branches) during word recognition from fluent speech. Moreover, since the sentences used by Morton and Long were spoken clearly and distinctly, the results show that contextual information is used to recognize words whenever it is available, and not just when the acoustic input is degraded or incomplete.

The phoneme monitoring technique has also been used to investigate the role of prosody (rhythm, stress, and intonation) in speech perception. According to Martin (1972), the rhythmic pattern of an utterance—defined by the location in time of stressed syllables—is generated from a hierarchical structure. Martin suggests that listeners are able to use this hierarchical structure to predict the temporal location of stressed syllables. In support of this hypothesis, Shields, McHugh, and Martin (1974) found faster reaction times to word-initial target phonemes in stressed syllables than in unstressed syllables. In addition, they showed that the reaction time (RT) advantage was due to the prosodic structure of the entire sentence, and not to differences between the target syllables themselves. The RT advantage disappeared when the target words were excised from the sentences, and presented in lists of words. In a similar vein, Cutler (1976) has shown that phoneme monitoring times are reduced when the intonation contour of a sentence "predicts" that the target word will carry stress. These studies show that the prosodic structure of a sentence can be used to predict the temporal location of a word, and direct a listener's attention to it. But note that the prosodic structure of a sentence, unlike its syntactic and semantic structure, does not suggest or limit word candidates.

Listening for Mispronunciations.   Cole and Jakimik (1978) have reported a series of experiments which used a listening for mispronunciations task (Cole, 1973) to examine the effect of prior context on word recognition from fluent speech. In these experiments, listeners were presented with spoken sentences or short stories in which words were mispronounced by changing a single consonant segment to produce a phonologically permissible nonsense word (e.g., "boy" to "poy"). Subjects were instructed to push a response button whenever a mispronunciation was heard, and the time to detect a mispronunciation was measured from the onset of the altered segment.

The results of a number of experiments, summarized in Cole and Jakimik (1978), showed that mispronounced words are detected faster when they are constrained by prior context. For example, in a replication of the experiment performed by Morton and Long (1976) in which the high and low transitional probability words were mispronounced (e.g., "branch" to "pranch" and "bed" to "ped"), it was found that reaction times were over 150 msec faster to mispronunciations of high transitional probability words. The results suggest that listeners detect a mispronunciation by recognizing the intended word (and the acoustic mismatch), and that this occurs faster when the mispronounced word is predictable from prior context. Cole and Jakimik also observed faster reaction times to mispronounced words that were implied in a previous sentence than to words that were not implied, and faster reaction times to mispronounced words that were suggested by the title of a story. The results suggest that word recognition involves the on-line use of various sources of knowledge.

Recently, in collaboration with Charles Perfetti, we presented mispronounced words in a short story to children in first, third, and fifth grade, and to college students. The story contained 36 mispronounced words, each of which was mispronounced twice in the story in exactly the same way. One occurrence of each mispronounced word was predictable from prior context and one occurrence was not predictable.

The predictability of the mispronounced words in the story was measured by a completion test that was administered individually to twenty college students. The experimenter read the story out loud, stopped before each word that was mispronounced in the story, and the subject guessed the intended word. Without exception, the predictable occurrence of each mispronounced word was guessed more often (average, 85%) than the unpredictable occurrence (average, 2%).

The following passage from the story illustrates the level of discourse, and provides examples of some of the mispronunciations:

> 'Now you must *ungress* (undress) and go to bed,' father said, 'You need your rest.'
>
> When Jamie was in his room he started to undress. First he took off his shoes and *thocks* (socks), then his pants, and finally his shirt. Then he put on his *padamas* (pajamas) and got in bed.

Before discussing the results, let us consider the sources of constraint that cause "pajamas" to be a predictable word. In this passage, "pajamas" is constrained by information in the preceding three sentences. It is important to know, for example, that Jamie has been told to go to bed; "pajamas" would have been unpredictable if he had been told to undress and put on a bathing suit. Thus, "pajamas" is a highly predictable word partly because of semantic constraints provided by the discourse structure of the story, and partly because of syntactic and semantic constraints provided by the words "Then he put on his...."

The results showed that mispronunciations were detected about 200 msec faster in predictable words than in unpredictable words by first, third, and fifth grade children and by college students. The effect of predictability was extremely robust—it was observed for all words, without exception. It appears that both children and adults use various sources of knowledge during the on-line recognition of words from fluent speech.

ASSUMPTION 2:
SPEECH IS PROCESSED
WORD BY WORD

We assume that listeners recognize words one after another. This assumption agrees with our experience of listening to fluent speech; we usually hear a speaker's words one after another as they are being said. Similar assumptions have been implicit in several psychological models of speech recognition (Cutler & Norris, in press; Foss, Harwood, & Blank Chap. 7; Marslen-Wilson & Welsh, 1978). We have made it an explicit and important part of our model, and despite its apparent simplicity, it is a powerful assumption.

What is gained by assuming that the words in an utterance are recognized one after another? First, by recognizing words in serial order, a listener can use the syntactic and semantic constraints provided by one word to recognize the following word. Second, each word's recognition locates the onset of the following word. Once a word has been recognized, the listener "knows" that the sounds which follow that word begin a new word.

Not all theorists agree with the assumption of word by word recognition. For example, Miller (1962) has argued that, while speech perception can be characterized as a series of discrete decisions, these decisions cannot be made fast enough to recognize speech word by word. Miller estimates that decisions in speech occur at about one decision per second in ordinary listening.

> "If we accept this as a rough estimate, it suggests that the phrase, usually about two or three words at a time, is probably the natural decision unit for speech .... we question whether a decision could be made about word N fast enough to limit the alternatives considered for word $N + 1$ [p. 82]."

Evidence for Word by Word Recognition

An experiment by Marslen-Wilson (1973) suggests that words are recognized soon after the acoustic input impinges on the listener, and that constraints provided by one word can be used to recognize an immediately following word. Marslen-Wilson tested 65 subjects for their ability to shadow (repeat verbatim) connected prose. From this group, seven "close" shadowers were found who could maintain the intelligibility of their speech while shadowing at mean delays of about 270 msec. Close shadowers were thus able to remain little more than a syllable behind the incoming speech. These subjects, along with seven more "distant" shadowers with latencies between 500 and 800 msec, were instructed to shadow 300-word prose passages presented at a conversational speaking rate (160 words per minute). Of the 402 errors made by the fourteen subjects, most were delivery errors (slurring, hesitations) or word omissions. The remaining errors were *constructive errors*, "in which subjects either added or changed entire words, or changed part of a word so as to make it into a different word." Of the 111 constructive errors, only three were structurally inappropriate. Errors made during shadowing, even at very short latencies, were both syntactically and semantically appropriate to the material being shadowed. For example, in the sentence "It was beginning to be light enough so I could see . . . ," two subjects inserted "that" following "so," one while shadowing at 254 msec behind the input, and the other at 559 msec. Marslen-Wilson argued that, since insertion of "that" is contingent on hearing "so," the subjects' word choice can be constrained by the preceding context provided by the word immediately preceding the error.

Cole and Jakimik (1978) employed the listening for mispronunciations task to show that semantic information provided by one word can be used to recognize an immediately following word. Pairs of sentences were constructed which were identical except for the word which preceded the mispronounced word, as in:

He noticed that a green shag garpet (carpet) covered the hallway.
He noticed that a green rag garpet (carpet) covered the hallway.

In one sentence in each pair, the mispronounced word was highly constrained by the preceding word (e.g., "gold ring," "mink coat," "broom swept," "baby cried"), but not in the other (e.g., "old ring," "pink coat," "groom swept," "lady cried"). Subjects were presented with one of the sentences in each pair and pushed a response key as quickly as possible whenever they heard a mispronunciation. Reaction times were over 180 msec faster when the mispronounced word was predicted by the preceding word.

Identical results have been observed with children when mispronounced words were presented in a short story. Ten of the words in this story (described in the previous section) were preceded, on one occurrence, by a word that highly constrained the identity of the mispronounced word (green grass, hall closet, ham sandwiches, gold necklace, back seat, singing songs, morning paper, teddy bear, picnic basket, french toast). On the other occurrence, the word preceding the mispronunciation did not provide as much semantic constraint (clean grass, tall closet, some sandwiches, old necklace, black seat, teaching songs, boring paper, crazy bear, plastic basket, (too) much toast). The two occurrences of each word were mispronounced in exactly the same way to form a phonologically permissible nonsense word (e.g., gold mecklace versus old mecklace), and reaction times were recorded from the onset of the altered segment.

The results are shown in Fig. 6.1. It can be seen that subjects of all ages detected mispronunciations faster when they were constrained by an immediately preceding word. The effect of predictability was highly significant when subjects or words were treated as random effects ($p < .001$ in

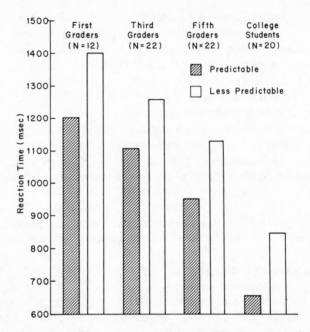

FIG. 6.1.   The effect of constraint provided by a word immediately before a mispronunciation.

all cases). The results provide rather convincing evidence that semantic constraints provided by one word are used during recognition of an immediately following word.

Cascading Context

The assumption of word by word processing leads to an interesting prediction: Any variable which causes a word to be recognized faster will also cause the immediately following word to be recognized faster. To see what we mean, consider the following sentences, which occurred in different versions of a story about a festival in the park:

We watched a tailor sewing *p*retty . . .
We watched a sailor sewing *p*retty . . .

In these sentences, the mispronunciation occurred in "pretty" ("tretty"). The critical feature of the experiment is that the mispronounced word is equally predictable (or unpredictable) in the two sentence versions. It is the word *preceding* the mispronounced word that is highly constrained in

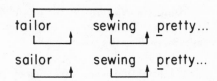

FIG. 6.2.   How context cascades.

one case but not the other; i.e., "tailor" predicts "sewing," while "sailor" does not.

The prediction of the model is conceptualized in Fig. 6.2. The lines drawn below each word to the beginning of the next word indicate that a word's recognition locates the onset of the next word. The arrow pointing from "tailor" to "sewing" indicates that recognition of "tailor" semantically constrains recognition of "sewing." The faster recognition of "sewing" when preceded by "tailor" should have a cascading effect, so that recognition of the mispronunciation in "pretty" should be faster in "tailor sewing pretty."

Four versions of the same story were recorded. The four versions were identical except for the words immediately preceding the mispronounced word, as shown below:

We watched a tailor sew pretty...
We watched a tailor sewing pretty...
We watched a sailor sew pretty...
We watched a sailor sewing pretty...

The design was completely between subjects, so that subjects in each group heard all of the sentences of the same type. There was no effect of verb form ("sew" versus "sewing"), so data were combined for the groups that differed only by this variable. As Fig. 6.3 shows, occurrence of a semantically constrained word before a mispronounced word speeds detection of the mispronunciation.

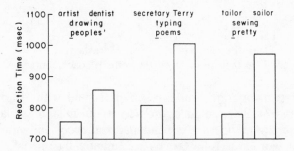

FIG. 6.3.   The effect of having a predictable word before a mispronunciation.

Somewhat similar results have been obtained by Blank and Foss (1978) using the phoneme monitoring technique. They presented subjects with sentences like the following:

The drunk concealed his aching eye *p*robably without even realizing he was doing so.

The drunk winked his bloodshot eye *p*robably without even realizing he was doing so.

Subjects were instructed to monitor for a word-initial target phoneme; in these sentences, the phoneme /p/, which occurred in "probably." Note that the word carrying the target phoneme is equally predictable in both sentences. It is the word *before* the target word ("eye") that is either relatively unpredictable, or constrained by two semantically related words.

According to the assumption of word by word processing, recognition of one word locates the onset of the following word, so that recognition of "eye" locates the /p/ in "probably" as the beginning of a new word. Thus, any variable that causes faster recognition of "eye" should produce faster identification of /p/ as a word-initial phoneme. We should therefore expect faster monitoring times to "probably" when "eye" is predictable from prior context. As predicted, monitoring times were faster when the word preceding the target was predictable from prior context.

Subsequent Context

Can listeners use information *following* a word during its recognition? If subsequent context is typically used during word recognition, then a mispronounced word should be recognized faster when it is *followed* by a semantically related word. To test this hypothesis, we presented subjects with sentences like:

Sylvia liked blaid (*p*laid) shirts/shoes...
While they talked, the paby (*b*aby) crawled/crashed...
The students liked their dasketball (*b*asketball) coach/course...

Subjects in two different groups were presented with 36 experimental sentences and 24 filler sentences, some without mispronunciations. Subjects in one group heard experimental sentences in which the mispronounced word was followed by a semantically related word, while subjects in the other group heard the sentences in which the word following the mispronounced word was less related.

Note that the sentences were constructed so that the mispronounced word had a low transitional probability; that is, it was not predictable from prior context. This was done in order to maximize any potential effect of subsequent context. The question is whether the listener will decide that a mispronunciation has occurred solely on the basis of phonetic information (e.g., "blaid" is not a word) or whether the listener will defer a decision until semantic information is available from a subsequent word.

The results revealed no difference in reaction times as a function of subsequent context. Listeners were able to detect the mispronunciation on the basis of the phonetic information before the semantic information from the following word was available. Although it is certainly the case that subjects in this experiment were primed to detect mispronunciations, and therefore responded as soon as they were able to detect a nonword, it is still interesting that a decision about a nonword could be made before semantic analysis of a subsequent word was performed. We suggest that in perception of conversational speech under good listening conditions, recognition of one word is complete before recognition of the following word begins.

Summary

Taken together, the results of the experiments reviewed in this section suggest that speech perception proceeds word by word. Constraint provided by one word was shown to produce faster recognition of an immediately following word. The effect of sequential constraint was shown to cascade, so that constraint provided by word A, which produced faster recognition of word B, also caused faster recognition of word C. Finally, the results showed that the effects of context are "left-to-right"; word C does not produce faster recognition of word B when B and C are semantically related.

ASSUMPTION 3:
WORDS ARE ACCESSED FROM
THE SOUNDS THAT BEGIN THEM

We have thus far emphasized the critical role of context in word recognition. We now switch our attention back to the stimulus. The point we wish to make is that, however important context may be, word recognition is still under stimulus control. It is important to keep in mind that even the most unpredictable words are recognized from fluent speech with great accuracy. Thus, no matter how strong our expectations, the acoustic input has the last word. Word recognition is conceptually guided, but data *driven*.

In this section, we focus on the recognition process at the point at which a word has just been recognized, and the listener is beginning to analyze the acoustic input at the beginning of the following word. We assume that the sounds which begin the incoming word are used to access word candidates.

Detecting Mispronunciations

The results of an experiment by Marslen-Wilson and Welsh (1978) provide some support for this assumption. They examined "fluent restorations" that subjects produced while shadowing speech that contained mispronounced words. Fluent restorations are "responses in which the subjects repeated the word in its normal form (e.g., repeating "travedy" as "tragedy") without any audible disruption of the fluency of their performance [p. 35]." Fluent restorations were more frequent when the mispronunciation occurred in the third syllable of a word (53%) than in the first syllable (45%). Marslen-Wilson and Welsh explain this result by assuming that, when the mispronunciation occurred in the third syllable, the word had been recognized prior to the occurrence of the mispronunciation. And,

> Once a single word-choice has emerged, the recognition system will have achieved its primary goal, and a less detailed assessment of the remaining input for that word will be required. This will have the effect of making the system less sensitive to deviations that occur after the point of identification [p. 57].

The results of an experiment by Cole, Jakimik, and Cooper (1978) are consistent with the explanation offered by Marslen-Wilson and Welsh (1978). A mispronunciation in the first segment of a monosyllabic word (e.g., "made" to "nade") was detected over twice as often as a mispronunciation in a final segment (e.g., "time" to "tine"). This result is consistent with the notion that a word can be recognized before its acoustic analysis is complete, and that there is less attention to phonetic detail following recognition.

Reaction Times to Mispronunciations

Experiments with the listening for mispronunciations task provide convincing evidence that words are accessed from acoustic information in the beginning of the word. In these experiments, reaction times to mispronunciations, measured from the onset of the altered segment, were compared for mispronunciations in either the first or second syllable of a word. According to the model, a mispronunciation should be detected faster in the second syllable of a word than in its first syllable. When a mispronunciation occurs in the second syllable of a word, the listener has already been presented with a correct first syllable, and has accessed the intended word (along with other word candidates with the same first syllable). The mispronunciation can be quickly detected based on prior context, the information in the first syllable, and the (partial) correct information in the mispronounced second syllable.

When a mispronunciation occurs in a first syllable, recognition is still constrained by prior context. However, the listener will have insufficient phonetic information to access the intended word, and unless there is a great deal of contextual constraint, the mispronounced first syllable will be used to access inappropriate words, that is, words which begin with the mispronounced syllable. In this case, the mispronunciation can be detected only after phonetic information from subsequent syllables fails to result in recognition. Thus, a mispronunciation in a first syllable can only be detected from recognition of *subsequent* syllables (since inappropriate words have been accessed), while a mispronunciation in a second syllable can be detected from *prior* context.

Faster reaction times to mispronounced second syllables have been reported by Cole (1973) and Cole and Jakimik (1978). These experiments showed that reaction times to mispronounced second syllables are about 180 msec faster than to mispronunciations in word-initial syllables. Interestingly, the reaction time advantage to mispronounced second syllables is largely independent of syllable stress. Listeners are more likely to *detect* a mispronunciation in a stressed syllable, but a mispronunciation in an unstressed second syllable is still detected about 180 msec faster than in a stressed first syllable.

Equally Predictable First and Second Syllables

The reaction time advantage for mispronounced second syllables is consistent with the assumption that words are accessed from the information in their first syllable. Another way of viewing this result is that a second syllable is more predictable than a first syllable. A second syllable is constrained both by prior context and by a correct first syllable, while a first syllable is constrained only by prior context. Therefore, if we make a second syllable as predictable as a first syllable—by letting the subject read the sentence that is about to be presented—the reaction time advantage for a mispronounced second syllable should disappear.

To test this hypothesis, we recorded 14 sentences in which a mispronunciation occurred in a stressed second syllable of a word, and 14 sentences in which phonetically matched mispronunciations occurred in stressed word-initial syllables. In the first part of the experiment, one group of subjects heard the 14 sentences with a mispronounced first syllable, along with 14 filler sentences with no mispronounced words, while a second group of subjects heard the filler sentences and the matched experimental sentences in which the mispronunciation occurred in the second syllable. Mispronunciations in the second syllable of a word were detected about 200 msec faster than mispronunciations in the beginning of a word (1006 msec versus 802 msec), and this difference was observed when both subjects ($F(1, 22) = 9.16$, $p < .01$) and words ($F(1, 13) = 35.77$, $p < .001$) were treated as random effects.

In the second part of the experiment, two additional groups of subjects heard the sentences. As before, one group heard sentences with mispronounced first syllables, while the other group heard sentences with mispronounced second syllables. But in this experiment, just before they listened to each sentence, the subjects were shown an index card which contained a printed version of the sentence. Although the subjects did not know the location of the mispronunciation, they did know, word for word, the content of the sentence. Thus, all syllables were equally (and perfectly) predictable. This manipulation completely eliminated the reaction time advantage for mispronounced second syllables. The mean reaction time to first syllable mispronunciations was 588 msec, compared to 584 msec to second syllable mispronunciations. Thus, when first syllables are as predictable as second syllables, they are detected as rapidly.

ASSUMPTION 4:
A WORD IS RECOGNIZED WHEN
THE SEQUENTIAL ANALYSIS
OF ITS ACOUSTIC STRUCTURE
ELIMINATES ALL WORD CANDIDATES
BUT ONE

We are now at that point in the recognition process at which the listener has accessed a set of word candidates from information at the beginning of an incoming word. Following Marslen-Wilson and Welsh (1978), we assume that the acoustic information within the word continues to be analyzed sequentially, and word candidates are eliminated from consideration as they become inconsistent with the sequential analysis of the stimulus. The intended word is recognized at that point at which the acoustic analysis is inconsistent with all word candidates but one. Thus, as Marslen-Wilson and Welsh (1978) note, "word-recognition reflects the emergence of a single choice, which in turn depends on the point at which the word in question diverges from all other words [p. 57]."[2]

If the information within a word is used to eliminate all word candidates but one, then word recognition should often occur before all of a word has been heard. A number of recent experiments provide converging evidence that a word can be recognized from fluent speech even before the sounds at the end of the word impinge upon the listener. According to Marslen-Wilson and Welsh (1978)

> Experiments in which subjects monitor sentences for word-targets specified in advance (Marslen-Wilson & Tyler, 1975...), and other studies which use the speech shadowing technique (Marslen-Wilson, 1973; 1975), enable us to measure the time it takes to recognize words in normal contextual speech contexts. The results showed that words in normal sentential contexts could be correctly identified and responded to with response latencies of 250–275 msec. If we assign 75–100 msec of these latencies to the processes involved in response integration and execution, then this means that the subjects were beginning to initiate their responses between 150–200 msec after the onsets of the words in question. That is, after they could only have heard the first two or three phonemes of the words—in most cases an initial consonantal phoneme or phoneme cluster or part of the following vowel.... These findings imply an extremely rapid access process, based at the most on partial information about the acoustic–phonetic properties of the word being recognized [p. 52].

---

[2]Is it reasonable to believe that the information within a word can be analyzed sequentially? It is well known that certain features of speech—such as formant transitions—carry information about successive phonemes in parallel. Liberman, Cooper, Shankweiler, and Studdert-Kennedy (1967) have argued that parallel transmission is necessary for speech perception, since phonetic information is presented too fast to be perceived phoneme by phoneme. It is certainly true that some acoustic features carry information about adjacent segments in parallel, but we suggest, in contrast to Liberman et al., that there is no logical reason that phonetic information within a word cannot be analyzed sequentially. Consider that speech is typically produced at about three to five syllables per second. If we assume that syllables contain three phonemes on the average, then speech is normally processed at the rate of 12 to 15 phonemes per second, or about 70 msec per phoneme. Since humans can process information in memory at the rate of about 10 msec per item (Haber, 1970), humans have the *capacity* to perceive an ordered sequence of phonemes from fluent speech as rapidly as it can be spoken. We are not suggesting that speech is perceived one phoneme at a time— that recognition of one phoneme is complete before the next begins. However, in *natural* speech, acoustic information about phonemes is ordered in time. In a syllable such as /di/ or /du/, the sequence stop-closure–stop-burst–formant-transitions provides an invariant ordering of events that can be used to identify the stop consonant. The temporal order of phonetic events in a syllable is therefore provided by the order of acoustic events. It is entirely possible, then, that phonetic information within a word may be analyzed sequentially, and that the results of this analysis can be used during word recognition from fluent speech.

The assumption that a word is recognized when the sequential analysis of its sound pattern eliminates all candidates but one was originally proposed by Marslen-Wilson and Welsh (1978) as part of a direct access model of word recognition. According to them:

> The model can make precise predictions for any specified word heard in isolation. The speed of recognition should be a direct function of the left-to-right sequential structure of the cohort of word candidates for a given initial sequence. Word recognition reflects the emergence of a single choice which in turn depends on the point at which the word in question diverges from all other words in its cohort [p. 57].

Thus, a word which has a relatively unique first syllable, like "umbrella," "shampoo," "vampire," or "whisper" should be recognized quickly compared to a word which shares a first syllable with many other words, like "compare," "contain," "perform," or "pretend." Stated another way, given the same amount of prior contextual constraint, a listener should be able to detect a mispronunciation faster in a word like "shampoo" than a word like "complain," since there are far fewer word candidates that will be accessed from the syllable /šæm/ than the syllable /kʌm/.

As part of her doctoral dissertation, Jakimik (1979) tested this hypothesis by examining reaction times to mispronounced second syllables of words as a function of the amount of constraint provided by the word's first syllable. In half of the sentences, the first syllable of a mispronounced word provided a great deal of constraint on the word's identity, since on the average, only 4.1 words began with the same syllable. In the other half of the sentences, the first syllable of the mispronounced word provided less constraint on the word's identity, since on the average, the first syllable was shared by 156.8 words. In addition, as the example sentences show, each mispronounced word occurred in two different sentences—once as a predictable word and once as an unpredictable word:

> It was necessary to *complain* to the manager in order to get anything done.
> [low transitional probability, low first syllable constraint]

> She was never satisfied and always *complained* about everything.
> [high transitional probability, low first syllable constraint]

> She said that she was going to *shampoo* her hair that evening.
> [low transitional probability, high first syllable constraint]

> Her oily hair needed to be *shampooed* every day.
> [high transitional probability, high first syllable constraint]

Overall, the two types of mispronounced words were matched for form class, stress pattern, and frequency of occurrence in English (Kučera & Francis, 1967). Each subject heard both types of mispronunciations, in either the predictable or the unpredictable sentences. Twenty subjects heard the 48 experimental sentences and 50 foils which either contained no mispronounced word or a mispronunciation in a first syllable.

The results, shown in Fig. 6.4, support the prediction of the model. Mispronunciations were detected significantly faster in words with an infrequent first syllable than in words with a frequent first syllable. The effect of first syllable constraint, although relatively small (73 msec for unpredictable words and 28 msec for predictable words) was significant by analysis of variance when both subjects ($F(1, 19) = 30.1$, $p < .001$) and words ($F(1, 44) = 4.1$, $p < 0.5$) were treated as random effects. Consistent with previous work reported in the second section, mispronunciations were detected faster in predictable words than in unpredictable words. The interaction between the predictability of the mispronounced word and the constraint provided by a first syllable did not reach significance.

PUTTING IT ALL TOGETHER

The experiments described in the previous four sections provide support for each of the assumptions of the model. The experiments reported in the present section demonstrate how these assumptions, considered together, can be used to describe the process of word recognition from fluent speech.

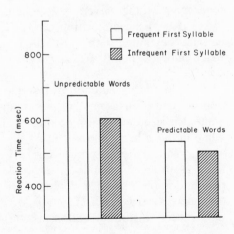

FIG. 6.4. The effects of first-syllable constraint and predictability.

Consider the sentence "They saw the cargo on the ferry," in which "go" is mispronounced as "ko." This sentence has two possible segmentations: The mispronunciation may be perceived as occurring within the word "cargo" or at the beginning of "go" in the sequence "car go." In order to examine the role of prior context in word recognition and segmentation, we spliced duplicated versions of the "cargo" sentence into two stories. One story was about two men sent to the docks to pick up a shipment of goods arriving on a ferry boat; this story directed a one-word segmentation of /kargo/. The other story was about a young man's parents who came to the dock to watch their son drive his car onto a ferry boat for the start of his summer vacation; this story directed a two-word segmentation of /kargo/. In both stories, the mispronunciation occurred in the sentence "Looking down from the pier, they saw the car*k*o on the ferry."

If we assume that listeners sequentially process speech word by word, and that contextual information—such as that provided by the theme of a story—is actively used to recognize words from the syllables under analysis, then reaction times should be faster when the mispronunciation occurs in the second syllable of a word, that is, in "carko." When the story is about two men looking for a shipment of cargo, the theme of the story and the sentence fragment "Looking down from the pier, they saw the car..." should provide sufficient constraint so that the syllable "car" will be used to access the word "cargo." Since the listener will have accessed the intended word from prior context and its first syllable, the mispronunciation should be rapidly detected in the story. When the story is about a young man's parents waiting to see their son's car go on the ferry, the same sequence of words, ending with "they saw the..." causes "car" to be recognized as a complete word. Given that "car" is recognized as a word, the listener will assume that the syllable "ko" begins a new word and will access words like "collide" and "collapse." The listener must wait for several subsequent syllables in order to recognize that "ko" is a mispronunciation of "go" and not the start of a new word actually beginning with "ko." Thus, given the identical acoustic input, reaction times should be faster to the mispronunciation in "cargo" than in "car go."

Note that the prediction of faster reaction times to the mispronunciation in "cargo" uses each of the assumptions of the model. In one story, context is used to determine that "car" is the first syllable of "cargo," while in the other, context causes "car" to be recognized as a complete word. Word by word processing is needed to explain how "car" is defined as the first syllable of a word in one story, and to explain how recognition of "car" as a complete word in the other story, causes "ko" to be perceived as the first syllable of a new word. Finally, faster reaction times to the mispronunciation in "cargo" depend on the assumption that information in the syllable "car" is used to access the intended word, and that the information in the word "cargo" is processed sequentially.

The experiment consisted of six stories that were written so as to demand either a one-word or two-word segmentation of "snowdrift," "address," and "cargo" in the following sentences:

1. "They saw the snowdrift (snow drift) by the window."
2. "He gave her address (a dress) with pleasure."
3. "They saw the cargo (car go) on the ferry."

The stories were recorded at a conversational speaking rate by a male speaker and had an average duration of about 3 minutes.

To control for acoustic factors, the three target sentences were each recorded *a single time* (with the mispronunciation), duplicated, and then spliced into the appropriate stories.[3] Splices were not detectable. Thus, exactly the same mispronunciation was presented in the same acoustic environment in two different stories. Mispronunciations were produced by changing /d/ to /t/ in "snow*d*rift" and "a*d*ress," and /g/ to /k/ in "car*g*o." A tone was placed on the alternate channel of the recording tape at the onset of the stop burst of the altered segment. Tone placement was performed before the sentences were duplicated, so tone placement was identical for the duplicated versions.

Subjects were randomly assigned to two groups of 13 subjects each. Subjects in one group heard the stories requiring perception of "snow drift" and "a dress" as two words and perception of "cargo" as one word, while subjects in the other group heard stories that required the alternate segmentation of these words. The stories were presented in the same order to subjects in each group. Subjects were told that they would hear short stories in which some of the words were mispronounced and that they should press the button in front of them as quickly as possible whenever they detected a mispronunciation.

The mean reaction times to the one-word and two-word segmentations of "snowdrift," "address," and "cargo" are presented in Table 6.1. It can be seen that reaction times are considerably faster when the story directed a one-word segmentation—i.e., when the mispronunciation was perceived as occurring in the second syllable of a word rather than at the beginning of a word. Mean reaction times were about 300 msec faster

---

[3]To insure that the prosodic structure of the three critical sentences did not bias a one-word segmentation, we presented an independent group of subjects with each of the sentences (in isolation), and asked them to indicate which of two possible segmentations of each they thought the speaker had intended. Across the three sentences, the two segmentations were heard equally often.

TABLE 6.1
Mean Reaction Times (in msec) to
One-Word and Two-Word
Segmentations of the Same Sequence
of Phonemes

Snowdrift	Address	Cargo
($n = 6$)	($n = 6$)	($n = 7$)
772	679	604
Snow drift	A dress	Car go
($n = 11$)	($n = 5$)	($n = 7$)
1039	1128	994

when the stories required perception of "cargo," "address," and "snow-drift" as single words. *T*-tests of the mean reaction times for each story pair revealed a nearly significant difference for "snowdrift" versus "snow drift," and significant differences for "address" versus "a dress," and for "cargo" versus "car go."

The final experiments reported in this chapter examine the assumptions of the model when alternate word-level segmentations are guided by the first few words of a sentence.

Consider the following pair of sentences:

The doctor said that nose*d*rops will help the cold.
The doctor said he knows *d*rops will help the cold.

Starting with the syllable [noz], the two sentences contain the same sequence of phonemes and the mispronunciation occurs in "*d*rops" (pronounced "trops"). By splicing a recording of the first four words of each sentence ("the doctor said that" and "the doctor said he") onto a duplicated recording of "nosetrops will help the cold," we create a pair of sentences in which the first few words of each sentence direct a one-word or two-word segmentation of the same physical stimulus.

If subjects are able to use contextual information provided by the first few words of a sentence to constrain word choice, we should again find faster reaction times when the mispronunciation is perceived as occurring in the second or third syllable of a word. For example, the occurrence of the complementizer "that" in the first sentence predicts that [noz] is likely to be the first syllable of a nominal compound (e.g., "nosebleeds," "nosedrops") or perhaps the first word in an adjective–noun phrase (e.g., "nose infection"). Since word choice is highly constrained, when "trops" is heard, the listener should be very fast in determining that it is a mispronunciation of "drops" in "nosedrops."

By comparison, in a sentence beginning "The doctor said he," the pronoun "he" specified that [noz] must be "knows." Recognition of "knows" as a word automatically determines that "trops" begins a new word. When a mispronunciation occurs in the beginning of a word, the listener must wait for *subsequent* phonetic information to determine that "trop" does not begin a legitimate word (e.g., "tropical"). Thus, if word recognition occurs in a rapid serial fashion, where recognition of one word constrains recognition of the next, reaction times to a mispronunciation of "drops" should be faster in the first version than in the second.

Note again that we used each of the assumptions of the model to predict the reaction time difference between the two sentences. Prior context was used to constrain recognition of [noz] as a complete word

TABLE 6.2
Sentences Requiring One-Word and Two-Word Segmentation of the
Same Sequence of Phonemes[a]

Sentence	Mispronunciation
1. The judge went to the fair*g*rounds for a divorce.	
The judge said he saw fair *g*rounds for a divorce.	(/g/ to /k/)
2. He just hated for*g*etting the right number.	
He was noted for *g*etting the right number.	(/g/ to /k/)
3. The doctor said that nose*d*rops will help the cold.	
The doctor said he knows *d*rops will help the cold.	(/d/ to /t/)
4. The color of the house*p*aint was rare.	
When I lived at the house *p*aint was rare.	(/p/ to /b/)
5. Antoinette watched the Corvette over*t*ake the bus.	
If you have to bring Annette over *t*ake the bus.	(/t/ to /d/)
6. The coach watched his quarter*b*ack go to the office.	
When Don gets his quarter *b*ack go to the office.	(/b/ to /d/)
7. My grandma's making home*m*ade preserves.	
The people staying home *m*ade preserves.	(/m/ to /b/)
8. Homework was the draw*b*ack in high school.	
Randy learned to draw *b*ack in high school.	(/b/ to /d/)
9. She saw some hand*s*ome statues through the window.	
She saw him hand *s*ome statues through the window.	(/s/ to /z/)
10. You should read the news*p*rint carefully.	
When you write the news *p*rint carefully.	(/p/ to /b/)
11. There's a little truck*s*top at the corner.	
If you see the truck *s*top at the corner.	(/s/ to /sh/)
12. The farmer put the chicken*f*eed in the pen.	
The farmer let the chicken *f*eed in the pen.	(/f/ to /v/)
13. You are always wel*c*ome back.	
If your sister's well *c*ome back.	(/k/ to /g/)
14. The truck plowed the growing snow*d*rift into the street.	
The wind made the falling snow *d*rift into the street.	(/d/ to /t/)

[a] Note: the mispronounced segments are italicized.

The doctor said that
The doctor said he   knows trops will help the cold.

FIG. 6.5.   Schematic   of   tape-   He was noted
splicing procedure.   He just hated   forketting the right number.

("knows") or the first syllable of one of a set of nominal compounds (e.g., "nosedrops"). Word by word processing was critical in explaining how "he" and "that" constrained recognition of [noz], and to explain how recognition of [noz] as "knows" caused "trops" to be treated as the first syllable of a new word. Finally, the reaction time difference was explained in terms of prior access of the two syllable word "nosedrops" based on information provided in the first syllable.

Two experiments were performed using the sentences shown in Table 6.2. The experiments were identical except that in the first, we used the tape-splicing manipulation shown in Fig. 6.5 to insure that mispronunciations were acoustically identical, while in the second experiment all sentences were recorded with natural intonation. Because the mispronunciations were not detected in four of the sentences used in the first experiment, we used a different consonant change to produce the mispronunciation when recording these sentences with natural intonation.

In each experiment, subjects were presented with the sentences intermixed with numerous filler sentences. Reaction times were always measured from the onset of the altered segment. The reaction time differences

TABLE 6.3

Speed of Detections (in msec) for One-Word and Two-Word
Segmentations of the Same Sequence in Spliced and Natural Sentences

	Spliced	Natural		Spliced	Natural
nosedrops	874	844	knows drops	1150	1250
quarterback	885	874	quarter back	995	1280
forgetting	954	781	for getting	1290	1090
chickenfeed	—	704	chicken feed	—	983
handsome	902	665	hand some	954	935
welcome	—	628	well come	—	854
drawback	879	841	draw back	994	1033
fairgrounds	910	1336	fair grounds	1418	1520
newsprint	—	621	news print	—	782
homemade	965	809	home made	1069	913
housepaint	974	758	house paint	1170	829
overtake	876	907	over take	1000	977
truckstop	—	758	truck stop	—	808
snowdrift	836	955	snow drift	1016	1000
Mean	906	820	Mean	1106	1018

shown in Table 6.3 reveal that the prediction of the model was confirmed. For the spliced sentences, mispronunciations were detected about 200 msec faster when they occurred in the second syllable of a word, and the effect was observed for all sentence pairs. The second-syllable reaction time advantage was 200 msec for unaltered, naturally recorded sentences, and the effect was observed for all 14 pairs. In both experiments, the effect was significant ($p < .01$) when subjects or words were treated as random effects.

SUMMARY AND CONCLUSIONS

In this chapter we have described a set of information processing strategies that transform speech into a series of words. The research described above provides at least partial support for each of the following statements:

Words are recognized through the interaction of sound and knowledge.
The words in an utterance are recognized one after another.
A word's recognition provides syntactic and semantic constraints that are used to recognize the following word.
A word's recognition locates the sounds which begin the following word.
The sounds in the beginning of a word are used to access word candidates.
The sounds in a word are processed sequentially.
A word is consciously recognized when the sequential analysis of sound eliminates all word candidates but one.

The model has a number of attractive features. First, it was formulated following a thorough examination of the acoustic stimulus. It confronts the question: How does a listener recognize words from partial acoustic information? This problem was dealt with by assuming that words are partially constrained by their acoustic structure, partially constrained by prior context, and are recognized through the interaction of these two sources of constraint. Second, the model confronts the question: How does a listener locate word boundaries? The problem of segmentation was dealt with by assuming that words are recognized one after the other, and that recognition of one word locates the onset of the following word. Third, the model provides a description of the moment by moment processing of fluent speech. It is possible to work through any sentence syllable by syllable (as we did in the introduction) or even phoneme by phoneme, and describe the number of word candidates that are active as each syllable (or phoneme) has been analyzed, and the point at which recognition occurs for each word. Fourth, the model is consistent with our experience of listening to speech. We typically recognize words one after another, as they are being spoken.

REFERENCES

Blank, M., & Foss, D. J. Semantic facilitation and lexical access during sentence processing. *Memory & Cognition*, 1978, *6*, 644–652.

Cole, R. A. Listening for mispronunciations: A measure of what we hear during speech. *Perception & Psychophysics*, 1973, *13*, 153–156.

Cole, R. A., & Jakimik, J. Understanding speech: How words are heard. In G. Underwood (Ed.), *Strategies of information processing*. London: Academic Press, 1978.

Cole, R. A., Jakimik, J., & Cooper, W. E. Perceptibility of phonetic features in fluent speech. *Journal of the Acoustical Society of America*, 1978, *64*, 44–56.

Cutler, A. Phoneme-monitoring reaction time as a function of preceding intonation contour. *Perception & Psychophysics*, 1976, *20*, 55–60.

Cutler, A., & Norris, D. Monitoring sentence comprehension. In W. E. Cooper & E. C. T. Walker (Eds.), *Sentence processing: Studies in honor of Merrill Garrett*. In Press.

Haber, R. N. How we remember what we see. *Scientific American*, 1970, *222*, 104–112.

Jakimik, J. *The interaction of sound and knowledge in word recognition from fluent speech*. Unpublished doctoral dissertation, Carnegie-Mellon University, 1979.

Klatt, D. H. Review of the ARPA speech understanding project. *Journal of the Acoustical Society of America*, 1977, *62*, 1345–1366.

Klatt, D. H., & Stevens, K. N. On the automatic recognition of continuous speech: Implications of a spectrogram-reading experiment. *IEEE Transactions. Audio Electroacoustics*, 1973, *AU-21*, 210–217.

Kučera, F., & Francis, W. N. *Computational analysis of present-day American English*. Providence, Rhode Island: Brown University Press, 1967.

Liberman, A. M., Cooper, F. S., Shankweiler, D. P., & Studdert-Kennedy, M. Perception of the speech code. *Psychological Review*, 1967, *74*, 431–461.

Marslen-Wilson, W. D. Linguistic structure and speech shadowing at very short latencies. *Nature*, 1973, *244*, 522–523.

Marslen-Wilson, W. D. Sentence perception as an interactive parallel process. *Science*, 1975, *189*, 226–228.

Marslen-Wilson, W. D. *Sequential decision processes during spoken word recognition*. Paper presented at the Psychonomic Society Meeting, San Antonio, Texas, 1978.

Marslen-Wilson, W. D., & Tyler, L. K. Processing structure of sentence perception. *Nature*, 1975, *257*, 226–228.

Marslen-Wilson, W. D., & Welsh, A. Processing interactions and lexical access during word recognition in continuous speech. *Cognitive Psychology*, 1978, *10*, 29–63.

Martin, J. G. Rhythmic (hierarchical) versus serial structure in speech and other behavior. *Psychological Review*, 1972, *79*, 487–509.

Miller, G. A. Decision units in the perception of speech. *IRE Transactions on Information Theory*, 1962, *IT-8*, 81–83.

Miller, G. A., Heise, G. A., & Lichten, W. The intelligibility of speech as a function of the context of the test materials. *Journal of Experimental Psychology*, 1951, *41*, 329–335.

Miller, G. A., & Isard, S. Some perceptual consequences of linguistic rules. *Journal of Verbal Learning and Verbal Behavior*, 1963, *2*, 217–228.

Morton, J., & Long, J. Effect of word transitional probability on phoneme identification. *Journal of Verbal Learning and Verbal Behavior*, 1976, *15*, 43–51.

Pollack, I., & Pickett, J. M. Intelligibility of excerpts from conversational speech. *Language and Speech,* 1963, *6,* 165–171.

Reddy, R. Speech recognition by machine: A review. *Proceedings of the IEEE,* 1976, *64,* 501–531.

Shields, J. L., McHugh, A., & Martin, J. G. Reaction time to phoneme targets as a function of rhythmic cues in continuous speech. *Journal of Experimental Psychology,* 1974, *102,* 250–255.

Warren, R. M. Perceptual restoration of missing speech sounds. *Science,* 1970, *167,* 393–395.

7 Deciphering Decoding Decisions: Data and Devices

Donald J. Foss

David A. Harwood

Michelle A. Blank
University of Texas at Austin

> *Decipherments are by far the most glamorous achievements of scholarship.*
>
> —M. Pope

What are the modules of linguistic information processing, what does each do, and how? Answers to these three questions would constitute a substantial contribution to the theory of mental processes, a decipherment of extraordinary glamour indeed. Alas, such a contribution will not be forthcoming in this paper, although we do hope to put some constraints on the form of such a theory and to demonstrate that some kinds of answers to these questions are more plausible than others. The questions presuppose that the information processing system as it applies to linguistic materials has a modular structure: That is, that there are certain underlying perceptual and cognitive mechanisms which can be distinguished functionally and structurally (Foss & Fay, 1975; Marr, 1976). It is plausible and even likely that the components interact in important ways. During the course of investigating the structure of these linguistic processing mechanisms, we will appeal to data concerning the actual units of perception developed while processing running speech. To the extent that we can identify such units we are also identifying some of the functions being computed by the modules (and thus, indirectly, the modules themselves).

The aspect of linguistic processing at issue here concerns primarily the "low level" processes, those that take the acoustic signal as input and yield an entry in the "mental lexicon" (word or morpheme) as output.

Thus, as a first approximation, the problem addressed in this paper is that of determining the number and nature of the modules that transfer the information from the acoustic to the lexical representation. Put another way, we are concerned with the problem of lexical access.

In the first part of this paper we will discuss one way that information may be represented in the mental lexicon, as well as the codes that may be computed as lexical items are retrieved. We will then describe a number of experiments concerned with the units of speech perception and with some of the variables that affect lexical access. These studies have in common their use of phoneme monitoring as a measuring technique. We will argue that results from these studies bear directly on questions about the codes that are computed during lexical access. An anomaly in the existing data will be described, and we will propose a new hypothesis, the Dual Code hypothesis, to account for the anomaly. This hypothesis helps to make clear which codes are computed and responded to during running speech, and it also permits us to describe in detail how phoneme monitoring is carried out by listeners. Finally, we will present some new data gathered to test the hypothesis. Although the data are only suggestive, they stimulate us to propose further tests that may be definitive.

THE LEXICON AND ITS ACCESS CODES

Consider the nature of representations in the mental lexicon. Associated with lexical items in the mental dictionary must be phonological, syntactic, and semantic information—just as in Webster's dictionary. In consequence, it is reasonable to suppose that the lexical level is the point at which many of the most important interactions occur during language processing.

Recently, a number of machine models of speech recognition have been developed (see Reddy, 1976; Klatt, 1977, for surveys). One intriguing model is the Hearsay II system, represented in Fig. 7.1. According to this model, the modules of information processing are in contact with one another via a " 'blackboard'—a structurally uniform global data base (Reddy, 1976, p. 513)." Speech is not processed by a set of serially operating mechanisms, but rather by a "set of cooperating asynchronous parallel processors [p. 513]." The communication among the various modules must occur in a common language. A common language is required since the syntactic system is not directly compatible with, say, the system of phonetic features. If the processors concerned with these two systems are to affect each other, they must be able to communicate, thus the requirement for a "uniform global data base."

Let us consider the idea that the language of the uniform data base in

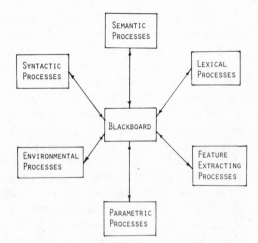

FIG. 7.1.   A "blackboard" model of speech recognition, a model in which parallel processors communicate via a common data base (after Reddy, 1976).

human speech perception is the language of the lexicon. (A similar hypothesis has been forwarded by Cole & Jakimik, 1979.) Thus, when the "feature extracting processes" have operated, the result will be a hypothesis about a lexical item. When this item is put on the "blackboard," its associated syntactic and semantic information will also be deposited there. If the syntactic information fits the needs of the syntactic processor, two things may happen. First, the hypothesis that the appropriate lexical item has been recovered is bolstered; and second, the operation of the syntactic module, and others, is modified in the light of this item. The hypothesis that the lexicon is the point where the disparate linguistic codes interact is shown schematically in Fig. 7.2.

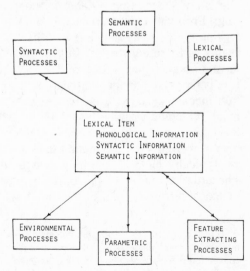

FIG. 7.2.   A "blackboard" model with the assumption that the lexical item provides the common data base for communication among the processors.

Although no theorist would doubt that disparate types of information are represented in the lexicon, and that this level of representation is at least a candidate for the level at which interactions of the above sort occur, theorists do differ on two fundamental issues: One concerns the types of information that are stored in the lexicon, and the other concerns the manner in which lexical items are accessed when an acoustic signal occurs. Disagreements about whether lexical items should be represented as collections of features, sets of procedures or production rules, members of fuzzy sets, etc., are instances in which the form of the representation is in dispute. Questions concerning the computations carried out by the modules that accept the acoustic input (i.e., questions about the transfer functions) are instances of the second dispute. Some theorists (e.g., Massaro, 1972) believe that a module takes the acoustic input and yields at the next intermediate stage a syllabic representation; others (e.g., Pisoni, 1976) opt for an intermediate phonetic stage. Theorists are in a particularly difficult position when there are questions both about the entities being computed by a mechanism and about the manner in which the computations are carried out. As has often been noted, we can only observe the input to the speech perception system; we can observe neither its "output" (the internal representation that results from the computations) nor the computational mechanisms and the intermediate representations to which they give rise.

There are, however, some aspects of lexical representation that seem indubitable. In particular, it is almost certainly true that lexical items have an internal structure that is captured quite well by the constructs "phonological segment" and "phonological feature."[1] Errors in the perception of speech (e.g., Miller & Nicely, 1955) and in speech production (e.g., Fromkin, 1973; Garrett, 1975), as well as the existence of alphabetic writing systems, are only a few of the compelling sorts of evidence for the reality of these constructs. But the fact that words in the mental lexicon have a phonological structure does not necessarily imply that this structure is recovered as the words are being processed by the speech perception mechanisms. At least two options are available here. On the one hand, we could assume that phonological information is stored with the lexical item and only becomes available to the listener once the word has been retrieved from the mental lexicon. Note that this is the assumption we typically make concerning semantic and orthographic information. The latter become available for further use by the listener only subsequent to lexical retrieval. On the other hand, we could assume that phonological

---

[1]For the present, the term "phonological" is being used in a purposefully vague way, intended to cover phonetic as well as phonological segments and features. A terminological convention is forthcoming later in the chapter.

information is computed by the speech perception mechanisms. According to this assumption, one of the modules of perception has as its output a phonological representation of the acoustic input. The phonological representation might then be used to help find the appropriate lexical item in the mental dictionary. Most theorists (e.g., Liberman, 1970; Pisoni, 1976) opt for the latter alternative, namely that a phonological (or at least a syllabic) representation of the acoustic input is developed during the process of perception. Thus, according to this point of view, the signal is transformed into a set of linguistic symbols which are then used to aid lexical retrieval.

Some computer-based word recognition systems do not attempt to compute an intermediate symbolic representation between the acoustic signal and the lexical representation. These systems can be divided into two broad classes, those that attempt to recognize isolated words, and those that attempt to recognize connected speech. The former operate by matching the input with a set of stored patterns. Such systems typically have vocabulary sizes of 200 words or fewer, can be highly successful (99%+ accuracy), and, importantly, their procedures cannot be extended to the task of recognizing connected speech. As Reddy (1976) notes, "Any attempt to extend the design philosophy of isolated word recognition systems . . . becomes an exercise in futility [p. 509]." Klatt's work (Chap. 9) exemplifies the computer-based approach to recognizing connected speech without including in the recognition system an intermediate phonological level between the acoustic and the lexical representations. For reasons that will become clear later, we do not believe that this class of theories has psychological validity.

Let us explore the alternative class of models, those that hypothesize the existence of an intermediate level of representation. We will first extend our picture of the blackboard model to that shown in Fig. 7.3. According to the theory exemplified in that figure, the acoustic input is operated upon by a perceptual module, resulting in a symbolic representation of the input that is intermediate between the acoustic and lexical representations (the "segments" computed by the "segmental recognition processes"). As suggested above, those theorists who believe that there is an intermediate representation differ about its nature. Some hold that the segments represented are syllabic, while others argue that they are (also) phonological. This is not an idle dispute. Determining the nature of the intermediate codes is simultaneously determining something about the nature of the perceptual modules themselves. Massaro has argued that the auditory input is stored in a preperceptual memory and that the output of the processes that operate on the data in this memory is a syllabic representation. Among the evidence supporting such a conclusion is Huggins' (1964) observation that switching speech from ear to ear leads to

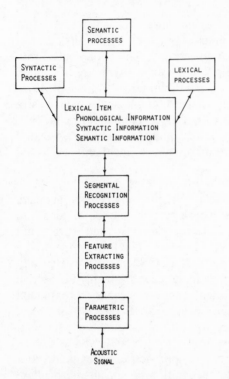

FIG. 7.3. A "blackboard" model with the assumption that phonological segments and features are computed prior to lexical access.

poorest perception of the message when the rates of alternation correspond to the rate of presentation of the syllables of the message. Massaro (1972) concluded, "Rather than parallel processing of phonemes, it is more parsimonious to assume that the syllable functions as the perceptual unit for speech perception [p. 140]."

There is little doubt that the syllable is an important unit in speech perception. But it is at least doubtful that the symbolic unit in terms of which lexical access occurs is the *unanalyzed* syllable. The phenomena involved in phonological fusion (Cutting, 1975), for example, seem to require that speech stimuli be represented at a phonological level. Other arguments to this effect have been presented elsewhere (Foss, 1974; Foss & Swinney, 1973), and further data supporting this position will be presented below. Studdert-Kennedy (1976) has suggested that we make a distinction between the acoustic and linguistic units of speech perception. He noted that most theorists agree that the acoustic unit of perception is the syllable—that it is a critically important stretch of the input over which calculations of the linguistic segments occur—but that they disagree about the linguistic units. Studdert-Kennedy's distinction is an excellent one to keep in mind.

PHONEME MONITORING

Our interest in the nature of the symbolic code used to access the mental dictionary during running speech was born of necessity as well as sired by curiosity. It grew from an interest in measuring the momentary processing difficulty that listeners have as they comprehend sentences. Behind this interest is the assumption that there are measurable momentary fluctuations in the demands placed upon the listener as he or she comprehends an utterance. These fluctuations may spring from many sources: from the necessity to access the present lexical item, from the necessity to determine the syntactic role of that item, from the requirement to make an inference, etc. Thus, at any moment it may be that the total processing demand upon the listener is composed of a number of component demands. Recently we discovered that William James had a similar pretheoretic intuition about sentence comprehension. Figure 7.4 is taken from his Principles. It shows how, at moment four in the sentence, when *same* has just been heard, the effects of the other words are also present. If we could map the envelope of difficulty that listeners have as they understand a sentence, then we would be in a position both to evaluate the effects of various syntactic, semantic, and pragmatic variables on the comprehension process, and to test in a careful way theories of sentence comprehension.

One way in which we can attempt to measure the momentary difficulty that listeners are having as they process sentences is to assess their ability to carry out an ancillary task. When such ability is relatively high, we conclude that the momentary processing difficulty is low, and vice versa. This is a common background assumption in many attempts to measure

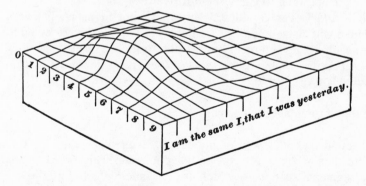

FIG. 7.4. The "thought's content" at moment four (when "same" is most prominent). Other words also affect the content at that moment. (Figure from William James, 1890, p. 283.)

information-processing capabilities, and it must be applied with caution (see Kerr, 1973, and Norman & Bobrow, 1975, for some discussion of the possible problems with this line of reasoning). The ancillary task of concern here is that of phoneme monitoring. In this task, listeners are presented with a sentence and asked both to understand it and to listen within it for a word beginning with a particular phoneme. They are instructed to push a button when the target phoneme is detected. The reaction time (RT) to make this response constitutes the major dependent variable of the experiment. When RTs are relatively long, it is assumed that the momentary difficulty of processing the sentence was high at the point where the target phoneme occurred. In other words, RTs are positively correlated with processing load. The phoneme monitoring task has been used in a number of experiments investigating the effects of a variety of variables on sentence comprehension. In general, the results have supported the (admittedly vague) background assumptions rather well. In particular, this technique has been used to investigate the units of speech perception, and it is to this topic that we now turn.

Responding to Targets and Units of Speech Perception

As is by now apparent, we agree with those theorists who believe that one of the modules of language processing computes a representation of the input in terms of its phonological segments. Somewhat paradoxically, there is seemingly strong evidence gathered in monitoring tasks for quite a different conclusion. Most readers of this paper are probably familiar with the set of arguments that were spawned by the interesting paper published by Savin and Bever (1970), but we want to review briefly the data and arguments and then to carry them forward.

Savin and Bever conducted an experiment in which listeners were presented with lists of nonsense syllables as in (1) and were asked to listen within each list for a target and respond to it. The targets specified were either an entire syllable (e.g., *sarg*) or the initial phonological segment of the syllable (e.g., /s/).

1. thowj tuwp sarg tiyf friyn. . .

They found that RTs were significantly faster when the target was the syllable than when it was the initial phoneme. This was true even for initial segments such as /s/ which are not much affected by the nature of the following vowel. As a result of this study, Savin and Bever concluded that the primary unit of speech perception was the syllable (or at least the consonant–vowel, CV). They did not dismiss the phoneme as a mere fiction, but, in our present terms, they rejected the idea that a processing module computed a symbolic representation at the phonological level during speech perception. At about the same time, Warren (1971) independently conducted a similar study and came to similar conclusions.

The trouble with the Savin and Bever study was not with its design nor with its data, but with the way in which the conclusions were drawn. This was demonstrated by Foss and Swinney (1973). They replicated Savin and Bever's work but with an important addition. Subjects were presented lists of two-syllable words as in (2) and were asked to monitor for either the initial phoneme of one of the words (e.g., /k/), the initial syllable of that word (e.g., can), or the entire word itself (e.g., candy).

2. rural ladder import candy woven...

Foss and Swinney found that RTs were slower to phoneme targets than to syllable targets, thus replicating Savin and Bever. But they also found that subjects were slower to syllable targets than to whole-word targets. If faster response times to syllables than to phonemes implicates the syllable as the unit of perception, then faster response times to words than to syllables implicates the two-syllable word as the perceptual unit. But this conclusion is totally unpalatable, as all would agree. The moral is that one simply cannot assume that the order of RTs reflects the order in which perceptual objects are developed by the listener. Many other factors must be taken into account in interpreting RT data of this sort.

In order to help interpret such data, Foss and Swinney suggested that a distinction be made between the perception of a linguistic unit and its identification. A unit is identified when a decision that can initiate a response has been made. A unit is perceived when it has been computed by a module of the perceptual system. This distinction can easily slip into vacuity if one is not careful, but it helps at least to make a methodological point: Because an investigator measures RT to some aspect of a stimulus does not mean that the processing system initiates a response as soon as that stimulus feature has been computed. Foss and Swinney argued that, in these experiments, words were identified before syllables, and syllables before phonemes. They suggested that phonemes were identified and responded to considerably after their perception and, indeed, after the words they compose have been identified.

In another experiment on this same issue, McNeill and Lindig (1973) manipulated both the "size" of the target (e.g., phoneme, syllable, word) and the size of the units in the list presented to the subjects. For example, when a word (e.g., novels) was the target, the list might also consist of words. But it might instead consist of three word sentences (e.g., novels affect Baptists); or, somewhat strangely, the list might consist of syllables (e.g., nov). In the latter case the subject was supposed to respond to nov when the target was *novels*. In addition, the list might consist merely of phonemes (e.g., /n/). Again, the subject was instructed to respond to /n/ when the target was *novels*. McNeill and Lindig found that RTs were fastest when the size of the target and the size of the items in the lists matched. Thus, when the list consisted of syllables, syllabic targets were responded to most rapidly; when the list consisted of words, word targets were responded to most rapidly. McNeill and Lindig (1973) concluded that "monitoring experiments have no implications at all . . . for the perceptual units of speech [p. 428]."

The neat pattern of results found by McNeill and Lindig is questionable, however. Foss and Swinney conjectured that the relative RTs to phoneme and syllable targets could be manipulated by changing the character of the lists to be searched. If the confusibility among the syllables was high, RTs in response to them might increase. This was later borne out in a study conducted by Healy and Cutting (1976). Also Mills and Martin (1976) showed in a different context that the findings of McNeill and Lindig are not general. Mills and Martin spliced the first syllable out of a two-syllable word and inserted it in a list of syllables. The spliced-in syllable was the target. Subjects took longer to respond to this target than to a syllable target that had been spoken in isolation. This suggests that the acoustic mismatch between the expected target and the actually occurring target also affected RTs in the McNeill and Lindig study.

It is not the intent here to review these experiments in detail. What is important is the observation that many, many factors contribute to the RTs that are observed in any monitoring study. Consequently, to repeat the moral, the pattern of RTs cannot simply be taken as reflecting the order in which calculations are carried out in the nervous system of the listener.

The studies conducted by Foss and Swinney were conducted in part to investigate the units of perception and in part to understand the monitoring task itself. We were trying to live up to Newell's (1973) "*First Injunction of Psychological Experimentation: Know the method your subject is using to perform the experimental task* [p. 294]." What the entire set of studies suggests is that the methods the subjects use are influenced by a large set of variables. But no theory of the method has yet resulted. The phoneme monitoring technique was among the first attempts to measure the effects of linguistic processing as it takes place. The difficulty of detailing what goes on in the task led Marslen-Wilson (1976) to remark pessimistically, "unfortunately the one line of research that did explore immediate processing has relied on a task, phoneme monitoring, whose relationship to linguistic processing variables is difficult to interpret . . . and whose use may have been based on incorrect assumptions about the nature of the processing system [p. 206]." Later in this chapter we will try to reinject some optimism by providing at least a part of the needed theory. The justification for the proposed theory is best understood when presented in the context of a substantive issue, namely the process of lexical access.

Phoneme Monitoring Studies of Lexical Access

Any theory of sentence comprehension must have as one of its components a theory of lexical access. This part of the comprehension process takes on special importance when one has adopted the hypothesis that the lexical item is the common source of information-sharing for many of the subprocessors, as suggested by the blackboard model of Fig. 7.3. A theory of lexical access must, of course, be responsive to the facts—if one value of a variable leads to slower access than does a different value, the theory must provide an explanation for this finding. Some studies investigating the effects of particular variables on lexical access have been carried out using the phoneme monitoring task. We will examine some of them both for what they tell us about the process of lexical access and for what they tell us about the monitoring procedure itself.

It has been shown, for example, that the sentence stress carried by a target-bearing word affects phoneme monitoring RTs. By inference, stress also affects lexical access time. Cutler and Foss (1977) showed that when a target word carries high sentence stress, RTs are shorter than when it does not. This is true for all types of words; both 'content' and 'function' words show the effect. Shields, McHugh, and Martin (1974) also showed that RT is faster when the target is carried by a stressed than by an unstressed syllable. This effect can be accounted for by relatively straightforward acoustic hypotheses.

More interestingly, Cutler (1976) demonstrated that targets on "stressed" words are responded to more rapidly than targets on "unstressed" words, even when the two words are equated for stress! To understand this paradox you must know that Cutler spliced physically identical target-bearing words into two sentneces. The syntactic contexts into which they were spliced were also identical. What varied, however, was the stress contour of the sentence. In one version of the test sentence the target-bearing word occurred in a position that would, in the normal course of uttering the sentence, receive high stress; in the other version the target occurred in a position that was going to receive low stress. Because of the tape-splicing operation, both targets received neutral (and identical) stress. Cutler found that RTs for the "expected high stress" words were shorter than those for the "expected low stress" words. She concluded that the stress contour of a sentence can direct the subject's attention to the points where the semantically most central words (the focus of the sentence) will occur. (Note that this line of reasoning assumes that listeners are identifying the words before the initial phonemes of them.) Thus, speed of lexical access can be affected by the way in which listeners deploy their processing resources. Such considerations are presently absent from our model of lexical access, a deficiency we will need to repair.

Another lexical variable that has been investigated with the phoneme monitoring technique is that of ambiguity. The existence of ambiguous words has long been one of the important sources of problems for machine recognition of language. And psychological evidence exists that the presence of an ambiguity in a sentence affects the processing of that sentence. An early experiment using the phoneme monitoring technique (Foss, 1970) manipulated ambiguity and found that RTs were longer after an ambiguous word than after a (relatively) unambiguous control word. Cairns and Kammerman (1975) reported a similar finding. Subsequently, both Foss and Jenkins (1973) and Cutler and Foss (1974) found that RTs in the monitoring task were longer after ambiguous than after unambiguous words, even when there was some prior context in the sentence which biased the interpretation heavily toward one of the meanings of the ambiguity. It remained for Swinney and Hakes (1976) to show that the ambiguity effect does go away when the biasing context is very strong.

It is important to note at this time that the interpretation of the entire set of ambiguity studies using the phoneme monitoring technique has been called into question. Mehler, Segui, and Carey (1978) have pointed out that the unambiguous control words in the above experiments tended to be longer (in syllables) than the ambiguous words. When this variable is controlled it appears to account for the "ambiguity" effect. That is, RTs after long words are faster than those after short words (see also Newman & Dell, 1978). Although we do not think that the matter is closed, the burden of proof surely lies with those who believe that there is a momentary increase in processing difficulty due to the difficulty of locating an ambiguous word in the mental lexicon. Recent studies (e.g., Swinney, 1976) have provided some new evidence in favor of this hypothesis.

A third variable that may affect lexical access and which has been investigated using phoneme monitoring is that of word frequency. It appears that in running speech, as well as in isolated word experiments, the frequency of a word in the language affects the time that it takes to access the word in the mental lexicon. In one experiment (Foss, 1969), subjects were presented with sentences containing either a high- or a low-frequency word of similar meaning and were asked to carry out the phoneme monitoring task. The target phoneme began the word following the high- or low-frequency word of interest. For example, in the sentences represented in (3) the target phoneme was /b/.

3. The $\left\{ \begin{array}{l} \text{itinerant} \\ \text{travelling} \end{array} \right\}$ bassoon player found himself without funds in a strange town.

Reaction times were longer when the targets occurred after low-frequency words than when they occurred after high-frequency words. To account for this result we need to make two assumptions. First, that the time to access a word is inversely related to its frequency (or its recency, cf. Scarborough, Cortese, & Scarborough, 1977). This is a commonplace assumption, consistent with considerable data, although the mechanisms responsible for the effect are still debated. Second, we assume that the listener does not identify word $n + 1$ in a sentence until an attempt has been made to identify word n. Thus, in our example, the identification of the word *bassoon* was held up until *itinerant* or *travelling* was processed (at least up to some point in the access system). Since processing the low-frequency item takes more time than processing the high-frequency one, identifying the target phoneme should also take longer in the former case. The details of this explanation need to be spelled out and, as we will soon see, the way in which we spell them depends upon the outcomes of other experiments and upon our theory of the phoneme monitoring task. To help us in this endeavor, let us consider one more set of findings.

Lexical access of a word may be affected by the semantic relationship that it has with the prior words in the sentence. Semantic relatedness is a fourth variable that has been investigated with the monitoring task. It has been known for some time that subjects in a lexical decision task (does this string of visually presented letters constitute a word?) are faster in saying that item $n + 1$ is a word if item n was semantically related to it. For example, Meyer and Schvaneveldt (1971) showed that it took less time to say that both members of the pair *doctor–nurse* were words than it did to say that both members of the pair *bread–nurse* were words. This has been interpreted as demonstrating that there is a network of interconnections among semantically related words (e.g., Collins & Loftus, 1975) and that activating one member of the network also activates its other members.

Although it may seem obvious that a similar effect of semantic relatedness would be found in sentences, there is not much evidence in the literature to support such a claim (Forster, 1976). However, Blank and Foss (1978) have found evidence that context aids lexical access during the comprehension of sentences. In their experiment, listeners were asked to comprehend sentences and to engage in the phoneme monitoring task. They were presented with four different sentence types, exemplified in (4)–(7).

4. The drunk concealed his aching eye probably without realizing he was doing it.
5. The drunk winked his aching eye probably without realizing he was doing it.
6. The drunk concealed his bloodshot eye probably without realizing he was doing it.
7. The drunk winked his bloodshot eye probably without realizing he was doing it.

In this set, the target phoneme is the /p/ in *probably*. Blank and Foss were interested in whether the time required to access the word *eye*, which occurs just prior to the target phoneme, would be affected by the prior context. Sentence (4) is essentially a control sentence in which the noun *eye* is preceded by relatively neutral words. In sentence (5), *eye* is preceded by a semantically related verb (*winked*), while it is preceded by a semantically related adjective (*bloodshot*) in sentence (6). Sentence (7) contains both of these related words. Pretesting determined that the verb and the adjective were approximately equal in the degree to which subjects thought them to be related to the critical noun. If the semantically related word speeds access to *eye*, then we expect that RTs to respond to the target phoneme will be shorter in sentences (5)–(7) than in sentence (4). The design of the study also lets us see whether the presence of two related words will aid lexical access more than the presence of a single related word. It also lets us begin to examine some of the temporal parameters of the activation process (if there is, indeed, any activation at all). Perhaps the adjective occurs too close in time to the noun it modifies for the activation to occur.

The results of the study are shown in Table 7.1. Reaction times to the target phoneme were shorter when the noun preceding the target was

TABLE 7.1
Mean Phoneme Monitoring Latencies
(msec)

Verb Context	Adjective Context	
	Unrelated	Related
Unrelated	482	462
Related	460	438

itself preceded by either a related verb or a related adjective. Furthermore, two sources of context led to faster RTs than either source alone; indeed, the effects were additive.

This result was not unexpected. Indeed, the outlines of the explanation were suggested some time ago. In his chapter on attention, William James discussed sentence comprehension in these words (1890, Vol. I): "Each word is *doubly* awakened; once from without by the lips of the talker, but already before that from within by the premonitory processes irradiating from the previous words [p. 450]." In the case of sentences like (5)–(7), the object noun (*eye*) was "awakened" by the "premonitory processes" radiating from the related words *winked* and *bloodshot*. Presumably, then, it required very little sensory input before the object noun was accessed. This viewpoint has been made explicit in Morton's (1969) logogen theory of lexical access. According to the logogen model, the lexicon consists of separate theoretical entities—the logogens—each of which is a threshold device. The information associated with a logogen is not made available to the listener until its threshold has been exceeded. Each logogen accepts both sensory inputs as well as inputs from semantically related logogens. That is, both of these types of information contribute to the logogen's "counter," raising it toward its threshold value. In particular, if logogens i and j are semantically related, and if i reaches its threshold, then its activation provides an input (via the "context system") to logogen j. In that case, the latter logogen does not require as much sensory input before it exceeds its threshold. As soon as logogen j is activated, then all of the information that is associated with it becomes available to the listener.

Returning to the Blank and Foss experiment, when subjects received sentences like (5)–(7) they were able to access the object noun more rapidly than when they heard sentences like (4). This means that they could begin to process the target-bearing word (e.g., *probably*) sooner in the former cases. And this, in turn, led them to identify the target phoneme sooner in those sentences. The present explanation is entirely consistent with the one given earlier when discussing the results of the frequency experiment.

Morton and Long (1976) have also investigated the effects of semantic relatedness upon lexical access. They used a somewhat different independent variable, although they employed phoneme-monitoring RT as the dependent variable. In their experiment, subjects were presented with sentences like (8) and (9), and were asked to push a button when they heard a word-initial /b/.

8. He sat reading a book until it was time to go home for his tea.
9. He sat reading a bill until it was time to go home for his tea.

The word carrying the target phoneme was either predictable from the context (e.g., *book*) or not (e.g., *bill*). Morton and Long found that the times to respond to the target were significantly shorter when the word carrying the target was predictable.

In order to observe effects of word predictability on responses to phonemes initiating those words, it is necessary to make two assumptions: first, that highly predictable words are more rapidly retrieved from the mental lexicon than are less predictable words; and second, that the listener identifies and responds to the target phoneme only *after* the word has been retrieved. Presumably the effects of predictability operate at the word level and not at the phonological level. Thus, the reasonable conclusion to draw from Morton and Long's data is that listeners operate upon a retrieved lexical item to determine whether it begins with the specified target phoneme. This is consistent with our earlier interpretations. Recall that Foss and Swinney (1973) made a distinction between the perception of a linguistic segment and its identification. They adopted the modular view of perception, "that there are processes that convert the neuroacoustic input into a neurophonetic representation, that there are other processes that transform the entities at the latter level into a representation at the neurophonemic level, and so on. . . . [T]hese processes do not operate straight through; they are subject to modification by feedback from higher-level analyses [p. 254]." Foss and Swinney went on to say that, "When speech processing has proceeded to the point where the phonetic-to phonemic transfer function can apply, then speech has been 'perceived' at the phonetic level [p. 254]." And they also suggested that subjects might be able to identify phonological segments during running speech only after the words carrying the segments had been identified. The results of their study supported this view. We now know, from the work of Healy and Cutting (1976), that the identification of various units can be affected by the context in which they occur—a very reasonable finding from a signal detection point of view. But according to Foss and Swinney's speculations, phonological segments are identified after the identification of words and syllables in a typical sentence-processing experiment. The results obtained by Morton and Long corroborate this line of reasoning.

But now the plot thickens. Some work conducted in our laboratory suggested that subjects can respond to target phonemes *prior* to the point at which the word carrying the target has been retrieved—and that this happened during running speech of similar phonological character to that used in the previous phoneme-monitoring studies (Foss & Blank, 1977). Let us now examine the results from a set of studies designed to follow up these earlier observations. They show, we believe, that listeners can indeed gain access to phonological information prior to the point where lexical retrieval has occurred.

Monitoring On and After Critical Words

The logic of these studies is as follows. If phonemes can be identified only after the lexical item they compose has been identified, then any variable that affects the time required to access the target-bearing word should also affect phoneme-monitoring RTs. In the present experiment, we manipulated a variable that should greatly affect access time—namely, whether or not the target-bearing word was in the listener's mental lexicon at all. Subjects were aurally presented with two basic sentence types, of which (10) and (11) are examples.

10. At the end of the last year, the government prepared a lengthy report on birth control.
11. At the end of last year, the gatabont prepared a lengthy report on birth control.

They were asked to listen for a word-initial target; in these examples it was /g/. Within some sentences [e.g., sentence (11)] the target-bearing item was not a real word, but was instead a nonsense item. The nonsense item was similar in many respects to its real word counterpart: same initial phoneme, same number of syllables, and same stress pattern. When listeners encounter an item like *gatabont* they cannot be successful in retrieving it from the mental lexicon since it is simply not there. According to Foss and Swinney and to Morton and Long, the subjects should be very slow in responding to a nonword-initial target phoneme. Both sets of investigators claimed that identification of a target phoneme will occur subsequent to identification of the lexical item.

In contrast, if subjects can identify a phonological segment prior to accessing the lexical item bearing it, then we might expect no difference in RT to respond to the /g/ in (10) versus (11).

A second variable was also manipulated in this experiment. On half the trials the target phoneme occurred *on* the nonsense word or its real word counterpart (this is the condition we have just discussed). On the other half of the trials the target phoneme occurred on the word immediately *after* the nonsense word or its counterpart (e.g., /p/ in *prepared* in the above examples). What should happen in this case? Recall that subjects are instructed to respond to word-initial target phonemes. Thus, position as well as identification information is required in order to carry out this task. In order to determine that a phoneme is word initial, the listener must know that the phoneme has been immediately preceded by a word boundary. Of course, if the target-bearing word has been retrieved from the mental dictionary, then the listener can determine its initial phoneme. If this were the only way that position information could be determined, it would argue that a subject could respond to a word-initial target phoneme only after accessing its carrier word. However, it is also possible for a phoneme to be identified as word-initial prior to retrieving the word it begins. Specifically, a listener can determine that a phoneme is word-initial if he or she knows that the just preceding phoneme is a word final. Thus, as soon as the listener has determined that the prior phonological information constitutes the end of a word, then a word boundary can be assigned. When this has occurred the listener then knows that the next phonological segment is word initial. It is possible in principle, then, to determine both position and identity information about a phoneme without retrieving its carrier word.

In the case of our experiment, the listener who is presented with sentence (11) will be in a difficult position when the /p/ occurs. Since the item *gatabont* is not in the mental dictionary, the subject cannot be certain where this "word" ends. Word boundary assignment will probably have to wait until further information from the word *prepared* has occurred. This means that subjects should be slower in responding to the /p/ after a nonword than after a real word.

To summarize, the experiment had four basic conditions. The target phoneme was either on or after the critical item. And the critical item was either a nonsense word or a real word counterpart to it. In the experiment, 32 undergraduate subjects listened to 36 experimental sentences. The latter were appropriately counterbalanced so that each sentence occurred in all four conditions across the study. After the subjects heard the sentences (plus a set of 36 fillers), they were given a recognition comprehension test to insure that they had paid attention to the meaning of the sentences.

The basic results from the study are shown in Table 7.2. The important thing to note about these results is the massive interaction. Reaction times were much longer (about 100 msec) when the target occurred after a

TABLE 7.2
Reaction Times (msec)

Target Position	Target Type	
	Word	*Nonword*
On	475	481
After	525	626

nonsense word than when it occurred after a real word. In contrast, the RTs were nearly identical when the target occurred on a real word as when it occurred on a nonsense word. The relevant interaction was highly reliable statistically (min $F'(1, 58) = 6.96, p < .02$).

The results from this experiment call into question the hypothesis that phoneme identification must wait until after lexical access or even an attempt at it. If the hypothesis were true, then RTs to targets on nonsense words would have been longer relative to their real-word controls both when the target occurred on the critical word as well as when it occurred after it. But RTs were not elevated when the target was on the nonsense word relative to when it was on its real word counterpart. Apparently phoneme identification can occur before lexical access. This can happen because listeners are using a top-down analysis for assigning word boundaries. Thus, when presented with the sentence, "At the end of last year, the g_____," listeners will identify *year* as a word and then attempt to identify a new word beginning with [ð]. There is no word in English starting with [ðəg], so listeners can determine that the next sequence is "the + word-initial /g/." This permits them to respond to the /g/ without accessing the item that it begins.

Perhaps, though, there is something about the use of nonsense words that led to these results. Although it would be difficult to tell a coherent story about why this might be so, we decided to see whether the on versus after effect would hold up when a study that employed real words only was conducted.

It was mentioned previously that studies using the phoneme monitoring technique have obtained data consistent with the hypothesis that word frequency affects lexical retrieval time in running speech. In those studies a word-initial target phoneme occurred immediately following the high- or low-frequency word of interest. It was found that RTs were longer after low frequency words. In the present study this work was extended, adding the conditions in which the target phoneme was also on the high- and low-frequency words. Four conditions exemplified by sentences (12) and (13) resulted.

12. Yesterday afternoon, the teacher borrowed the article from the reference library.
13. Yesterday afternoon, the tutor borrowed the article from the reference library.

The target phoneme was either on the critical word (the /t/ in *teacher* or *tutor*) or immediately after it (the /b/ in *borrowed*). The critical words differed in frequency (mean frequency in the Kucera and Francis, 1967, count was 125.5 for the high frequency items versus 3.9 for the low frequency items), but were similar in meaning, began with the same phoneme, and had the same number of syllables.

If high-frequency words are accessed more rapidly, and if lexical access is normally a prerequisite for identifying a word-initial phoneme, then it follows that phoneme-monitoring RTs should be shorter when the target phoneme is on a high-frequency word than when it is on a low-frequency word. If, on the other hand, lexical access is not required for phoneme monitoring, then we would again expect to see no difference in RTs when the target is on the high- versus low-frequency word. Of course, RTs should be shorter when the target is after a high-frequency word relative to when it is after a low-frequency word, just as they were in the earlier study (Foss, 1969).

As in the previous experiment, the present study had four basic conditions. The target phoneme occurred either on or immediately after the critical word; and the critial word was either high or low frequency in the language. Forty subjects listened to 40 experimental sentences, appropriately counterbalanced so that each sentence occurred in each of its four versions across the experiment. The procedure was very similar to that used in the earlier study employing nonsense words.

The results of the experiment are shown in Table 7.3. Reaction times were longer when the target phoneme occurred after a low-frequency word than when it occurred after a high-frequency word. This difference was statistically reliable (min $F'(1, 74) = 4.26$, $p < .05$). In contrast, there was essentially no difference in RTs to target phonemes that occurred on high- versus low-frequency words.

Conceptually, then, the results of this experiment were identical to those of the previous experiment. The frequency of the item carrying the target (nonsense item, low- or high-frequency word) has no effect on the time that subjects take to respond to the target. In contrast, the frequency of the item just prior to the target-bearing word has a significant impact upon the time to respond to the target.

These results are in sharp contrast to those expected by Foss and Swinney and by Morton and Long. They also appear to be at variance with the results observed by the latter investigators. Recall that Morton

TABLE 7.3
Reaction Times (msec)

Target Position	Word Frequency	
	High	Low
On	397	403
After	482	514

and Long found that subjects were faster in responding to target phonemes when they were carried by words that were predictable from the context (i.e., high transitional probability words). The reasonable interpretation of their data is that listeners operate upon a retrieved lexical item to determine whether it begins with the specified target phoneme. The lexical items are retrieved more rapidly when the context is appropriate. The reasonable interpretation of the two experiments described here is that listeners need not wait until the lexical item has been retrieved before responding to word-initial target phonemes. Instead they are able to respond at an earlier point in the comprehension process. In terms of the model that we have been using up to now, our data suggest that listeners can under some circumstances identify and respond to a phonological representation of the input before the lexical item carrying the phonological segments is represented on the "blackboard."

THE DUAL CODE HYPOTHESIS

Let us suppose that the reasonable interpretation of our data is correct, that subjects can respond to phonological segments before lexical access has occurred. This conclusion bolsters further our contention that *the speech perception mechanisms compute a representation of the input in terms of phoneme-sized units*. In other words, it supports the idea that one of the modules of the speech perception system computes a phonological representation. Consider this conclusion along with our earlier one that each lexical item has its phonological code stored with it and that this code is "written on the blackboard" when the lexical item has been retrieved. We seem to have two phonological codes, one that exists prior to lexical access and one that becomes available when lexical access occurs. Is this an embarrassment of riches? No; for as may already be apparent, the codes are not really the same.

Our view of speech perception, like that of the majority of theorists, holds that there are both analytic and synthetic aspects to the process. Let us focus upon the analytic aspects of perception; they are represented by the parametric processes and the feature extraction processes of Fig. 7.3. These processes result in a set of segments (or perhaps more accurately, in a set of feature bundles). Note that these feature bundles can be detailed representations of the input. They may represent such aspects of the stimulus as whether or not the segment is aspirated. In addition, details sufficient to determine the speaker's accent are present in this code. Let us call a representation at this level a "phonetic" representation. Thus, the module of perception takes an acoustic representation of the stimulus as input and yields a phonetic representation as output. Of course the phonetic representation need not be fully specified. This point is obvious when we note that speech is often heard in noisy environments and that therefore the cells in the phonetic feature matrix may have missing entries. (The analogy to the phonetic feature matrix of Chomsky & Halle, 1968, is clear, we presume.)

According to the present hypothesis, then, the point at which the phonetic representation occurs is prior to the point at which the lexical item is identified. When the lexical item has been accessed within the mental lexicon, then all of the phonological information associated with that entry is made available to the listener (put on the blackboard). Certain redundancies of the phonetic representation may no longer be present (e.g., whether a voiceless stop is aspirated or not), while critical missing entries from the phonetic matrix may now be filled in. Let us make a terminological distinction. We called the former representation—the one occurring prior to lexical access—the phonetic representation. It is composed of phonetic segments. Call the latter representation—the one occurring subsequent to lexical access—the phonological representation. It is composed of phonological segments. Although the distinction is borrowed from Chomsky and Halle (1968), it is probably obvious that the terms are being used here in a somewhat different way than they used them.

Given the above distinction, it now makes sense to ask, which phoneme is identified when the subject responds in the phoneme monitoring task? That is, does the subject respond to the phonetic or to the phonological phoneme? The answer is: either. The code responded to may vary according to experimental circumstances; for example, when the phonetic code is completely specified, then the subject may (or may not) respond to it. When the phonetic code does not contain enough information to permit identification of the target segment, then the response must be made on the basis of the phonological code if it is to be made at all. The view that there are two codes to which the listener may respond in the phoneme monitoring task will be called the Dual Code hypothesis.

Informally at least, the Dual Code hypothesis can account for the experiments that we have described. In our experiments, the subjects were responding on the basis of the phonetic code. These listeners did not have to gain access to the target-bearing items in their lexicons before they were able to initiate their responses to the target phoneme. In Morton and Long's experiment, the subjects were typically responding to the phonological code. Lexical access occurred before the phonetic information was identified, and a response was initiated on the basis of the phonological code. But why should this difference between the two experiments exist? Why, that is, do the subjects in our experiments find it possible to respond to the phonetic code while those in Morton and Long's seemingly do not? This question spawns another, related one. How can it ever be the case that a listener can respond to the phonological code before the phonetic one?

One answer to these questions may be forthcoming if we again borrow an idea from Morton's (1969) logogen theory of lexical access. Consider the subject in a phoneme monitoring experiment. When a target is specified, the subject may develop a target image within both the phonological and the phonetic codes. As soon as the subject detects that one of these images has been matched, he or she will initiate a response. (We can think of this part of the task in decision-theoretic terms as well. The phonetic and phonological targets must be matched to some criterion before a response will occur.) When semantically related contextual information has partially activated a logogen, only a minimum of phonetic information may be required before that logogen exceeds its threshold. Thus, the phonological code associated with a logogen can become available (on the blackboard) and will match the phonological target image even though the phonetic representation of the input may still be incomplete—it has not matched, and may never match, the phonetic target image with enough fidelity to lead to response initiation.

In the sentences used by Morton and Long, some of the target-bearing words were preceded by semantically related context. These target-bearing words required a minimum of phonetic input before their logogens were raised above threshold. The phonological code rapidly became available and the subjects responded to it; at the same time, insufficient phonetic information was identified for a response to be made to that code. In the sentences used in our experiments, no relevant semantic context was present. Hence, activation of the logogen did not occur prior to the identification of the (phonetic) target phoneme. The subjects therefore responded to the phonetic code and we observed no effect of frequency.

To summarize, we have proposed that there are two codes to which the subjects might respond in a phoneme monitoring experiment, one a phonetic code and the other a phonological code. The former is the product of a perceptual module that operates upon the acoustic stimulus and yields its product prior to lexical access. The latter becomes available to the listener as a consequence of lexical access. Under some circumstances, the phonological code may be more fully specified than the phonetic code and the subjects may respond to it. In other circumstances, the subjects can respond to the phonetic code. When listeners respond to the phonetic code, we will not see the effects of variables that affect speed of lexical access; when they respond to the phonological code we will see the effects of such variables. Although this story may be a step in the right direction, we will soon see that it is not the entire journey.

Tests of Dual Coding: Task Variable

Clearly the most important difference between the experiments conducted by Morton and Long and those reported here has to do with the presence or absence of relevant semantic context prior to the target-bearing word. However, other differences existed between these studies as well, and one of them is worth noting. In their study Morton and Long asked subjects to repeat back each sentence after they had heard it. Thus, they used a rote recall task as a check on whether or not the subjects were attending to the sentences as well as to the monitoring task. In our studies we used a different task, one that we have called the recognition comprehension task. In this task the subjects heard the entire set of sentences and then were presented with a typed subset of them, along with some foils, and were asked to say which had occurred during the monitoring phase of the experiment. In some of our studies we used only the data from those subjects who scored above chance on this recognition test. The difference in comprehension tasks is one that could make a difference in the code to which the subject responded.

Suppose that the phonetic code is stored in a fast-decaying short-term memory, perhaps the precategorical acoustic store investigated by Crowder (1972). Suppose further that the requirement to recall the sentence verbatim also puts a demand upon this storage device. In such a case it is reasonable to conjecture that the listener will have a harder time responding to the phonetic code. The recall task will interfere with the phonetic representation, biasing the listener toward responding to the phonological code. This interpretation is consistent with the pattern of results in the above experiments. Subjects in Morton and Long's study were given the rote recall task; they also appeared to be responding to the phonological code. When the discrepancy between our findings and those of Morton and Long was first noted, we replicated their experiment using our recognition comprehension task. We observed the same effect that they had, namely that RTs were shorter when the target-bearing word was predictable from the context, but the magnitude of the effect was reduced relative to the effect they reported. This is consistent with the idea that the comprehension task was influencing the code to which the subject was responding. But of course it is not really appropriate to compare magnitudes of effects across half a continent and an ocean, so we redid Morton and Long's study again, this time using our comprehension task for half the subjects and their test for the other half. In this study, we borrowed 20 of the sentences used by Morton and Long, examples of which are repeated here as (14) and (15). For any given subject, ten sentences had the target on the probable noun while ten had it on the improbable noun, e.g., the /b/ in *book* or *bill*. Sixty subjects were tested, 30 with each comprehension task.

14. He sat reading a book until it was time to go home for his tea.
15. He sat reading a bill until it was time to go home for his tea.

In this experiment, then, we were investigating whether the type of comprehension task would affect the degree to which a listener would respond to the phonetic as opposed to the phonological code. We suspected that listeners given the rote recall task might be forced to respond to the phonological code, while those given the recognition test might be able to respond to the phonetic code. If this were true, then the difference between RTs on probable versus improbable nouns would be smaller for the latter subjects.

The basic results from this study are shown in Table 7.4. As can be seen, there is no apparent difference in the data due to the type of comprehension test employed; subjects responded equally faster to the probable noun than to the improbable one in each case.

There were, however, some indications in the data that the comprehension tasks were having differential effects on the subjects' performance. For one thing, the within-group variability was greater in those subjects presented with the recognition comprehension test. This is consistent with the idea that there was more variability in the type of code to which subjects in that group were responding. Perhaps some of those subjects were responding to the phonetic code, while all of the subjects given the rote test were responding to the phonological code. Admittedly, this is not a strong argument. It is somewhat bolstered by the following observation. Subjects who are responding to the phonetic code ought to have two things in common. They should respond relatively quickly, and they should not differ in the time it takes them to respond to the probable versus the improbable nouns. Subjects who are responding to the

TABLE 7.4
Reaction Times (msec)

Comprehension Test	Noun Type	
	Probable	Improbable
Recognition	405	449
Recall	409	456

phonological code, on the other hand, should respond relatively more slowly and they should show a difference in the time it takes them to respond to the probable versus the improbable nouns (since they are typically responding to a code that occurs subsequent to lexical access). Therefore, in a condition in which some subjects are responding to the phonetic code and some to the phonological code, we expect to see a correlation between absolute RT and the magnitude of the difference in RTs to respond to the probable and improbable nouns. For subjects in the recognition group we observed such a correlation: $r = .42$, ($p < .05$). For subjects in the rote recall group no such correlation obtained, $r = -.09$.

Test of Dual Coding: Stimulus Variable

Ideally, we would like to manipulate the code to which a listener will respond in the phoneme monitoring task. Success at doing so would bolster our Dual Code theory considerably. There is little evidence (albeit there is a shred) from the above experiment that the comprehension task is a successful way to carry out such a manipulation. What other means could be used to affect the probability that the listener will be able to respond to the phonetic code? Consider a listener who is presented with a sentence in a noisy environment. Noise should affect the success that the low-level stimulus analyzing mechanisms have in extracting stimulus parameters. Thus, under noisy conditions it seems unlikely that the listener will be able to develop a fully specified phonetic representation. In consequence, lexical access will depend more heavily upon other factors such as context or word frequency. It also follows that subjects ought to have a higher probability of responding to the phonological code when noise is present that when it is absent, since the phonetic representation will not match the phonetic target.

In order to test this idea, we designed the following experiment with the aid of Sally Doyle. We took the sentences from the earlier experiment on word frequency—examples of which are repeated here as (16) and (17)—and presented them along with noise to a new group of subjects. We also replicated the earlier frequency study, by presenting the sentences in the quiet as well.

16. Yesterday afternoon, the teacher borrowed the article from the reference library.
17. Yesterday afternoon, the tutor borrowed the article from the reference library.

Recall that the target phoneme was either on the high- or low-frequency word (e.g., the /t/ in *teacher* or *tutor*), or immediately after it (e.g., the /b/

in *borrowed*). Each subject received sentences in all four of these conditions. Half of the 80 subjects heard the sentences through noise, half heard them in the quiet.

Earlier it was found that there was no difference in phoneme monitoring RTs when the target was on the high- and low-frequency words. There was a difference when the target occurred after these two types of words. Now, however, when the sentences were heard in noise, we expected to see the effects of frequency when the target was on the high- versus the low-frequency words as well as when the target was after these words. We reasoned that the subjects were more likely to respond to the phonological code in the noise condition. Since high-frequency words should be accessed more rapidly, their phonological codes should be available to the subject more rapidly than the phonological codes for the low-frequency words. Ideally we would have liked to have seen the earlier interaction between frequency and target position disappear completely. But we were happy to settle for an effect of frequency in the on condition when noise was present.

The results from this study are presented in Table 7.5. Subjects in the no-noise condition behaved just as had the earlier subjects. There was no effect of frequency when the target was on the high- versus the low-frequency noun, and there was a substantial effect of frequency when the target was in the after position. The noise had a major effect on overall RTs; subjects took over 150 msec longer to respond in the noisy conditions. But the pattern of results in the noise condition was identical to that observed in the no-noise condition. Once again we observed an effect of word frequency when the target was in the after position; in addition, there was no effect at all of frequency when the target was in the on position.

This result was somewhat disconcerting. The Dual Code theory appears to be a promising way to account for some superficially discordant data, yet a prediction derived from this model seems to be at variance

TABLE 7.5
Reaction Times (msec)

Noise Condition	Target Position	Word Frequency	
		High	*Low*
No noise	On	436	445
	After	514	540
Noise	On	582	586
	After	661	727

with the facts. However, a somewhat closer look at our data suggests that the facts may not be quite what they appear. Although this is a recent experiment and has not been thoroughly followed up (e.g., with speech-sounding noise rather than the 'pink' noise we used), one thing seems clear: The subjects in the noise group performed more poorly on the comprehension test than did the subjects in the no-noise group. Subjects in the former condition made significantly more errors on the recognition test. What this observation suggests is that subjects in the noise group were devoting more of their processing resources to the monitoring task—indeed, to examining the phonetic code—such that they were able to identify the target phoneme from the phonetic code in the on condition. In consequence, they were not able to process the sentences very well, as demonstrated by their poorer performance on the comprehension task. Clearly it is inappropriate to compare phoneme monitoring times across conditions in which the resources devoted to sentence comprehension are not equivalent. The task presupposes that subjects in the various conditions are attempting to comprehend the message to an approximately equal degree.

Admittedly, the above comments are highly speculative (and perhaps forced). At least it is clear how to proceed in this case. We need to convince our subjects in the noise group to give a higher priority to the comprehension task. When they do, they will have fewer resources to devote to the monitoring task. When that happens then (a) they should have a much lower probability of responding to the targets; and (b) when they do manage to respond, they will have a higher probability of responding to the phonological code.[2]

RESOURCE ALLOCATION: THE EXECUTIVE

Behind this line of reasoning, with its appeal to resource allocation, is the assumption that there is some executive whose job it is to schedule the resources in order to meet the high-level goals of the comprehender. In order to account for our data, then, we should explicitly introduce the executive or the scheduling system into the theory. This is done in the model shown in Fig. 7.5. This model keeps many of the features of the earlier ones. In particular, the blackboard concept is still being used, with the lexical item being the element that gets put on the blackboard. It is the

---

[2]Recently, Blank (1979) has investigated predictions from the Dual Code model in experiments where the target items alone were replaced by noise (i.e., she combined phoneme monitoring with the phonemic restoration technique). Her results corroborate very well predictions derived from the model.

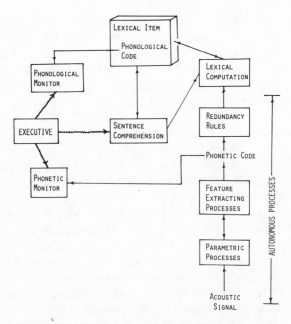

FIG. 7.5. Expanded "blackboard" model showing the "executive" and
some of the processes that it sueprvises (see text).

central box at the top of the figure. We have omitted for visual clarity the
other inputs to the blackboard (such as the environmental processes) that
were shown in Fig. 7.1, but they are still meant to be present in Fig. 7.5.

On the right side of the figure are represented the bottom-up or analytic
speech perception mechanisms. As can be seen, the phonetic code is one
of the major products of this part of the model. These mechanisms are
marked as being autonomous processes. What this means is that, relatively speaking, they do not require supervision from the executive, i.e.,
they do not constitute a drain on the listeners' resources. This latter claim
is meant to be a relative one. It is possible that all of these processes
require some of the listeners' limited resources, but that the operation of
these perceptual mechanisms is so overlearned that they need but a minute fraction of them. To make an analogy, detecting their operation from
RT data would be like detecting whether someone's doorbell light was on
by visually inspecting the rate at which their electric meter turns.

On the left of the figure is represented the executive and the two
monitoring devices that the executive can construct when the subject is
presented with the phoneme monitoring task: the phonetic and the
phonological monitors. Each scans the appropriate coded representation
of the input: The phonetic monitor looks at the phonetic code, the
phonological monitor at the phonological code which is made available to

the listener upon retrieval of a lexical item. (Other lexical codes, the syntactic and semantic ones, are not depicted on the blackboard, again simply for visual clarity.) Both of the monitors, as well as the process of constructing a representation of the sentence (the acts of comprehension subsequent to lexical access), are shown to be under supervision of the executive. What this means is that all of them require substantial amounts of the listener's available resources. Furthermore, it seems reasonable to suggest that the executive is single-minded, that here is where the cognitive bottleneck is likely to occur. In other words, the executive may allocate to task x whatever proportion of the available resources are required to carry out this task. If x is the top-level goal in the executive's hierarchy, then x will get all of the resources it needs, up to the amount available, to do the job. The executive may also be thought of as subject to two kinds of interrupts. A primary interrupt can grab the executive's attention, i.e., when such an interrupt occurs the executive must immediately allocate resources to the device calling for them. This is how we think about the "autonomous" processes. A secondary interrupt is a signal to the executive (e.g., a flag is set), but service for that device awaits the executive's pleasure (determined by the hierarchy of goals).

Given this model, we can speculate about why the subjects in the noise group of our last-described experiment performed the way they did. Suppose they interpreted the experiment as a test of their detection abilities. In that case the monitoring task was first on the executive's hierarchy. Most of the available resources were devoted to the phonetic monitoring task. Perhaps next on the hierarchy was the phonological monitoring task, and finally came sentence comprehension. Subjects in the noise condition were able to respond rapidly to the phonetic code when the prior word boundary had been established. This led to no difference in RTs in the on condition, even when noise was present, although it led to a decrement in comprehension.

Naturally, we are interested in subjecting these ideas to further test. We have already mentioned one way in which the noise experiment could be modified to better test the present point of view. There are other manipulations that we would like to carry out to test the revised Dual Code model. Consider, for example, what would happen if a subject were given two or more targets to monitor for within the same sentence. This would put an additional burden on the executive if the listener attempted to monitor the phonetic code. In fact, if we assume that the phonetic code is one that decays rapidly, the listener may not be able to examine it for two or more targets before it "fades." Thus, listening for multiple targets should increase the probability that subjects will respond to the phonological code rather than to the phonetic code. In that case we should observe the effects of variables that affect lexical access when the target is on the word of interest as well as when it is after it.

There are already some data in the literature which suggest that the requirement to monitor for two targets does increase the probability that the subject will respond to the phonological as opposed to the phonetic code. Rubin, Turvey, and Van Gelder (1976) reported the results of two experiments in which subjects were asked to monitor "word"-initial target phonemes. The subjects were presented with lists of monosyllabic words and nonwords. Rubin et al. found that RTs were significantly shorter when the target phoneme was carried by a word than when it was on a nonword. Note that this study bears a superficial resemblance to the word versus nonword experiment reported earlier in this paper, the one in which subjects responded to targets on and after words and nonwords. But we observed no difference when the target was in the On position, a finding seemingly at odds with that reported by Rubin et al. However, among the prominent differences between our study and theirs is the fact that their subjects were asked to monitor for two phonemic targets (/b/ and /s/) while ours monitored for a single target. According to the present analysis, monitoring for two targets should reduce the probability of the subject's being able to respond to the phonetic code. Consequently, the status of the target-bearing item (word or nonword) is more likely to show up in their study than in ours. This analysis receives considerable support from data gathered by Rubin (1975). He conducted a modified replication of the Rubin *et al.* experiment, giving subjects only a single target to monitor for. Under that circumstance, no difference in monitoring time was observed when targets were on words versus nonwords, just as predicted. These results encourage us to carry out parallel experiments using sentences only.

Before leaving this topic we want to mention briefly one more bit of evidence that can be interpreted as supporting the concept of the executive and the Dual Code hypothesis. The data come from a very nice set of studies carried out by Newman and Dell (1978). These investigators showed that RTs in the phoneme monitoring task are affected both by the length of the word preceding the target and by the similarity of the preceding word's initial phoneme to the target. In particular, they manipulated the number of features that were shared by the target phoneme and by the initial phoneme of the preceding word. RTs were slower as the number of shared features increased. Newman and Dell correctly noted that this finding supports a bottom-up analysis of the stimulus.

In our present terms, Newman and Dell's results support the phonetic monitoring mechanism as well as the existence of the executive. The executive examines the contents of the phonetic monitor (see Fig. 7.5) and finds that the contents of the phonetic code nearly match the target specification. This may cause the executive to devote additional resources to analyzing that segment of the input. When the critical input (the one similar to the target) is examined more thoroughly, it is found that the threshold for the target has not been exceeded. By then, however, other demands on the executive have piled up. By the time they have been serviced and the executive can return to the monitoring task, time has passed, thus yielding the results observed by Newman and Dell.

SUMMARY

In this paper we have tried to argue for the hypothesis that there is a processing module which computes a representation of the speech input in terms of phonetic segments. That is, one of the products of the speech perception system is a representation in a phonetic code. The primary evidence supporting such a conclusion comes from experiments in which listeners gain access to phonetic segments prior to accessing the lexical item that such segments compose. This evidence has come from a new set of studies using the phoneme monitoring technique. We would like to suggest, then, that McNeill and Lindig were premature in their conclusion that monitoring experiments have no implications for the perception of speech. If we avoid reasoning naively from absolute values of RTs to claims about the units of perception, we may be able to gain additional insight into the complex mechanisms of speech perception using monitoring tasks.

In earlier papers it was suggested that listeners may never be able to gain access to "low level" products of their perceptual mechanisms. This conclusion appears to have been incorrect. How far we can push subjects in this direction is unclear. But we have taken to heart Miller's (1972) observation: "Thus, what is accessible and what we can become aware of in using language are not immutable givens, fixed once and for all, but can change with maturation and experience [p. 379]." It may be that we can find strong evidence in RT studies that phonetic features are computed by one of the perceptual modules. Indeed, a previous experiment (Foss & Dowell, 1971) can be reinterpreted in just these terms.

Finally, we want to emphasize strongly the tentative nature of the present story concerning the mechanisms involved in phoneme monitoring and what they can tell us about the perceptual processes of speech. This chapter is offered very much in the spirit of a progress report. We do feel, however, that the beginnings of a theory of our method have been presented and that this theory bears upon some general problems of speech perception.

ACKNOWLEDGMENT

The work reported here has been supported by grant MH 29891 from the National Institute of Mental Health. We would like to thank Ron Cole, Anne Cutler, Sally Doyle, and Bjorn Lindblom, each of whom has made a contribution to this paper. David Harwood is now at M.I.T.

REFERENCES

Blank, M. A. *Dual-mode processing of phonemes in fluent speech*. Unpublished doctoral dissertation, University of Texas at Austin, 1979.

Blank, M. A., & Foss, D. J. Semantic facilitation and lexical access during sentence processing. *Memory & Cognition*, 1978, *6*, 644–652.

Cairns, H. S., & Kamerman, J. Lexical information processing during sentence comprehension. *Journal of Verbal Learning and Verbal Behavior*, 1975, *14*, 170–179.

Chomsky, N., & Halle, M. *The sound pattern of English*. New York: Harper & Row, 1968.

Cole, R. A., & Jakimik, J. Understanding speech: How words are heard. In G. Underwood (Ed.), *Information processing strategies*. New York: Academic Press, 1979.

Collins, A. J., & Loftus, E. F. A spreading-activation theory of semantic processing. *Psychological Review*, 1975, *82*, 407–428.

Crowder, R. G. Visual and auditory memory. In J. F. Kavanagh & I. G. Mattingly (Eds.), *Language by ear and by eye*. Cambridge, Mass.: MIT Press, 1972.

Cutler, A. Phoneme-monitoring reaction time as a function of preceding intonation contour. *Perception & Psychophysics*, 1976, *20*, 55–60.

Cutler, A., & Foss, D. J. *Comprehension of ambiguous sentences: The locus of context effects*. Paper presented at the 46th annual meeting of the Midwestern Psychological Association, Chicago, 1974.

Cutler, A., & Foss, D. J. On the role of sentence stress in sentence processing. *Language and Speech*, 1977, *20*, 1–10.

Cutting, J. E. Aspects of phonological fusion. *Journal of Experimental Psychology: Human Perception and Performance*, 1975, *1*, 105–120.

Forster, K. I. Accessing the mental lexicon. In R. J. Wales & E. Walker (Eds.), *New approaches to language mechanisms*. Amsterdam: North-Holland, 1976.

Foss, D. J. Decision processes during sentence comprehension: Effects of lexical item difficulty and position upon decision times. *Journal of Verbal Learning and Verbal Behavior*, 1969, *8*, 457–462.

Foss, D. J. Some effects of ambiguity upon sentence comprehension. *Journal of Verbal Learning and Verbal Behavior*, 1970, *9*, 699–706.

Foss, D. J. On the time-course of sentence comprehension. In *Problemes actuels en psycholinguistique/Current problems in psycholinguistics*. Paris: Editions du C.N.R.S., 1974.

Foss, D. J., & Blank, M. A. *On the alchemy of speech perception during sentence processing: Dross into gold or the reverse?* Paper presented at the 49th annual meeting of the Midwestern Psychological Association, Chicago, 1977.

Foss, D. J., & Dowell, B. E. High-speed memory retrieval with auditorily presented stimuli. *Perception & Psychophysics*, 1971, *9*, 465–468.

Foss, D. J., & Fay, D. Linguistic theory and performance models. In D. Cohen & J. Wirth (Eds.), *Testing linguistic hypotheses*. Washington, D.C.: Hemisphere Publishing Corp., 1975.

Foss, D. J., & Jenkins, C. J. Some effects of context on the comprehension of ambiguous sentences. *Journal of Verbal Learning and Verbal Behavior,* 1973, *12,* 577–589.

Foss, D. J., & Swinney, D. A. On the psychological reality of the phoneme: Perception, identification, and consciousness. *Journal of Verbal Learning and Verbal Behavior,* 1973, *12,* 246–257.

Fromkin, V. A. *Speech errors as linguistic evidence.* The Hague: Mouton, 1973.

Garrett, M. F. The analysis of sentence production. In G. H. Bower (Ed.), *The psychology of learning and motivation,* (Vol. 9). New York: Academic Press, 1975.

Healy, A. F., & Cutting, J. E. Units of speech perception: Phoneme and syllable. *Journal of Verbal Learning and Verbal Behavior,* 1976, *15,* 73–84.

Huggins, A. W. F. Distortion of the temporal pattern of speech: Interruption and alternation. *Journal of the Acoustical Society of America,* 1964, *36,* 1055–1064.

James, W. *The principles of psychology.* New York: Henry Holt, 1890.

Kerr, B. Processing demands during mental operations. *Memory & Cognition,* 1973, *1,* 401–412.

Klatt, D. H. Review of the ARPA speech understanding project. *Journal of the Acoustical Society of America,* 1977, *62,* 1345–1366.

Liberman, A. M. The grammars of speech and language. *Cognitive Psychology,* 1970, *1,* 301–323.

Kucera, H., & Francis, W. N. *Computational analysis of present-day American English.* Providence, R.I.: Brown University Press, 1967.

Marr, D. *From computational theory to psychology and neurophysiology: A case study from vision.* M.I.T. Artificial Intelligence Laboratory, Working Paper 131, 1976.

Marslen-Wilson, W. Linguistic descriptions and psychological assumptions in the study of sentence perception. In R. J. Wales & E. Walker (Eds.), *New approaches to language mechanisms.* Amsterdam: North-Holland, 1976.

Massaro, D. W. Preperceptual images, processing time, and perceptual units in auditory perception. *Psychological Review,* 1972, *79,* 124–145.

McNeill, D., & Lindig, K. The perceptual reality of phonemes, syllables, words and sentences. *Journal of Verbal Learning and Verbal Behavior,* 1973, *12,* 419–430.

Mehler, J., Segui, J., & Carey, P. Tails of words: Monitoring ambiguity. *Journal of Verbal Learning and Verbal Behavior,* 1978, *17,* 29–35.

Meyer, D. E., & Schvaneveldt, R. W. Facilitation in recognizing pairs of words: Evidence of a dependence between retrieval operations. *Journal of Experimental Psychology,* 1971, *90,* 227–234.

Miller, G. A. Reflections on the conference. In J. F. Kavanagh & I. G. Mattingly (Eds.), *Language by ear and by eye.* Cambridge, Mass.: MIT Press, 1972.

Miller, G. A., & Nicely, P. E. An analysis of perceptual confusions among some English consonants. *Journal of the Acoustical Society of America,* 1955, *27,* 338–352.

Mills, C. B., & Martin, J. G. *Listener expectancies and acoustic cue structure in target reaction time.* Paper presented at the annual meeting of the Psychonomic Society, St. Louis, 1976.

Morton, J. Interaction of information in word recognition. *Psychological Review,* 1969, *76,* 165–178.

Morton, J., & Long, J. Effect of word transitional probability on phoneme identification. *Journal of Verbal Learning and Verbal Behavior,* 1976, *15,* 43–52.

Newell, A. You can't play 20 questions with nature and win: Projective comments on the papers of this symposium. In W. G. Chase (Ed.), *Visual information processing.* New York: Academic Press, 1973.

Newman, J. E., & Dell, G. S. The phonological nature of phoneme monitoring: A critique of some ambiguity studies. *Journal of Verbal Learning and Verbal Behavior,* 1978, *17,* 359–374.

Norman, D. A., & Bobrow, D. G. On data-limited and resource-limited processes. *Cognitive Psychology*, 1975, *7*, 44–64.

Pisoni, D. B. Speech perception. In W. K. Estes (Ed.), *Handbook of learning and cognitive processes*. Hillsdale, N.J.: Lawrence Erlbaum Associates, 1978.

Pope, M. *The story of archaeological decipherment: From Egyptian hieroglyphs to Linear B*. N.Y.: Charles Scribner's Sons, 1975.

Reddy, D. R. Speech recognition by machine: A review. *Proceedings of the IEEE*, 1976, *64*, 501–531.

Rubin, P. E. *Semantic influences on phonetic identification and lexical decision*. Unpublished doctoral dissertation, University of Connecticut, 1975.

Rubin, P., Turvey, M. T., & Van Gelder, P. Initial phonemes are detected faster in spoken words than in spoken nonwords. *Perception & Psychophysics*, 1976, *19*, 394–398.

Savin, H. B., & Bever, T. G. The nonperceptual reality of the phoneme. *Journal of Verbal Learning and Verbal Behavior*, 1970, *9*, 295–302.

Scarborough, D. L., Cortese, C., & Scarborough, H. S. Frequency and repetition effects in lexical memory. *Journal of Experimental Psychology: Human Perception and Performance*, 1977, *3*, 1–17.

Shields, J. L., McHugh, A., & Martin, J. G. Reaction time to phoneme targets as a function of rhythmic cues in continuous speech. *Journal of Experimental Psychology*, 1974, *102*, 250–255.

Studdert-Kennedy, M. Speech perception. In N. J. Lass (Ed.), *Contemporary issues in experimental phonetics*. New York: Academic Press, 1976.

Swinney, D. *Does context direct lexical access?* Paper presented at the 48th annual meeting of the Midwestern Psychological Association, Chicago, 1976.

Swinney, D., & Hakes, D. Effects of prior context upon lexical access during sentence comprehension. *Journal of Verbal Learning and Verbal Behavior*, 1976, *15*, 681–690.

Warren, R. M. Identification times for phonemic components of graded complexity and for spelling of speech. *Perception & Psychophysics*, 1971, *9*, 345–349.

8 Analyzing Spoken and Written Language

Michael I. Posner

Vicki L. Hanson
University of Oregon

In discussing papers presented to the Carnegie Symposium on visual perception a half dozen years ago, Allen Newell (1973) argued that the speakers were playing 20 Questions with nature. He appeared to feel the number of admissable queries in that game was being exceeded, and it was time to establish a different strategy for the analysis of mind. The strategy he proposed was the development of detailed information-processing models appropriate to complex tasks such as reading or listening. These models could be used to integrate the findings of experiments and would themselves be tested by comparison to human performance.

We mention this piece of recent history because our comments will reflect its influence. We will deal with the chapters by Bond and Garnes by Cole and Jakimik, and by Foss, Harwood and Blank, by applying Newell's proposed strategy of using complex computer models to integrate and summarize findings in both speech perception and reading. This approach was recently taken by Rumelhart (1977), who adopts the Hearsay Speech Understanding System (see Chap. 9) as a model of both speech perception and reading. The ease with which such models can be transferred between reading and speech recognition suggests their value as tools for integrating experimental results and in pointing out similarities between the two tasks.

Applying a model like Hearsay points out the similarities of the abstract information-processing elements used in reading and listening. But a century of empirical studies of audition and vision should caution us to be sensitive to differences in the organization, evolutionary history, and function of processes based upon these specialized senses. The well-known empirical differences between the ease of acquiring the skills of speech and reading (e.g., Kavanagh & Mattingly, 1972) suggests that such models may not do justice to the way in which the specific characteristics of sensory systems impose constraints upon the efficient use of more abstract information-processing mechanisms (Rozin & Gleitman, 1977). In examining these chapters we hope to point out places where comparisons between reading and listening are most likely to be helpful in understanding the general characteristics of language perception and places most likely to reveal factors unique to speech as a vehicle for language.

ECOLOGICAL VALIDITY

The three chapters on which we comment all depart from the recent tradition of most research on speech perception. They emphasize the processing of speech as it occurs during comprehension, rather than concentrating on phoneme perception. This broad approach affords the opportunity to observe the degree to which principles involved in the comprehension of speech are unique to that mode of presentation. This approach also accords with the recent emphasis favoring ecological validity in our methods (Neisser, 1976).

Few methods could be more ecologically valid for the study of speech perception than listening to conversations and examining the sorts of errors that people make. After all, speech is used primarily as a means of communication between individuals. Garnes and Bond have done a service in presenting us with 900 case histories of mishearings or errors during conversation.

Nonetheless, ecological validity carries with it certain difficulties. One of the problems with the Garnes and Bond analysis is that we have no clear data on the relative frequency of various kinds of errors. Nor do we believe that all of those reported were in fact errors. For example, if a person says *assorted* and the listener hears *a sordid*, is the listener in error or did the listener make one of the possible correct interpretations of the acoustic stream produced by the speaker? We believe that many of the errors presented by Garnes and Bond are of the type in which a perfectly correct segmentation of the acoustic stream was made by the listener. The perception is in error only in that it is not what the speaker intended. These are beautiful examples of the problem of segmentation. Cole and Jakimik properly emphasize the skill humans have in correctly interpreting ambiguous word strings, but we do not always succeed in doing so correctly, as shown by these errors observed by Garnes and Bond.

Garnes and Bond also report errors that may be due to strong influences of context. For example, the statement, "They had a *ten year* party for Marlene," spoken at a university function, might easily be misheard (in accordance with findings on the effects of need on perception) as "They had a *tenure* party for Marlene." These mistakes in which a general perceptual context affects the interpretation and segmentation of speech are related to the kinds of evidence that have led students of semantic memory to argue that language is in constant interaction with more general stored frames or scripts (Minsky, 1975).

SERIAL TASKS

While Garnes and Bond focus on field studies with both their surface validity and their difficult interpretive problems, Cole and Jakimik partially sacrifice ecological validity in order to gain experimental control of the speech message. In their task, the subjects are required to detect mispronunciations that are produced by the experimenter. There is no possibility that the speaker and listener are simply disagreeing about the segmentation of the same acoustic stream. In one important way, the Cole and Jakimik experiments are valid simulations of the normal listening task. Rather than involving a single phoneme or word in isolation, they involve listening to a continuous stream of information. The task for the subject is to detect as quickly as possible any departure from the correct pronunciation of a lexical item.

The use of serial tasks by Cole and Jakimik allows them to investigate the importance of transition probabilities between words on their subjects' performance. A few years ago, the study of transition probabilities within and between words through the use of approximations to English was perhaps the most popular approach to language (e.g., Miller, 1951). Under the influence of information theory, experimenters looked at the effect of the amount of information in a word upon its perception. This statistical approach to the surface structure of the English language was submerged in part by Chomsky's logical argument that such an approach would never be adequate to the task of generating permissible sentences in the language. Cole and Jakimik find that highly predictable words are recognized more rapidly in their mispronunciation task: an example of the general principle that reaction time is related to the uncertainty of the stimulus event.

One disadvantage of the approach to transition probabilities taken by Cole and Jakimik is that it examines mainly qualitative effects, instead of asking, for example, the contributions to the reduction of uncertainty of words at varying distances from the target word. There are already a number of quantitative efforts to do this for visual materials (see Garner, 1962, for a review). Since most of the nonlinguistic work on uncertainty and reaction time has found very similar principles in vision and audition, there is little reason to expect reading and listening to speech to differ.

We are also struck with how similar the proposition concerning the active nature of listening in the Cole and Jakimik paper is to many recent proposals made by those studying reading of sentences and paragraphs. Similarly, there has been as much dispute about the unit(s) of reading as there has been about the unit(s) of listening, although there seems little doubt that the word plays a very important role in both tasks. Given these expected similarities between speech perception and reading, one result obtained for the detection of mispronunciations at first seems quite different than one would expect to find in reading. In reading, one frequently overlooks misspellings. Indeed, one would expect that a reader would be most likely to miss a spelling error in words that are most predictable from their context. Thus proofreaders frequently have trouble finding errors in highly predictable items.

There has been some conflict in the visual literature on the ease of detecting target letters as a function of context. Krueger (1970) has found that it is easier to detect letters within meaningful passages than when scrambled. On the other hand, Healy (1976) has shown that detection of the letter "t" in the word "the" occurred more often in scrambled than in coherent text. Recently Schindler (1978) has done a good deal to resolve this discrepancy. He has shown that one is more likely to miss target letters that occur in high-probability function words within prose material than in scrambled text, but that there is a reversal when one deals with low-probability content words. These results in reading may reflect eye position, but if reading and listening are similar, they suggest that the results obtained by Cole and Jakimik may be more fragile and delicate than one first expects when examining their series of experiments.

The Cole and Jakimik results raise a paradox with respect to the reading literature because they find that an increase in the ability to predict the correct word from context makes it easier rather than harder to detect a mispronunciation. Recall that they find subjects are quicker in responding to mispronunciations that occur in predictable (high-transitional-probability words) than in unpredictable words, and are quicker in later syllables than in earlier syllables. But Marslen-Wilson and Welsh (1978) show that, when subjects shadow speech that contains mispronunciations, they are more likely to reconstruct the correct pronunciation of a word when it is predictable from context, than when it is unpredictable. Further, Marslen-Wilson and Welsh find that, in terms of error in a mispronunciation detection task, there is very little if any difference between items having high and low transitional probabilities. For the error measure, Cole and Jakimik find similar results.

These results, taken together, do not support a universal improvement in all processing as a function of word predictability, but instead the results appear to depend on the task. If the subjects are not warned about mispronunciations and are asked simply to pronounce (shadow) what they hear, they will generally fail to detect mispronunciations in predictable words. However, if they are asked to detect mispronunciations, they will not be more accurate following a constraining context, but they will be quick in responding. If they are asked to detect a particular phoneme, they will also be quick in responding when it occurs in a predictable word (Morton & Long, 1976). What do these results mean? The answer seems straightforward for the phoneme monitoring task. If subjects on some trials are able to predict the word that carries the target phoneme, they ought to be faster in being able to decide what the first phoneme is. For the mispronunciation task, Cole and Jakimik propose that a mismatch between the expected and the spoken word aids in mispronunciation detection. Since subjects are intending to press the key whenever their expectations of what should occur are violated, a keypress ought to be facilitated by a mismatch between a highly predictable item and the input. Overall, these results indicate that in listening, as in reading, the basic effect of context, as found by Marslen-Wilson and Welsh, is to aid perception of a word that fits with the context. The detailed means by which this facilitation in perception affects performance depends heavily on the task.

One of the more interesting aspects of the Cole and Jakimik paper is the idea that items are processed one word at a time. This proposition helps them to provide a method of segmentation of the complex acoustic input stream. It is an interesting and worthwhile idea. However, it also reveals one of the problems that staying at one level of analysis produces. They talk in terms of the word as a unit that is recognized or identified. Thus they conclude from an experiment in which the forward transition probabilities matter more than backward transition probabilities that subjects have processed the material word for word. What is meant is that subjects have sufficiently heard each word such that receiving more context following its occurrence will not aid in detecting mispronunciations. However, one should not conclude from this that the backward transitional probabilities are not helping at all. Suppose one receives a pair of sentences either like *the bark is peeling* or *the bark is loud*. Notice that the word *peeling* or *loud* is not likely to improve either phoneme monitoring of the /b/ in *bark* or detection of the mispronunciation *tark*. However, there is no question that the information provided by the word *peeling* or *loud* worked backward to change some aspects of the assignment of meaning to the word BARK. If the term "recognition" is used to mean the full processing of the word including semantics, it would clearly be wrong to argue that backward context is unimportant.

There is also a problem with assuming that a word by word analysis completely solves the segmentation problem. The segmentation of the acoustic input will be different in the sentences "They threw a ten-year party for Marlene for her decade of service to the company," and "They threw a tenure party for Marlene when she acquired the position on the university faculty." In the first sentence, the acoustic input would be interpreted as "ten-year" while the same acoustic segment in the second sentence would be interpreted as "tenure." Subsequent context can therefore have an effect on word segmentation.

The use of serial tasks draws attention to the statistical constraints between sequential items in word strings. One can easily overlook the complex processes that each item in the string produces. In the Cole and Jakimik analysis the word is seen as an atom, accessible as a whole. As in physics, it is possible to smash the word-atom, showing that it consists of a number of independent codes which themselves have important influence on tasks like listening and reading. Though there are important theories at the level of the word, there are new principles to be learned when the word is fragmented into codes, as Foss et al. point out.

SMASHING THE WORD

Foss, Harwood and Blank are driven to look inside the word by puzzling and paradoxical results which occur in the phoneme monitoring task. It is clear that phoneme monitoring is often based not on the acoustic input stream, but on lexical look-up. This finding is entirely consistent with Cole and Jakimik's point of the important interaction between top-down and bottom-up processes. Even as simple a task as determining the beginning phoneme of a word seems to be crucially dependent upon higher level expectancies. But Foss et al. go further by supposing that there are two different ways in which the subject may detect a target phoneme in a sentence. To prove this he tries to show that the two putative codes can be manipulated independently. If the time for lexical lookup is delayed by switching from a meaningful to a nonsense word, models in which phoneme monitoring is based on lexical lookup must find at least some delay in that task. Finding none, Foss argues that, at least under some conditions, it is possible to base the phoneme monitoring task on a lower level of analysis, which is evidence for a phonetic[1] code uninfluenced by meaning.

---

[1]We use the term "phonetic" in a loose sense to refer to the segmental structure of words. We do not imply, by using the term "phonetic" (rather than "phonemic"), that the segmental representation of a word captures fine acoustic and phonetic distinctions such as the differences in /t/ in /tip/, /step/, and /pit/.

The multicode view that Foss et al. present, and in particular their use of independent manipulability as a way of establishing the code, is similar to work that has been going on in the study of visual words (Posner, 1978). It might be useful to compare the results obtained in the two modalities.

Perhaps the best evidence that distinct codes can be accessed while making perceptual judgments is found in research on the word superiority effect (Reicher, 1969). The most important finding is that in a number of conditions every single letter of a visual word is better perceived than a single letter in isolation. This finding seems best understood if we think that subjects use the phonetic or name code of a visual word to identify the letters of which it is composed, but use the visual code when a single isolated letter is presented. This view is beautifully supported by Polf (1976). She applied a speed–accuracy tradeoff method to force subjects into rapid choices among two alternative letters, either of which might have been in a just prior flash. With very rapid responses, the subjects appear to use a visual code. Under these conditions letters are handled more accurately when presented in isolation than when embedded in a word. When responses were delayed the situation was quite different. Isolated letters were never as accurately identified as when embedded in words. One explanation of this effect is to suppose that words are rapidly encoded into phonetic form. Isolated letters are dealt with visually and thus their identification is impaired by the masking stimulus which follows them. One might well expect a similar phenomenon in audition. Isolated portions of a word might show masking by a subsequent sound which would not be effective in masking the word as a whole. Thus subjects could identify each part of a spoken word better than that same part in isolation.

Detailed comparisons of the coding principles involved in reading and listening to words would be very helpful. Studies of language represent a special opportunity for investigating higher levels of nervous system organization, because there are overlearned correspondences between items completely different in input energy. It is a pity that the tradition of separating studies by sensory system is so strong that cross-modal comparisons are rarely made.

COMMON PHONETIC CODE

A basic underlying question in comparing visual and auditory language is whether the phonetic code for processing visual words is the same as the phonetic code discussed by Foss et al. Conceptually, both codes are similar in that they refer to nonphysical aspects of the stimulus and require abstraction of features which are language related. Neither code requires prior lexical access. Posner (1978) has reviewed the evidence for the independent manipulability of the visual and phonetic codes while processing printed words. The auditory and phonetic codes for spoken words are more difficult to separate than the visual and phonetic codes for printed words, because the auditory input and its phonetic recoding are necessarily similar. Nonetheless, Hanson (1977) has shown that the same model applies to the processing of speech as to the processing of printed words.

What is lacking, however, is convincing evidence that the phonetic code used for processing visual words is the same as the phonetic code used for processing auditory words. Reserach in progress looks at this question. Hanson (1978) had subjects monitor auditory or visual words for the presence of the phoneme /s/ under task conditions which, according to arguments advanced by Foss et al., would produce responding on the basis of the phonetic code. When subjects monitored the auditory input, there was facilitation in task performance when both the auditory and the simultaneously presented visual word contained the target phoneme, and there was interference in task performance when only the visual word contained the target. Thus, when performing a phonetic analysis of auditory words, visual inputs were influencing decisions. This influence suggets a processing system common to both modalities.

If the visual and auditory phonetic codes are the same, then tasks requiring higher levels of analysis should produce the same results regardless of input modality. For the processing of single words, there is evidence for the common semantic processing of visual and auditory inputs. One line of evidence comes from research where visual and auditory words are simultaneously presented and subjects are asked to attend only to the words on one modality. Studies have indicated that there is a mutual influence of unattended visual and auditory words for semantic categorization tasks (Hanson, 1978) and for pronunciation tasks (Lewis, 1972) when words in the unattended modality are semantically related to the items in the attended modality. Memory research has indicated that recall and recognition of words is independent of modality of input, even though information regarding input modality is still available for durations of several minutes (Bray & Batchelder, 1972; Hintzman, Block & Inskeep, 1972). Activation of modality-specific pathways may, however, facilitate access to these higher levels of analysis (Kirsner & Smith, 1974).

CONTROL OF CODES

Foss et al. conclude their chapter by examining the controlability of internal codes by subjects. It seems natural to assume that if codes can be manipulated independently by the experimenter, then they can be chosen in the absence of such manipulations by the subject. This does not seem to be completely true. Recent work using visual words by Carr, Davidson, and Hawkins (1978) shows the limitations in the ability of subjects to select between lexical and phonetic codes. By manipulating the percentage of pronounceable nonwords in a list, the investigators make it sensible for subjects in one condition to attend to the lexical code and in another condition to attend to the phonetic code. They expected that subjects in the latter condition would show no difference between words and pronounceable nonwords, but that in the former condition they would. Although they were able to induce some differences in processing for pronounceable nonwords, they were unable to induce any flexibility in the handling of words. It thus appears that many of the routines which select codes for items—although presumably learned in the first place—are not easily amenable to control by the subject. Certainly the question of cognitive control over component codes is an important one. It is both surprising and exciting that some of the component processes involved in dealing with single words seem not to be amenable to the subject's control.

CONCLUSIONS

Figure 8.1 presents an overview of the three chapters reviewed. Each of them focuses on a different level of the speech perception process. Garnes and Bond deal with speech as a communication process. Cole and Jakimik focus on problems that arise from the need to segment a continuous

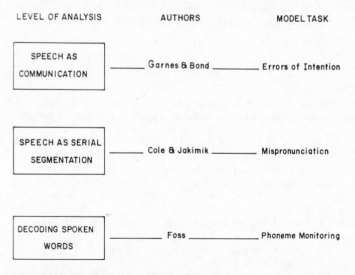

FIG. 8.1. Conceptualization of the papers by Bond and Garnes, by Cole and Jakimik, and by Foss, Harwood, and Blank.

acoustic signal into a string of words. Foss, Harwood, and Blank deal with the internal codes derived from a single word. Each paper defines a model task that can be used to explore the speech perception process at the level intended. The view of a complex task like speech perception as involving many independent subprocesses is in accord with models like Hearsay. The effort to develop a model task to tap at each level of analysis is in accord with recent attempts to focus on the common elementary mental processes involved in many forms of information processing activity (Chase, 1978).

As we have tried to point out, there are difficulties in viewing any task as a pure measure of only one subprocess. Nonetheless, the combination of detailed models that serve to interrelate experimental results with analytic tasks does seem to provide a research strategy that is both consonant with Newell's requirement and allows room for the development of new facts about the human information-processing system.

After examining these chapters in relation to studies of reading, we propose as a working hypothesis that the same phonetic code is derived from listening and reading. If so, then all tasks relying upon phonetic codes, or upon lexical or semantic derivatives of them, will reveal very similar principles in speech perception and reading. This view leads us to expect that many of the findings reported here should agree in some detail with results obtained from studies of reading. Our analysis suggests that in general this is true, but in many cases the data comparing reading and listening are simply not available. We would like to see future research directed to the working hypothesis that reading and listening use the same phonetic code. We hope that the data obtained by testing this issue will be useful in constructing models that relate the two tasks.

REFERENCES

Bray, N. W., & Batchelder, W. H. Effects of instructions and retention interval on memory of presentation mode. *Journal of Verbal Learning and Verbal Behavior*, 1972, *11*, 367–374.

Carr, T. H., Davidson, B. J., & Hawkins, H. L. Perceptual flexibility in word recognition: Strategies affect orthographic computation but not lexical access. *Journal of Experimental Psychology: Human Perception and Performance*, 1978, *4*, 674–690.

Chase, W. G. Elementary information processes. In W. K. Estes (Ed.), *Handbook of learning and cognitive processes* (Vol. 5). Hillsdale, N.J.: Lawrence Erlbaum Associates, 1978.

Garner, W. R. *Uncertainty and structure as psychological concepts*. New York: Wiley, 1962.

Hanson, V. L. Within-category discriminations in speech perception. *Perception & Psychophysics*, 1977, *21*, 423–430.

Hanson, V. L. *Common coding of visual and auditory words*. Unpublished doctoral dissertation, University of Oregon, Eugene, 1978.

Healy, A. F. Detection errors in the word the: Evidence for reading units larger than letters. *Journal of Experimental Psychology: Human Perception and Performance,* 1976, *2,* 235–242.

Hintzman, D. L., Block, R. A., & Inskeep, N. R. Memory for mode of input. *Journal of Verbal Learning and Verbal Behavior,* 1972, *11,* 741–749.

Kavanagh, J. F., & Mattingly, I. G. (Eds.). *Language by ear and by eye: The relationships between speech and reading.* Cambridge, Mass.: MIT Press, 1972.

Kirsner, K., & Smith, M. C. Modality effects in word identification. *Memory & Cognition,* 1974, *2,* 637–640.

Krueger, L. E. Search time in a redundant visual display. *Journal of Experimental Psychology,* 1970, *83,* 391–399.

Lewis, J. L. Semantic processing with bisensory stimulation. *Journal of Experimental Psychology,* 1972, *96,* 455–457.

Marslen-Wilson, W. D., & Welsh, A. Processing interactions and lexical access during word recognition in continuous speech. *Cognitive Psychology,* 1978, *10,* 29–63.

Miller, G. A. *Language and communication.* New York: McGraw-Hill, 1951.

Minsky, M. A framework for representing knowledge. In P. H. Winston (Ed.), *Psychology of computer vision.* New York: McGraw-Hill, 1975.

Morton, J., & Long, J. Effect of word transitional probability on phoneme identification. *Journal of Verbal Learning and Verbal Behavior,* 1976, *15,* 43–52.

Neisser, U. *Cognition and reality.* San Francisco: Freeman, 1976.

Newell, A. You can't play 20 questions with nature and win: Projective comments on the papers of this symposium. In W. G. Chase (Ed.), *Visual information processing.* New York: Academic Press, 1973.

Polf, J. *The word superiority effect: A speed–accuracy analysis and test of a decoding hypothesis.* Unpublished doctoral dissertation, University of Oregon, Eugene, 1976.

Posner, M. I. *Chronometric explorations of mind.* Hillsdale, N.J.: Lawrence Erlbaum Associates, 1978.

Reicher, G. M. Perceptual recognition as a function of meaningfulness of stimulus material. *Journal of Experimental Psychology,* 1969, *81,* 276–280.

Rozin, P., & Gleitman, L. R. The structure and acquisition of reading II: The reading process and the acquisition of the alphabetic principle. In A. S. Reber & D. L. Scarborough (Eds.), *Toward a psychology of reading: The proceedings of the CUNY Conferences.* Hillsdale, N.J.: Lawrence Erlbaum Associates, 1977.

Rumelhart, D. E. *Introduction to human information processing.* New York: Wiley, 1977.

Schindler, R. M. The effect of prose context on visual search for letters. *Memory & Cognition,* 1978, *6,* 124–130.

III MACHINE-MOTIVATED MODELS

9 Machine Models of Speech Perception

Raj Reddy
Carnegie-Mellon University

INTRODUCTION

Can we build a system that can recognize and interpret speech? Many approaches to this problem begin with the study of the best existence proof we have—human speech perception. Given the immense complexity of the problem, these approaches have tended to focus on some narrow aspect of the overall problem. The many studies in acoustic–phonetics and mechanisms of hearing fall into this category. While such studies have provided a wealth of extremely useful information, the global question of how a human recognizes and interprets speech is not yet well understood.

Our own approach to the problem has been to study machine models and system organizations that can recognize natural continuous speech. These efforts have led to two interesting systems: the HEARSAY system and the Harpy system. In this chapter I describe the models of speech perception used in these systems and discuss their strengths and weaknesses.

Since the goal of our research is to recognize fluent speech—not to model human speech perception—my discussion is limited to machine models of speech perception. I will pay little or no attention to the applicability of these models to human speech perception. The reader is referred to the chapters in this volume by Klatt and Newell (Chaps. 10 and 11) for a discussion of the psychological implications of the Harpy model and to Rumelhart (1977) for an earlier discussion of the HEARSAY model.

Early attempts at automatic speech recognition were limited to recognition of isolated words by single speakers. Systems of this class are already commercially available (Martin, 1977). Our own research has been directed toward systems capable of recognizing connected speech from multiple speakers and operating in real time. Because of the horrendous problems involved in recognizing natural continuous speech (Reddy, 1976; Cole & Jakimik, Chap. 6), it is necessary to make various simplifying assumptions before the problem of machine recognition becomes tractable. These simplifying assumptions include limits on vocabulary size and restrictions on the structure of the language.

To be successful, a speech perception system must make effective use of many diverse sources of knowledge in decoding an unknown utterance. These sources of knowledge include the characteristics of speech sounds (*acoustic-phonetics*), variability in pronunciation (*phonology*), the stress

TABLE 9.1
Design Choices for Speech
Understanding Systems

Task characteristics
    speakers: number, male/female, dialect
    vocabulary and syntax
    response desired
Signal-gathering environment
    room noise level
    transducer characteristics
Signal transformations
    digitization speed and accuracy
    special-purpose hardware required
    parametric representation
Signal-to-symbol transformation
    segmentation?
    level transformation occurs
    label selection technique
    amount of training required
Matching and searching
    relaxation: breadth-first
    blackboard: best-first, island-driven
    productions: best-first
    locus: beam search
Knowledge source representation
    networks
    procedures
    frames
    productions
System organization
    levels of representation
    single processor/multiprocessor

and intonation patterns of speech (*prosodics*), the sound patterns of words (*lexicon*), the grammatical structure of language (*syntax*), the meaning of words and sentences (*semantics*), and the context of the conversation (*pragmatics*). One of the main problems in speech perception is the conversion of these diverse sources of knowledge into action, i.e., an effective sequence of operations that transforms the signal into an interpretable sequence of symbols. In addition, there is the problem of incorporating these sources of knowledge into system organizations that are *extensible*. Extensible systems are those in which changes to the vocabulary, syntax, and task specification are easily accomplished.

What makes speech perception a challenging and difficult area of artificial intelligence is the fact that error and ambiguity permeate all the levels of the speech decoding process. In speech, there are many sources of variability that contribute to the errorful nature of the decoding process. In spontaneous (nonmaximally differentiated) connected speech, many expected features (and phonemes) may be missing. Variability due to noise and speaker differences leads to errors. Incomplete and/or inaccurate representation of knowledge sources leads to more errors. Thus, speech perception systems must accept the inevitability of errors and handle them in a graceful manner.

The number of design decisions involved in formulating a complete machine model can be truly staggering. Table 9.1 illustrates the large number of design choices which confront a system designer. For each of the 10 to 15 decisions, we have between two and 10 possible alternative choices. Thus, the space of solutions contains over a million alternative system configurations. In this chapter we present only two of these.

THE HEARSAY SYSTEM

The model used in the HEARSAY system was formulated in the early seventies based on the experience gained in attempting to build connected speech recognition systems (Reddy, 1967; Vicens, 1969; Reddy, 1976). The key problem was to find an effective paradigm whereby different knowledge sources could effectively contribute to the analysis and interpretation of an unknown utterance. The problem was further compounded by the fact that each knowledge source used a different set of symbols. For example, knowledge about grammatical structure and knowledge about word pronunciation are not easily represented using the same set of symbols. The question, then, is how to design a system in which all the diverse sources of knowledge, each using a different set of symbols, can communicate and cooperate with each other while decoding an utterance. A system organization based on independent cooperating knowledge sources using a global "blackboard" formed the basis of several HEARSAY system implementations. The HEARSAY-I system was the first speech understanding system developed at Carnegie-Mellon University (Reddy, Erman, Fennell, & Neely, 1973; Reddy & Newell, 1974). Many of the limitations of this first implementation of the model were overcome in the HEARSAY-II system (Erman & Lesser, 1978). In this chapter I describe one of the implementations of the HEARSAY-II system.

The Blackboard Model

The model used in the HEARSAY system is based on a "blackboard" analogy. Each knowledge source (KS) is viewed as an information gathering process which places ("writes") all its hypotheses on a globally accessible "blackboard." These hypotheses can then be used by other KSs to validate and/or reject an hypothesis and to create new hypotheses at other symbolic levels. Figure 9.1 gives a schematic diagram of the blackboard model.

The HEARSAY-II system represents knowledge as a set of self-activating, asynchronous, parallel processes. The modular structure of the system makes it easier to add new KSs into the system. The most

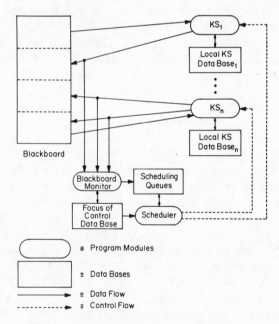

FIG. 9.1.   The HEARSAY-II system architecture.

interesting part of the system is the organization of the blackboard itself. All the partial analyses are represented in the blackboard as a generalized three-dimensional network. The three dimensions of the network are the distinct information levels (e.g., "phrase," "word," "syllable," and "phone"), the temporal coordinates within the utterance, and the alternative hypotheses.

The current state of the partial solution is represented as *hypotheses* on the blackboard. A hypothesis is an interpretation of a portion of the speech signal at a given level. Given the error and uncertainty of the analysis, the same portion of speech may have several competing alternative hypotheses. The problem is to find the best sequence of hypotheses that is globally consistent with the constraints imposed by the knowledge sources.

Hypotheses generated by one KS are used to generate hypotheses by another KS. For example, hypotheses at the "syllable" level may be used to generate hypotheses at the "word" level. These interacting hypotheses are related to each other across the different levels by using an and/or-directed graph structure. Hypotheses are used to predict or eliminate other hypotheses. Figures 9.2 and 9.3, shown in the following subsection, provide concrete examples of these concepts.

Knowledge Source Activation and Focus of Attention

The goal of all speech understanding systems is to find the most plausible interpretation of an utterance that is consistent with all the sources of knowledge. However, given the error and uncertainty associated with the hypothesis-generation process, several competing hypotheses must be considered in the global context of the entire utterance to determine which one is most promising. The problem of selecting one or more hypotheses for further processing leads to search.

The search space of alternative hypotheses must be considered along two dimensions in the HEARSAY-II system: the *time* dimension and the *information level* dimension. One can decide to examine the utterance left-to-right (FIFO-type strategy) or one can start with reliable hypotheses ("islands of reliability") and extend these hypotheses to consider preceding or following words. One can decide to verify the presence or absence of a predicted word or one can attempt to create longer phrases by concatenating grammatically compatible smaller phrases.

In the HEARSAY-II system, scheduling and activation of KSs is based on a complex focus-of-attention strategy. The priority of a KS waiting for execution is based on concepts such as best-first, validity, significance, efficiency, and goal satisfaction (Hayes-Roth & Lesser, 1977).

An Example of the HEARSAY-II Recognition Process

The example given in this section is drawn from a version of the HEARSAY-II system demonstrated in 1976 at the end of the five year Advanced Research Projects Agency (ARPA) project. The task for the system is to answer questions about a document-retrieval task from a collection of computer science abstracts. The system accepts sentences such as "Please help me," "Are there any articles by Feigenbaum and Feldman?" and "List the articles." The vocabulary contains about 1,011 words. The grammar for this task is highly restricted. It has a dynamic branching factor of about 33 and an entropy branching factor of about 5.[1]

Figure 9.2 illustrates the different levels and knowledge sources operating in the system. The system contains six different symbolic levels of abstraction: parameter, segment, syllable, word, word-sequence, and phrase. There are a total of twelve KSs active at these levels. We will briefly outline the function of each of these KSs here. A more complete description is given by Erman and Lesser (1978).

SEG: This module performs digitization, ZAPDASH (zero-crossings and peaks in smoothed and differenced waveforms) and LPC (linear prediction analysis) parameter extraction, segmentation, and labeling. (A further description of these processes is provided in the next section.)

POM, MOW, WORD-CTL: These three KSs are used to generate bottom-up word hypotheses, syllable hypothesization, word hypothesization, and policy controlling the number of hypotheses to be generated in each time area.

WORD-SEQ: This module is used to generate a small set of word-sequence hypotheses from word hypotheses.

WORD-SEQ-CTL: This KS controls the amount of hypothesization that WORD-SEQ does by creating "goal" hypotheses.

PARSE: This KS can parse a word sequence of arbitrary length, using full constraints given by the language, to determine whether the sequence is an acceptable part of some sentence in the language.

PREDICT: This KS is used to predict words that can immediately precede or follow a given phrase.

VERIFY: This KS is used to verify the existence or reject a predicted word in the context of the predicting phrase, using knowledge about juncture rules and word pronunciations.

CONCAT: This KS is used to create new and longer phrases using a verified word and its predicted phrase.

STOP: This KS halts the recognition process if there are no more

---

[1]See Goodman (1976) for a discussion of the measures of complexity of languages.

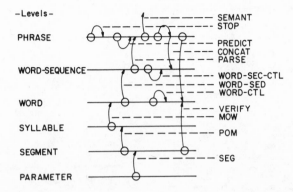

FIG. 9.2.   The levels and knowledge sources used in HEARSAY-II.

partial hypotheses worthy of being extended or if a predefined amount of computing resource is used up.

SEMANT: These KSs are used to generate the semantic interpretation of complete or partial phrases and to maintain a model of conversation.

Figure 9.3 contains some of the hypotheses generated at each of the levels during a recognition cycle. The waveform of the spoken utterance, which was "Are any by Feigenbaum and Feldman?", is shown in Fig. 9.3a. The correct word boundaries (determined by human inspection) are shown in Fig. 9.3b. The remaining sections of Fig. 9.3 contain hypotheses created by the KSs on the blackboard.

Figure 9.3c shows the results of the segmentation and labeling process. The segment boundaries are indicated by vertical lines. The best rated phone hypotheses are shown for each segment. Thus for the first segment, only the silence phone "—" is hypothesized. For the second segment, four phones—UW, AA, ER, and AW—are hypothesized. Note that this is the beginning vowel segment of the word ARE.

Figure 9.3d shows some of the syllable hypotheses. The POM knowledge source provides syllable class definitions using seven symbols: AA-like (A), IY-like (I), UW-like (U), liquid (L), nasal (N), plosive (P), and fricative (F). For example the syllable-class hypothesis PIN stands for the possible presence of a syllable unit containing a plosive (P) followed by an IY-like vowel (I), followed by a nasal-like segment (N). Figure 9.3e shows some of the bottom-up word hypotheses generated using the syllable class hypotheses. Note that four of the six words (ARE, BY, AND, FELDMAN) in the utterance are correctly hypothesized. The numbers next to the words represent a likelihood value for each hypothesis. The values can range from 0 to 100, with 100 being a perfect match.

Up to this point, the whole hypothesis generation process has been

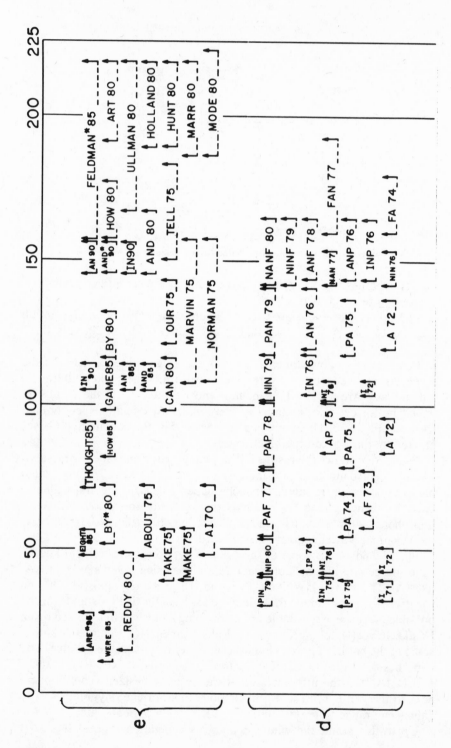

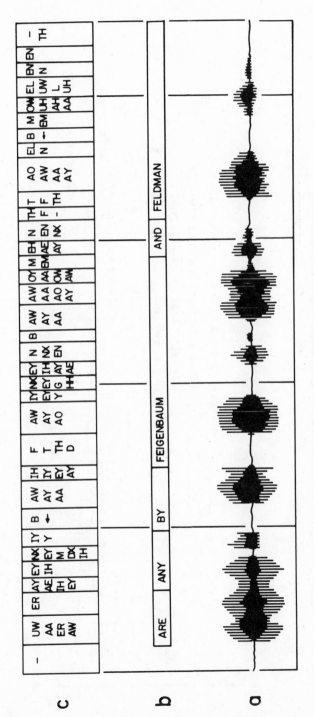

FIG. 9.3. Example of the HEARSAY recognition process.

223

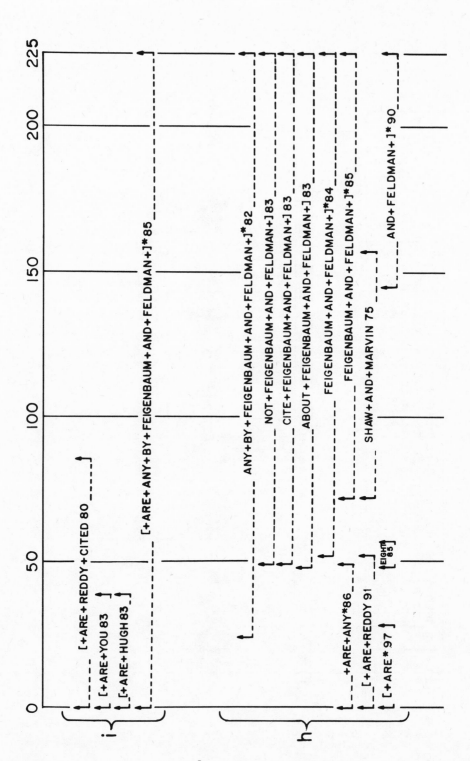

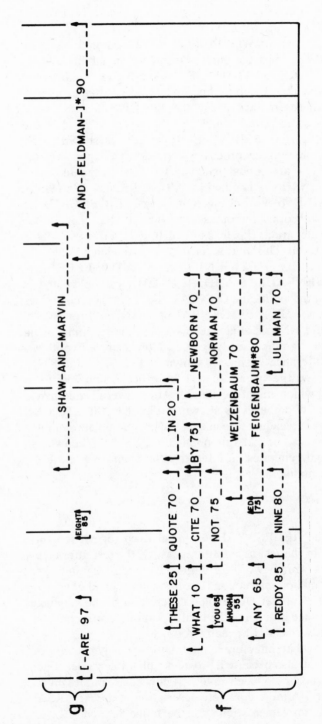

FIG. 9.3. (Cont.)

225

"bottom-up." At this point the WORD-SEQ knowledge source becomes activated and produces four partial phrases (islands of reliability) shown in Fig. 9.3g such as [+ ARE and AND + FELDMAN. (The symbols [and] are used to represent the beginning and end of an utterance, respectively.) These hypotheses in turn cause the PREDICT and VERIFY knowledge sources to be activated, which cause words such as ANY and REDDY to be hypothesized to the right of [+ ARE, as shown at the bottom of Fig. 9.3f. Note that this process is "top-down." Upon verification, ANY and REDDY are concatenated to [+ ARE to create longer sequences such as [+ ARE + ANY and [+ ARE + REDDY (Fig. 9.3h). Similarly, AND + FELDMAN from Fig. 9.3g causes FEIGENBAUM to be predicted (along with other hypotheses) to the left (Fig. 9.3f). After verification and concatenation, this leads to FEIGENBAUM + AND + FELDMAN in Fig. 9.3h. This phrase is further extended to the left, causing phrases such as BY + FEIGENBAUM + AND + FELDMAN and ABOUT + FEIGENBAUM + AND + FELDMAN to be created as shown in Fig. 9.3h. At this point, the CONCAT knowledge source notices that [+ ARE + ANY and BY + FEIGENBAUM + AND + FELDMAN can be merged because ANY is adjacent to BY and the resulting single enlarged phrase remains grammatically correct. Now a single hypothesis covering the entire utterance exists, as shown in Fig. 9.3i. The STOP knowledge source allows the system to search further to find additional sentence hypotheses which might be better. After several attempts at creating new sentence hypotheses as shown in Fig. 9.3i, the STOP KS does stop system activity, leading it to accept the only complete sentence hypothesis as the correct one. At this point, the SEMANT knowledge source is activated and generates an interpretation from a structure for use by the discourse module.

Performance

The final version of the HEARSAY-II system achieved correct semantic interpretation of 90% of the test set of utterances. Of the test utterances, 73% were recognized correctly word-for-word. The processing time averaged about 85 Mipss (million instructions executed per second of speech) on a DEC System 10 computer. A detailed description of the language, test data, and performance is given in the final report of the speech understanding project (Reddy & CMU Speech Group, 1977).

The HEARSAY model architecture is interesting not only because the entire system worked, but also because it provides a plausible model of how complex interactions occur between diverse knowledge sources in the presence of uncertainty. A more complete description of the HEARSAY model and its various implementations can be found in Reddy et al.,

(1973), Lesser, Fennell, Erman, and Reddy (1975), Lesser and Erman (1977), and Erman and Lesser (1978).

THE HARPY SYSTEM

The Harpy system is the result of combining and improving the best features of two earlier systems previously developed at Carnegie-Mellon University: HEARSAY-I (Reddy et al., 1973) and DRAGON (Baker, 1975). The network representation and delayed decision-making features of the Harpy system were derived from DRAGON. The best-few search technique and the segmentation and labeling techniques are extensions of techniques used in the HEARSAY-I system.

The Locus Model

The Harpy system views the speech interpretation problem as a problem of search. The role of knowledge is to constrain the number of alternatives considered at each stage of analysis. This is accomplished in the Harpy system using *locus search*. The *locus model* is a beam search technique in which all except a beam of near-miss alternatives around the best path are pruned from the search tree at each segmental decision point. This process constrains exponential growth and eliminates backtracking. All the KSs are compiled into a single integrated network. This permits all the relevant constraints provided by the different sources of knowledge to act together in any given instance. The search process itself is segment-driven and not event-driven as in HEARSAY-II. The problems of focus of attention are eliminated by proceeding left-to-right and considering only (a beam of) the best-few alternatives in parallel. Figure 9.4 gives an overview of the locus model.

An Example of the Harpy Recognition Process

The principal task used in the Harpy system demonstration is the 1011-word vocabulary document-retrieval task discussed in the preceding section. The Harpy system was also tested using several other simple tasks such as connected digit recognition. We illustrate the recognition process of the Harpy system using the grammar network shown in Fig. 9.5.

Internally, Harpy represents all the legal sentences as a finite-state graph structure. Figure 9.5 shows the graph of the grammar used in the news retrieval task. The legal sentences of the language are organized as a network of nodes, where each node holds a word in the vocabulary. The nodes are interconnected such that any path through this word network

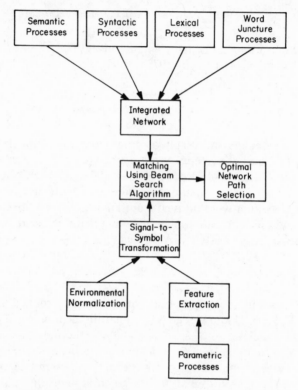

FIG. 9.4. The locus model used in the Harpy system.

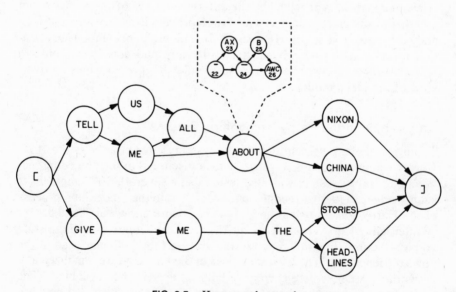

FIG. 9.5. Harpy word network.

constitutes an acceptable sentence, e.g., "Tell me about Nixon," "Give me the headlines," and "Tell me all about China."

The set of alternative pronunciations of a word can be represented as a network of acoustic–phonetic symbols, called "phones." Phones are the smallest element of speech knowledge represented in the Harpy network. Each path through the network represents an acceptable pronunciation of the word. The insert in Fig. 9.5 shows the possible pronunciations for the word "about" and illustrates how the pronunciation network is really a further specification of the word network shown in Fig. 9.5. In Fig. 9.6 we replace each word in the word network with its pronunciation network. This procedure generates a new finite-state graph, in which each path is a pronunciation of a legal sentence of the language. This network is modified to incorporate word juncture phenomena, such as insertions and deletions of phones. The resulting network, shown in Fig. 9.6, is a compilation of all the relevant KSs into a single, integrated network representation.

Figure 9.7 gives the complete oscilloscopic trace of an utterance during recognition. The unknown sentence is digitized, segmented, matched with phone templates, and compared with the sentences in the language using the knowledge network. The utterance with the best score is chosen as the sentence and displayed at the bottom of the waveform. We briefly described each of these steps in the recognition process using the example shown in Figs. 9.7 and 9.8.

Digitization. All of the recognition experiments were conducted in a computer terminal room environment (approximately 65 dbA) using an Electrovoice head-mounted close speaking microphone (model number RE51). The signal was band-pass filtered at (85 Hz-4.5 kHz) using a Kronhite filter (model number 3750R) and sampled at a 10 kHz sampling rate. The time-sharing operating system was modified to accept high data rate signals without any data loss. Utterance beginning and end detection was done using amplitude and zero-crossing measurements of the signal (Gill, Goldberg, Reddy, & Yegnanarayana, 1978). The digitized waveform is shown in Fig. 9.7. Note that the second line of the waveform is a continuation of the first and the third is a continuation of the second.

Segmentation. The continuous speech signal is segmented into discrete components using ZAPDASH parameters. The segmentation process is described in detail by Gill et al. (1978). A recursive top-down segmentation procedure is used to identify segments based on features such as silence, voicing, frication, peak detection, and dip detection. Figure 9.7 shows a typical segmentation achieved by the system. Note that segmentation boundaries are marked by vertical bars and that vowels

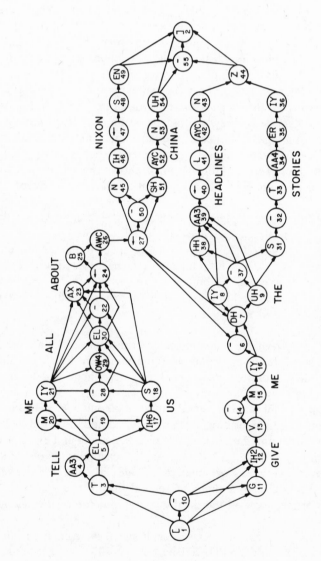

FIG. 9.6.　Harpy phone network.

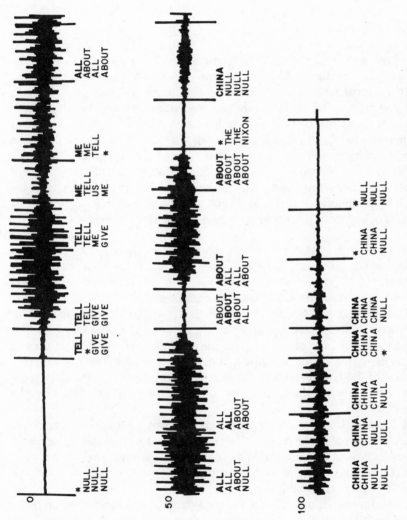

FIG. 9.7. Waveform display of the recognition process. Shown are segmentation, word labels associated with segments, and the words selected by the backtrace.

are usually divided into two or more segments. There is one missing segment boundary at the juncture of the words *all* and *about*—the /l/–schwa boundary is missing. But given the constraints of the language, the system recovers from such errors.

Phone Template Matching.   Spectral characteristics of each segment are determined by using linear prediction analysis (LPC) over the midposition of the segment. The average segment length is about 5 centiseconds, resulting in a factor of five improvement in computation over systems which perform LPC analysis each centisecond. For each segment, the LPC coefficients of the segment are matched with speaker-dependent templates using the LPC minimum distance residual metric as described by Itakura (1975). In certain versions of the Harpy system, only those templates which are permissible in that context are computed. Note that implicit in this discussion is the assumption that, given enough allophone templates, it is reasonable to attempt labeling of segments using pattern-matching techniques. This was by no means an accepted approach to phone labeling until the proven success of the Harpy system.

Recognition and Match.   Figure 9.8 illustrates the steps in the matching and search process. Figure 9.6 shows the knowledge network in which the sentence "Tell me all about China" is legal. Note that, given this network, only four phone labels are permissible in the sentence initial position, namely IH2 (an allophone of /I/), G, —, and T. The values of the acoustic match distance are given to the right of the boxes in Fig. 9.8. Note that the silence phone /—/ has the smallest distance of 0.23 for the first segment (indicating the closest match), /T/ has a distance of 1.46, /G/ a distance of 1.57, and /IH2/ a distance of 2.26. These are the only legal phones for this position, so none of the other phone distances are evaluated.

As the acoustic matches are generated, Harpy begins the recognition process. The goal of the recognition task is to find an optimal sequence of phones satisfying two criteria. The sequence must represent a legal path through the knowledge network and should consist of phones with high acoustic match probabilities.

The beam search used by the Harpy system is a heuristic search technique which locates a near-optimal sequence of phones that is consistent with the network. Beam search is a technique in which a group of near-miss alternatives around the best path is examined. By searching many alternatives simultaneously, this method avoids the need for backtracking. The search is executed by creating and examining a tree structure of phones whose connections are consistent with transitions in the knowledge net. Each ply (or column) in the recognition tree given in Fig. 9.8

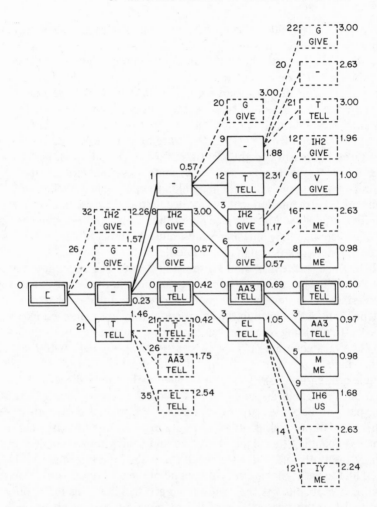

FIG. 9.8. Harpy recognition process using beam search.

represents the matching associated with one segment of the digitized utterance.

The root node of the tree is the sentence beginning state [of the network in Fig. 9.8. Harpy begins the search by taking all the legal phones that can follow from the sentence-initial state and entering them in the recognition tree. Referring to Fig. 9.8, each box in the second ply (column) gives the phone and the word associated with the candidate state. Next, a path probability is calculated for each candidate. This is a cumulative value based on the path probability of the previous node and the acoustic match probability of the current node. The path probability value is indicated on the left side of each box. The path with the best probability (boxes with double lines in Fig. 9.8) is determined. In the second ply, the /—/ state has the best value. All the remaining candidates are then compared with it. Those candidates that fall below a threshold of acceptability are pruned from further searching. The pruned states are indicated by dotted boxes in Fig. 9.8. The successors of each surviving candidate are expanded, based on the information in the knowledge network.

As can be seen from Fig. 9.8, there are four successors to the /—/ state and three successors to the /T/ state. Note that, although not shown in Fig. 9.6 as a specific pointer, each state can transition to itself. This permits two or more adjacent segments to be matched to the same state. Thus, the segmentation can introduce extra segment markers without significant penalty. Missing a segment, however, causes problems; in the Harpy system, likely missing states must be created as optional states when the network is originally created.

When the successor states are copied onto the recognition tree as candidates for matching with the next segment in the segment list, two or more states may generate the same successor. Instead of retaining two independent paths through the same node, they are collapsed into a common path, avoiding redundant computation. In Fig. 9.8 both the /—/ and the /T/ states generate /T/ as a successor. Only the path with the highest prior value is relevant at this point. The deleted path is indicated by a double broken-line box. The lesser valued paths can be discarded, because their path probabilities can never exceed the one with the highest value. The path probabilities are calculated as before, the best path is established, and unpromising alternatives are pruned. The forward search continues, expanding the recognition tree and saving those connections that satisfy the threshold, until we reach the end of the utterance.[2]

Of all the paths that survive at the end of the utterance, the one with the best path probability is the solution we are seeking. This is the only path that satisfies the two criteria of the recognition process. It provides the best interpretation of the acoustic matches, while satisfying the constraints of the knowledge network.

A backtrace through the recognition tree reveals the desired solution, indicating the phone and word assignments associated with the best path. Since the pointers for each surviving path in the beam of the recognition tree are retained until the end, this turns out to be a straightforward look-up operation and does not involve any search. Note that what ap-

---

[2]It was not possible to show the entire recognition tree. Figure 9.8 shows only a portion of the tree, i.e., up to the fourth segment of the waveform shown in Fig. 9.7. Examining Fig. 9.7, we see under each segment the words associated with the best four words in the candidate list for that segment.

pears to be the best choice for each segment in the forward search may not, in fact, be part of the globally best sequence discovered during the backtrace. Thus, local errors introduced by segmentation and acoustic matches are recovered by delaying commitment to a particular path until the forward search is completed. Therefore the forward search may be errorful without affecting the final solution. Referring to Fig. 9.7 again, *the final word choice* selected by the backtrace is indicated in darker print than the rest of the candidate choices. Note that on line two of the waveform, the assignment of ALL and ABOUT involves the second best choices.

Occasionally, the heuristics associated with the beam search miss the optimal path, but because the acoustic matches are less than perfect, attempting to find the optimal path at great cost and effort leads to little or no improvement in the overall performance.

TABLE 9.2
Performance of the Harpy System

Targets (from 1971)	Harpy Performance (1976)
Accept connected speech	yes
from many	5 (3 male, 2 female)
cooperative speakers of the General American Dialect	yes
in a quiet room	computer terminal room
using a good quality microphone	ordinary microphone
with slight tuning/speaker	substantial tuning (20–30 utterances/speaker)
requiring only natural adaptation by the user	no adaptation required
permitting a slightly selected vocabulary of 1000 words	1011 words, no postselection
with a highly artificial syntax and highly constrained task	combined syntactic and semantic constraints → avg. branching factor of 10
providing graceful interaction	modest interaction capabilities
tolerating < 10% semantic error	9% sentence error—5% semantic error
in a few times real-time[a] [on a 100 MIPS machine]	80 times real-time on a[a] .35 MIPS PDP-KA10 using 256K of 36-bit words with a simple program organization costing about $5 per sentence
and be demonstrable in 1976 with a chance of success	operational 13 August 1976

[a] A few times real-time on 100 MIPS processor is anywhere from 200 to 500 MIPSS (millions of instructions executed per second of speech). The actual performance of Harpy was about 28 MIPSS, i.e., 80 times real-time on a .35 MIPS processor.

Harpy Performance

Harpy was the only system whose performance met or exceeded all the original stated objectives of the five year ARPA speech understanding effort (Klatt, 1977). Table 9.2 presents the original stated goals and the performance of the Harpy system in 1976. Since then, the system has been further improved and it now runs about ten times faster. The system was also tested on several other simpler tasks. Detailed performance of the system on these tasks is given in the final report of the speech understanding project (Reddy and the CMU Speech Group, 1977) and in Lowerre and Reddy (1978).

There are several important factors that contributed to the success of the Harpy system. Foremost among them are the representation of knowledge in a single integrated network and the beam search technique. Several speech-related decisions that led to improved performance were the use of a large number of allophone templates, dynamic adaptation to new speakers, compiled phonological rules, LPC analysis, and the Itakura distance metric.

DISCUSSION

In the previous sections we presented two different models of speech recognition, the HEARSAY-II and the Harpy systems. One is based on the view that speech recognition is best viewed as an information gathering process. The other is based on the classic heuristic search paradigm using a special beam-search heurisitc.

Table 9.3 shows the principal differences between the two models. At a gross conceptual level, the role of knowledge and its representation (in the long-term memory) appears to be the same in both cases: The role of knowledge is to generate hypotheses or to verify (or prune) them. In both cases, knowledge functions as condition–action rules. The difference between the two systems is in the implementation of knowledge. Knowledge implementation is procedural in HEARSAY and exists as a state space representation in Harpy.

The two systems differ substantially in the way in which hypotheses are represented in the working memory (the short-term memory). In HEARSAY, the partial sentence hypotheses are represented as a multilevel and/or tree structure. In Harpy, they are explicitly instantiated in terms of states traversed which implicitly provide hypotheses associated with all the levels of the state.

The flow of control and the order of search differ in interesting ways in the two models. In the HEARSAY system, the hypotheses propagate

TABLE 9.3
Differences between the HEARSAY II and Harpy Systems

	HEARSAY-II	Harpy
Knowledge sources (LTM)	C–A rules procedural hypothesize-test	C–A rules state space hypothesize-test (prune paths)
Blackboard (STM)	multi-level (3D) AND-OR tree	implicit coding of levels (2½ D) explicit instantiations
Order	island-driven even-driven (pattern-directed)	left-to-right segment-driven (signal-directed)

from islands of reliability using an event-driven best-first search strategy. In Harpy, the hypotheses propagate from left-to-right using a segment-driven best-few beam search strategy.

Other Systems

At this point it is interesting to compare these systems with the principal characteristics of two other systems: The Bolt Beranak and Newman (BBN) Hear What I Mean (HWIM) System and the IBM system. In the HWIM system (Wolf & Woods, 1978), emphasis was placed on the acquisition and utilization of the best available speech knowledge. Given the ill-structured nature of the existing knowledge, it was not possible to code and debug all the knowledge and to generate an integrated system with the expected performance within the time constraints of the ARPA project. The flow of control in the HWIM system was also island-driven, but the focus of attention and knowledge source activation strategies were explicitly programmed in the HWIM system, whereas in the HEARSAY system they are data-directed.

In the IBM system, the primary emphasis has been to use information-theoretic statistical models of knowledge. The flow of control is essentially left-to-right using a best-first search strategy. This system was used to run the same document-retrieval task that was used by the Harpy system (Bahl, Baker, Cohen, Cole, Jelinek, Lewis, & Mercer, 1978). The system achieved over 98% sentence accuracy. However, several differences in the two experiments make a direct comparison of the results difficult. The 9% sentence error reported for the Harpy system was for five speakers (three male and two female) in a computer terminal environment using an ordinary microphone with only minor tuning of the system for each speaker. The IBM system reports less than 2% sentence error rate for a single speaker in a sound-proof booth using a high quality microphone with extensive tuning and requiring over 100 times more computation than was used in the Harpy system. The results are nevertheless interesting because they show that very high performance can, in fact, be achieved in controlled environments, given enough computer power.

Limitations of the HEARSAY Model

In spite of the many elegant and aesthetically pleasing aspects of the Hearsay model, such as KS independence, parallel asynchronous data-directed activation of KSs, and the blackboard data structure, there are several problems with the current implementation of the model. Here we present only a few key problem areas. (A more detailed discussion of several related issues is given by Lesser & Erman, 1977).

The Focus-of-Attention Problem.   At any given point in the analysis of an utterance, there are many competing hypotheses at different levels and at different time periods waiting to be extended. Of these, the KS scheduler must select one (or a few if a parallel processor is available) for consideration. The goal is to select and activate KSs which are most likely to lead to successful recognition. In the current implementation this is based on concepts such as competition, validity, significance, efficiency, and goal satisfaction. The effective use of these concepts requires that the system have several meta-level knowledge sources which are presently ill-defined.

The Stopping Problem.   The concept of an information-gathering process is highly seductive, and yet the very fact that independent KSs are going their merry ways gathering new information leads one to wonder if the process will ever stop. In the current implementation, the STOP knowledge source attempts to take control after the first acceptable sentence hypothesis is created on the blackboard or after a given amount of computing resource has been expended. By comparing the current best interpretation of the utterance to other competing partial interpretations, a substantial pruning of hypotheses takes place. Segmentation and labeling provide enough information to calculate a maximum rating for a hypothesis if expanded to cover the utterance. Hypotheses whose expanded rating falls short of the current best hypotheses are pruned. Stopping occurs if no hypotheses have an expected rating greater than the current best interpretation. Unfortunately, there is always a small possibility that the correct interpretation is just beyond the horizon.

The Monitoring Problem.   Data-directed asynchronous activation of KSs leads to the interesting process of distributed control in the HEAR-

SAY system. However, the continuous evaluation of preconditions (the stimulus frame) of each KS turns out to be computationally expensive. In the current implementation, a clever representation of the stimulus frame substantially reduces the effort required. Monitoring, however, continues to require a nontrivial share of the total resources.

The Knowledge-Sharing Problem. Often the same knowledge is needed in different parts of the system. For example, knowledge about word pronunciations is needed by the word hypothesizer, word verifier, and word juncture validation procedure. The juncture procedure itself is used by WORD-SEQ, VERIFY, and MOW knowledge sources. Thus it becomes clear that not only must KSs be able to share hypotheses in the short-term memory (blackboard) but also parts of long-term memory (knowledge). At present this is done in an ad hoc way on a case-by-case basis. A more satisfactory solution is needed.

Limitations of the Harpy Model

In spite of its superior performance and apparent simplicity, there are several questions about the Harpy system regarding the generality and extensibility of the approach, the cost of knowledge integration, and the importance of delayed decisions.

Generality and Extensibility. The current implementation of Harpy cannot handle problems such as hesitation pauses, repetition, non-grammaticality, and new words unknown to the system. Neither can any other system at present. However, systems such as Hearsay are potentially capable of handling such problems without any change in the overall approach. It appears that the Harpy system can also handle these problems using multiple (increasingly less constrained) networks. But as one begins to modify the Harpy system in this direction, many of the apparent differences between the Hearsay and Harpy approaches begin to diminish.

There are also questions about whether the finite-state grammar representation used by Harpy would be acceptable for natural language input. If one is willing to place a restriction on the length of a sentence, any language can be modeled using a finite-state graph (FSG) representation. A simple FSG in which any word can follow any other word would accept all legal sentences but would permit many illegal sentences as well. However, one need not take such a drastic step. If one is willing to accept some loss of constraints with the accompanying relaxation of the language to accept some illegal sentences, the language can usually be represented by a suitable FSG.

How can Harpy handle sentences that are not part of its grammar? In general it cannot, but neither can any other system or human. Ungrammaticality results in an incorrect interpretation or no interpretation at all. In the latter case, Harpy and HEARSAY-II would output sentence fragments. A theory for consistently interpreting errorful sentence fragments was developed and resulted in the construction of the SEMANT knowledge source (Fox & Mostow, 1977). SEMANT produces the best consistent interpretation of sentence fragments and ungrammatical sentences in restricted domains. It acts as a post-processor for both Harpy and HEARSAY-II.

To be able to handle new words and new sentence constructs that are not part of one's vocabulary or grammar, one needs a knowledge acquisition facility. We have been developing concepts that would permit Harpy-like systems to acquire new words and new constructs. This requires an ability for the system to recognize that an unknown utterance is inconsistent with its internal knowledge and then to activate partial matching and word spotting type networks which are substantially less constrained. If all the words are known but they are ungrammatical (as in "sleep roses dangerously young colorless"), the new sentence, if desired, can be assimilated into the word network. If one or more words are unknown, then one needs a "speak and spell" program to learn the new words or variations of existing words.

The Cost of Knowledge Integration.   The knowledge compiler for the 1011-word document-retrieval task takes over 12 hours of DEC-10 computer time. The net effect, of course, is that at the time of execution the system runs very quickly. However, as the system is being developed it is not utilized enough to make the cost of compiling worthwhile. Alternative implementations where KSs are interpreted dynamically might be attractive in such cases.

Delayed Decisions.   At present the entire search tree, generated by the beam search technique, is kept around so that a globally consistent decision might be made at the end of the utterance. As the work by Cole and Jakimik (Chap. 6) demonstrates, human perceivers do not wait until the end of an utterance to make decisions about the words that occur at the beginning. A modification of the present search process in which only a limited delay is permitted (adequate to provide enough context) might be interesting (Newell, Chap. 11).

CONCLUSION

The machine models of speech recognition presented in this chapter are interesting not only because they have led to integrated working systems but also because they have led to interesting speculations about alternative models for human speech perception (Klatt, Chap. 10; Newell, Chap. 11). Several new improvements to the existing models are needed before they can begin to approach human performance. In most of the existing systems, the acquisition, assimilation, and debugging of knowledge are essentially manual. Automated knowledge acquisition and learning techniques are essential for future progress in this area.

Most of the current systems have little or no facilities for graceful interaction and error recovery. Graceful interaction in systems requires, among other things, models of the task, models of the user, and models of conversation. Progress in this area is essential for future accpetance of this class of systems.

Current systems tend to be brittle and do not react gracefully in the presence of noise and degradation of speech quality. There are few answers in the literature to questions such as: How does the system performance degrade with quantization noise, additive noise, and multiplicative noise? Studies of human perception in the areas of knowledge acquisition, graceful interaction, and the presence of noise would be extremely helpful to progress in this field.

ACKNOWLEDGMENTS

I would like to thank Jim Baker, Lee Erman, Gary Goodman, Rick Hayes-Roth, Vic Lesser, and Bruce Lowerre, whose contributions were essential to the final success of the HEARSAY and Harpy systems. I would also like to acknowledge the contributions of several other members of the Carnegie-Mellon speech group. (Reddy & CMU Speech Group, 1977). I would also like to thank Ron Cole, Lee Erman, and B. Yegnanarayana for their comments on this chapter.

REFERENCES

Bahl, L. R., Baker, J. K., Cohen, P. S., Cole, A. G., Jelinek, F., Lewis, B. L., & Mercer, R. L. Automatic recognition of continuously spoken sentences from a finite state grammar. *Proceedings of the IEEE International Conference on Acoustics, Speech and Signal Processing*, Tulsa, Oklahoma, 1978, 418–421.

Baker, J. K. The DRAGON system—An overview. *IEEE Transactions on Acoustics, Speech and Signal Processing*, 1975, *23*, 24–29.

Erman, L. D., & Lesser, V. R. The Hearsay-II speech understanding system. In W. A. Lea (Ed.), *Trends in speech recognition*. Englewood Cliffs, N.J.: Prentice-Hall, 1979.

Fox, M. S., & Mostow, D. J. Maximal consistent interpretations of errorful data in hierarchically modelled domains. *Proceedings of the International Joint Conference on Artificial Intelligence*, 1977, *1*, 165–171.

Gill, G., Goldberg, H., Reddy, R., & Yegnanarayana, B. *A recursive segmentation procedure for continuous speech*. Technical Report, Department of Computer Science, Carnegie-Mellon University, Pittsburgh, Penn., 1978.

Goodman, G. *Analysis of languages for man-machine voice communication*. Unpublished doctoral thesis, Stanford University, Stanford, Calif., 1976.

Hayes-Roth, F., & Lesser, V. R. Focus of attention in the Hearsay-II speech understanding system. *Proceedings of the International Joint Conference on Artificial Intelligence*, 1977, *1*, 27–35.

Itakura, F. Minimum prediction residual principle applied to speech recognition. *IEEE Transactions on Acoustics, Speech and Signal Processing*, 1975, *23*, 67–72.

Lowerre, B., & Reddy, D. R. The Harpy speech understanding system. In W. A. Lea (Ed.), *Trends in speech recognition*. Englewood Cliffs, N.J.: Prentice-Hall, 1979.

Lesser, V. R., & Erman, L. D. A retrospective view of the Hearsay-II architecture. *Proceedings of the International Joint Conference on Artificial Intelligence*, 1977, *2*, 790–800.

Lesser, V. R., Fennell, R. D., Erman, L. D., & Reddy, D. R. Organization of the Hearsay-II speech understanding system. *IEEE Transactions on Acoustics, Speech and Signal Processing*, 1975, *23*, 11–23.

Martin, T. B. Practical applications of voice input to machines. Proceedings of the IEEE, April 1977, *64* (4), 487–501.

Reddy, D. R. Computer recognition of connected speech. *Journal of the Acoustical Society of America*, 1967, *42*.

Reddy, D. R. Speech recognition by machine: A review. *Proceedings of the IEEE*, April 1976, *64* (4), 501–523.

Reddy, D. R., & CMU Speech Group. Speech understanding systems: Summary of results of the five-year reserach effort at CMU. Department of Computer Science, Carnegie-Mellon University, Pittsburgh, Penn., 1977.

Reddy, D. R., Erman, L. D., Fennell, R. D., & Neely, R. B. The Hearsay speech understanding system: An example of the recognition process. *Proceedings of the International Joint Conference on Artificial Intelligence*, Stanford, Calif., 1973, 185–194.

Reddy, D. R., & Newell, A. Knowledge and its representation in a speech understanding system. In L. W. Gregg (Ed.), *Knowledge and cognition*, Potomac, Md.: Lawrence Erlbaum Associates, 1974.

Rumelhart, D. *Introduction to human information processing*. New York: Wiley, 1977.

Vicens, P. *Preprocessing for speech analysis*. Technical report, AI Memo 71, Stanford University, Stanford Calif., 1968.

Vicens, P. J. *Aspects of speech recognition by computer*. Unpublished doctoral thesis, Department of Computer Science, Stanford University, Stanford, Calif., 1969.

Wolf, J., & Woods, W. A. The HWIM speech understanding system. In W. A. Lea (Ed.), *Trends in speech recognition*. Englewood Cliffs, N.J.: Prentice-Hall, 1979.

10

Speech Perception: A Model of Acoustic-Phonetic Analysis and Lexical Access

Dennis H. Klatt
Massachusetts Institute of Technology

INTRODUCTION

Recent spectrogram-reading experiments (Cole, Rudnicky, Reddy, & Zue, Chap. 1) have shown that the acoustic signal is rich in phonetic information. Without knowing anything about the words that are present, an expert spectrogram reader can produce a broad phonetic transcription that agrees with a panel of phoneticians from 80 to 90% of the time, depending on the scoring method used. Furthermore, perceptual experiments by Liberman and Nakatani (personal communication) indicate that listeners can transcribe nonsense names embedded in sentences (and obeying the phonological constraints of English) with better than 90% phonemic accuracy.

These experiments call into question the view that the speech signal is so impoverished of phonetic information that speech perception usually proceeds "top-down," with syntactic and semantic knowledge sources hypothesizing lexical candidates to be compared with aspects of the acoustic signal for verification. Of course there are listening conditions where noise or distortions force the listener to rely more heavily on expectations and higher-level knowledge to hypothesize words, but I believe that a bottom-up method of lexical access is an essential part of the normal speech decoding process. This chapter will be concerned with the process of lexical hypothesis formation from acoustic data. Little will be said about how such a bottom-up component of the speech understanding process interfaces with other components of a complete model of sentence perception.

There have been several recent efforts to build computer-based speech understanding systems that accept spoken input sentences within some limited domain, and respond with the correct answer better than 95% of the time (see Klatt, 1977 for a review). Of particular interest are the Harpy system (Lowerre & Reddy, 1978), which represents a large but finite set of sentences by a network of expected spectra, and the HWIM system (Klovstad, 1978; Wolf & Woods, 1978), which takes into account the phonological recoding of words and word sequences in normally spoken sentences. Examination of these systems has changed my views about how speech is normally perceived. Perhaps it is not wise to draw conclusions about the functioning of the human brain from analogies to computer algorithms, but the theoretical advantages of combining some of these strategies into a perceptual model are compelling.

A typical three-step machine method of lexical access is shown in Fig. 10.1a. Parameters are extracted from the speech waveform, a phonetic transcription is derived, and then lexical hypotheses are proposed. Parameters might include formant frequencies (Zue & Schwartz, 1978), articulatory configurations (Wakita & Kasuya, 1977), or spectra (Lowerre & Reddy, 1978). The phonetic representation might be a distinctive feature matrix (Medress, 1969) or a lattice of segmental alternatives (Wolf & Woods, 1978). Lexical search might proceed in an analysis-by-synthesis mode at the syllable level (Weeks, 1974) or by precompiling phonological knowledge into a network of expected phonetic sequences for words, using scoring penalties for incorrect, missing, or extra segments in the input (Klovstad, 1978). The relative advantages among these choices are discussed in Klatt (1978a).

This chapter presents an alternative method of lexical access from acoustic input. In the next section, eight problems associated with word identification in running speech are identified. In the third and fourth sections, two new computer systems, SCRIBER and LAFS, are proposed as potential engineering solutions to these problems. The LAFS system is then modified to form the perceptual model described in the fifth section.

The SCRIBER phonetic transcription system described in detail in the third section and shown here in Fig. 10.1b is proposed as an alternative to the more traditional methods of phonetic analysis. Knowledge of auditory psychophysics (such as critical bands, loudness, forward and backward masking, etc.) is used to derive an appropriate spectral representation for speech. Phonetic decoding rules then take the form of a network of expected sequences of static spectra for each possible transition between phonetic segments.

The LAFS system shown in Fig. 10.1c is proposed as a method for generating lexical hypotheses directly from a spectral representation of speech without first recognizing phonetic segments. Acoustic–phonetic

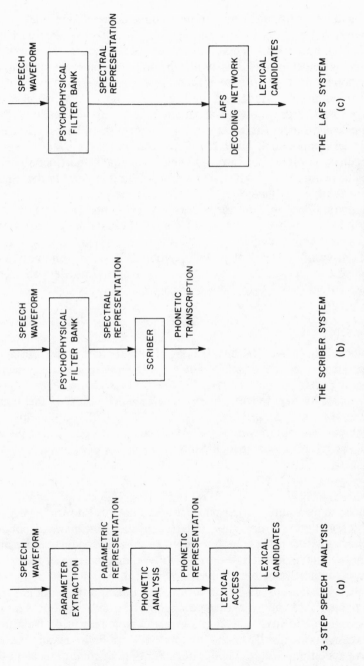

FIG. 10.1. The block diagram of part (a) describes typical machine analysis procedures for bottom-up lexical access. Parts (b) and (c) outline the structure of two models of the early stages of speech perception to be described in later sections.

245

knowledge and word-boundary phonology are precompiled into a decoding network of expected spectral sequences for all possible word sequences from the lexicon. This sytem avoids making possibly errorful early phonetic decisions and thus avoids the problems inherent in using an errorful phonetic transcription to search the lexicon.

The fifth section is concerned with modeling how humans generate lexical hypotheses from acoustic information. A new perceptual model of bottom-up lexical access is described that incorporates both SCRIBER and LAFS as components. The model departs from most current views of how speech is perceived, in that phonetic segments and phonological rules play a role only in LAFS network compilation, and not in the direct analysis of the speech waveform during lexical search.

In a sixth and final section, the perceptual model proposed in the fifth section is compared with other models. One of these models, analysis by synthesis at the lexical level, is described in some detail in order to establish the relative advantages of precompilation of acoustic–phonetic and phonological relations to active synthesis of the same knowledge.

THE PROBLEM

Before describing SCRIBER and LAFS, eight problem areas are identified that have plagued designers of speech recognition and speech understanding systems for decades. All have to do with the identification of words in spoken sentences, given some representation of the input acoustic waveform. The problems listed in Table 10.1 are endemic to speech communication; they must be overcome by any speech processing system or model of human speech perception.

1. Acoustic–Phonetic Noninvariance

The acoustic manifestations of a phonetic segment are known to vary in different phonetic environments (Klatt, 1978b; Liberman, Cooper, Shankweiler, & Studdert-Kennedy, 1967). While many acoustic cues are largely context independent and thus form invariant properties of a given phonetic segment (Blumstein, Stevens, & Nigro, 1977; Cole & Scott, 1974; Fant, 1974; Stevens, 1975), there are also context-dependent cues to the same phonetic distinctions. Listeners seem to be able to process these latter cues when the invariant cues are artificially removed (Delattre, Liberman, & Cooper, 1955), and are probably able to make use of context-dependent information under normal listening conditions as well. What decoding strategy permits the listener to interpret cues that depend on phonetic context (so as to make optimum use of all the information contained in the speech waveform), especially when phonetic environ-

TABLE 10.1
Eight Problem Areas that Must Be Dealt with by
any Model of Bottom-up Lexical Access

1. Acoustic–phonetic noninvariance.
2. Segmentation of the signal into phonetic units.
3. Time normalization.
4. Talker normalization.
5. Lexical representations for optimal search.
6. Phonological recoding of words in sentences.
7. Dealing with errors in the initial phonetic representation during lexical matching.
8. Interpretation of prosodic cues to lexical items and sentence structure.

ment itself is not known with any certainty? More importantly, what are the perceptually relevant acoustic cues to each phonetic contrast, and how are cues combined?

2. Segmentation into Phonetic Units

Is segmentation an independent process, preceding phonetic labeling, or is it simply an automatic consequence of the phonetic decision process itself? If the speech waveform could first be segmented reliably into chunks corresponding to phonetic segments, the job of identifying each segment would be much simplified. Unfortunately, segmentation criteria depend on detailed knowledge of articulatory–acoustic relations, the permitted phonetic categories of the language in question, and other phonological constraints (see Klatt, 1978a, and Cole et al., Chap. 1 for examples). Ambiguities in segment boundary locations are produced when the various articulators move asynchronously, as is often the case. A particular difficulty with feature-detector models of phonetic perception, such as the model described by Pisoni and Sawusch (1975), is the problem of interpreting detector outputs in order to align the columns of the derived feature matrix and see how many segments are present.

No matter how segmentation is accomplished, it appears that errors are inevitable. When a system commits itself to an error in an early stage of the analysis, such as a segmentation error, it is difficult for other components to recover and find the correct analysis. If a way could be found to defer or avoid segmentation decisions, overall system performance might improve.

3. Time Normalization

Segmental durations are influenced by many factors, including speaking rate, locations of syntactic boundaries, syllable stress, and features of adjacent segments (Klatt, 1976b, 1979; Lehiste, 1970). A segment can vary in duration by a factor of two or three depending on its environment in the utterance. This kind of temporal variation clearly rules out the use of spectral prototypes of fixed duration in phonetic recognition. Some sort of time warping, time normalization, or method of ignoring the time dimension must be devised.

In addition, there are cases where the duration of an acoustic event can play a decisive role in a phonetic contrast of English (e.g., /ɛ/–/æ/ or /s/–/z/), but the durational dividing line between the two phonetic categories is sensitive to the factors listed above. Thus there are really two parts to the time-normalization problem: (1) how to ignore irrelevant variations in segmental durations; and (2) how to incorporate durational information in selected segmental decision strategies when durational perturbations due to syntax, semantics, and stress are not known at this level. A phonetic transcription system can be designed to solve the first half of the time-normalization problem, but can never be entirely successful at the interpretation of durational cues to segmental contrasts. We are faced with the classical chicken-or-egg problem; phonetic decisions depend in part on lexical and syntactic factors that cannot be resolved until the phonetic decisions have already been made. This appears to be another example where the principle of delayed commitment is applicable: If possible, one should not make phonetic decisions prior to lexical hypothesis formation. The decoding of durational cues to syntactic structure and semantic emphasis is discussed more fully below under problem 8—interpretation of prosodic cues.

4. Talker Normalization

Talkers differ in the length and general shape of their vocal tracts, in the articulatory–acoustic targets they use for each phonetic segment type, in their coarticulatory strategies as a function of stress and speaking rate, and in the dialect they employ (Stevens, 1972c). In addition, speech is heard in many different kinds of noise, reverberation conditions, and telephone channels. The variability created by these factors does not seem to cause great difficulties for the listener, but little is known about the perceptual strategies used to normalize for different talkers and listening environments.

5. Lexical Representations for Optimal Search

It is often tacitly assumed that the lexical representations used for matching during speech perception come from the same stored lexicon that is used for speech production (Liberman & Studdert-Kennedy, 1978), and that this single lexicon contains fairly abstract forms for morphemes (forms of the kind discussed by Chomsky & Halle, 1968). However, it seems clear that speech analysis routines cannot be expected to derive these abstract phonemic forms using bottom-up analysis (reasons are suggested by the examples of Table 10.2). The actual lexical representations used during matching are probably more nearly phonetic or acoustic in nature. These forms are either derived on the fly by generative rules, or (as is more likely given the computational efficiency) precompiled into some optimal form for rapid lexical search. The precise nature of the lexical representations used in bottom-up speech analysis is not known.

6. Phonological Recoding

The expected phonetic realization of a word depends on the sentence context in which it appears (Oshika, Zue, Weeks, Neu, & Aurbach, 1975). Consider, for example, the phonetic string observed for the spoken utterance "Did you hit it to Tom?" shown in Table 10.2. No word boundaries are indicated in the phonetic transcription, because acoustic cues to word-boundary locations are rarely present within phrases (although the utilization of separate prevocalic and postvocalic allophones of liquids and voiceless plosives helps to constrain the possible locations of some word boundaries). Each of the simplifications listed in Table 10.2 can be described by general phonological rules. During speech production, such rules are assumed to operate on an underlying abstract phonemic representation for each word or morpheme. For example, an (optional) word-boundary phonological rule /d/ # /y/ → [ǰ] transforms the word-final phoneme /d/ and the word-initial /y/ into the phonetic segment [ǰ] in "would you."

In most models of lexical access, such modifications must be viewed as a kind of noise that makes it more difficult to hypothesize lexical candidates, given an input phonetic transcription. To see that this must be the case, note that (a) pronunciation variants cannot be stored in the diction-

TABLE 10.2
Examples of Word-Boundary Phonology

"would you hit it to Tom"

[W ʊ j ə h ɪ ɾ ɪ t ə t ɑ m]

1. Palatalization of /d/ before /y/ .
2. Reduction of unstressed /u/ to schwa in "you."
3. Flapping of intervocalic [t] in "hit it."
4. Reduction to schwa and devoicing of /u/ in "to."
5. Reduction of geminate [t] in "it to."

ary, since one doesn't want to accept [jə] for "you" in the word sequence "are you"; and (b) each phonological rule example of Table 9.2
results in irreversible ambiguity—the [ǰ] observed in the sample phonetic
transcription of Table II could be the first or last segment of a word like
"judge", or it could be the surface manifestation of an underlying /d/ #
/y/. The number of phonological phenomena is quite large, and their effects on unstressed syllables can be dramatic, as suggested by the examples in Table 10.2. Phonological recoding, both within words and across
word boundaries, must be accounted for in a perceptual strategy. The
significant amount of ambiguity introduced by cross-word-boundary
phonological rules seems to support a top-down analysis-by-synthesis
model of lexical access unless knowledge of the effects of these rules can
be precompiled into an appropriate bottom-up decoding structure.

7. Dealing with Phonetic Errors

Even an ideal phonetic transcription component will make errors in the
presence of environmental noises, talker variability, and other factors.
Thus the lexical matching component must be able to find the (hopefully
correct) best scoring word, even when no words match the input perfectly. The derivation of scoring algorithms for segmental substitution,
omission, and insertion errors is difficult because some phonetic confusions are likely only in particular phonetic and stress environments. Very
little is known about perceptually motivated scoring algorithms and decision strategies appropriate for lexical search.

8. Interpretation of Prosodic Cues

Prosodic cues (fundamental frequency contour, pattern of segmental durations, and intensity contour) are used by the talker to distinguish between stressed and unstressed syllables, to delimit syntactic units, to
indicate contrastive stress or emphasis, and to signal psychological state
or attitude toward the utterance (Klatt, 1976b; Lea, 1973; Lehiste, 1970;
Lieberman, 1967). For purposes of lexical access, cues to the stress pattern can be quite useful. Many lexical alternatives can be ruled out if they
do not have the right pattern of stressed, unstressed and reduced syllables.

Unfortunately, perturbations to prosodic contours that depend on syntactic, semantic, and psychological variables confound the situation and
make interpretation of the stress pattern difficult. In addition, interpretation of syllable stress from prosodic variables is complicated by segmental
factors. Some phonetic segments are inherently more intense, or they are
of greater duration, or they perturb the fundamental frequency contour.

The listener appears to make stress judgments that are relative to these intrinsic properties of segments. As noted earlier, segmental decisions such as /ɛ/–/æ/ depend on duration cues that can only be interpreted with certainty after the stress pattern is known; it seems that segmental judgments and stress judgments must be computed simultaneously and interactively.

Of the eight problems outlined above and in Table 10.1, the first four are addressed by the SCRIBER phonetic transcription system. The second computer system to be described, the LAFS lexical access algorithm, not only takes advantage of the solutions embodied in SCRIBER, but also adds strategies that effectively deal with the final four problems. Sections describing the computational algorithms of SCRIBER and LAFS are followed by a discussion of the relations between these components and models of speech perception.

SCRIBER: A PROPOSED SOLUTION TO AUTOMATIC PHONETIC ANALYSIS

This section is concerned with the specification of a new computer algorithm for generating a phonetic transcription of the acoustic waveform corresponding to an unknown English sentence. The system is called SCRIBER, and is presently under development in the Speech Communication Laboratory at Massachusetts Institute of Technology. This preliminary report is concerned only with the design philosophy of the system since there are no results to report as yet.

A tentative set of about 55 output phonetic categories has been selected. The inventory of phonetic segment types is large enough to preserve distinctions useful in lexical decoding (e.g., postvocalic allophones of the liquids, unstressed and unreleased allophones of the plosives, etc.), but it is by no means intended to represent a narrow phonetic transcription.

Representation of Acoustic–Phonetic Knowledge

As an engineering approximation, it is assumed that transitions between phonetic segments can be represented succinctly and accurately by sequences of a few static spectra. For example, Fig. 10.2 illustrates a sequence of four spectra used to characterize the transition between [t] and [a] in the phrase "the top of the hill." Such a transition from the middle of one phone to the midpoint of the next is called a diphone. It has been argued that the coarticulatory influences of one phone on its neighbors do not usually extend much further than half-way into the adjacent phones

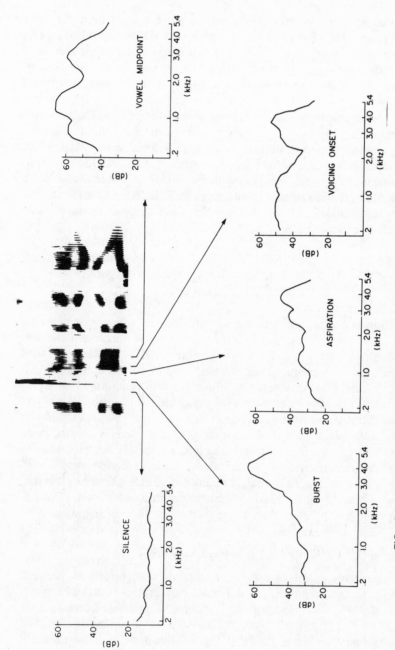

FIG. 10.2. A broadband spectogram is shown of the phrase "to the top of the hill," in order to indicate times at which spectra were computed so as to characterize the transition from the middle of closure for [t] to the middle of the vowel [a] in the SCRIBER phonetic decoding network.

(Gay, 1978; Peterson, Wang, & Sivertsen, 1958). To the extent that this approximation is true (see Lehiste & Shockey, 1972 for supporting perceptual evidence), diphone concatenation captures much of the context-dependent acoustic encoding of phonetic segments.

There exist a number of special cases that require attention in a diphone system. For example, a vowel followed by a nasal can be nasalized to a variable degree. The SCRIBER system is designed to produce, as output, the intended nonnasalized vowel. The technique employed is to define two (or more if necessary) alternative spectral sequences that describe the same diphone—one with a nasalized vowel, and one without. Similar solutions are required to decode other optional coarticulatory phenomena and to deal with certain unstressed allophones.

The choice of the diphone as the unit used to relate acoustic and phonetic levels is not central to any of the models to be described. A diphone dictionary is a convenient tabular way of cataloging acoustic–phonetic relations, but the same relations could, in principle, be described by rules (if the appropriate rules were known) or in terms of a dictionary describing the spectral manifestations of larger units such as triphones (Wickelgren, 1969), demisyllables (Fujimura & Lovins, 1978), or syllables (Studdert-Kennedy, 1976).

The spectral representation that has been chosen is based on the psychophysical considerations given in Table 10.3 (Klatt, 1978a). A short-term spectrum is computed every 10 msec using a set of 30 overlapping critical-band filters. Several examples of these spectra are shown in Fig. 10.2. It is up to the experimenter to select sufficient sample spectra to characterize each possible phonetic transition of English. There are 55 phonetic segment types in the inventory of SCRIBER, but many of the 55-by-55 possible acoustic transitions do not occur. Only about 2000 *diphones* are phonologically permissible in English. Each of these diphones is thus characterized by a sequence of three or four spectral templates, as in Fig. 10.2.

There can be template sharing for portions of diphones that are acoustically similar. For example, Fig. 10.3 indicates expected spectral sequences for the prestressed aspirated consonant [t] followed by any stressed vowel of English. The decoding structure summarizes the obvious fact that the closure (silence) spectrum for [t] is the same before any vowel, and the observation that onset spectra for [t] are virtually identical before all front vowels, identical before all back unrounded vowels, and identical before all rounded vowels (Klatt, 1978b; Zue, 1976). As indicated in the figure, spectral characteristics observed during aspiration are dependent on both [t] and the vowel, since formant onset values depend on the vowel (Klatt, 1978b). In general, a new spectral template is defined

TABLE 10.3
Psychophysical Considerations in the Design of a Spectral Representation
for Speech Processing

1. Include frequency components from at least 270 to 5600 Hz, because this is the minimum passband for which there is no measurable loss in intelligibility when compared with systems containing wider bandwidths (French & Steinberg, 1947).
2. Include a dynamic range of at least 50 dB, so as to adequately represent spectra of both the intense and weak speech sounds.
3. Provide a temporal resolution of about 10 msec, because this is the best current guess as to the shortest spectral window employed by the auditory system, and because otherwise certain rapid formant transitions and brief plosive bursts might be missed.
4. Take into account the observation that our ears cannot resolve individual harmonics of a voiced sound if the harmonics are spaced within a critical bandwidth of about a quarter of an octave (Houtgast, 1974; Plomp and Mimpen, 1968; Sharf, 1970).
5. Take account of the fact that the contribution to intelligibility from different portions of the spectrum is not uniform (French & Steinberg, 1947). The relative importance to speech intelligibility of different frequency components is in good agreement with a theory stating that each critical bandwidth contributes about equally to intelligibility, at least over the range from 270 to 5600 Hz.
6. Design the slopes of the critical band filters so as to account for the spreading of masking (i.e., low frequencies mask weak, higher-frequency components better than vice versa, so the filters have more gradual low-frequency skirts).
7. Express the output of each filter in dB (because decibels are an approximately equal-interval scale for loudness), and quantize filter outputs to about 1 dB (because the just-noticeable difference for changes to formant amplitudes change is 1 dB or more, depending on the circumstances, as in Flanagan, 1957).
8. Process only the *magnitude* of the spectrum, because the phase of the spectrum is too unpredictable to be used in phonetic decoding.
9. Use a number of overlapping critical-bandwidth filters, sufficient to discriminate spectral changes caused by formant frequency changes of about 3–5%, because this is the just-noticeable difference for a formant frequency shift (Flanagan, 1957).
10. Employ a preemphasis filter based on a pure tone threshold curve which indicates that there is an effective emphasis of frequencies in the 2–3 kHz range. Use equal-loudness contours to compute the growth in loudness with increases in signal intensity (Zwicker, Terhardt, and Paulus, 1978).

for each distinctive spectrum that is observed in a phonetic transition. If the transition is rapid, templates may be defined as often as every 10 or 20 msec, while for gradual spectral changes, few templates are defined per unit time.

A complete spectral sequence phonetic decoding network is compiled automatically from transition definitions of the type shown in Fig. 10.2. The network is highly interconnected, since all possible phonetic transitions must be represented by spectral sequences. However, there exists a relatively simple recognition strategy for utilizing this compact representation of acoustic–phonetic knowledge.

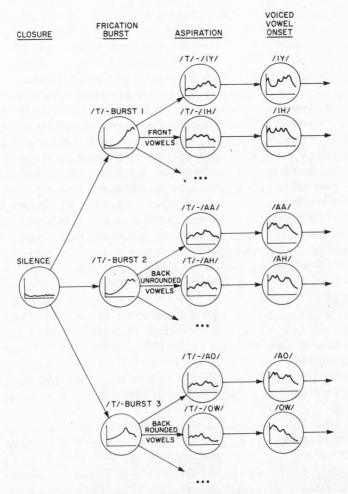

FIG. 10.3.   A small portion of the SCRIBER spectral-sequence phonetic decoding network is shown to illustrate the defining characteristics of pre-stressed prevocalic [t]. Each state of the network (circle) is characterized by a spectral template (dB versus frequency, as shown inside the circle). Not shown are durational constraints in the form of a feedback path to each state indicating the expected number of input 10-msec spectra that can be associated with each state during recognition.

Recognition Strategy

Once a network has been created, the input waveform is analyzed by computing a spectrum every 10 msec (using overlapping 25.6 msec chunks of windowed waveform). The recognition strategy consists of comparing this input spectral sequence with spectral templates of the network. The idea is to find the path through the network that best represents the observed input spectral. This path defines the optimal phonetic transcription.

A Euclidean distance metric involving differences in dB in selected frequency bands is used to compute matching scores for each input spectrum with the spectral templates, in a manner very similar to the strategy employed in the HARPY sentence recognition system (Lowerre & Reddy, 1978). The metric has some perceptual validity for static spectral comparisons (Lindblom, in press), but it will no doubt have to be modified to take into account changes in average speech spectrum and noise background associated with a new speaker or a new recording environment (Klatt, 1976a). Modifications may also be needed for comparison of template sequences so as to emphasize dynamic over static properties of the speech signal. For example, a long vowel probably should not contribute much more to dynamic distance than a brief plosive burst.

Input spectra are processed one at a time and used to try to extend the most promising "phonetic hypotheses." A hypothesis consists of (a) a pointer to a state in the decoding netword; (b) the duration of the input that has been associated with that state; (c) a cumulative spectral matching score; and (d) the last two phones of the implied phonetic transcription. A hypothesis is extended by assigning the new 10-msec input spectrum to the current state in the network or to one of the network states that can be reached from this state. A hypothesis will generate several daughter hypotheses if alternative paths from the current network state score reasonably well.

When the best scoring hypothesis in the (ordered) list of all current alternatives reaches a place in the network calling for the output of a phonetic symbol, it is assumed that the earlier of the two previous phonetic symbols that have been saved with the hypotheses is correct. The phonetic symbol is output and all hypotheses are not possessing this symbol are pruned from further consideration. A large number of best scoring hypotheses are pursued in parallel during a Harpy-like "beam search" of all alternative paths having scores that are within some fixed distance of the best scoring path to date (Lowerre & Reddy, 1978). Given this strategy, SCRIBER evaluates nearly all reasonable phonetic transcriptions of the input and selects the optimum transcription.

Phonetic Noninvariance

How does SCRIBER deal with the first four problems listed in Table 10.1? As a solution to the acoustic–phonetic noninvariance problem, SCRIBER incorporates diphone definitions. Any acoustic cue that is dependent on immediate phonetic context can be represented in a SCRIBER decoding network. Thus, for example, the burst spectrum for [t] is expected to have its most prominent spectral peak at lower frequencies before rounded vowels than before unrounded vowels (as shown in Fig. 10.3), and systematic differences in formant motions following [t] release into various vowels are described by individual aspiration templates for each [t]–vowel diphone. To the extent that acoustic invariance is present, states in the network are combined (for example, the [t] burst is represented by the same template before all front vowels in Fig. 10.3).

Diphone prototypes have been defined in terms of sequences of spectra in order to test the simplest possible hypothesis concerning which acoustic cues are most salient to each phonetic decision. It is hoped that, if the right metric can be devised for comparing spectra, SCRIBER will perform well and there will be no need to postulate a representational level between spectra and phonetic segments. The alternative is to interpose certain kinds of property detectors or phonetic feature detectors that extract particular attributes from the spectra. Such a level will not be included in SCRIBER unless the simpler model fails to account for various natural acoustic–phonetic distinctions (see Stevens, 1972a, for a partial list). Thus while sequences of spectra are not acoustic cues in the usual sense, they imply a theory in which spectra form a Gestalt or holistic unanalyzed representation rather than the input to a system of feature analyzers.

Segmentation

There is no explicit segmentation step in the SCRIBER decoding strategy. In a sense, all possible segmentations (alternative assignments of input spectra to network states) are evaluated in parallel. Because the input is not segmented before phonetic labeling, there is no need to develop strategies for correcting errors in segmentation. The final transcription provides an implicit segmentation since each 10-msec input spectrum has been associated with a particular state of the best scoring path through the network. Therefore, durations of acoustic events can be computed if relevant to a phonetic contrast (see next paragraph).

Time Normalization

The sequence-of-spectra concept is attractive for a number of reasons. For example, if desired, one could allow acoustic events to have any arbitrary duration without penalty, and irrelevant durational variability would be ignored. However, it is well known that duration is important for a number of phonetic contrasts, and some mechanism for incorporating durational constraints in the network representation is essential. To achieve this goal, the system is augmented in the following way. The expected duration of the input to be associated with each spectral template of a phonetic transition definition can be added to the diphone definitions for those cases where duration is deemed important. The result is that any state in the network of Fig. 10.3 can be assigned an explicit feedback path specifying the expected number of input spectra that can be associated with that state during recognition. For example, the number of input spectra associated with the burst spectrum plus the number associated with the aspiration spectrum in Fig. 10.3 should be about 5 (50 msec, i.e., the voice onset time should exceed about 25 msec) for a pre-stressed [t] to be recognized. In those cases where duration is determined to be important to a phonetic contrast, differences between expected and observed durations of the input assigned to a spectral template contribute to the distance score for a hypothesis. In this way, durations of acoustic events can be measured and compared with an accuracy that seems consistent with the relatively large (25 msec or more) durational just-noticeable differences observed during sentence perception (Klatt & Cooper, 1975).

Rate of spectral change is not represented by this means, because it appears that cases where rate seems important—e.g., in distinguishing between /ba/ and /wa/ (Liberman, Delattre, Gerstman, & Cooper, 1956)—depend more on the duration of the initial [w]-like spectrum, and thus can be better represented by specifying the expected duration of an initial steady state spectrum, and specifying that a certain spectral sequence be traversed. Rate of formant transitions or rates of other spectral changes are difficult to represent in discrete networks of this sort. One cannot easily constrain the relative duration of each component template of a transition definition—only the overall duration of the transition and/or the duration of any initial or final steady states. If rate turns out to be a perceptually important *independent* acoustic cue, this would constitute evidence against the template-sequence approach outlined here.

As argued earlier, variations in segmental durations due to speaking rate, syntactic factors, stress, and phonetic environment make it very difficult to rely on absolute durational constraints to distinguish among phonetic segments. The SCRIBER system can be set up to ignore irrelevant variations in segmental duration, but higher level variables that influence segmental durations contribute durational ambiguity that simply cannot be overcome. Duration ratios among adjacent acoustic events may serve as useful speaking-rate–invariant cues for certain phonetic contrasts (Port, 1978), but a minimum-use-of-duration strategy still seems wise in any attempt to build a phonetic recognizer. The inability to make effective use of durational (and fundamental frequency) cues to segmental contrasts is one of the primary reasons why I feel that a phonetic transcription component is not an appropriate driver for lexical search.

Talker Normalization

One criticism of previous template models of speech recognition is that they cannot be modified very easily to handle different talkers. There is considerable variation in the details of spectra characterizing phonetic segments spoken by men, women, and children. On the other hand, acoustic patterns observed for adult talkers are more similar in a critical-band spectral representation than one might expect (Searle, Jacobson, & Rayment, 1979). This observation lends support to a talker normalization procedure proposed by Lowerre (1977). He restricted the Harpy sentence-recognition network to contain only 98 different spectral template types, and all sentences had to be represented in terms of sequences of spectra drawn from these 98 templates. Templates were modified incrementally toward spectra seen for a new speaker in the following way: If a sentence could be recognized using templates representative of an ''average talker'' (the sentence error rate was about four times as great as when talker-specific templates were available), then the observed input spectra were used to modify those spectral templates of the network that were matched during recognition.

An added advantage of this approach is that it captures some idiosyncratic aspects of acoustic targets employed by each talker in realizing different phonetic segments. For example, if the speaker habitually uses a fronted /u/, the appropriate template(s) converge toward spectra that reflect this habit. The network is intended to represent the acoustic–phonetic characteristics of a particular dialect of English, while the spectrals templates represent acoustic targets that are talker-dependent. The separation of the SCRIBER system into talker-dependent templates and a talker-independent knowledge network has important theoretical implications. Speech processing by man and machine would be considerably simplified if such a separation could be experimentally validated.

In the SCRIBER system, more than 98 spectral templates will be required to make fine phonetic contrasts (about 300 may be sufficient), but the dynamic talker-normalization procedure of Harpy can still be applied. In addition, several generalized methods of talker normalization will be investigated, such as starting with an average female template if the new talker seems female, or modifying all templates on the basis of average spectral properties of a new voice, or estimating vocal tract length, or saving template sets for familiar voices.

When compiled into a decoding network, SCRIBER is not particularly large. A complete 2000-diphone inventory requires an average of about two new states per diphone, resulting in a network of about 4000 states and 6000 paths. (This is substantially smaller than the 15,000-state Harpy sentence-decoding network that can recognize 10^8 different sentences.) Sentence decoding then involves a large number of similar computations that can be performed in real time on a present-day fast digital processor such as the Floating Point Systems AP-120B.

Advantages of SCRIBER

The main advantages of SCRIBER are

1. the possibility of embedding all acoustic–phonetic knowledge concerning English (including phonological constraints on permitted phonetic sequences) into a single uniform network representation;
2. the ability to produce a phonetic transcription by simultaneously evaluating the scores for most of the likely alternative phonetic transcriptions;
3. no need for explicit phonetic segmentation.

Knowledge appears in a transparent form (the dictionary of spectral sequences for each phonetic transition) that makes optimization relatively easy. If it is successful, SCRIBER has possible applications as a limited-performance phonetic typewriter, as a "front end" for a computerized speech understanding system, as an aid for the deaf, and as a part of a model of speech perception (discussed in the fifth section).

LAFS: A PROPOSED SOLUTION TO THE PROBLEM OF LEXICAL ACCESS

The LAFS (lexical access from spectra) system is a computer algorithm for efficient accurate lexical search. LAFS avoids explicit phonetic transcription by precompiling knowledge of acoustic–phonetic relations into lexical definitions, in a way that is based on SCRIBER. The system deals with ambiguity generated by phonological recoding rules by precompiling knowledge of the rules into a decoding network.

Lexical Representations

The first step in the design of LAFS is to construct a tree of expected *phonemic* sequences for all words of the lexicon, as shown in Fig. 10.4a. An abstract phonemic lexicon is assumed as a starting point, because of the many theoretical advantages of postulating abstract underlying forms for words and morphemes (Chomsky & Halle, 1968), even though the psychological lexicon may not include some of the more abstract, less productive rules (Ohala, 1974). The phonemic lexicon is organized into the form of a tree (Fig. 10.4a), such that words having the same initial

STEP 1: LEXICAL TREE (PHONEMIC)

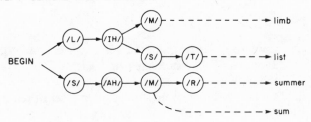

STEP 2: LEXICAL NETWORK (PHONETIC)

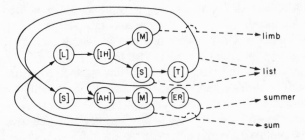

STEP 3: LEXICAL ACCESS FROM SPECTRA (SPECTRAL TEMPLATES)

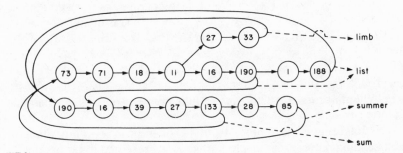

FIG. 10.4. The LAFS lexical-access-from-spectra decoding network that is shown in part (c) is derived by first constructing a tree of phonemic representations for all words in the lexicon, a portion of which is shown in part (a), and then connecting all word terminations to word beginnings and applying a set of phonological rules in order to form a phonetic sequence lexical decoding network, as shown in part (b). The numbers inside the states in the spectral sequence decoding network of part (c) refer to spectral templates from an inventory of about 300.

phoneme sequence share nodes (phonemes) and branches until the words diverge in phonemic representation. Initial portions of words are shared so as to save storage, increase search speed, and facilitate application of phonological rules. Of course, a pair of words cannot share tree nodes if the words react differently to phonological rules due to stress differences or other factors.

Precompiled Phonological Rules

Phonological rules are used to derive phonetic forms for each word. Rule application often depends on characteristics of adjacent words, so the lexical tree is first modified in the following way: The end of each word in the tree is attached to all word-beginning states. Then a set of phonological rules are applied to replace each phoneme by an appropriate phonetic allophone, delete or replace some segments, and modify the connectivity pattern (Klovstad, 1978). The result is a phonetic-sequence lexical decoding network of the type shown in Fig. 10.4b, representing expected phonetic properties of all possible (grammatical and ungrammatical) word sequences of the lexicon. Cross–word-boundary phonological phenomena that must be described include the possible insertion of a silence or juncture phone such as the glottal stop, normal phonetic coarticulation, and various simplifications such as palatalization, flapping, [t]-deletion, etc. (Oshika et al., 1975).

For example, the effect of the [s t # s] → [s] phonological rule in Fig. 10.4b is to create an extra path from near the end of words ending in [s t] to the second phonetic segment of words beginning with [s], so that a word pair such as "list some" can be recognized when spoken in the normal way, i.e. without the [t]. Since the rule is optional, the network must represent both alternatives, and the path from the final [t] of "list" to words beginning with [s] is therefore not broken. In the past few years, phonologists have developed formal rules of considerable predictive power (Chomsky & Halle, 1968; Cohen & Mercer, 1975; Oshika et al. 1975; Woods & Zue, 1976) that should prove useful in the context of lexical access.

If lexical access is attempted from a phonetic transcription, even given this decoding network in which words are represented in terms of phonetic segments, and phonological rule phenomena are represented by the connectivity pattern, one still requires a sophisticated matching strategy to select words corresponding to the derived phonetic string. A metric is needed to determine penalties for mismatches and for segmental intrusions or deletions, because the automatic phonetic analyzer will make many errors of these types. Experience with the Bolt Beranek and Newman (BBN) lexical decoding network has shown that metrics to handle errors are very important, in that unexpected transcription errors may result in a fatal rejection of the correct word (Wolf & Woods, 1978).

The ideal way to deal with transcription errors would be to go back to the acoustic data to see if the expected phonetic sequence for a word scores reasonably well. A phonetic transcription intentionally throws away this information, reducing large amounts of acoustic data to a sequence of discrete phonetic elements, and thus, it has been argued, making the lexical search problem computationally tractable. Why not avoid the problem of recovering from errorful intermediate phonetic decisions by not making phonetic decisions at all? To accomplish this goal within LAFS, each state transition in Fig. 10.4b is replaced by a mininetwork of spectral templates. Each mininetwork is obtained from the SCRIBER diphone dictionary.

The result is shown in Fig. 10.4c, a lexical-access-from-spectra decoding network that has no intermediate phonetic level of representation. The network is quite large, but only on the order of three teims as large as the lexical decoding network made up of phonetic segments that is shown in Fig. 10.4b (i.e., there are, on the average, about three new states required to represent a phonetic transition).

Recognition Strategy

The LAFS network of Fig. 10.4c is very similar in structure to SCRIBER, and the decoding strategy of SCRIBER (i.e., find the best path using a simple spectral metric) can be applied. A lexical decision confirming the presence of word X is made when all alternative word sequence hypotheses not containing this word are unlikely to increase in score as more of the input waveform is processed. Hypotheses not containing the identified word are then pruned from further consideration, in order to minimize the number of alternative word sequences that need to be considered in parallel.

In a system containing a large lexicon, one cannot postpone a lexical decision very long because too many alternative partial phrases would then have to be considered. Hopefully, in most practical applications, decisions can be held in abeyance for up to 0.5 seconds after the end of the hypothesized word, and the lexical hypothesis buffer need not grow any larger than about 1000.

Interpretation of Prosodic Cues

Not only is it possible to evaluate all reasonable lexical alternatives simultaneously in LAFS, but one can specify tighter durational constraints, voice-onset-time constraints, and stress-related constraints on acoustic events associated with words in LAFS than in SCRIBER, because one knows more about the expected stress pattern and phonetic environment. For example, a shorter vowel duration is expected in "batter" than in "bat," although both contain the same stressed vowel; such a constraint is easily applied in LAFS, but cannot be handled by a phonetic decoder.

The LAFS system also offers a mechanism for preliminary hypotheses to be formed concerning the syntactic structure of the sentence and the locations of semantically important words. Since the LAFS network is derived from lexical representations, one can specify not only the expected phonemic string and the expected durational pattern, but also the expected fundamental frequency (F_0) contour and the intensity envelope that would normally be seen in a stressed (or unstressed) sentence environment. Differences between expected and observed prosodic variables either signal that the lexical candidate is inconsistent with the input, or that the differences might be interpretable as cues to syntactic structure. For example, an unusually long final syllable in a word would indicate the presence of a phrase or clause boundary. Other possibilities include identifying the first part of a compound by a shorter than usual word duration, or detecting an emphasized word by a higher than usual fundamental frequency peak. Assuming that the network contains absolute values of prosodic cues to be expected, some form of normalization will be required to compensate for average speaking level, speaking rate, and fundamental frequency range employed by the current talker before direct comparison of observed and expected data is possible.

While duration and intensity contour ought to be effectively interpreted at a lexical level, there is reason to question whether F_0 can be processed in this way. A word receives a number of alternative F_0 contours, depending on sentence type (statement/question), syntactic position, and emotional nuances imparted by the speaker. Thus to interpret F_0 within LAFS, it may be necessary to have some current hypothesis in mind as to the prosodic interpretation of the previous input.

Morphemes versus Words

If the lexicon is broken down into morphemes (e.g., books = book + s, baseball = base + ball), there can be considerable savings in both storage and processing time. Allen (1973) has assembled a morpheme dictionary that can represent at least ten times as many English words as there are morphemes. LAFS should probably be organized in terms of the more common morphemes, but for recognition purposes, a lexical decoding network must keep separate representations for morphemes that change pronunciation when bound together (e.g., applicability = apply + able + ity). Even so, an English lexicon containing, for example, 15,000 morphemes would result in a phonemic tree of only about 50,000 states, and the resulting LAFS decoding network would have less than 150,000 states.

Relation to Harpy

The Harpy speech recognition system (Lowerre, 1976; Lowerre & Reddy, 1978) represented a finite set of sentences in terms of a network of words, represented words in terms of phonemic sequences, used a few phonological rules to select allophones and modify the connectivity pattern across word boundaries, and represented each of 98 phonetic segment types in terms of a single spectral template. While LAFS is based on these concepts, it differs from Harpy in several ways. For example, the set of acceptable input sentences is unbounded in LAFS. More importantly, LAFS has augmented abilities to characterize acoustic characteristics of phonetic transitions via diphone and triphone definitions. LAFS incorporates a better motivated spectral representation and distance metric than the Harpy linear prediction spectrum and minimum residual error metric. Finally, complex phonological recodings within words and across word boundaries can be expressed within LAFS, and prosodic cues can be interpreted.

Advantages of LAFS

LAFS has been designed to deal with all eight problems identified in Table 10.1. The first four problems (acoustic–phonetic noninvariance, segmentation, temporal variability, and talker variability) are addressed by using the spectral-sequence diphone definitions and recognition strategy employed by SCRIBER. The fifth problem, how to represent words of the lexicon for optimal search, was solved by converting abstract phonemic forms into spectral sequences. The sixth problem, how to take into account phonological recoding across word boundaries, was solved by applying a set of phonological rules to augment and adjust the connectivity pattern of the lexical network. The seventh problem, how to recover from errorful phonetic decisions, has been nullified by not making intermediate phonetic decisions. Error recovery is still an issue, in that background noises or mispronunciations can corrupt the input. Recovery from these distortions depends on the ability of the beam-search strategy to find the best path through the lexical network, even when no words score very well. The eighth and final problem, interpretation of prosodic cues, has been solved by storing expected prosodic attributes of words in the lexical decoding network and by interpreting deviations from these expectations either (1) as an indication that the lexical hypothesis is not compatible with the input; or (2) as cues to syntactic and semantic structure.

Thus, in theory, a LAFS processor has the capability of representing all of the acoustic–phonetic and phonological knowledge needed to recognize words in spoken sentences. Lexical hypotheses can be generated rapidly and more accurately in a LAFS structure than in any two-step model (phonetic recognition followed by lexical access) containing the same acoustic–phonetic and phonological knowledge. Two-stage models violate that principle of delaying absolute decisions until all of the relevant information is available, and errors thereby introduced cannot always be overcome. LAFS will make fewer errors than SCRIBER for another reason: LAFS does not evaluate all phonologically possible phonetic sequence alternatives—only phonetic sequences that make up English words—and the consideration of fewer alternatives means fewer chances to make an error. The cost of recasting LAFS as a two-stage model would be both a decrement in performance and a need to add strategies for comparing errorful phonetic strings with expected phonetic strings; these strategies are totally unnecessary in a model that does not make phonetic decisions.

IMPLICATIONS FOR MODELS OF SPEECH PERCEPTION

Do the computational strategies of SCRIBER and LAFS have any relation to plausible models of speech perception? I believe that it is worthwhile to seriously entertain this possibility. A perceptual model based on LAFS may turn out to be too simple-minded to stand the test of time, but it can serve as an excellent framework for asking new kinds of experimental questions.

Figure 10.5 presents one such model of speech perception in the form of a block diagram. The model consists primarily of a LAFS bottom-up lexical hypothesis component. Tentatively, it is also postulated that the model also include a SCRIBER phonetic transcription component that is used for adding new words to the LAFS decoding network, and perhaps also for early verification of top-down lexical hypotheses.

Normal Mode of Lexical Access

An input speech waveform (position 1 in Fig. 10.5) is transformed into a sequence of spectra (2) by a spectral analysis component analogous to the peripheral auditory system. The LAFS lexical-access-from-spectra component reads information off the resulting "neural spectrogram" temporary store (a name coined by J. C. R. Licklider to draw an analogy with a

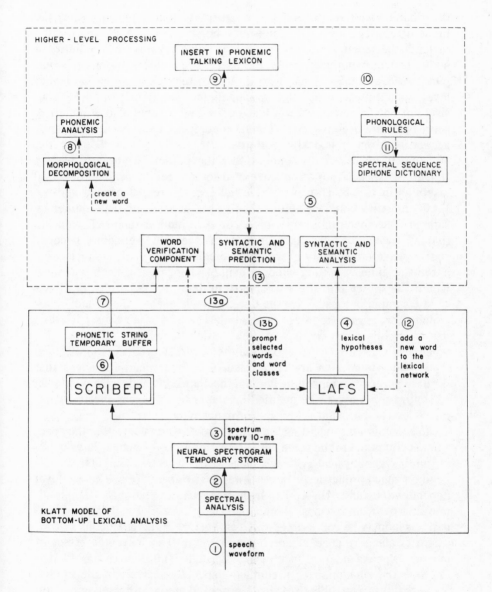

FIG. 10.5.   Block diagram of a proposed perceptual model of lexical access (enclosed in solid lines) and how it interfaces with higher level components (enclosed in dashed lines). The numbers are included to aid the reader in following the explanation of information flow in the text.

broadband spectrogram) in a single left-to-right pass, by processing the input in 10-msec sequential chunks. The box labeled "LAFS" in Fig. 10.5 includes the spectral sequence lexical decoding network and the buffer of active lexical hypotheses generated by the recognition strategy. As output, LAFS produces lexical hypotheses (3) that are analyzed by higher level syntactic and semantic components (4). The output of LAFS consists not only of a sequence of best-scoring words, but also of matching scores that are used by the higher level components to decide whther to accept a bottom-up lexical hypothesis.

There is no reason to suppose that the peripheral auditory system transforms speech into a sequence of discrete spectra sampled every 10 msec, as in LAFS. However, both the spectral representation and the LAFS network could be reformulated as a quasi-continuous model by sampling the spectrum every 1 msec, or even more fequently. It appears that there would be little change in performance if this were done, because speech waveforms do not change that rapidly, and spectra sampled using a 10-msec time weighting window cannot change very much when the window is shifted only 1 msec forward in time.

More important issues are the duration and shape of the window over which short-term spectra are computed. The 25.6 msec Kaiser window that is employed in LAFS has an effective duration of about 10 msec. This value was chosen so as to maximize the accuracy of a spectral estimate while still retaining an ability to track the rapid spectral changes that occur in speech. To model the human, the choice of window (or windows) will ultimately have to be justified on the basis of psychophysical data, physiological data, and LAFS performance data.

A second issue concerning the neural spectrogram is whether the spectrum is computed in the same way no matter what the signal. Physiological and psychophysical evidence suggests that spectral computations depend on signal properties in several ways: The spread of masking is level dependent (Egan & Hake, 1950); the response to stationary signals diminishes over time (Kiang, Watanabe, Thomas, & Clark, 1965); and sudden onsets may be represented differently (Leshowitz & Cudahy, 1975). There is also evidence of nonlinear processes that have the effect of enhancing peaks in vowel spectra (Houtgast, 1974). Research is needed to improve the simulation of preliminary spectral analysis in the model, because it is not possible to evaluate proposed metrics for the comparison of spectral sequences until issues of spectral representation are settled.

Other Cues to Segmental Contrasts.   Up to this point, emphasis has been placed the utility of a spectral sequence in characterizing each possible phonetic transition. I believe that spectral sequences are the raw material on which speech perception strategies are based (not formants or the outputs of various kinds of property detectors), but some qualifying remarks are in order. At least two other independent dimensions are known to play a limited role in the perception of certain phonetic contrasts.

One is the fundamental frequency of vocal fold vibrations (F_0). For example, F_0 is usually lower in voiced obstruents than in a following vowel, while following a voiceless obstruent, F_0 is usually higher at voicing onset than it is later in the vowel (Lea, 1973). This kind of F_0 cue can influence a voiced–voiceless decision (Haggard, Ambler, & Callow, 1970). In addition, a strictly spectral explanation, such as the hypothesis that an F_0 increase changes the amount of low-frequency energy in the spectrum, cannot account for the perceptual influence of the F_0 contour (Massaro & Cohen, 1976).

A second acoustic dimension that can influence a phonetic decision, but which is not subsumed by the proposed spectral-sequence prototype for a phonetic transition, is the degree to which the spectrum is periodic (as in a vowel), aperiodic (as in a voiceless consonant), or contains both low-frequency periodicity and high-frequency aperiodic noise (as in a voiced fricative or voiced /h/). Differentiating between, for example, a voiced /h/ and a vowel on the basis of spectral cues alone can be difficult. Perceptual data on the importance of a "degree-of-periodicity" cue are not available. Nevertheless, a measure of the degree of periodicity in the spectrum above about 1 kHz might be a useful acoustic parameter. It appears that the auditory system would have no difficulty in computing such a periodicity measure at high frequencies (Searle et al., 1979).

The Role of Formant Frequencies.   No mention has been made of formant frequencies and formant motions as possible cues for phonetic perception. In the acoustic theory of speech production, formant frequencies play a central role, characterizing the natural resonant modes of the vocal tract for a given articulatory configuration (Fant, 1960). However, automatic extraction of formant frequency information from the speech waveform is a difficult engineering task. It is still tacitly assumed by many that formant frequencies are psychologically real dimensions employed in perceptual decoding strategies (Carlson, Fant, & Granstrom, 1975; Delattre et al., 1955). We have no perceptual data that would refute this assumption, but there are several reasons to question its plausibility. For example, occasional formant tracking errors should result in dramatic errors in phonetic perception, whereas observed phonetic errors demonstrate a strong tendency to be acoustically similar to the intended vowels and consonants (see, e.g., Miller & Nicely, 1955). As we have argued, absolute decisions at any level below the word (parametric representation, phonetic feature representation, or segmental representation) should be avoided if at all possible for optimal lexical decoding.

Metrics for Spectral Comparisons

Assuming that a reasonable characterization of the information residing in the neural spectrogram can be established, simple metrics for determining the similarity between phonetic segments can be proposed and evaluated against psychophysical data. The objective is to simulate, for example, perceptual distance data (Singh, 1971) and also category boundary shifts as acoustic cues are manipulated. For example, one can simultaneously manipulate several acoustic dimensions of synthetic speech-like stimuli (Massaro & Cohen, 1976; Stevens and Klatt, 1974) and try to account for cue tradeoffs. The simplest static metric might consist of summing the squares of the differences in dB across a set of critical-bandwidth filters. The simplest dynamic metric might consist of summing the static distance over time. If these and other kinds of simple metrics are falsified by perceptual studies, we would have evidence in favor of an intermediate level of analysis, perhaps one involving property detectors.

Several alternative talker-normalization procedures were proposed for LAFS. One involved continual modifications to the spectral templates used in the network, on the basis of experience with the speech of the current talker. In order to retain this knowledge in long-term memory, a set of templates could also be saved for each familiar talker and for prototypical male and female talkers. Other techniques include computational procedures for modifying templates on the basis of vocal tract length estimates, average speech spectrum estimates, and average background noise spectrum estimates. All of these techniques are theoretically well motivated and thus potentially psychologically valid.

Experiments that examine the limits of listener's abilities to normalize for unusual spectral distortions may help to constrain the nature of the normalization process. For example, it seems that listeners are remarkably insensitive to changes in the relative amplitudes of spectral peaks caused by playing speech through fixed filters, but the limits of this ability have not been quantified when formant amplitude relations are disturbed dynamically.

Learning New Words

In the event that the higher level components determine that an unfamiliar word has been spoken (see Fig. 10.5, position 5), a phonetic representation of this speech interval (6), produced by SCRIBER or perhaps by an augmented LAFS model, is recovered from a temporary phonetic buffer (7), submitted to morphological analysis (8), converted to a phonemic representation (9), and stored in the primary lexicon along with syntactic, semantic, and morphological properties. The new word is then incorporated into the spectral-sequence decoding network of LAFS through activation of procedures that include processing the abstract phonemic representation by a set of phonological rules (11), and expanding the resulting alternative phonetic forms into expected spectral sequences (12) that are then integrated with the LAFS network.

Addition of a new form to the network includes attaching it to the appropriate bound morphemes. For example, assuming that the talker has learned the pluralization rule of English in the form of a productive rule, she/he would have to look at the final phoneme of a new word, determine the distinctive feature categories to which it belonged, and define a network path from the end of the new word to the appropriate plural morpheme subnetwork.[1] The advantage of placing common bound morpheme suffixes, like the regular plural, in a special subnetwork is to insure that they be preceded only by the appropriate words.

Verification of Top-Down Lexical Predictions

There exist listening situations where specific words can be anticipated on the basis of situational context and prior dialog. In this case, one need not wait for LAFS to complete its bottom-up analysis, but instead, the higher level components can scan the input as it arrives so as to make an early lexical decision and prepare for the next word.

The way that this is accomplished is not at all clear. LAFS might be modified to work interactively with syntactic and semantic routines (see Newell, Chap. 11, for an extreme version of this alternative), or there may exist a special mechanism for top-down lexical prediction and verification. Both alternatives are shown in Fig. 10.5. A top-down lexical

---

[1] Derivation of phonological and morphological facts about new words appears to require a sophisticated network-building "demon." A computationally equivalent more plausible embodiment of precompiled knowledge might be to realize cross-word phonological recoding as a set of subroutines (rather than activate a demon to modify every word pair in the network that satisfies the preconditions for rule applicability). To learn a phonological rule would be equivalent to creating this subroutine. For example, when evaluating the score for a portion of the network corresponding to a postvocalic /st/ cluster for "list," one would scan the list of phonological rules that apply to postvocalic segments, detect the /st # s/ → [s] rule, and thereby jump to the appropriate nodes of the network. The computational cost of scanning possible rules is offset by the need for a less powerful demon. This is a standard tradeoff between computational speed and storage requirements, that comes up often in computer programming, but we have no idea how the nervous system has solved the tradeoff problem.

hypothesis (13) is sent to a special word verification component (13a) that scans the phonetic transcription produced by SCRIBER to compute a matching score that can be used to disconfirm the presence of an expected word, even if the complete phonetic representation has not been received. This alternative has the advantage of preserving the autonomy of LAFS from syntactic/semantic influences (Forster, 1976). The second (nonexclusive) alternative, path (13b), is discussed below. Both are presented in dashed lines because of my limited interest in pursuing here the implications of this part of the model, and because there are other ways in which top-down lexical predictions could be verified.

Lexical Ambiguity in Noise.   As presently conceived, LAFS does not output a word until a certain amount of additional input is scanned. LAFS must wait long enough to resolve lexical ambiguities introduced when subwords like "see" are contained in words like "cement," or alternative word sequences like "see mental loudmouths" and "cement allowed mountains" cover part of the phonetic input equally well. Unfortuantely, the search space increases rapidly with delayed commitment. There is an exponential growth in alternative hypotheses with increased delay in commitment, so an autonomous LAFS probably cannot be allowed to defer decisions until several additional morphemes worth of input is scanned, but rather must try to make commitments with a minimum delay, no matter what the cost in performance.

Thus it is not at all clear how well an autonomous LAFS model (or any autonomous model of bottom-up lexical hypothesis formation) can perform in the context of a morpheme lexicon as large as in unconstrained English, or in the context of commonly encountered background noises. Speech can be understood in a moderately high noise background. The performance of an autonomous LAFS is likely to degrade significantly in noise (perhaps to a point where its output is essentially useless for moderate amounts of noise).

Given these observations, my present intuitions favor an interactive LAFS network in which particular lexical items or classes of items can be facilitated by a predictive syntactic/semantic module (path 13b of Fig. 10.5). The matching scores for these words are increased in proportion to the confidence of the top-down predictions, analogous to the logogen model of Morton (1970). If message redundancy is high and these constraints can narrow the lexical search, fewer errors will be made in general, and performance should not degrade as rapidly in the presence of noise and ambiguity. The alternatives ways to integrate acoustic and semantic cues to lexical items are discussed in greater detail in Marslen-Wilson and Welsh (1978) and in Morton and Long (1976). However, it is important to emphasize that the present paper is not concerned with this issue, since the principles embodied in LAFS—i.e., lexical access from a network of spectral sequences for words—can be incorporated in either an autonomous module or an augmented interactive data structure.

In conclusion, steps have been taken in this section to transform LAFS into a plausible perceptual model. This has required few modifications to the LAFS network representation of knowledge or to the recognition strategy. However, additional components have been postulated for add-ing new words to LAFS, and it has been argued that a method is needed for applying predictive constraints within LAFS to narrow the search space.

DISCUSSION

Why propose a new model of lexical access? Modeling efforts can serve several purposes: (1) to unify seemingly disparate facts into a cohesive theory; (2) to detect gaps in the knowledge available to support any model; and (3) to define testable alternatives to mechanisms described in previous models. The present model of the early stages of speech perception is far too speculative to qualify as a theoretical synthesis of available data. In the following paragraphs, the model is discussed with reference to the latter two objectives.

Precompiled Knowledge

The most important idea to come out of recent efforts to build computerized speech understanding systems is that one can precompile detailed relations between acoustic and lexical events into an efficient high-performance decoding structure for speech analysis. Precompilation is a fundamental computational technique that is clearly potentially applicable in other domains. For example, during the development of speech production strategies, the motor commands to the articulators to realize a particular phonetic segment must be adjusting as a function of the current state of the articulatory apparatus, i.e., as a function of the previous phonetic segment. These adjustments can be learned as rules in a feature-based system, but they might also be precompiled and stored in the form of a network of motor instructions for all phonologically possible phonetic sequences of English.

Phonological Rules

It is well known that words have different phonetic realizations, depending on the sentence context. Phonological recoding seems to occur so as to simplify the task of the talker. Do these simplifications add a significant burden to the listener by increasing the ambiguity of speech? There is no doubt that ambiguity is generated, because it is not possible to write a unique inverse decoding rule for most phonological rules. How much ambiguity depends on whether the listener must consider all applicable inverse decoding rules at all phonetic positions in an unknown utterance, or whether a psychological equivalent of LAFS rule-precompilation occurs.

It may be possible to determine experimentally whether phonological recodings are learned as generalized rules and precompiled into a decoding structure. For example, "list some" is likely to have a deleted [t], while "list one" may not. Reaction time experiments are needed to see if word strings subjected to phonological recoding and simplification require greater processing time. One would predict an insignificant increase in lexical access time if rule effects have been precompiled into a decoding structure like the LAFS spectral-sequence decoding network. However, if rules are not precompiled and the effects of phonological recoding make lexical access considerably more difficult by introducing many alternative underlying phonetic strings, reaction time is likely to increase. Careful experimentation may reveal which, if any, phonological phonemea are detrimental to speech decoding.

Phonetic Segments

The lexical recognition procedures of LAFS call into question the status of phonetic segments as units to be recognized during the bottom-up lexical hypothesis formation. The psychological reality of phonetic segments has been emphasized in the past on grounds of linguistic parsimony, in order to reduce the size of the knowledge store, in order to minimize the processing burden on the listener, and to serve as an interface between talking and listening. The model that we have proposed demands re-examination of these arguments.

A number of experiments have been devised to determine which units are involved in speech perception. For example, the LAFS model is consistent with reaction time data that indicate quicker reaction times for word processing over phoneme monitoring (Rubin, Turvey, & Van Gelder, 1976; Savin & Bever, 1970). It has been suggested that the listener cannot access the phonemes that were used to recognize a word, but a clear alternative possibility is that word recognition does not usually involve phoneme recognition as an intermediate step. The absence of phonetic identification in LAFS is also consistent with the phonetic restoration effect (Warren, 1970), because all that is available from the output of LAFS is the best scoring word. The LAFS model is also consistent with studies which indicate the perceptual migration of clicks to word boundaries (Ladefoged & Broadbent, 1960), with details of word advantage effects on a voice-onset-time continuum (Ganong, 1978), and with information-theoretic arguments to the effect that listeners should not be required to make too many serial decisions per unit time (Miller, 1962).

Of course, we do not propose to discard the phonetic segment entirely in the perceptual model. Phonetic analysis skills are essential for adding words to the lexicon used for talking and for adding morphemes to LAFS. At an earlier developmental stage, phonetic analysis skills are probably essential for learning to talk (see following text for a discussion of developmental issues).

Phonetic Features

The model is intentionally provocative in its attempt to define a speech analysis system that does not make use of either simple acoustic property detectors or sophisticated phonetic feature detectors in any module (except that features serve as names for sets of phonetic segments that participate in particular phonological rules of higher-level components). Phonetic feature analyzers are included in most current models of speech processing (Blumstein et al., 1977; Jakobson, Fant, & Halle, 1953; Oden & Massaro, 1978; Pisoni, 1976; Pisoni & Sawusch, 1975). Evidence cited in support of feature analyzer concepts includes (1) the structure of perceptual confusion matrices (Miller & Nicely, 1955; Shankweiler & Studdert-Kennedy, 1967); (2) the phenomena of cross-adaptation (Cooper, 1978); (3) data on the perception of competing acoustic cues (Massaro & Cohen, 1976); and (4) categorical perception of consonants. Recent reviews of this literature (Ades, 1978; Ganong, 1979; Parker, 1977; Studdert-Kennedy, in press) suggest that all of the effects noted are consistent with *acoustic* properties of phonetic segments taken as a whole, and that one is not *required* to conclude that segments are represented in terms of distinctive features at early stages of speech perception. There appear to be no data that would rule out either SCRIBER or LAFS as components of perceptual processing.

Along the same line, recent analyses of data of speech production error suggest that segments are manipulated as unanalyzed wholes during the initial stages of speech production (Shattuck-Hufnagel & Klatt, 1979). The authors have shown that exchange errors of the type "*m*it or *h*iss" involve the movement of whole segments rather than the movement of component distinctive features. Is it possible that distinctive features are nothing more than names for sets of phonetic segment types that participate in phonological rules during both speech production and perception? Distinctive feature theory will always serve as a set of unifying principles for the organization of languages and the definition of natural phonetic contrasts for humans to produce and perceive (Chomsky & Halle, 1968;

Jakobson, Fant, & Halle, 1953; Stevens, 1972a), but it really has not been established that this representation is employed by the language user at acoustic and articulatory levels.

Perhaps the promulgation of LAFS as a creditable psychological model will stimulate the design of new types of experiments that can distinguish between feature-based, segment-based, and word-based accounts of acoustic–phonetic processing and lexical access. While I offer below a few suggestions on this point, note the cautionary words of Licklider (1952), who pointed out that certain classes of feature-analysis systems and template-based systems are functionally equivalent, in the restricted mathematical sense that either can compute the same input–output transformation.

The model described here represents speech by sequences of acoustic events. Identification is determined by how well the input matches individual category prototypes. Our approach is thus similar to one advocated by Oden and Massaro (1978), except that our prototypes are defined in terms of sequences of spectral templates, rather than in terms of the outputs of feature detectors. In order to distinguish between a spectral-sequence model and a feature-detector model, two hypotheses must be tested: (1) whether metrics can be developed to predict psychophysical similarity between phones on the basis of general spectral and temporal properties; and (2) whether rate of spectral change is an important *independent* variable in speech perception.

Stevens (1972a) and others have argued that certain properties (such as the distinction between a rapid onset versus a gradual onset, or simultaneous versus sequential acoustic onsets) are natural psychophysical dimensions along which languages divide their phonetic inventories. It will be interesting to see whether the spectral representation and distance metrics proposed here can account for these and other natural phonetic contrasts, or whether special property detectors (or prototypes more complex than a sequence of spectral templates) must be postulated.

Relation to Other Models of Speech Perception

Analysis by Synthesis.   An analysis-by-synthesis strategy was first formulated at the level of phonetic segments and features in order to overcome the noninvariance problem (Halle & Stevens, 1962; Stevens, 1972b; Stevens & Halle, 1964). The theoretical advantages of analysis-by-synthesis concepts applied at the lexical level have been hinted at earlier when identifying problem areas. Since the literature does not contain a description of how such a lexically based model might work, the following paragraphs describe one possible realization.

A block diagram of an analysis-by-synthesis model is shown in Fig.

10.6. The speech waveform corresponding to an unknown utterance arrives at the left in the diagram, and the best scoring word string leaves at the right. It is assumed that peripheral cochlear spectral analysis and central neural processing result in a spectral representation for the incoming speech. This representation is placed in a temporary "echoic" memory store having characteristics that are not unlike those listed earlier in Table 10.3.

Results of backward recognition masking experiments suggest that only about 200–300 msec of speech can be retained in this memory store at any given time (Massaro, 1975). Certain kinds of transient acoustic information contained in the neural spectrogram may be lost unless they are quickly recoded into phonetic form, although prosodic information such as aspects of the fundamental frequency contour, intensity envelope, segmental durations, and vowel quality are presumably recoded and placed in a short-term memory store to permit relative comparisons across greater time spans of the input.

Phonetic feature analyzers read off information from the neural spectrogram. The phonetic feature detectors are thought to place their outputs in a matrix, where the columns represent a division of the time dimension into phonetic segments and the rows represent differnet phonetic features. Each entry in the matrix indicates whether or not a particular segment has a given feature, or is left unspecified. The phonetic feature specification for a segment may be incomplete for two reasons: Either sloppy articulation or environmental noise has led to an ambiguity, or some decisions involving complex context-dependent acoustic–phonetic

ANALYSIS-BY-SYNTHESIS MODEL OF SPEECH PERCEPTION

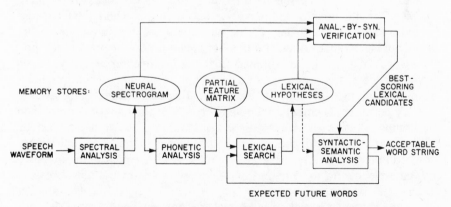

FIG. 10.6.   Simplified block diagram of an analysis-by-synthesis model of speech perception. Memory buffers are represented by ovals, processes by rectangles, and information flow by arrows.

relations are not attempted in the preliminary phonetic transcription. If specified, features are usually thought to be binary, representing the presence or absence of some attribute in the partial feature matrix representation of Fig. 10.6. Alternatively, there may be an advantage in using continuous scales to represent the degree of confidence in each future decision, in order to provide more information for lexical hypothesis formation.

Information drawn from the phonetic feature matrix is used to search through the lexicon for possible sentence-initial words (or morphemes). Lexical candidates expected on the basis of the situation and previous dialog may be "facilitated" so that even if the feature match is not perfect, these highly probable words will be included in the lexical hypothesis memory store.

Due to the errorful and incomplete nature of the preliminary phonetic feature representation of the input speech, a rather large number of lexical candidates are likely to be found—perhaps an unreasonably large number (Klatt & Stevens, 1973). Syntactic/semantic routines would be hardpressed to chose the correct initial word and succeeding words, given this amount of ambiguity. Thus the model of Fig. 10.6 includes an analysis-by-synthesis component that accepts both bottom-up and top-down lexical hypotheses and returns to the acoustic and phonetic data to verify the presence of details to be expected given the whole word (Klatt, 1975). Verification takes into account not only the acoustic manifestations of phonetic expectations, but also perturbations caused by the prosodic cues that are expected given the lexical stress pattern and syntactic cateogry or categories.

Once the best scoring sentence-initial lexical candidate has been accepted by the syntactic/semantic module, the whole process is iterated, starting from the position in the partial feature matrix where the first word ended. (The limited capacity of the partial feature matrix memory store probably means that sentence processing must proceed in near real time.) The words of a candidate sentence must also fit together properly. Given a knowledge of the previous word in a hypothesized sentence fragment, phonological rules contained in the verification component can be used to specify permitted segmental recoding across word boundaries and thus to determine whether the word pair is compatible with the acoustic data. Significant cross-word phonological and coarticulatory interactions are common in sentences. Words rarely appear in a canonical form specified by the lexicon, and some means of dealing with word variability is essential.

As the sentence is elaborated, greater reliance is made on predictions given by syntactic/semantic expectations. These expectations might be used to order the lexical candidates in the lexical hypothesis memory store, or to indicate to the verification component that verification need not be as detailed, or to indicate that not all candidates need evaluation if the expected word scores reasonably well. While the process should rarely reach a dead end (signifying an incorrect analysis), when it does, memory stores are searched to try to backtrack to the next-best alternative partial sentence.

The block diagram of Fig. 10.6 is just a framework or philosophy for speech understanding, not a complete model. None of the components have been fleshed in with very great detail, particularly the partial feature analysis stage and how the lexicon is searched to find lexical candidates bottom up. It is hoped that this paper will stimulate efforts to refine feature-based analysis-by-synthesis theories of speech perception that deal with the eight problem areas of Table 10.2, and that the paper will help to generate critical experiments to determine whether feature-based analysis-by-synthesis theories are more realistic models of human sentence perception than the model of Fig. 10.5.

Analysis by synthesis is a powerful (though expensive) method of weeding out false word candidates. The power derives from the fact that segment durations, intensity contour, and fundamental frequency contour must make sense, given the large number of factors that contribute to the expected patterns. Similarly, all of the acoustic cues that contribute to phonetic distinctions make more sense when a lexical hypothesis is under consideration. However, these advantages can be incorporated directly in a LAFS structure. Precompilation of knowledge is an attractive form of analysis by synthesis; the LAFS strategy permits the evaluation of far more lexical possibilities in parallel than if a single analysis-by-synthesis module were to be activated by one top-down lexical hypothesis at a time.

For familiar words, precompilation of acoustic–phonetic and phonological knowledge is a big winner. However, there probably are situations where precompilation is not the best solution, and other strategies (such as analysis-by-synthesis) may be invoked by the listener. For example, when listening to speakers with foreign accents or unfamiliar dialects, understanding improves when one has deduced a theory of the phonetic recoding, but it may not be desirable to compile this special knowledge into LAFS.

The Motor Theory.   Liberman et al. (1967) and Studdert-Kennedy, Liberman, Harris, and Cooper (1970) have argued that the acoustic encoding of phonetic elements in spoken utterances is so complex that it requires a special decoder. The decoder attempts to determine an articulatory sequence that could have produced the observed acoustic pattern. This motor theory of speech perception postulates an intermediate articulatory representation between the acoustic data and the phonetic interpretation. The need for referral to a motor component in speech perception has been further elaborated by Liberman and Studdert-Kennedy (1978). A model based on this philosophy has never been specified in very great detail. However, no matter what form the model takes, in principle all of the complex acoustic–articulatory–phonetic relations implicit in a motor theory can be precompiled into a network of expected spectra for each phonetic transition. If this were done, the resulting network would hopefully be indistinguishable from SCRIBER. In a sense, SCRIBER can be viewed as a computationally equivalent passive form of an active motor theory.

Is it possible to reformulate SCRIBER or LAFS to include an intermediate articulatory level? An acoustic-to-articulatory transformation can be computed, at least approximately (Atal, 1975), and could form an intermediate step in a modified LAFS model of lexical access in which states become articulatory configurations. Such a system would have no computational advantage over the present LAFS, since both can compute the same decoding transformation with about the same computational cost, but an articulatory LAFS might be more suitable for the interface between speech perception and speech production. A lexical-access-from-articulatory-sequences model seems worthy of investigation for this reason, but it does not appear that a lexical decoding network based on articulation could be used simultaneously for speech production. The representation is not sufficiently abstract—all of the coarticulatory and phonological details that are a consequence of low-level articulatory dynamics are already represented in the decoding network, whereas the lexicon used for talking is almost certainly phonemic (Fromkin, 1971; Shattuck-Hufnagel & Klatt, 1979).

The Logogen.   Morton (1970) has proposed a model of lexical access in which each word in the lexicon has an associated "logogen" that specifies defining characteristics of the word along various acoustic and semantic dimensions. If enough of these features are satisfied during sentence processing, the word is recognized. A logogen model can account for many kinds of experimentally determined interactions between acoustic and semantic cues to lexical identity (Morton & Long, 1976), by postulating a threshold mechanism whereby top-down expectations can push a word over threshold before all acoustic cues are seen. There is no description of how acoustic cues are processed in a logogen model. The model is clearly compatible with the general acoustic-to-lexical analysis framework outlined here. In fact, LAFS could be considered as a more specific characterization of how the bottom-up part of a logogen model would function.

A logogen model has some difficulty in accounting for details of word reaction time data (Marslen-Wilson & Welsh, 1978). However, the autonomous LAFS model is similarly deficient in that there must be a delay before identifying each word (because one has to wait until at least the next word is over to be confident of selecting the best path in the beam search), and this is also inconsistent with reaction time data.

Context-Sensitive Allophones. Wickelgren (1969, 1976) proposed a theory of speech perception in which a large set of context-dependent allophones are used to derive a phonetic representation for an unknown utterance. For each phoneme X, a set of context-dependent allophones aXb were defined for all possible preceding phonemes, a, and all possible following phonemes, b. While such an approach solves the noninvariance problem, it does not address most of the other problems listed in Table 10.1. The solution to the noninvariance problem proposed by Wickelgren is slightly more powerful than the diphone approach (and considerably more costly in terms of number of basic elements to be recognized). It suggests a way in which SCRIBER and LAFS can be improved in those cases where diphones do not capture all of the context dependency of speech. If, for example, the acoustic characteristics of /ɪ/ in a word like "will" cannot be predicted from diphones obtained from "*wi*th" and "h*ill*" because the /w/ and /l/ collectively velarize the /ɪ/ to a greater extent, then a special context-dependnet allophone, or "triphone," can be defined in terms of a sequence of spectral templates and placed in the network in place of the two concatenated diphones.

Sequential Word Recognition. Cole and Jakimik (Chap. 6) have used a mispronunciation detection task to show that sentence perception generally involves the direct left-to-right decoding of words, one after the other. The advantage of such a strategy is that the end of one word defines the beginning of the next word in time, thus reducing the potential ambiguity of looking for words starting at other phonetic positions in the sentence. LAFS incorporates this advantage of direct left-to-right processing of a sentence, and it adds the further advantage of being able to deal with phonological recoding across word boundaries.

The Hearsay II Blackborad. Hearsay II is one of several computer-based speech understanding systems developed during the ARPA speech understanding project (for a review, see Klatt, 1977). The Hearsay II blackboard model of speech perception is described by Erman (1979). In this model, or framework for speech understanding, a set of knowledge sources work asynchronously toward the decoding of a sentence by taking their input from a common blackboard and placing the results of their analyses back on the blackboard. LAFS could function as a component of such a blackboard model. Alternatively, the theories being considered in parallel by LAFS could be placed on the blackboard for examination by other modules, even before LAFS has made a final decision. The latter possibility forms the basis for a number of attractive alternative models of speech perception, but they all will have to face such inherent problem as how to schedule activity among the modules that interact with the blackboard, and how to deal with the halting problem (Newell, Chap. 11).

Is Speech Special?

If our model is correct, one need not postulate the existence of innate feature detectors sensitive only to the phonetic contrasts of spoken language (Eimas & Miller, 1978). Instead, certain natural discriminations (so natural as to be made by infants) would be the consequence of properties of the spectral sequence representation of auditory signals.

However, speech could be special in several other respects. For example, speech stimuli may be distinguished from nonspeech stimuli because they are the only signals that receive high enough matching scores in the outputs of LAFS and SCRIBER to be processed as language. Also, the steps involved in constructing and augmenting a LAFS decoding network are complex. Is LAFS representative of general cognitive strategies (in which precompiled knowledge networks play a prominent role), or does speech acquisition require the postulation of special innate structures for the development of LAFS and supporting higher level components?

Developmental Issues

The earliest representation of words by an infant is probably in the form of a crude direct encoding of what appears on the (hard-wired?) neural spectrogram. Perhaps only a few of the most prominent spectral details within a word are remembered at first. The actual memory representation for words may thus be quite similar to a LAFS sequence-of-spectra representation right from the beginning. On the basis of further experience, spectral details are filled in, but only when needed to differentiate between new words.

In order to learn to talk, a phonemic analysis of the input speech must then be discovered by relating the processes of listening (acoustic events) and talking (articulatory commands). The creation of a phonemic talking lexicon is no doubt facilitated by the presence of partial acoustic–phonetic invariance. It seems that many invariant (or nearly invariant) cues must be present if the child is to discover the phonemic structure of his/her native language. However, according to the views expressed here, the acquisition of phonemic analysis capabilities and of a phonemic talking lexicon does not lead to any fundamental changes in bottom-up lexical access of familiar words via LAFS.

Relations between the two representations used for talking and listening are then internalized by associating spectral sequences with each phoneme or phoneme pair so as to create the diphone dictionary required for top-down augmentations of LAFS. The final steps needed to acquire an adult-like LAFS decoding network are the acquisition of morphological decomposition skills and the discovery of how word sequences are modified by phonological rules. The perceptual model thus acknowledges the psychological reality of linguistic units and of rules that never appear explicitly in LAFS. Just how sophisticated these processes are, however, is a subject for experimentation (Ohala, 1974).

Elaboration of a concrete model of speech acquisition along these lines would be an important contribution to the general theory of speech perception. Hopefully, many testable alternatives can be isolated by comparing this account of language development with other current theories.

The Validation Issue.   The presence of both LAFS and SCRIBER in the proposed perceptual model makes it much more difficult to determine the psychological validity of either. Depending on the perceptual task (nonsense-syllable identification, repeated listening to the same pair of words, or listening to unpredictable sentences made up of familiar words), the listener may engage either or both mechanisms. Similarly, analysis by synthesis or another form of top-down verification employing generative rules that are computed on the fly may be invoked when listening to some speakers. Nevertheless, I believe that the efficient decoding of normal conversational speech depends critically on mechanisms found in LAFS, whether or not these are the only mechanisms used in speech perception.

Conclusions

The perceptual model shown in the bottom half of Fig. 10.5 has been proposed and compared with a number of alternative models. I have established the theoretical advantages of a spectrally based decoding network approach to speech analysis, and have suggested several kinds of experiments that might settle the issues that have been raised concerning its perceptual reality. The essential features of the model are:

1. precompilation of phonological rules that describe phonetic recoding of words in sentences, so as to avoid having to consider application of inverse rules indiscriminately;
2. no calculation of a phonetic level of representation during lexical search, because calculation of such an intermediate representation

must introduce errors (due in part to the greater number of alternatives in a phonetic transcription and in part to an inability to interpret durational and FO cues to segmental contrasts) thus violating the principle of delayed commitment;

3. representation of acoustic–phonetic knowledge in terms of sequences of spectra for each possible phonetic transition, rather than postulating the existence of invariant attributes for phones or the existence of low-level property detectors and phonetic feature detectors until such time as simpler assumptions are proven unworkable.

This model, summarized in Fig. 9.5, is offered as the most complete, most simply structured current theory of the initial stages of acoustic-phonetic analysis and lexical search.

ACKNOWLEDGMENT

Preparation of this manuscript was supported by an NIH grant. My sincere thanks go to R. Cole, A. Liberman, M. Liberman, D. Pisoni, R. Reddy, B. Repp, and K. Stevens for numerous suggestions for improvements to an earlier draft. I alone take responsibility for the views expressed here.

REFERENCES

Ades, A. E. Theoretical notes: Vowels, consonants, speech and non-speech. *Psychological Review*, 1978, *84*, 524–530.

Allen, J. Speech synthesis from unrestricted text. In J. L. Flanagan & L. R. Rabiner (Eds.), *Speech synthesis*. Stroudsberg, Penn.: Dowden, Hutchinson and Ross, 1973.

Atal, B. S. Toward determining articulatory positions from the speech signal. In G. Fant (Ed.), *Speech communication* (Vol. 1). Stockholm: Almgrist and Wiksell, 1975.

Blumstein, S. E., Stevens, K. N., & Nigro, G. N. Property detectors for bursts and transitions in speech perception. *Journal of the Acoustical Society of America*, 1977, *61*, 1301–1313.

Carlson, R., Fant, G., & Granstrom, B. Two-formant models, pitch and vowel perception. In G. Fant & M. A. A. Tatham (Eds.), *Auditor' an ilysis and perception of speech*. New York: Academic Press, 1975.

Chomsky, N., & Halle, M. *The sound pattern of English*. New York: Harper & Row, 1968.

Cole, R. A., & Scott, B. Toward a theory of speech perception. *Psychological Review*, 1974, *81*, 348–374.

Cohen, P. S., & Mercer, R. L. The phonological component of an automatic speech recognition system. In D. R. Reddy, (Ed.), *Speech recognition: Invited papers presented at the 1974 IEEE symposium*. New York: Academic Press, 1975.

Cooper, W. E. *Speech perception and production: Selected studies on adaptation*. Cambridge, England: Cambridge University Press, 1978.

Delattre, P. C., Liberman, A. M., & Cooper, F. S. Acoustic loci and transitional cues for consonants. *Journal of the Acoustical Society of America*, 1955, *27*, 769–773.

Egan, J. P., & Hake, H. W. On the masking pattern of simple auditory stimulus. *Journal of the Acoustical Society of America,* 1950, *22,* 622–630.

Eimas, P. D., & Miller, J. L. Effects of selective adaptation on the perception of speech and visual patterns: Evidence for feature detectors. In R. D. Walk & H. L. Pick (Eds.), *Perception and experience.* New York: Plenum Press, 1978.

Erman, L. The Hearsay-II speech understanding system. In W. A. Lea (Ed.), *Trends in speech recognition.* Englewood Cliffs, N.J.: Prentice-Hall, 1979.

Fant, G. *Acoustic theory of speech production.* The Hague: Mouton, 1960.

Fant, G. *Speech sounds and features,* Cambridge, Mass.: MIT Press, 1974.

Flanagan, J. L. Estimates of the maximum precision necessary in quantizing certain dimensions of vowel sounds. *Journal of the Acoustical Society of America,* 1957, *29,* 533–534.

Forster, K. I. Accessing the mental lexicon. In R. J. Wales & E. C. T. Walker (Eds.), *New approaches to language mechanisms.* Amsterdam: North-Holland, 1976.

French, N. R., & Steinberg, J. C. Factors governing the intelligibility of speech sounds. *Journal of the Acoustical Society of America,* 1947, *19,* 90–119.

Fromkin, V. The non-anomalous nature of anomalous utterances. *Language,* 1971, *47,* 27–52.

Fujimura, O., & Lovins, J. B. Syllables as concatenative phonetic units. In A. Bell & J. B. Hooper (Eds.), *Syllables and segments,* 1978.

Ganong, F. Dicholic feature recombination errors and distinctive features. Unpublished manuscript, 1979.

Ganong, F. A word advantage in phoneme boundary experiments. *Journal of the Acoustical Society of America,* 1978, *63,* S20 (A).

Gay, T. Articulatory movements in VCV sequences. *Journal of the Acoustical Society of America,* 1977, *62,* 183–193.

Haggard, M., Ambler, S., & Callow, M. Pitch as a voicing cue. *Journal of the Acoustical Society of America,* 1970, *47,* 613–617.

Halle, M., & Stevens, K. N. Speech recognition: A model and a program for research. *IRE Transactions and Information Theory,* 1962, *IT-8,* 155–159.

Houtgast, T. Auditory analysis of vowel-like sounds. *Acoustica,* 1974, *31,* 320–324.

Jakobson, R., Fant, G., & Halle, M. *Preliminaries to speech analysis.* Cambridge, Mass.: MIT Press, 1953.

Kiang, N., Watanabe, T., Thomas, E., & Clark, L. *Discharge patterns of single fibers in the cat's auditory nerve.* Cambridge, Mass.: MIT Press, 1965.

Klatt, D. H. Word verification in a speech understanding system. In R. Reddy (Ed.), *Speech recognition.* New York: Academic Press, 1975.

Klatt, D. H. A digital filter bank for spectral matching. In C. Teacher (Ed.), *Conference Record of the 1976 IEEE International Conference on Acoustics Speech and Signal Processing.* IEEE catalog No. 76Ch1067-8 ASSP: 1976. (a)

Klatt, D. H. Linguistic uses of segmental duration in English: Acoustic and perceptual evidence. *Journal of the Acoustical Society of America,* 1976, *59,* 1208–1221. (b)

Klatt, D. H. Review of the ARPA speech understanding project. *Journal of the Acoustical Society of America,* 1977, *62,* 1345–1366.

Klatt, D. H. SCRIBER and LAFS: Two new approaches to speech analysis. In W. A. Lea (Ed.), *Trends in speech recognition.* Englewood Cliffs, N.J.: Prentice-Hall, 1978. (a)

Klatt, D. H. Analysis and synthesis of consonant–vowel syllables in English. *Journal of the Acoustical Society of America,* 1978, *64,* Supplement 1, S43 (A). (b)

Klatt, D. H. Synthesis by rule of segmental durations in English sentences. In B. Lindblom & S. Ohman (Eds.), *Frontiers of speech communication research.* New York: Academic Press, 1979.

Klatt, D. H., & Cooper, W. E. Perception of segment duration in sentence contexts. In A.

Cohen & S. G. Nooteboom (Eds.), *Structure and process in speech perception*. New York: Springer-Verlag, 1975.

Klatt, D. H., & Stevens, K. N. On the automatic recognition of continuous speech: Implications of a spectrogram-reading experiment. *IEEE Transactions on Audio and Electroacoustics*, 1973, *AU-21*, 210–217.

Klovstad, J. W. *Computer-automated speech perception system*. Unpublished doctoral dissertation, Massachusetts Institute of Technology, 1979.

Ladefoged, P., & Broadbent, D. E. Perception of sequence in auditory events. *Quarterly Journal of Experimental Psychology*, 1960, *13*, 162–170.

Lea, W. A. Segmental and suprasegmental influences on fundamental frequency contours. In L. Hyman (Ed.), *Consonant types and tone*. University of Southern California Occasional Papers in Linguisics, 1973, No. 1.

Lehiste, I. *Suprasegmentals*. Cambridge, Mass.: MIT Press, 1970.

Lehiste, I., & Shockey, L. On the perception of coarticulation effects on English VCV syllables. *Journal of Speech and Hearing Reserach*, 1972, *15*, 500–506.

Leshowitz, B., & Cudahy, E. Masking patterns of continuous and gated sinusoids. *Journal of the Acoustical Society of America*, 1975, *58*, 235–242.

Liberman, A. M., Cooper, F. S., Shankweiler, D. S., & Studdert-Kennedy, M. Perception of the speech code. *Psychological Review*, 1967, *74*, 431–461.

Liberman, A. M., Delattre, P., Gerstman, L., & Cooper, F. S. Tempo of frequency change as a cue for distinguishing classes of speech sounds. *Journal of Experimental Psychology*, 1956, *52*, 127–137.

Liberman, A. M., & Studdert-Kennedy, M. Phonetic perception. In R. Held, H. Leibowitz, & H.-L. Teuber (Eds.), *Handbook of sensory physiology* (Vol. VIII). Heidelberg: Springer-Verlag, 1978.

Licklider, J. C. R. On the process of speech perception. *Journal of the Acoustical Society of America*, 1952, *24*, 590–594.

Lieberman, P. *Intonation, perception and language*. Cambridge, Mass.: MIT Press, 1967.

Lindblom, B. Phonetic aspects of linguistic explanation. *Studia Linguistica*, in press.

Lowerre, B. T. *The HARPY speech recognition system*. Unpublished doctoral dissertation, Carnegie-Mellon University, 1976.

Lowerre, B. T. Dynamic speaker adaptation in the HARPY speech recognition system. In H. F. Silverman (Chairman), *Conference Record of the 1977 IEEE International on Acoustics, Speech and Signal Processing*. IEEE catalog No. 77CH1197-3 ASSP: 1977, 788–790.

Lowerre, B. T., & Reddy, D. R. The Harpy speech understanding system. In W. A. Lea (Ed.), *Trends in speech recognition*. Englewood Cliffs, N.J.: Prentice-Hall, 1978.

Marslen-Wilson, W. P., & Welsh, A. Processing interactions and lexical analysis during word recognition in continuous speech. *Cognitive Psychology*, 1978, *100*, 29–63.

Massaro, D. M. Backward recognition masking. *Journal of the Acoustical Society of America*, 1975, *58*, 1059–1065.

Massaro, D. M., & Cohen, M. M. The contribution of fundamental frequency and voice onset time to the /zi/–/si/ distinction. *Journal of the Acoustical Society of America*, 1976, *60*, 704–707.

Medress, M. *Computer recognition of single-syllable English words*. Unpublished doctoral dissertation, Massachusetts Institute of Technology, 1969.

Miller, G. A. Decision units in the perception of speech. *IRE Transactions and Information Theory*, 1962, *IT-8*, 81–83.

Miller, G. A., & Nicely, P. E. Analysis of perceptual confusions among some English consonants. *Journal of the Acoustical Society of America*, 1955, *27*, 338–353.

Morton, J. A functional model for memory. In D. A. Norman (Ed.), *Models of human memory*. New York: Academic Press, 1970.

Morton, J., & Long, J. Effect of word transition probability on phoneme identification. *Journal of Verbal Learning and Verbal Behavior,* 1976, *15,* 43–51.

Oden, G. C., & Massaro, D. W. Integration of featural information in speech perception. *Psychological Review,* 1978, *85,* 172–191.

Ohala, J. J. Experimental historical phonology. In J. M. Anderson & C. Jones (Eds.), *Historical linguistics II: Theory and description in phonology.* Amsterdam: North Holland, 1974.

Oshika, B., Zue, V. W., Weeks, R. V., Neu, H., & Aurbach, J. The role of phonological rules in speech understanding research. *IEEE Transactions, Acoustics, Speech and Signal Processing,* 1975, *ASSP-23,* 104–112.

Parker, F. Distinctive features and acoustic cues. *Journal of the Acoustical Society of America,* 1977, *62,* 1051–1054.

Peterson, G. E., Wang, W., & Sivertsen, E. Segmentation techniques for speech synthesis. *Journal of the Acoustical Society of America,* 1958, *30,* 739–742.

Pisoni, D. B. Speech perception. In W. K. Estes (Ed.), *Handbook of learning and cognitive processes.* Hillsdale, N.J.: Lawrence Erlbaum Associates, 1976.

Pisoni, D. B., & Sawusch, J. R. Some stages of processing in speech perception. In A. Cohen & S. G. Nootebaum (Eds.), *Structure and process in speech perception.* New York: Springer-Verlag, 1975.

Plomp, R., & Mimpen, A. M. The ear as a frequency analyzer II. *Journal of the Acoustical Society of America,* 1968, *43,* 764–768.

Port, R. F. Influence of tempo on stop closure duration as a cue for voicing and place. *Journal of Phonetics,* 1979, *7,* 45–56.

Rubin, P., Turvey, M., & van Gelder, P. Initial phonemes are detected faster in spoken words than in spoken non-words. *Perception and Psychophysics,* 1976, *19,* 394–398.

Savin, H. B., & Bever, T. G. The nonperceptual reality of the phoneme. *Journal of Verbal Learning and Verbal Behavior,* 1970, *9,* 295–302.

Searle, C., Jacobson, J. Z., & Rayment, S. G. Stop consonant discrimination based on human audition. *Journal of the Acoustical Society of America,* 1979, *65,* 799–809.

Shankweiler, D. P., & Studdert-Kennedy, M. Identification of consonants and vowels presented to left and right ears. *Journal of Experimental Psychology,* 1967, *19,* 59–63.

Sharf, B. Critical bands. In J. V. Tabias (Ed.), *Foundations of modern auditory theory* (Vol. 1). New York: Academic Press, 1970.

Shattuck-Hufnagel, S. R., & Klatt, D. H. The limited use of distinctive features and markedness in speech production: Evidence from speech error data. *Journal of Verbal Learning and Verbal Behavior,* 1979, *18,* 41–56.

Singh, S. Perceptual similarities and minimal phonetic differences. *Journal of Speech and Hearing Research,* 1971, *14,* 113–124.

Stevens, K. N. The quantal nature of speech: Evidence from articulatory–acoustic data. In E. E. David & P. B. Denes (Eds.), *Human communication: A unified view.* New York: McGraw Hill, 1972. (a)

Stevens, K. N. Segments, features, and analysis by synthesis. In J. F. Cavanaugh & I. G. Mattingly (Eds.), *Language by eye and by ear.* Cambridge, Mass.: MIT Press, 1972. (b)

Stevens, K. N. Sources of inter- and intra-speaker variability in the acoustic properties of speech sounds. In A. Rigault & R. Charbonneau (Eds.), *Proceedings of the Seventh International Congress of Phonetic Sciences.* Mouton: The Hague, 1972. (c)

Stevens, K. N. On the potential role of property detectors in the perception of consonants. In G. Fant & M. A. A. Tathem (Eds.), *Auditory analysis and the perception of speech.* New York: Academic Press, 1975.

Stevens, K. N., & Halle, M. Remarks on analysis by synthesis and distinctive features. In W. Wathen-Dunn (Ed.), *Proceedings of the AFCRL Symposium on Models for the Perception of Speech and Visual Form.* Cambridge, Mass.: MIT Press, 1964.

Stevens, K. N., & Klatt, D. H. Role of formant transitions in the voiced–voiceless distinction for stops. *Journal of the Acoustical Society of America*, 1974, *55*, 653–658.

Studdert-Kennedy, M. Speech perception. In N. J. Lass (Ed.), *Contemporary issues in experimental phonetics*. New York: Academic Press, 1976.

Studdert-Kennedy, M. Speech perception. In *Language and Speech*. In press.

Studdert-Kennedy, M., Liberman, A. M., Harris, K. S., & Cooper, F. S. Motor theory of speech perception: A reply to Lane's critical review. *Psychological Review*, 1970, *77*, 234–249.

Wakita, H., & Kasuya, H. A study of vowel normalization and identification in connected speech. In M. F. Silverman (Chairman), *Conference Record of the 1977 International Conference on Acoustics, Speech and Signal Processing*, IEEE Catalog No. 77CH1197-3 ASSP, 1977, 417–421.

Warren, R. M. Perceptual restoration of missing speech sounds. *Science*, 1970, *167*, 392–393.

Wickelgren, W. A. Context-sensitive coding, associative memory and serial order in (speech) behavior, *Psychological Review*, 1969, *76*, 1–15.

Wickelgren, W. A. Phonetic coding and serial order. In *Handbook of perception* (Vol. VII). New York: Academic Press, 1976.

Weeks, R. V. Predictive syllable mapping in a continuous speech understanding system. In L. D. Erman (Ed.), *Contributed Papers of the IEEE Symposium on Speech Recognition*. IEEE Catalog No. 74CH0878-9 AE, 1974.

Wolf, J. J., & Woods, W. A. The HWIM speech understanding system. In W. A. Lea (Ed.), *Trends in speech recognition*. Englewood Cliffs, N.J.: Prentice-Hall, 1978.

Woods, W. A., & Zue, V. W. Dictionary expansion via phonological rules for a speech understanding system. In C. Teacher (Chairman), *Conference Record of the 1976 IEEE International Conference on Acoustics, Speech and Signal Processing*. IEEE Catalog No. 76CH1067-8 ASSP, 1976.

Zue, V. W. Acoustic characteristics of stop consonants: A controlled study. *Lincoln Laboratory Technical Report No. 523*, Cambridge, Mass., 1976.

Zue, V. W., & Schwartz, R. Acoustic processing and phonetic analysis. In W. A. Lea (Ed.), *trends in speech recognition*. Englewood Cliffs, N.J.: Prentice-Hall, 1978.

Zwicker, E., Terhardt, E., & Paulus, E. Automatic speech recognition using psychoacoustic models. *Journal of the Acoustical Society of America*, 1979, *65*, 487–498.

11 Harpy, Production Systems, and Human Cognition

Allen Newell
Carnegie-Mellon University

1. INTRODUCTION

The story is by now familiar: In 1971, following upon the report of a study group (Newell, Barnett, Forgie, Green, Klatt, Licklider, Munson, Reddy, & Woods, 1971), an intensive effort was launched by the Advanced Research Projects Agency of the Department of Defense (ARPA) to advance the art of speech recognition by computers to handle connected speech. Five years of effort by a small community of organizations led in late 1976 to a demonstration of several speech understanding systems with substantial capabilities (Medress & committee, 1976).

These systems, for example, Hearsay-II at CMU (Erman & Lesser, 1977) and HWIM (Hear What I Mean) at (BBN) (Woods, Bates, Brown, Bruce, Cook, Klovstad, Makhoul, Nash-Webber, Schwartz, Wolf, & Zue, 1976) were cast mostly within the mainstream of artificial intelligence (AI) systems. They followed directly on the initial image of how to formulate the recognition of speech using multiple sources of knowledge as a problem of heuristic search, though they explored different issues within that conceptual frame. One system, Harpy at CMU (Lowerre, 1976; CMU Speech Group, 1977), proved to be the dark horse. Conceived originally by Jim Baker (1975) as a Markov process, the original system was christened Dragon—to indicate that it was an entirely different kind of beast from the AI systems being considered in the rest of the speech effort. Harpy turned in a superior performance, significantly better than either that of Hearsay-II or HWIM. Harpy was the only one of the systems to meet a set of prominent performance specifications laid down in the original study group report (though Hearsay-II came within shooting distance). Harpy is generally viewed as an engineering-oriented solution to the speech understanding task, as opposed to an artificial-intelligence-oriented solution. (This is not necessarily the view held by its designers and friends around CMU.) In any event, Harpy appears the likely source of a generation of applied limited speech understanding systems for connected speech.

Harpy provides a fine opportunity to play out the scientific tactic of *sufficiency analysis*. Here we have a system, bred out of technology, which accomplishes an important human intellectual function. Harpy, as it exists, has limitations, and its extension is an open question technically. But it has so advanced the art of recognition in an area deemed exceedingly difficult for many years, that the mechanisms it embodies rate being taken seriously.

Sufficiency analysis is based on the following proposition:

> Important confirming evidence for a psychological theory is whether a system designed according to the theory is sufficient to perform the intellectual functions the theory purports to explain, providing that the mechanisms involved are reasonable according to general knowledge of human capabilities.

Psychology generally ignored questions of sufficiency prior to the development of artificial intelligence, which produced systems that could perform various intellectual tasks. The usual form of sufficiency analysis is to start with an AI system that does perform some task, and analyze whether its mechanisms are reasonable in the light of general psychological knowledge. For example, modern chess playing programs (Slate & Atkin, 1977) examine several thousand positions per second, which is orders of magnitude beyond what humans can do; thus, although they are sufficient for good chess play, they are not acceptable as a theory of human play. Sufficiency is only one type of evidence, but one of substantial power when dealing with complex processes of unknown character.

This paper, then, is an attempt to take Harpy seriously as a model of human speech perception. As a psychological model, Harpy comes unrecommended by its developmental history. Many may prefer to trust the inference from motive: If Harpy was developed without regard to its psychological relevance, indeed with exclusively engineering concerns, then it must have little to say about psychology. My trust is in the opposite inference: that the structure of the task under realistic constraints dictates many features of the mechanisms that cope with it. In any event, the game here is to take Harpy seriously and see where we arrive. No elaborate defense of the methodology of sufficiency analysis is required.

We are not without existing basic models for speech perception, at least in general outline (Studdert-Kennedy, 1976). The two most prominent are the Motor Theory developed by the scientists at the Haskins Laboratory (Liberman, Cooper, Shankweiler, & Studdert-Kennedy, 1967) and the scheme of Analysis by Synthesis, initially put forth by Halle and Stevens (1962). Both models build on the indubitable fact that the character of the speech signal is shaped strongly by the system that produces it. Other schemes are not so strongly influenced by motor concerns, such as the logogen model of Morton (Morton & Broadbent, 1967) and the proposals of Cole and Jakimik (Chap. 6). The theory to be put forth here is not motivated by any of these, being generated directly from Harpy. What other theories it resembles ultimately remains to be seen; it is not specifically designed to be different.

Though interested in Harpy from its inception, not until I read a paper by Dennis Klatt (1977) reviewing the ARPA Speech Understanding Program where he listed some psychological conjectures based on Harpy, did I realize how important it was to try a sufficiency analysis. Klatt (Chap. 10) has far more credentials than I to attempt the task of this paper. In any event, I agreed to try my hand at it, believing it to be an important exploration, whether or not the resulting psychological theory looks plausible.

I have an abiding interest in a class of system architectures called production systems, both from a psychological viewpoint (Newell, 1973; Newell & Simon, 1972) and an AI viewpoint (Newell, 1977; Rychener & Newell, 1978). It had always been an idea to look at Harpy from a production system viewpoint, as one approach to sufficiency analysis. Indeed, it also seemed interesting to look at the Hearsay-II organization in terms of production systems (though not with any psychological concerns), and a thesis has just recently been completed along such lines (McCracken, 1978). But not until some recent progress this fall in developing a new production system architecture for human cognition did this connection become strong enough to demand explication of Harpy in production system terms. What started out to be a general sufficiency analysis has become the more narrow enterprise of mapping Harpy into a specific production system architecture. The aim and the caveats are still the same, but a specific vehicle has been chosen.

What is gained by mapping Harpy into a production system architecture rather than analyzing it directly? There is a good deal of evidence that production systems are a good system organization within which to represent human cognition (Anderson, 1976; Hunt & Poltrock, 1974; Newell & Simon, 1972). Beyond this, the new architecture is specifically shaped to be a plausible organization that reflects human behavior qualitatively in a range of short-term tasks that have been much studied in psychological literature (e..g, the Sternberg, Brown-Peterson, and memory span paradigms). Thus, to map Harpy into this architecture is to demonstrate that Harpy is a plausible model of speech perception. This (desired) result does not quite follow immediately. The resulting system, call it PS. Harpy, needs to be checked on a number of grounds, e.g., can full speech be recognized in realistic times. But the mapping will go a long way towards facilitating such an analysis, since the interpretation of the architecture in human cognitive terms is quite definite.

One criticism should be immediately forestalled. Production system architectures are universal computational machines. There is no doubt at all that Harpy can be programmed as a production system. Thus, what counts is the nature of the mapping, especially whether the resulting processing is plausible given the human limits we already know about.

Given the above remarks, the organization of this chapter is straightforward. Section 2 introduces the specific production system architecture that purports to be the architecture of the human mind. Section 3 summarizes the essentials of Harpy and lays out the questions a sufficiency analysis should address. Section 4 gives a preliminary analysis of Harpy as a production system. This will raise a major issue, the representation of intensity, which will be the topic of Section 5. Section 6 then presents a refined analysis, taking into account the results of Section 5. To this point, then, we have finally produced a PS.Harpy that satisfies (some) sufficiency issues. Section 7 explores briefly how PS.Harpy deals with a few empirical phenomena about speech perception. Finally, Section 8 concludes with an assessment of what has been accomplished.

2.   THE PRODUCTION SYSTEM ARCHITECTURE

In preparation for mapping Harpy into a psychological theory of speech perception, I lay out a proposed structure of the architecture within which human cognition occurs. This architecture is an instance of a class of system organizations, called production systems, which have received a good deal of attention in artificial intelligence (Waterman & Hayes-Roth, 1978) and cognitive psychology (as already noted). In general, production systems need no defense here, though they are by no means generally accepted. The specific version that I will use was only recently developed. In its own way, it is as novel as the material on Harpy. Unfortunately, we will have to present it here as a given, limiting description to its main outlines and not providing justification for details of its structure. An extended paper on this organization, which is called HPSA77 (for Human Production System Architecture, version 1977), is currently in process (Newell, in preparation).

Basic Production System Architecture

Consider a system with the gross characteristics shown in Fig. 11.1. There is a large memory of productions (PM, for *production memory*). Each *production (P)* consists of a set of *conditions* (C_i) and a set of *actions* (A_j). The conditions of each production look into a *working memory* (WM) of data *elements* (E_k). The data elements are *symbolic structures* of some sort. Each condition is a template of some kind that can ask whether it matches a given data element. A production is satisfied, at a given moment, if all of its conditions find matching elements in the WM. Such a set of matching elements constitutes a possible *instantiation* of the production.

At a given moment, some set of productions is satisfied. In fact, a production may be satisfied in many ways, corresponding to distinct instantiations. The total set of instantiations for all productions is called the *conflict set*. From it, an instantiation is selected and its actions executed, i.e., the selected production is fired. The actions (the A_j) of a production (properly instantiated by whatever variables are bound by the matching) make a sequence of modifications to WM, adding, deleting and modifying elements.

The behavior of a production system is completely specified by this so called *recognition–act cycle:*

1. Match all the productions of the production memory against the working memory to determine the conflict set.
2. Select the successful production by a process of conflict resolution.
3. Execute the actions of the resulting production.

The cycle is repeated indefinitely. All of the conditional behavior of this system is expressed in this cycle; the actions themselves are unconditional operations that affect WM.

The total system shown in Fig. 11.1 consists of the central cognitive structure (PM and WM) plus the structures to interact with the external world. Data from the external world flows into the WM, and actions that affect the external world are evoked by elements that are placed in WM. Also required, but not directly represented in Fig. 11.1, are capabilities for modifying production memory. In current versions this is realized by actions that create productions out of WM elements.

Conflict resolution is governed by several types of rules. Many types of rules exist (McDermott & Forgy, 1978), but three are worth noting here.

The first type is *refraction,* which inhibits a rule from firing a second time on the same data. The need for some type of refraction arises from the tendency of production systems to go into one-instantiation loops.

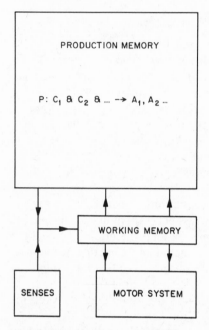

PRODUCTION MEMORY

$P: C_1 \ \& \ C_2 \ \& \ ... \ \rightarrow A_1, A_2 \ ...$

WORKING MEMORY

SENSES   MOTOR SYSTEM

FIG. 11.1.   Production system architecture

Given that a production fires at one cycle (i.e., is satisfied and wins out in conflict resolution), it clearly is primed to fire again unless something changes. The actions can change things, or the architecture can have refractory rules that inhibit repeated firings—but something is required.

The second type of conflict resolution rule is *recency,* which prefers instantiations that bind to elements that have more recently entered working memory. If WM is thought of as ordered from left to right in Fig. 11.1, with new elements entering from the front, then recency means that productions that bind to elements early in the WM preferentially win out. Recency provides a mechanism for focus of attention and continuity of effort. The result of a production that has just fired becomes the most recent element in WM, and some production involving it has a good chance of being the next one to fire.

The third type of conflict resolution is *special case order,* which prefers a production that is a special case of another. Special case order reflects the heuristic that productions conditional on more data (i.e., a superset) are based somehow on more information and should be fired first. Special case order seems well suited to adding new productions to the production memory (i.e., learning), where it permits new, generally more discriminative productions to dominate existing ones.

The structure of Fig. 11.1 can be mapped onto the standard picture in cognitive psychology of human mental structure as follows. The production memory is *long term memory* (LTM). It contains both data and program—all the knowledge that the human remembers for more that a few seconds. A set of productions is clearly a program (a set of if–then statements). It holds data by taking the actions as the data expressions and the conditions as the access path to the data. The production memory is thus very large, holding hundreds of thousands to millions of productions. Working memory corresponds to *short term memory* (STM). It holds data, but only for a short period of time. Limitations on its capacity and duration are such that the human exhibits the sort of short term fragility that psychology has extensively investigated (eg, see Crowder, 1976; Murdock, 1974). The data elements correspond to *chunks,* which have structure and can be decoded into component chunks. The recognition–act cycle corresponds to the fundamental cycle of human cognitive activity, which takes of the order of 100 msec, give or take a factor of a few. Recognition is a parallel process, since it must select the satisfied productions out of the entire production memory each cycle. The execution of a single sequence of action confers a serial aspect to the processing. The *sensory* and *motor* aspects are not detailed, but they act concurrently.

I have sketched only the basic features of a production system architecture. Many aspects have been left unspecified: the exact nature of the actions; the types of templates in the conditions; the details of conflict resolution; the forms of data elements; the timing properties of the recognition–act cycle. There are substantive reasons for not being entirely specific, in addition to expository limits. We do not know yet what exact variant of the architecture best describes the human cognitive structure, even assuming a production system to be the correct scheme (a proposition that many may not wish to subscribe to in any event). Thus, a particular variant (HPSA77) is described in the following discussion as the starting point for my investigation into Harpy. And even here, many aspects remain open to be possibly specified further in the attempt to discover how to structure a production system architecture in a Harpy-like way to recognize speech.

There are good reasons for considering together the class of architectures based in Fig. 11.1. Many variations of such architectures have been tried (Baylor & Gascon, 1974; Forgy & McDermott, 1977; Moran, 1971; Newell, 1973; Rychener, 1976; Young, 1973). Experience shows them to be equivalent in many ways. The common features of Fig. 11.1 do indeed impose a common gross behavior, and the further specifications affect mainly details.

To make these notions concrete, Table 11.1 shows a collection of productions which can illustrate a variety of features. They are written in a specific architecture, called OPS2, which we are currently using for our artificial intelligence research (Forgy & McDermott, 1977). The task is a

TABLE 11.1
Example Production Systems

A1: (Probe =X) (Digit =X) → (Say "Yes")
A2: (Probe =X) − (Digit =X) (Digit =Y) → (Say "No")
B1: (Probe =X) (Digit =Y) → (Test =X =Y)
B2: (Test =X =X) → (Say "Yes")
B3: (Test =X =Y) − (Test =Z =Z) → (Say "No")
C1: (Probe 6) (Digit 6) → (Say "Yes")
C2: (Probe 6) − (Digit 6) → (Say "No")
D1: (Probe 6) → (Say "Yes")
D2: (Probe K) → (Say "No")
E1: (Probe =X) & =Z (Digit =Y) → (<Delete> =Z) (Test =X =Y)
F1: (Digit =X) & =Y → (Say =X) (<Delete> =Y)
WM: ((Probe 6) (Digit 1) (Digit 6) (Digit 4))

simple Sternberg item classification (Sternberg, 1969), where only the essential features of the task are present, without any controlling context of evocation and response, and without any potentially disruptive additional data elements and productions. The PS has acquired a set of digits, each coded as (Digit···); they are sitting in WM shown at the bottom of the figure). The system is to say yes if the probe digit, coded as (Probe···), is a member of the set, no otherwise. The elements may have arrived in WM from the external world or from the execution of other productions (e.g., if the set were being held in LTM).

Consider productions A1 and A2, which form a production system that can perform this simple task. The elements to the left of the arrow, →, are the conditions. A1 has two conditions; A2 has three. The elements to the right of the arrow are the actions; each production has a single action, A1 to say yes, A2 to say no. The terms with the equal sign (=X, =Y, etc.) are variables, which may be instantiated so as to make the condition, which is a template, match a data element. With the given WM, A1 will be satisfied if =X takes the value 6. The conditions in a production can match elements anywhere in WM, e.g., A1 matches to the first and third. A2 cannot be satisfied with WM as shown; thus there is only one satisfied production and therefore it fires. If WM contained (Probe 5) instead of (Probe 6), then A1 would not be satisfied and A2 would, leading to saying no. A2 makes use of a negative condition, −(Digit =X), which is satisfied only if (Digit =X) cannot be satisfied. Thus, the recognition match consists of a number of mechanisms (variables and negated elements, here) which collectively define its power.

The need for avoiding loops is apparent with A1. Nothing keeps it from being satisfied on each cycle so that the behavior of the PS would be "Yes Yes Yes···" indefinitely. OPS2 uses a rule of *absolute refraction*, in which an instantiation can never be executed a second time on WM elements that have not been changed. This effectively stops such behavior. Production *E1* (towards the bottom) shows another way of avoiding the immediate loop, namely, by removing one of the elements necessary for the production (i.e., *E1*) to fire. *E1* also illustrates the use of an action (deletion) other than adding an element to WM. It also shows the labeling of an entire condition element with a variable, by &=*Z*, which is needed in conjunction with the <delete> function. *A1–A2* does not directly illustrate the other conflict resolution rules. But if the negation were removed from *A2* (and ignoring whether it would make sense), then both *A1* and *A2* could be satisfied by the WM shown. *A2* would win by virtue of special case order, since it would bind to all the same data elements as *A1*, but also to another one, thus being the more specialized production. Recency would occur if one of the productions bound to memory elements that had entered WM more recently than those for another productions. OPS2 uses a strictly lexicographic ordering on memory elements to determine recency if the productions bind to several elements in WM (as both *A1* and *A2* would). *B1–B3* in Table 11.1 provides an alternative PS for performing the same task. Instead of producing the answer directly, *B1* creates temporary data elements, (Test···), which *B2* then tests. As matters stand in OPS2, *A1–A2* is a much more efficient way of doing the task than *B1–B3*.

HPSA77: Further Specifying a Cognitive Architecture

In the attempt to discover the production system architecture that best matches the evidence on human cognition, four additional assumptions have been made. Each is a related group of details of the architecture, built to respond to some major type of human behavioral data. I present these with a minimum of discussion, though they all rate extended treatment. They specify the architecture only somewhat further; many additional details still remain open. These four design decisions are intended to be the initial part of a more extended sequence of design decision that will ultimately fully determine the architecture.

On the Serial Limitation and the Basic Cycle Time.   The basic structure of a production system architecture is to be a parallel-recognition–serial-action system. From this flows the basic serial character of high level cognition. This first additional assumption delimits the locus of seriality further:

D1.1. There is a single mechanism available for instantiating, binding, and using variables so that only one instantiation involving variables can be executed at a time.

Productions (such as *B1* in Table 11.1) that contain variables in their conditions that are used to instantiate expressions on their right hand sides are very different from productions, such as *C1*, that contain no variables. *B1* must line up to use a limited mechanism; *C1* need not. I call this mechanism the *use-variables* (UV) mechanism, and leave entirely open the locus of the limitation; whether in the instantiation of the variables in the condition to the WM element; in the binding of the variables to the value for future use: in the copying of the action element; or in each act of replacement of a variable by its value in an action.

Along with assumption D1.1 goes another:

D1.2. All the instantiations of a selected production are executed at once, before the next recognition occurs.

What is selected by the conflict resolution is one of the satisfied productions, and it locks out all other productions until all of its instantiations pass through the use-variables mechanism. This makes the actual computational cycle consist of a recognition, a selection of a production, and the execution of several sequences of actions, corresponding to each instantiation of the production. For example, *B1* is satisfied in three ways on WM, one for each (Digit···) element. Thus if *B1* fired, it would put three new elements in WM. Note that D1.2 is not a complete specification; it does not specify in what order the instantiations are executed, if that is important.

Since there may conceivably be a large number of instantiations of a single production, there may have to be a limit to the extent of the lockout:

D1.3. An arbitrary limit may exist to the number of instantiations or actions that may be executed before the next recognition phase begins.

To illustrate, if WM had a thousand (Digit···) elements, there might be only seven of them that could generate (Test···) elements before going back to the recognition phase.

A final assumption that limits the power of the recognition match belongs in this group. Each condition can seek an element anywhere in WM that satisfies it. In most production systems, variables are freely permitted throughout the conditions. Thus the recognition phase is capable of detecting patterns of elements satisfying various equality conditions among the components of working memory elements. *A1* in Table 11.1 provides an example, since $=X$ occurs in two separate condition elements, and hence only if two separate WM elements are equal on this component with *A1* fire. This appears too powerful an ability in the human cognitive system, and we restrict it as follows:

D1.4. The same variable cannot appear in more than a single condition element.

A variable can, of course, be used in more than one action element. D1.4 limits only the condition elements, which express the power of the match. However, a variable can occur more than once *within* a single element. *B2* in Table 11.1 provides an example, and thus contrasts with *A1*, which now becomes inadmissable. Multiple occurrences of a variable must occur at some place, if the system is to be capable of performing equality tests.

The assumptions D1.1–D1.4 were all dictated by the attempt to come to grips with what can broadly be called Sternberg phenomena (see Sternberg, 1969)—linear dependencies of reaction time on set size, with coefficients well below 100 msec per item (the classical Sternberg item classification tasks yields about 40 msec per item). Interpretation of these fast rates as search times through the sets raises the possibility of a computational cycle time of the order of 40 msec. This appears to imply too much computational power in a few seconds. The assumptions grouped under D1 draw the teeth of this implication by offering a different explanation for the Sternberg coefficient, namely that it corresponds to the operation of the UV mechanism. With the duration of UV set at about 40 msec per instantiation, HPSA77 provides an explanation for many of the important phenomena in the Sternberg paradigm. For instance, in Table 11.1, *A1–A2*, which would permit size-independent behavior, is not a possible method, whereas *B1–B3*, which shows linear behavior, is. On the other hand, *C1–C2* will also accomplish the task directly and is variable free; the problem is that *C1* and *C2* cannot be constructed on the fly for each new trial.

Creation of New Elements. The normal assumption in a production system architecture is to permit actions to create new elements in WM, and for these to persist for a substantial period of computation. It is easy to show that this ability would provide the human with cognitive powers sufficient to obviate most of his well known short-term memory difficulties. Briefly stated, the only restraint on using mnemonic devices like "one is a bun, two is a shoe,..." to solve all the short-term memory problems is that the human cannot create the necessary temporary structures sufficiently rapidly and reliably. On the other hand, if no new elements can be created at all in the short term, little computation of any sort can be done. For instance, *B1* in Table 11.1 would be inadmissible.

The solution seems to be to permit actions to create data elements in working memory, but to limit their life severely. One alternative is to treat all data elements uniformly. Another, which is taken by HPSA77, is to distinguish *new* data elements from *old* data elements that have already been learned by the system, and to permit different lifetimes for each type. Thus data elements themselves can be said to become *established* in LTM. Because in a production system architecture the only LTM is production memory, the set of established (old) data elements corresponds to those that occur as actions of productions. New data elements are then those that do not so occur. They can arise either from instantiations of actions that contain variables or (possibly) from the external world. Note that an action that contains variables is not a data element, since it cannot exist as an element in WM; it is a generator of data elements, some of which may already exist as actions of other production and some of which may be new.

A convenient way to view such a system is in terms of activated elements:

> D2.1. Working memory is a set of activated elements; an element of LTM *enters* WM when it becomes active and *leaves* WM when it ceases to be active.

This makes WM a set. Multiple occurrences of an element cannot exist in WM, since it only constitutes an activation on the set of elements in LTM. For instance, there could not be a second copy of (Digit 2) in the WM of Table 11.1. If repeated digits were given, more complex data elements would be required, such as (Digit 4 first) and (Digit 4 second).

> D2.2. Elements that are already established in LTM have relatively long residence times in WM, of the order of seconds.
>
> D2.3. Elements that are not already established in LTM have relatively short residence times in WM, of the order of a quarter of a second.

In terms of activation, one can think of established elements continuing to exist in LTM (ensconced) in productions, even though they cease to be active, whereas new unestablished elements cease to exist when they cease to be active. For example, the (Test···) elements of *B1* in Table

11.1 would all quickly disappear; they would remain just long enough to do their computational job.

D2.4. The time to create new elements that exist permanently in LTM is of the order of several seconds.

The relative times are still left quite open, especially the longer ones. A new element can arise in the system whenever an action element is created with a variable instantiated to a new value. Thus the UV mechanism does create new elements; they simply do not last long. Whether new elements can be created from the outside remains an open question. HPSA77 also remains entirely open at this point on the mechanism for permanent creation, and whether there are separate mechanisms for creation of new elements and for creation of new productions. They are clearly tied together in some respects, but establishment of data elements may involve only very specialized production-creating mechanisms.

With the assumptions of D2, the architecture appears to behave properly with respect to certain short term memory behavior. In the Brown–Peterson (Peterson & Peterson, 1959) paradigm of short-term rapid forgetting under rehearsal-free conditions, HPSA77 has difficulty in remembering the target words, as do humans. Furthermore, its problem is essentially one of interference. It can recall the familiar components with which it was presented, but cannot differentiate which ones were actually in the specific stimulus. Thus it shows perfect performance on the initial trial, release from proactive inhibition, and similar phenomena, in qualitative agreement with human behavior (Crowder, 1976).

Forward Order of Experience.   It is a commonplace that people recall their experience in the same time order in which they experienced it, in the forward time direction. This creates a difficulty for production system architectures generally speaking, and probably for many other architectures (but not for all, e.g., Estes, 1972). Production system architectures tend to be stack machines, in that WM is ordered with new elements entering at the front. In our exposition of the basic architecture, the recency rule for conflict resolution conveys this characteristic. But this makes the "natural" character of forward experiencing difficult to understand and to implement. For instance, *F1* in Table 11.1 is the obvious way of repeating back the digits in WM— but it does so in opposite order. The following assumptions deal with this problem:

D3.1. Productions themselves remain in a state of activation after the production is executed.

D3.2. Activation of productions lasts a relatively long time, of the order of many seconds (or even much longer).

D3.3. An activated production will become satisfied again if an element enters WM that satisfies a single one of its conditions.

These assumptions imply that if a single element from the past is recalled, then it can possibly trigger productions that were executed at the original time, thus iteratively producing a stream of elements running forward in time that reconstruct the original memory as experienced. This will be a genuine reconstruction, since what is reproduced is what could be recognized by productions existing at the time of the experience. Nothing is said about how long the state of activation lasts, except that it is not short-lived. This lack of specification is dictated (as in the other assumptions) by the desire not to specify more of the architecture than is necessary to solve a specific difficulty (here forward experiencing), leaving as much freedom as possible for future issues.

This assumption of activating productions as well as data elements may seem quite radical. Interestingly, it is very close in spirit to the absolute refractory conflict resolution rule use in OPS2—namely, as long as all the elements that satisfied a production remain in WM, a production will become a candidate for re-execution if a single element to which it binds becomes reasserted. Stated somewhat tersely this is: Over the period in which WM lasts, D3 is equivalent to absolute refraction.

Some short-term memory reporting phenomena seem to be explained in a qualitatively satisfactory manner with D3. In simple digit span experiments, reporting digits back in forward order is much easier than in backward order. HPSA77 does memory span experiments by recognizing the material on input, thus activating a bunch of productions (i.e., those that do the recognition). Recall occurs by first recalling an anchor point (e.g., the initial item in the sequence) and then trying to recapture the sequence running forward, by refiring the original recognizing productions. This not only produces appropriate forward recall behavior, but makes backward recall more difficult.

Sensory Processing. Figure 11.1 shows the main cognitive engine. It is necessary to fix how information from the senses flows into it and how motor actions issue from it. The sensory aspects are especially crucial for the topic of this paper (though from a motor theory of speech perception, motor aspects may be almost as important). In the usual view of human memory structure, a set of sensory buffers (the Sperling memory, the auditory buffer, etc.) exist, which lie outside the central system of Fig. 11.1 and feed WM already-symbolized data. Thus there is another memory or memory-access system that makes contact between the sensory features and some sort of lexicon converting the features to (verbal linguistic) symbols, which are then subject to further cognitive processing (the logogen memory is an example; Morton & Broadbent, 1967). HPSA77 makes a different assumption:

D4.1. All sensory contact with cognitive knowledge occurs via WM.

This imples that much of the conversion of sensory information to symbols occurs in WM. D4.1 does not specify where the boundary is, i.e., at exactly what place and in what form knowledge is encoded outside the system of Fig. 11.1 and enters WM. What arrives might reasonably be called sensory *features*. D4.1 claims only that the knowledge coded in the form of productions in PM can't be used in the preprocessing stages that produce such features. Thus, these features, though they might be symbols or data elements in the WM, cannot yet represent words or other semantic constructs, which are encoded in productions. This seems to imply, and we will take it thus, that the sensory buffers are part of WM.

D4.2. Productions that do not require the use-variable (UV) mechanism are free to execute asynchronously and concurrently, subject perhaps to lockout restrictions if common structures are accessed.

This assumption is the other side of the coin of D1.1 and is not really independent of it. Having located the serial constraint in a specific mechanism (UV), if that mechanism is not evoked there should be no serial constraint. The concurrent productions are easily characterized: They do not contain variables. The qualification in D4.2 refers to the possible existence of an entirely separate source of limitation on concurrency, which arises when two active elements wish to touch the same structure. The caveat is included only to acknowledge the potential existence of such constraints, not to make any substantive pronouncement on them.

These assumptions on the sensory system do seem to be quite radical compared with the other assumptions that have been made, at least in certain superficial appearances. For instance, if one thinks of the amount of low-level information involved in perception, then WM must contain hundreds of thousands of active elements, though they may exist there for only a short time. Likewise, many thousands of variable-free productions may be firing simultaneously in the processing of such features, although any time a production is selected that involves variables it must line up in front of the UV mechanism and wait its turn to have its variables instantiated, bound, and used.

There are many sensory phenomena to which the D4 group of assumptions is at least superficially responsive. They involve issues of how the

cognitive system penetrates into perception and how various tasks involving perception of sets of elements show size independence, in marked
contrast to the linear size dependence shown by tasks such as the
Sternberg paradigm. A simple way to indicate the scope of these assumptions is by reference to a recent theory put forth by Shiffrin and Schneider
(1977; Schneider & Shiffrin, 1977). HPSA77 can be taken to be a more
explicit version of the Shiffrin and Schneider theory, in which the
variable-free productions map into their *automatic processing* and the
variable-containing productions map into their *controlled processing*.[1] It
is more explicit because it provides a total control structure with common
underlying mechanisms, while assigning specific mechanisms to the two
types of processing (automatic and controlled), and it offers an explanation for why controlled processing is serial. It is useful here to note the
correspondence, because generally speaking HPSA77 will cover the same
ground as the Shiffrin and Schneider theory and offer similar explanations
for various phenomena.

Summary on HPSA77. The preceding architecture is the starting
point for understanding how Harpy can be seen as a model of human
speech perception. By its construction, HPSA77 is a plausible model for
the structure of human cognition. The evidence for this is not detailed
here, but is taken as a working assumption. As noted already, HPSA77 is
deliberately an incomplete specification, preserving as many degrees of
freedom as possible while still explaining various phenomena. For instance, no mechanisms for production creation have yet been posited.
Some parts of the architecture may need substantial elaboration when we
come to the speech task, but this introduction is sufficient to let us move
on to the presentation of Harpy itself and what is implied by a sufficiency
analysis of it.

3. SUFFICIENCY ANALYSIS OF HARPY

Harpy is no more a single specific system than is the basic production
system of Fig. 11.1. Starting with Dragon, there has been a continuous
tree of evolution with some dozens of variations, some of which have
proved abortive and some of which have survived. I extract from this
variety the "essential Harpy." Raj Reddy has given a more complete picture in Chap. 9 (see also Lowerre, 1976), so it is possible to be brief.

---

[1]For instance, productions *D1–D2* in Table 11.1 illustrate roughly what is possible in a
typical situation where automatic processing is possible. Because the probe set and the
target set remain disjoint over many trials, variable-free productions such as *D1* and *D2*,
which permit direct response, can be acquired.

Summary of Harpy

Figure 11.2 gives one picture of the Harpy algorithm. Ultimately, at performance time, there exists a great set of states. Each state has associated with it a phone template for the character of the sound to be heard if in that state, and a set of transitions to states that can immediately follow it in time. Thus a state encodes the understanding that a certain sound has been heard, along with the expectations for what acoustic input should arrive next.

Taking the transitions to have probabilities associated with them and the template comparison process to yield a probability that the phone was heard at that point, the Harpy algorithm can be viewed as finding the maximum likelihood path through the network formed by iterating the state system indefinitely though time at some basic time grain. The actual path equation is:

$$P_{i,\,t+1} = C(A_i,\, D_{t+1}) \times \text{Max}_j(P_{j,\,t} \times T_{j,\,i}) \tag{3.1}$$

where $P_{i,\,t}$ = probability of state S_i at time t

$\quad C(A_i,\, D_t)$ = comparison of A_i, the template for state S_i, with the acoustic data signal, D_t, at time t

$\quad T_{j,\,i}$ = probability of state S_i arising immediately after state S_j

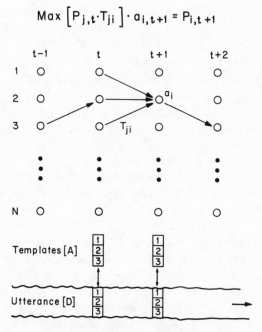

FIG. 11.2.   The Harpy algorithm

Taken in full (as performed by Dragon), the algorithm is a simple dynamic program that sweeps across the entire rectangle of states and time, keeping only the maximum as it goes and cumulating the probability score. At the end (tf), the maximum $P_{i,\ tf}$ constitutes the final point on the solution, and a backtrace through the rectangle using saved back-pointers yields the optimal path, hence the maximum likelihood utterance.

Harpy consists of a number of modifications of (3.1). First, the empirical evidence shows that the transition probabilities can be dispensed with, i.e., replaced by 0s and 1s. This simplifies the path equation to:

$$P_{i,\ t + 1} = C(A_i, D_{t + 1}) \times \text{Max}_{j\ in\ Ti}\ (P_{j,\ t}) \tag{3.2}$$

where T_i = transition set of $T_{j,\ i} = 1$.

Now a substitution of logarithms produces:

$$L_{i,\ t + 1} = C(A_i, D_{t + 1}) + \text{Max}_{j\ in\ Ti}\ (L_{j,\ t}) \tag{3.3}$$

where $L_{i,\ t} = \log(P_{i,\ t})$.

The next major amendment is to introduce *beam search*. Thus, as shown in Fig. 11.3, only a variable fraction of the states (the beam) are kept at each point in the search. This is about 1% for current Harpy and thus represents a significant computational reduction. Restriction to a beam does imply the possibility of missing the solution path, since if one of its intermediate states is poor enough to drop out of the beam, the path is gone forever.

With the notion of the beam comes the decision process to determine the cutoff:

$$e = \text{beam cutoff at } t:$$
$$\text{reject all } L_{i,t} \text{ more than } e \text{ from the maximum.} \tag{3,4}$$

The exact form of the cutoff is important. Neither a fixed number nor a fixed fraction works well. The current version keeps all states whose likelihoods are within a fixed range of likelihood from the best. This admits a variable number of states to the beam, but the criterion remains constant.

If Harpy has a beam of F states at time t, it undergoes expansion at $t + 1$ to $F \times B$ states, where B is the number of transitions (i.e., the average size of the connection set, T_i). This expanded beam must then be clipped to bring it back into line. If the best likelihood (L^*) were known in advance, then the threshold of $(L^* - L < e)$ could be applied as each transition was generated. However, L^* is not known with certainty until all transitions have been generated; hence a slightly more complex computation is required.

The next essential feature of Harpy is the variable size of the basic time step. This has two parts. First, the grain of the computation was originally fixed (at 10 msec). Thus the Harpy algorithm worked directly with con-

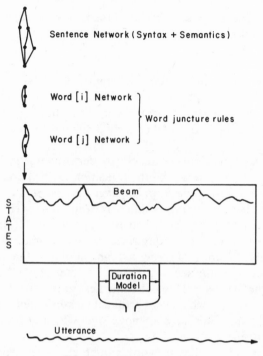

FIG. 11.3. The beam search

tinuous unsegmented speech. Currently, Harpy has an independent pre-processing step that segments the signal into variable duration units on the basis of similarity of the parametric representation. Segments run from 30 msec to over 100 msec, and average about 50 msec. The use of a variable segment implies that the beam cutoff threshold cannot remain constant over all segments. Harpy currently makes it proportional to the duration of the segment (i.e., $e = e' \times$ duration), but this is not wholly satis-factory. There is also a separate determination for each step, whether the path through a state will remain in the state or will exit according to the possibilities in the T_i, the transition set. This is done by a mechanism that decides whether the next segment is sufficiently similar to the current one. It can be viewed as an implicit loop-back of S_i to S_i at each point, except that separate criteria are used for proceeding other than that im-plicit in $C(A_i, D_t)$.

The nature of the comparison between acoustic template and data is that a set of 14 components (LPC coefficients) characterize the speech around the point in question and a metric (called the Itakura metric) is computed between these 14 parameters and a corresponding set of 14 parameters that make up the template. This metric is a general quadratic form in the parameter vectors, but once the acoustic template is fixed the expression just becomes a weighted sum:

$$C(A, D) = \text{Sum}_{k = 1:14} \ W_k \times D_k \qquad (3.5)$$

There is a fixed set of templates (currently 98), which corresponds to an acoustic definition of phones. These are modified for each speaker on a running basis from words he speaks. Very little data is required for this, so that a running calibration takes only a second or two of speech per phone.

The above summary covers the Harpy performance system. The network (i.e., the state system with the transition matrix) does not occur as an act of god, but is derived from language knowledge in a specific way. Given some generative representation of a grammar (Harpy grammars have all been context-free, so called BNF, grammars), a finite grammar network can be generated for any fixed period of time, though it grows combinatorially. Figure 11.4 shows a fragment of a grammar net, containing several potential utterances, such as "Tell me about China" and "Tell us about all the stories." This net embodies grammatical knowledge. In the Harpy framework, which uses artificial task-oriented grammars, such a net also embodies the semantic knowledge, which has been woven into the grammar itself.

Similarly, each lexical item (word) can be characterized by a network of states, representing which phones can follow which other phones in the various pronunciations of the word. Figure 11.5 gives an example for the word "please" (the curly brackets give minimum and maximum default durations). These nets embody both lexical and phonological knowledge. Due to the finite character of words, these nets have a fixed size, unlike

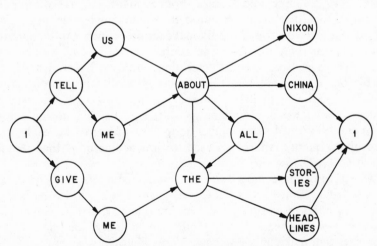

FIG. 11.4. Fragment of grammar net

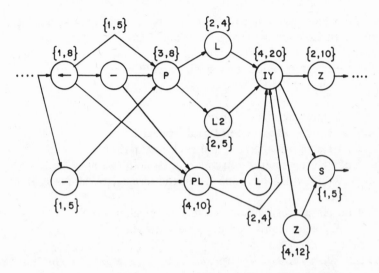

FIG. 11.5.   Example of phonetic network of the word "please"

the grammar nets, which grow exponentially in the duration of the utterance.

The single-level performance net is created by replacing each node of the grammar tree, which represents a lexical item, with the corresponding net of phones. When this occurs a number of rules must be applied to account for coarticulation effects that arise because of the abutment of the end of one word with the beginning of another. Such rules are not needed within the word network; i.e., the net is the final result of having already applied such rules. These rules modify the total net, both adding links and deleting links at word junctures, thus producing a final network that is no longer a simple expansion. In Harpy, this network is produced as a distinct act of compilation. Some additional state minimization operations are performed, which do not change the qualitative performance but increase the efficiency somewhat.

The main structure of Harpy has now been filled out. There are a number of minor features in Harpy to increase its efficiency, and a number of improvements in the works to increase its accuracy. These latter are ultimately of importance, but we can examine the present Harpy as a plausible speech perception mechanism for humans to discover where the critical issues lie.

Issues of Sufficiency Analysis

Given Harpy as it stands, we can ask how plausible it is as a model of human speech perception, looking only at its gross characteristics. What seems to fit the requirements of perceiving speech in terms of what we know about humans? What seems to be its most outlandish aspects? My purpose in this section is to raise these questions rather than answer them. They will sensitize us to the important issues as we try to map Harpy into a production system model of speech perception in the next section. For ease of reference I list the questions:

S1. Can Harpy recognize speech?
S2. Can Harpy be extended to full speech?
S3. Can Harpy recognize full speech in time?
S4. Does Harpy require too much immediate memory?
S5. How does Harpy cope with the creativity and variability of speech?
S6. Can Harpy respond adequately to speaker variability?
S7. Is language acquisition possible with Harpy?

S1. Can Harpy Recognize Speech?   A sufficiency analysis starts with a system that can perform the intellectual function in question. Thus Harpy can indeed recognize connected speech, and at a nontrivial level of accuracy and sentence complexity. That is what it means to meet the ARPA specifications of 90% semantic accuracy, 1,000 words vocabulary, several speakers, little training per speaker, etc. This is the strong point. However, we must recognize that Harpy is not the only scheme that can recognize speech. Both Hearsay-II and HWIM, as well as a number of other systems (Jelenek, 1976; Nakagawa, 1976; Ritea, 1975), can also recognize connected speech. Differences in capability could be assigned to factors that are not relevant to the psychological plausibility of the systems, such as development effort or whatever. Another system concept could be adopted as a starting point for a sufficiency analysis, say the multiple knowledge source philosophy of Hearsay-II, which has some very attractive features as an A1 system. Such a course might well be worth pursuing and is in no way precluded by the present analysis. Indeed, Klatt's contribution to this book (Chap. 10) draws on many different mechanisms from the entire ARPA Speech Understanding Systems research effort; his strategy may well be the preferred one.

Two generalized features of Harpy recommend it as basis for a perceptual system. The first is the question of search. The real time aspect of speech argues against there being very much open-ended search. However much one might want otherwise, it seems unlikely that a technical solution to the speech problem exists that does not involve search. The uncertainties are too strong. The fundamental character of Harpy lies in its transformation of the search from an exponential process to a linear one. This is accomplished, not by magic, but by fiat, i.e., by forcing all the incoming perceptual information into a finite (though large) set of states.

An absorption of uncertainty must occur in this forcing, and errors are generated thereby. Whether more or less than in other schemes is not determined just by the choice of search scheme, but involves many other aspects of the total scheme. The gain with Harpy is to bring the search under control, so that search can be safely indulged in as a real-time process. This seems to me a great virtue and recommends Harpy-like schemes over others, such as Hearsay-II and HWIM, where the search control comes about in different ways.

The other generalized feature that appeals to me about the Harpy scheme is the uniformity of its structure and the consequent simplicity of its algorithm. Successful technologies for doing complex tasks seem to arise by finding a unit or element that is capable of restrained diversity, but which can be multiplied indefinitely to attain the complexity desired. The technology of DNA/RNA is an example; so is computer technology, in each of its successive stages. This may just be another way of stating the presumption of hierarchy—that all complex systems require a hierarchical structure (Simon, 1962). But it seems to add to this an assumption of uniformity and combinational involution within a level, which the usual formulation does not dwell upon. In any event, the uniform structure of Harpy makes it seem like a structure that could indeed arise as a natural technology for perceiving speech.

Having said a few pleasant things about Harpy, let us now move on to the problems and issues.

S2. Can Harpy Be Extended to Full Speech? All speech systems, Harpy included, have only worked with limited language, limited vocabulary, limited grammar, etc. Though a presumption of sufficiency must be admitted, it may not survive as one proceeds to open speech. However crude, it seems worthwhile to make some estimates of how big Harpy would be for full speech.

The first critical parameters are the total number of states, S, the branching factor of the net, B, and the depth that must be searched, D. The accuracy of recognition is also critical; we will implicitly be holding this constant (though the assumption that Harpy scales is pretty tenuous). The current net is 15,000 states and covers a 1,000 word vocabulary with a grammar that has an average branching factor[2] of 10, extending over a depth of about two seconds (six words), yielding a grammar net of 1,800 nodes. To compute these quantities in general, we must combine a

---

[2]There is much variation and some inconsistency in branching factor estimates. They arise in part because of the difference between taking arithmetic and geometric means and in part from the actual paths taken through grammars differing statistically from random paths.

characterization of the grammar in terms of words with a characterization of the words in terms of phones.

At the word level, a language may be characterized as having a vocabulary of V words with a redundancy of r, i.e., the fraction r of the words in any sentence that may be deleted without loss. The redundancy characterizes the aggregated constraint from the grammar and static semantic restrictions. Then, for an utterance of length Dg words, the number of nodes in grammar tree, Tg, can be expressed as:

$$Tg = Bg^{Dg} = V^{(1 - r)Dg} = [V^{(1 - r)}]^{Dg} \tag{3.6}$$

The grammar net arises from this tree by identifying many nodes. This can be thought of as compressing the branching factor by an additional factor of c in determining the growth rate of the grammar net. In Harpy, the grammar tree is 10^6 (for six words), and the net has only 1,800 nodes, yielding a total compression of about 550, or a compression factor per word of $c = .35$. Note that this does not represent an increase in the redundancy of the language; the effective branching factor is still $V^{1 - r}$. No one knows how c extrapolates to a full language. If, from ignorance, we take c as a constant, then for the states in the grammar net we get:

$$Sg = [cV^{(1 - r)}]^{Dg} \tag{3.7}$$

The total states in the Harpy net arise by replacing each node of the grammar net by a lexical net, which both expands the states and lengthens the depth. To first order, the average lexical net is independent of vocabulary size and grammatical structure (though words do get longer as vocabulary increases). There are Sw states per word; thus we get for the total states in the Harpy net:

$$S = SwSg \tag{3.8}$$

The average branching factor, B, of this net (the average size of the transition set T) arises from the branching factor within words, Bw, and the branching factor of the grammar, Bg, which is $V^{(1 - r)}$ from (3.6). The latter takes place only over word durations, not over each state transition. Since the words are on the average Dw transitions long, we get for the effective branchiness (i.e., transitions):

$$B = BwBg^{1/Dw} = BwV^{(1 - r)/Dw} \tag{3.9}$$

These formulas characterize the language by the vocabulary, V, the redundancy, r, the relevant sentence depth, Dg, and the data for words in terms of phones: $Bw, Dw,$ and Sw. The phone representation of a word can be taken as roughly constant, with the values $Dw = 5$ phones per word, $Sw = 8$ states, and $Bw = 2$, all taken from Harpy. Dg can also be taken as constant, since it represents not the average length of a grammatical utterance, but the maximum length of phrase that carries some significant constraint. $Dg = 6$ (3 words/sec $\times$ 2 sec) is consonant with Harpy. For vocabulary and redundancy we can adopt ranges of values. A full vocabulary lies between 10^4 and 10^5. The redundancy of regular English lies between .5 and .75, as derived in various ways (Luce, 1960). Vocabulary and redundancy always enter into the calculations as $V^{(1 - r)}$, the effective grammar branching factor *(Bg)*. Therefore we need only consider values of Bg: $Bg = 10$ to 320 spans the full range. In Table 11.2, we show the various combinations of V and r that combine to produce a given Bg.

Table 11.2 shows the calculations for S and B as a function of Bg. The first column is for current Harpy; the others are the extrapolations. We see that S ranges from the order of 10^3 states, for a vocabulary of 10^4 words and a redundancy of .75, to a horrendous 10^{13} states, for a vocabulary of 10^5 and a redundancy of only .5. A million states does not perhaps seem out of the question, but it is clear that the number of states can go out of sight rather easily. By contrast, we see that there is relative small variation in the figures for branching factor, from 3 to 6.

These calculations do not doom a Harpy-like scheme. Additional ideas about how the number of states can be reduced are not reflected here. These calculations do tell us to watch the total numbers as we consider how Harpy is mapped into human cognition.

S3. Can Harpy Recognize Full Speech in Time?   The computational task of Harpy is easily expressed, given the basic parameters. The amount of computation is proportional to the states considered (i.e., the beam, F) times the branching factor (B) times the number of steps (D). Each unit of computation involves a comparison of a template to the data, a step in the logic of maximization and selection, and an accessing of a transition and a new state. It is best expressed in amount of computation per second of speech:

$$\text{Computation} = F \times B \times D \qquad (3.10)$$

The effort to do the backtrace is negligible compared to computing the forward beam, so is not included in (3.10).

D is fixed for a second of speech at about $5 \times 3 = 15$ steps per second. We know the beam cutoff fraction (f) for the existing Harpy (.01) but do not know how it would extrapolate. What matters is how good the acoustic separation is and how many candidates there are. The criterion keeps all those candidates within a band at the top. Assuming this fraction remains constant for full speech lets us plot on Table 11.2 the various amounts of computation for variations in S and B. This yields a minimum amount of computation per second of 10^4 units, according to Table 11.2.

TABLE 11.2
Estimates of Critical Parameters for Harpy

Vocabulary	*Redundancy*					
10^5	.80	.74	.68	.62	.56	.50
5×10^4	.79	.72	.66	.60	.53	.47
10^4	.75	.67	.60	.52	.45	.38
5×10^3	.73	.65	.57	.49	.41	.32
10^3	.67	.57	.47	.37	.27	.17
Grammar branching (Bg)	10	20	40	80	160	320
Grammar states (Sg)	2×10^3	1×10^5	8×10^6	5×10^8	3×10^{10}	2×10^{12}
Harpy states (S)	1×10^4	9×10^5	6×10^7	4×10^9	2×10^{11}	1×10^{13}
Branching factor (B)	3.2	3.5	4.2	4.8	5.5	6.3
Computation units	7×10^3	5×10^5	4×10^7	3×10^9	2×10^{11}	1×10^{13}
Beam (F)	2×10^2	9×10^3	6×10^5	4×10^7	2×10^9	2×10^{11}
Integrated beam (Fx)	4×10^3	3×10^5	2×10^7	1×10^9	7×10^{10}	5×10^{12}
Fixed parameters	$Bw = 2$	$Dw = 5$	$Sw = 8$	$Dg = 6$	$c = .35$	$f = .01$

This is an amount of computation, not the time to make the computation, since it remains open how big the unit is and how much concurrency might occur. There are limits to the amount of concurrency possible, but that depends on the computational scheme.

S4. Does Harpy Require Too Much Immediate Memory?   The Harpy algorithm demands that a set of states, the beam, be carried through time. The beam is about 200 states for current Harpy. Assuming the beam fraction to remain the same at .01 yields the estimates shown in Table 11.2. At the least a few hundred states seem to be needed. This implies a requirement for immediate memory in the human. Of course, this need not be standard verbal short-term memory (the seven plus or minus two variety), but the requirement may still be hard to meet.

The requirement is actually more than the momentary set of states in the beam, because the past beam must be remembered (in terms of back-pointers), so as to recover the optimal path for the final recognition. Thus the immediate memory requirement is probably more like the total integrated beam, which is $F \times D$, where D is the total steps, namely 30. These figures are also shown in Table 11.2.

The requirement for immediate memory is not just for space, as discussed above, but also for duration. The backtrace does not commence until the forward sweep has covered the whole utterance. This is an essential feature of the algorithm, since it is the way in which the results of the search is obtained. In Harpy, this duration is of the order of two seconds. In any event, this duration is an additional requirement on the nature of immediate memory.

More subtle requirements on memory organization arise from the iterative nature of speech. The acoustic data arrives continuously over time at exactly the same receptor organs. Thus, ipso facto, the signal must move to other organs in order to be remembered (or, equivalently, to make way for the new signal). This suggests pipeline computation. But a pipeline implies that computational capacity exist at each stage of the pipeline, and may imply a large duplication of computational mechanism. Actually, current implementations of Harpy do not pipeline. Having only a single processor, they pass the data through the processor and then lay it out in (memory) space to be retrieved later for the backtrace. The active computation is really an instantaneous effort on the front of the speech wave, and all of the past remains quiescent until the backtrace. Thus the memory organization problem is really how to get the memory for backpointers moved out so that it does not clog up the current computation. The duration of processing before backtrace is not likely to be constant; rather, it would seem to depend on the actual dependencies in the speech.

This variability may also be a complication in dealing with the memory organization.

S5. How Does Harpy Cope with the Creativity and Variability of Speech? Harpy works with a fixed network. Hence an immediate concern is whether Harpy by its nature is inadequate to understanding freely expressed speech. There leaps to mind the long-standing arguments of the linguists about the creativity of language. Along with this come questions of fragmentary and ungrammatical utterances.

There are real issues here, but one must first lay to rest the proposition that finiteness always brings with it a failure of creativity. Linguistic creativity has never seemed impossible because the alphabet is finite or even because the vocabulary is finite. It has always been understood that iteration of finite means (here, selection from a finite vocabulary) is potentially sufficient to deal with creative expression (here, creative reception). Harpy can be viewed merely as an *extended vocabulary* that takes into account the redundant structure necessary to extract speech from the noisy signal (not to understand its semantics), so that the finally recognized utterance is an iteration of trips through the net. Thus, it is no more (and no less) true of Harpy than of any system that the set of utterances is limited to a finite (hence "noncreative") set.

The real issues of creativity and variability seem best dealt with as requirements to handle certain specific situations. First, a human can understand grammatical utterances that he has not heard before. Does Harpy depend on the net encompassing all grammatical possibilities? Does the view above of Harpy as an extended vocabulary plus the use of very large nets suffice? Second, a human can understand any sequence of words from its vocabulary, if clearly spoken. Such utterances surely lie outside the Harpy net. How can Harpy recognize such utterances? Third, humans cope with utterances that have genuinely new elements, exhibiting thereby various forms of cognitive assimilation and inference. How can Harpy do likewise? Fourth, humans are able to incoporate immediate increments of linguistic knowledge; e.g., a new word or notation may be explicitly defined en passant during conversation. Such knowledge cannot be in the existing network when given. Currently Harpy needs a formal representation of the grammar and a substantial compilation phase. How can it handle such short-term knowledge? Fifth, humans cope with some grammatical errors and fragmentary utterances. These must also surely lie outside the Harpy net. How will Harpy cope with such "structural" errors, as opposed to continuous errors in the acoustics (which the template match using the Itakura metric at least addresses)?

These requirements may be solved by a variety of different

mechanisms. I group them together since they all involve somehow the fixed Harpy network and how it is to be transcended.

S6. Can Harpy Respond Adequately to Speaker Variability?   There should be a sufficiency issue surrounding the Harpy mechanisms for expressing speaker variability by means of unique phone sets for each speaker. The Harpy scheme does not require much memory, so long as there are a fixed set of phone labels and all that varies are the templates. But there are time lags on obtaining the variability, and presumably there are limits to how much variability can be handled by this mechanism. Though Harpy shows some adaptiveness for individual speaker's phonetics, it has no mechanisms to deal with individual differences in phonological and grammatical rules.

S7. Is Language Acquisition Possible with Harpy?   Any sort of elaborate structure or complex preparation raises the issue of how such a structure is acquired. Though the homogeneous structure of the network, made up of simple elements (nodes, transition links, templates), seems relatively nonproblematical a priori, the elaborate compilation process raises a red flag. The computational aspects of that process must be taken into account. Even more, the acquisition of the compilation process must be accounted for. This becomes an especially binding issue for the human system, since it acquires language very early, when its cognitive powers are apparently still primitive. The natural assumption is that the basic acquisition of language must be a feature of the underlying cognitive system and not the result of extended intelligent strategic action.

For the current Harpy, the compilation process involves having additional representations for all the components of language: a grammar, a lexicon, and acoustic–phonetic rules for word junctions. Actually a lexical item for Harpy is already an integrated representation of all the different ways in which the word can be pronounced. Conceivably this knowledge is held in rule form, so that a new word can be expanded into a net by some generation process, just as is the grammar net. The alternative is that knowledge about variability of pronunciation arrives in piecemeal fashion, so that the net representation of a lexical item must either be regenerated or modified. The same is true of the grammar net, of course. Though the acquisition of additional grammatical constructions may be rare, each lexical item added to the vocabulary requires an extension of the grammar net (as well as of the total compiled network).

Summary.   I have enumerated some of the main sufficiency questions. These arise directly from the structure of the Harpy algorithm.

They need to be treated no matter how we map Harpy into the human cognitive system. However, they are not the only questions that will occur. Once we consider a specific identification, additional questions may demand treatment, depending on the shape of the mechanisms that are employed to realize the Harpy algorithms.

It should not be inferred that all these problems are Harpy's alone. Analogs of some of them will exist for other schemes. For instance, one of the underlying objections to Analysis by Synthesis has always been a sufficiency issue of how there could possibly be enough computational capacity for it to run in a blind generate-and-test mode, even if it did have a good test (the synthesis).[3]

The questions of creativity, and the amount and duration of immediate memory, will arise in all cases. In fact, one of the gains to be made from attempting a sufficiency analysis of Harpy is just to get these issues to claim their proper share of attention in competition with various empirically striking phenomena.

I have taken Harpy as it currently is. There are many things still to be done to Harpy to decrease its computational complexity (both time and space), increase its accuracy, and increase its flexibility (both in performance and in acquisition). These considerations can branch off in many directions. It is not worth following them until they become critical to the analysis. Therefore, I will come back to possible modifications of the Harpy structure after I have attempted to map Harpy into a model of human perception and have specific difficulties that demand solution.

4.   HARPY AS A PRODUCTION SYSTEM:
PRELIMINARY ANALYSIS

I now turn to the central task of the paper: to find a way for the human to perceive speech by performing a Harpy-like computation. The key to doing this is to take Harpy seriously and not worry too much about outrageous aspects of the scheme until the mapping is complete. Then I can ask whether the difficulties so revealed can be alleviated. Thus I have termed this section a preliminary analysis.

I assume HPSA77, the architecture described in Section 2, which shares the properties of a basic production system architecture and adds four (complex) assumptions, D1–D4. Not all these assumptions are equally critical for us. Having developed the architecture independently, so it qualitatively fits a modest range of behavior, it is appropriate to posit

---

[3]It never proved persuasive that Halle and Stevens (1962) also posited a plausible generator, since it was a genuine *deus ex machina*.

the entire architecture. However, nothing is sacred about HPSA77. If the requirements of Harpy point in a different direction, we will follow Harpy and modify HPSA77.

The Essential Idea: Transitions are Productions

The basic elements of the mapping can be immediately set out:

M1. The states in Harpy correspond to symbols or data elements.

M2. The state-dependent transitions correspond to productions with prior states in their conditions and successor states in their actions.

M3. Most transitions correspond to variable-free productions.

M4. The parametric representation of the acoustic signal arises in WM as a data element.

M5. The comparison of templates to data elements occurs by means of the recognition match.

There is no automatic guarantee that a mapping with these gross properties can actually be constructed. There are many open issues: Can variable-free productions represent the computation? Can the recognition match perform the required act of comparison? How are the acoustic parameters actually to be represented? And so on. Still, some important things about sufficiency follow from these five mapping propositions. It is worthwhile noting them before plunging into the detailed considerations of the full mapping.

The mapping localizes the speech perception productions where HPSA77 independently claims perceptual processes belong, namely, in the productions corresponding to Shiffrin and Schneider's automatic processing. One important consequence is that concurrent processing is available, something that is clearly needed. The fundamental act of firing a production will correspond to the basic computational act of making a transition in Harpy. Thus the beam will be sitting in WM and will consist of elements holding states and the values associated with the state. Concerns about the size of the beam then translate directly into concerns about WM size and duration. The speed of computation becomes tied directly to the cycle time of the recognize–act cycle. Note that in HPSA77 the cycle time is not yet pinned down, either for automatic or controlled productions. (Assumption D1 dealt only with avoiding the implication from the Sternberg coefficient of too short a cycle time.)

An important feature of the mapping is that it breaks the network apart. What exists is a set of individual productions. They come together dynamically to produce the Harpy computation. The act of construction of the net is the act of adding many individual productions. Thus, it appears unnecessary to engage in a major act of compilation. Too much comfort should not be taken from this, because many aspects of the acquisition process remain problematical, such as creating appropriate individual productions, modifying or screening the behavior of inappropriate productions that have already been learned, etc. Still, the problem is cast in a somewhat different computational light.

A last general implication is that the perception of speech does not take place in a separate component from the rest of cognitive processing. Though of necessity most processing must be done by variable-free productions, variable-containing productions can also participate to the extent they can be executed in limited time. Thus a way exists for modest amounts of general computation to be brought to bear during perception.

With this overview, I can proceed to carry out the mapping in detail.

The Detailed Mapping

Many issues must be dealt with in making the mapping. I will introduce them one by one in an attempt to make clear what aspects of the model are responsive to what issues. I will sometimes cope only partially with an issue. By laying them out concretely, it will be possible to accumulate the set of partially satisfied issues at the end of this preliminary pass.

It is possible to foresee what will drive the mapping. Harpy requires a lot of computation, much more than can be accomplished serially in the time available. The only device in HPSA77 for concurrent computation is the execution of distinct variable-free productions. Thus it is necessary to incorporate as much of the computation as possible into the recognition match. Getting a large number of elements in working memory for a few (powerful) productions to iterate over cannot work. Thus, even when we do not know exactly the form that the full computation can take, we know enough to try to express the computational functions in the productions themselves.

II. Performing State-Dependent Transitions. We can try a single production for each transition. Equation 3.3 suggests that we write:

$$P_{i,j}: (\text{State } S_i) \rightarrow (\text{State } S_j) \qquad \text{for each } i \text{ and each } j \text{ in } T_i \quad (4.1)$$

The WM contains elements for the states (State S_i). We have tagged the elements with an identifier (State $\cdots$), though it is not clear it is needed. A transition to a new state occurs if a current state element (State S_i) is in WM. Thus the beam resides in WM as a set of active state elements.

12. Incorporating the Likelihoods into the Transition. Formulation (4.1) is inadequate, since all that S_i encodes is the unique state identifier, and not the accumulated likelihood value, $L_{i,\ t}$. On the other hand, the likelihoods themselves are just values of some sort and are not identified per se with their states. We can modify (4.1) by making the data element for a state hold both the state identification and the cumulative likelihood value, (S_iL):

$$P_{i,\ j}: (\text{State } S_i = L) \to (\text{State } S_j\ [=L]) \tag{4.2}$$

By encoding L and S in the same element we maintain the association between them. However, (4.2) leaves open how the new L is determined, since its value will generally be different from the original likelihood of S_i which is bound to the variable $=L$, though partially dependent on it. We indicate this unfinished character of the mapping by the use of brackets, $[=L]$. Note that we have introduced a variable into (4.2), $=L$, to pick up the likelihood from WM. Thus, our system is no longer variable free. Before taking care of this difficulty, we need to get the rest of the path computation expressed. Note also that (4.2) leaves open how likelihoods are represented, specifying only that the representation can be bound to a variable.

13. Taking Account of the Current Acoustic Data. The acoustic data enters into obtaining the new likelihoods, and we can express this dependency symbolically within the brackets:

$$P_{i,\ j}: (\text{State } S_i = L)\ (\text{Data } = D) \to$$
$$(\text{State } S_j\ [= L + C(A_i, = D)]) \tag{4.3}$$

The WM now contains an element that holds the acoustic parameters, (Data D_t). As with the state elements, we have tagged the acoustic data with an identifier, (Data $\cdots$), though its necessity is not clear. In order to let the acoustic data enter into the determination of the new likelihood on the right-hand side, we have had to introduce another variable, $=D$, into the system, which must ultimately be removed. Again, we have left open the representation of the acoustic data (D_t), assuming only that it can be bound to a variable $(=D)$.

14. Encoding the Back-pointers to Permit the Backtrace. Back-pointers can be encoded by remembering the state pairs of each transition that is generated. This can be done just by expanding the state element once more.

$$P_{i,\ j}: (\text{State } S_i = = L)\ (\text{Data } = D) \to$$
$$(\text{State } S_jS_i\ [= L + C(A_i, = D)]) \tag{4.4}$$

The = in the initial template (State $S_i = = L$) is a don't-care mark, which indicates that the prior state is not relevant to whether a match occurs. It need not count as a variable, in terms of variable-free productions, since no value is bound and used on the right-hand side. However, for this to be the case does imply a further specification of the UV mechanism, namely, that the constraint is on binding or using and not just on multiple instantiation.

This formulation implies that backtracing will occur by pairwise linking back through the state elements, though we leave open for the moment just what calculation has to be performed. This proposed mechanism has a potential flaw. If a state were ever repeated, then the back-pointer would not be unique; either a loop or a jump might occur. In current Harpy this is avoided because a back-pointer array is kept for each time step. But there is as yet no explicit time indexing in the WM representation, so confusion is possible.

The PS described by (4.4) will carry out the generative component of the forward sweep. The set of states that are developing in the WM at a given instant constitutes the beam at that instant. But the WM holds the entire beam history, with each new wave of the beam showing up at the front of WM (i.e., as the most recent set of state elements). The productions must still become variable-free, so that as many as are satisfied can fire; thus, the entire beam can be computed at the time its acoustic data element arises in WM.

The system so far has only been responsive to generating the alternatives. I now begin to put in the selective mechanisms.

15. Taking the Maximum Over All States in the Path Equation. Taking the maximum is one way of cutting down the set of paths to be carried forward. Consider not computing at all the maximum called for in equation (3.3). The result would be to carry forward several paths to the same state. These would then have duplicate histories for the remainder of the utterance. They would expand the total set of states that are candidates for retention in the beam. Cutting back the beam to fixed size would presumably get rid of some of them, but the net effect would still be to cause some fraction of the beam to consist of useless paths. Providing that the maximum state would be taken at the end and that one could correctly trace out the back path, the only result would be an effective diminution of the beam. Stated otherwise, if the fraction lost was stable, then the maximum could be dispensed with if compensated by a beam of increased width with its consequent extra computing costs.[4] Thus, one possible solution for taking the maximum is to ignore it.

---

[4]This holds only for systems, such as Harpy, that use a beam search, where beam clipping performs the same function (up to some point) as taking the maximum.

However, it is possible that we need not follow this course. The recognition match takes the maximum automatically, under the proper mapping. To see this, consider in detail what happens when two states, say S_i and S_j, lead to the same state, S_k. Each then will lead on to duplicate common paths, which will differ only in the likelihoods that are brought forward, one reflecting the history through S_i, the other the history through S_j. We can plot the state elements that will be generated in WM at the critical junction, moving on to (say) S_m and then S_n:

$$(\text{State } S_k \ S_i \ L_i) \Rightarrow (\text{State } S_m \ S_k \ L'_i) \Rightarrow$$
$$(\text{State } S_n \ S_m \ L''_i) \Rightarrow \ldots \tag{4.5}$$

$$(\text{State } S_k \ S_j \ L_j) \Rightarrow (\text{State } S_m \ S_k \ L'_j) \Rightarrow$$
$$(\text{State } S_n \ S_m \ L''_j) \Rightarrow \ldots \tag{4.6}$$

Suppose L_i were less than L_j (so that, with maximization, only the S_j–S_k–S_m–S_n path would survive). Then L'_i will be less than L'_j, L''_i less than L''_j, and so on through the future. Now the generation productions will certainly generate both of the state elements at the left side, coming into state S_k. They may generate both of the middle elements in (4.5) and (4.6) because their state elements for the conditions are still dissimilar (one has S_i, the other S_j, in the second place). Furthermore, the output elements (the middle elements) are also dissimilar, one having L'_i, the other L'_j; so they will not coalesce into the same WM element. But will they generate both of the elements at the far right? These are generated by (4.4) operating on the two middle state elements, respectively. These input elements differ only in L'_i and L'_j and are both being matched to the same production (since the acoustic data is the same for both):

$$P_{m, \, n}: (\text{State } S_m = \, = L) \, (\text{Data } = D) \rightarrow$$
$$(\text{State } S_n \ S_m \ [= L + C(A_m, = D)]) \tag{4.7}$$

Could conflict resolution accept one (with $= L$ bound to L'_j) in preference to the other (with $= L$ bound to L'_i)? If a preference does occur, then it is likely that the secondary item will never get to fire. Both recency and special case order are candidates to accomplish this. If the difference between L'_j and L'_i is to be one of recency, this implies something strong about the encoding of likelihoods—namely, that it be analogous to activation. If the difference is to be one of special case order, then no such far reaching implication seems to exist. Let us hold this choice in abeyance for the moment, but assume that some mapping decision will be made so that only one of the two instantiations fires. Then the potential dilution of the beam with duplicates will come to a halt almost immediately after the convergence of states. Possibly some tag ends will exists (the middle element of equation 4.5), but this will not prove bothersome. We will have to return to make this decision in final form, but can leave it for the moment.

16. Clipping the Beam to Keep a Specified Beam Width. From equation (3.4), the clipping conditions involve rejecting all those state elements (State S_i S_j L) where L is more than e from the best. The cutoff varies so as to maintain a given robustness in the beam. Clipping can be achieved by two alternative mechanisms: (1) failing to fire a production on data elements that do not warrant it (i.e., should be clipped); or (2) recognizing unsatisfactory elements in the WM by general clipping productions that mark the elements to inhibit further generation. General clipping productions would probably contain variables. As noted earlier, it is not possible in general to use such productions to evaluate state elements, since they would not be able to fire in parallel. Thus, let us explore the other alternative, which is to incorporate as much of the evaluation as possible into production selection.

Consider modifying production (4.4). First, the likelihood variable ($=L$) can be replaced by a match to a constant, so that degrees of matching can be introduced. Second, C, the comparison operation, can be moved to the condition side; thus $=D$ can be replaced by the template and the recognition match itself be used to make the comparison. We get:

$$P_{i, j}: \text{(State } S_i = L) \text{ (Data } A_i) \rightarrow$$
$$\text{(State } S_j S_i [L - r(L) + r(A_i)]) \tag{4.8}$$

where $r(X)$ = the residual from matching to X.

Two important assumptions have been made in (4.8). To explain them, consider that (4.8) was matched against:

$$\text{WM: } (\cdots \text{ (State } S_i S_k L') \cdots \text{(Data } D_f) \cdots) \tag{4.9}$$

Normally, in HPSA77, a match will occur if and only if L and L' are the same, and similarly if A_i and D_t are the same. The first new assumption is that L and L' will match if they are "close," and similarly, A_i and D_t will match if they are "close." What constitutes "close" remains open, except that ultimately the closeness of A_i and D_t must agree with the template metric used in the Harpy algorithm (although clearly it need not be the Itakura metric, used in the current Harpy, as others may be equally well suited). The second assumption is that the residual of the match of a condition, call it $r(X)$, is available on the action side. The brackets on the right-hand side of (4.8) remind us that we have not settled how the computation there will go: but both residuals show up there as appropriate input to determining the new likelihood.

These assumptions indeed appear radical. However, Harpy works with continuous quantities, and the incorporation of quantities into a symbolic system, such as HPSA77, must occur someplace. The scheme implicit above may not be right. There are alternative paths that might be traveled. The most obvious one is to retain the exact match and to introduce multiple productions with quantitative symbols that range over discrete levels of likelihood. The chief drawback to this latter type of scheme, even beyond the explosion of productions, is its limited precision. Therefore I will pursue the more radical path. However, as with the assumption about conflict resolution for taking the maximum, I will accept the result and proceed with the remainder of the mapping. When all assumptions have been made I will be in a better position to analyze their joint nature and impact.

The same likelihood symbol, L, appears in all productions of (4.8). This amounts to adopting a uniform basis for the measurement of likelihoods. Conceivably, this could be biased for different transitions by using $L_{i, j}$ instead of L. But it is unclear whether this is useful.

One result of this formulation is the apparent elimination of the variables in system (4.4), thus returning to variable-free productions that can run concurrently. Whether this is effective depends on how the residuals are handled. They clearly sense something of the elements matched, and they may turn out to be variables in sheep's clothing. Note that $L - r(L)$ is just L', which is to say we have substituted L' for L. How is this different from simply matching to $= L$ and substituting? In any event, this cannot be evaluated until we finally settle how the computation in the brackets is done.

17. Extrapolating Speech Over Gaps in the Input.   An important problem should be noted in (4.8). (Data A_i) can fail to match, independent of the satisfaction of the accumulated likelihood, however it will ultimately be sensed. This produces a situation of sudden death in which a single unfortunate gap in the acoustic data can terminate the optimal path. This gap need not be caused by internal noise in the system, but for example might be from external noise (e.g., a door slam). This problem is explicitly recognized in the current Harpy system, where the criteria on the cutoff is often expressed in terms of how many cycles it permits a path to survive when it is receiving no support from the acoustic evidence at all.

Let us return to the idea of selecting the beam after the forward generation has developed the new state elements in WM. Then generation need not be dependent on the acoustic data. However, we must be sure that selective evaluation is done by variable-free productions. This must yield two sets of productions, one for generation, one for evaluation:

$$P_{i, j}: (\text{State } S_i = L) \rightarrow (\text{State } S_j \ S_i \ [L, \ r(L)]) \tag{4.10}$$

$Q_{i, j}$: (State S_j S_i L) (Data A_i) →

$\quad$ (State S_j S_i [$L - r(L) + r(A_i)$])   (4.11)

If L is close enough to L' (the likelihood in the state element), the productions of (4.10) will take every member of the beam and make all the transitions, thus yielding the full expanded beam. We have left open (as far as possible) what value is actually produced for the likelihood of the new element. This is indicated by the brackets. Once a state element is in WM, the productions of (4.11) can be evoked if both L is close enough to L' and A_i is close enough to D_t. Here the brackets on the right side express the resultant in the same form as (4.8).

Even if the acoustic data is too far from A_i for (4.11) to match, then (4.10) will continue to carry the expansion forward. If at some subsequent point the match becomes good enough, then (4.11) can again be evoked to do whatever the brackets indicate to raise the value of the likelihood.

As it stands, (4.11) produces extra elements which differ only by the value of the likelihoods. I leave open whether this causes any difficulty and whether the issue can be avoided by interpreting (4.11) to modify an element rather than replace it.

The obvious difficulty with the system (4.10)–(4.11) is that (4.10) would appear to generate forever, unconstrained. This means that the bracket computation must do something that diminishes the likelihood of the new state elements, so that if unreinforced they will eventually fall too far below L to be satisfied. The obvious way to imagine this happening is for the value of the likelihood to be common through all these forward steps and to gradually decay if left alone. The obvious production to replace (4.10) would be:

$P_{i, j}$: (State S_i = = L) → (State S_j S_i = L)   (4.12)

The value of $=L$ decays autonomously if left alone.

It is clear that (4.12) has re-introduced variables—just what seems prohibited. Replacing $=L$ with [$L - r(L)$], which produces the same value as a reduced L', would seem to be just a notational difference.

All is not yet lost. Consider the following scheme (which will add to the accumulating list of promissory notes if adopted). We ignore the residual in (4.10), but do use a diminished value of stipulated likelihood. Thus we get:

$P_{i, j}$: (State S_i = L) → (State S_j S_i J_i)   (4.13)

where J_i = the stipulated diminished likelihood.

If $P_{i, j}$ matches at all, then the prior value of the likelihood is lost, to be replaced by a stipulated value (J_i). Now we assume that the chance of $P_{i, j}$ being satisfied does depend on the closeness of the match. Thus there is some probability $p(r(L))$ that (4.13) will fire, and this diminishes with increasing $r(L)$. If J_i is set so that the probability is p, then the probability of a particular forward path surviving undergoes exponential decay, i.e., $1, p, p^2, p^3, \ldots$ for successive steps forward. If p times B, the branchiness of the transitions, is less than one, then the entire expansion from a state element will converge to zero as long as there is no (positive) interference from the acoustic signal. Note that p can be made to vary as a function of the state (i.e., J_i is a function of state), so that high probability paths can be distinguished a priori from rare paths.

There are some discomforting features in this solution. One is that the choice is actually probabilistic, so that the best path has some absolute chance each time of disappearing. Furthermore, attempts to attain high survival rates translate into long survival times.[5]

A second, even more discomforting, feature is that all history is wiped out as each new generation is selected. L', the cumulated likelihood of the state up to this moment, does not pass to the new state elements. L' affects only the chance of survival on the one trial. This might conceivably be tolerable when all the forward branches are data-free extrapolations across a complete acoustic gap. But this same production will be used for all generation, and so will have the same property of losing the past. Despite these difficulties, let us hold this solution as one possibility, along with the chance of finding some way of retaining the accumulated likelihood value as the system moves forward.

Before leaving this issue, note one more potential difficulty to the whole notion of splitting generation and evaluation into separate productions. It is possible for the productions to get out of synchronization. Although a (4.11) production cannot operate until its corresponding (4.13) production has fired, there is no such absolute constraint in the other direction and generation might get ahead of evaluation in some uncomfortable way. Given that all productions are executing concurrently, there may be no difficulty, but the potential hazard sets a red flag.

18. Adding Likelihoods to Comparisons. If we accept productions (4.13) and (4.11) as an adequate representation of the recognition system, then the problem of combining continuous quantities is focussed in (4.11), and in particular in the bracket computation $[L, r(L), r(A_i)]$ plus what can be transmitted from the condition of a production to the actions without evoking the UV mechanism. I have already come across the difficulty in dealing with residuals that they appear to be variables after all.

The productions of (4.11) turn out to be potentially a special case where

---

[5]This problem also plagued the fixed (10 msec) step-size version of Harpy in implementing variable length segments entirely through self-looping transitions. For then segment length must be geometrically distributed, for exactly the same reason as survival durations above.

the UV mechanism might be avoided, though we may not wish to exploit it—namely, the action expression is identical to the condition expression except for the change in value of the likelihood. If we view the action element as new, then there appears no way to avoid using a variable to communicate the information across the production. But if we view the action element as being the same element as the condition element, then the action is only one of modifying what is there. The possibility of conceiving it this way depends on how likelihoods are encoded. If the updated likelihood is a new arbitrary symbol, then again there seems no way out of treating it as a substitution. If the updated likelihood is truly a changing of value, then a different operation is conceivable. It is worth noting that this possibility seems less open to us in dealing with (4.10). The action element (State S_j S_i $[L, r(L)]$) is a new element in WM and hence does not pre-exist to be modified. This difference is not fortuitous, but follows directly from splitting (4.8) to separate the creative-generative aspect from the evaluative aspect.

If I take the path that maps Harpy successfully, then I can invent an action, call it *increment,* which lets me add the residual $r(A_i)$ to L. I need also to indicate that this happens on a given element identified at the input. To remain consistent with the characterization of productions as variable-free, the action element is prefixed with $=$. Thus I replace production (4.11) by:

$$Q_{i,\,j}: (\text{State } S_j\ S_i\ L)\ (\text{Data } A_i) \Rightarrow$$
$$=(\text{State } S_j\ S_i\ \text{Increment } (r(A_i))) \qquad (4.14)$$

This use of $=$ does not constitute use of a variable, since the identity is being carried by the element as a whole.

Besides placing additional requirements on the encoding of likelihoods, I have also specified more narrowly the critical aspects of the UV mechanism. Assumption D1 does not specify what aspect is really limiting—the instantiation of variables, the transportation of value, the creation of new elements, or the replacement/substitution of values in these new elements. These different aspects have quite different properties (e.g., how processing time varies with the number of variables, variable occurrences in conditions, action elements, and variable occurrences in actions). But it was not necessary to specify the effect so tightly. The present assumption seems to put the burden on the creation of new elements, though it still leaves open various other aspects.

If we use (4.13), a small discrepancy between it and (4.14) needs to be cleared up. If (4.13) diminishes the likelihood from some initial value L, then the state elements that (4.14) will deal with will have likelihood J_i. Consequently, instead of (4.14) we should use:

$$Q_{i,j}: (\text{State } S_j \ S_i \ J_i) \ (\text{Data } A_i) \Rightarrow$$
$$= (\text{State } S_j \ S_i \ \text{Increment } (r(A_i))) \tag{4.15}$$

This scheme represents adequately the process of constructing cumulative likelihoods either on the original scheme in which such likelihoods would be accumulated step by step or the new scheme in which each step leads to a history-losing resetting of the likelihood to a standard value (the J_i).

I9. Matching the Template and the Acoustic Parameters.   As shown in equation (3.5), the Itakura metric ultimately reduces to a dot product match, in which the terms from the template really correspond to orthogonal components, rather than corresponding components to the acoustic parameters. There is nothing in the type of match used in production system architectures that looks like a weighted sum, especially with negative weights, which is implied by the notion of orthogonal components to a positive vector (the acoustic parameters). Rather than attempt to cope with such a metric, it seems better to deny that the Itakura metric is other than a computational device for current Harpy, and to look for matches that seem more appropriate to the sort of matching structure available. Certainly the experience with Harpy and other speech efforts (Goldberg, 1975) shows that no one metric and/or set of parameters is uniquely suited for recognition. There seems to be general agreement on the nonessential nature of the Itakura metric. For instance, current research on Harpy involves consideration of new metrics (see also Klatt, 1977).

Having said this, little more can be added. The template A_i in (4.15), of course, is not a single symbol (even with an associated quantity). A_i consists of an expression with symbols for each parameter:

$$(\text{Data } A_1 A_2 A_3 \cdots A_{14}) \tag{4.16}$$

It is almost entirely open in the system what happens when two such expressions are matched, i.e., what sort of summary quantity emerges. This summary, which is the residual $r(A_i)$, must be the desired metric, and it must be recoverable to be used in the increment operation.

I conclude that there is no evident obstacle with respect to the metric, but that some key facts are probably missing.

I10. Avoiding Confusion with Old Data.   An important simplification of our Harpy production system is that the data elements are not specifically indexed on time. The back-pointers, for instance, are simply associated with states and not with states at specific times, which is how the current Harpy encodes the memory. What keeps PS.Harpy from getting all confused, either going around in circles or applying the acoustic data to states at different times?

The answer must lie in the recency conflict resolution rules, which keep the attention of the system focussed on the front of WM, and in the refraction rules, which keep productions from repeating themselves exactly. To first order, these mechanisms are constructed exactly to keep processing straight over time and they can be presumed to perform adequately here.

If there is any implication here, it is that these conflict resolution rules have to be extended to variable-free productions and are not just a feature of the UV mechanism. Refraction must apply to variable-free productions. Normally, recency cannot apply to a variable-free production, because any two such productions can fire concurrently, hence without conflict; and a single such production cannot have more than a single instantiation. However, if we permit don't-care elements ($=$) in the condition, then a single variable-free production can have several potential instantiations. It can only be permitted one, and that one should be determined by recency.

III. Performing the Backtrace. The backtrace productions depend on the data representation of the back-pointers, which has already been fixed in the state element; and on the form of the desired final result, which has not been specified yet. To do the latter would go beyond the recognition phase, and hence beyond the direct concern of this paper. It is sufficient to show that the appropriate grammatically analyzed word sequence can be recovered. This is just the path through the grammar net with access to the words from the abstract nodes of the grammar.

We need a production system that provides a way to initiate the backtrace, to link back through the states, and to obtain access to the symbols for the words (our surrogate for obtaining a final integrated structure to use in the larger cognitive context).

Harpy initiates the backtrace when the utterance is complete. This is a default design decision based on the (temporary) structuring of Harpy's task environment to work on one utterance at a time. The clue to the end of an utterance is a relatively long period of silence. This maps into the detection of a specific acoustic data element (silence not being the absence of perceived sound, but the perception of a distinct acoustic environment). Thus, we get:

$$U1: (\text{State} = S = L)\,(\text{Data } A_s) \rightarrow (\text{Utterance } S_{\text{end}} = S) \qquad (4.17)$$

This production will be triggered whenever the prolonged-silence data element (Data A_s) occurs during the analysis of an utterance (so that state elements are active in WM). $U1$ contains a variable ($=S$) for the state, within the state element. According to Harpy, the state element to be picked is the one with the highest likelihood (i.e., the maximum of the most recent beam), and this cannot be known in advance.

$U1$ will instantiate all the state elements in the beam that are close enough to L. Furthermore, nothing restricts $U1$ to matching only the · front wave of the beam; instantiations may come from anywhere. According to assumption D1.2, all of these instantiations should be executed. This could be a problem, since only the maximum element is to be selected for the backtrace. According to assumption D1.3, there may be a limit on the set actually to be executed, though D1.3 does not specify any details of the restriction. If we are to use $U1$ to initiate the backtrace, we need to specify these restrictions so that (1) the maximum state element is always evoked; and (2) whatever other elements are evoked will not bother the operation of the backtrace. It is plausible that the executed set should always contain the best matching instantiation, which would solve the first part. This does, however, add to the specifications of D1.3. Though distinct from the assumption to be made in Section I5 to take the maximum, it seems quite similar to it in spirit.

What happens to all the other state elements that might be evoked? Conflict resolution should assure that the maximum likelihood element will dominate in the immediate selection. But the others could cause difficulty as they float in WM. One possibility is that the HPSA77 includes the ability to control the lockout, within limits, so only a single instantiation can be kept if desired. Let us put off making a design decision here and simply assume that only the maximum element need be considered.

The action side of $U1$ provides an element, (Utterance S_j S_i), which is analogous to the state elements, but labeled as the final utterance. It will hold the whole chain back to the beginning. $U1$ provides the last element if the chain, which is a special state, S_{end}.

The obvious way to trace back through the path is with a single general linkage production:

$U2$: (Utterance $= = S$) (State $= S$ $= S'$ $=$) $\rightarrow$

(Utterance $= S$ $= S'$)   (4.18)

Unfortunately, $U2$ is not admissible according to assumption D1.4. It uses the same variable in two conditions, and indeed this identification is the heart of the production. The situation here is exactly analogous to the situation in the Sternberg paradigm which was used as an example in Table 11.1. There, $A1$–$A2$ would have provided a direct solution to classifying the probe item, if the identity test could have been done on the fly, i.e., by the two occurrences of $= X$ using the recognition match. The solution is indicated there by the production system $B1$–$B3$, which first creates a testing chunk that brings together the two symbols to be compared. Thus, we get a revision of *U2* and add a testing production, *U3*:

$$U2: \text{(Utterance} = =S) \text{(State} =S'' =S' =) \rightarrow$$
$$\text{(Test} =S =S' =S'') \tag{4.19}$$

$$U3: \text{(Test} =S =S' =S') \rightarrow \text{(Utterance} =S =S') \tag{4.20}$$

We have again the problem of many instantiations, since (4.19) is satisfied for all state elements (there being no constraining conditions on its variables). Since (4.20) will select out only the one that moves back a step, there is only the problem of the lockout while all the instantiations of (4.19) are being executed. The irrelevant test elements will not get in the way (providing, as assumed, there is no capacity limit on WM). We can defer the question of whether the lockout problems are severe and take *U1–U3* as producing the utterance chain.

The action of *U1–U3* will come to an end when the chain runs out. There will be a state element of the form (State S_i S_{start} L), which will lead to an utterance element of the form (Utterance S_i S_{start}), as a distinguished element to start the chain.

Finally, we have to retrieve the words. The states are associated uniquely with nodes in the grammar (though many states lead to the same node). These nodes define uniquely the word associated with the node. Since we are considering a compiled network, we can assume that there is a direct link back from the states to the relevant codes for the words.

$$W_i: \text{(Utterance } S_i =) \rightarrow \text{(Word } Wx) \tag{4.21}$$

where Wx = The word associated with S_i.

The word is not indexed on i (i.e., Word_i), since many states will home to the same word. Actually, there is no need for every state to associate to a word. Several schemes are possible; e.g., either (or both) of the end states have W_i productions, but the interior states do not. There is nothing in our present context that lets us design this part of the scheme further, so we simply leave this aspect open. Nothing is affected in the path generation by whether or not W_i productions exist for a given state.

The productions *U1–U3* and the W_i constitute the backtrace production system. It has some interesting aspects. First, *U1–U3* contain variables. Consequently, the backtrace runs as a serial process. It will actually ripple back at the basic cycle time of the system, since each step must be finished before the next one is started. Second, it evokes the words backwards, from the most recent towards the past. This seems on the surface to be a violation of the normal way of experiencing input, i.e., forward. Thus there may be an interaction with the design decision D3 in HPSA77, which was responsive to making forward experiencing natural.

I12. Matching Variable Duration Phones.   In Harpy the segments are of variable duration and a template match can be extended to the next segment if it is sufficiently similar. There seems to be little difficulty in achieving this. The acoustic data arises in WM as (Data $D_{1,t} D_{2,t} \cdots D_{m,t}$), though nothing yet indicates whether it existed in some further decomposed form in WM or whether it arises *de novo* from sensory mechanisms. Consider the simplest version, where components are fixed (complex) acoustic features, which rise in WM autonomously whenever the feature exists in the acoustic stream. (It remains open how much specialized, but cognitive-context free, processing occurs to develop the feature.) At some instant a set of them will trigger off an acoustic recognition production:

$$R_k: D_1 D_2 \cdots D_m \rightarrow (\text{Data } D_1 D_2 \cdots D_m) \qquad (4.22)$$

This production has the effect of creating a separate memory of the existence of a set of features, independent of the D_i themselves. It resolves the memory problems mentioned under sufficiency issue S4, namely that speech by its nature originates in a repeatedly used fixed structure, and some sort of transfer of information to a new place must occur.

The R_k productions will fire whenever they are satisfied. A given characterization (Data $D_1 \cdots D_m$) will last as long as no other $R_{k'}$ is sufficiently similar to fire. Thus the variable duration will simply happen. The time course will be governed by the set of R_ks that are available, how dense a net they throw over the space of acoustic-feature vectors. With this scheme the two varieties of variable duration merge into one. Even though the D_i move around somewhat, the refractory conflict resolution should keep the same production from firing repeatedly.

Potential difficulties certainly exist with this scheme. There is a strong dependency on the nature of the recognition match metric. Without some investigation of this metric, it is unclear whether the right partitioning of the acoustic space is possible. This is simply another way of stating the concern of Section I9 that the recognition match be able to provide an adequate acoustic metric. However, this scheme seems basically sound enough as an initial pass.

I13. Initiation of Recognition.   In Harpy, speech processing is initiated by a small communication protocol: The speaker initiates with a written command (LISTEN!); the system returns a visually displayed command (READY!); after which it starts to receive, taking the first significant sound intensity to be the start of the utterance. Analogous to doing the backtrace only when the whole utterance is complete, this arrangement reflects the specialized experimental environment. However, I can capture the essence of the arrangement by defining a collection of *initiation* productions:

$$V_k: (\text{Data } A_k) \to (\text{State } S_j\ S_{\text{start}}\ L_k) \tag{4.23}$$

The V_k go directly from sound patterns to putting the initial state element into WM. These latter then make contact with the appropriate $P_{i,j}$. There may be any number of the productions; in fact, compared to the rather small number of transitions from a state symbol well into an utterance, the context for initiation may be quite broad.

Missing from the V_k is any notion of the initiation depending on some external state, some expectation. An alternative formulation to (4.23) would enter a single state element (State $S_{\text{start}} \cdots$), which would then trigger the equivalent of (4.23) as regular $P_{i,j}$ productions. Entering the single initial state element would easily be made dependent on expectations. However, there is little point here in expanding the system in this way.

I14. Precision of Likelihoods. Interestingly, nothing has yet forced the question of the precision of the likelihoods and the comparison. Yet this must ultimately be a major item in the plausibility of the model. Harpy currently uses an eight-bit encoding of the likelihood (256 distinct values). Experiments with Harpy showed that accuracy decreases significantly if only six bits are used.

So far, the restraints placed on this representation of likelihood have no interaction with a requirement that likelihoods be precise to at least eight bits. Thus we need to be much more specific about representing likelihoods before we can even express this demand in a useful way.

I15. Summary: Encoding Likelihoods. I have now taken care of most of the major mapping issues. In the course of this, a number of explicit promissory notes have been accumulated. I list them under the issues where they achieved their final form:

I4. Avoid confusions on backpointers.
I5. Maximize by means of recency or special case order.
I6. Match on closeness of likelihoods and acoustic parameters.
I7.1. The probability of match might depend on the closeness.
I7.2. Replacement or creation of elements in evaluation.
I7.3. Synchronization problems between generation ($P_{i,j}$) and evaluation ($Q_{i,j}$).
I8. Increment an element according to the residual.
I9. Summing residuals produces desired acoustic match metric.
I11.1. Controllable lockout or no intrusion of extra backtrace starters.

I11.2. Limited lockout on stepping through the backtrace.
I13. Likelihoods must be precise to eight bits.

Much of this list concerns how one passes from signals, which are continuous quantities, to symbols, which are expressions over discrete alphabets. How does one encode the likelihoods to have the correct properties? It was important to get all the aspects of this basic theme together, rather than to deal with each piecemeal. A moment's consideration shows that the problem is much larger than the perception of speech. It concerns the general transformation of all sensory signals into symbolic form. Thus, it will pay to turn aside and look at the general encoding of stimulus intensity. Though it will be done briefly, it will at least provide some basis for a design choice that may work out over a wider domain than just speech. With the larger perspective, I will then be able to complete the mapping constructed in this section.

5. THE REPRESENTATION OF INTENSITY

Continuous magnitudes show up in human cognition in several places and almost surely in different representations. We know something of the sensory transduction into neural pulse rates, which are an analog representation of stimulus intensity. We also know that humans use a wide variety of symbolic notations for quantities, such as familiar radix notation, as well as more imperfect collections of discrete quantity names ("big," "little"). That there is signal to symbol transduction is beyond doubt; there may be several such transductions. It is a feature of all representations of the same underlying domain (here the continuum), that they are capable of mimicking each other. To first order this is built into their being representations of the same thing. Thus, we should not expect it to be easy to determine empirically what representations are being used when we have only, or mostly, behavioral evidence available.

Types of Representations

Within a production system architecture, there are several possibilities for representing quantities.[6] For short I can call these the *counting, population, radix, value, dual-value,* and *activation* representations.

A counting representation makes use of the ability of an expression to

---

[6]An extended treatment of the development of quantitative symbols within a production system framework has been produced by Klahr and Wallace (1976). However, it focuses on issues that do not help us with the encoding of initial intensity information.

hold various numbers of tokens. Thus given a primitive symbol X, the expressions (X), (X X), (X X X) encode 1, 2 and 3 respectively. Given that new quantitative symbols can be defined, then (X3 X4) is 7, where X3 is (X X X), etc. This is an analog representation for the integers, making use of the physical properties of symbolic expressions.

A population representation uses the occurrence of N data elements in WM as a representation of the number N. Thus, if WM held (X A) (X B) (X C) this would be taken as meaning three Xs. The representation is similar to a counting representation, but without any easy way to localize, store, or manipulate the representations. It would seem hardly worth mentioning, except that it showed up in issue I7 as a possible representation of likelihood to deal with gradual extinction of the pure generation productions of 4.13.

A radix representation is a symbolic representation that has a collection of primitive quantitative symbols (the basis), such that various expressions involving the primitive symbols in known roles can be interpreted as quantities. The common number notation provides a standard example. The digits 0, 1, . . ., 9 are the basis, and an expression (9 4 2 3 6) is interpreted as the number $9 \times 10^4 + 4 \times 10^3 + 2 \times 10^2 + 3 \times 10 + 6$. There are similar representations that have somewhat different properties. For instance, let a quantity be represented by $(S_1 S_2 \cdots S_n)$ where S_1 is the best estimate that can be given with one primitive symbol, S_2 is a correction in either direction to yield the best estimate in two symbols, S_3 is another correction, again in either direction, and so on. This is radix-like, but may not have uniqueness of representation; for example, $(S_1 + S_2)$ and $(S_3 - S_4)$ may represent the same quantity.

A value representation admits symbols that can be treated as if they were continuous quantities. Expressions such as $(S\ 4.32)$ or $(T\ -3)$ are admissible, along with $(S\ X)$ or $(T\ TEMP)$. This begs the question of how the quantitative symbols represent quantities. When one uses such notations in programming languages (e.g., Lisp) there is another underlying representation (the bit array). But the issue can be finessed and it can simply be assumed that a quantitative value can be used at any place that a symbol can occur. These values can be treated as if there were some analog representation with only finite accuracy.

A dual-value representation associates with every symbol a quantitative value. Each position in an expression has both a symbolic name ($S1$) and a value (4.32), e.g., ($S1$: 4.32 $S4$: -3). This contrasts with a pure value representation where numbers are simply one alternative. It agrees with the value representation in simply assuming some encoding of continuous magnitude for the quantitative symbol.

An activation representation associates with elements in WM a quantity, namely their activation, which is a continuous magnitude. This is not available in LTM (in fact, positive activation defines existence in WM). Thus it shares with the dual-value representation the feature that elements have both symbols and quantities, but contrasts with it by the quantity only being available in the short term.

All six of these representations come in various flavors and with various restrictions. One major dimension is the representation of negative numbers and of fractions. For instance, in its natural form, activation only represents positive numbers. A second dimension is the set of operations involved. Counting and radix representations do not add any new operations at all, but pose the problem of how to achieve the use of quantitative symbols through the existing capabilities of the architecture. Value and dual-value representations both require adding primitive matching predicates (or metrics) and primitive actions. Activation, as it currently exists, works through conflict resolution rather than the recognition match; it is thus quite different in its operational character from the others. However, this might be enriched in various ways to make the activation capable of being sensed and manipulated. This might even lead to providing some capability for long term storage.

In this paper there is only space to explore a single alternative for how to represent magnitude. The most appealing is the activation representation. The range of alternatives have been enumerated to indicate that other paths are possible as well.

The two purely symbolic representations (counting and radix) suffer operationally from the requirement that most of the speech computation must be done by variable-free productions. How can such productions accomplish symbolic arithmetic? At a more general level, it seems odd to have a biological system that moves from a purely symbolic machine toward quantitative symbols as composed expressions. Surely the evolutionary movement has been in the other direction. No such objections exist for the value and dual-value representations. What raises concern here is that they will provide too much power. If, following "natural" programmer instincts, the full arithmetic set of operations (add, subtract, multiply and divide) is provided, then how will the difficulty the human has in doing arithmetic be explained? Even restriction to addition and subtraction still provides substantial power. One recommendation for activation is that it is already part of the architecture, being the one way in which continuum notions are already available. Also, it seems somewhat easier to provide limited capabilities, that do not blossom into awesome computational powers. None of these arguments are conclusive, for there are many variations possible of each representational type. Thus, the selection of an activation representation is a designer's choice.

Activation Encoding of Intensity

We can formulate this design decision as another step in the HPSA77 specification:

D5.1. Sensory information is encoded into the activation of WM elements.

HPSA77 already assumes that there is an amount of activation associated with each element in working memory. The actions, whether those on the right side of productions or those external to the production system, endow an element with an initial activation level which undergoes some time course of decay, until the element is no longer capable of aiding in evoking a production. Conflict resolution according to recency is in terms of activation. The way that activation of all the WM elements that support a production combine to yield its *effective* recency is a major degree of freedom available to make activation an appropriate way of encoding sensory intensity. Currently in OPS2 the combination rule is lexicographic order, but this is known to be unsatisfactory.

A useful way of determining whether activation will behave correctly to encode intensity is to explore how it handles the phomenena of simple stimulus detection and estimation, sensory psychophysics. This will help avoid making too many inappropriate assumptions in mapping Harpy. This can be done expeditiously by considering some models that appear moderately successful in handling psychophysical data.

Two of these are the so called *Timing* and *Counting* models (Green & Luce, 1975; Luce & Green, 1972; McGill, 1967). These both assume that intensity is encoded as a series of pulses on neural channels, with the pulse rate being monotonically related to the intensity. The basic measurement act is accumulating numbers of pulses and the times they take, over one or many channels. The basic decision procedures involve fixing times or counts, taking the measurements, and thresholding them against criteria. Sometimes, as in magnitude estimation, the measurements themselves must be converted into a response; hence some kind of genuine transduction must occur. The two models differ in what they hold constant (times or counts) and correspondingly what they measure (counts or times, respectively). Both, however, share the property that they inherently couple accuracy and time, since more accuracy can be achieved by taking a longer time to accumulate evidence. Thus, they directly create the opportunity for time–accuracy tradeoffs. This arises from the basic choice of representation in which intensity is coded by means of pulse rate (equivalently, pulse interval).

As analyzed in the literature, the models in general assume away the issues of central concern here. That is, they assume a homunculus to carry out the various operations and calculations required. The procedures to be carried out are determinate and, though they require processing and control, do not require intelligence. One is tempted to describe them as simple procedures, but that judgment is relative to the means at hand, to the architecture. The work on these models has focused on asking how well they explain the range of known psychophysical phenomena. My focus is on whether HPSA77 plus D5 just mentioned can implement these models in an appropriate way, on how it can explain the homunculus. If it does, then we inherit, so to speak, their explanations (as well as their flaws).

Consider a version of the timing model: On each of J channels, count a fixed number of k pulses and sum (or average) their total times. This yields an estimate of the stimulus intensity associated with that bundle of channels. In HPSA77+D5, without further assumptions, there is no way to measure times directly, no master clock. What is available is the decay of activation. Thus to measure time, a signal fires a production that activates a timer symbol (Clock), simply a symbol whose activation will be used to measure time.

$$T1: \text{(Signal)} \rightarrow \text{(Clock)} \tag{5.1}$$

The detector production is attempting to sense the existence of an event (the pulse) on another channel (Z) and to obtain the time measurement from (Clock).

$$T2: \text{(Clock) } (Z) \rightarrow [\text{time measure}] \tag{5.2}$$

A choice is available about whether the measurements will be taken with respect to the decrease in activation from the top or in absolute amount of activation. The latter looks less attractive, since the system itself would seem to be bathed in a bed of noise, so that no absolute base line is detectable. Furthermore, attending to the capabilities needed for Harpy, note that the main sensing technique is the residual formed during the match. Thus, if (Clock) on the condition side represents the maximum activation, the residual of the (Clock) condition and the (Clock) in WM provides a measure of the decay of WM (Clock), and hence of how long it has been ticking as a clock.[7] Thus, there is a revision of $T2$:

$$T2: \text{(Clock) } (Z) \rightarrow \text{(Time } [r(\text{(Clock)})]) \tag{5.3}$$

---

[7] Note that (Clock) in $T2$ is not the same element as (Clock) in WM, so they can have different activations; we could not have used Clock (that is, the same symbol) in both expressions.

The residual from the match is not itself a symbol. That is, it seems unlikely that a signal to symbol transformation occurs within the recognition match, such that match deviations show up as quantitative symbols somehow. Rather, the residuals seem more akin to activation, something that can be used to modify the activation of other symbols.

To pin this down, a precise set of rules for sensing and manipulating activation must be invented. This is necessary to move beyond informal use of brackets. There is now enough context to simply lay out a particular scheme and examine its properties. These add additional specifications to design decision D5.

Redefine brackets to mean the manipulation of activation. Thus, $X[\cdots]$ means that the expression in $[\cdots]$ has to do with the activation on X. If it occurs as part of a condition, it has to do with sensing the residual; if it occurs as part of an action element, it has to do with setting or modifying the activation of the element. There are variables in brackets, e.g., $X[=y]$. These bind to activation, not to the symbols themselves. Activation variables can only be used to set or modify the activation of existing symbols. Whether those symbols are newly created or not is determined independently in the usual way in HPSA77. The use of activation variables does not evoke the UV mechanism; hence activation variables may occur in either variable-free or variable-containing productions.

I will start by assuming that only the actions of setting and incrementing can be performed on the right hand side of a production. Thus $X[=y]$ will set X to have activation $=y$; $X[+ =y]$ will increment the existing activation of X by $=y$; and $X[- =y]$ will decrement it. The operations of differencing (obtaining the residual) and thresholding (match or no match) are performed by the recognition match (hence occur on the condition side of a production); they do not occur as actions. I leave open the issue of independent control of thresholds in the condition elements, i.e., setting an activation level for the condition elements and symbols to be used in the match. I do assume that the activation of an element, say (A B C), is composed (simple summation) from the activation of its components plus some activation proper to the expression itself. Thus, the basic production evocation also provides for the operation of accumulation. The ability to assign activation variables is important; it amounts to a strong control assumption about independent access to the components of activation. It permits some conditions to be used to gate or control the firing of a production, while other conditions sense activation. Without this, with just the total accumulated residual available to modify the action elements, there would always be a mixture of effects to cope with.

The above assumptions can be summarized as follows:

D5.2. The activation of an element is the activation of its components plus an activation proper to the element itself.

D5.3. Activation can be sensed by the recognition match; anywhere a normal variable can occur, an *activation variable* can also occur to sense the residual of the match to the component of the template. Activation variables do not involve the use-variables (UV) mechanism.

D5.4. Activation can be set, incremented, and decremented by actions, using either constant amounts of activation or sensed residuals (values of activation variables).

These assumptions do not appear to modify HPSA77, but only to further specify it. One of the strongest specifications is to a particular form of recency conflict resolution. The scheme strongly suggests, though it does not appear to absolutely demand, that the recency ordering be based on the total accumulated activation from all the condition elements. This is only one form of recency rule and, in fact, not one that has been explored extensively.

We can now turn back to formulating the Timing model. We get a new version of *T2:*

$$T2: (Clock)[=t](Z) \rightarrow (Time\ X[=t])\ (Decide) \qquad (5.4)$$

The activation variable $=t$ is set to be the residual of (Clock) in the template, set at some standard value, and of (Clock) in WM; this becomes the activation level of X within the expression to hold the time. (Decide) is a control signal telling the decision production that it is time to decide. This latter production can make the decision based on what (Time X) says:

$$T3: (Decide)\ (Time\ X) \rightarrow \cdots \qquad (5.5)$$

T3 does not admit of a settable threshold. One way of accomplishing this is by a second condition element:

$$T3: (Decide)(Threshold\ V)(Time\ X) \rightarrow \cdots \qquad (5.6)$$

By manipulating the activation on V, one gets evocation or not, corresponding to how big the residual is on X. Another way to set thresholds, of course, would be to introduce threshold-setting operations directly. But we will try to get by without this extra apparatus.

Productions *T1–T3* handle only a single pulse on a single channel. Accumulating time for multiple counts for a single channel can be done either by holding off reading (Clock) until the kth pulse or by adding in a residual with each pulse and quitting after k pulses. In either case, this requires counting the pulses on Z. There are serious limitations to this within HPSA77, which correspond directly to the limitations of humans to do lots of very fast counting. If we postulate a good mechanism for counting at one place in HPSA77, we must then show why it could not be used in other places as well. Small amounts of counting can be achieved in several ways, such as by state transitions or by recognizing counting patterns such as (X X X). But large counts remain an open issue. (It is unclear whether large counts occur in the Timing model; most existing work involves less than ten pulses per channel.)

Let us simply choose one way: counting by state transitions and then reading the (Clock). We get the following modification:

$T1$: (Signal) $\rightarrow$ (Clock)(Count T_0)   (5.7)

$T2_i$: (Z)(Count T_i) $\rightarrow$ (Count T_{i+1}) $i = 0, 1, \ldots, k - 1$ (5.8)

$T2_k$: (Clock)$[=t](Z)$(Count T_k) $\rightarrow$ (Time $X[+ =t]$) (Decide)   (5.9)

$T3$: (Decide)(Threshold V)(Time X) $\rightarrow \cdots$ (5.10)

The T_i are simply $k+1$ arbitrary counting symbols, analogous to the S_i used for speech states.

The final mechanism required is to accumulate over multiple channels. This can be done either by accumulating the activation from all channels into a single place or by keeping separate accumulators and using the accumulation feature of the condition elements at decision time. Looking at the separate-accumulator version, there are J channels, Z_j, so the $T2_i$ get multiplied to run off J separate counters—but using the same (Clock)—and $T1$ gets multiplied to initialize the J counters. There must also be J (Decide) elements to record each channel reaching the kth count, and $T3$ must fire only if all channels have finished. We get the final system:

$T1_j$: (signal) $\rightarrow$ (Clock)(Count$_j$ T_0)   (5.11)

$T2_{i, j}$: (Z)(Count$_j$ T_i) $\rightarrow$ (Count$_j$ T_{i+1})   (5.12)

$T2_{i, k}$: (Clock)$[=t](Z_j)$(Count$_j$ T_k) $\rightarrow$
(Time $X_i[+ =t]$) (Decide$_j$)   (5.13)

$T3$: (Decide$_1$)$\cdots$(Decide$_J$)(Threshold V) (Time X_1)$\cdots$
(Time X_J)$\rightarrow \cdots$ (5.14)

There are still some discomforting things about (5.11)–(5.14), such as the multiple counters and the large number of condition elements in $T3$. But we have hardly explored the space of productions systems to accomplish this task, and substantial tuning of the system is possible. We need not pursue the details further.

However, some remarks are appropriate about general plausibility and sufficiency. The productions are variable-free, so that the entire process can occur concurrently, which is clearly necessary. However, important demands on precision of activation are set by this scheme, and they may prove too stringent. The extensive character of the productions, with all the separate counters and counter states, may have consequences for establishing such systems, a matter that I haven't gone into at all. Though I did not present a version of the Counting model, its character follows along similar lines, given the development above. Thus, whether a Timing model or a Counting model is used is clearly a matter of software, and is not, so to speak, wired in. This is what Green and Luce (1975) found—namely, that payoffs could swing human subjects from one kind of behavior to the other. Though incidental to their focus of fitting specific models, such considerations are critical from an architectural concern.

In any event, I can rest here. This excursion was intended only to provide a crude indication that adopting decision D5 would be a reasonable choice. Formulations 5.11–5.14 show that decision D5 has a chance of being commensurate with the Luce and Green Timing model for psychophysics, and thus of being a plausible model of sensory intensity generally.

6. HARPY AS A PRODUCTION SYSTEM: FINAL VERSION

Accepting the design decision of the prior section on the representation of intensity, which identifies sensory magnitude with activation level, I can rework PS.Harpy.

The Final Version

The main issue is what activation to identify with the likelihood in the state expressions, (State S_i S_j L). There are three immediate possibilities: the special symbol L; the state, S_i; or the state expression (State S_i S_j L) itself. As usual, the right choice is not completely clear. However, L seems redundant with the state expression, and the use of the state symbol would appear to produce a classic type-token problem, if the same state were to be considered at more than one time in the utterance. Use of the expression itself has the virtue of simplifying the state element by eliminating L, since it is redundant. To be explicit, we add another mapping assumption:

M6. Likelihoods are encoded as the activation on the state element.

With this stipulation, I can simply write down the new production system for PS. Harpy:

$$P_{i,\,j}: \text{(State } S_i =)[=l] \rightarrow \text{(State } S_j\ S_l)[=1 - k_{i,\,j}] \tag{6.1}$$

$$Q_i: \text{(State } S_i =)(\text{Data } A_{i1} \ldots A_{im})[=d] \rightarrow$$
$$=\text{(State } S_i =)[+ =d] \tag{6.2}$$

$$R_k: D_1\ D_2 \cdots D_m \rightarrow (\text{Data } D_1\ D_2 \cdots D_m) \tag{6.3}$$

$$U1: \text{(State } =S =)(\text{Data } A_s) \rightarrow (\text{Utterance } S_{\text{end}} =S) \tag{6.4}$$

$$U2: \text{(Utterance } = =S)(\text{State } =S'' =S') \rightarrow$$
$$(\text{Test } =S =S' =S'') \tag{6.5}$$

$$U3: \text{(Test } =S =S' =S') \rightarrow (\text{Utterance } =S =S') \tag{6.6}$$

$$W_i: \text{(Utterance } S_i =) \rightarrow (\text{Word } Wx) \tag{6.7}$$

$$V_k: \text{(Data } A_k) \rightarrow (\text{State } S_j\ S_{\text{start}})[l_k] \tag{6.8}$$

Production 6.1 arises from (4.13). It generates the next state elements without regard for the acoustic data. Representing likelihoods by activation now permits a decrement on pure extrapolation that retains the memory of the likelihood of the input state. The decrement itself can be a function of the transition (S_i to S_j), as expressed in $k_{i,j}$. Thus, the worries about history-free generation that attended our initial formulation have vanished. Depending on the size of the decrement ($k_{i,j}$), acoustically unsupported extrapolation will eventually come to a halt.

Production 6.2 arises from (4.15). It operates to select out those forward paths that are supported by the acoustic data. It does this by boosting the likelihood by the amount of the acoustic match ($+ =d$). This increment is added to the existing likelihood element and not to a newly created element. All (6.2) does is enhance good paths. The actual clipping of the beam occurs because state elements with too low an activation level will not evoke their $P_{i,j}$ productions to get extended.

Note that (6.2) has Q_i, not $Q_{i,j}$ as in (4.15). The productions are the same; the question is whether one can get by with a single production for each state (S_i) or must have one for each transition, that is, for each second state symbol (S_j) in the production. The underlying question is whether a variable-free production will be called on to execute on multiple instantiations. But if Q_i is satisfied by many state elements (with the same S_i, but different S_j), then recency conflict resolution will let it fire on only one, the maximum. Hence, a single Q production can be used per state.

Similarly, it can be seen that the argument in issue I5 goes through that the maximum will be taken for sets of transitions to identical states, as required by equation (3.3). Two state elements leading to the same state will occur as (State $S_k\ S_i$)[$=l_i$] and (State $S_k\ S_j$)[$=l_j$] with $=l_i < =l_j$. $P_{k,m}$, which extends the path to (State $S_k\ S_m$), will fire in any event. Recency (maximum activation) will assure that the activation level of the match will be that of $=l_i$, the maximum input likelihood.

Production 6.3 arises from (4.22) without change. It operates to segment and chunk the context-free representation of the auditory input. If the features D_i are sufficiently activated to evoke an R_k, then an acoustic description of the segment (Data $D_1 \cdots D_m$) occurs in WM with high activation, being the most recent one.

Productions 6.4–6.7 arise from (4.17)–(4.21) without change, except to delete the likelihood symbol. They perform the backtrace and create a sequence of words-in-context in WM. As discussed earlier, this sequence is the putative output of the process of speech recognition, to be used in various cognitive ways.

Production 6.8 arises from (4.23) without change, except to accommodate the activation encoding of likelihood. It initiates speech processing.

The system of productions 6.1–6.8 constitutes the final form of the mapping of Harpy into HPSA77. It is not a complete system of productions, for it does not perform all the tasks needed for Harpy. It takes the isolated acoustic parameters as given input, but these must come from somewhere. It produces a conventional output from the backtrace rather than one appropriate to some actual task to be performed. It provides only for the performance system of perceiving speech, not the system outside the net that contains grammatical, lexical, and phonological knowledge or the system that compiles this prior knowledge into the state network. Though a small point, no additional control structure has been provided to let speech perception occur in the midst of the general cognitive life of the perceiver. For instance, WM is filled with other symbols concurrently with recognizing the utterance. Still, this production system, PS.Harpy, is complete enough to permit some assessment of the enterprise.

Analysis of Basic Sufficiency Questions

With (6.1)–(6.8) in hand, I consider the basic sufficiency questions posed in Section 3.

PS.Harpy is an attempt to map faithfully the current Harpy into HPSA77. By so limiting our aim, we obtained a well-defined task, which did not mix questions of interpreting the mechanisms of Harpy either with new ideas for speech processing or with modifications to explain known human speech phenomena. We also preserved maximally the sufficiency of the system to perceive speech (to the limit of Harpy). Redesign and embellishment begins to loose Harpy's demonstration of adequacy and to evolve toward being simply another (new) proposal for a speech system.

However, as I now confront the various ways in which PS.Harpy is inadequate, either on sufficiency grounds (in this section) or explanatory grounds (in the next section), I can consider how PS.Harpy could be modified and extended. There is nothing sacred about an exact mapping of Harpy, especially about the particular sequence of mapping decisions used. The chief virtue of (6.1)–(6.8) is to provide an initial point in an approximating sequence of theories of human speech perception, a point that has certain desirable properties, namely sufficiency in the sense we are using the term.

S1. Can PS.Harpy Recognize Speech?   PS.Harpy is as adequate as Harpy, providing that the mapping is completed in a way that achieves the remaining details of Harpy. In issue I15 we listed a number of promissory notes and open choices. Making decision D5 and mapping assumption M6 has resolved many of these issues. But the remaining ones constitute the requirements for appropriate further specification. They are the still open questions about the performance side of sufficiency.

   I4. Avoid confusions on back-pointers.
   I7.3. Synchronization problems between generation ($P_{i,j}$) and evaluation (Q_i).
   I9. Summing residuals produces desired acoustic match metric.
   I11.1. Controllable lockout or no intrusion of extra backtrace starters.
   I11.2. Limited lockout on stepping through the backtrace.
   I13. Likelihoods must be precise to eight bits.

We must simply accept these six items as continued promissory notes, awaiting much greater detail on how a PS.Harpy would be implemented. There is no doubt that some of them (e.g., the accuracy one) could threaten the entire edifice. Most of the others are subject to being solved by design improvements, such as the synchronization and lockout problems.

S2. Can PS.Harpy Be Extended to Full Speech?   From the analysis of Table 11.2, we can compute the number of productions that are required. The $P_{i,j}$ contributes one per transition (SB) The Q_i contributes one per state (S). The R_k constitute the phonetic alphabet. The number of phone templates, 98, of the current Harpy is not a good guide, since one way of compensating for a weak metric is to expand the alphabet of templates. The International Phonetic Alphabet (with perhaps several hundred symbols when expanded) might be a more suitable guide. Thus, there might be at most a few thousand of these. This would provide of the order of ten to twenty variations per phoneme, which seems quite sufficient. The backtrace requires one production for each word-in-context (i.e., Sg) plus three more ($U1–U3$). Finally, the initialization productions (V_k) can be viewed as providing multiple entries to a subset of the grammar nodes.

There is no way to estimate this number; perhaps taking it of the order of the vocabulary (V) would not be too far off. Thus, in toto:

$$\text{Number of productions} = SB + S + [\text{Phonetic alphabet}] + (Sg + 3) + V \qquad (6.9)$$

The actual numbers are shown in Table 11.3 for the same range of effective vocabulary (Bg) considered earlier. (V is not uniquely determined by Bg, so I assumed reasonable values of redundancy around .6.) At the low end, there are less than 10^5 productions, which might be tolerable. At the high end, there are 10^{14} productions, which seems utterly out of the question. It is clear I need to consider what might modify these numbers.

The simplest extrapolation of Harpy takes the basic structure as fixed. The language itself, as characterized by V (vocabulary), r (redundancy), and the word parameters (Bw, Dw, Sw), is also fixed. Thus, the potential candidates for modification are Dg (depth before backtrace), c (grammar compression) and f (beam fraction). Considering (6.9), the controllable item is Sg (since $S = SwSg$), which depends on c and Dg. We know very little about c; those working on Harpy think it might decrease some with increasing language (Reddy, personal communication). We might examine a drop by a modest fraction (15%). Dg, on the other hand, has been set in Harpy to the full length of the utterance (2 sec on average) without much analysis. This might well be substantially shorter. We might examine cutting Dg to one second, i.e., three words. Table 11.4 shows the revised figures for Harpy. Looking at the high end ($Bg = 320$), we see that Sg has come down to 10^6, making S less than 10^7, so that, as shown in Table 11.5, we get 5×10^7 for the number of productions. The other numbers are correspondingly lower, as the size of the language decreases. These are still large numbers, but they are conceivable.

S3. Can PS.Harpy Recognize Full Speech in Time? Two quantities must be computed: the total amount of computation and the total elapsed time given the concurrency available. As to the amount of computation, we need to fill in the content of the unit computation on each Harpy cycle. A $P_{i,j}$ will be executed for every transition from the existing beam, getting FB firings. However, roughly speaking, the Q_i will be executed only on those state elements that are sufficiently close to become part of the new beam, getting F. (This is only a rough estimate: The beam also contains elements that have not been boosted by a Q_i production (pure extrapolations); and not all boosted elements will be included in the beam.) In addition, one R_k fires in recognizing the acoustic wave as a speech sound. In the backtrace, there are two executions, *U2* and *U3*,

TABLE 11.3
Vital Statistics for PS Harpy

Grammar branching (Bg)	10	20	40	80	160	320
Productions	7×10^4	5×10^6	3×10^8	2×10^{10}	4×10^{12}	1×10^{14}
Firings (Harpy cycle)	6×10^2	4×10^4	3×10^6	2×10^8	2×10^{10}	1×10^{12}
Firings (sec of speech)	9×10^3	6×10^5	7×10^7	3×10^9	2×10^{11}	2×10^{13}
WM load	4×10^3	3×10^5	2×10^7	1×10^9	7×10^{10}	5×10^{12}
Fixed parameters	$Bw = 2$	$Dw = 5$	$Sw = 8$	$Dg = 6$	$c = .35$	$f = .01$

TABLE 11.4
Estimates of Critical Parameters for Advanced Harpy

	10	20	40	80	160	320
Grammar branching(Bg)	3×10^1	2×10^2	2×10^3	1×10^4	1×10^5	9×10^5
Grammar states (Sg)	2×10^2	2×10^3	1×10^4	1×10^5	9×10^5	7×10^6
Harpy states (S)	3.2	3.6	4.2	4.8	5.5	6.3
Branching factor (B)	1×10^1	9×10^1	9×10^2	8×10^3	7×10^4	7×10^5
Computation units	2×10^{-1}	2×10^0	1×10^1	1×10^2	9×10^2	7×10^3
Beam (F)	3×10^0	3×10^1	2×10^2	2×10^3	1×10^4	1×10^5
Integrated beam (Fx)						
Fixed parameters	$Bw = 2$	$Dw = 5$	$Sw = 8$	$Dg = 3$	$c = .30$	$f = .001$

TABLE 11.5
Vital Statistics for PS Harpy Based on Advanced Harpy

Grammar branching (Bg)	10	20	40	80	160	320
Productions	5×10^3	2×10^4	9×10^4	7×10^5	6×10^6	5×10^7
Firings (Harpy cycle)	4×10^0	1×10^1	7×10^1	6×10^2	6×10^3	5×10^4
Firing (sec of speech)	6×10^1	2×10^2	1×10^3	1×10^4	9×10^4	8×10^5
WM load	3×10^0	3×10^1	2×10^2	2×10^3	1×10^4	1×10^5
Fixed parameters	$Bw = 2$	$Dw = 5$	$Sw = 8$	$Dg = 3$	$c = .30$	$f = .001$

and possibly another one, a W_i (call it three in total). These occur much later, but can be associated with a unique Harpy cycle. The initiation productions, V_k, contribute nothing per cycle, constituting in essence a distinct cycle. Thus we get:

Production firings $= FB + F + 1 + 3$ per Harpy cycle   (6.10)

The actual numbers are shown in Table 11.3. Again, at the high end the numbers come out very large, i.e., 10^{12} firings per Harpy cycle. These can be multiplied by about 15 Harpy cycles per second to get the computation per second of speech, as shown.

If we consider how this can be cut down, the same assumptions as used above reduce S. In addition, the beam fraction f is also controllable (though it does not affect the number of productions). This is directly responsive to how good the acoustics are—the more discriminative and reliable, the smaller f can be. The best indication of the human potentiality for pure speech sounds comes from the performance of VZ (see Cole, Rudnicky, Zue, & Reddy, Chap. 1). Reddy estimates that this might result in a factor of 10 improvement in f, which is to say $f = .001$ instead of the current .01 for Harpy. Extrapolated estimates are shown in Table 11.4 for Harpy and in Table 11.5 for PS.Harpy. For the maximum case, there are now about 5×10^4 firings per Harpy cycle. Again, these figures are high, but not out of the question.

Given the complete concurrency of the PS.Harpy scheme, it is not clear that an important constraint can be derived from the number of production firings. PS.Harpy is posited to be capable of firing any number of variable-free productions concurrently.

The second computation needed is the amount of elapsed time to recognize speech. The key issue is what production firings must occur sequentially, either because the output of one is the input to another or because they use the limited resource of the UV mechanism. Fig. 11.6 lays out the pattern of production firings. The development of the acoustic signal by the R_k paces the computation, but occurs concurrently. Only the first occurrence, if any, contributes to the elapsed duration. A single firing of a V_k is required to initiate the forward sweep. The forward sweep itself consists of pairs of associated $P_{i,j}$ and Q_i productions. These occur in series: P generates, then Q boosts, to provide for the next P to generate. The forward sweep consists of D Harpy cycles, so there will be D firings of P productions and D firings of Q productions. The backtrace must follow this same path, after a single firing of $U1$ to initiate it. $U2$ and $U3$ pairs execute in series for D steps. Both $U2$ and $U3$ are variable-containing productions. However, their sequential nature arises from the data dependence as well as from the limited resource of the UV

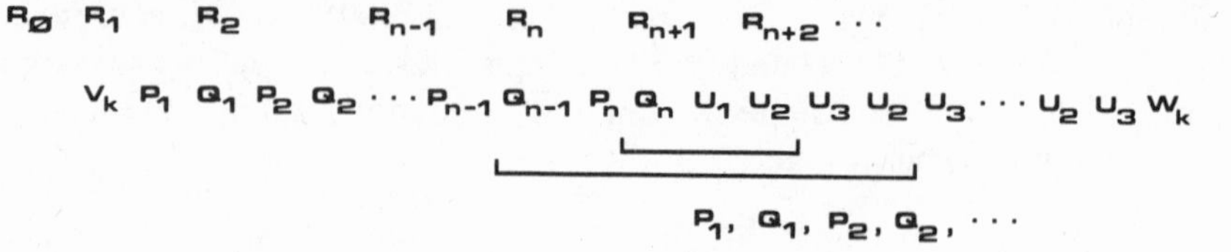

$R_{\emptyset}$ R_1 R_2 R_{n-1} R_n R_{n+1} R_{n+2} $\cdots$

V_k P_1 Q_1 P_2 Q_2 $\cdots$ P_{n-1} Q_{n-1} P_n Q_n U_1 U_2 U_3 U_2 U_3 $\cdots$ U_2 U_3 W_k

P_1, Q_1, P_2, Q_2, $\cdots$

FIG. 11.6.   Elapsed time to perceive an utterance

mechanism. The W_i, which bring down the word codes, are variable-free productions and operate concurrently with the main backtrace. Presumably the last one occurs after the last cycle of the backtrace and could add to the elapsed duration. thus, using $T[X]$ to stand for the duration of a production of type X, we get:

$$\text{Duration} = T[R] + T[V] + D \times T[P] + D \times T[Q] + T[U1] + D \times T[U2] + D \times T[U3] + T[W] \tag{6.11}$$

How long these production firings take depends on the detailed timing assumptions about the recognition–act cycle: the recognition time, the action time, the timing effects when variables are involved (i.e., UV is evoked). These assumptions have not been made yet in HPSA77, though the UV mechanism was assumed to add around 40 msec per instantiated action (independent of recognition time) and recognition time was assumed to be probably longer. In particular, nothing was specified about possible processing time differences between variable-free and variable-containing productions. Besides the uncertainty on component time assumptions, there is also the question of how many instantiations will be created by $U2$ before the lockout terminates and lets $U3$ fire.

Even with these uncertainties, (6.11) can be expressed in terms of basic recognition and action times. The times are subscripted according to whether they are variable free (vf) or variable containing (vc); and let L be the number of instantiations that occur within the lockout for $U2$.

$$\text{Duration} = (2D + 3)T[\text{Recog}_{vf}] + (2D + 3)T[\text{Action}_{vf}] + (2D + 1)T[\text{Recog}_{vc}] + (LD + D + 1)T[\text{Action}_{vc}] \tag{6.12}$$

Some insight into (6.12) can be obtained by transforming it to express the duration required per second of speech. Humans keep up with speech input (and in fact with speeded speech); which implies that they must process speech in less than real time on the average. Equation (6.12) represents the amount of time to process D segments. However, it cannot just be normalized, since if continuous speech is being processed, the forward sweep of one recognition phrase can be processed concurrently with the backtrace of the prior one. This is shown on Fig. 11.6 by the bottom line of Ps and Qs occurring under the Us in the main computation. What counts then is which of the two sequences takes longer, the $P\text{-}Q$ sequence or the U sequence. Assuming it is always one or the other (just for simplicity here) we get:

$$\text{Processing time per segment} = \text{Max}(2T[\text{Recog}_{vf}] + 2T[\text{Action}_{vf}],$$
$$2T[\text{Recog}_{vc}] + (L + 1)T[\text{Action}_{vc}])$$
$$(6.13)$$

We have suppressed terms that are proportional to $1/D$; they are small and have no effect on which component is the maximum.

It seems extremely unlikely that the times for recognition or action of variable-free productions will be less than those that use the UV mechanism. Consequently, it can be seen that the backtrace will always dominate (6.13). Thus, we can simplify:

$$\text{Processing time per segment} = 2T[\text{Recog}_{vc}] +$$
$$(L + 1)[\text{Action}_{vc}])$$
$$(6.14)$$

Segments in Harpy run about 50–70 msec (depending on whether one counts the input segments or their lengthening by the algorithms that perseverates in a state). Taking recognition time as 80 msec and action time as 40 msec, just for a sample calculation, we get $(200 + 40L)$ msec for 50–70 msec of speech, or a ratio of over three times real time at a minimum. This says a second of speech takes at least three seconds to recognize. This is too high by a factor of three. If we check the minimum component (the forward sweep), we see that it consists of two recognition times and two action times per segment, but of variable-free productions. Turning the question around and asking what primitive times would be acceptable, we get about 25–35 msec per total production (a recognition plus a single action) for variable-free productions. This might be acceptable, given that the UV mechanism is not involved. In any event, given the uncertainties in the specifications, we should not be unduly concerned with discrepancies of the order we have here. From a sufficiency point of view, these are quite satisfactory. However, this does post notice that a strong constraint on the theory is available from a consideration of speech rates.

As important as the quantitative measures are the qualitative questions of what might affect the duration of the computation. The duration is strongly dependent on the segmentation of the speech signal by the R_k productions. If they produce more or less segments per second, the recognition time will respond proportionately. Beyond this we need to distinguish clearly questions of total duration, as seen in (6.12), and questions of processing rates, as seen in (6.13). In one, the forward sweep and backtrace add to determine a total time; anything that affects either component induces an effect to the total time. In the other, only the maximum component counts; anything that affects the lesser component has no effect on the total at all.

Looking at the forward sweep, it is possible that not all the Q_i fire. They will not fire during gaps and they may not fire in other cases as well; for instance, high likelihood paths may race ahead without needing to wait until the Q-boost occurs. This would speed recognition durations; it would seem not to effect processing rates since the forward sweep is the minority component.

Whether the backtrace could be speeded up is a complex matter, though clearly important since it appears to be the limiting process. The obvious tactic is to build backtrace productions that pick up several chained state elements at a time. This is precluded by D1.4, which will not let a variable occur in more than one condition element. This is a good example of the force of D1.4. If there were no such limitation on the power of the match, then productions with, say, 15 chained condition elements could pick up the entire speech path in a single cycle. However, one can pick up several such chains as free paths and encode them all in a test element, just as $U2$–$U3$ operate. Then the correct test element could be selected out in one recognition cycle. It takes time to do intermediate chunking, so detailed investigation is needed to discover what the real possibilities are. Beyond this, there may be strategies for heuristically guessing the path, possibly by trading accuracy against time. For instance, one could jump directly from the end of a word (as picked up by the backtrace) to the front of the word, avoiding all the intermediate states. At some point in this reduction, the backtrace may drop below the forward sweep, and thus no longer be the critical determiner of processing rate.

There seems little point in exploring this space of algorithms in detail here. I have established that processing rates do not remove PS.Harpy from consideration. Indeed, they make PS.Harpy seem quite plausible, in comparison with the size estimates. This is not surprising, moreover, since the use of concurrent processing trades off memory for time.

S4. Does PS.Harpy Require Too Much Immediate Memory? Two memory loads need to be considered: the maximum amount of information stored at any point; and the total duration over which storage must occur. As to the total load, essentially this will just be the extended beam, one data element for each state in the beam over long enough to initiate the backtrace (*FD* elements). It might be thought that more must be remembered, since the backtrace itself takes time and the speech keeps coming in. But the backtrace runs concurrently with the (new) forward wave, so this requirement does not occur.

As to the total duration of any element, this must be the interval to initiate the backtrace, as above, plus the time it takes the backtrace to get through the whole history to the initial element. Since the utterance is fully recognized the moment the backtrace is complete, this is just the total processing time for the D segments, i.e., (6.11). As in the discussion above of processing time, until we have a closer estimate of the recognition and action times we cannot draw strong quantitative conclusions. Above, we did get an minimum estimate of three times real time for the backtrace, with something less than this for the forward sweep. That might add up to anywhere from four to six times real time for the total duration. This would yield four to six seconds of immediate memory, since we have been assuming D to be about a second of speech. This is again too large a value, and in about the same way as the processing rate. But it can certainly be taken as within the range of plausibility, given the uncertainty in the calculations.

S5. How Does PS.Harpy Cope with the Creativity and Variability of Speech? In the original discussion of (S5) we posed the issue of creativity and variability in speech perception by enumerating several concrete tasks that required transcending the fixed network in some way. Two basic capabilities seem to be involved: (1) how to make use of knowledge about speech that is already in the fixed network, but embedded in a way that seems to preclude its use; and (2) how to make use of added knowledge that has not yet been integrated into the network. This latter knowledge could already exist in long term memory (assimilated as productions), or it could just have been acquired and be only in WM (not yet existing as productions). To first approximation we can ignore this difference, since any way of affecting the perception subsystem will work through data elements placed in WM.

Consider the first capability: making use of the knowledge already in the net. Such knowledge is encoded as subnets (or sets of subnets generated according to systematic rules). The knowledge can be hidden in the net because access to the knowledge is not available; there is no transition in the net from existing states in WM to the given subnet. Knowledge might also be effectively hidden if gaining access to it, though possible, leads to undesirable effects, such as taking outgoing transitions to inappropriate states.

On the access side, the V_k productions already provide a basic solution. They give access to an arbitrary Harpy-net state from an acoustic clue. Thus, given the appropriate V_k, PS.Harpy can make use of any subnet; it is not restricted to entering through the transitions already available in the net. The net effect of such V_k evocations is to add to the size of the beam. But such additions would come on at relatively low likelihoods and get eliminated quickly, unless subsequent states pick up strongly or (importantly) unless all the existing next states are failing to gain any support, so that the new path rises rapidly towards the top on a relatively weak beam.

At first glance it would seem that, once in the net, no bad side effects could come from continuing as long as possible. Thus, knowledge could not become unavailable because it leads to following inappropriate paths. After all, PS.Harpy wishes to understand whatever linguistic utterance is being heard. Perhaps the V_k are all the mechanisms that PS.Harpy needs to make use of all the knowledge in the net.

Two counters to this are immediately apparent. First, nothing has been said about the mechanisms for acquiring the V_k. This is a valid concern. What little I have to say about it is best taken up under sufficiency issue S7. Second, knowledge may be available that sharply restricts the speech (e.g., only three words were spoken). Following the natural transitions in the network violates such knowledge; hence, a priori useful pieces of the network become unavailable. Again, this is a valid concern. Such restricting knowledge is necessarily of a transitory nature, and the problem of using it belongs to the second major concern we expressed earlier, to which we now turn.

Consider, then, the second capability: making use of knowledge outside the network. Such knowledge could be the original linguistic knowledge from which the network was compiled; or it could be extra linguistic task knowledge (as in our earlier example). A basis for this capability lies in the ability of productions to execute indirectly. Consider first the knowledge about transitions, which is contained in the $P_{i,j}$ productions. I encode it in an element, (Indirect $(S_j \ S_i)$), which other productions can place in WM. Then the following two productions perform the same function as the $P_{i,j}$:

$$X1: \text{(State } =S \ =)(\text{Indirect } (=S' \ =S'')) \rightarrow$$
$$(\text{Test}' \ =S \ =S' \ =S'') \tag{6.15}$$

$$X2: (\text{Test}' \ =S \ =S' \ =S) \rightarrow (\text{State } =S' \ =S)[l] \tag{6.16}$$

If a state element (State $S_i \ S_h$) shows up in WM and a corresponding (Indirect $(S_j \ S_i)$) element is also in WM, they will inject into WM the result of a state transition: (State $S_j \ S_i$). From this point on, it will be indistinguishable from any other elements in the beam; the Q productions will boost it, other Ps will add further transitions, etc.

The one way in which $X1$ and $X2$ do not mimic the $P_{i,j}$ is in the assignment of likelihood. With the design choice of encoding likelihoods as activation, there is no way to symbolize this in the encoded element and assign a specific activation to the new state element, as the P productions do. $X2$ assigns a likelihood, but it does so independently of which particular state transition it is making.

This issue of independence also infects the situation with respect to the knowledge in the Q_i. The whole purpose of the Qs is to boost the activation level. We can have productions X_k which provide such boosts:

$$X_k: (\text{State} = S =)(\text{Evaluation} \cdots)[=e] \rightarrow = (\text{State} = S =)$$
$$[+ =e + l_k]$$ (6.17)

However, the effects of these productions do not stem from their acting as indirect interpreters of the external knowledge (the evaluation elements), but only from the *activation* they have associated either with these elements (the $=e$) or with themselves (the l_k).

Putting to one side the complexities that arise from these limitations, the X productions provide a way of injecting external knowledge that has been generated (to WM) by some cognitive process (e.g., operating on "Only three words will be spoken") into the ongoing process of recognizing speech. These cognitive processes (themselves production systems) are outside our consideration here, except for how they interface with the speech system. The difficulty that remains is that the Xs imply knowledge of the actual states of the Harpy network. These states would seem to be "internal" symbols of some sort and a legitimate concern is how cognitive productions gain this knowledge so they can create the appropriate WM elements.

Solutions to this latter problem would propel me into a full-scale design effort for the system that compiles productions. Such an extension exceeds the bounds of this paper. However, one direction for such a design is to unpackage the pure state symbols, S_i, and replace them by descriptive elements that preserve much of the source knowledge. For example, instead of S_i one might have (Node $H\, G_i\, F_i\, E_i$), where the H is a symbol that describes the role of the state (beginning, interior, or ending state for a word); G_i is a symbol from the grammar net; F_i is a symbol from the phone net for word; and E_i is a symbol for the unique conditions that cause state splitting because of word juncture, etc. Then the X productions are modified to detect aspects of (Node $\cdots$) that they can reasonably know about (e.g., a grammar node symbol).

The X productions contain variables, and this produces an important limitation. Although they can be sensitive to the entire beam, they cannot operate in lieu of the variable-free beam computation. Only a few executions of the Xs are possible within any small period of time.

These mechanisms make available some capability for accessing knowledge embedded in the network and for mixing in external knowledge. I can now dispose quickly of the various tasks posed in sufficiency issue S5 from the standpoint of basic sufficiency, i.e., whether these tasks imply fundamental processing difficulties for PS.Harpy.

First, to understand grammatical utterances that have not been heard before, the problem for PS.Harpy is to extract from the net subpieces as large as are familiar. The V_k permit some of this. In addition, a small amount of aid can be obtained from the X productions working on the generative knowledge of the grammar that can be presumed to exist. But no mechanism has been suggested that permits large amounts of extra-net knowledge to be brought to bear. So whether the suggested mechanisms (along with very large nets) are sufficient must remain open.

Second, to understand an arbitrary sequence of clearly spoken words from the vacabulary is partly the question of whether the vocabulary knowledge that exists in PS.Harpy can be brought to bear. The mechanism of the V_k suggests this is possible. But recognition without grammar is clearly a task with less restraint. Performance of both PS.-Harpy and of humans would be expected to decline (and it does in fact for both); nothing here permits seeing whether special difficulties for PS.-Harpy, serious enough to threaten a sufficiency analysis, exist in that decline.

Third, to understand utterances that have genuinely new elements requires an involvement of the cognitive system that is beyond discussion here. The responsibility of the perception subsystem would be to obtain a sequence of (essentially ungrammatical) words, and we have covered this in the second task. The ability to permit a small amount of additional analysis based on the knowledge developed by the cognitive system during the course of inference is clearly permitted, but it is strictly limited in character.

Fourth, to incorporate immediate increments of linguistic knowledge is exactly what we have discussed for the X productions. We have to go much beyond this analysis to see whether the mechanism is sufficient.

Fifth, to cope with grammatical errors and fragmentary utterances, several ingredients are available. Such errors cause the acoustic sequence to break contact with the net. They will leave a short grammatical fragment available to be picked up by the backtrace. (The break point itself will not reflect the error sharply, due to the extrapolative character of the $P_{i,j}$, but that probably matters little.) The V_k will soon initiate another sequence, if only the recognition of isolated words. I can assume, though I haven't put it in explicitly, that the backtrace will be triggered by such initiation. Thus, the net effect is to present the cognitive system with a sequence of short fragments for interpretation. This act of interpretation lies outside the scope of PS.Harpy. Whether the preliminary recognitions that PS.Harpy does provide are sufficient for the abilities humans exhibit on ungrammatical utterances cannot be determined at this level of analysis.

S6. Can PS.Harpy Respond Adequately to Speaker Variability? Harpy has a single mechanism for coping with speaker variability at the acoustic level—namely, computing unique phone templates and switching to a user-unique template set. Though nothing prevents adding new words or grammatical rules and constructing speaker-unique networks, these approaches have not been seriously explored.

PS.Harpy doesn't change this picture in most respects. On the positive side, the learning does not appear to be so monolithic (more on that in sufficiency issue S7). Individualized versions of any of the productions are possible, simply by the addition of speaker-dependent condition conditions. An R_k can be of the form:

$$R_k: (\text{Speaker } Z)D_1 \cdots D_m \to (\text{Data } D_1 \cdots D_m) \qquad (6.18)$$

The speaker identification, Z, can clearly be an individual name or a description of a class of speakers.

Adjustments on the cues that evoke a given (Data $\cdots$) are also possible:

$$R_k: (\text{Speaker } Z)D^*_1 \cdots D^*_m \to (\text{Data } D_1 \cdots D_m) \qquad (6.19)$$

The D^*_h are idiosyncratic acoustic features, which are not just chunked by the R_k, but are also mapped into values, the D_h, which are already tuned to the learned structure of the net.

Similar modifications are possible for the P and Q productions. Indeed, from the viewpoint of participation in the perceptual computation, modification of any of these aspects seems essentially equivalent. Furthermore, the modifications do not have to be total, since in any event they would be represented by the aggregate of a bunch of individual production creations themselves.

On the negative side two items, at least, are serious. The first is that the only modifications possible are in productions. No factorization of the speech system into mechanism plus parameters exists such that setting a (small) number of parameters will accommodate the perceptual system to the speaker. Further, this character is built deeply into PS.Harpy (though not into Harpy itself), since parameterization implies the use of variables. For a production to make use of parameter values requires that it handle that value indirectly (as in $X2$ and $X3$). We all have, I think, strong feelings that factorization is essential for short term adaptation. Thus, the proposed scheme of adaptation seems cumbersome in the extreme in this respect.

The second difficulty is how the productions are to be learned. The mechanism above addresses the final structure for expressing speaker-dependent performance. This learning question is indeed important. We have tripped over it several times already, deferring it to sufficiency issue S7. Before turning to it, at last, we can summarize by saying that PS.-Harpy leaves the sufficiency issue of speaker adaptation about in the same state it is for Harpy, but without strong indications of deep trouble.

S7. Is Language Acquisition Possible with PS.Harpy? Harpy's large, highly detailed, precompiled network seems especially vulnerable in a sufficiency analysis. Unfortunately, two issues limit our treatment. First, the context of learning involves a vastly enlarged cognitive world that must be treated concurrently with PS.Harpy. Though the question of interest is whether the compiled network violates some basic features of the human processing system, it cannot be explored very well without bringing in the entire framework within which learning takes place. Such an investigation cannot be avoided ultimately, but it can hardly be attempted as an add-on to this chapter.

Second, the development of the underlying production system architecture (HPSA77) has not yet been extended to long-term learning. This requires design decisions about the formation of new productions and their addition to production memory. Much current research on productions systems does involve systems that learn by adding productions (e.g., Rychener & Newell, 1978; Waterman, 1975). Some of this work is directly psychological (Anderson, Kline, & Beasley, 1977; Anzai, 1978; Langley, 1978; Neves, 1978). The basic learning assumption is made throughout that productions are created by the actions of other productions, deliberately. This does not yet seem the right design decision for HPSA77. Consequently, the basic learning decision remains in abeyance. As in the first issue, such decisions cannot be avoided ultimately, but they are too much to add to this chapter. The positing of the intensity aspect (D5), which was necessary to complete the performance model of PS.-Harpy, already required a detour.

Nevertheless, some aspects can be explored. The final learning of the net is clearly in terms of productions. PS.Harpy will have to construct and store away in production memory 10^5 or so productions (see Table 11.5). Three questions at least are to be asked about this:

1. Can that many productions be created and installed in the time available?
2. Is the information available to construct the productions?
3. Are the occasions available to construct the productions?

Note that other a priori obvious questions do not arise. For instance, PS.-Harpy does not face a problem of how to install a production vis a vis the existing productions. Production memory is just an unstructured set of productions, so adding a production entails no complexities.

On the amount of time to learn, times for human verbal learning, which are of the order of 2–10 sec per chunk (Simon, 1974) provide for a trial calculation. The appropriate identification is that a chunk corresponds to a production (actually, such a correspondence lies buried in decision D3, though we have not made that explicit here). Taking the upper figure of 10 sec gives 10^6 sec of learning time, which is of the order of 300 hours. Though only a small fraction of a day would be devoted to such learning, this is still not an alarming number. (On the other hand, if we upped the number of productions by many additional orders of ten, we clearly could be in trouble.)

The usual concern about such learning rates based on verbal learning is whether they are too slow (the process being somehow too "rote"). Shifts to faster learning pose no threat here. More of concern is the evidence that learning "automatic" responses takes thousands of trials (Neisser, Novick, & Lazar, 1963; Shiffrin & Schneider, 1977). These responses should correspond to variable-free productions. However, so little is understood (or even conjectured) about what is being learned in these situations and why it takes so long, that we can do no more than note the issue.

On the other two questions of whether the information and the occasions are available, the X productions (6.15–6.17) cast this issue in a specific form. If appropriate data structures, such as (Indirect$\cdots$) and (Evaluation$\cdots$), get into WM, then the system can behave as if it has the productions. Thus the act of constructing a production for the net is the act of going from the X productions plus the data elements to a production that has removed the indirect addressing capability but retains the speech-relevant parts. To illustrate with the simplest case, given an X_k and a working memory that contains an appropriate state element for S_h and evaluation data element, the problem is to get the corresponding Q_h production. That is, from (6.20) and (6.21), one must get (6.22):

$$X_k: \text{(State } = S =)\text{(Evaluation (Data } D_1 \cdots))[=e] \rightarrow$$
$$=\text{(State } = S = \text{(State } = S =)[+ =e + l_k] \qquad (6.20)$$

$$\text{WM: } (\cdots \text{(Evaluation (Data } D_1 \cdots)) \cdots \text{(State } S_h \; S_j) \cdots) \qquad (6.21)$$

$$Q_h: \text{(State } S_h =)\text{(Data } D_1\cdots)[=e] \rightarrow =\text{(State } S_h =)[+ =e] \quad (6.22)$$

It can be seen that all the requisite structures are available to perform the construction of Q_h. Whether there is anything hard about it depends on aspects of the production-learning process that have not been specified, such as whether details of X_k are available or are inaccessible within production memory. The problem of the creation of the $P_{i,j}$ and the R_k is analogous, though additional complexities come in for the $P_{i,j}$ (which must merge two productions, $X1$ and $X2$).

This view essentially makes learning occur out of the attempts of the cognitive system to cope with language by means of deliberate action (though it says nothing of what relation that deliberate action bears to the ability to articulate what is going on). Thus, the occasions for learning arise whenever the X productions are engaged in coping with some language behavior that PS.Harpy knows but hasn't already assimilated into the net.

This analysis pushes the questions of sufficiency back to where the knowledge comes from that gets into WM. In major part, this question is no longer concerned with PS.Harpy and the peculiar network characteristics it incorporates. Thus we can safely leave it. One question that does remain is whether the assumption about knowing the state symbols poses any special difficulties. I dealt with this briefly in sufficiency issue S5, and have little more to say about it here, except to note that it could cause genuine problems.

Summary on Sufficiency Analysis.   I have looked at the central issues in whether PS.Harpy is ruled out of court on sufficiency grounds, i.e., because it uses mechanisms that are obviously beyond human capabilities. As might be expected, the analysis was at some points inconclusive. The closest I came to outright rejection were in the numbers of productions, etc. Projections on how Harpy-like schemes might improve brought the numbers down to the merely huge. Still, the size of the net must remain a point of genuine vulnerability for a Harpy-like model. The other major direction for vulnerability, the fixed net, showed itself to be somewhat porous on inspection, in that mechanisms could be found for approaching the various issues. But the analyses were fragmentary and far from satisfactory. For myself, PS.Harpy seems not rejectable on sufficiency grounds, but the reader will have to make his or her own judgment.

7. SOME SPEECH PHENOMENA

PS.Harpy, being a theory of speech perception embedded in a theory of general cognition, should make a prediction (right or wrong) on almost any speech phenomenon. This theoretically pleasant state of affairs is thwarted in several ways: PS.Harpy is still incomplete; a prediction can depend on the content of productions that we don't know in enough detail; we are unable to extract the prediction from the system; or, contra assumption, the phenomenon to be predicted really does lie outside the domain proper of PS.Harpy. Let me discuss a few phenomena of speech perception to see what position, if any, PS.Harpy takes and how inferences occur. Detailed treatment is outside the scope of this paper. In the following, I do not always distinguish Harpy from PS.Harpy, though sometimes predictions would hold for any implementation of Harpy and sometimes only for PS.Harpy.

These implications of PS.Harpy are drawn informally, and in two distinct ways. First, assertions are made about the behavior that will occur from PS.Harpy (sometimes in conjunction with other productions). This inference should be, but is not, demonstrated either formally (which is hard) or from running programs. Second, there are almost always multiple ways to do a task within a programming system—that is, within an architecture such as HPSA77. The assertion that a given method (i.e., production system) is used requires showing that other potential methods are not used. In general this is very hard to do, since it means considering the class of all methods for doing a given task. One purpose of the rather explicit derivation of the mapping in Section 4 was to indicate where alternative productions systems did or did not seem possible. In the material below, I rarely go even this far.

P1. Automatic Extrapolation of Speech. A common phenomenon is that the listener automatically predicts the speaker. The conversational form of this is finishing sentences for speakers. A basis for this phenomenon is shown explicitly in the Shannon guessing game and implicitly (presumably) in all the results that show better memory as a function of increased constraint (approximation to meaningful, grammatical discourse) (Miller & Selfridge, 1953). The phenomenon is stronger than the experimental results, because it says the hearer does such prediction en passant while listening and not as if it were an additional task.

PS.Harpy clearly shows a tendency to do this in the $P_{i,j}$ productions, which extrapolate forward without the speech input. This is not quite enough, however, since the actual prediction of the utterance within PS.-Harpy requires that the backtrace occur. As we noted, Harpy adopts relatively artificial conditions for backtrace initiation (the end of the total utterance). If we assume, consistent with $U1$, that one criteria is silence (i.e., a pause), then the backtrace will be initiated whenever the speaker pauses unduly. The extrapolated speech is as much a candidate for the maximum as actually heard speech, so that automatic prediction will occur over pauses, etc. Whether PS.Harpy will run ahead of the speaker will depend on the speaker's rate, since PS.Harpy's rate is determined by its internal cycle time.

The extrapolated states undergo decay. Hence, an important question is whether PS.Harpy will extrapolate for long enough to produce the observed phenomena. In general, only a few cycles of extrapolation seem possible or the beam will become too diluted with unsupported paths. Recall that Harpy operates to assure only about four cycles, which is approximately 200 msec, or about one word's worth. This seems not enough. However, a closer look reveals that the decay rate is set to eliminate paths in competition with heard speech, which is getting boosted. When there is no input, so that all paths are extrapolations, then the duration will be as long as state elements will win in competition with nonspeech activities. Furthermore, if the decrements are governed by a priori confidence (the $k_{i,j}$ of formulation 6.1), then the maximum likelihood path will emerge. We do not have enough information to make quantitative predictions about how long it will last. From the precision estimates of eight bits, we can get an upper bound of 256 cycles, which is of the order of five seconds; this at least might permit a few words (a second of speech). Note that the amount of speech predicted will depend on how predictable (i.e., constrained) the speech is. When there are a few highly probable alternatives, the $k_{i,j}$ will be small, the decay will be slight, and the path will survive a long time.

P2. Phonemic Restoration Effect. A strong point of PS.Harpy should be the penetration of cognition into perception—having moved perceptual processing relatively far into the cognitive engine. Perhaps the best evidence for such cognitive penetration is the phonemic restoration effect (Warren, 1970; see Warren, 1976, for a review). If a noise occludes a phoneme (which in the experimental demonstrations is actually not there at all) in an utterance where higher linguistic context dictates the identity of the phoneme, then the phoneme will actually be heard; that is, it cannot be distinguished from the other phonemes in the utterance. The occluding noise itself is not precisely localizable; in particular, knowing the experimental arrangement (that the noise filled a gap with no actual phoneme present) does not help to identify which phoneme was restored.

PS.Harpy will exhibit the phonemic restoration effect. The $P_{i,j}$ generate state elements that pass over a noise. The sequence of state elements that it produces in no way reveals what phoneme is not present, i.e., that no acoustic support occurred for the gap. We have not presented productions for performing the task of phoneme (or sound) identification, but no basis would exist for making the discrimination.

The question of time localization and order judgments is a large one that we cannot enter into here. However, it is apparent that in PS.Harpy the only immediate basis for time and order judgments is activation, and the only basis for remembering order and localization beyond the duration of initial activation is integration with other elements, integration into the web of experience. Thus the sounds in an utterance are heard physically in order, which results in their being activated in order; but they are remembered in order because of their integration into the state-element sequence of the understood utterance. It follows that the occluding noise (buzz or click) cannot be localized with respect to the utterance because it is not integrated into the utterance, just as is required by the phoneme restoration effect.

Why then should a gap of silence be readily both detected and localized, which is the case? There are two possible answers within PS.-Harpy. One is that prolonged silence (a gap) is the cue in *U1* for initiating the backtrace. Hence, not only is a gap universally detected (independent of the net), but its location is well marked. According to this mechanism, silence gaps will be especially distinguished with respect to their detection and localization. The more general possibility is that any speech sound (as opposed to a buzz or click) may be integrated into the net and hence be perceived and localized. Silence is a speech sound (it generates a (Data $\cdots$) element), and hence would be treated this way. This is not enough: The speech sound may not be part of the extended beam at the point of occurrence; furthermore, the path incorporating the sound must be retrieved by the backtrace. This second possibility is less sharp than the first. We raise it because one must find in the system all the different ways in which a phenomenon could be generated, not just the more obvious ways.

If I ask what would allow the noise to be localized (and of course it is localized phenomenally within some interval), it would happen when the system could create a structure that encodes the noise relative to other events. For PS.Harpy, this means firing a production on it (which is the only way to encode it). More specifically, it means firing a variable-containing production, since no variable-free production can link two items that are contingent with respect to one another. (That is, to be variable-free is to involve only pre-established items.) Thus, localization cannot occur concurrently when the noise occurs. The noise gets recognized (by the equivalent of R_k productions), but simply sits in WM waiting for some variable-containing production to attend to it. One would expect this to happen at some break points in the processing, namely when the backtrace has a chance to enter. Thus we are brought again to the criteria for initiating the backtrace (*U1*), which have not been completely spelled out. But it is not unreasonable to consider that these are sometimes at grammatical boundaries etc., as has been found (Fodor & Bever, 1965).

Could PS.Harpy be modified so that extrapolations could be distinguished from interpretations of actual input? This cannot be done in the $P_{i,j}$, because at the time of deposition it is not known which case the state element will belong to. However, it might be done in the Q_i, which could replace the state-element with one that was marked as boosted by acoustic input. This would still be a variable-free production. There will now be, on occasion, pairs of state elements, some marked, some not. The backtrace would have to weave its way among these, but this does not seem difficult to accomplish. From this one would have to predict that a person could learn to localize missing phonemes, providing a training regime, analogous to original language learning, could be devised to always maintain the discriminations. The incompleteness of HPSA77 with respect to learning new productions, and especially learning new variable-free productions, does not permit going any further with this problem here.

P3. The Absence of Active Parsing. It is a feature of Harpy, inherited by PS.Harpy, that there is no parsing stage. Recognition happens in a single (forth and back) pass, and when it is done the hearer understands both the utterance and its grammatical and semantic structure. No amount of self observation on the part of the hearer will yield any insight into how the grammatical structure is achieved. All this is in accord with phenomenological observations, at least to first order.

PS.Harpy predicts that there are limits to this automatic aspect of parsing, which are provided by what is in the Harpy net. As mentioned earlier, this will not consist of the entire grammar, but will be built up to provide the discrimination to recognize speech. That is, as long as useful constraint exists for recognition, the "compiled" grammar net will grow. But it will not grow in terms of any criteria of grammatical or semantic completeness. Thus in complex novel constructions, such as deeply embedded sentences, we would expect there to be recognition of the short phrases but the cognitive unraveling of the larger structure.

With this result, which seems to be substantially correct as a first approximation, goes a series of potential problems to explain differences in reaction time to understand various types of sentence. One recalls the earlier attempts to determine experimentally times for transformations (Miller & Isard, 1963). Though discredited in their original aim, such results could pose a problem.

P4. Ambiguous Utterances. As Harpy stands (also PS.Harpy), a single best utterance is selected by the backtrace. How then does ambiguity occur? Observe that PS.Harpy always generates many alternative paths. Many of these will be the same path through the grammar net, and thus will be equivalent. But variant readings of an utterance that are good matches to the acoustic utterance will also exist in the WM. Whether PS.-Harpy becomes aware of them, in terms of being able to engage in further processing, depends on whether the backtrace will pick up more than one of the paths. There would seem to be no difficulty creating such alternative production systems. Thus, the detection of ambiguity is dictated in part by the cognitive set to see the multiple readings. At the current level of specification of PS.Harpy, we have no way of determining whether the standard backtrace for the human is the one Harpy uses (finding only the one best) or is some variant that will see multiple solutions if they are close enough to the best case.

With a large beam, many readings would be possible. A human is only able, at best, to get a few readings. Why can't PS.Harpy read out many readings, thus showing a capability well beyond that of humans? First, though the beam is full of alternative paths, we don't have good statistics on how many of them are alternative readings at the grammar-net level, as opposed to alternative readings about how the speaker sounded. Assuming that many grammatical readings are latent in the final beam, PS.-Harpy would suffer from severe response interference in trying to read them out. While the backtrace was obtaining one, the others would all be decaying and the decay would be worse when more readings were attempted.

Detecting ambiguity when it occurs takes time in PS.Harpy, just as it does in humans. The extra time is due to the extra trip by the backtrace productions, not to any extra forward-wave processing. In particular, there is no need to reprocess the sentence to "become aware" of the alternative readings. The extra time exists only when the ambiguity occurs; it is not an effect that arises because of the possibility of ambiguity, not an ensemble effect. It would surely seem possible to induce a person to take extra time because of the possibility of ambiguity, but PS.Harpy would have to explain this as being due to a superimposed cognitive strategy for extra processing of the utterance.

The ambiguity is picked up at the point of backtrace, which may not necessarily be at the end of the utterance. Thus we would expect any temporal disruption to occur just a little after the point of ambiguity became clear. In garden path sentences, for instance, no extra time would be expected until the end of the path had been reached.

P5. Categorical Perception.   The phenomenon of categorical perception has played an important role in the psychology of speech perception (see Studdert-Kennedy, 1976, for one recent overview). Its defining generalization is that perception of speech sounds seems to be categorical, in that discrimination appears to occur by identification (labeling the sound as being in a predefined class), rather than by measurement of differences along acoustic attributes. Importantly, consonants show categorical perception much more than do vowels. It is also now known that categorical perception occurs for domains other than speech and possibly even for nonhumans. Thus it appears that the phenomenon of categorical perception is losing its status as a key phenomenon in understanding speech perception.

However, it is still useful to see what PS.Harpy has to say about the phenomenon. Given a speech context, the attempt to compare two sounds (as in the so-called ABX paradigm) leads fundamentally to the identification of state elements and their associated grammar nodes, that is, to categorical perception. Without a speech context the sounds must be encoded according to some different encoding structure, e.g., chirps, buzzes, etc., and there would not necessarily be categorical perception (as holds for humans). Thus, PS.Harpy shows the basic phenomenon.

Why then would vowels be different? Vowels and consonants are not differentiated within PS.Harpy, at least at the level of formulation developed so far. One possible mechanism stems from the vowels being longer. Such a difference, in itself, does not explain anything. But if the categorical processing of vowels were handled in a short time, then time is available for processing the vowels according to other encodings, e.g., as continuous sounds. This agrees with several indications that degrading and shortening vowels makes their perception more categorical, PS.-Harpy takes no longer to process a vowel than a consonant, considering only the processing from the R_k level up. Normally, in running speech, the extra time from the long segments simply contributes to the total time available to process the entire forward sweep. In speech-sound discrimination experiments, which consist of short single-syllable words, the extra time is available, while the sound is still being heard, to analyze it as a nonspeech sound.

From PS.Harpy's viewpoint, whatever phenomenon is shown by categorical perception is not unique to speech. Though I have not explored the matter carefully here, nothing in the PS.Harpy scheme is specific to speech. Rather, the presuppositions involve a time-sequenced input to which attention can be devoted continuously, the existence of strong structure (the grammar net), and the existence of stable structure and long learning times (to get the variable-free productions built). But insofar as other domains share these properties, they too can exhibit categorical perception in the same way.

P6. Word Recognition versus Letter Recognition. The basic phenomenon is that reaction time to recognize a letter within a word is longer than to recognize the word itself (Savin & Bever, 1970). This is counterintuitive on the grounds of a hierarchical recognition process, which should require the components to be recognized before the higher unit. The phenomenon has been shown repeatedly by now, and an attempt has been made to generalize it to the proposition that the recognition of any task-defined unit is faster than recognition of its components (McNeill & Lindig, 1973), which not only makes it apply at all levels (such as phrases versus words, words versus syllables, syllables versus phonemes, etc.), but also gives it a short-term character in terms of momentary task set. There is some controversy about this latter extension (Warren, 1976).

How will PS.Harpy perform in such tasks? The forward sweep proceeds independent of concern with what task is to be performed. In some sense, it recognizes the whole utterance. There certainly is no staging above the segment level (the Data···)) at which components become available. However, the task is not complete until the backtrace extracts and identifies the desired information. With the standard backtrace, we would expect the utterance to be identified and the components to be extracted from it, by decoding the word or whatever. What prevents this result from propagating upward indefinitely (e.g., the paragraph is recognized before its component sentences) is that the backtrace is triggered on relatively short utterance durations. Whenever the backtrace operates, there will the components (what is identified by the backtrace) be identified before their superordinate units. From what has been said earlier about the criteria for inclusion in the recognition net, it should be apparent that no simple structural property determines when the backtrace operates, but rather a conglomeration of conditions that can be summed up by the phrase "the demands of recognition." So one should not expect to find neat divisions of units from components according to recognition times.

The structure of PS.Harpy permits some prediction of whether results quite different from the reported ones might be found. The backtrace would seem to be rather easily modifiable. What could be achieved by a different backtrace? It might certainly attempt to pick up a feature of the word directly, rather than afterward. It would seem difficult by this means to have the component become faster than the higher unit, but something approaching parity might be attained. Given extensive learning in a highly stable situation (for example, of the kinds demonstrated by Neisser in his search task in Neisser, Novack, & Lazar, 1963, and by Shiffrin & Schneider, 1977), one could produce limited inversions of the effect. Though we do not have yet a model for such learning, one would have to predict that an "automatic" response could be learned that would tap onto the existence of the component as it emerged in the forward sweep.

P7. The Word-Frequency Effect.   The basic phenomenon is that familiar words are recognized more easily (accurately in noise, quickly) than rare words (see Gregg, 1976, for a general overview). In word identification in noise, the errors are similar to the presented stimulus word. Sometimes the frequency level of the errors is independent of the frequency level of the presented word (Broadbent, 1967); sometimes it seems to reflect its frequency level (Frederiksen, 1971). When the experiment defines small closed populations of words (as opposed to the full vocabulary of the subject), the word-frequency effect essentially disappears.

Consider first how long it takes PS.Harpy to respond to a word in an isolated-word recognition experiment. As it stands, the forward wave will travel with the word and then the backtrace will pick out the identification. With only a single word involved, the states in the final beam could hold the word identification directly. In discussing the backtracing component, we had no basis for deciding which states should be able to evoke the grammar node, hence the word identity; it is surely reasonable to assume that boundary states lead back to the word. Hence, the backtrace operates in a single step and the time is determined by the forward wave. Thus, in the standard program there would seem to be no differential reaction-time effect of word frequency.

This leaves the source of the effect in some special feature of the task, namely speeded word identification. There seem to be two possibilities: (1) the backtrace can be initiated sooner; or (2) the forward sweep can go faster. In any case, the differential effect must arise from something that is a function (up to correlation) of word frequency. Within the current PS.-Harpy, only the $k_{i,j}$ in the $P_{i,j}$ extrapolation productions is a possible source. However, systematic structural differences in words as a function of frequency is also a possibility (Landauer & Streeter, 1973).

Consider triggering the backtrace early. There is no way for the system to examine the whole beam en passant to decide when to do this. However, a fixed criteria could be used. That is, if a path came up above a level determined by an examining production, then the system would initiate finding the word and responding. If the $k_{i,j}$ were a function of frequency, then the high frequency words would be more likely to satisfy this criteria, hence to be recognized early.

The errors that occur in such speeded trials would follow the a priori distribution of errors in the beam at some early time. There would not seem to be any reason why the frequency level of the true candidate would affect the frequency level of the error that was made. This is essentially what Broadbent found. On the other hand, the errors that are made will be similar to the input signal, since they are selected out of the beam that is built in response to the signal, again as found.

Consider the alternative of speeding up the forward sweep. This is composed entirely of a sequence of $P-Q$ pairs, paced by the concurrent firings of R_k to encode the signal. The $P-Q$ pairs form a serial sequence. Without creating a different algorithm, there seems no way to remove a $P_{i,j}$, which is the generative step. However Qs are not required. It may be possible for the Ps to race ahead to obtain a complete path. Assuming this would lead to triggering the backtrace early, this would lead to speeded recognition. This would happen, if at all, only on high frequency words (with slow $k_{i,j}$ decay), hence producing the differential effect.

Consider next the accuracy of responding under noise. To explore this fully requires extending the model back to the genesis of the R_k to discover how noise can enter into the processing—another excursion we cannot afford. One simple view says that noise in general leads to a failure of the (Data$\cdots$) to make contact at all, rather than supporting strongly a false path. Thus recognitions in noise will have relatively heavy contributions from unsupported extrapolations by the $P_{i,j}$. This returns us to the dependency for such extrapolations on the $k_{i,j}$, so that if they are an appropriate function of frequency (as seems natural), then there is a basis for the word-frequency effect.

The result of Pollack, Rubenstein, and Decker (1959) that, if the population is explicitly given, then the (basal) word frequency does not count needs also to be explained. These results involve the threshold for detection. This is not the situation in which the modified executive, described above, operates. Rather substantial time is available to make use of the short-term knowledge of the vocabulary. Operating simply as a test to reject candidates suggested by the backtrace already seems sufficient to produce a strong counteraction to the word-frequency effect. Additional shaping of the forward wave may also be possible, in the manner briefly discussed under sufficiency issue S5.

P8. The Unit of Speech Perception. Much of the work in speech perception has revolved around the attempt to discover the "unit,"—that is, whether recognition is organized around the acoustic segment, the feature, the phoneme, the syllable, or the word. Some of the phenomena already discussed (such as the word/letter recognition effect) have been seen as parts of this larger theoretical question. PS.Harpy, by providing a complete set of mechanisms for recognition, provides in some sense a complete answer to this question. The (Data$\cdots$), which are acoustic segments of variable duration and learned character, certainly exist. At recognition time, the state structure does not have any hierarchical organization, so no higher units exist. However, there is a structure from which this state network is derived. This does have hierarchical structure, hence units. In Harpy this is a two-level affair, the lexical and the grammatical level. But this part of the organization of PS.Harpy could be different in many ways and still make little difference to the operational structure of (6.1)–(6.8).

In any event, it should be realized that the question of the unit of speech perception becomes slightly anachronistic once complete computational organizations for perception are proposed. They invariably have a more complex reality, which then becomes the central object of scientific interest.

8. CONCLUSION

I have now achieved my goal: I have produced a theory of human speech perception based on Harpy that is sufficient to perceive connected speech and is not implausible in terms of human information processing capabilities.

But what is it that I have achieved in fact? There are several aspects that need to be discussed.

Sufficiency. Harpy (or, better, Harpy-extended) is not known to be sufficient to recognize full human speech. This is an important limitation of the results obtained here. However, it is not basically of concern to me. Harpy's current and potential power are sufficient unto the day thereof. As we learn more about how to recognize speech, Harpy may prove to be a technical dead-end, and other mechanisms, say more akin to Hearsay-II, will emerge. That will be all right with me.

More important, the projection of Harpy into PS.Harpy has produced estimates for the complexity of the computation: how many productions, how much computation, and how much working memory. These numbers seem uncomfortably large, though not out of the question with the improvements that might be possible in a Harpy-like technology (e.g., in the depth, D, the beam fraction, f, and the compression, c).

It is possible to conclude from these numbers that Harpy is not a good basis for human speech perception. However, such a conclusion should produce an uncomfortable feeling. For there is no system around (and no design for one) that takes any less computation. Indeed, to my knowledge, Harpy is the best scheme computationally (in terms of millions of instructions per second of speech). And PS.Harpy already exploits to the extreme that great computational loophole, parallel computation. Nothing comes for free, of course, so what PS.Harpy has purchased in time, it has paid for in hardware (the large number of productions). I would hope that those who reject PS.Harpy as a theory on computational grounds would discuss the computational alternatives in some quantitative detail.

We also do not have a complete picture of the information-processing limits of the human. Some numbers for the human are reasonably large (e.g., neuron populations, which get above 10^8 with no difficulty); some numbers are pretty small (e.g., the symbolic computation cycle is highly unlikely to be less than 20 msec). So it is hard to know when numbers are out of range. However, the biggest gap in our knowledge would seem to be about the structural limits on the nature of learning—on what form things must take in order to be learned. Here my analysis is completely inadequate.

PS.Harpy as a Psychological Theory. Sufficiency analysis is only one item of evidence. The psychological literature is replete with speech-perception related phenomena, all of which can serve to test a theory and refine it further. We discussed a small collection of such phenomena. My analysis dealt only with the basic findings and at a qualitative level. PS.-Harpy exhibits many of the right characteristics, though difficulties could crop up on any of them as the theory attempts to make more thorough and detailed predictions.

PS.Harpy was not defined with any of these specific phenomena in mind. Thus, in a subjective sense, all of these predictions count for the theory. However, as noted, the informal derivations were suspect in a couple of ways. In particular, demonstrating that PS.Harpy must show a given behavior in a task requires considering the class of all methods for the task that can be devised within the architecture. Other methods always exist, and it must be shown that they would not be learned or would not be selected on this occasion, etc. Without such analysis, there seems too high a chance of selecting out the one method that has the desired properties. That such a (desired) method exists is important, but it is only half the argument. Thus, I consider the analyses in Section 6 simply heuristic. Primarily, they make the case that PS.Harpy is a serious contender as a psychological theory. I don't wish to underplay the extent to which PS.Harpy appears to have the right properties. I consider the indications in Section 6 remarkable, especially since they were in essence simply "read off" the existing system.

On HPSA77. It is regrettable that HPSA77 had to be introduced without more analysis and support. Nevertheless, PS.Harpy, now that it is complete, stands on its own as a plausible theory. Its could have been proposed de novo, just from the notion of a basic production system architecture, such as has been current in psychology for some time. Assumption D3, on the activation of productions, probably would have dropped out, as it has played little role in the present analysis.

What was gained in mapping Harpy into HPSA77, rather than just considering the psychological implications of Harpy directly? I addressed the question briefly at the beginning, but the issues can be seen more clearly now. On the positive side, the psychological interpretation of HPSA77 is well tied down. This shows in the ability to make time predictions for speech based on behavior in memory experiments. The prediction was not completely tight here, because the timing specifications have not yet been made for HPSA77; but the tie between these two classes of phenomena is quite clear. If I had not had HPSA77, or some equivalent, I would have continually found myself with open fields of possibilities for how to realize the futures of Harpy in the human. My plight would have been much more like the diagram presented in Klatt's paper (Chap. 10), which, whatever its merits, is relatively free in introducing functional boxes. Finally, we actually ended up with an explicit model for speech perception, (6.1)–(6.8), which would have been impossible without some such constraint as HPSA77 provides. Of course, if the model is basically wrong, then such minor virtues are little consolation. On the negative side, many of the explanations of speech phenomena depended only on the features of Harpy and not on how these were implemented. Here, use of HPSA77 may obscure the essential structure of the explanation, though the more explicit theoretical structure might make it easier to derive.

Critical Weaknesses of PS.Harpy. The analysis dealt rather completely with the performance of perception. The most vulnerable aspect of the performance system is the backtrace. In part this is the (apparent) clash with the design decision D3 on positing activation on productions so that experiencing in the forward direction was possible. No specific difficulties were uncovered, but philosophically it seems wrong to have the speech system routinely working backwards through the utterance, when the human has difficulties doing it for deliberately held memory-span tests. The backtrace productions are variable-containing productions, entirely analogous to the performance productions that would exist for the memory-span task. One possibility is that the linked structure of the analyzed speech utterance, which does not exist for the typical memory-span task, makes a critical difference.

There are other issues with the backtrace as well. It operates like an executive routine, and variations in it were proposed freely in discussing the psychological phenomena. A more thorough analysis is required to understand what is possible and what is not. This is a place where the lack of an analysis of the entire class of methods produces a sense of unease. This same freedom implies that there may be schemes for doing the backtrace that work forward in various ways, or that do parts of the task concurrently with the forward sweep. Such variations, were they to exist, might change some of the conclusions of the paper.

The second major deficiency in analysis of PS.Harpy is the lack of detail on the acoustic side. Having jettisoned the Itakura metric used in Harpy as a candidate for detailed mapping, it was left open what sort of metric would do. It was not appropriate to invent a new metric in this paper. This had the effect of truncating the entire acoustical analysis.

Related to this, the functional boundary between the cognitive system and a distinct sensory-perceptual system remains open, though the theory localizes it firmly in WM. Two principles help determine this boundary. First, any effect of cognition on perception must occur in WM; this forces various perceptual products to be symbols in WM. Second, anything that happens in WM is open to cognitive manipulation and modification by the acquisition of new productions; this forces various perceptual products to reside outside of WM. Beyond this, there is no implication about how much specialized perceptual processing might happen. That PS.Harpy stopped with the R_k is of little moment. If I were willing to assume the (Data$\cdots$), I could have jettisoned the R_k; similarly, prior stages of chunking and processing by productions could have occurred in WM to produce the symbols taken as input by the R_k. What data would help define this boundary isn't evident. The phoneme restoration effect, perhaps the most obvious candidate, was explained already within PS.Harpy. In any event, I was unable to provide a serious assessment of the adequacy of the recognition match to handle the measure of closeness between the template and the acoustic parametric signal. With this lack, PS.Harpy has to remain silent on many speech phenomena.

There was almost no analysis on the details of the process of compilation and how PS.Harpy would learn the network. With this went a loss of plausibility constraint on the forms of the productions. Could they have been learned? For instance, could the $k_{i,j}$ (in the $P_{i,j}$ productions) be learned? The failure here stems in part from HPSA77 not having adopted yet any design decision with respect to learning new productions. Why this is the case is too extended a story for this paper. But also in part the failure stems simply from the learning context opening up the analysis to new tasks and new contexts, which would have multiplied the effort of this paper many fold. Insofar as the concerns about Harpy rest on its fixed, compiled nets, then the analysis of this paper has only set the stage for the real sufficiency analysis still to come.

Relation to Other Theories.   We limit ourselves to only a couple of remarks about other theories. First, with respect to Klatt's effort, being developed and presented concurrently with this (Klatt, Chap. 10), my general debt has already been expressed. His tactic, which is to draw on a range of new mechanisms, to compose what seems like an appropriate total scheme, seems eminently sensible to me—in some sense a better tactic than my own, which accepts one system in toto. His theory provides a clearer picture of some of the essentials for adding new words, etc., aspects that were left hanging in PS.Harpy. On the other hand, he posits functional boxes freely around his system, compared with PS.-Harpy, which really does fit almost everything within a known control structure. Furthermore, he weakens the sufficiency aspects of his system considerably, since it now is simply a new design for a speech understanding system.

PS.Harpy is not a motor theory. That is clear. The sufficiency of Harpy shows that analysis by synthesis is not necessary at the point of performance—though limitations on Harpy's extendibility could show that demonstration to be in error. Given that PS.Harpy is both sufficient and plausible psychologically, the generalized sufficiency-like arguments behind both the motor theory and analysis-by-synthesis simply lose their force. What might be true at the learning level is an entirely different matter, though neither of these motor theories make use of learning arguments. Likewise, whether there is a role at the cognitive level for speech production involvement in the recognition of difficult speech is also an open question.

Extension to the Rest of Perception. I have concentrated here on speech perception, though I took a small excursion part way into psychophysics in Section 5 in order to ground a given design decision. Having specified HPSA77 this far (i.e., to PS.Harpy), treatment of other senses is highly constrained. While it is possible that vision, for example, could be handled entirely differently, the main line of approach would certainly be simply to include the visual sensory buffer (the icon) as part of WM (already assumed in D4), and to do the visual recognition in essentially the same manner as I have done speech, taking into account the different structural features of the task (two dimensions, size, knowledge structure, etc.). Such an undertaking might not be quixotic at all. Technologically, the group around Raj Reddy at Carnegie-Mellon University are following exactly this path. A recent thesis (Rubin, 1978) has shown what has to be done to adapt Harpy techniques to natural scene analysis and has demonstrated its basic feasibility.

Methodological Notes. Some comments on the methodological aspects of this study are in order.

The first is the fruitfulness of sufficiency analysis. This paper was meant to demonstrate the usefulness of this technique. I am satisfied with the exercise in this respect and hope others are induced to consider sufficiency issues more intensively.

The second is the power of the mapping. Starting with Harpy and an architecture, a full-blown psychological theory of speech perception was manufactured in short order. I can testify personally to the power of this device, since the entire theory was force-generated in a few days, starting with just the mapping assumptions M1–M5, and unwinding essentially as it appears in the paper.

The third is the benefit of having a theory of the architecture of human cognition. The argument needs to be made more generally in connection with HPSA77; but this paper seems to me a data point about how useful such a construct is. Of course, it pays to have the *right* architecture, but I wish to note explicitly the power an architecture provides for making scientific progress. HPSA77 is a design probe and, although it is wearing rather well at the moment, it cannot possibly survive the attempt to extend it to cover all of cognition. But it seems to be a good vehicle.

The fourth is how a complete model of cognition has something to say about a very wide range of phenomena. PS.Harpy offers explanations of many phenomena, not because it was specifically designed to cover them, and not because additional assumptions are added each time, but because it was designed to be a full system for the perception of speech, and hence must exhibit behavior in all speech situations.

The fifth is the role of minimally specified theories to keep design decisions open to accommodate new results in new task domains. This runs counter to some popular notions about rushing headlong for falsifiability. It also seems as if the theory were being adapted post hoc to meet each new result. But it seems a remarkably sensible strategy when a complex system such as the human brain has to be modeled. Far from being post hoc, there is an accumulation of design specification (i.e., of theoretical constraint) with each act of accommodation. As long as the theory has sufficient precision, all the chickens will come home to roost eventually. This tactic does lead to the temporary inability to predict behavior in various tasks, because of underspecification. PS.Harpy shows this in several ways. But this should just be seen as selecting an appropriate approximating sequence for developing a theory. After all, the empirical results that will cause difficulty are patient—they will lie in wait for a very long time.

ACKNOWLEDGMENTS

I am grateful for comments on an earlier draft by John McDermott and Don McCracken. I am also grateful for many discussions on Harpy with Raj Reddy.

The research in this paper was supported in part by the Public Health Service Grant (MH-07722) from the National Institute of Mental Health and in part by the Defense Advanced Research Projects Agency (DOD), ARPA Order No. 3597, and monitored by the Air Force Avionics Laboratory under Contract F33615-78-C-1151.

The views and conclusions contained in this document are those of the author and should not be interpreted as representing the official policies, either expressed or implied, of the Defense Research Projects Agency of the U.S. Government.

REFERENCES

Anderson, J. R. *Language, memory and thought.* Potomac, Md.: Lawrence Erlbaum Associates, 1976.

Anderson, J. R., Kline, P. J., & Beasley, C. M. *Theory of the acquisition of cognitive skills.* (ONR Technical Report 77-1.) New Haven, Conn.: Yale University, 1977.

Anzai, Y. Learning strategies by computer. *Proceedings of the Second National Conference, Canadian Society for the Computational Study of Intelligence,* University of Toronto, Canada, July 19–21, 1978.

Baker, J. The Dragon system: an overview. *IEEE Transactions Acoustics, Speech and Signal Processing,* 1975, *ASSP-23,* 24–29.

Baylor, G., & Gascon, J. An information processing theory of aspects of the development of weight seriation in children. *Cognitive Psychology,* 1974, *6,* 1–40.

Broadbent, D. Word frequency effect and response bias. *Psychological Review,* 1967, *74,* 1–15.

CMU Speech Group. *Speech understanding systems: Final report.* Department of Computer Science, Carnegie-Mellon University, 1977.

Crowder, R. G. *Principles of learning and memory.* Hillsdale, N.J.: Lawrence Erlbaum Associates, 1976.

Erman, L., & Lesser, V. A retrospective view of the Hearsay-II architecture. *Proceedings of the Fifth International Joint Conference on Artificial Intelligence,* 1977, MIT, 790–800.

Estes, W. K. An associative basis for coding and organization in memory. In A. W. Melton & E. Martin (Eds.), *Coding processes in human memory.* Washington, D.C.: V. H. Winston & Sons, 1972.

Fodor, J. A., & Bever, T. G. The psychological reality of linguistic segments. *Journal of Verbal Learning and Verbal Behavior,* 1965, *4,* 414–420.

Forgy, C., & McDermott, J. OPS2: A domain-independent production system language. *Proceedings of the Fifth International Joint Conference on Artificial Intelligence,* 1977, 933–939.

Frederiksen, J. R. Statistical decision model for auditory word recognition. *Psychological Review,* 1971, *78,* 409–419.

Goldberg, H. G. *Segmentation and labeling of speech.* Unpublished doctoral dissertation, Carnegie-Mellon University, 1975.

Green, D. M., & Luce, R. D. Speed–accuracy trade off in auditory detection. In S. Kornblum (Ed.), *Attention and performance IV.* New York: Academic Press, 1975.

Gregg, V. Word frequency, recognition and recall. In J. Brown (Ed.), *Recall and recognition.* New York: Wiley, 1976.

Halle, M., & Stevens, K. N. Speech recognition: A model and a program for research. *IRE Transactions of Information Theory,* 1962, *IT-8,* 155–159.

Hunt, E. B., & Poltrock, S. E. The mechanics of thought. In B. H. Kantowitz (Ed.), *Human information processing: Tutorials in performance and cognition.* Hillsdale, N.J.: Lawrence Erlbaum Associates, 1974.

Jelenek, F. Continuous speech recognition by statistical methods. *Proceedings of the IEEE,* 1976, *64,* 532–556.

Klahr, D., & Wallace, J. G. *Cognitive development: An information processing view.* Hillsdale, N.J.: Lawrence Erlbaum Associates, 1976.

Klatt, D. Review of the ARPA speech understanding project. *Journal of the Acoustical Society of America,* 1977, *62,* 1345–1366.

Landauer, T. K., & Streeter, L. A. Structural differences between common and rare words: Failure of equivalence assumptions for theories of word recognition. *Journal of Verbal Learning and Verbal Behavior,* 1973, *12,* 119–131.

Langley, P. BACON. 1: A general discovery system. *Proceedings of the Second National Conference, Canadian Society for the Computational Study of Intelligence,* University of Toronto, Canada, July 19–21, 1978.

Liberman, A. M., Cooper, F. S., Shankweiler, D. S., & Studdert-Kennedy, M. Perception of the speech code. *Psychological Review,* 1967, *74,* 431–461.

Lowerre, B. T. *The Harpy speech recognition system.* Unpublished doctoral dissertation, Carnegie-Mellon University, 1976.

Luce, D. The theory of selective information and some of its applications. In D. Luce (Ed.), *Developments in mathematical psychology.* Glencoe, Ill.: The Free Press, 1960.

Luce, D., & Green, D. M. A neural timing theory for response times and the psychophysics of intensity. *Psychological Review,* 1972, *79,* 14–57.

McCracken, D. *A production system version of the Hearsay-II speech understanding system.* Unpublished doctoral dissertation, Carnegie-Mellon University, 1978.

McDermott, J., & Forgy, L. Production system conflict resolution strategies. In D. W. Waterman & F. Hayes-Roth (Eds.), *Pattern-directed inference systems.* New York: Academic Press, 1978.

McGill, W. J. Neural counting mechanisms and energy detection in audition. *Journal of Mathematical Psychology,* 1967, *4,* 351–376.

McNeill, D., & Lindig, L. The perceptual reality of phonemes, syllables, words and sentences. *Journal of Verbal Learning and Verbal Behavior,* 1973, *12,* 419–430.

Medress, M., and committee. Speech Understanding Systems: Report of a Steering Committee. *SIGART Newsletter,* No. 62, pp. 4–8, 1976.

Miller, G. A., & Isard, S. Some perceptual consequences of linguistic rules. *Journal of Verbal Learning and Verbal Behavior,* 1963, *2,* 217–228.

Miller, G. A., & Selfridge, J. A. Verbal context and the recall of meaningful material. *American Journal of Psychology,* 1953, *63,* 176–185.

Moran, T. *The symbolic imagery hypothesis: An empirical investigation via production system simulation of human behavior in a visualization task.* Unpublished doctoral dissertation, Carnegie-Mellon University, 1971.

Morton, J., & Broadbent, D. E. Passive versus active recognition models, or is your homunculus really necessary? In W. Wathen-Dunn (Ed.), *Models for the perception of speech and visual form.* Cambridge, Mass.: MIT Press, 1967.

Murdock, B. *Human memory: theory and data.* Hillsdale, N.J.: Lawrence Erlbaum Associates, 1974.

Nakagawa, S. *A machine understanding system for spoken Japanese sentences.* Unpublished doctoral dissertation, Kyoto University, 1976.

Neisser, U., Novick, R., & Lazar, R. Searching for ten targets simultaneously. *Perceptual and Motor Skills,* 1963, *17,* 955–961.

Neves, D. M. A computer program that learns algebraic procedures by examining examples and by working test problems in a text book. *Proceedings of the Second National Conference, Canadian Society for the Computational Study of Intelligence,* University of Toronto, Canada, July 19–21, 1978.

Newell, A. Production systems: Models of control structures. In W. C. Chase (Ed.), *Visual information processing.* New York: Academic Press, 1973.

Newell, A. Knowledge representation aspects of productions systems. *Proceedings of the Fifth International Joint Conference on Artificial Intelligence,* 1977, MIT, 984–988.

Newell, A. *A production system architecture for human cognition.* (in preparation).

Newell, A., Barnett, J., Forgie, J. W., Green, C., Klatt, D. H., Licklider, J. C. R., Munson, J., Reddy, D. R., & Woods, W. A. *Speech understanding systems: Final report of a study group.* New York: North-Holland/American Elsevier, 1973. (Reprinting of 1971 study).

Newell, A., & Simon, H. A. *Human problem solving.* Englewood Cliffs, N.J.: Prentice-Hall, 1972.

Peterson, L. R., & Peterson, M. J. Short-term retention of individual verbal items. *Journal of Experimental Psychology*, 1959, *58*, 193–198.

Pollack, I., Rubenstein, H., & Decker, L. Intelligibility of known and unknown message sets. *Journal of the Acoustical Society of America*, 1959, *31*, 273–279.

Ritea, B. Automatic speech understanding systems. *Proceedings of the 11th IEEE Computer Society Conference*, 1975, 319–322.

Rubin, S. *The ARGOS image understanding system.* Unpublished doctoral dissertation, Carnegie-Mellon University, 1978.

Rychener, M. *Production systems as a programming language for Artificial Intelligence applications.* Unpublished doctoral dissertation, Carnegie-Mellon University, 1976.

Rychener, M., & Newell, A. An instructable production system: basic design issues. In D. A. Waterman & F. Hayes-Roth (Eds.), *Pattern-directed inference systems*. New York: Academic Press, 1978.

Savin, H. B., & Bever, T. G. The nonperceptual reality of the phoneme. *Journal of Verbal Learning and Verbal Behavior*, 1970, *9*, 295–302.

Schneider, W., & Shiffrin, R. M. Controlled and automatic human information processing: I. Detection, search, and attention. *Psychological Review*, 1977, *84*, 1–66.

Shiffrin, R. M., & Schneider, W. Controlled and automatic human information processing: II. Perceptual learning, automatic attending, and a general theory. *Psychological Review*, 1977, *84*, 127–190.

Simon, H. A. The architecture of complexity. *Proceedings of the American Philosophical Society*, December 1962, *106*.

Simon, H. A. How big is a chunk? *Science*, 1974, *183*, 482–488.

Slate, D. J., & Atkin, L. R. CHESS 4.5: The Northwestern University chess program. In R. W. Frey (Ed.), *Chess Skill in Man and Machine*. New York: Springer-Verlag, 1977.

Sternberg, S. The discovery of processing stages: Extensions of Donders' method. In W. G. Koster (Ed.), *Attention and performance II. Acta Psychologica*, 1969, *30*, 276–315.

Studdert-Kennedy, M. Speech perception. In N. J. Lass (Ed.), *Contemporary issues in experimental phonetics*. New York: Academic Press, 1976.

Warren, R. Perceptual restoration of missing speech sounds. *Science*, 1970, *167*, 392–393.

Warren, R. M. Auditory illusions and perceptual processes. In N. J. Lass (Ed.), *Contemporary issues in experimental phonetics*. New York: Academic Press, 1976.

Waterman, D. A. Adaptive production systems. *Proceedings of the Fourth International Joint Conference on Artificial Intelligence*, Tbilisi, USSR, 1975, 296–303.

Waterman, D., & Hayes-Roth, F. (Eds.), *Pattern-directed inference systems*. New York: Academic Press, 1978.

Woods, W., Bates, M., Bruce, B., Cook, C., Klovstad, J., Makhoul, J., Nash-Webber, B., Schwartz, R., Wolf, J., & Zue, V. *Speech understanding systems: Final report.* Cambridge, Mass.: Bolt Beranek & Newman, 1976.

Young, R. *Children's seriation behavior: A production system analysis.* Unpublished doctoral dissertation, Carnegie-Mellon University, 1973.

12

Copycat Science
or
Does the mind really work by table look-up?

Donald A. Norman
Center for Human Information Processing
University of California, San Diego

I have been asked to review three papers from this book, by Reddy, Klatt and Newell. But my real task is more than that. For these three people looked at a large segment of the problem of understanding speech, and their work has implications far beyond the topic of speech understanding. I find myself impressed, and depressed.

One thing I cannot stand is a copycat science. But I now predict a new wave of theory in psychology. Theoretical psychology, the great usurper.

There is a bird that lets other birds lay eggs in its nest. Then it sits patiently on the intruding eggs, comforting them until they hatch. And even as the intruder chick dominates the natural chicklings, the pseudoparent fails to understand what has happened. I name that bird "psychology."

I can see the journal articles now:

Empirical Tests of the Harpy Beamwidth Assumption
Phoneme Monitoring and Evidence for Precompilation
in Speech Recognition
Attentional Demands During Backtrace: A Test of Psychological Validity
A Critique of Pure Spectrum

Psychology has a tendency to be a "copycat science," to copy the current ideas of neighboring disciplines into its own. And so I see a new era in which bottom-up models such as these will be thrust upon the psychological scheme, led by the impressive set of papers under review. This is not necessarily bad: There is no reason why one science should not benefit by the examples and advances of another. But whether the format of Harpy should be such an influential force should be determined by

381

reason, by analysis, and with full understanding of the implications. I do not believe we yet know enough to take a mechanism for machine recognition of speech and translate it into a model of human cognition. But I will conclude my paper by stating that Harpy may indeed help re-assess the current understanding of human cognitive abilities in a useful way.

ON HARPY

These papers by Reddy, Klatt and Newell have been critically influenced by Lowerre's doctoral dissertation on the development of the system of speech recognition called Harpy (Lowerre, 1976). The lessons of Harpy are generalized to a far greater degree than I would have imagined. Suddenly, we have two major proposals for models of speech recognition systems that emphasize both the role of bottom-up sensory analyses, and the use of precompiled, table look-up computational schemes, thereby minimizing the role of higher order knowledge in the understanding of speech. My job is to discuss the validity of these models, and to understand their implications for speech recognition.

Harpy is an impressive system. It can accomplish the goals set up for speech recognition systems in 1971: to recognize connected speech from many cooperative speakers, in a quiet room, using a good microphone, with slight tuning for each speaker. It has a vocabulary of slightly over 1,000 words, and it achieves 95% accuracy on naturally formed sentences from that vocabulary for a specific document-retrieval task. It works fast enough, in principle, to do the job in real time. (For an excellent review of Harpy and of other speech understanding systems, see Reddy, Chap. 9 and Klatt, 1977.)

Does this performance qualify Harpy as a model of human speech understanding? Well, people do a lot better than Harpy, several orders of magnitude better (one to two orders of magnitude better in vocabulary size, many orders of magnitude better in number of speakers that can be recognized—with no need for special adjustment (tuning) for each speaker, orders of magnitude better in the lack of restrictions upon subject matter, upon the signal-to-noise ratio, and upon syntax that is understandable). More importantly, Harpy is counterintuitive; it seems to violate our expectations about the nature of the system that is necessary to understand speech. Harpy lacks flexibility. Harpy does not take into account changing conditions of knowledge from many different sources. Harpy has a built-in, efficient, precompiled network of special paths, designed to meet previously specified goals for speech understanding systems. Why, then, is Harpy so important? Because it works, and a working system is a strong argument for a method.

My favorite piece among artificial intelligence structures is the Hearsay speech understanding system. Hearsay is based on the basic principle that a system can incorporate many different sources of information and that these modules can interact in a flexible and graceful manner. Unlike Harpy, Hearsay fulfills my psychological intuitions about the form of a general cognitive processing structure. My colleagues and I have used Hearsay as a source of theoretical ideas. But now I see the father of Hearsay (Reddy) being overturned by a child of Hearsay (Harpy). And Reddy, and Klatt, and Newell embrace the principles of Harpy as valid models of both artificial speech understanding systems and of human speech recognition. Why does an implausible model win such converts? Because it works? Surely there must be more to it than that.

To be fair to psychology, I have to admit that psychologists have very difficult tasks. We wish to explain cognitive behavior in terms of its underlying mechanism. But what mechanism? Not neurological, for there is a fundamental mismatch between behavior of neurological components and the resulting phenomena. Not philosophical, for we seek empirical validation. The resulting set of psychological theories are not wholly satisfactory; they are a mixed bag of concepts. Here is a representative list of recent psychological concepts: short-term memory, means–ends analysis, utility theory, exhaustive search, limited resource models, conscious and nonconscious stages of analysis. The list combines strategies, mechanisms, descriptive models, and metaphors—all mixed together. Moreover, every concept on the list is suspect: Each concept is less firmly supported by data than is usually admitted. Some concepts have no support, others have both confirmatory evidence and contradictory evidence.

What is the proper level of psychological theory? What level of explanation gives us power unique to our discipline, with some sensible basis in observation? I do not know the answer. I do not know what a proper psychological theory should look like. This is a disturbing admission, not only because I am a psychologist, but because I claim to be a theoretical psychologist, a person struggling to reach the proper level of psychological behavior. One problem I face is that there is a many-to-one mapping from theory to data. Our field has become too sophisticated in our ability to devise models, because all too often the models are surprisingly weak. Our most specific and powerful models are about very simple aspects of behavior. Whenever we look at more complex behavior, the models tend to be either descriptive, or vague in the mechanisms. Alternatively, they are very precise (as in the recent surge of models of memory representation and use), but untestable. Instead of testing the models themselves, one can only test small asides or irrelevant aspects. Psychology being what it is, these small inessential tests get performed (and published) with great regularity. Given this state of our theories in psychology, perhaps it is not so surprising that Harpy is being taken so seriously by my colleagues.

Will Sufficiency Suffice?

Boom. Success. Harpy. Psychology, here is your answer. Forget your verbal, qualitative, hand-waving models. Here is a model that works. Klatt reconsiders how speech is understood. Newell extrapolates. Reddy combines.

Harpy: a model of speech recognition that appears to work. Now, on closer examination, it doesn't work very well. But it does work well enough to be impressive, well enough to let it claim a reasonable level of sufficiency. (How can I help but be impressed by a system that claims to recognize 1,011 words in naturally spoken speech from a variety of speakers, when two of those valuable words are "Donald Norman"?)

In the preceding chapters we have seen three people take the work of Harpy very seriously as a general model of speech recognition and as a specific model of human psychology. Reddy, Klatt, and Newell, three distinguished scientists from the fields of artificial intelligence, speech, and computer science/psychology take Harpy seriously. From what evidence?

Is it enough to say that since Harpy recognizes speech it therefore passes the critical test of sufficiency? Will sufficiency suffice? And, how sufficient is Harpy? It has a limited vocabulary. It recognizes only a limited number of persons. It does not make use of higher-level knowledge. Harpy also has a long list of deficits, many of them stated by Reddy (Chap. 9) and by Klatt in his earlier review (Klatt, 1977). Is the success of Harpy large enough for us to assume that minor corrective efforts will achieve a more satisfactory level? Or is there still a large gap between the performance of Harpy and the performance of humans? I think the latter: Impressive though Harpy may be, it definitely falls short of human performance; the gap is large enough to require fundamental changes.

But meanwhile, nothing succeeds like success. For years, the literature on the perceptual systems, on pattern recognition, and on speech recognition has contained numerous models and suggestions. One thing seemed quite clear, however: Any successful system was going to have to combine information from a variety of sources, information about the acoustic signal, about the speaker, about the syntax and semantics of the language, about the topic matter, the world, computational postulates—everything.

Now comes a successful speech recognition devide that appears to ignore most of these aspects of the problem, concentrating instead on essentials, getting from speech waveform to word, efficiently. What does this mean for the psychology of speech understanding? Are all these ideas wrong?

In the three preceding papers, we have three highly respected scientists telling us about the effect that Harpy, the successful speech system, has had upon their lives. Reddy realizes the problems of Harpy, but tells us not to worry: Everything will turn out all right. Harpy can be modified to make it sensitive to context, to take advantage of other knowledge sources, to compile its efficient networks on the fly, as they are needed. Did Reddy hear me say I preferred Hearsay to Harpy, that Hearsay was a psychologically more realistic system? Then, says Reddy, have no fears, for the modified Harpy will combine the best of all worlds, looking like Hearsay in the way it uses higher level knowledge, looking like it does now in its efficient use of computational algorithms.

Klatt tells us that he has learned from Harpy that precompiled spectral patterns and their interactions can do wonders for the task of recognizing words. It minimizes continual feedback loops and hypotheses, and eliminates the interaction among various sources of knowledge prevalent in other schemes.

Newell also believes. His model of how the mind works is a production system: If a production system is a model of the mind, and if Harpy is a model of speech recognition—and if the mind can do speech recognition—then Harpy better be a production system. And so Newell proceeds to show us that Harpy could indeed be a production system.

Will sufficiency suffice? Well, it will if there are no alternatives, or if there are sufficient constraints on the task or the mechanisms so that few or no alternatives remain. We do not know whether speech has so many constraints that there is only a small class of mechanisms able to explain it. We also do not know enough about neural structures to know what kinds of computational systems are possible. And the competition is weak. Yes, other speech recognition systems have been studied, and some of these perform better than Harpy at some aspects of the task. But these systems are all closely related. Sufficiency does not suffice if the competition is weak, or if the task is simplified, or if major phenomena are not yet covered. At the moment, when talking about speech, we do not know the answers.

ON NEWELL, ON KLATT, AND ON REDDY

A few years ago, at an earlier Carnegie-Mellon Conference, Allen Newell wrote an important review of the papers in his session. Newell claimed that "You Can't Play Twenty Questions with Nature and Win." He started off by stating that his favorite experimental scientists had just presented clean, elegant data: but of what? What difference would it make to the scientific scene fifty years hence?

I cannot resist the temptation to repeat the argument. Here are three of my favorite scientists. I charge them with ignoring nature and going all out for the final theory. Now, this is not always such a bad idea. Sometimes it works. In the game of Twenty Questions, sometimes you can get to the target by asking a few tentative initial questions and then directly trying a possible answer. It's a bad strategy, but very rewarding when it succeeds.

Comments on Newell's Paper

Allen Newell, I charge you with ignoring nature. You are playing All-or-None. You have proposed that a production system is a model of the mind. You have looked at the success of Harpy and realized that it can be modeled with a production system. And so you have given us the model of the mind, complete with Harpy-like speech recognition. Then, the question you have asked yourself, and the reader, is whether you succeeded: Will the production-system model really work? Well, I think that there are other issues that must be discussed. Suppose I grant you the production system Harpy. In principle, it can be done. Harpy is a big network, and a network can be described as a set of node–arc–node triples: essentially a Markov net of transitions among states. Production systems certainly can and do perform conditional state transitions. Whether or not all the details are correct, and whether or not it can be done fast enough is a different story, but for the moment, suppose that the major goal of your paper is correct: Harpy can be realized as a production system. Then what? What if I don't agree that the mind is a huge production system?

Newell has said, and I agree, that nothing can succeed like success, for success is the demonstration of sufficiency. And scientific theory must pass two criteria: sufficiency and necessity. Sufficiency means that the assumptions and mechanisms of the theory will actually do the task expected of it: The theory has *sufficient* power. Necessity means that the particular mechanisms and methods are actually necessary, that the task requirements of the theory could not be performed without those particular assumptions. For engineering purposes, sufficiency is essential, whereas necessity is not important. For the purpose of explanation in a scientific domain, necessity is a critical feature of a theory. But when only one theory exists which is capable of meeting the sufficiency criterion, what is one to do?

I am critical of Newell's attempt, but very sympathetic to it as well. I think it is absolutely essential that our theories be able to pass the sufficiency test. They must also pass the necessity test, but I do not know how to get the experimental evidence that will let us do this. The speech system is complex. Reddy, Klatt, and Newell have all understood the limitations of existing knowledge. All have listed explicitly the problems of existing systems, all have asked for help in gathering evidence to support them. I can't criticize their efforts, at least not any more than they themselves have already done. If we want to know how human systems work, we need to collect data that tell us about immensely complex psychological mechanisms. And now I am back to my problem of not knowing at what level psychological theories should exist. What data can we collect? What level of theory is appropriate?

Newell has the courage of his convictions. I think that is an important point in his favor. Moreover, Newell resists any easy solution to the problem. It would have been simple for him to have devised special-purpose routines and procedures to operate upon the speech waveform, to convey information about continuous variables, and to handle the problem of matching and binding variables. But production systems already exist, and Newell has imposed upon himself the task of determining whether or not these existing systems can handle the speech recognition job. Newell tried to put everything within the mechanism of his production system, which assumes a basic cycle time of 80 to 100 msec per cycle, and an "instantiate and bind" time of about 40 msec, done serially, whenever there is a variable in the condition side of a production. These times are much too slow, and so Newell was forced by these assumptions to state that the left-hand side of a production could not contain any variables.

Were I trying to do this job, I would not have restricted myself so much. I would not have had the courage of my earlier theoretical conviction. I would not have used data from psychological tasks of one sort to try to explain the psychological task of speech recognition. I think Newell's attempt must be commended for its intellectual honesty and for the brilliance and power of the approach. I would have said that he couldn't succeed, and in fact I still do not know whether or not he does. It does look like a production system can be built, but whether it can handle speech at the proper rate will not be determined until someone actually constructs the system. There are too many assumptions and unknowns in the computations. But Newell's paper convinces me that a production system model is indeed a powerful mechanism—that it is either capable of understanding speech, or very close to being capable.

I think Newell was wrong to ignore our knowledge of the specialized computation that is done in the sensory systems, including the sensory cortex. I would be surprised if there were not specialized mechanisms for speech. If one wishes to use a production-system model of the mind, I still see nothing wrong with allowing the matching side of the production to be handled by special purpose devices. I think the correct model will have specialized sensory matching (feature detection). Speech, vision, smell, taste, touch, and temperature—all should have specialized matching operations, each probably different from the others. These specialized mechanisms would do two things.

They would strengthen the psychological validity of the model, and they would certainly strengthen the power of the system, allowing Newell to relax the restrictions that he has imposed upon himself.

Comments on Klatt's Paper

Klatt suggests that it is possible in most cases to go directly to a lexical representation of words from the acoustical spectrum. This is a novel approach for those in the business of analyzing speech: it is usually thought that the analysis of speech requires layers of abstraction. For example, speech sounds are transformed into phonemes, and phonemes into words. Klatt believes that these steps are unnecessary because all relevant information can be incorporated into a decision network modeled on that used by Harpy. (Actually, the networks are originally constructed using phonemes, but it is the system designer, not the system, who has done the phonemic analysis.)

Klatt has given us two models. The basic model, the main subject of the paper, combines two cooperative methods. One method, called LAFS (Lexical Analysis from Spectrum), takes the sound information and goes directly to the lexical representation wherever that is possible. Whenever LAFS fails, Klatt suggests that a second method operates, doing a phonetic analysis, a morphological decomposition and phonemic analysis. This mode of operation is presumed to be necessary only when the lexicon does not contain the target item, or when the spectral information is severely deficient.

The second model given to us by Klatt is not intended to be taken seriously, at least not now. But I find myself intrigued. The model, analysis by synthesis, adds just those features so badly missing from Klatt's other model, from Harpy, and from Newell's analysis: the use of context, of meaning, of information beyond the word. This modern version of the analysis by synthesis model makes heavy use of top-down processing and tries to work cooperatively with several sources of contextual information. Although the arguments for the analysis by synthesis model are given in a very persuasive manner, its details are absent, and the theme of Klatt's paper is that LAFS—which relies on bottom-up analyses—is the model he prefers.

Klatt is trying to see how far he can push the bottom-up analysis of the signal. He knows full well that this will not be the complete story, but he nevertheless believes that this type of speech analysis can be much more useful than has heretofore been thought, another lesson learned from Harpy. My problem in analyzing the system is simple: Will it work? How do I know? How does anyone know? The arguments seem reasonably persuasive, but there are many missing steps. What happens in the presence of noise? What happens with badly pronounced words, or what happens when the system gets off track for one reason or another? (How will the system react to someone who stutters?) We are assured that the system can handle minor perturbations in input (such as a cough or other short bursts of noise), but what of longer duration noise problems, or simply a low signal-to-noise ratio? The answer is that one cannot tell until the system is built.

Will Klatt's system work? Klatt has given us some problems that he hopes to solve. Let us see how well he does.

Klatt's Performance on the Standard Problems of Speech Recognition. Three of the major problems for any speech recognition system appear to be handled very well by Klatt's model. These are:

1. acoustic–phonetic noninvariance;
2. phonetic segmentation; and
3. time normalization.

The problem of acoustic–phonetic noninvariance is solved by explicit storing of all possible combinations of sounds. The number of possible pronunciations that must be stored is large, but is still only in the few thousands. To my knowledge this suggestion was first made by Wickelgren (1969), and I find it somewhat amusing to see this suggestion resurfacing, to see it being taken seriously, and to find that it is perhaps correct. I think Wickelgren too will be amused.

The next two issues—phonetic segmentation and time normalization—turn out to be pseudo-issues. They are solved by being ignored. The form of the match process used by Klatt goes directly to lexical items, bypassing any need for time normalization or phonetic segmentation. If phonetic segmentation is needed, it can be derived *after* the lexical item has been identified.

Three of Klatt's issues are not handled well. These are:

1. talker normalization;
2. ambiguity caused by errors in analysis; and
3. interpretation of prosodic cues.

Talker normalization is a major unsolved problem. It will require either many spectral templates, or several basic prototypes, or some new method. The way that sound spectra vary with speakers is still an unsolved problem. Klatt's hope is that only a few basic sets of spectra need to be stored, and that it is necessary only to match the speaker to the closest set. Will it work?

The problem of ambiguity that will be caused whenever there are errors in the preliminary phonetic representation is not handled well. The system seems to rely too much on the proper identification of the first segments of each lexical item. It seems to me that this leads to a system that can have problems when there are no matches, or ambiguous, multiple matches. Top-down information will probably have to be added to the model in order to disambiguate problems caused by these errors.

Prosodic cues are not handled well, either. The same factors that led to solving the time normalization problem and the acoustic–phonetic noninvariance problem make the prosodic analysis difficult. Some of the stress and temporal information has been discarded to simplify the analysis. Klatt hopes that this information can be pulled out anyway—that a metric can be devised to determine the mismatch between the actual sound spectrum and the one expected, and that this metric can then tell us about prosodic information. Again, will it work?

To summarize, Klatt proposes an interesting system. I am more impressed with the fact that Klatt has taken Harpy so seriously than I am with the details of the actual proposal. This marks a rather dramatic change in the approach I expect from him, and it makes me take Harpy much more seriously as a possible model of human speech understanding than I would otherwise have done. Even if Harpy were the very best speech understanding system around, I would normally view it as a model of how machines, but not people, might recognize speech. But now that I have read Klatt's proposal, I wonder.

Comments on Reddy's Paper

Reddy's work has influenced much of the current speech understanding work, especially the Hearsay and Harpy systems described in Chap. 9, and so my comments about Reddy have been incorporated throughout this paper. His work has been very influential, both in the development of all of the speech systems discussed here and in my own personal understanding of speech understanding and of the nature of complex interacting systems. Though I will not discuss Reddy in specific terms, his work has had an enormous impact on many of the papers presented in this book. In addition, he has provided the participants with a description of progress in the study of speech understanding at Carnegie-Mellon University, including the development of the Harpy system. Reddy has sketched the virtues and the deficits of various speech understanding systems, suggesting the new directions that will be travelled by systems now under study, and listing the kinds of data from experimental psychology that would be useful to guide further development.

ARCHITECTURE OF MIND

What is the architecture of the mind? What is in the nature of the biological substance of the brain that it can implement subroutines, call procedures, have memory stacks, pass and bind variables? How did these functions evolve?

What about the specialized nature of the sensory receptors? We have a very specialized hearing apparatus, one that does very interesting things. Current speech understanding systems, at best, approximate the ear's operations. Those of you who are simply casual observers of the speech understanding industry may be surprised to learn that the ear does not have a bank of third-octave filters. It does not do a Fourier analysis of the signal. Rather, there are some elegant mechanical lever systems, some lovely fluid mechanics, some beautiful travelling waves on the basilar membrane. The critical bands displayed by detection and masking studies can indeed by *approximated* by banks of third-octave filters, but the approximation substitutes a discrete set of filters with fixed center frequencies for a continuous system—the approximation may or may not destroy critical features of the analysis. Then there are about 30,000 nerve fibers leaving each cochlea and going to the brain, ascending to the sensory cortices, but interacting with each other all the way. The ear responds to intensity over an amplitude range of approximately ten billion to one. Our ability to localize sounds requires precision of approximately 10 microsec in comparing signals from the two ears. We do not yet know how pitch is abstracted from the auditory system, but for the range of speech signals in the few hundred Hertz range it seems clear that detecting the location along the basilar membrane at which there is maximum aplitude of vibration is *not* the mechanism. We know that there are specialized cells in the acoustic cortex that are capable of detecting specific kinds of signals, including the on-set and off-set of transient signals and perhaps even special frequency glides. Although we do not know the details of these operations, we do know that there are very specialized and exquisite sensory mechanisms for analysis of arriving signals. Thus, it seems strange to devise a theory of human speech understanding without taking into consideration something about the specialized mechanisms.

Are we really ready to speculate about the processing mechanisms of the brain? I think not. I think today we are very knowledgeable about a certain class of computational device: the von Neumann computer. We also know quite a bit about analog computation. For those people interested in building artificial devices that understand speech, it does not matter much how the brain actually operates, how human psychology is implemented. For those who are concerned with human mechanisms, I suspect we are going to need a new kind of computer metaphor. Indeed, I suspect that both computer science and psychology are going to need a new class of computer architecture as they explore symbolic processing. I am not sure what these machines will be, except they are bound to have heavy and fundamental use of pattern-directed operations, of processes that are fundamentally parallel in nature. We might need structures with variable levels of activation. The fields of psychology and artificial intelligence need some active exploration of alternative structures.

Memory versus Computation

One important point that the three preceding chapters emphasize is that efficient computation can be performed if only the appropriate combinations of possible input sequences have been precomputed. In most of our modeling of intelligent systems, we have been tempted to define powerful systems that use a few simple primitive mechanisms to derive all that follows. The difficulty with this approach is that it requires extensive computation, and computation takes time. One can save time by trading memory storage for computation—computing beforehand a set of possible alternatives, storing them away in memory. Then, at the time of application, one simply does a pattern match search of memory and finds the appropriate action. The amount of memory required is large, but the savings in computation time is considerable. In an earlier era of computation, large amounts of memory frightened us. But why should we not be able to store hundreds of thousands of special purpose patterns?

Consider the necessary storage required for an English vocabulary. There are tens of thousands of words, and there must be specific information about each one. Each has a spelling pattern, a pronunciation pattern, a meaning, and perhaps special syntactic information. Why not attach a set of 10 to 20 spectral patterns to each word to define all possible pronunciations? Granted that words are distorted and pronounced differently in different contexts, but it is also true that considerable savings in memory space can occur if one takes advantage of the overlapping pronunciations of words, of overlapping underlying morphemes. Is it too much to think that a person stores a thousand or a hundred thousand special combinations to understand spoken speech? Remember, understanding and producing language is one of the most complex things that we do. It takes a child a decade or more to speak as well as an adult. Ten years of extensive practice in understanding and producing sounds seems like an adequate amount of time to learn the several hundred thousand combinations.

The Human Computer

I am impressed by how bad a computer humans really are. It is true that we perform such wondrous tasks as speaking and listening, playing chess and Go, and creating theoretical physics and philosophy. But I have trouble remembering a modern twelve-digit telephone number, and I fear that the limit of my intellectual ability is the game of tic-tac-toe, at least if I play it by pure planning without any use of prior knowledge.

There are large numbers of tasks that I do without any conscious control, and speaking is one of them. I have very little control over how I speak or what I say. I usually do not know the words I speak until I have spoken them. Sometimes I listen to myself and am surprised by what I hear being uttered. Whenever I think about human cognitive performance, I am surprised at how bad we are at controlling our cognitive activities. I am impressed with how bad a computer the human is.

I do not think humans are capable of much deductive thought, nor are they capable of much extensive planning. I am becoming convinced that we perform best when we do not need conscious processing, when we have previously stored large patterns of possible behaviors, when we operate by table look-up rather than by computation. Much of the evidence for this comes for the many studies of chess performance done at Carnegie-Mellon University. This research has shown that experts play chess by utilizing a large number of stored patterns, and maybe that is how we listen and talk. Perhaps the human system is designed so that it is very efficient at the use of memory, finding specialized routines and executing them. Maybe our conscious resources are restricted to high-level control.

The complaint against the storage of specialized routines is that so many of them are required. But how many are too many? It takes years of training to become an expert. I have estimated that 5,000 hours of practice are necessary to become a professional at any activity. And even after these 5,000 hours, one is still not at world-class performance, simply at excellent performance.

One criticism of any suggestion that requires so much to be learned is that it is implausible. But this is not necessarily such a bad assumption. The elements required to be learned are simply ones, much less complex than the normal items studied in verbal learning experiments. It is not implausible that these elements be learned much more quickly than are individual words of the lexicon (to take a reasonable example). But note:

Even if there were 100,000 elements to be learned, and even if each took 10 seconds, that is only 3,000 hours—well within the range I believe necessary to learn a complex task to expert proficiency. (As I write this paragraph I admit a feeling of recognition: I am doing just the sort of calculation done by Newell to demonstrate the sufficiency argument of his system. I have no idea if my rough computation is valid, but it certainly is a nice feeling to be able to make several rough but plausible assumptions and have the results turn out in a nice, consistent manner.)

We should not be scared of the numbers. Maybe there is a lesson to be learned from Harpy. Maybe Harpy-like models that heavily emphasize matching and de-emphasize computing are indeed appropriate models of human performance.

CONCLUDING REMARKS

The relative success of the Harpy speech understanding system comes as a surprise to many people. It does not use elegant mechanisms; it relies on precompiled network structures rather than on computation. Its performance is good enough for a number of eminent people to take it seriously as a model of human speech recognition.

At first glance, Harpy appears indefensible as a model of human performance. On further inspection, however, Harpy may be a lesson for all of us. Maybe the human computer is good at matching, bad at computations. Maybe people do learn hundreds of thousands of special-purpose data patterns. The Hearsay speech recognition system, with its blackboard and its cooperative interactions between independent knowledge sources, is an elegant model for psychology. In practice, however, it was excessive in its computational demands. Maybe this is a lesson for theoretical psychology. Maybe complex tasks cannot be done by extensive computation.

I think that Klatt's attempt to push the bottom-up analysis is important, for it will tell us just how far one can go with these table look-up mechanisms. I think that Newell's attempt to analyze Harpy as a production system is important, for it will tell us the limits of that method of computation.

But I believe that Harpy has problems. It has problems in its generality and extensibility. It uses a finite state grammar, and this is inadequate for English. It does not know how to handle nongrammatical utterances or novel words. It does not integrate knowledge from outside sources. Still, Harpy is sufficient, and perhaps sufficiency suffices. At the very least, Harpy's success, and the articles by Klatt and Newell, have forced us to reconsider the relative weights given to different aspects of computation.

Should Harpy be the prototype of a new generation of psychological models? (Copycat psychology, here we go.) Maybe yes, maybe no. There is a lesson to be learned from Harpy: People may not do as much computation and reasoning as has heretofore been supposed. But then again, we must remember that Harpy is an artificial intelligence solution to a problem that is largely based around signal analysis. Note well the words "artificial" and "signal." Perhaps the lesson has to do with the inability to perform large amounts of computation on traditional digital computers when there is an obvious need for speed. But there are other lessons too, lessons that do apply to psychology. We have always accepted the need for phonetic and/or phomenic analysis in speech perception. Is there really such a need? The papers under discussion in this chapter argue a strong no: Phonetic analysis is not necessary.

Copycat psychology, remember that speech perception is largely a perceptual activity. There are specialized neural systems in the brain specifically designed for sound analysis. The need is for accuracy, quick and efficient accuracy. You do not want to burden the cognitive processor (if there is one) with low-level decisions about sensory events. So, do not confuse the solutions that seem to apply to the understanding of the speech waveform with solutions that are needed for the understanding of cognition in general. Yes, they are related. Yes, speech (and all perception) uses considerable amounts of general cognitive processing. But don't go overboard. Use Harpy as a lesson. Use the models proposed by Klatt and by Newell as possible prototypes of human computation for other purposes. But learn the lessons with some reason, with intelligence. Copy wisely.

REFERENCES

Klatt, D. H. Review of the ARPA speech understanding project. *Journal of the Acoustical Society of America*, 1977, *62*, 1345–1366.
Lowerre, B. T. *The HARPY Speech Recognition System*. Unpublished doctoral dissertation, Carnegie-Mellon University, 1976.
Wickelgren, W. A. Context-sensitive coding, associative memory, and serial order in (speech) behavior. *Psychological Review*, 1969, *76*, 1–15.

IV

PRODUCTION OF FLUENT SPEECH

13

Syntactic Coding of Fundamental Frequency in Speech Production

John M. Sorensen
Massachusetts Institute of Technology

William E. Cooper
Harvard University

The order in which conjoined words are arranged reveals much about their meaning (Cooper & Ross, 1975; Malkiel, 1959). In English, we tend to place first in a conjoined phrase a word which denotes salience (*figure and ground*, not **ground and figure*), temporal primacy (*stop and shop*, not **shop and stop*), and any of a number of other semantic properties. In the title of this book, we find the ordering *Perception and Production*, not *Production and Perception*. Does this choice reflect the salience of perception, aptly capturing the fact that perception is dealt with here more extensively than production?[1] If so, why does perception occupy the limelight, not only in this volume, but in psycholinguistics generally (see for example, Fodor, Bever, & Garrett, 1974; Clark & Clark, 1977)?

The answer seems to lie in the fact that speech perception has been more amenable to direct experimental attack than speech production. In perceptual research, the stimulus can be well defined acoustically, but the stimulus in speech production has remained elusive. Still, as we will endeavor to show in this chapter, a large portion of the speech production process can be studied experimentally. Moreover, we believe that, in terms of temporal primacy, research on production should be conducted prior to related work on the perception of fluent speech, since the latter is informative only insofar as it takes as its object of study the set of stimuli which are actually utterable by the speaker.

---

[1]Other factors may also play a role in the choice of the ordering *perception and production*. In particular, there is a strong tendency for words pertaining to input to precede words pertaining to output, as in *enter and exit, in and out*. This tendency is also exhibited in compound words, including *sensori-motor*.

We began a long-term study of speech production because we came to an impasse in studying perception. We wanted to know if listeners could use time and frequency information to recover and predict structural relations among the constituents of an utterance. Preliminary work showed that listeners could detect such information in the case of timing (Klatt & Cooper, 1975; Lehiste, 1973) and could, moreover, utilize time and frequency information in making post hoc decisions about syntactic structures (Lehiste, Olive, & Streeter, 1976). In trying to pursue this question in detail, however, we quickly found that too little was known about what the speaker produces to formulate proper questions for perceptual study. Accordingly, we decided to study speech production, not only to guide our research on the perception of speech, but also to investigate production as a complex system in its own right.

One of the main assumptions of our research is that a speaker formulates many aspects of the syntactic structure of an utterance before formulating its phonetic representation. This direction of information-flow, from syntactic to phonetic coding, means that information computed in a syntactic representation is available to influence subsequent stages of phonetic processing. If this assumption is correct, we may infer abstract properties of the speaker's syntactic code from concrete acoustical analyses of the speechwave. As we will see below, experiments on many different aspects of speech production provide strong support for the assumption of syntactic-to-phonetic coding.

Evidence for Syntactic Control of Speech Production

When we began our work on speech production, we decided to consider the speech attribute of duration, because it provided an opportunity to study syntactic influences by means of relatively simple acoustic analysis. Previous work indicated that syntactic structure influences both the durations of pauses (e.g., Goldman-Eisler, 1968; Grosjean & Deschamps, 1975) and the durations of words and syllables (e.g., Klatt, 1975; Lindblom & Rapp, 1973; Martin, 1970). Our studies have examined these syntactic effects on duration in more detail, in order to provide information about the abstract properties of the speaker's grammatical code.

Segmental Lengthening. One such study involved an analysis of segment and pause durations in a class of structurally ambiguous sentences (Cooper, Paccia, & Lapointe, 1978). An example of this type of sentence appears below, with its two distinct meanings indicated in parentheses:

a. My Uncle Abraham presented his talk naturally.
   (Of course Abraham presented his talk.)
b. My Uncle Abraham presented his talk naturally.
   (Abraham presented his talk in a natural manner.)

In this example, the ambiguity arises because the adverb *naturally* can modify either the entire sentence, as in the (a) reading, or merely the verb phrase, as in the (b) reading. For this sentence, measurements of duration were obtained for the key segment /taw/ of *talk* and for the following pause. A group of ten speakers who produced these sentences showed consistent lengthening in the (a) reading for both the word segment and pause. Similar results were obtained for five additional subtypes of structural ambiguity.

A unified structural representation of the various ambiguities revealed that the lengthening effects could be accounted for in terms of the number of constituents that contribute to phrase-final lengthening—lengthening of a syllable that occurs at the end of major phrases (e.g., Klatt, 1975; Sorensen, Cooper, & Paccia, 1978). In the example above, *talk* marks the end of two major phrases in the (a) reading but of only one phrase in the (b) reading; *talk* occurs at the end of the verb phrase and the direct object noun phrase in (a) but occurs only at the end of the direct object noun phrase in (b). Given a top-down processing model of speech production (Cooper, in press), lengthening is applied at the ends of a number of successively narrow domains of grammatical coding. In this view, *talk* is longer in (a) than (b) because phrase-final lengthening is applied at two separate stages of coding rather than one.

Further consideration of structural ambiguities and their effects on speech timing indicated that the hierarchical representation of phrase structure captured the results better than accounts based on simple linear coding. In effect, by analyzing structural ambiguities in terms of syntactic representations, we were able to make inferences about some of the major dominance relations among phrases that are included in the speaker's coding (for a more extensive discussion, see Cooper & Cooper, 1978).

Blocking. Another means of obtaining information about the speaker's domains of syntactic coding is to study how phonological rules may be blocked at syntactic boundaries. It is assumed that, at some processing level, phonological rules are applied over some specified syntactic domain, and that the phonetic information which lies outside of this domain cannot be considered when the rules are applied. Consider, for example, the phonological rule of alveolar flapping, which commonly operates in speech to flap an intervocalic alveolar stop preceded by [r] or

[n], when it occurs in a falling stress pattern. As the following examples indicate, this rule may apply both within and across word boundaries.

sanity   [sænɪti] → [sænɪɾi]

sort of   [sortʌv] → [sorɾʌv]

For present purposes, the important feature of this rule is that its application across word boundaries requires an interaction between the phonetic segments on both sides of the boundary. In order for the rule to operate, the phonetic information on both sides of the word boundary must be available to the speaker during the same domain of processing. If the speaker concludes a major domain in coding at the word boundary, the rule should be blocked from applying.

Blocking of phonological rules has been demonstrated for alveolar flapping (Egido & Cooper, 1978) and for other effects of phonological and phonetic conditioning (Cooper, Lapointe, & Paccia, 1977; Cooper, Egido, & Paccia, 1978). An example for alveolar flapping appears below, in which the key words are italicized for convenience.

    a. Steven said that *late applications* should be sent to the Dean's office.
    b. Even if they're *late applications* should be sent to the Dean's office.

A major clause boundary occurs in (b) but not in (a) after the word-final /t/ in "late," and experimental results show that speakers apply the rule of flapping to the /t/ in "late" much less frequently in (b) than in (a). In addition, this blocking effect occurs independently of any pausing which may accompany the word boundary in (b). Rather, the blocking effect seems to indicate that the speaker has concluded a domain of syntactic processing at the end of *late* in (b) and is thus unable to look ahead to consider the following phonetic segment, in order to determine whether or not flapping may be applied.

The work on speech timing and blocking of phonological rules has laid a foundation for the studies presented here on fundamental frequency (hereafter F_0). As we will discuss below, F_0 is a more complex acoustic phenomenon than duration, taking longer to analyze and to interpret. In the long run, however, F_0's complexity offers an advantage. It may provide much more information about the speaker's syntactic code than does duration. This possibility is the prime motivation for our study of F_0, and our results to date suggest that F_0 can indeed provide new information about syntactic processing.

The organization of the rest of this chapter is as follows: We will next introduce F_0 as an acoustic phenomenon and discuss methods of acoustical measurement. In the following three sections, we present new experimental studies and discuss their psychological implications. In the final section, we consider the relation of this work to research on speech perception, and outline the practical benefits of the study for communications engineering.

F_0 AND ITS MEASUREMENT

In speech production, F_0 is defined as the rate at which the vocal cords open and close during voiced portions of speech. This rate of opening and closing is expressed in hertz (Hz). An important distinction should be made at this point between F_0 and the perceptual correlate of F_0, known as "pitch." Unlike F_0, pitch depends not only on the rate of vocal cord vibration, but also on factors such as speech intensity. It is important to note the difference between F_0 and pitch because, to a large degree, the linguistic literature relevant to F_0 is usually concerned with a variable termed "intonation," defined as the variation of pitch in a sentence (for a review, see Crystal, 1969, Chap. 2). As Crystal points out, this literature is primarily devoted to such language variables as sentence mood (i.e., whether a sentence is interrogative, imperative, declarative), focus, semantic relations, and how these variables affect a listener's judgments of pitch patterns. Our work can be distinguished from most of these prior studies in that (1) only acoustically measured values of F_0 are used as data; and (2) our attention is typically focused on testing possible influences of F_0 that reflect the speaker's computation of syntactic structures.

The acoustic analysis and interpretation of F_0 is considerably more complex than that for segment duration. There are two major reasons why this is so. To begin with, data reduction is a necessity because the F_0 of a word is a contour, not a single datum, as shown in Fig. 13.1. There is far too much data to consider in the entire contour shape of a sentence or even of one word. However, measures of the highest and lowest F_0 values of a word often yield valuable information, and our work to date has focused on measuring such "peaks" and "valleys" of F_0 on specific words in sentences spoken by a number of different speakers. These measurements are then analyzed using statistical techniques to assess any significant trends. The test performed most often is a two-tailed t-test for matched pairs. This statistic computes the difference in a matched pair of data across a number of subjects. We can thus include both male and female speakers in our experiments, even though there is often a large difference between the ranges of their typical F_0 values.

The second obstacle in analyzing F_0 is the problem of obtaining reliable measurement. Since F_0 information exists in both frequency and time, an

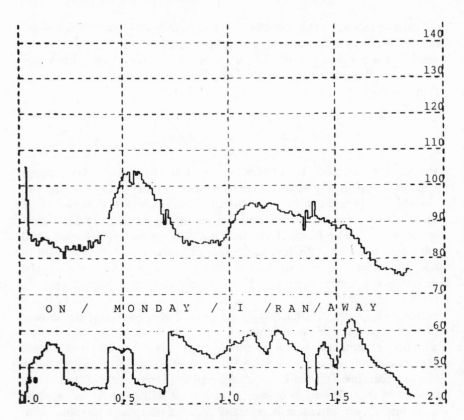

FIG. 13.1.   Sample F_0 plot obtained from the FPRD program for the sentence "On Monday I ran away," spoken by a male speaker of American English. The numbers alongside the right-most vertical line indicate frequency in Hz, and the numbers along the bottom horizontal line indicate time in seconds.

The upper contour represents the F_0 plot, and the lower contour indicates the amplitude of the corresponding glottal cycles. The amplitude contour aids in demarcating individual words from one another. In addition, the amplitude trace is useful in systematically ruling out spurious values of F_0, since spurious values of F_0 are typically associated with low values of amplitudes.

algorithm to recover F_0 from the speech signal can utilize time-domain and/or frequency-domain techniques of signal analysis. (For a review and comparison of several algorithms, see Rabiner, Cheng, Rosenberg, & McGonegal, 1976). Frequency-domain techniques, as well as certain time-domain techniques, provide an "estimate" of F_0 over a small portion, or "window," of the speech signal, typically 5–20 msec in duration. The output F_0 contour from such a program is a set of points, spaced 5–20 msec apart, with each point representing the estimated F_0 over that window. We have found such a time-domain program (Gold & Rabiner, 1969) adequate in a study of fall–rise patterns in F_0 (Cooper & Sorensen, 1977). However, we have since determined that a very different type of time-domain program provides an even better method of obtaining F_0 contours, for reasons discussed below.

Amplitude-versus-time plots of a speech wave reveal a certain "semiperiodic" nature in the voiced segments of the signal. The longest portion of the waveform that repeats itself corresponds to one opening and closing of the vocal cords, and is termed a "glottal cycle." Figure 13.2 shows a typical speech wave trace. If, in a series of glottal cycles, each cycle has a duration of exactly 8 msec, then F_0, the fundamental frequency of that portion of speech, is exactly 1/(8 msec) or 125 Hz. A straightforward method for calculating F_0 thus involves demarcating each consecutive glottal cycle, calculating its duration, and then inverting the duration, thereby obtaining a glottal-cycle-by-glottal-cycle computation of F_0. The difficulty lies in developing a computer algorithm that demarcates each glottal cycle. Fortunately, there is a feature associated with a glottal cycle that is stable enough to be detectable in nearly all speech samples. This feature is a correlate of the closure of the vocal cords, which produces a long, sharply sloping "stroke" in the speechwave (Henke, 1974). A "stroke" is defined as any portion of the speechwave between a local maximum and a local minimum. The slope of a stroke may be either positive or negative in polarity. Henke has developed a program known as FPRD (*Fundamental Period*), which searches for this stroke in speech samples which have been analog low-pass filtered at 900 Hz and digitized at 10 kHz. For reasons which do not concern us here, the strokes chosen by FPRD as the longest and steepest in each glottal cycle are called "Level-4" strokes.

Figure 13.3 shows an amended version of Fig. 13.2, where we have indicated which strokes were chosen by FPRD as the Level-4 strokes in this speech sample (FPRD's ability to indicate which strokes are chosen as the Level-4 strokes is very helpful, as we will see below.) FPRD then

FIG. 13.2. Sample amplitude versus time trace of a typical speechwave, showing the semiperiodic nature of a voiced vowel. The duration of each glottal cycle is denoted by "T," and can be estimated by measuring the distance between any two similar locations of adjacent cycles.

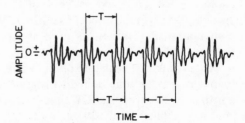

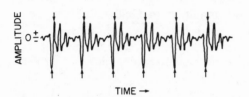

FIG. 13.3. Amended version of Fig. 13.2. The maximum and minimum of the "strongest" stroke in each glottal cycle are marked by small arrows. These strokes were identified as the Level-4 strokes by the FPRD program.

calculates, to the nearest microsecond, the duration between zero-crossings of adjacent Level-4 strokes. These glottal cycle durations are subsequently inverted and plotted on a graph of F_0 versus time. A small horizontal hash-mark represents the inverted duration of one glottal cycle, and these hash-marks are connected by straight vertical lines, forming the type of piece-wise continuous contour shown in Fig. 13.1. A measure of the relative energy associated with each glottal cycle is also plotted directly below each value of F_0.

The FPRD program has a number of attractive features. First, it allows us to obtain values of F_0 at specified locations in a word. This cannot be accomplished by the programs mentioned earlier which provide "estimates" of F_0 over a "window" of time, since it is usually not possible to tell precisely where in a word the estimate of F_0 was calculated. Second, since the program indicates which strokes were chosen as the Level-4 strokes, the experimenter can determine the cause of occasional spurious F_0 values. Such errors occur more often in regions of speech that have very low amplitude, or in regions of fast F_0 transition such as the onset of voicing after a stop consonant, so the experimenter first consults the amplitude contour found on the F_0-versus-time plot produced by FPRD. In our studies, we set an arbitrary criterion: To be considered as data, values of F_0 must have an associated amplitude whose magnitude is at least 50 percent of the peak amplitude of the nearest vowel. However, if the amplitude of a glottal cycle meets this criterion, and an F_0 value or values still appear to be unusual, then the experimenter can review the original speechwave to learn which strokes were (incorrectly) identified as Level-4 strokes, and determine (with the aid of computer-controlled cursors) what the proper value(s) of F_0 should be for that portion of the speech signal. Finally, because FPRD works in the time domain, it is computationally fast. In its current implementation on a now-obsolete ten-year-old PDP-9 computer, it requires only about eight times real time to process input speech and obtain an F_0 contour. This is as fast or faster than most other time-domain programs. Typical frequency-domain algorithms require at least 30 times longer than FPRD to produce an F_0 contour (Rabiner et al., 1976).

F_0 DECLINATION

The general direction of F_0 in a sentence is downward. This general fall has been termed "F_0 declination" by a number of researchers (Cohen & t'Hart, 1967; Maeda, 1976).
There are two closely linked issues surrounding F_0 declination:

1. Given the proper *domain* of application of F_0 declination, what is its *form*? (That is, does it exhibit some consistent shape on a graph of F_0 versus time?)
2. Given the proper *form* of declination, what are the syntactically defined (if any) *domains* of application?

We began our own studies by examining the form of declination, believing that we needed to know more about this issue before dealing with other attributes of the F_0 contour.

Declination Form

In this subsection, we present three studies aimed at providing a better description of the form of F_0 declination. Previous work by Maeda (1976) and by others cited therein modeled "intonation contours" by a number of characteristic F_0 movements, or "attributes," superimposed on a straight, falling "baseline." Any "baseline" model of declination is only useful insofar as, in combination with the other attributes, it predicts where actual values of F_0 lie. Unfortunately, neither Maeda, ourselves, nor anyone else has yet arrived at a description of a baseline with such strong predictive power.

Rather than try to formulate such a baseline, we have adopted a slightly different approach. Breckenridge and Liberman (1977) note that a line connecting the F_0 peaks in a sentence declines at a faster rate than a line connecting the F_0 valleys. We have thus attempted to describe a separate "topline" and "bottomline." Unlike the baseline concept which, with a set of attributes, should be able to predict the location of all F_0 values; the topline and bottomline only predict where the peaks and valleys of F_0 should occur. The topline and bottomline are weaker predictive models of F_0 declination, but at this stage in our knowledge they provide very useful information about the form of F_0 declination.

In order to study syntactic influences on F_0, it would be valuable to study a corpus of casual, spontaneous speech. However, such a corpus does not provide enough control of the speaking materials to render critical testing of hypotheses. Accordingly, an experimental procedure has been developed by Cooper (1976) to test influences of syntax on speaking variables in a tightly controlled setting. This procedure has yielded a considerable amount of information concerning syntactic control of timing in speech production, and it is now being used to study F_0. The procedure involves the construction of sentence materials matched for stress, phonetic environment, semantics, and other nonsyntactic influences. These sentence materials are usually constructed in pairs, and from two to four pairs of sentences are typically used to test a particular hypothesis.

Area undergraduate college students serve as paid volunteer subjects, and are tested individually in a sound-insulated room. The subjects are presented with approximately seven to ten sentence lists during an experimental session, which lasts no more than one hour. Each of the sentence lists represents a separate experiment and contains several camouflaged filler sentences, similar to the test sentences. Filler sentences always occur as the first and last sentences on a given list. Subjects are given frequent rest breaks and encouraged to take drinks of water at any time during the experiment.

The subjects are told to read each sentence silently until they understand it and then to read it once out loud for practice, without any contrastive or emphatic stress or intonation. The practice reading allows the experimenter to check for any unusual stress or intonation. The subjects then read each sentence twice for recording onto a Presto A908 tape recorder via an Altec 684A voice microphone. If the subject departs from his intended utterance in any way, he stops, says the word *repeat*, and utters the sentence token again. These sentences are analyzed for F_0 with the FPRD program already discussed.

As a prerequisite to interpreting the results, it is useful to compare the act of practiced reading, as in our experiments, with spontaneous speaking. First, the tendency of the F_0 contour to decline throughout declarative utterances—one of the major phenomena on which this study is based—typically accompanies spontaneous speech as well as practiced reading. Accordingly, it is reasonable to assume that the kinds of inferences drawn from experiments with read speech exhibiting this phenomenon would also apply to spontaneous speech. On the other hand, it seems that a chief difference between spontaneous speech and read speech involves the amount of preplanning on the part of the speaker. With practiced reading of the sort used here, our results may show a consistent trend toward greater preplanning than in most spontaneous speech. Our results may thus be more indicative of the preplanning *capabilities* of the speaker than of the preplanning that typically accompanies adult conversations. Nonetheless, the study of such capabilities should form a useful foundation for any theory that attempts to account for the characteristics of spontaneous speech.

Study 1

A first experiment was designed to test whether the topline and bottomline fall at different rates in controlled sentences, as suggested by Breckenridge and Liberman (1977). Sentences were constructed in which a single phrase (*Mr. and Mrs. Jacob E. Baxter*) was placed in a total of five different positions in strings containing the same number of syllables, as in the following examples:

a. *Mr. and Mrs. Jacob E. Baxter* wanted to move into the suburbs last summer.
b. We wanted to move to the suburbs last Spring with *Mr. and Mrs. Jacob E. Baxter.*

The five test sentences and two matched fillers were presented to ten subjects, using the experimental procedure outlined above. Values of F_0 were recorded at four locations in each sentence: The peak (highest) in F_0 of the first, stressed syllable in *Jacob*; the peak of the stressed syllable *E*; the peak of the stressed first syllable in *Baxter*; and the valley of the unstressed second syllable in *Baxter*. The results revealed a strong tendency for the difference between the average value of each peak and the value of the valley to decrease as the key phrase was located later in the sentence. If the topline and bottomline were parallel to one another, we would expect no such shrinkage between the values of the peaks and valley to occur. The existence of shrinkage indicates that a single baseline may not be adequate to capture the F_0 contour's declination and that separate descriptions of the topline and bottomline are required. For a number of reasons, including the fact that F_0 peaks are easier to measure and are perceptually more salient than F_0 valleys, we have focused our attention on the form of the F_0 topline.

Study 2

In the main experiment, designed to investigate the form of the topline function, four sentences were constructed with approximately the same syntactic structure and number of syllables. We intentionally included some variation in these parameters, to determine the degree to which a topline function is invariant. In addition, we used a number of different vowels in order to normalize effects of inherent differences in F_0 due to vowel type. All the vowels measured for F_0 were bounded on either side by stop consonants, fricatives, or nasal consonants, in order to simplify the task of segmenting them from the contour produced by the FPRD program. The test sentences, with the key words italicized are:

1. The *book* on the *table* was a *gift* from my *mother*.
2. The *man* in the *truck* sent *roses* to his *niece*.
3. The *students* on the *bus* threw *gum* at the *teacher*.
4. The *ducks* in the *park* will eat *popcorn* and *peanuts*.

These sentences were presented with three matched fillers to 10 subjects, using the experimental procedure outlined above. F_0 contours were obtained using FPRD of the first occurrence of each sentence spoken by each speaker. The peak in F_0 was obtained for each of the stressed vowels in the underlined key words. The first peak was labeled P_1, and so on through P_4. The location of the measured peak relative to the beginning of the signal buffer was also recorded in seconds. The time of occurrence of P_1 was labeled t_1, and so on.

The first step in data manipulation was to normalize the times of occurrence in each sentence by setting t_1 equal to zero seconds, and appropriately shifting t_2 through t_4. The mean values for P_1 through P_4 and t_1 through t_4 were then obtained for each sentence across all ten subjects. These data are given in Table 13.1 and shown graphically in Fig. 13.4. After a considerable study of the data, a surprisingly elegant rule emerged.

The Topline Rule

The rule predicts the F_0 values of P_2 and P_3 at given locations t_2 and t_3 based on the values of P_1, t_1, P_4 and t_4. We discovered this rule when we considered that point on the graph of F_0 versus time which occurs halfway between the first and last peaks on the frequency axis and one-fourth distance from the first peak to the last peak on the time axis. The line drawn through this "key point" and the point at t_4, P_4 constitutes an excellent model of speakers' F_0 topline.

The key point is conceptually useful because it indicates that half the fall between the first and last F_0 peak occurs during the first fourth of the sentence. However, we do not attach any special significance to the location of the key point in terms of the speaker's production of the sentence. In other words, although the rule can be described as the line connecting the key point and (t_4, P_4), it could be alternatively described, for example, as a line with a slope $2/3$ $[(P_4 - P_1)/(t_4 - t_1)]$, passing through the point (t_4, P_4). The points (t_1, P_1) and (t_4, P_4) are used to define this rule, rather than, say, the points (t_1, P_1) and (t_2, P_2), because the former pair of

TABLE 13.1
Pooled Data from Main Topline Experiment with Sentences 1–4

Sentence	Measure	P_1	P_2	P_3	P_4	t_1	t_2	t_3	t_4
1	$\bar{X}$	182	165	148	131	0	.44	1.01	1.59
	S_x	57	46	40	36	0	.05	.06	.14
	c.o.v.	.31	.28	.27	.27	—	—	—	—
2	$\bar{X}$	170	158	147	136	0	.37	.94	1.58
	S_x	55	42	37	36	0	.04	.11	.14
	c.o.v.	.32	.27	.25	.26	—	—	—	—
3	$\bar{X}$	188	150	145	141	0	.35	1.07	1.52
	S_x	65	41	39	37	0	.03	.09	.11
	c.o.v.	.35	.27	.27	.26	—	—	—	—
4	$\bar{X}$	180	152	150	147	0	.46	1.06	1.65
	S_x	60	42	39	40	0	.04	.11	.13
	c.o.v.	.33	.28	.26	.27	—	—	—	—

points represents the temporal endpoints over which the rule predicts the F_0 value at any intermediate point in time.

The function described by the above line has been named the Topline Rule (hereafter TR). Whatever the method of description of the rule, it appears to predict the value of an F_0 peak, given only its particular location in a sentence, and the location and F_0 of the first and final peaks. The TR is shown graphically in Fig. 13.5. The most stringent test of the TR's validity is determining how well it predicts the values of P_2 and P_3 in individual utterances. The calculation of the error between actual and predicted values of peak F_0 in an individual utterance goes as follows:

A. Compute the equation of the line with slope = $\frac{2}{3}$ $[(P_4 - P_1)/(t_4 - t_1)]$, passing through the point (t_4, P_4). Call the slope mTR and the intercept bTR.

B. The expected value of an F_0 peak (P_e) can be calculated from its obtained time of occurrence (tn); i.e.,

$$P_e = (mTR \times tn) + bTR$$

C. The percent of error is then defined as $(P_0 - P_e)/P_e$, where P_0 is the obtained value of the F_0 peak occurring at tn. A positive percent error indicates that the peak obtained is higher than the line given by the TR; a negative percent error, that the peak obtained is below the line.

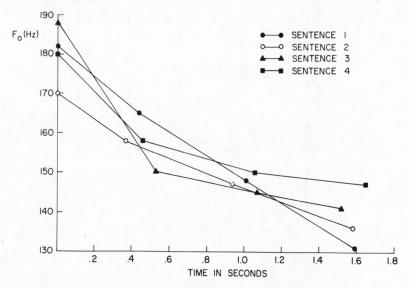

FIG. 13.4.   Graphical version of the pooled data presented in Table 13.1. Graphs such as this were useful in formulating the Topline Rule.

The percent error terms are presented for all utterances in Table 13.2. As outlined above, the TR was calculated for each utterance, values of t_2 and t_3 were used to generate the expected F_0 peak values, and these were compared with the obtained F_0 values of P_2 and P_3 to arrive at the final percent error terms.

A careful study of the data indicates that the TR is a better predictor of the F_0 topline than Table 13.2 might initially seem to indicate. An ideal sentence in this study would have the same vowel occurring in all four nouns measured for peak F_0, in order to control for differences in the inherent values of F_0 among vowels. However, sentences such as "the *man* in the *van* sent *pansies* to his *fans*" introduce an atypical "singsong" rhythm and have thus not been included in the experiments here.

One striking illustration of how inherent F_0 affects the TR and the error terms is found in sentence 3. The P_1 word, *students,* and the P_4 word, *teacher*, were measured for F_0 in the vowels /u/ and /i/, respectively. These vowels have a characteristically high F_0, as noted by Peterson and Barney (1952). If P_1 and P_4 are higher than average due to these vowels, then the line given by the TR will be shifted upwards. In such an instance, one would predict that the percent error terms would tend to be negative, since the values of P_{expected}, on the line given by the TR, would tend to be higher than the values of P_{obtained}. This is especially true in the case of sentence 3, since the vowels measured for P_2 and P_3 have low inherent

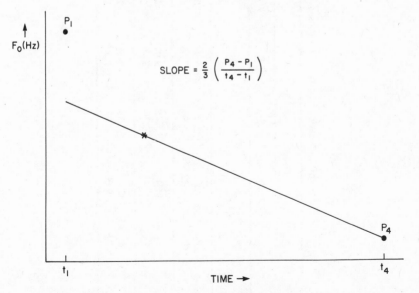

FIG. 13.5. Graphical representation of the Topline Rule: The "key point" is denoted by an asterisk.

TABLE 13.2

Percent Error Calculations between Predicted and Obtained Values of P_2 and P_3 in the Main Topline Experiment

Sentence		M.B.	M.S.	B.F.	P.D.	P.L.	J.H.	B.G.	J.M.	N.D.	M.D.
								Speaker			
1	P_2	2.16	11.4	2.80	4.81	−7.08	12.9	15.3	16.3	−3.12	4.85
	P_3	−3.35	1.02	3.65	2.48	1.18	3.30	14.3	4.39	4.77	1.78
2	P_2	−5.72	15.7	5.95	3.57	−8.73	10.3	6.91	7.36	−.468	2.12
	P_3	−4.22	5.94	7.88	3.10	−3.56	−1.53	6.84	4.92	−.703	−3.50
3	P_2	−11.4	−5.46	−9.01	−2.86	−10.6	−2.67	.690	−5.59	−6.57	−12.4
	P_3	−5.64	−3.39	−9.69	−4.14	−.012	−.640	−3.14	−2.45	3.07	−9.50
4	P_2	−12.8	7.33	−2.57	2.70	−9.61	4.56	−4.14	7.11	−8.98	.236
	P_3	−9.08	3.67	−15.2	−1.65	−2.03	6.65	.693	4.10	−5.80	−4.72

F_0. From Table 13.2, we see that, of the twenty error terms for P_2 and P_3 in sentence 3, 18 are indeed negative.

One way to lessen the effects of differences in inherent F_0 is to calculate, respecting the sign of the error terms, the mean percent error of P_2 and P_3 for each subject across all four sentences. These means are shown in Table 13.3. The largest magnitude percent error is -9.01%, for P_2 of subject P.L. Furthermore, the grand mean percent error across subjects is .383% for P_2 and $-.257\%$ for P_3. Over a medium-sized corpus of speech samples, normalizing for inherent F_0 differences among vowels and different speaker characteristics, the TR predicts the value of sentence-intermediate F_0 peaks with an accuracy of better than $\pm0.5\%$. The TR thus represents the topline in a manner that is more than adequate for the theoretical and practical considerations dealt with below.

Study 3

In this experiment we extended our study of the Topline Rule to include sentences which differ from those of Study 2 in their structure, length, and number of F_0 peaks to be measured. Ten speakers who did not participate in Study 2 read the list of experimental sentences presented below, following the procedure outlined earlier. The test sentences consisted of four matched pairs, with each pair containing the same three key words but differing in length:

5a. The *deer* could be *seen* from the *car*.
5b. The *deer* by the canyon could be *seen* from the window of the *car*.
6a. The *cat* was *asleep* in the *tree*.
6b. The *cat* that Sally owned was *asleep* on the large branch in the *tree*.
7a. The *host* could have *packed* all the *plates*.
7b. The *host* at the party could have *packed* all the glasses with the *plates*.
8a. The *fox* has *escaped* from his *cage*.
8b. The *fox* that Sidney caught has *escaped* sometime last night from his *cage*.

The three italicized key words in each sentence were measured for peak F_0 (P_1, P_2, P_3) and time of occurence of the peak (t_1, t_2, t_3) in all eight sentences. The Topline Rule was again used to predict the F_0 value of the sentence intermediate peak. In this case, the points (t_1, P_1) and (t_3, P_3) generated the topline function based on the TR. Then, given the obtained time of occurence (t_2) for P_2, a predicted value of P_2 was calculated, and then compared with the obtained value for P_2. This procedure is identical

TABLE 13.3
Pooled Data for Percents of Error between Predicted and Obtained Values of P_2 and P_3 in the Main Topline Experiment

		M.B.	M.S.	B.F.	P.D.	P.L.	J.H.	B.G.	J.M.	N.B.	M.D.	Grand
						Speaker						
P_2	$\bar{X}$	-6.94	7.24	-.708	2.06	-9.01	6.27	4.69	6.30	-4.78	-1.30	.383
	S_x	6.80	9.13	6.56	3.39	1.49	6.91	8.40	9.00	3.75	7.64	8.19
P_3	$\bar{X}$	-5.57	1.81	-3.34	-.053	-1.11	1.95	4.67	2.74	.334	-3.99	-.257
	S_x	2.52	4.01	10.9	3.45	2.11	3.77	7.62	3.48	4.69	4.63	5.63

to that of Study 2, except that only one peak value is predicted by the Rule and subsequently compared with the obtained value. The mean percent of error across short sentences (the (a) versions) and long sentences (the (b) versions) are presented for all ten subjects in Table 13.4. The grand mean percent error is well below 1% for both the short and long sentence versions.

Finally, we should mention that the formulation of the Topline Rule presented above was not our first version of the Rule. We had previously attempted to derive a Topline Rule which was drawn through the point (t_1, P_1). This necessitated the TR to be described as two line segments, rather than a single line segment. One of these two earlier versions consisted of the line segment connecting (t_1, P_1) to the "key point", and a second segment connecting the key point and (t_4, P_4). The other version included the segment connecting (t_1, P_1) and $(t_1 + \frac{1}{2}(t_4 - t_1), P_4 + \frac{1}{3}(P_1 - P_4))$, and the segment connecting this latter point with (t_4, P_4). In both versions, while it is true that the *second* line segments are colinear with the single line version of the TR, the first line segments are not. However, the differences among the predictions of the two-line vs. single-line models are minimal, and we have opted for the single-line version because of its greater simplicity (for further discussion, see Cooper and Sorensen, 1979).

Invariance of the Topline Rule

In summary, the data from these studies indicate that, in several types of declarative sentences, the Topline Rule predicts the value of an F_0 peak from values of the first and last F_0 peak and the distance in time between them. The TR shows some evidence of being invariant across the following language variables:

1. *Sentence length.* The sentence length $(t_3 - t_1)$ in sentences 5–8 varied by a factor of three or more between the short and long sentence versions. The sentence length of sentences 1–4 was intermediate to that of the short and long versions of sentences 5–8.

2. *Number of F_0 peaks predicted.* Sentences 1–4 contained two sentence-intermediate peaks, while sentences 5–8 contained one.

3. *Grammatical category of the word predicted.* Given that the first and last F_0 peaks occur on Nouns, and that they occur as the second and last words in the sentence, the TR accurately predicted the F_0 peaks in Nouns (sentences 1–4), Verbs (sentences 5, 7, 8), and Adjectives (sentence 6).

4. *Structural differences.* Sentence 4 contained only one prepositional phrase. Sentences 6 and 8 contained relative clauses, and there

TABLE 13.4

Pooled Data for Percent of Error Values between Predicted and Obtained Values of P_2 in Topline Experiment with Sentences 5-8

Sentences		C.A.	M.B.	W.L.	F.H.	B.S.	C.K.	J.S.	D.S.	C.P.	C.M.	Grand
							Speaker					
(A) versions	$\bar{X}$	2.45	1.50	-3.90	-1.38	4.58	.063	-2.98	1.11	3.49	.533	.547
	S_x	6.16	6.43	1.77	7.38	6.19	7.86	9.71	6.93	3.04	8.68	6.52
(B) versions	$\bar{X}$	5.31	-.387	-1.61	6.86	2.29	-3.30	-1.39	-3.74	1.10	-.698	.484
	S_x	3.77	7.12	3.13	14.1	5.31	4.29	9.07	7.63	5.00	7.37	7.26

was considerable variation in the verbs of sentences 5–8. Sentences 5 and 7 contained two auxiliaries, sentence 8 contained one, and sentence 6 none.

5. *Sex of speakers.* Of the total of 20 speakers participating in the two studies, six were female and 14 were male. No consistent variation in the error terms as a function of sex of the speaker was noted.

Psychological Implications

How does the speaker program an F_0 declination in fluent speech? One possible model of this process based on these studies is as follows: At the beginning of an utterance, the speaker's look-ahead mechanism informs him of approximate sentence length, which is somehow used to generate the approximate F_0 value of the first peak. The approximate value for the last peak is also known to the speaker, as evidenced by its constancy across sentences of different length (see below). Once the speaker begins talking, feedback (auditory or otherwise) informs him of the value of the first peak, which together with the value of the last peak and approximate estimated sentence duration can be used to generate the Topline Rule. The speaker then endeavors to produce those peak values of F_0 based on the rule.

Examination of peak F_0 values provides evidence that a look-ahead mechanism is at work in the speakers' processing. Table 13.5 gives the mean values for P_1 and P_3 across the long and short versions of sentences 5–8. The average difference in P_1 in long versus short sentences was 13.5 Hz, while for P_3 the average difference was −2.1 Hz (i.e., P_1 was higher and P_3 slightly lower in the long sentences). Other researchers (McAllister, 1971; O'Shaughnessy, 1976) have also noted the tendency for F_0 to start higher at the beginning of a longer constituent. The results of two-tailed t-tests showed significantly higher values of P_1 in long sentences of sentence pairs 5, 7, and 8: pair 5, $t = 2.67$, $p < .05$; pair 7, $t = 3.78$, $p < .005$; pair 8, $t = 2.94$, $p < .02$; df = 9 in all tests. A nonsignificant trend in the same direction was observed in pair 6: $t = 2.07$, $.07 > p > .05$, df = 9. It appears that the speaker plans the general shape of the F_0 declination to the extent that, when given a long sentence, he begins speaking with a higher F_0 than he would have if he was about to produce a short sentence. The speaker is fully aware of his upcoming utterance in this task, and though this is not always the case in spontaneous speech, the result indicates that the speaker's preplanning, when it occurs, exerts a systematic influence on the first F_0 peak in an utterance.

In contrast, none of the four sentence pairs showed a significant difference in the values of P_3. This near constancy of P_3 may also be due in part to the speakers' planning and look-ahead mechanisms. Maeda (1976)

TABLE 13.5
Pooled Data for P_1 and P_3 in Topline Experiment with Sentences 5-8

	Speaker									
	C.A.		M.B.		W.L.		F.H.		B.S.	
	Long	Short	Long	Short	Long	Short	Long	Short	Long	Short
$\bar{P}_1$	184	171	255	253	294	279	154	144	112	111
$\bar{P}_3$	140	144	164	175	237	239	109	110	77	81

	C.K.		J.S.		D.S.		C.P.		C.M.	
	Long	Short	Long	Short	Long	Short	Long	Short	Long	Short
$\bar{P}_1$	267	240	189	176	193	172	133	134	353	319
$\bar{P}_3$	229	227	117	124	137	128	115	117	250	251

has obtained data which indicate a high degree of consistency both in the final F_0 value in a sentence (the final F_0 valley) and in the amount of F_0 fall on the final stressed word. While the constant final valley may be caused by some physiological floor effect, the amount of final fall typically produced by the speaker may be necessary in order to signal a domain boundary. Therefore, knowing the approximate low F_0 values he commonly produces, the speaker could plan the proper F_0 peak value in order to produce an appropriate amount of F_0 fall.

Declination Resetting: The Domain of the Topline Rule

Over what domain does a speaker apply F_0 declination? We will make no attempt here to answer this question experimentally. However, based on the studies of declination form, we are able to spell out several of the major theoretical issues concerning the domain of the speaker's F_0 declination. In the studies concerned with the form of declination, the test sentences were designed with coinciding main clause boundaries and utterance boundaries. To approach the issue of whether the domain of F_0 declination is syntactically defined, we must now consider utterances containing more than a single main clause, such as:

9. *Dick* will *take* the *jeep* and *Clark* will *drive* the *truck.*

Assume for a moment that the TR formulated in the previous section generalizes to a sentence such as (9) and that the domain of declination is the entire utterance. Figure 13.6a shows schematically an idealized series of peak F_0 values and the resulting F_0 topline based on these assumptions (cf. Fig. 13.5). Figure 13.6b shows a second series of F_0 values, assuming that the domain of declination is the main cause. Note that there is a "resetting" of the speaker's F_0 declination at the boundary between the two main clauses. Figure 13.6b illustrates the strongest version of the resetting hypothesis—namely, that each clause has an identical declination, indicated by the identical slopes and starting values of the toplines. This can be termed "complete" resetting. Resetting of this type would be most evident in a comparison of values of the peak in F_0 (P_1) of the word prior to the boundary (in this case, *jeep*), with the peak in F_0 (P_2) of the word following the boundary (in this case, *Clark*).

Experiments have been conducted with sentences such as (9), and P_2 was found to be significantly higher than P_1. However, declination resetting is only one possible explanation of this result. Figure 13.7a shows an amended version of Fig. 13.6a. Although the entire sentence here contains only one F_0 declination, P_2 (F_0 peak on *Clark*) is higher than P_1 (F_0 peak on *jeep*). P_2 in this figure represents a "local" peak above the topline. A

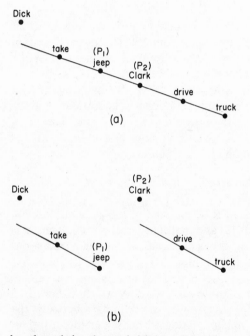

(a)

(b)

FIG. 13.6. Two possible representations of the F_0 topline in a sentence containing two main clauses, "*Dick* will *take* the *jeep* and *Clark* will *drive* the *truck*." The (a) version depicts the topline, assuming that the domain of application of F_0 declination includes the entire utterance. In the (b) version, two toplines are shown, reflecting the alternative assumption that F_0 declination is programmed over the domain of a single main clause. The resetting of the declination between the two clauses is represented here as "complete resetting," in which the two toplines have equal slope and starting value.

An important, testable consequence of the declination resetting in the (b) version specifies that the value of peak F_0 in *Clark* (P_2) is higher than the value of peak F_0 in *jeep* (P_1), whereas the reverse relationship holds between P_1 and P_2 in the (a) version. The relationship between P_2 and P_1 in the (b) version would still be apparent if the peak F_0 on *Clark* (P_2) lies on the topline rather than above the topline. As noted previously, our data suggest that the F_0 peak on the first stressed syllable of a main clause lies above the topline.

local peak in clause-initial position is a typical feature in F_0 contours (we have already seen this in the last experiment in which the first peak in the clause occurred above the line predicted by the TR). In Fig. 13.7a, this local F_0 peak may be a correlate of extra stress placed on the word (Fry, 1955) due to its status as a proper noun and as the subject of the clause. In addition, Fig. 13.7b indicates one of the many degrees of "partial" resetting, where a new declination begins in the second clause, but with a decreased slope and/or decreased starting value. Such "partial" resetting can also manifest itself in higher values of P_2 and P_1.

In view of these many alternatives, we have designed a better test of resetting, involving sentences such as:

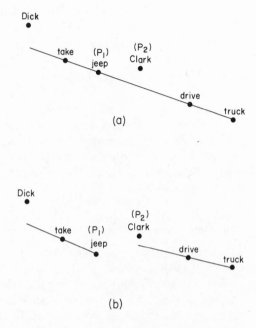

FIG. 13.7. Two additional representations of the F_0 topline of the same sentence considered in Fig. 13.6. The (a) version in this figure differs from that of Fig. 13.6a in that the peak F_0 of *Clark* (P_2) lies above the topline, as would be the case if this word receives special stress either because it serves as the subject of the second main clause or because of its status as a *proper* noun. The (b) version in this figure differs from the corresponding (b) version in Fig. 13.6 in that this version depicts partial, rather than complete resetting.

10. Jim and his friend *Ted saw Sue* and *John saw Bill* and his friend Tina.

In (10), peak F_0 can be measured in each of the six italicized words. The three words before the main clause boundary are matched with three words after the boundary for grammatical status as proper noun subject, verb, and proper noun object, respectively. If the matched words after the boundary show higher F_0 than those before the boundary, strong evidence would be obtained for the presence of declination resetting at main clause boundaries.

Intuitively, this outcome seems likely, but the case favoring a *syntactically* defined domain of declination would still not be complete. Perhaps resetting is triggered by the presence of a breathing pause which also accompanies the syntactic boundary. In work with speech timing, we have shown that a number of effects located at syntactic boundaries are attributable to syntactic coding and not to pausing (for a review, see Cooper, in press; also Egido & Cooper, 1978). However, it is at least conceivable that pausing is a relevant variable in the case of F_0 resetting. The acoustical analysis of F_0 and pause durations in sentences like (10) has not yet been carried out, so we cannot answer this question at present. Whatever the outcome, this study will allow us to make inferences about the nature of the speakers' domain for processing F_0 declination.

FALL-RISE PATTERNS

Across word boundaries, the F_0 contour may follow one of a number of patterns, such as fall–rise, flat–rise, etc. Previous acoustical analyses of F_0 have demonstrated the presence of the fall–rise pattern at major syntactic boundaries (e.g., Lea, 1973), yet the sentence materials were not sufficiently well matched to permit the testing of specific hypotheses. In this section, we present experiments on fall–rise patterns which help characterize the types of syntactic boundaries that produce such patterns. In particular, we show that this pattern is especially manifest at word boundaries that coincide with major syntactic boundaries and with sites of certain transformations.

Fall-Rise Patterns at Major Syntactic Boundaries

In a series of experiments reported in detail elsewhere (Cooper & Sorensen, 1977), we examined the presence of fall–rise patterns at major syntactic boundaries, including the boundaries between two main conjoined clauses, a main clause and an embedded clause, and between a preposed phrase and the rest of its clause. In order to study fall–rise patterns, we obtained three measurements of F_0 near the site of the syntactic boundary: the peak (P_1) and valley (V) in F_0 of the last stressed syllable prior to the boundary, and the peak (P_2) in F_0 of the first stressed syllable following the boundary. Within a single sentence, a fall–rise pattern was examined by performing significance tests on values of P_1 versus V and P_2 versus V. Across matched sentence pairs, tests were performed comparing the amount of fall and rise $(P_1 - V$ and $P_2 - V$ respectively). Sample sentences from Cooper and Sorensen (1977) appear here:

11. Anthony was sur*prised* and *Ray*mond became upset.
    [Main clause–Main clause]
12. Anthony was sur*prised* An*drea* became upset.
    [Main clause–Embedded clause]
13. At Brockton's city *park Cher* scolded the children.
    [Preposed phrase–Main clause]

In all cases, significant within-sentence fall–rise patterns were obtained. In matched comparisons between main–main and main–embedded boundaries, we found that fall–rise patterns were most pronounced at the boundaries between two main clauses. These boundaries also show the largest magnitude of pausing, segmental lengthening, and blocking of cross-word phonetic rules (Cooper & Cooper, 1978). Moreover, the fall–rise patterns observed at boundaries between two main clauses were local, in that they did not represent the speaker's resetting of the entire declination function. Comparisons of P_1 and P_2 within sentences revealed consistently higher values for P_1, as predicted by the hypothesis that the patterns were local, and not a reflection of declination resetting. Although it is reasonable to expect higher P_2 values on the basis of stress (since P_2 words were proper nouns, whereas P_1 words were common nouns), P_1 values were higher than P_2 values, which clearly indicates that the fall–rise patterns were local in character.

The study of fall–rise patterns at major boundaries can provide a basis for more elaborate experimentation, in which these patterns are examined in terms of graded variations in syntactic boundary strength (Cooper & Cooper, 1978). The magnitude of such fall–rise patterns should provide a good measure of boundary strength, especially when used in conjunction with the magnitude of other phenomena influenced by syntax, including segmental lengthening, pausing, and the occurrence of blocking.

Fall–Rise Patterns at Deletion Sites

In a transformational grammar, underlying and surface levels of structure are mediated by transformational rules which may operate to add, move, or delete elements (Chomsky, 1965). If we are able to confirm that F_0 patterns of a specialized sort (e.g., fall–rise patterns) are produced at deletion sites per se, we provide evidence that the speaker must have computed some underlying structure in order to derive the notion "deletion" from that structure.

Our experiments on F_0 patterns in deletion contexts have been restricted to contexts produced by transformational rules of gapping, rules which can delete material from within a phrase (Jackendoff, 1971; Ross, 1970). Gapping rules were chosen for study because, unlike many other putative deletions, they have strong support in the linguistic literature as bona fide deletions (Sag, 1976). Moreover, intuition suggested that deletion sites produced by gapping are accompanied by significant fall–rise patterns in F_0.

Verb Gapping. Verb gapping operates to delete an occurrence of a verb under identity with a prior occurrence of the same verb (Ross, 1970). In the present experiment, matched sentence pairs were constructed to provide a direct comparison between F_0 patterns in deletion versus non-deletion contexts.

Eight subjects participated in this experiment. Eight test sentence-pairs and six fillers were used in the experiment. The test sentences appear below. In each case, the key words to be measured for F_0 are italicized. The (a) sentence versions contain no deletion, while in each (b) version, there has been a deletion of the verb in the second clause. For example, if the deleted verb in sentence 14b were reinserted, the sentence would read as follows:

The seamstress wove your hat and the maid *wove* your scarf.

A similar analysis applies to each of the (b) sentence versions in sentences 15b through 22b. The test sentences were identical to those used by Cooper et al. (1978) in an experiment on blocking of palatalization. However, the Cooper et al. study involved eight different subjects.

14a. The seamstress wove your hat and then *made* your scarf.

b. The seamstress wove your hat and the *maid* your scarf.

15a. The porter took your bags and *weighed your* luggage.

b. The porter took your bags and *Wade your* luggage.

16a. The chef fixed the soup and then *made your* sandwich.

b. The chef fixed the soup and the *maid your* sandwich.

17a. The head teacher will help your daughter and then *aid your* son.

b. The head teacher will help your daughter and the *aide your* son.

18a. The bus driver will take your brother and then *guide your* sister.

b. The bus driver will take your brother and the *guide your* sister.

19a. The hostess will show your aunt and then Tom will *guide your* uncle.

b. The hostess will show your aunt and the touring *guide your* uncle.

20a. Aunt Bessie took your fruit and my uncle *weighed your* vegetables.

b. Aunt Bessie took your fruit and my uncle *Wade your* vegetables.

21a. The intern will help your father and the nurse will *aid your* mother.

b. The intern will help your father and the nurse's *aide your* mother.

Acoustical analysis of P_1, V, and P_2 was conducted as in previous experiments. The results show fall–rise patterns in both deletion and nondeletion contexts, with the fall–rise pattern being more pronounced at the deletion sites. Furthermore, the comparison of P_1 and P_2 values indicated that the fall–rise patterns were local, rather than a reflection of declination resetting. In particular, the average values of P_2 were lower than those of P_1 in 15 of the 16 test sentences, and the overall value of P_2 was 3.9% lower than that of P_1.

Comparisons of the deletion and nondeletion contexts showed that the average fall from P_1 to V was almost twice as great in the deletion contexts, averaging 8.1% for the deletion sentences, versus 4.5% for the nondeletion sentences. The average rise from V to P_2 was also consistently greater in the deletion contexts.

Considering each point individually, comparisons showed that the values for P_1 were approximately equal for deletion and nondeletion contexts, whereas the values for V and P_2 were consistently lower for the deletions. This pattern of results can be summarized by the schematic diagram in Fig. 13.8. Because the values of P_1 were approximately equal in deletion and nondeletion contexts, the greater F_0 fall in deletion contexts is not attributable to a general stress heightening. In conclusion, the results of this experiment provide initial evidence for the notion that fall–rise patterns are more pronounced at deletion sites. However, other data on deletions must be considered before we can verify the claim that it is the deletion per se which is responsible for the fall–rise in F_0, since the sentences produced by verb gapping also differ from nondeletion sentences in their surface structures. In particular, sentences with verb gapping exhibit a surface noun-phrase–noun-phrase sequence, whereas nondeletion sentences exhibit a verb–noun phrase sequence. Accordingly, we extended our study to another type of gapping in which this surface sequence was not present.

Noun Gapping. In order to determine whether the fall–rise patterns obtained for verb gapping generalize to other types of deletion, we designed an experiment to examine fall–rise patterns at sites of noun gapping, another form of gapping which can delete a noun under identity with a prior occurrence of the same noun (Jackendoff, 1971). The following sentences were read by eight subjects, none of whom served in the verb gapping test. The two sentence pairs included deletion and nondeletion contexts. In the (b) versions of each test sentence pair here, the noun *juice* is deleted under identity with its occurrence in the first clause.

22a. Janet had prune juice today before lunch and I had *grape juice* last week.
   b. Janet had prune juice today before lunch and I had *grape just* last week.
23a. Janet made prune juice the day before yesterday and *grape juice* last week.
   b. Janet made prune juice the day before yesterday and *grape just* last week.

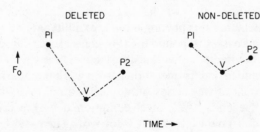

FIG. 13.8. Schematic representations of the fall–rise patterns obtained in the experiment on verb gapping.

The results showed significant fall–rise patterns only for the gapped contexts of the (b) versions. In addition, a comparison of P_1 and P_2 revealed that the fall–rise patterns for the gapped contexts were local effects and not due to declination resetting. The fall in F_0 from P_1 to V in the gapped sentences averaged 18%, compared to only 1.3% in the non-gapped sentences. As in the case of verb gapping, the values of V were consistently lower in the gapped sentences. Values for P_1 were somewhat higher in (22a) than in (22b), but values of P_1 in pair 23 were nearly equal. Values for P_2 were nonsignificantly higher in both gapped sentences.

In conclusion, the results of the experiments on gapping with both nouns and verbs indicate that these deletion sites are accompanied by significant fall–rise patterns in F_0. It is at least conceivable that the patterns are attributable to a degree of awkwardness inevitably accompanying these locations. While we cannot rule out this possibility entirely, one piece of evidence against it involves the fact that the values of P_1 were approximately equal for the deletion and nondeletion contexts in both experiments. Since the fall–rise patterns are more pronounced in deletion contexts for both noun and verb gapping, we suspect that those patterns reflect the speakers' programming of deletion sites per se, implying that the speaker's syntactic representation includes both underlying and surface levels of coding.

BLOCKING OF CROSS-WORD F_0 EFFECTS

In addition to the presence of declination resetting and fall–rise patterns, the influence of the speaker's syntactic code on F_0 may be exhibited by the blocking of F_0 effects which normally occur across word boundaries. In previous work, it has been shown that durational effects and phonological rules may be blocked across word boundaries when such boundaries coincide with a major syntactic break (Cooper, Lapointe, & Paccia, 1977; Egido & Cooper, 1978). It appears that the blocking phenomenon provides a tool for probing the speaker's domains of syntactic processing, and we have already been able to make some new inferences about these domains from studies such as those cited.

Recently, we have extended the work on blocking to determine whether this phenomenon is exhibited for F_0 effects that normally operate across word boundaries. In general, very little is known about cross-word F_0 effects, so we began by considering a well known within-word effect and tested its operation across word boundaries. The effect chosen for the bulk of this series of studies is a fall in F_0 during the first 50 or so milliseconds of a vowel conditioned by the presence of a prior voiceless consonant (e.g., /k/). Prior work (Lea, 1973; Stevens, Henke, & Sorensen, unpublished data) has shown this effect within words, and we conducted a pilot study to determine whether it operates across word boundaries, as when /k/ is word-final and the vowel is at the beginning of the next word. The results indicated the presence of a cross-word effect. After /k/, the F_0 for the word-initial vowel showed a falling contour during the first 50 msec. With this information, we were now ready to construct experiments to test whether the cross-word effect could be blocked at major syntactic boundaries.

Experiment 1. In the first experiment, we constructed four pairs of sentences whose members contained a word boundary between a word ending in /k/ and a following word beginning in a vowel. The members of each pair differed according to whether the critical word boundary coincided with a major clause boundary or with a minor boundary between an adjective and head noun of a noun phrase. Previous work with other cross-word effects had shown that this structural contrast between major and minor syntactic boundaries was sufficient to reveal a blocking effect (Cooper, Egido, & Paccia, 1978; Egido and Cooper, 1978).

The test sentences appear below with the key words italicized. In each pair, the (a) sentence contains the major syntactic break at the key word boundary.

24a. Unless they're *black earrings* won't look good with Jan's outfit. [S–S]
 b. I said that *black earrings* would look good with Jan's outfit. [Adj.–N]
25a. Because they're *sick eagles* will be removed from the aviary. [S–S]
 b. On Tuesday *sick eagles* will be removed from the aviary. [Adj.–N]
26a. Although I usually don't like my cereal *thick oatmeal* with brown sugar is good. [S–S] [I usually don't like my cereal to be thick]
 b. Although I usually don't care for cereal *thick oatmeal* with brown sugar is good. [Adj.–N] [I like oatmeal]
27a. Unless they're *black otters* are easy prey to sea lions. [S–S]
 b. In Russia *black otters* are easy prey to sea lions. [Adj.–N]

Ten speakers read these test sentences from a list interspersed with filler sentences. Acoustical measurements of F_0 were obtained at four successive locations: (1) the offset of voicing preceding the word-final /k/; (2) the onset of voicing for the word-initial vowel; (3) 50 msec after the onset of voicing for this vowel; and (4) 100 msec after the onset of voicing for this vowel.

The results for the ten speakers are summarized in Fig. 13.9. The (b) sentences exhibited a falling F_0 contour during the first 100 msec of the word-initial vowel, indicating the presence of a cross-word phonetic effect as in the pilot study. The (a) sentences, however, exhibited a sharply rising F_0 during the first 50 msec of the vowel. This sharp rise appears to reflect some type of start-up effect in F_0 at the beginning of a new clause. Since this effect is quite large, there is no way to tell whether the cross-word F_0 effect from the word-final /k/ has been blocked or not in the (a) sentences.

Experiment 2. Accordingly, we designed a second experiment in which further gradations of syntactic boundary strength were included, in the hope that a stronger phrase boundary would reveal an effect of blocking without producing a confounding start-up effect of F_0 rise. The four test sentences shown below were spoken by the same ten speakers as in the previous experiment. The (a)–(d) sentences range from strong to weak syntactic boundaries.

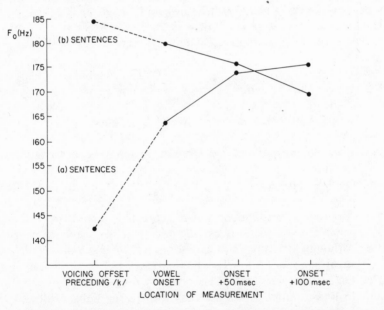

FIG. 13.9. Graphs of pooled data for the (a) and (b) versions of sentences 24–27. Solid lines connect the average F_0 values measured at the three locations beginning with the vowel onset. Dotted lines connect the average F_0 values measured at the voicing offset preceding /k/, with the values measured at the vowel onset. Dotted lines were used here to indicate a discontinuation of voicing between these two locations. The temporal intervals between points connected by solid lines are drawn to scale, whereas the intervals between points connected by dotted lines are not.

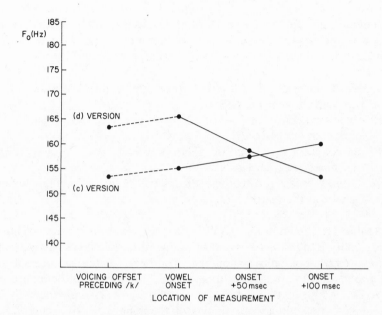

FIG. 13.10.   Graphs of pooled data for the (c) and (d) version of sentence 28.

28a. Unless you're coming *back Allen* will park in Terry's driveway. [S–S]

 b. I told the man in *back Allen's* new car was in the driveway. [NP–rel]

 c. Diane will try to *back Allen's* new car into the driveway. [V–NP]

 d. I told Diane the *back alley* was made into a driveway. [adj.–N]

Acoustical measurements were obtained for the same four locations as before. As in the previous experiment, a significant start-up F_0 rise during the vowel's first 50 msec was obtained for both the (a) and (b) sentences. For the verb–noun phrase boundary in (c), however, the F_0 was virtually flat for the vowel, as expected if blocking occurred in the absence of any other F_0 effects.

In contrast, the (d) version with the minor adjective–noun boundary exhibited the falling F_0 contour indicative of an F_0 conditioning effect caused by word-final /k/. The difference between the (c) and (d) sentences, shown graphically in Fig. 13.10, suggested that the F_0 effect is indeed blocked at major syntactic boundaries. However, we shall see momentarily that this is not the only possible interpretation.

Experiment 3. A third experiment was conducted to focus on the difference between the adjective–noun and verb–noun phrase boundaries.

Ten new speakers uttered two pairs of sentences in which a key word boundary coincided with the contrast between the minor adjective–noun boundary (b) and the more major verb–noun phrase boundary (a).

29a. We found out that Joey will *make eggs* and hot muffins for his brother's lunch. [V–NP]
  b. We found out that Joey used *fake eggs* and live rabbits in the magic show. [Adj.–N]
30a. Janice discovered that the Baxters will *make ice* in their freezer for ninety people. [V–NP]
  b. Janice discovered that the Bruins use *fake ice* for their hockey games in the Garden. [Adj.–N]

The results are shown in Fig. 13.11. As in the previous experiment, the F_0 contour during the first 100 msec of the word-initial vowel was virtually flat for the verb–noun phrase boundaries of the (a) sentences, whereas the F_0 contour showed a falling pattern for the adjective–noun boundaries in (b). Again, it appears that the F_0 contour of the vowel is influenced by the presence of a preceding word–final /k/ in the minor adjective–noun boundary, but is not influenced by the presence of this same segment in the major verb–noun-phrase boundary.

It is tempting to conclude that the flat F_0 contour for the verb–noun phrase boundary represents the blocking of the /k/ conditioning effect. However, it is also possible that the differences between the minor and more major boundaries can be attributed to differences in inherent stress. With an adjective–noun sequence, speakers typically produce a rising F_0 on the adjective and a falling F_0 on the noun (e.g., Maeda, 1976; O'Shaughnessy, 1976). Thus, it is not clear on the basis of these data alone that the /k/ actually exerts a cross-word effect in the adjective–noun case. Since the boundary between a verb and noun phrase is typically flat in F_0, it is difficult to ascertain whether the difference obtained in this experiment should be attributed to blocking or to inherent differences in F_0 as a function of phrase structure.

Experiment 4. To select between these alternatives, we conducted a fourth experiment in which a converse F_0 conditioning effect of the voiced stop consonant /g/ was examined. Previous work indicated that, in within-word contexts, /g/ produces an F_0 rise during the following vowel; whereas as we have seen, /k/ produces an F_0 fall on the following vowel (Lea, 1973). We reasoned as follows: If the results for Adjective–Noun boundaries in previous experiments were due to inherent stress rather than to a /k/ conditioning effect, then the falling F_0 pattern should also be observed with word-final /g/, whereas the F_0 should rise at the beginning

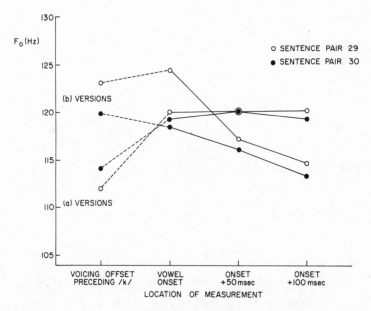

FIG. 13.11. Graphs of pooled data for the (a) and (b) versions of sentences 29 and 30. The only difference in format between this figure and Figs. 13.9 and 13.10 involves the range of F_0 values plotted along the ordinate.

of the vowel following /g/ if a cross-word conditioning effect is present. We also included test sentences with Verb-Noun Phrase boundaries, to assess whether the F_0 conditioning effect of /g/ (if it exists at all) is blocked by such a boundary.

Ten new speakers uttered two pairs of test sentences containing adjective–noun and verb–noun-phrase boundaries.

31a. Sandy asked George to *dig onions* out of the basket on the porch. [V–NP]
  b. Sandy tossed all the big onions into the basket on the porch. [Adj.–N]
32a. Sandy asked George to *dig apples* out of the basket on the porch. [V–NP]
  b. Sandy tossed all the *big apples* into the basket on the porch. [Adj.–N]

The F_0 contours were measured as in previous experiments, and the data are shown graphically in Fig. 13.12. The blocking hypothesis predicted a cross-word phonetic effect in the (b) versions, such that the F_0 would rise during the first 100 msec. Figure 13.12 indicates a rise in F_0 for

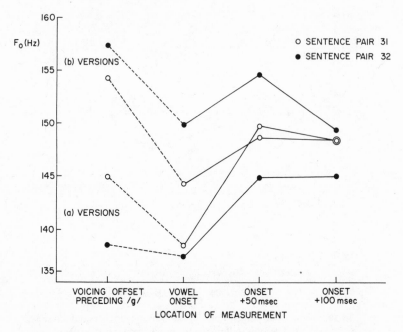

FIG. 13.12. Graphs of pooled data for the (a) and (b) versions of sentences 31 and 32. The range of F_0 values along the ordinate here differs from that in Fig. 13.11, but the scale of the two figures is identical.

both (b) versions during the first 50 msec of the vowel; Sentence (32b) contains an unexplained fall during the second 50 msec.

The blocking hypothesis also predicts that the F_0 contours in the (a) versions should be flat. The data do not support this prediction. In fact, the rise in F_0 for the (a) versions is greater in magnitude than for the (b) versions. We can conclude that the cross-word phonetic effect of /g/ is not blocked at either the adjective–noun or verb–noun phrase boundaries. This conclusion is not surprising, because most subjects exhibited continuous voicing across the boundary. In work with other cross-word phonetic effects, it has been shown that the presence or absence of blocking at syntactic boundaries does not correlate with the magnitude of pause duration (Egido & Cooper, 1978). However, when the speakers produce no pause whatsoever, as with most of the present utterances, it seems likely that the speakers had simultaneous access to phonetic information on both sides of the boundary.

Conclusions on F_0 Blocking. In summary, the results of our experiments on F_0 blocking have provided new information about F_0 effects, but they leave unanswered the question of whether blocking, in the sense described earlier, occurs for these effects. What we have learned from these experiments is that the /k/–/g/ voicing influence on the F_0 of a vowel does operate across word boundaries and that clause boundaries are accompanied by rather dramatic rises in F_0. To learn more about blocking, we will need to examine other cross-word conditioning effects of F_0.

IMPLICATIONS FOR PERCEPTION AND SPEECH SYNTHESIS

At the outset of this chapter, we noted that research on speech production provides necessary guidelines for research on speech perception. We are now able to provide some examples of this working principle. Thanks to the recent studies of F_0 in speech production, we can begin to ask perceptual questions like the following:

1. When a speaker resets his F_0 declination, can the listener detect and utilize this information in recognizing that the speaker is beginning a new structural domain?
2. Do listeners normalize their perception of F_0 in accord with the form of declination produced by the speaker?
3. Can listeners detect and utilize local fall–rise patterns of F_0 in recovering information about syntactic boundaries and deletion sites?

In general, we are primarily interested in learning whether listeners can use syntactically governed inflections of F_0 to recover and predict structural relations in on-line perception of sentences. To date, not a single strand of experimental evidence can be brought to bear on this issue. However, we now have a fairly clear idea of how to proceed with experimental studies concerning the questions outlined above. The stimuli for these experiments will consist of electronically modified versions of natural sentences, to permit precise acoustic control of the F_0 parameter. An analysis-by-synthesis system can be utilized for this purpose (Gold, 1977). This system allows an experimenter to extract a set of parameters (such as the F_0 contour) from the speech signal, modify one or more of them, and synthesize the new waveform. The technique introduces very little unnaturalness in the altered signal.

With this technique, it will be possible, for example, to present listeners with sentences that differ minimally in the presence or absence of F_0 resetting. If listeners are asked to press a response key as soon as a main clause has been completed, will their response times be faster when F_0 resetting is present in string-identical utterances? If so, we can conclude that listeners are at least capable of utilizing this F_0 information. To find out whether listeners *normally* use this information in on-line sentence perception is more difficult, and we have not yet devised a perceptual task which will provide this vital information. This shortcoming is shared by virtually all tasks currently used to test on-line sentence perception, including phoneme monitoring (Cutler & Norris, 1979; Foss, 1969), listening for mispronunciations (Cole, 1973; Cole & Jakimik, Chap. 6), and studies of click detection and reaction time (Bever & Hurtig, 1975). In essence, listeners do not normally listen for the presence of a particular phoneme (as in phoneme-monitoring), for the presence of a mispronunciation (as in listening for mispronunciations), or for the presence of an extraneous click (as in click detection), though certain results with these paradigms indicate that the methods do reflect some important aspects of perception in its typical form. In the same vein, listeners do not consciously judge the presence of clause boundaries, as required by our task. Still, the task is useful in finding out whether listeners are at least capable of utilizing F_0 information to aid in their making structural decisions.

Turning to the question of perceptual normalization for F_0 declination, we find one very tantalizing piece of available data. Breckenridge and Liberman (1977) conducted a study in which listeners were asked to judge the relative pitch of two stressed nonsense syllables in a sequence containing both stressed and unstressed nonsense syllables. The sequence mimicked the rhythm of a natural sentence, and systematic variations of the F_0 or amplitude were introduced electronically. The results of their experiments indicated that the listener normalizes for F_0 declination in making pitch judgments. Since the pitch judgments involved only two syllables per utterance, we cannot determine how closely the listener's built-in normalization for declination matches the form of declination reported above. However, it will be possible to extend Breckenridge and Liberman's procedure to longer utterances, with up to four or five variations in pitch. Listeners should have little trouble learning to assign integer values of one to four for these pitch values, and in so doing it should be possible to determine how closely they track the producer's declination.

In discussing the perception of F_0, we have emphasized the processing of syntactically governed F_0 inflections, since these have been the main focus of our speech production work. However, it should be noted that the perception of F_0 is also relevant to other issues, including the perception of naturalness and integrity of the speech signal (Delgutte, 1976; Maeda, 1976; Nooteboom, Brokz, Dooderman, de Jong, t'Hart, van Katwick, de Rooij, Slis, & Williams, 1975; O'Shaughnessy, 1976; t'Hart & Cohen, 1973). This research has examined perception of F_0 from the standpoint of computer programs which synthesize speech by rule. Current synthesis programs produce speech which contains a halting, arhythmic quality, typically arising from improper or inadequate prosodic rules.

Our work suggests that some prosodic features are computed over syntactically defined domains. Efforts can be directed at implementing rules which consider these syntactic domains in their assignment of segmental timing and F_0 inflections. In addition, rules should be implemented to capture the prosodic features derived from our experiments, such as the Topline Rule. It is generally believed that such rules will improve the naturalness of synthesized speech, rendering it more practical for widespread application.

IMPLICATIONS FOR SPEECH RECOGNITION BY MACHINE

Some speech recognition programs have utilized syntactic parsing to guide low-level stages of phonetic recognition. For example, Lea (1975) has based a syntactic analysis component of a recognition algorithm on the detection of fall–rise patterns of F_0. This program is capable of correctly detecting more than 80% of major syntactic boundaries, and the syntactic representation is used to guide phonetic recognition. Such topdown processing is based on the observation that the phonetic segments immediately bordering the sites of major syntactic boundaries are the most reliably represented in the speechwave. That is, their acoustical representation is relatively invariant. This notion has received support from our own studies on blocking (Cooper, Lapointe, & Paccia, 1977; Cooper, Egido, & Paccia, 1978; Egido & Cooper, 1978), which indicate that major syntactic boundaries block phonetic conditioning effects. These conditioning effects camouflage the phonemic identity of the segments involved and produce machine errors in recognition. Thus, by directing the initial stages of phonetic recognition to the stressed syllables lying nearest to major syntactic boundaries, the likelihood of making correct phonetic identification of some segments is optimized. This information can then be used in constraining the possible set of choices encountered in phonetic recognition of other segments. This schema is not intended to mimic human perception (which is guided more by immediate temporal constraints), but it does provide one means of minimizing errors in phonetic recognition by machine.

CONCLUSION

Our studies of fundamental frequency have aimed at discovering relatively abstract properties of the speaker's syntactic code by examining a concrete, measurable property of the speech wave. Because of F_0's complexity, we are only beginning to capture the essence of its attributes and their relation to syntactic coding. In grappling with this problem, we have found it useful to place strong restrictions on the scope of our hypothesis-testing and our data base. This narrow focus has allowed us to make some sense of the complex F_0 contours observed in fluent speech. There undoubtedly exists more information in these contours than we have been able to consider; nonetheless, these studies provide some basis for research aimed at discovering the mental computations of the speaker.

We have indicated that the syntactic code may influence F_0 in a variety of ways, exemplified by phenomena such as declination resetting, fall–rise patterns, and perhaps the blocking of cross-word F_0 effects. In studying these phenomena we have already been able to make some inferences about psychological notions such as the speaker's domains of processing, the application of look-ahead, and the existence of more than a single level of syntactic coding. In addition, the findings have provided guidelines for related studies of speech perception and for applications to problems in communications engineering.

ACKNOWLEDGMENTS

This work was supported by NIH Grants NS 13028 and NS 15059 as well as by the M.I.T. Research Laboratory of Electronics. We thank Dr. William Henke for providing the FPRD computer program and much helpful advice. JMS is now at Bolt Beranek and Newman, Inc., 50 Moulton St., Cambridge, MA 02138.

REFERENCES

Bever, T. G., & Hurtig, R. R. Detection of a nonlinguistic stimulus is poorest at the end of a clause. *Journal of Psycholinguistic Research*, 1975, *4*, 1–7.
Breckenridge, J., & Liberman, M. Y. *The declination effect in perception*. Unpublished manuscript, 1977. (Available from Bell Laboratories, Murray Hill, N.J.)
Chomsky, N. *Aspects of the theory of syntax*. Cambridge, Ma.: MIT Press, 1965.
Clark, H. H., & Clark, E. V. *Psychology and language*. New York: Harcourt Brace, and Jovanovich, 1977.
Cohen, A., & t'Hart, J. On the anatomy of intonation. *Lingua*, 1967, *19*, 177–192.
Cole, R. A. Listening for mispronunciations. *Perception and Psychophysics*, 1973, *14*, 153–156.
Cooper, W. E. Syntactic control of timing in speech production: A study of complement clauses. *Journal of Phonetics*, 1976, *4*, 151–171.
Cooper, W. E. Syntactic-to-phonetic coding. In B. Butterworth (Ed.), *Language production*. New York: Academic Press, in press.
Cooper, W. E., & Cooper, J. M. *Syntax and speech coding*. Book in preparation, 1978.
Cooper, W. E., Egido, C., & Paccia, J. M. Grammatical control of a phonological rule: Palatalization. *Journal of Experimental Psychology: Human Perception and Performance*, 1978, *4*, 264–272.
Cooper, W. E., Lapointe, S. G., & Paccia, J. M. Syntactic blocking of phonological rules in speech production. *Journal of the Acoustical Society of America*, 1977, *61*, 1314–1320.
Cooper, W. E., Paccia, J. M., & Lapointe, S. G. Hierarchical coding in speech production. *Cognitive Psychology*, 1978, *10*, 154–177.

Cooper, W. E., & Ross, J. M. World order. In R. Grossman, J. San., & T. Vance (Eds.), *Papers from the parasession on functionalism in linguistics.* Chicago: Chicago Linguistic Society, 1975.

Cooper, W. E., & Sorensen, J. M. Fundamental frequency contours at syntactic boundaries. *Journal of the Acoustical Society of America,* 1977, *62,* 683–692.

Cooper, W. E., & Sorensen, J. M. *Fundamental frequency in sentence production.* Book in preparation, 1979.

Crystal, D. *Prosodic systems and intonation in English.* Cambridge: Cambridge University Press, 1969.

Cutler, A., & Norris, D. Monitoring sentence comprehension. In W. E. Cooper & E. C. T. Walker (Eds.), *Sentence processing: Psycholinguistic studies presented to Merrill Garrett.* Hillsdale, N.J.: Lawrence Erlbaum Associates, 1979.

Delgutte, B. *Fundamental frequency contours of French: A perceptual study.* Unpublished master's thesis, Massachusetts Institute of Technology, 1976.

Egido, C., & Cooper, W. E. Blocking of alveolar flapping in speech production: The role of syntactic boundaries and deletion sites. *Journal of Phonetics,* in press.

Fodor, J. A., Bever, T. G., & Garrett, M. F. *The psychology of language: An introduction of psycholinguistics and generative grammar.* New York: McGraw-Hill, 1974.

Foss, D. J. Decision processes during sentence comprehension: Effects of lexical item difficulty and position upon decision times. *Journal of Verbal Learning and Verbal Behavior,* 1969, *8,* 457–462.

Fry, B. D. Duration and intensity as physical correlates of linguistic stress. *Journal of the Acoustical Society of America,* 1955, *27,* 765–768.

Gold, B. Digital speech networks. *Proceedings of the IEEE,* 1977, *65,* 1636–1658.

Gold, B., & Rabiner, L. Parallel processing techniques for estimating pitch periods of speech in the time domain. *Journal of the Acoustical Society of America,* 1969, *46,* 442–448.

Goldman-Eisler, F. *Psycholinguistics: Experiments in spontaneous speech.* New York: Academic Press, 1968.

Grosjean, F., & Deschamps, A. Analyse contrastive des variables temporelles de l'anglais et du francais: Vitesse de parole et variables composantes, phenomenes d'hesitation. *Phonetica,* 1975, *31,* 144–184.

Henke, W. L. Signals from external accelerometers during phonation: Attributes and their internal physical correlates. *Quarterly Progress Report of the M.I.T. Research Laboratory of Electronics,* 1974, *114,* 224–231.

Jackendoff, R. S. Gapping and related rules. *Linguistic Inquiry,* 1971, *2,* 21–35.

Klatt, D. H. Vowel lengthening is syntactically determined in a connected discourse. *Journal of Phonetics,* 1975, *3,* 129–140.

Klatt, D. H., & Cooper, W. E. Perception of segment duration in sentence contexts. In A. Cohen & S. G. Nooteboom (Eds.), *Structure and process in speech perception.* New York: Springer-Verlag, 1975.

Lea, W. A. Segmental and suprasegmental influences on fundamental frequency contours. In L. M. Hyman (Ed.), *Consonant types and tone.* Los Angeles: Southern California Occasional Papers in Linguistics, 1973, No. 1.

Lea, W. A. *Prosodic aids to speech recognition: VII. Experiments on detecting and locating phrase boundaries.* Sperry Univac Report #PX 11534, 1975.

Lehiste, I. Phonetic disambiguation of syntactic ambiguity. *Glossa,* 1973, *7,* 107–121.

Lehiste, I., Olive, J. P., & Streeter, L. A. Role of duration in disambiguating syntactically ambiguous sentences. *Journal of the Acoustical Society of America,* 1976, *60,* 1199–1202.

Lindblom, B., & Rapp, K. *Some temporal regularities of spoken Swedish.* Papers from the Institute of Linguistics, University of Stockholm, 1973, *21.*

Maeda, S. *A characterization of American English intonation.* Unpublished doctoral dissertation, Massachusetts Institute of Technology, 1976.

Malkiel, Y. Studies in irreversible binomials. *Lingua,* 1959, *8,* 113–160.

Martin, J. G. On judging pauses in spontaneous speech. *Journal of Verbal Learning and Verbal Behavior,* 1970, *9,* 75–78.

McAllister, R. Predicting physical aspects of English stress. *Quarterly Progress and Status Report,* Speech Transmission Laboratory, Royal Institute of Technology, Stockholm, Sweden, 1971, *1,* 20–29.

Nooteboom, S. G., Brokz, J. P., Dooderman, G. J. N., de Jong, Th. A., t'Hart, H., van Katwijk, A. F. V., de Rooij, J. J., Slis, I. H., & Williams, L. F. *Research on speech perception in the I.P.O. 1975.* IPO Annual Progress Report. Eindhoven, Holland, 1975.

O'Shaughnessy, D. *Modelling fundamental frequency, and its relationships to syntax, semantics, and phonetics.* Unpublished doctoral dissertation, Massachusetts Institute of Technology, 1976.

Peterson, G. E., & Barney, H. L. Control methods used in a study of the vowels. *Journal of the Acoustical Society of America,* 1952, *24,* 175–184.

Rabiner, L. R., Cheng, M. J., Rosenberg, A. E., & McGonegal, C. A. A comparative performance study of several pitch detection algorithms. *IEEE Transactions on Acoustics, Speech, and Signal Processing,* 1976, *ASSP-24,* 399–418.

Ross, J. R. Gapping and the order of constituents. In M. Bierwisch & K. E. Hiedolph (Eds.), *Progress in linguistics.* The Hague: Mouton, 1970.

Sag, I. A. *Deletion and logical form.* Unpublished doctoral dissertation, Massachusetts Institute of Technology, 1976.

Sorensen, J. M., Cooper, W. E., & Paccia, J. M. Speech timing of grammatical categories. *Cognition,* 1978, *6,* 135–153.

Stevens, K. N., Henke, W. L., & Sorensen, J. M. Unpublished data, Massachusetts Institute of Technology, 1975.

t'Hart, J., & Cohen, A. Intonation by rule: A perceptual quest. *Journal of Phonetics,* 1973, *1,* 309–327.

14 Performing Transformations

David Fay
University of Illinois, Chicago Circle

For nearly two decades, psycholinguists have been concerned with specifying the relationship between linguistic competence and linguistic performance. More specifically, the concern has been to determine what role, if any, is played by a transformational grammar in the everyday use of language. From the point of view of transformational linguistics, this concern is a natural one, for, as Chomsky (1965) has put it, "a reasonable model of language use will incorporate as a basic component, the generative grammar that expresses the speaker–hearer's knowledge of the language, [even though] this generative grammar does not, in itself, prescribe the character or functioning of a perceptual model or a model of speech production [p. 9]." However, despite the considerable effort devoted to demonstrating the use of transformational rules in linguistic performance, virtually no evidence has been produced to date (see Fodor, Bever, & Garrett, 1974, for a review).

There are two responses one might make to this dilemma. One approach is to question whether a transformational grammar, at least in its present form, correctly characterizes the speaker–hearer's knowledge of language. If it doesn't, then it is not the right generative grammar to incorporate into theories of language performance. This position has been advocated recently by Bresnan (1978). She argues that transformational grammar needs to be made more "realistic," in the sense of being more in accord with the available psychological evidence. This can be done, she suggests, by eliminating from the grammar of English many of the transformations found in classical transformational theory (as in Chomsky, 1965, for example). Bresnan tries to show that even on internal linguistic

441

grounds, such a move is desirable. This seems a promising approach and has received much attention in recent years (Brame, 1976; Freidin, 1975; Wasow, 1977). However, it is still too early to tell whether it will be successful and whether it will help to solve the psycholinguist's problem.

Taking a different approach, one might conclude that the lack of psychological evidence for transformations does not reflect the incorrectness of the grammar; rather, it reflects incorrect assumptions about how the grammar is, in Bresnan's terminology, "realized" in the language user.

In this chapter, we explore this latter approach. In contrast to previous discussions of this kind (Bresnan, 1978; Fodor et al., 1974), the focus is exclusively on speech production rather than comprehension. My argument is that a transformational grammar should be directly realized in a model of speech production. I proceed by first considering what it means to directly realize a grammar in a psychological model. Evidence from errors made in spontaneous speech is then reviewed, and it is shown how the errors support a Direct Realization Model (DRM). Because of the unorthodox nature of the evidence and the unfamiliarity of the Direct Realization Model, some discussion is devoted to the ways in which the model can be evaluated against competing accounts of the data. Finally, certain assumptions made by the model are supported by independent lines of evidence.

A DIRECT REALIZATION MODEL OF SPEECH PRODUCTION

According to Bresnan (1978), a realization of a grammar in a psychological model "should map distinct grammatical rules and units into distinct processing operations and informational units." For a given grammar, this mapping can be accomplished in many different ways. To take a simple example, consider the phrase structure grammar in Table 14.1.

One possible realization of this grammar in a production model would be one in which the rules are utilized in precisely the form in which they appear in the grammar. However, to construe these rules as real-time operations, they must be supplemented with a set of control processes which operate with the stored rules to produce sentences. In the case at hand, we might imagine that the process starts with the symbol S which is placed in a working memory. The list of rules is then searched until one is found which has on its left side one of the symbols listed in working memory. (At the initial stage, of course, this can only be rule 1: S → NP   VP.) When the appropriate rule is found, it is interpreted as an

TABLE 14.1

1.	S	→	NP VP
2.	NP	→	DET N
3.	VP	→	V N
4.	V	→	ate
5.	DET	→	the
6.	N	→	men
7.	N	→	dinner

operation which replaces a symbol in working memory with the symbols on the right side of the rule. In addition, the replacing symbols are surrounded with brackets labelled by the symbol that was replaced. This process iterates until no more symbols can be found in working memory which match the left hand side of some rule. An example of such a derivation is given in Table 14.2.

What has been done here is to take a realization mapping of the grammar into a performance model that preserves not only the substance of the grammatical rules, but also their form. In other words, a performance theory of this type would be just a formalization of the set of procedures which a linguist might use to check what output is given by the grammar in Table 14.1. This type of mapping, which preserves the form as well as the substance of the rules of grammar, will be called a *direct realization* mapping.

A realization mapping that preserves the substance of the rules, but not the form, will be considered an *indirect realization*. A simple example of

TABLE 14.2

Step	Rule	Contents of Working Memory	
1	—	S	
2	1	(NP VP)	
		S	
3	3	(NP (V N))	
		S VP	
4	4	(NP ((ate) N))	
		S VP V	
5	7	(NP ((ate) (dinner)))	
		S VP V N	
6	2	((DET N) ((ate) (dinner)))	
		S NP VP V N	
7	5	(((the) N) ((ate) (dinner)))	
		S NP DET VP V N	
8	6	(((the) (men)) ((ate) (dinner)))	
		S NP DET N VP V N	

TABLE 14.3

ate:	(S\NP)/N
the:	NP/N
men:	N
dinner:	N

an indirect mapping of the grammar in Table 14.1 is based on the set of rules in Table 14.3.

The rules of Table 14.3 are to be interpreted in the following way. They consist of a lexicon of the language. Associated with each word in the lexicon is a category label, either basic (e.g., N) or derived (e.g., NP/N). A derived category label is of the form X/Y or X\Y where X and Y can be either basic or derived categories. The label X/Y is to be interpreted as a category that can combine with category Y placed to the right to make a new category, X. For example, a word of category NP/N will combine with a word of category N on the right to make a phrase of category NP. Thus, category NP/N is equivalent to the category Determiner in the standard phrase structure grammar notation. X\Y receives the same interpretation except that Y is placed to the left to give an X. It is easy to show, by working through the rules in Table 14.3, that they give the same output as those in Table 14.1, except for differences in the category labels. A sample derivation is given in Table 14.4.

The rules in Table 14.3 then are simply a recasting of phrase structure rules into another form.[1] From the point of view of a linguist, they represent the same theory as the grammar of Table 14.1; the two are simply notational variants that generate the same set of sentences and associated structural descriptions. But from the perspective of processing models, they lead to different realizations of the grammar.

The natural processing order for the rules in Table 14.3 is to start with lexical items and then build up the structure until an S node is reached, as shown in Table 14.4. This is because the category of each word indicates directly what it combines with. Contrast this with the case of phrase structure rules in which the natural interpretation is to process from the highest node down to the words, since the rules indicate how categories expand. In other words, a phrase structure grammar seems most compatible with top-down processing, while the rules in Table 14.3 suggest bottom-up processing.

As these simple examples show, it is possible to realize the same grammar in different ways. A realization that preserves the form of a

---

[1] Rules of this form comprise what is termed a categorial grammar (see Lyons, 1968; Partee, 1975).

TABLE 14.4

Step	Contents of Working Memory					
1	(the)					
	NP/N					
2	(	(the)	(men))			
	NP	NP/N	N			
3	(	(the)	(men))	(ate)		
	NP	NP/N	N	(S\NP(/N		
4	(	(	(the)	(men))	(	(ate)	(dinner)))
	S	NP	NP/N	N	S\NP	(S\NP)/N	N

grammar is a direct realization; one that doesn't, is an indirect realization. Since performance systems presumably evolve in such a way as to optimize reliability, efficiency, modifiability, etc., one realization may satisfy these criteria better than another. Hence, the realizations of a particular grammar will not necessarily be psychologically equivalent.

This point has been made previously by Newell and Simon (1972) in a discussion of models of problem solving and, more recently, by Rips, Smith, and Shoben (1975) with respect to semantic memory models. Rips et al. agree with the observation of Hollan (1975) that a feature model like the one they propose could be recast into an informationally equivalent network model. But, as they point out, the operations needed to retrieve information from memory will depend on the form in which the information is represented. Consequently, one model may be superior to another when both structure and process are taken into account. In the same way, the processes that operate with grammatical rules will depend on the form in which the grammar is realized.[2]

The thesis of this chapter is that speech production involves a direct realization of a transformational grammar. The transformational grammar to be realized is the so-called "standard theory" of *Aspects of the Theory of Syntax* (Chomsky, 1965). What then would a direct realization of a

---

[2]It should be noted that the difference between direct and indirect realization models is more a matter of terminology than a conceptual distinction. The fact that current transformational grammars use phrase structure rules in the base component, rather than rules of the type given in Table 14.3, is a result of convention and historical accident. Consequently, which form of a grammar is called a direct realization and which an indirect realization is also accidental in this sense. I introduce the notion of *direct* realization to emphasize that a model of how a grammar is realized involves a commitment to the form in which the rules of the grammar are utilized. At the same time, the terminology highlights the fact that realizations that take on quite different forms may be realizations of the same grammar. Thus, an Augmented Transition Network (Woods, 1970) model of speech production, were one to be developed, might well turn out to be simply an indirect realization of a transformational grammar.

transformational grammar consist of? Since we will be concerned here only with syntactic processes in speech production, the question reduces to: How is the syntactic structure of a sentence determined?

A direct realization of a transformational grammar would initially apply phrase structure rules and lexical insertion transformations to produce a deep structure. Nothing more will be said about these rules here. Rather, the focus will be on transformational rules, whose role is to transmute deep structures into surface structures. It is the claim of the DRM that the deep structure underlying an utterance and each structure produced by the application of a transformation corresponds to a psychological structure. The transformations then are mental operations (that is, changes in mental structure), and the logical ordering of rules in the grammar corresponds to a temporal ordering of the operations that result in an utterance. Moreover, the DRM requires that transformations be employed in just the form in which they appear in the grammar. Many more details need to be specified, of course, in order to see precisely how a directly realized transformational grammar would work. I will return to some of these details below, but first we will consider some data that suggest the use of transformations in speech production.

Evidence for Transformations

This section will provide evidence that a model of speech production should consist of a direct realization of a transformational grammar. Since the arguments and evidence have been discussed in detail elsewhere (Fay, in press), just the main points are considered here.

The Direct Realization Model states that transformations are carried out as psychological operations during speech production. If this is correct, we should be able to observe errors in speech which result from the malfunctioning of these rules. Such errors have been found in a collection of approximately 5,000 errors of all types recorded by the author and his friends over the last six years. The errors were written down at the time they occurred, along with as much linguistic and situational context as seemed relevant. When possible, the intended utterance was determined by querying the speaker; otherwise, it was determined from the linguistic context, including, most often, the speaker's spontaneous corrections. In the author's collection of errors, only about 100 could be construed as syntactic, and many of these involve relatively superficial processes like number agreement or case marking. Despite the small numbers, however, syntactic errors clearly fall into classes about which certain generalizations hold. It is these generalizations, rather than the individual errors they are based on, that I am most interested in accounting for in the theory outlined in this chapter.

Among the many possible types of errors predicted to occur by the DRM, particularly revealing ones would be those in which some rule fails to move a word from its deep structure position. The resulting utterance will contain a trace of the underlying order of elements in the form of the misplaced word.

One rule that might produce such errors is WH-movement. This rule moves a WH-word or phrase (e.g., *who, what, which boy, how many of your toes*) from the position it occupies in underlying structure to one of two positions. If the sentence is a direct question as in (1), the WH-phrase is moved to the front; if it is an indirect question as in (2), it is moved only as far as the verb.

1. Which brand of cigarettes does Tom smoke?
2. I don't know which brand of cigarettes Tom smokes.

The reason WH-movement is an important rule to examine is that it lies at the heart of the transformationalist position. While the existence of other transformations has become controversial of late, even among transformational grammarians, WH-movement has remained untouched thus far by the controversy. The reasons are not hard to find.

Consider the following facts. A verb like *amuse* must be followed by a direct object which refers to a human. Hence, (3) is grammatical, but (4) and (5) are not.

3. Tom amuses his friends.
4. *Tom amuses.
5. *Tom amuses the wall.

However, this generalization is violated in certain WH-questions as in (6), which lack the required object after the verb.

6. Which friends does Tom amuse?

But notice that in sentences like (6), in which *amuse* is missing its direct object, a phrase of the appropriate semantic type appears at the beginning of the sentence. Note further that when such a phrase appears sentence-initially, *amuse* cannot be followed by a direct object, as shown in (7).

7. *Which friends does Tom amuse Sam?

How are these facts to be explained?

Transformational grammar holds that this correlated appearance and disappearance of the direct object of *amuse* is more than coincidental.

The systematic relation between *amuse* and its object is represented by generating the object next to *amuse* in deep structure. If the object is a WH-phrase, it can then be moved to the front of the sentence by WH-movement.

What is important about this example is that a phrase structure grammar, the principal competitor to the transformational theory, cannot handle such correlations at all. This follows from the fact that the gap between the WH-phrase and the verb *amuse* may stretch over an indefinite number of words, as suggested by (8)–(10):

8. Which friends did Mary say Tom amuses?
9. Which friends does Sam believe Mary said Tom amuses?
10. Which friends does Dick pretend that Sam believes Mary said Tom amuses?

Although phrase structure grammars can literally generate such sentences, they cannot do so without at the same time generating ill-formed sentences like that in (7) (Bresnan, 1978).

For other rules, the so-called bounded transformations, the same arguments do not hold. Other less direct reasons must be given to justify their inclusion in the grammar (Chomsky, 1965). It is these transformations whose existence has recently been called into question (Freidin, 1975; Oehrle, 1975).

If there is any rule for which we should find evidence in speech production, then, it is WH-fronting. If such evidence were lacking, we would have to seriously question whether any version of transformational grammar were realized in speech production.

Fortunately, the required evidence is provided by errors in spontaneous speech, as shown in (11) and (12).

11. Target: Linda, which ear do you talk on the telephone with?
    Error: Linda, do you talk on the telephone with which ear?

12. T: Look at how fast those clouds are moving.
    E: Look at those clouds are moving how fast.

When we compare the related simple declaratives in (13) and (14), we see that the misplaced WH-phrases in the errors occupy deep structure positions.

13. I talk on the telephone with my left ear.
14. Those clouds are moving very fast.

The DRM provides a very simple explanation for these errors. Suppose that the speaker has omitted the transformation of WH-fronting in a direct question, in (11), and an indirect question, in (12). In that case we should expect to find the WH-phrase in deep structure position, as we do. This explanation is strengthened by the fact that no errors have been observed in which a WH-phrase is misplaced into any other position than that which it occupies in deep structure.

Further evidence for the application of transformations to a deep structure level can be found in a different type of error associated with WH-fronting. As Ross (1967) has noted, this rule is subject to a constraint which, roughly speaking, guarantees that all the material contained in the WH-phrase will be moved by the rule, not just the WH-word. In example (12), for instance, it would be an error to move *how* from the phrase *how fast*, without moving *fast* as well. Yet just this kind of error occurs, as shown in (15) and (16).

15. T: Go ahead and do what else you're going to do and I'll be there in a minute.
    E: Go ahead and do what you're going to do else and I'll be there in a minute.
16. T: Who else did I think had left?
    E: Who did I think else had left?[3]

Once again, an element has been left in deep structure position; it has not been moved by the operation of WH-movement. And once again, the misplacement is always to deep structure position.

The data presented thus far suggest that deep structure is a psychologically real stage in the construction of an utterance. And by implication, transformations must apply to those deep structures.

But even if one accepts the notion that deep structure is computed during speech production, one might argue that some type of operation other than transformations converts these structures into an utterance. This kind of argument has been made previously by Fodor et al. (1974), with respect to sentence comprehension. They were led to this position by their observation that there was evidence for the computation of surface and deep structures during sentence comprehension, but none for the transformational rules that should relate them.

This objection can be answered by observing errors in which the internal operations of a transformation itself are revealed. Since the inception of transformational grammar (Chomsky, 1955/1975), transformations have

---

[3]This error is from Garrett (1975).

been analyzed into component operations called elementary transformations. These operations include substitution, deletion, and adjunction (or copying). In particular, it has been suggested (Chomsky, 1965) that any rule that moves material around in a sentence should be written not as an elementary movement transformation, but rather as a combination of copying and deletion. Analyzed this way, an element to be moved is first copied into its new location, and then the original is deleted.

Given the assumption of DRM that transformations are directly realized as operations in speech production, and the knowledge that operations in speech production can be skipped, as shown earlier, the prediction follows that errors will occur in which one of the elementary transformations comprising a rule will be omitted.

Consider, for example, the rule of particle movement, which moves a particle from its position next to a verb to a new position to the right of an adjacent noun phrase. In Table 14.5, we have given the rule as expressed in standard notation (Bach, 1974).

As can be seen, the rule consists of two parts—the structural analysis and the structural change. The structural analysis says that the rule can apply to any phrase marker that can be analyzed into a verb, followed immediately by a particle, followed immediately by a noun phrase. The variables X and Y indicate that anything at all can precede the verb and follow the noun phrase. The way in which this rule factors a tree into its parts is shown by the dotted lines in Fig. 14.1.

The structural change specifies how a rule alters the tree it applies to. In Table 14.5, the structural change indicates that a copy of a particle is to be attached as a sister to the noun phrase, and the particle from which a copy is made is to be deleted. The effect of these operations is shown in Fig. 14.2.

Since particle movement consists of two elementary transformations, copying and deletion, it is possible for one, but not the other, to be skipped. If the deletion is skipped, a particle will be duplicated. Just this kind of error occurs as shown in (17).

17. T: Would you turn on the light?
    E: Would you turn on the light on?

TABLE 14.5
Particle Movement

Structural analysis	X	-	V	-	PRT	-	NP	-	Y
	1		2		3		4		5
Structural change	1		2		0		4+3		5

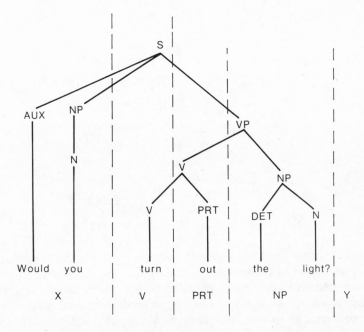

FIG. 14.1.   Factorization by the particle movement transformation of the tree underlying *would you turn the light out?*

18. T: A boy who I know has hair down to here.
    E: A boy who I know a boy has hair down to here.[4]
19. T: And when they chew coca, which they chew all day long, they ...
    E: And when they chew coca, which they chew coca all day long, they ...

The examples in (18) and (19) reveal the same phenomenon with the rule of relative clause formation. Here the movement involved is not as obvious. The rule is supposed to move a noun phrase in a relative clause to the front of its clause and attach a WH-marker. Later rules change the WH-marked word into a WH-word. If this rule copies correctly, but doesn't delete the original, the result will be as in (18) and (19). Observe, once again, that an element, in this case a noun phrase, is stranded in its deep structure position. Errors of this type involving other rules are discussed in Fay (in press).

We pause here to review the type of argument being made for the Direct Realization Model. I started by assuming that transformational

---

[4]This error is from the Appendix in Fromkin (1973).

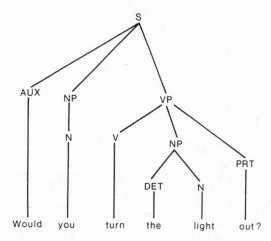

FIG. 14.2.   The result of applying particle movement to the tree in Fig. 14.1.

rules, in precisely the form in which they are stated in the grammar, are applied as mental operations to mental structures in the form of phrase structure trees. On the reasonable assumption that required operations are skipped on occasion, it was possible to predict the types of errors that might be found in spontaneous speech. Since the predicted errors were observed, the assumptions were supported.

There are, of course, many objections that could be raised at this point. For example, the DRM clearly makes the prediction that all the syntactic planning of a sentence must be complete before the sentence is uttered. This follows from the way in which many transformations, WH-movement for example, take a whole sentence as their domain. Some may find this prediction objectionable, however, because of the common intuition that speech is planned "left-to-right." Others may find it difficult to imagine how the semantic interpretation rules in the grammar could be realized in a production model, especially if they must apply to surface structure, as is argued in recent versions of transformational theory. Rather than attempt to discuss these interesting questions here, I focus on a single issue: the question of whether other models of production might equally well explain the available error data. It might be that virtually any model of production can provide a reasonable fit to the error data. The only way to settle this question is to examine competing models in the light of the data.

There is one serious impediment to this exercise, however. There has been so little work done on speech production, either in psychology or artificial intelligence, that it is far from clear what the competing models will be. Despite these limitations, it will be instructive to consider in some detail one alternative to the DRM as outlined here. As I will attempt to show, this alternative has great difficulty in explaining the available data.

But before evaluating the DRM in relation to an alternative model, it is necessary to describe a control process that operates with the grammar in the DRM to produce sentences.

Friedman's Algorithm: A Control Process

It will be helpful to make the Direct Realization Model more explicit than has been necessary thus far. I am aided in this by the fact that the syntactic component of a transformational grammar has previously been implemented as a computer program by Friedman (1971). Her program successfully generates sentences, demonstrating that a fully explicit Direct Realization Model for speech production is at least feasible.

Earlier, a distinction was made between the grammar that is realized in a production model (or computer program) and the control processes that operate with the grammar to produce sentences. As suggested above by the brief discussion of the form of transformational rules, the grammar incorporated into the DRM can be made fully explicit. However, the manner in which the rules are applied has yet to be specified. I can remedy this by describing Friedman's algorithm for applying a transformation to a phrase structure tree. It seems to be a natural one, and it will be adopted as part of the DRM.

Friedman's algorithm involves two pointers. The "rule pointer" indicates a term in the structural analysis of the transformation being applied. The "tree pointer" points to a node of the phrase marker being analyzed. Initially, the rule pointer is set on the first symbol of the structural analysis of the transformation being applied, and the tree pointer is set at the topmost node of the tree. The symbol on the tree node currently being examined is compared to that indicated by the rule pointer. If they are the same, one part of the structural analysis has been located; the rule pointer is then advanced to the next symbol and search begins again. If the symbols differ, the left branch from the current node is taken, and the tree pointer is set to the next node encountered. This process is repeated until the correct node is found or the bottom of the tree is reached, in which case the rule doesn't apply. (The special provisions necessary to handle variables in the structural analysis will not be described, nor the backup procedures employed in case of false parsings.)

The operation of this tree-parsing algorithm can be illustrated by applying the passive rule given in Table 14.6 to the tree shown in Fig. 14.3.

The inessential variables in this statement of the rule have been suppressed in order to simplify the exposition. Friedman's algorithm would start by searching for an NP, the first symbol in the structural analysis of the passive rule. The search is initiated at the S node in Fig. 14.3 and then moves down the left branch, which an NP node is found.

TABLE 14.6
Passive

NP	-	AUX	-	V	-	NP
1		2		3		4
4		2		be+en+3		by+1

Next an Aux is sought by backing up to the S node and examining the next branch to the right. After the Aux node is located, search begins for a V, again at the S node. This time the rightmost branch is taken to the VP node. Since this is not a V, the left branch is taken, and a V is successfully located. Search proceeds in this manner until each symbol in the structural analysis has been found in the tree. The numbers on the nodes in Fig. 14.3 correspond to the order in which the nodes are examined.

As long as each symbol of the structural analysis is found in the tree, the algorithm guarantees that the tree will be exhaustively analyzed, as required by the definition of a transformation. The passive rule, for example, could not apply to a tree if the constituent intervened between a verb and the first NP following it.

As even this simple illustration shows, there are many operations performed by the algorithm in applying a transformation, and many pieces of information to keep track of. As a consequence, there are many opportunities for error. Most errors, of course, will result in the rule failing to apply at all. But, on occasion, the rule will misapply. We turn now to a class of errors of this sort. We will show how the errors are predicted from a DRM incorporating Friedman's algorithm. We will then be in a position to test an alternative account in some detail.

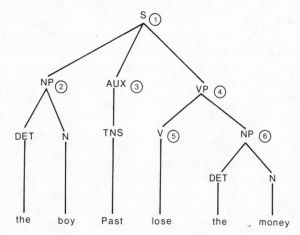

FIG.14.3. The structure underlying *the boy lost the money*. The numbers show the order in which nodes are searched by Friedman's algorithm.

TABLE 14.7

someone PAST tell me about all of it	Underlying form
all of it PAST be+en tell me about by someone	*Passive
all of it PAST be+en tell me about	Agent deletion
it all PAST be+en tell me about	Quantifier postposition
it all be+PAST tell+en me about	Affix hopping
it all was told me about	Morphophonemics
it was all told me about	Auxiliary shift

Consider the errors given in (20)–(22).

20. T: If that was done to me . . .
    E: If I was done that to . . .[5]
21. T: It's a generalization that holds and something oughta be said about it.
    E: It's a generalization that holds and oughta be said something about.
22. T: I was told about all of it.[6]
    E: It was all told me about.

Put informally, what is happening in these errors is that a passive construction is formed with the object of a preposition rather than the direct object of a verb. The remarkable similarity of the errors suggests they should be given a unified explanation.

In the DRM, these errors are obtained as illustrated by the derivation for (22) given in Table 14.7.

As the derivation shows, the passive rule takes the wrong NP to the subject position. Note that the NP includes the quantifier *all*. Because it moves to the front of the sentence, *all* interacts with later rules, rules which would not have affected it had it not been moved. Once the passive rule has applied, agent deletion removes the semantically empty *by*-phrase to form what is often called an "agentless" or "short" passive. Next, a rule moves *all* to the right of the subject and deletes *of* (Emonds, 1976). This rule is motivated by alternations like that in (23).

---

[5]This error is cited in Hausser (1971).

[6]The speaker was not clear about the precise wording of the target in this example; in addition to that given in (22), the following were suggested as possible targets:

(i) I was told about it all.
(ii) I was told all about it.

The argument to be given is not materially affected by which one is taken to be the true target.

23. a. All of the men wore trenchcoats.
    b. All the men wore trenchcoats.
    c. The men all wore trenchcoats.

Next, the standard rule of affix hopping moves affixes onto an adjacent verb, and then morphophonemic rules spell out the verb forms. Finally, a rule that Baker (1971) has called auxiliary shift hops the auxiliary verb *was* to the left of the quantifier. The errors in (20) and (21) can be derived in a similar fashion using the transformations of the standard theory.

Let us now consider in more detail how the passive rule might have misapplied. In Fig. 14.4 we show the tree underlying (22) at the point at which passive applies.

In parsing this tree, the algorithm will locate first an NP, then an Aux, then a V. Once the Verb has been found, the tree pointer should be moved back up to the VP node and then down to the next node to the right, looking for an NP. Suppose that the tree pointer is moved down, not the next branch to the right, but the branch to the right of that one. This type of error may be called a branching error. The result will be to send the tree pointer down toward the NP that is to be incorrectly moved, and so suggests a way of producing the passive errors.

Observe, however, that the first node encountered after the branching error is a prepositional phrase node, which is not the NP being sought. Its left branch is then taken to the preposition node. But since the P node is not an NP, and doesn't have an NP under it, the algorithm would have to conclude that the passive rule doesn't apply. Thus, it looks like these errors cannot be accounted for after all as a simple error in the application of a transformation. While a branching error seems a plausible mistake for the parsing algorithm to make, it appears not to give the right results.

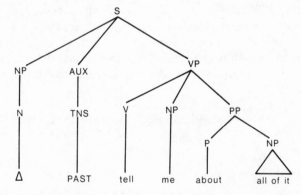

FIG. 14.4.   The underlying structure of *I was told about all of it* to which the passive rule applies.

Fortunately, appearances are deceiving. There is nothing wrong with the algorithm; rather, it is the passive rule which is incorrect. Note that as the rule is stated in Table 14.6, the NP to be moved into subject position must immediately follow a verb. However, this cannot be correct, since passives like those in (24)–(26) are perfectly good.

24. The postman was snarled at by the dogs.
25. The president's speech was commented on by BBC.
26. A general is looked to for moral leadership by his troops.

Thus, the passive rule must be reformulated to include an optional preposition after the verb (Akmajian & Heny, 1975), as shown in Table 14.8.

Once this change is made, it is plain that the parsing algorithm can make a branching error as noted above and yet still apply the passive rule to sentences with the appropriate structure. In the tree shown in Fig. 14.4, the algorithm will take the right-most branch from the VP node and a PP node will be encountered. The left branch is then taken from the PP node to the preposition, which fits the P term in the structural analysis of the passive rule. The algorithm will continue by searching for an NP on the right branch of PP and will find it. Since the structural analysis of the passive rule is satisfied, it applies, giving errors like those observed.

Note that this explanation of the errors depends crucially on two factors. First, branching errors must be a type of error that can occur in the application of transformations. It is important that independent evidence of their existence be found in a different set of constructions. Second, explanation of passive errors assumes that they will occur only in a narrow range of structures, ones which just happen to fit the structural analysis of the passive rule after a branching error is made. The postverbal prepositional phrase is one such construction. Another is the double object construction as in (27).

27. The governor appointed a woman Health Commissioner.

If a branching error is made in the application of the passive rule in this type of sentence, the second NP after the verb would be moved into subject position, as in (28), rather than the first NP, as in the correct (29).

TABLE 14.8
Passive Rule

NP	-	AUX	-	V	-	(P)	-	NP
1		2		3		4		5
5		2		be+en+3		4		by+1

28. ∗Health Commissioner was appointed a woman by the governor.
29. A woman was appointed Health Commissioner by the governor.

Hence, the account of passive errors given here clearly predicts that errors like that in (28) will be observed. On the other hand, this account predicts that an NP can be incorrectly moved from a position immediately adjacent to the object NP (with a preposition possibly invervening) and from no other position; otherwise, the structural analysis of the passive rule will not be satisfied after the branching error occurs. For instance, there is no simple branching error that will produce (31) from an application of passive to the structure underlying (30).

30. John persuaded Mary to climb a tree.
31. ∗A tree was persuaded Mary to climb by John.

Therefore, we should fail to observe errors like that in (31), and likewise in many other cases of this sort.

I do not, as yet, have evidence directly supporting the predictions made by this account of passive errors. Even in the absence of such data, though, it is still desirable to evaluate the account, and the DRM it derives from, against other models of production, an exercise to which we now turn.

EVALUATING AN ALTERNATIVE MODEL

Let us first note that the Direct Realization Model is actually composed of two relatively independent components. As pointed out earlier, the model assumes both a grammar—in this case, the standard theory of *Aspects of the Theory of Syntax*—and a set of control processes. Each of these components will be evaluated in turn, using as a test case the DRM analysis of passive errors just elaborated. It should be recognized, however, that empirical tests of either of the independent components will ordinarily require assumptions to be made about the character of the other.

It is in the area of the grammar incorporated by the DRM that the model is most easily tested and most vulnerable. This follows from the fact that the DRM must be compatible not only with whatever performance facts are available, but also with the known linguistic facts. Were a linguist to come up with decisive arguments against whatever grammar was assumed by the DRM, the model would be falsified, at least in that form. Processing aspects of the DRM are not subject to this double jeopardy. In general, arguments about which linguistic analysis is correct will not bear directly on the control processes assumed by the DRM.

If the DRM survives arguments against it based on linguistic data, it must also succeed in explaining the performance data. This will not always be easy, as can be seen by examining an alternative account of the passive rule errors discussed previously. Suppose that instead of basing the DRM on the standard theory, it is based on a case grammar as proposed by Fillmore (1968). This is a particularly interesting comparison, since two recent computational models of production (Chester, 1976; Simmons & Slocum, 1972) have been realizations of case grammars.

The case treatment of passives differs from the standard analysis in two main ways. First, the underlying order of elements is different, so that somewhat different transformations are required in derivations. Second, transformations generally move around case constituents rather than the usual NPs or VPs. These differences can best be appreciated by examining a sample derivation. Consider the following simple active sentence.

32. Kristin mailed a letter to the President.

As indicated in Fig. 14.5, its underlying structure in case grammar consists of an S node expanded as modality and proposition, rather than directly into noun phrase and verb phrase. Proposition is in turn expanded as a verb and a set of cases: agentive, objective, dative, instrumental, and so on. Each case branches into K (which may be empty) and a noun phrase. The K constituent contains case affixes, postpositions, and, most importantly for English, prepositions.

This underlying structure is transformed into the surface form of (32) in the following steps. A subject creation rule moves the agentive con-

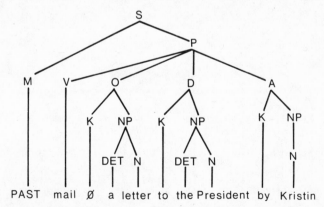

FIG. 14.5.   The structure underlying *Kristin mailed a letter to the President* in case grammar.

stituent into subject position as shown in Fig. 14.6. A subject preposition deletion rule then removes the K constituent from subject position and, with it, the preposition associated with agentives in underlying structure. Finally, an object preposition deletion rule gets rid of the K constituent of the objective phrase, giving the surface form in Fig. 14.7.

A passive version of (32) can be derived by having the subject creation rule move the objective case into subject position. At the same time, the verb is marked as passive. This has several consequences that need not concern us here (see Fillmore, 1968). The surface passive form is produced by deleting the empty K node in subject position, with the subject preposition deletion rule.

From these derivations, it is apparent that the case treatment of passives differs from the standard account both in the type of constituent moved to subject position (objective versus NP) and in its handling of prepositions. As we will see, these differences are crucial in the account that can be given of passive errors.

How might passive errors be derived in case grammar? Recall that the standard passive rule refers to the geometrical properties of the tree to identify what is to be moved (i.e., "move the first NP after the verb"). The case rule, on the other hand, refers only to a category label (i.e. "move objective case"). This difference is what distinguishes the rules in the types of errors that can arise in their application. Whereas the standard rule fails in reading the geometry of a tree, the so-called branching error, the case rule will have to make case reading errors. The natural way then for the case rule to move the wrong constituent, in the passive errors considered earlier, is to misread some case constituent as an objective case. It will then be moved to subject position by the subject creation rule, thus accounting for why the wrong NP appears in that position.

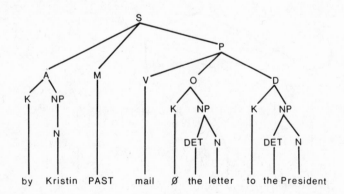

FIG. 14.6.   The result of applying a subject creation rule to the structure in Fig. 14.5.

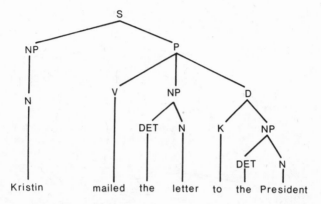

FIG. 14.7. The surface structure of *Kristin mailed a letter to the President*.

However, further examination of this approach shows that it won't work. Note that the subject creation rule applies to the whole case constituent rather than just to the NP it contains. As a consequence, a preposition will be moved into subject position along with the wrong NP, and subsequently will be deleted by the subject preposition deletion rule. A derivation of this sort is given in Fig. 14.8 for the passive error in (20). As indicated by the derivation, the case grammar approach predicts that when the wrong NP is moved to subject position in passives, the preposition normally associated with it will disappear. This follows automatically from the way in which the rules of case grammar interact. Contrary to this prediction, prepositions show up in their original deep structure position in all the observed passive errors.

There are two ways out of this bind for the advocate of a DRM based on case grammar. The first is to reformulate the passive rule so that it moves an NP rather than a case constituent. But this is to give up precisely what differentiates case grammar from the standard theory. Alternatively, one might allow the rule to enter the wrong case constituent and pick out the objective constituent it is looking for. If a dative constituent is examined, for example, the parsing algorithm would have to fail to recognize that dative is not objective, incorrectly allow the passive rule to penetrate into the dative constituent, and finally fail to recognize that NP is not objective. Positing multiple errors of this sort within a single utterance seems highly implausible, not to mention unparsimonious. I think it can be concluded then that the standard analysis of passives provides a simpler, more satisfactory account of passive errors than the case approach. In this instance at least, the DRM as outlined earlier survives a test of the assumption it makes about the nature of the grammar of English. The more general point made by this exercise is that the grammar

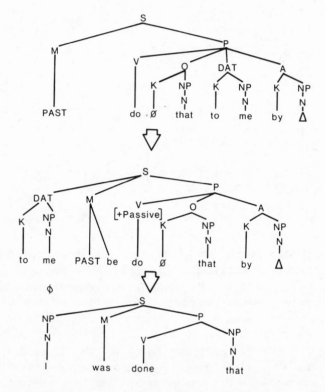

FIG. 14.8.   A derivation based on the erroneous application of the subject creation rule to the dative constituent.

incorporated into the DRM can be evaluated against plausible alternatives even on the basis of the rather scanty data presently available.

Consideration of alternative accounts of passive errors raises a methodological issue concerning the use of speech errors as data. Obviously, any model can account for any set of errors if no constraints are placed on the way in which the model can be perturbed to produce errors. For example, it was assumed above that a case grammar explanation of passive errors which relied on multiple errors should be ruled out. Likewise, in all of the derivations of errors under the DRM model we have allowed only one error to occur. The reason for this is simple, but fundamental. Unless some constraints are put on explanations of errors, they are vacuous. The requirement that a model must be able to explain an error by a single malfunction in performance is both a strong constraint and a reasonable one. It is strong enough to make it difficult to give an account of errors and thus to provide some explanatory power to those accounts. And it is a reasonable limitation given the low probabilities of multiple errors occurring in the same utterance.[7] The general point is that only by constraining theories of errors in some such way will they be falsifiable.

I have given an example of how the grammar assumed by the DRM can be evaluated against other grammars using speech errors. Is it possible also to evaluate the control processes incorporated into the DRM in this way? It turns out to be very difficult to do so given the type of data currently available. One can change the control processes substantially and get identical predictions about error types. For example, I have assumed that the parse of a phrase structure tree starts at the top and proceeds down left branches as deep into the tree as is necessary to find the appropriate node. Only after the node is not located on the path through left branches is any right branch searched. That is, the search is basically left-to-right.

Other search schemes are easily imagined (see Knuth, 1973). All those examined thus far, however, seem to make equivalent predictions about errors. To take one example, imagine that search through a tree is right-to-left, rather than the reverse. In the application of the passive rule to the tree in Fig. 14.4, for example, the rightmost element of the structural analysis of the passive rule, repeated here for convenience as (33), would be searched for first.

33. NP—AUX—V—(P)—NP

Search would proceed from the top of the tree down *right* branches to the NP that is object of the preposition. Next, a preposition would be sought and found on the left branch of the prepositional phrase. The tree pointer would then travel up to the VP node and, in the correct parse, down to the object NP looking for a verb. Since there is no verb, the backup procedure is called which straightens things out by reparsing the tree. However, if the parsing algorithm makes a branching error at the VP node, the tree pointer will find the V it is looking for. The passive rule will then be satisfied and it will apply, although incorrectly. In this way, the observed passive errors will be produced. Other types of tree search give the same result.

It appears then that the control processes do not yet carry much of an explanatory load in the DRM as outlined here. The apparent way to

---

[7]Since (1) independent errors should occur in the same utterance with a probability that is the *product* of the individual probabilities of occurrence; and (2) single syntactic errors seem to be quite infrequent, we should hardly expect to find any double errors at all. Hence, it seems appropriate, at this stage of investigation, to rule out accounts based on multiple errors. Of course, were reliable estimates of error rates available, more complex accounts would be viable as long as they correctly predicted relative frequencies of error types.

remedy this would be to expand the range of evidence used to test the model from observational data to experimental data. While this is a desirable step for obvious reasons, it is also one that raises difficult methodological problems. As is often observed, it is not at all clear how to approximate spontaneous speech in a controlled experimental setting. In any event, it appears that the evaluation of control processes is very much a task for the future.

This ends our discussion of the direct evaluation of the syntactic rules assumed by the DRM. I have attempted to show that clear tests may be made of the grammar realized by the DRM against both linguistic and performance data. The control processes are not so easily tested though, and their examination probably awaits the application of experimental methods to syntactic planning in speech production.

FURTHER EVIDENCE FOR THE DRM

The primary concern of this paper has been the nature of the syntactic operations carried out in the construction of an utterance. We have seen glimpses of the deep structures that these operations are applied to in the form of errors in which rules failed to deform the underlying structures in the normal fashion, thus unmasking the underlying order of elements.

If these underlying structures are really computational stages in speech production, then there should be independent evidence for their existence. By the same token, there should be other arguments for the existence of surface structure, which is the level that results from the application of all transformations. I conclude this paper by citing lines of investigation which back up the DRM on these points.

The effects of surface structure in speech production ought to be most apparent in the phonetic realization of an utterance. Cooper, Paccia, and LaPointe (1978) have investigated this possibility by examining the segmental durations of an utterance. They show that durations are controlled, at least in part, by the surface structure of an utterance. In particular, large breaks in surface constituent structure are coded in an utterance by the lengthening of the syllable immediately preceding the break. This is just what might be expected under the DRM. While other evidence for surface structure could be cited (Fay, 1975), the work of Cooper et al. is sufficient to indicate the way in which the DRM articulates with and is supported by other aspects of speech production.

Independent support for the deep structural assumption of DRM is much harder to come by. However, there is one piece of evidence that, while far from conclusive, suggests the existence of an underlying order that is different from surface order. The evidence comes from errors in spontaneous speech in which two words exchange positions in an utterance (Fay, 1975; Garrett, 1975). Actually, constituents at all levels of phrase structure, from word to sentence, undergo exchanges. Moreover, the exchanged constituents are of the same type—nouns exchange with nouns, verbs with verbs, and so on—showing that there is a labelled structure underlying an utterance at some stage in its construction.

The question that naturally arises is: What level of structure is disturbed by exchanges? It has been argued elsewhere that these errors occur at the level of surface structure (Fay, 1975). This is indicated by the fact that they must follow the application of certain transformations and must precede morphophonemic and phonological rules; were the errors to occur before transformations or after the phonological rules, they could not take the form they do.

While almost all of the errors in my corpus were of this sort, there was one that hinted at a deeper level of syntactic structure. This error is given in (34):

34. T: You don't know what you're in for.
    E: You don't know what's in for you.

A derivation of the target utterance is given in Table 14.9. As can be seen, subject–verb agreement is determined first. This is indicated by marking the verb [+2], which will cause the later morphophonemic rules to choose the second-person form of the verb. WH-fronting then moves a WH-word to the front of the indirect question. Affix hopping subsequently attaches the present-tense marker to the verb, which is eventually spelled out as *are* by morphophonemic rules.

It is important to note that subject–verb agreement must precede WH-fronting. This is because a WH-word that serves as a subject can be moved indefinitely far away from the verb that agrees with it. An example of this is shown in (35).

35. a. Which man does Bob believe Ted suspects ‗_____ loves Alice?
    b. Which men does Bob believe Ted suspects _____ loves Alice?

TABLE 14.9

You don't know (Q you PRES be in for WHAT)	Underlying form
You don't know (Q you PRES be[+2] in for WHAT)	Subject–verb agreement
You don't know (WHAT you PRES be[+2] in for)	WH-fronting
You don't know (WHAT you be[+2]+PRES in for)	Affix hopping
You don't know what you're in for.	Morphonemics

Observe that the verb *love* agrees in number with the WH-phrase which has been moved all the way to the front of the sentence. Were subject–verb agreement to follow WH-Fronting, it would be difficult to have the agreement rule pick out correctly the subject a verb is to agree with.

Consider now the error in (34). An account might be given of it as an error occurring at the level of surface structure (i.e., the level just before the application of morphophonemic rules in Table 14.9). The displacement of *you* to the end of the sentence could be explained quite simply. It is already known that quantifiers and adverbs float to new positions in an utterance (Fay, 1975); perhaps pronouns are to be added to this error type. But how can the verb marking be explained? The verb should have been marked to agree with its subject *you* at some stage earlier than surface structure as indicated in Table 14.9. Yet it agrees with *what* instead. The only apparent explanation for the utterance at the level of surface structure is to assume that two independent errors have taken place. First, *you* is displaced to the end of the sentence; then, subject–verb agreement incorrectly applies at surface level to change the verb to agree with *what*.[8] As was argued above, this kind of multi-error account is highly suspect.

There is a much simpler approach, one that assumes an underlying level of syntactic structure. A derivation of the error within this framework is given in Table 14.10. If we assume that two noun phrases, in this case *what* and *you*, can exchange places with each other not only at the surface level as suggested above, but also at an underlying level, before any transformations have applied, then all the properties of the error fall out automatically. In particular, the application of subject–verb agreement after the exchange explains why the Verb agrees with *what* rather than *you*. And the exchange itself explains why *you* goes to the position occupied by *what* in underlying structure, rather than to any other position. This latter fact is not explained at all in the surface structure account given above.

By assuming an underlying level of syntactic structure, it is possible to construct an explanation for this error that accounts for all of its properties. This can be done while positing the occurrence of only a single error. Moreover, there is no need to add pronoun displacement to the inventory of possible error types. The explanation offered here then, supports the assumption made by the DRM of a deep structure level

---

[8] Actually, it is not clear that subject–verb agreement would make the verb agree with *what*, since *what* is not in subject position. Rather, it is in complement position, a position to which the agreement rule does not refer. Thus, it may be that the surface structure account requires the existence of yet another error underlying the utterance in (34), an error in the application of subject–verb agreement.

TABLE 14.10

You don't know (Q you PRES be in for WHAT)	Underlying form
You don't know (Q WHAT PRES be in for you)	*Exchange error
You don't know (Q WHAT PRES be[+3] in for you)	Subject–verb agreement
You don't know (WHAT PRES be[+3] in for you)	WH-fronting
You don't know (WHAT be[+3]+PRES in for you)	Affix hopping
You don't know what's in for you.	Morphophonemics

underlying an utterance. From this evidence we can see that the syntactic processes of the DRM are anchored at both ends. The existence of both deep and surface structures is supported by evidence other than that which originally motivated the model.

CONCLUSION

I have tried to present the case for the DRM as a model of speech production. There is a certain amount of data directly in support of it, although by no means as much as might be desired. Moreover, it seems to provide a better account of the available data than at least one plausible alternative. In addition, key assumptions made by the model are supported by work on other aspects of speech production.

But perhaps the most appealing feature of the DRM is that it provides a partial solution to the problem of how the syntactic component of a grammar relates to the language user. If this solution is correct, it suggests many interesting extensions of the DRM into other areas of speech production, including phonological and phonetic processes, word formation, lexical access, and, of course, semantics. If these extensions support the framework outlined here, one can foresee the emergence of a comprehensive, yet detailed, model of speech production in the not-too-distant future.

REFERENCES

Akmajian, A., & Heny, F. *An introduction to the principles of transformational syntax.* Cambridge, Mass.: MIT Press, 1975.

Bach, E. *Syntactic theory.* New York: Holt, Rinehart, and Winston, 1974.

Baker, L. Stress level and auxiliary behavior in English. *Linguistic Inquiry,* 1971, *2,* 167–181.

Brame, M. *Conjectures and refutations in syntax and semantics.* Amsterdam: North-Holland, 1976.

Bresnan, J. A realistic transformational grammar. In M. Halle, J. Bresnan, & G. Miller (Eds.), *Linguistic theory and psychological reality.* Cambridge: MIT Press, 1978.

Chester, D. The translation of formal proofs into English. *Artificial Intelligence*, 1976, *7*, 261–278.

Chomsky, N. *Aspects of the theory of syntax*. Cambridge: MIT Press, 1965.

Chomsky, N. *The logical structure of linguistic theory*. New York: Plenum, 1955/1975.

Cooper, W., Paccia, J., & LaPointe, S. Hierarchical coding in speech timing. *Cognitive Psychology*, 1978, *10*, 154–177.

Emonds, J. *A transformational approach to english syntax: Root, structure-preserving and local transformations*. New York: Academic Press, 1976.

Fay, D. *Some investigations of grammatical category in performance devices*. Unpublished doctoral dissertation, University of Texas at Austin, 1975.

Fay, D. Transformational errors. In V. Fromkin (Ed.), *Errors of linguistic performance: Slips of the tongue, ear, pen, and hands*. New York: Academic Press, in press.

Fillmore, C. The case for case. In E. Bach & R. T. Harms (Eds.). *Universals in linguistic theory*. New York: Holt, Rinehart, and Winston, 1968.

Fodor, J., Bever, T., & Garrett, M. *The psychology of language*. New York: McGraw-Hill, 1974.

Freidin, R. The analysis of passives. *Language*, 1975, *51*, 384–405.

Friedman, J. *A computer model of transformational grammar*. New York: American Elsevier, 1971.

Fromkin, V. Speech errors as linguistic evidence. The Hague: Mouton, 1973.

Garrett, M. The analysis of sentence production. In G. Bower (Ed.), *Psychology of learning and motivation* (Vol. 9). New York: Academic Press, 1975.

Hausser, R. A theory of systematic deviants. In *Report to NSF: On the theory of transformational grammar*. Grant GS-2468, Emmon Bach and Stanley Peters, Principal Investigators, 1971.

Hollan, J. Features and semantic memory: Set-theoretic or network model? *Psychological Review*, 1975, *82*, 154–155.

Knuth, D. *The art of computer programming, Vol. 3: Sorting and searching*. Reading, Mass.: Addison-Wesley, 1973.

Lyons, J. *Introduction to theoretical linguistics*. London: Cambridge University Press, 1968.

Newell, A. and Simon, H. A. *Human problem solving*. Englewood Cliffs, N.J.: Prentice-Hall, 1972.

Oehrle, R. *The grammatical status of the English dative alternation*. Unpublished doctoral dissertation, Massachusetts Institute of Technology, 1975.

Partee, B. Montague grammar and transformational grammar. *Linguistic Inquiry*, 1975, *6*, 203–300.

Rips, L., Smith, E., & Shoben, E. Set-theoretic and network models reconsidered: A comment on Hollan's "Features and semantic memory." *Psychological Review*, 1975, *82*, 156–157.

Ross, J. R. *Constraints on variables in syntax*. Unpublished doctoral dissertation, MIT. Bloomington: Indiana University Linguistics Club, 1967.

Simmons, R., & Slocum, J. Generating English discourse from semantic networks. *Communications of the ACM*, 1972, *15*, 891–905.

Wasow, T. Transformations and the lexicon. In A. Akmajian, P. Culicover, & T. Wasow (Eds.), *Formal syntax*. New York: Academic Press, 1977.

Woods, W. Transition network grammars for natural language analysis. *Communications of the ACM*, 1970, *13*, 591–606.

15

The Latency and Duration of Rapid Movement Sequences: Comparisons of Speech and Typewriting*

Saul Sternberg

Stephen Monsell[1]

Ronald L. Knoll

Charles E. Wright
Bell Laboratories, Murray Hill, New Jersey

I. INTRODUCTION

We communicate verbal information in three principal ways: We write, we speak, and we use keyboards. Maximum information rates in speech and typing are higher than in writing (Seibel, 1972), and as more of our work uses computers, keyboard entry is becoming increasingly important. This chapter reports some new findings about the temporal patterns of rapid movement sequences in speech and typewriting and what these patterns might mean in relation to the advance planning or "motor programming" of such sequences. We shall be concerned with how response factors affect the time to initiate a prespecified rapid movement sequence after a signal (the "simple-reaction" time) when the goal is to complete the sequence as quickly as possible, as well as how such factors affect the rate at which movements in the sequence are produced.[2] The response factor of central interest will be the number of elements in the sequence.

Most existing research on skilled performance has been concerned with *perceptual*–motor skills. For example, in most studies of typing

---

*Reprinted, with permission, from G. E. Stelmach (Ed.), *Information processing in motor control and learning*. New York: Academic Press, 1978.
[1]Current address: Committee on Cognition & Communication, University of Chicago.
[2]Some similar questions about handwriting are addressed in Wing (1978).

behavior, performance has been measured when new segments of text are read concurrently with the typing of segments that have just been read (see, e.g., Butsch, 1932; Shaffer, 1976). Nonetheless, it has been argued that a major source of errors in typing is in the control of finger movements rather than in the perception of what is to be typed (see, e.g., Shaffer & Hardwick, 1969; Van Nes, 1976). Partly for this reason and partly because we believe it is desirable to study aspects of skilled performance in isolation, we have tried in these experiments on speech and typewriting to study movement processes uncontaminated by the concurrent perception of new material.

These studies began with two accidental findings (reported in Monsell & Sternberg, 1976). The first was that the number of words in a brief rapid utterance influenced the time to initiate the utterance, even though the talker knew what he would have to say well in advance of the reaction signal. This finding seemed surprising, particularly in view of the claim based on previous studies (Eriksen, Pollack, & Montague, 1970; Klapp, 1971, 1976) that the latency (or reaction time) for saying a single word, known in advance, is not affected by the number of syllables it contains. The second finding was that the functions relating the duration of these rapid utterances to the number of words they contained were concave upward rather than being linear, indicating that words in longer sequences were produced at slower rates.

Our interest in the effect of the length of a movement sequence on its latency was based partly on the possibility that it reflects a latency component used for advance planning of the entire sequence: The length effect would then measure the extra time required to prepare extra elements. The idea that changes in reaction time might reflect changes in *sequence preparation* in this way seems to have been first proposed by Henry and Rogers (1960), who found that simple-reaction time increased with the number of elements in a sequence of movements made with one arm. According to their model, part of the reaction time includes the time to gain access to stored information concerning the whole sequence: a process akin to loading a program into a motor buffer, with sequences containing more elements requiring larger programs, and larger programs requiring more loading time. Numerous studies have since been made of effects of factors such as the extent, duration, and "complexity" of arm and hand movements on their latency. Both simple-reaction and choice-reaction paradigms have been used. However, as indicated in the reviews of this work by Hayes and Marteniuk (1976) and by Kerr (1978), both paradigms have given rise to conflicting and controversial findings. We consider briefly three issues that are relevant to these conflicts and to the experimental methods we decided to adopt.

Element Invariance and
the Measurement of Response Complexity

One issue that arises in examining previous work is the proper index of response complexity. An increase in the extent or duration of a movement sequence may not necessarily increase the amount of planning required, as measured by the number of "instructions" or "subprograms" in a "program". (Once this issue is raised, it suggests an explanation for the contrast mentioned above: The latency of an utterance could be influenced by the number of words in the utterance but not by the number of syllables in a word if the "programming unit" was a suprasyllabic sequence such as a word or a stress group, rather than something smaller such as a syllable or an articulatory gesture.)

The aspect of response complexity we have manipulated in our experiments is the number of elements (spoken words, keystrokes) in a movement sequence, which we varied over a wide range (from one to five) relative to previous studies. To minimize the probability that effects of the number of elements in a sequence on its latency or duration are trivial consequences of differences in the elements themselves, we have tried to insure that the elements are as fixed as possible, regardless of the sequence in which they are embedded. Insofar as the approximation to this *element-invariance requirement* is a good one, the wide range enables us to study the form of the function relating latency to the number of elements, and to investigate the relation between the "programming units" and the elements we manipulate. In addition, insofar as the form of the function is simple (e.g., linear), the data would suggest that the invariance requirement is approximately satisfied.

Before leaving this issue it is helpful to be somewhat more precise about the requirement of element invariance. Let us divide elements in a sequence into four classes: interior elements (i) both preceded and followed by other elements, beginning elements (b), terminating elements (t), and single elements (s) neither preceded nor followed by others. Now consider the elements that are present in sequences of increasing length: s, bt, bit, $biit$, $biiit$. To study the form of the function relating latency (or duration) to the number of equivalent elements in a sequence, we can restrict ourselves to the *changes* in performance that result from equivalent *increases* in length, starting from a short sequence.

Suppose that we start with sequences of length $n = 2$. Then all increases in length can be regarded as resulting from the addition of i-elements. We therefore need to assume that i-elements are all equivalent. In addition, since elements already present must not change as we increase sequence length, all b-elements must be assumed equivalent regardless of sequence length, and similarly for t-elements. There is no need for b- and t-elements to be equivalent to i-elements or to each other. If we start with sequences of length $n = 1$ rather than $n = 2$, however, we must also assume the equivalence of s- and b-elements and of i- and t-elements (or, alternatively, of s- and t-elements and of i- and b-elements). One can imagine this requirement not being met, especially given the evidence, from speech, of bidirectional coarticulation effects (see Kent & Minifie, 1977). Insofar as our data cause us to question this equivalence, we must restrict our attention to the performance functions for $n \geq 2$.

Response Effects in Simple Reactions versus Choice Reactions

A second issue raised by previous work is whether choice reaction or simple reaction is the more appropriate paradigm for investigating the effects of the characteristics of a response on the planning of that response. One argument (e.g., Klapp, 1976) assumes that after sufficient practice one movement sequence (simple reaction) can be fully prepared in advance of the signal, but that more than one (choice reaction) cannot; therefore, choice-reaction latencies are more likely to reflect response-planning operations. However, there is little independent evidence favoring either of the assumptions. Certain response variations have been observed to produce larger effects on latency of the choice reaction, and this fact has been taken as evidence that advance planning between signal and response plays a larger role there than in the simple reaction. However, this inference depends on the idea that the only locus of response-factor effects is response planning; the inference is not justified if response factors also influence additional operations that might be required for choice reactions but not for simple reactions, such as "translation" from stimulus to response or "response selection."

There are two kinds of "compatibility" effects in the choice-reaction paradigm that suggest the influence of response factors on operations other than response planning. Consider first the finding that the latency of a particular response to a particular stimulus depends on the mappings of the other possible responses on the other possible stimuli (e.g., Duncan, 1977). This suggests that changes in latency produced by varying the attributes of a specified response to a specified stimulus are likely to depend on S–R (stimulus–response) mappings of other pairs—a dependence that might be hard to explain solely in terms of the planning of that response.

Consider second the effects of compatibility of entire stimulus and response ensembles ("SE–RE compatibility," as contrasted with the "S–R compatibility" of mappings of the same stimulus and response ensembles; Brainard, Irby, Fitts, & Alluisi, 1962): The change in latency induced by switching from one R-ensemble to another depends on the S-ensemble. This indicates that at least one of the processing stages between stimulus and response is influenced by the identities of both (Sternberg, 1969a, Sec. 5.3); hence, any effect of response factors might arise at least in part in that stage and could therefore depend on (interact with) stimulus factors—another dependence that might be hard to explain in terms of response planning.

Considerations like these not only weaken the argument just mentioned for using the choice-reaction paradigm, but also show that the effects of response (or stimulus) factors cannot be assigned conclusively to response (or stimulus) processes without suitable control experiments. While this caveat applies to simple- as well as choice-reaction paradigms, we believe the hazards to be greater in the choice situation, where it is likely that a more complex series of processes determines the latency and that stimulus-response interactions are larger. Indeed, in those studies we know of where the same variations in S–R mapping were examined in both choice-reaction and simple-reaction paradigms, S–R compatibility effects that were substantial in the former proved to be vanishingly small in the latter (Callan, Klisz, & Parsons, 1974; Anzola, Bertolini, Buchtel, & Rizzolatti, 1977).

Another consideration that arises in the choice-reaction paradigm is the possibility of effects of *response–response compatibility*. Evidence has been accumulating that the other possible responses in an experiment influence the latency of a specified response, not merely by virtue of their number, but also their kind. Thus, in the case of binary choice, the latency of a response is shorter if it is paired with another that could be performed at the same time (Berlyne, 1957), or that is performed by a finger on the opposite hand (Kornblum, 1965), or that involves a movement in the same direction (Megaw, 1972), or that contains the same initial phoneme (Sanders, 1970). Given the available evidence, these effects cannot be unequivocally distinguished from S–R or SE–RE compatibility and conclusively assigned to response processes. But insofar as similar effects are observed with arbitrary stimulus ensembles and arbitrary S–R mappings, an interpretation in terms of response processes is compelling. We believe that ultimately an account of the planning and execution of responses will have to explain R–R compatibility.[3] For the present, however, such considerations complicate the interpretation of response effects: In the choice-reaction paradigm, the influence of altering one of the responses on the latency of that response could depend on the identity of the other (not performed) response.

Our approach, then, has been to study the effects of sequence length on latency in the simple-reaction paradigm; we believe that contributions to these effects from stimulus discrimination and S–R translation processes are minimized in that paradigm, and it permits us to defer the issue of R–R compatibility. If under these conditions there remains an orderly dependence of latency on the nature and number of elements in the entire movement sequence, this dependence would seem particularly worth investigation, since there would appear to be fewer alternatives that compete with the hypothesis of advance planning of the entire sequence than in the choice-reaction paradigm. However, we do not wish to argue that just because we use the simple-reaction paradigm, any effects of response factors on latency can be immediately assigned to a response-planning process that occurs after the signal but before the start of the response. It is still necessary to pit this hypothesis against the promising alternatives that remain, such as delays associated with operations that are required to maintain a description of the response in short-term verbal memory, failure of the invariance requirement discussed above, or effects of sequence length on the time to retrieve the first element from a previously loaded motor-program buffer. Indeed, as we shall attempt to show, the results we have obtained thus far tend to favor a somewhat different hypothesis from the one that first attracted us to the problem.

Relation Between Advance Planning and Feedback Control

A third issue raised by previous work, and one that dominates much writing on motor processes, is the relation between the advance planning of a movement sequence and the influence of feedback during the execution of that sequence. Clearly the existence of any sensory delay requires that brief movement elements be controlled independently of the peripheral feedback they produce (e.g., Welford, 1974). The idea of a central motor

---

[3]A study by Rosenbaum (in press) can be regarded as a first attempt to provide a process model of R–R compatibility effects. He has argued, with experimental support, that under some conditions only the movement "features" not shared by the pair of responses in a binary choice-reaction task are prepared after the signal, whereas the features they do share are prepared before the signal. Note that "R–R compatibility" has usually been applied to simultaneously performed responses.

program for the control of entire sequences seems to have arisen from the observation that sensory delays were too great to permit feedback ("closed loop") control even from one element to the next, in rapid performance (e.g., Lashley, 1951; but see also Adams, 1976).

The "program" concept has been restricted in recent years by the idea that the *only* way organisms deal with limited feedback delays in executing rapid movements is to preplan entire sequences (e.g., Schmidt, 1972), rather than, for example, planning some movements concurrently with the execution of earlier movements. Thus, in his influential definition, Keele (1968; see also Russell, 1976) proposed that " a motor program may be viewed as a set of muscle commands that are structured before a movement sequence begins, and that allows the entire sequence to be carried out uninfluenced by peripheral feedback [p. 387]."

This definition has seemed to suggest to some investigators that advance planning generates only command sequences that can be executed without any feedback ("open loop"), rather than, for example, programs that include instructions for sensing and responding to feedback, programs that can themselves be altered in response to feedback, or even programs that consist of ordered sets of "response images" (e.g., Greenwald, 1970; Adams, 1976) to which feedback from the movement sequence is compared. Miles and Evarts (1979, Part 1) review evidence favoring the importance of feedback during "programmed" movement sequences.

We believe it is inappropriate to restrict the "program" concept to cases of sequence control without feedback. Suppose that for a particular kind of movement sequence we had a hierarchical analysis in terms of sequences of units, each consisting of a sequence of subunits, and so forth. At each level of the hierarchy, control would have to be exercized over the selection, sequencing, and timing of the subunits, as well as over other attributes. At each level of the hierarchy and for each attribute, separate and largely independent questions could be raised, first about the roles of central and sensory sources of feedback, and second, about the time relations between preparation and execution. Possible roles of feedback include, for example, serving as a cue that triggers the onset of the next subunit in a sequence, or providing information used in an error-correction process. Possibilities for the scheduling of preparation range from preparing each subunit after the previous one has been executed, through preparing later subunits while earlier ones are being executed, to preparing the whole sequence in advance.

We feel that questions about the existence and extent of advance planning are separable from questions about the precise role played by feedback, and we suspect that the methods appropriate for answering them are very different. In our view the experiments to be described in this chapter bear principally on the issue of the time relation between planning and execution.[4]

II. EXPERIMENTS ON SPEECH

With minor deviations, the procedure on each trial of the three speech experiments to be described was as follows: First a short list of digits or words was presented sequentially and visually, at a rate of about 1 sec per item. The lengths and compositions of the lists were varied from trial to trial by means of a different balanced randomization for each subject. The list was followed by a fixed delay of about 4 sec that subjects could use for rehearsing silently and preparing to respond. On about 85% of the trials a visual "recite signal" (an illuminated rectangle) appeared at the end of the delay. This signal was preceded at 1-sec intervals by two brief "countdown" signals (the first signal auditory, and the second visual), which were included to minimize the subject's time uncertainty about when he might be required to respond. On the remaining 15% of the trials the recite signal was omitted; subjects were not to respond on these "catch trials," which were included so as to prevent anticipations on signal trials.

Instructions, feedback, scores, and cash bonuses were designed to encourage subjects to *complete* the reciting of each list as soon as possible after the signal, while maintaining a low error rate. (The error rates were in fact negligible and will not be discussed.) The subjects were four female high school students who were well practiced in experiments requiring rapid reciting.

Using an energy-sensitive speech detector with a low threshold, we made two measures of each response: its *latency*, measured from signal onset to the start of the utterance, and its *duration*. (The subjects were attempting to minimize the sum of these two measures.) Each subject had about 200 trials per day.

Numbers in Ascending Sequence

In our initial studies we had used lists of randomly ordered letters or digits. We later observed the same effects with well-learned sequences that place a minimal load on memory. Thus, in the first experiment pre-

---

[4]The experiments on speech were selected from a larger series described in Monsell and Sternberg (1976) and to be reported in greater detail elsewhere by Monsell and Sternberg. The experiment on typewriting was selected from a series to be reported in greater detail elsewhere by Sternberg, Knoll, and Wright.

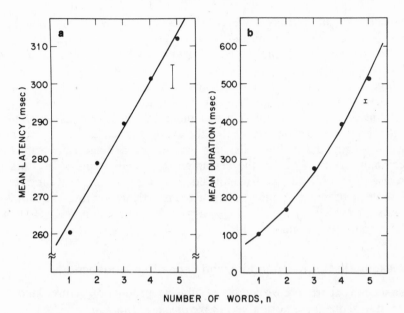

FIG. 15.1.   Ascending numbers experiment: The results are averaged over four subjects and over starting numbers; about 140 observations per point. a. Mean latencies, estimate of standard error ($\pm SE$), and fitted linear function (Table 15.1). b. Mean durations, estimate of $\pm SE$, and fitted quadratic function (Table 15.1). Note the difference between the ordinate scales. See Table 15.1, footnote (a), for the fitting procedures. The SE estimates in Figs. 15.1–15.6b were chosen to be appropriate for revealing badness of fit. They are therefore based on mean squares for high-order interactions from analyses of variance in which *subjects* was treated as a fixed effect. Table 15.1 appears on p. 493.

sented here the lists were subsequences of one to five items drawn from the natural number sequence 1, 2, ..., 9, and starting with one of the five nunbers 1, 2, ... , 5. On the single day of testing there were about seven trials per subject for each of the 25 possible lists.[5]

Figure 15.1a shows that mean latency increased approximately linearly with the number of words (n) in the list at a rate of 12.6 msec/word. Thus, the time to start saying *two–three–four–five–six*, for example, was about 50 msec greater than the time to start saying *two*. Latency functions were similar across starting digits (slopes of the fitted functions are 10.2, 10.1, 15.3, 14.0, and 13.3 msec/word for lists starting with 1, 2, 3, 4, and 5,

---

[5]A feature that distinguishes this experiment from our other experiments is that although beginning items are balanced in lists of different lengths, populations of interior and terminating items differ systematically across lengths, thereby violating the element-invariance requirement of Section I. This could bias the results somewhat, especially for duration data.

respectively) and across subjects (slopes are 10.1, 9.5, 19.4, and 11.3 msec/word for the four subjects). Linear regression accounts for 98.7% of the variance among mean latencies; deviations from linearity were not statistically significant.[6]

Figure 15.1b shows that the increase of duration with list length is distinctly nonlinear; the quadratic function shown fits well however, accounting for 99.8% of the variance among mean durations.[7] Acceleration of the duration function implies that the average articulation rate depends on list length: the longer a list, the greater the average time from the beginning of one word to the beginning of the next (this idea is made precise in Sec. V). Subjects responded well to the request that they complete their utterances rapidly: Their average articulation rate of about 9.4 words/sec is high relative to previously reported maximum rates (Hudgins & Stetson, 1937; Landauer, 1962).

Weekdays in Normal, Random, and Repeating Sequence

In a second experiment we compared subjects' production of three kinds of weekday sequences: normal (e.g., *Wednesday–Thursday–Friday–Saturday*), random, without replacement (e.g., *Monday–Friday–Wednesday–Sunday*), and repeating (e.g., *Monday–Monday–Monday–Monday*). The cyclic structure of the days of the week allowed us simultaneously to match populations of beginning words, terminating words, and interior words across list lengths (even in the familiar normally ordered lists) and across conditions. Lists contained from one to five words, and the two days of the experiment provided about 25 trials per length per condition per subject.

Mean latency (Fig. 15.2a) again increased approximately linearly with list length. Slopes of the fitted linear functions do not differ significantly across conditions. The average latency slope is actually *smaller* for weekdays (8.8 msec/word) than for digits (12.6 msec/word) despite their

---

[6]To test whether the latency effect could result from a small but increasing proportion of extreme observations with longer lists, we examined the latency distributions. Mean quantiles for each list length and mean standard deviations were obtained by averaging separate estimates from latency distributions for each subject and starting digit. The slopes of linear functions fitted to the mean 20% and 80% points of the distributions were 10.2 and 14.1 msec/word, respectively, indicating that the entire distribution, and not simply the upper tail, is affected by list length. The greater rate of change for the higher quantile reflects a small increase in dispersion with list length; mean standard deviations of latencies increase from about 22 msec ($n = 1$) to 30 msec ($n = 5$).

[7]We chose a quadratic function partly because of its success in describing other duration data for $1 \leqslant n \leqslant 5$. Although departures from the fitted quadratic function are small, they are statistically significant in this experiment (but not in the others to be reported). See footnote 5 for a possible explanation of this difference between experiments.

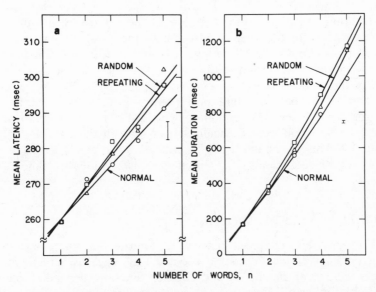

FIG. 15.2. Weekdays in normal, random, and repeating sequences: The results are averaged over four subjects; about 100 observations per point. a. Mean latencies, estimate of $\pm SE$, and fitted linear functions: normal, $259.9 + 7.8(n - 1)$; random, $259.9 + 9.6(n - 1)$; and repeating, $259.9 + 9.1(n - 1)$. b. Mean durations, estimate of $\pm SE$, and fitted quadratic functions: normal, $168.8 + 174.1(n - 1) + 8.6(n - 1)^2$; random, $168.8 + 174.0(n - 1) + 16.6(n - 1)^2$; and repeating, $168.8 + 201.2(n - 1) + 12.7(n - 1)^2$. The three fitted functions in each panel were constrained to pass through a common fitted value at $n = 1$.

greater syllabic length, but this between-experiment difference is not reliable.

Despite the similarity of latency functions, durations were, of course, much greater for lists of weekdays than for lists containing the same number of digits. Mean durations (Fig. 15.2b) are significantly nonlinear, but very well described by quadratic functions;[8] these functions differ significantly across conditions.

For understanding our results, the relation between the repeating condition and the others will be of particular interest. One way to make this comparison is to subtract from each coefficient of the fitted function for the repeating condition the mean of the corresponding coefficients for normal and random conditions. The resulting differences are 0.4 ± 0.9 msec/word for the slope of the latency function, 0.1 ± 4.0 msec/word^2 for

---

[8]The percentages of variance among the mean durations accounted for by fitted quadratic functions are 99.92, 99.96, and 99.98% for normal, random, and repeating conditions, respectively, and 99.99% for the means over conditions.

the quadratic coefficient of the duration function, and a significant 27.2 ± 3.2 msec/word for the linear coefficient of the duration function.[9] The only reliable effect of constructing an utterance from repetitions of the same word rather than from distinct words is to increase the linear coefficient of the duration function.

When we compare the duration function for numbers to the average function for the weekdays conditions (see Table 15.1), we find that the large duration difference is localized primarily in the constants (101.1 versus 168.8 msec) and linear coefficients (57.6 versus 183.1 msec/word). The quadratic coefficients (12.2 versus 12.6 msec/word^2) are almost identical.

Words of One and Two Syllables

Because they were produced in separate experiments, comparison of the data from number and weekday lists could only suggest whether and how the coefficients of the latency and duration functions depend on number of syllables per word. For more precise estimation of these effects we ran an experiment that was larger and that incorporated deliberate variation of word length.

Lists varied in length from one to four words; the words in a list were either all one-syllable words, or all two-syllable words. The vocabulary consisted of 72 common nouns, and was constructed so that all the two-syllable words were stressed on the first syllable and contained (an approximation to) one of the one-syllable words as the first syllable. (Examples of such embedded pairs are *bay–baby, rum–rumble, track–tractor, cow–coward,* and *limb–limit.*) Our aim was to bring our manipulation as close as possible to the addition of an unstressed syllable to a given stressed syllable. On each of the eight days of the experiment a subject worked with lists drawn from sets of nine words of each length that were changed from day to day; the sets were chosen so that a subject encountered the two members of any embedded pair on different days.

Each list was presented on three successive trials; because repetitions had little effect on either latency or duration, the data were averaged over repetitions. Each subject contributed about 12 observations per list length per word length per day.

Latency functions in this experiment (Fig. 15.3a) were significantly nonlinear, but since this is the only experiment among many, using lists of up to six words, in which we have observed such nonlinearity, we feel justified in describing the latency data in terms of parameters of the fitted linear functions. Slopes of these functions (in units of milliseconds per

---

[9]When quantities are stated in the form $a \pm b$, b is an estimate of the standard error of a, based on between-subject variability.

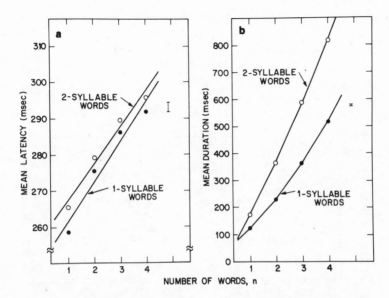

FIG. 15.3.   Experiment comparing words of one and two syllables: The results are averaged over four subjects and eight days; about 400 observations per point. a. Mean latencies, estimate of ± *SE*, and fitted linear functions (Table 15.1). b. Mean durations, estimate of ± *SE*, and fitted quadratic functions (Table 15.1).

word) for one- and two-syllable words are almost identical, confirming the suggestion derived from the other two experiments; the difference is 0.9 ± 1.1 msec/word. However, the *mean* latency was influenced to a small but statistically significant extent by number of syllables: Mean latency for lists composed of two-syllable words was 4.5 ± 1.3 msec longer. (Experiments by other investigators have perhaps not been sensitive enough to detect differences as small as this; hence the earlier claim of no effect.) In an idealized description of these data one can take the slope difference to be zero and assert, therefore, that the effects of syllables per word and words per list are *additive:* Each factor has the same effect regardless of the level of the other.

The relation between latency functions for the lists containing one- and two-syllable words is stable with increasing practice, as shown by Fig. 15.4. Both means and slopes decrease to what appear to be asymptotes, and while there is no consistent ordering of slopes across days, the mean latency for lists of one-syllable words is smaller on seven days out of eight.

As one would expect, and despite its small effects on latency, number of syllables had a large effect on the duration function (Fig. 15.3b). Data from both conditions are again well described by quadratic functions. The large duration difference is localized (see Table 15.1) primarily in the

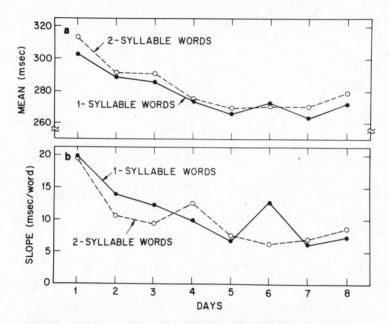

FIG. 15.4. Effects of eight days of practice on two aspects of latency (Fig. 15.3a) for lists of length one to four of one- and two-syllable words. a. Mean latency averaged over four list lengths, versus days; about 200 observations per point. b. Slope of fitted linear latency function, versus days.

constants (1-intercepts; 122.4 versus 173.4 msec) and linear coefficients (91.9 versus 180.4 msec/word); the quadratic coefficients (13.6 versus 12.0 $msec/word^2$, with a difference of 1.6 ± 0.9 msec/word^2) are almost identical, confirming the earlier findings.

Some Findings from Other Experiments

Here we list a few of our findings from other experiments that are especially pertinent to the interpretation of the latency effect.

Asymptote of the Latency Function. As the length of well-learned sequences is increased beyond about six words, the latency ceases to increase in an orderly manner and tends, instead, to fluctuate about an asymptotic value. (For novel sequences the range of the latency effect is of course limited in a different way: Once the immediate memory span is exceeded, both latency and error rate increase drastically.)

Insensitivity to an Additional Load on Short-Term Memory. In one experiment subjects memorized two lists on each trial: The first was to be recited rapidly, and the second was to be recited at a leisurely pace afterwards. The combined length of the two lists was never greater than five items. The presence and length of the second list had virtually no effect on the latency for reciting the first list (or on its duration). The latency therefore depends not on the load on short-term memory before or after the signal, but on the amount that must be said rapidly.

Invariance across Recite Signals of Different Modalities.   In an experiment comparing visual and auditory recite signals, the difference between slopes of the resulting latency functions for lists of one to five words was negligible and nonsignificant.

Invariance across Changes in Time Uncertainty.   In the experiments described here, we attempted to minimize subjects' time uncertainty about when the recite signal might occur by using fixed foreperiods and countdown signals. In an experiment in which this procedure was compared to one with a highly variable foreperiod, we found that although the increase in time uncertainty was effective, in the sense that it caused an increase in the mean of the latency function, the change in its slope was negligible and nonsignificant.

Effect of Interpolating Words without Primary Stress.   We have studied the effects of inserting unstressed connectives (*and, of, or*) between the successive nouns in a list, and of inserting words with little stress (*by, and, is a, minus*) between the successive (stressed) digits in a list. Neither of these operations increased the slope of the latency function (in milliseconds per noun or per digit) above its normal value; however, they did increase the mean latency. Thus, whether a list is augmented by extra unstressed syllables, or by separate words that carry little or no stress, the result is the same: There is a small increase in the mean, but no effect on the slope.

III. HYPOTHESES ABOUT THE LATENCY EFFECT

The findings presented thus far provide us with two principal facts to be explained. First, the latency for rapid reciting of a prespecified utterance increases approximately linearly and at a rate of about 10 msec/word (or primary stress), over a range of one to five words. Second, over the same range, the more words in the utterance, the slower the rate at which it is recited. We begin with a discussion of some of the alternative hypotheses that we have considered for the latency effect and that have guided our experiments.

Time Sharing: Readiness versus Rehearsal

The first two hypotheses reflect the possibility that the latency effect results from the load imposed by lists of increasing length on a short-term memory store, as traditionally conceived.[10] Suppose that while the subject awaits the signal he divides his time between maintaining his memory of the list (by covert rehearsal, for example), and being ready to respond to the signal. If the reaction signal occurs when he is in the *maintenance state,* then it takes time to shift into the *ready state.* Increasing the list length may increase either the proportion of time spent in the maintenance state or the time taken to switch out of it. Given this hypothesis, and assuming that the subject has control over which state he is in, one would expect that increasing the time uncertainty associated with the reaction signal would make it more likely that the subject was in the maintenance state when the signal occurred and would thus increase the size of the latency effect (indexed by the slope of the latency function). The invariance of the slope, found when time uncertainty was manipulated experimentally, argues against this hypothesis. (In addition, the subjects asserted that they were not consciously rehearsing as the time approached when the signal might be presented.)

Capacity Sharing and the Load on Short-Term Memory

A related possibility is that the longer the list, the more of a limited "capacity" (rather than time) has to be devoted to maintaining it in memory, and this reduces the capacity available for either processing the recite signal or having the first item ready. Several of our findings argue against this hypothesis (as well as the previous one). First, the similarity of latency functions for weekdays in normal, random, and repeating sequences shows that the capacity required to retain the list in memory is unimportant. Second, Baddeley, Thomson, and Buchanan (1975) have shown that the limit on the number of unrelated words that can be retained in short-term memory can be described in terms of the time it takes to say those words, so that brief words require less of the memory capacity than long words. Yet we have shown that the slope of the latency function is independent of word duration. Finally, by using an auxiliary memory load, we showed that increasing the number of words to be maintained in short-term memory, without changing the number to be recited fast, does not influence the latency.

---

[10]Here and elsewhere (where we use the term "ordinary short-term memory") we refer to the "short-term store" of Atkinson and Shiffrin (1968), or "primary memory" (see, e.g., Craik & Levy, 1976; Crowder, 1976).

Competition among Distinct Response Elements

According to the element-competition hypothesis, adequate preparation for the reaction signal requires that all the distinct elements from which the response is to be constructed be mentally "primed" or "activated" before the response begins (Lashley, 1951; Wickelgren, 1969). Suppose that all the primed elements then compete with any element that has to be produced, and that competition increases latency. The first element in a longer list has more competitors and hence a longer latency. Such a mechanism is particularly appealing because it can also readily explain the finding that the average rate at which the elements in longer lists are produced is lower. This hypothesis can be rejected on the basis of the typical latency effect found in the repeated weekdays condition, where list length was increased not by enlarging the set of *types* (and hence the number of *distinct* elements to be primed), but by adding to the number of *tokens* of the same type. Insofar as the primed elements are smaller than words, the absence of an effect of syllables per word on the latency-function slope can also be taken as negative evidence.

Information Transmitted

A fourth hypothesis is based on the observation that the amount of selective information in the response, in the sense of Shannon (see Garner, 1962), increases with the length of the list. Suppose that even though the list is specified in advance, the subject must resolve response uncertainty in selecting what to say at the time of response initiation. According to one version of this hypothesis (*sequence uncertainty*), the list must be selected from the set of all lists of the same length drawn from the same vocabulary. According to another version (*first-item uncertainty*), the first word must be selected from among all the words in the list. Under either version, if latency increased with the amount of information transmitted by the response, one would expect that for random lists, latency would increase with length. However, since an increase in the number of *repeated* words should not cause a corresponding increase in the amount of information, results from the weekdays experiment argue against this hypothesis.

Sequence Preparation (Version 1): Motor-Program Construction or Activation

According to the final and, we think, the most acceptable pair of hypotheses among those we consider, a representation of the entire response appropriate for controlling its execution (a *program*) is constructed before the response starts. The program consists of a set of linked *subprograms*, one for each *unit* of the response. The measure of the length of the program is the number of subprograms it contains. We suppose that the program is retained in a special *motor-program buffer* that is distinct from ordinary short-term memory. This memory state (or code, or structure) is not sensitive to factors such as familiarity of the response, similarity or identity among its elements, its duration as such, or the extent to which short-term memory is otherwise occupied.

The first version of the sequence-preparation hypothesis is in the spirit of the "memory drum" model proposed by Henry and Rogers (1960): Either part or all of a process by which the program is constructed, or else a process of activating a previously constructed program (by "loading" it, for example), is not (and perhaps cannot be) started before the signal. Furthermore, this process is completed before the response begins, and has a duration that increases linearly with the number of units in the list. Either the duration of the process is independent of subprogram length, or subprogram length is independent of unit size; otherwise we would have seen an effect on the latency slope of syllables per word.

Why should a process of program construction or activation not be completed *before* the signal, when the subject knows in advance exactly what has to be said? We offer two speculative reasons:

1. Constructing or activating a motor program might be inherently tied to its execution: Once the program is ready to be used, execution follows automatically and is hard to inhibit. If the preparation process took place before the signal, the subject would then respond on catch trials. To avoid this, preparation must await the signal. If program activation involved loading the program into a delay-line memory, for example, and execution occurred when the information emerged at the other end of the delay line, the system would have the required property that activation causes execution.

2. The contents of the motor buffer might be subject to rapid decay, in which case the program would have to be set up immediately before use. (Furthermore, processing of the reaction signal might interfere with maintenance of information in the motor buffer.)[11]

---

[11]Neurophysiologists have argued that parts of the nervous system that may be implicated in the sequencing and timing of rapid movements can retain information only briefly. Also, certain neural structures, such as the parallel fibers in the cerebellum, appear to function as delay lines—though the delays they generate may be too short for present purposes (see Kornhuber, 1974; Eccles, 1969).

Sequence Preparation (Version 2): Subprogram Retrieval

According to the second version of the sequence-preparation hypothesis, the construction and any necessary activation of the program as a whole are accomplished before the signal. However, only after the signal occurs is the subprogram for the first unit retrieved or located in the program. Mean retrieval time increases linearly with the number of subprograms contained in the buffer. This could arise because the retrieval is accomplished by means of a sequential search (analogous to mental search processes that have been proposed for other domains; e.g., Sternberg, 1969b) through the set of subprograms or through a directory of subprogram "addresses." Alternatively, retrieval time could increase with the number of subprograms because capacity has to be shared between a parallel search or a direct access process, and maintenance of the motor program; the property of linearity is less readily associated with such mechanisms, however. Possible reasons why retrieval of the first subprogram might have to await the signal are similar to the two reasons given above.

The retrieval version of the sequence-preparation hypothesis has a feature not shared with Version 1: It not only explains the latency effect, but also leads naturally to an account of the slower production rate for longer lists, if the same retrieval mechanism is assumed to apply to each of the other units in the list as to the first. Insofar as the relations between latency and duration data are consistent (inconsistent) with such an account, they support the retrieval (activation) version.

Suppose, for example, that the mechanism responsible for the length effect is a simple search process.[12] Then there are two obvious ways in which latency and duration might be related. If the same set of subprograms is searched, regardless of how many units have already been produced, then we expect that the mean time between the production of one unit and the next will increase linearly and at the same rate with list length as the latency does. On the other hand, if the contents of the buffer shrink as the response proceeds, then it is easy to show that the mean time between one unit and the next (averaged over the list) will again increase

---

[12]The idea that in proceeding through a set of linked subprograms a search is used (rather than a process involving direct access by one subprogram to the next) would be superfluous if subprograms were stored in the same order in which they were to be used. An example of a theory of the control of serial order that is more congenial to the search idea is Wickelgren's (1969) context-sensitive associative theory of speech production, whose units could be stored in a random order and still support an ordered serial response, because each unit is stored with tags that indicate the preceding and following units.

linearly, but at half the rate at which the latency increases. [These statements are valid without further assumptions if the search process is
exhaustive (Sternberg, 1969b); if it is *self-terminating* they depend on the
order of search meeting certain requirements.] A similar argument can be
made if the mechanism is based on capacity sharing; in that case we have
a variety of element competition (see Sec. III) that applies to identical as
well as distinct elements. We shall consider the duration data below, in
light of these issues.

IV. ELABORATION OF THE SEQUENCE-PREPARATION HYPOTHESES

Nature of the Programming Unit in Speech

Both versions of the sequence-preparation hypothesis incorporate the
idea that the response latency increases by some amount for each part
(subprogram) of the motor program, where each subprogram controls one
of the *units* in the response.[13] What is the nature of these response units?
(They need not correspond to what we have called *elements*—convenient
but arbitrary response segments.) Recall that variation in the number of
syllables per word had no effect on the latency increment per word. Since
this manipulation indirectly alters the duration of a word, the number of
articulatory gestures it contains, and the number of syllables, the unit
cannot be a *speech segment of specified duration*, the *articulatory gesture*, or the *syllable*. Two of the remaining alternatives are the *word*, and
the *stress group* or "*metric foot*" (a segment of speech associated with a
primary stress). We have seen that the increase in latency with list length
depends on the number of words in the list with primary stress and not on
whether other words, with little or no stress, are inserted. Our present
conclusion is that each subprogram controls a stress group, and we shall

---

[13]An alternative possibility for the construction version of the hypothesis is that the
latency depends on the length of a higher-level program from which the motor program is
constructed. Consider the following analogy: There is a "source program" (e.g., a series of
coded representations in short-term memory) and an "object program" (the motor program)
that is compiled from it and held in the motor buffer. Compiling requires fetching source
units, translating them, and sending the resulting object units. Object units need not correspond one to one with source units. The rate of compiling could primarily reflect the rate of
fetching, the rate of translating, or the rate of sending. In the construction version of the
hypothesis, we cannot assign the latency effect unambiguously to one of these. Thus, the
latency might, for example, depend on the number of words (a possible source unit) or the
number of stress groups (a possible object unit). For the activation or retrieval versions of
the hypothesis, however, the latency effect should reflect object units.

tentatively assume this in the following sections. The fact that the unit that underlies performance in our experiments appears to be articulatory rather than semantic seems to us to support further the interpretation of the latency effect in terms of a motor program.

A Basis for the Syllables Effect

We have seen (Sec. II) that although there was no effect on the latency-function *slope* (in milliseconds per stress group) of increasing the number of syllables per word or of inserting unstressed words, these operations did add an approximately constant increment to the latency for lists of each length, thereby increasing the latency-function *mean*. How can this increase be explained in the context of the sequence-preparation hypotheses? One possibility is that whereas activation (of the entire program) or retrieval (of the first subprogram) is completed in a time determined by the number of units, each unit has to be further *unpacked* into its constituents (syllables or articulatory gestures, for example) before it can be executed. Unpacking can be regarded either as advance planning or as retrieval, at a lower level of the response hierarchy.

Suppose that duration of the unpacking process increases with the *size* (number of constituents or duration) of a unit. Since only the first unit must be unpacked before the utterance begins, the unpacking operation prolongs the latency by the same amount for all list lengths. The latency function therefore increases in mean, but not in slope, when we increase the unit size. One implication that could be used to test the unpacking idea is that for a list of specified length whose units are of mixed size, the latency should depend only on the size of the first unit.

V. ANALYSIS OF THE DURATION FUNCTION

Quantitative Representations for Duration Data

Our second principal finding is that the duration function accelerates with sequence length, which suggests that the average interval between the starting times of successive elements is greater for longer sequences; this property also characterizes typewriting (see Sec. VI). We have seen in Section III that the quantitative characterization of the duration effect may help to select among alternative hypotheses for the latency effect. In the present section we introduce some concepts and notation that will facilitate the analysis and comparison of duration data in speech and typing.

The existence of the duration effect suggests that it might be useful to examine the individual time intervals between successive elements that add together to generate the observed duration. Such examination, however, requires measuring the interval between single time points associated in an invariant manner with individual elements (a *measurement-invariance requirement*); this is difficult in experiments involving rapid speech, but easy for typewriting, where the exact time of each key depression can be readily determined.[14] Let these times in a sequence of length n be $T_{1n}, T_{2n}, \ldots, T_{nn}$, with the reaction signal specifying the time origin so that T_{1n} is the latency, L_n. (Note that if we regard each response element as *ending* with the key depression, then the measured latency in typing incorporates the duration of the first element, unlike the latency measure in speech, which does not incorporate the duration of the first word.) The $n - 1$ time intervals between successive elements are then $T_{2n} - T_{1n}, T_{3n} - T_{2n}, \ldots, T_{nn} - T_{n-1, n}$, which we denote $R_{2n}, R_{3n}, \ldots, R_{nn}$, respectively. A useful measure of production rate that can be estimated from the duration, $D_n = T_{nn} - T_{1n}$ of an entire sequence of length n, and which is easy to relate to the $n - 1$ time intervals between successive elements, is the *mean* such time interval,

$$R_{.n} = \frac{1}{n-1} \sum_{k=2}^{n} R_{kn} = \frac{1}{n-1} \sum_{k=2}^{n} (T_{kn} - T_{k-1,n}) = \frac{1}{n-1} (T_{nn} - T_{1n})$$

$$= \frac{1}{n-1} D_n \quad (n \geqslant 2) \tag{15.1}$$

We use R because $R_{.n}$ and R_{kn} are measures of *rate;* note, however, that they denote time per response element, not elements per unit time.

The rate function $R_{.n}$ provides an alternative representation of duration data that has some useful properties. First, if D_n increases as a quadratic function of length, then, as we shall see below, $R_{.n}$ increases linearly.[15] This simplicity of form, together with the fact that $R_{.n}$ has a smaller range of variation than D_n, makes any systematic deviations from the fitted function more apparent and facilitates comparisons between functions. In addition, in those instances where the duration variance

---

[14]As a starting point, one can decompose the movement sequence in typing a list of letters into a series of elements, each ending at the moment a key depression is detected. Then, by definition, the single measured time point always marks the end of a movement element, and so the requirement of an invariant relation between time point and element is satisfied. It is possible, however, that this initial decomposition of the movement sequence is not the best one theoretically, even though it facilitates measurement; one test is whether the data are orderly and easily interpretable. We believe that for the movement sequences in rapid speech, the appropriateness of any particular decomposition is even less obvious.

[15]An alternative measure with this property, but less desirable in other respects, is the first difference function, $D_n - D_{n-1}$, which is similar to the derivative.

increases most dramatically with n, we have observed the $R_{.n}$ variances to be more homogeneous.

Estimation of $R_{.n}$ as defined in Equation 15.1 is straightforward for typing data, but to apply that definition to our speech experiments the duration measures first need correction. Let T^*_{kn} and T_{kn} represent, respectively, the starting and ending times of the kth word in a response of length n. For the response as a whole, the measured starting time T^*_{1n} (appropriate for a measure of latency) and the measured ending time T_{nn} do not mark corresponding points in the first and last response elements; these measures therefore fail to meet the measurement-invariance requirement mentioned previously in this section.

Let us identify the *end* of each word as the desired (invariant) time point. Then the measured duration $D^*_n = T_{nn} - T^*_{1n}$ includes not only the sum $D_n = T_{nn} - T_{1n}$ of the $n - 1$ intervals from the end of one word to the end of the next, but also the time $T_{1n} - T^*_{1n}$ from the start to the end of the first word. To estimate D_n from D^*_n we must therefore subtract an estimate of this extra time. If we assume that the duration of the first word is independent of n, then $D^*_1 = T_{11} - T^*_{11}$ provides the desired estimate, so that $D_n = D^*_n - D^*_1$, and we have

$$R_{.n} = \frac{1}{n-1}D_n = \frac{1}{n-1}(D^*_n - D^*_1) \qquad (n \geqslant 2) \qquad (15.2)$$

If D_n is actually quadratic, but the duration of the first word depends on n, then it is likely that D^*_n would differ systematically from a fitted quadratic function and that $R_{.n}$ would be systematically nonlinear. (A dependence of the duration of the first word on n, particularly on $n = 1$ versus $n > 1$, could come about from failure of the element-invariance requirement discussed in Sec. I.) Note that Equation 15.2 can be regarded as a generalization of Equation 15.1; in a case such as typewriting, $D^*_1 = 0$, so $D_n = D^*_n$.

Now let us consider a quadratic duration function, as fitted to the data in Figs. 15.1b, 15.2b, and 15.3b:

$$D^*_n = \alpha + \beta(n - 1) + \gamma(n - 1)^2 \qquad (n \geqslant 1) \qquad (15.3)$$

We have written D^*_n as a function of $n-1$ rather than n because the parameter α then represents D^*_1 (which is zero for the case of typewriting) and because the rate and duration functions are then related in a simple way; from Equations 15.2 and 15.3 we get

$$R_{.n} = \beta + \gamma(n - 1) \qquad (n \geqslant 2) \qquad (15.4)$$

Thus, a quadratic duration function implies a linear rate function: The quadratic coefficient, γ, in D^*_n represents the amount by which the average interval between one element and the next increases for each element added to the response, whereas the linear coefficient, β, represents a "base" value of the average interelement time, to which the successive increments are added. If the duration function were linear, we would have $\gamma = 0$, and the rate function would then be a constant.

Analysis of Durations in Experiments on Speech

Latency and duration functions that were fitted to the data from the three speech experiments are summarized in the top four lines of Table 15.1. As already noted, the quadratic coefficients in the four duration functions are remarkably similar in magnitude, despite substantial differences in word duration. This implies that the rate at which the mean time between successive words increases with sequence length is the same for words containing different numbers of syllables. To reveal this more clearly, we have displayed the observed and fitted rate functions $R_{\cdot n}$ for our third experiment (see Fig. 15.6a). When we describe the production rate as a function of the number of words (rather than, for example, the number of syllables), the two rate functions are almost perfectly parallel, just as for the latency functions (see Fig. 15.3a), despite their considerable difference in mean: The slope difference between the fitted functions is only 1.6 ± 0.9 msec/word.[16] That is, the effects on the mean time between successive words of the number of syllables per word and the number of words in the response are almost perfectly additive: The first term, β, depends only on word length, whereas the second term, $\gamma(n - 1)$, depends only on number of words. The simplicity of our results, when described in this way, supports the view that it is the number of words or stress groups in the response, not the number of syllables or articulatory gestures, that determines the decline in production rate with response length—the same response unit that we have seen (in Sec. IV) to be implicated in the growth of latency.

The results in Table 15.1 also show that the rate and latency effects— measured by the parameters γ and θ, respectively—are remarkably close in magnitude. This is consistent with the proposal that the two effects are actually the same and are generated by a common mechanism, as is assumed in the subprogram-retrieval version of the sequence-preparation hypothesis with a nonshrinking buffer (Sec. III). However, although similar in many ways, our results from measurements of typewriting force us to question the generality of identical effects.

---

[16]Both sets of data are slightly concave downward and, although we have not found this to be true in all our speech experiments, we have observed this effect often enough to make us suspect that it is real. Examination of the first differences, $D_n - D_{n-1}$ makes us suspect that the nonlinearity of $R_{\cdot n}$ results from a violation of the element-invariance requirement (see Sec. I) which causes the estimation error discussed in Section V: The measured duration, D_1^*, of a single isolated word may be somewhat longer than the duration of the first word in a list that contains more than one word.

TABLE 15.1
Fitted Latency and Duration Functions from Four Experiments[a]

Experiment or Condition	Latency Function $L(n) = \eta + \theta(n-1)$	Duration Function $D(n) = \alpha + \beta(n-1) + \gamma(n-1)^2$
Speech		
Ascending numbers	$263.3 + 12.6(n-1)$	$101.1 + 57.6(n-1) + 12.2(n-1)^2$
Weekdays (mean)	$259.9 + 8.8(n-1)$	$168.8 + 183.1(n-1) + 12.6(n-1)^2$
Monosyllabic nouns	$261.5 + 11.1(n-1)$	$122.4 + 91.9(n-1) + 13.6(n-1)^2$
Disyllabic nouns	$267.4 + 10.1(n-1)$	$173.4 + 180.4(n-1) + 12.0(n-1)^2$
Typewriting		
Alternating hands	$229.7 + 14.9(n-2)$	$71.9(n-1) + 15.2(n-1)^2$
One hand	$231.2 + 4.1(n-2)$	$142.9(n-1) + 14.1(n-1)^2$

[a] Values are in milliseconds. The element count, n, represents the number of words (speech experiments) or the number of letters (typing experiment) in the response. Parameters θ and η of $L(n)$ were fitted by least squares to data for $n \geq 1$ (speech) or for $n \geq 2$ (typing). Estimates of β and γ were determined by least-squares fitting of a line to the rate function R_n. For speech, the constant α was then determined by least-squares fitting of a quadratic function with specified β and γ; for typing, α was set at zero, corresponding to the measured duration of a single response.

VI.   AN EXPERIMENT ON TYPEWRITING

For several reasons, we decided to study the sequences of rapid finger movements in typewriting using essentially the same paradigm as in the speech experiments. First, typing readily permits measurement of the individual time intervals between successive response elements, in addition to overall response duration. Second, although potential artifacts due to measurement error may never be entirely eliminated, they are at least likely to be different in typing than in speech. In speech, for example, measurement delays might be influenced by loudness, sequence length might influence the volume of air in the lungs, and it is difficult to apply an objective criterion of response accuracy. These problems are obviously not critical in typing, but others might be, such as variations in the starting position of the hands or in the movements used to press a particular key. Third, we wished to see to what extent our findings generalized to a very different performance with a different training history. It can be argued that the production of a spoken word is much more complex than the pressing of a key, because it requires the exquisitely precise timing and coordination of a large number of diverse muscle systems that control respiratory, laryngeal, and multiple articulatory mechanisms (see, e.g., Kent & Moll, 1975; MacNeilage & Ladefoged, 1976). Furthermore, while normal speech rates are far slower than those obtained in our experiment, typists are trained to achieve high rates outside the laboratory.

Procedure

The procedure was similar to that used in the speech experiments. On each trial a row of from one to five different letters was first displayed for 1.0 sec. The display was followed by a fixed delay of 2.4 sec. On 80% of the trials a brief tone burst occurred at the end of the delay, signalling the subject to start typing the letter list. This reaction signal was preceded at 0.7-sec intervals by two brief noise bursts, which served as "countdown" signals. Keypress responses on the remaining 20% of the trials, on which the reaction signal was omitted, were regarded as errors. Again, the procedure was designed to encourage subjects to complete their responses as soon as possible after the signal while maintaining a low error rate. (The mean percentage of trials on which errors occurred was 2.3%; these few errors will not be considered further.) The time recorded for the depression of a key was determined by when it was detected by an electronic keyboard.[17]

Each letter list was presented on three successive trials; because repetitions had little effect on either latency or duration, the data were averaged over repetitions. Lengths and compositions of the lists were varied from one group of three trials to the next by means of a different balanced randomization for each subject.

Since Lahy's (1924) pioneering "Motion Study in Typewriting" and similar work reported by Coover (1923), it has been known that letter bigrams that are typed by fingers on alternate hands can be produced at faster rates than bigrams typed by fingers of the same hand. To explore responses containing elements whose durations differed, as we did in speech by manipulating the number of syllables per word, we used pure one-hand sequences in some blocks of trials and pure alternating-hand sequences in others; in both conditions, left and right hands were used equally often. All sequences were drawn from the same 16 letters, and average bigram frequencies in English were equated in the two conditions; we used only bigrams that actually occur in English.

The subjects were four female professional typists employed at Bell

---

[17]Our keyboard had "N-key rollover," which permits it to detect a keypress with a negligible delay after it occurs, regardless of whether other keys remain depressed (see Kallage, 1972).

Laboratories, with test rates in prose typing of about 90 words per minute (or about 7.5 strokes per second). The data to be presented were obtained on two days of testing, after one day of practice with the same types of material. During the two days, each subject provided about 50 observations for each of the five list lengths per condition.

Latencies of Typing Responses

Figure 15.5a and Table 15.1 show that response latency again increased with sequence length, but in a different manner in the two conditions. The nonlinearity (latency for $n = 1$ falls below a fitted line) that is present in both sets of data is significant for the one-hand condition only. We have chosen to fit linear functions to the data for $2 \leqslant n \leqslant 5$ in both cases, however, to achieve comparability and because the standard error of the slope for the alternating-hand data, based on between-subject differences, is reduced by a factor of 2 when L_1 is omitted.[18] To emphasize the omission of L_1, in Table 15.1 we represent the fitted lines as functions of $n - 2$ instead of $n - 1$; the constant terms then represent intercepts at $n = 2$. Despite the irregularity of the function for the one-hand condition, estimated slopes are very similar across subjects: The mean and standard error are 4.1 ± 1.3 msec/letter for this condition (significantly greater than zero) and 14.9 ± 1.7 msec/letter for the other, with a difference of 10.8 ± 1.8 msec/letter that is highly significant.

Why should either of our latency functions show a discontinuity between a single keystroke and multiple keystrokes? And why should such an effect occur more strongly in typing than in speech? One possibility is that as sequence length is changed from $n = 1$ to $n = 2$, the response elements fail to satisfy the element-invariance requirement (see Sec. I). In particular, a single keystroke may not be equivalent to either a beginning or terminating keystroke, especially in the one-hand condition. One possible reason for the contrast with our speech data is that while the production of even a single monosyllabic word typically involves multiple articulatory gestures and therefore requires precise control over timing and coordination, this may be true only of sequences of two or more keystrokes, because of the relative simplicity of a single keystroke.

There is no reason to believe that the letter strings in the two conditions place systematically different loads on ordinary short-term memory; the difference between the latency functions therefore provides further evidence against the time-sharing and capacity-sharing hypotheses discussed in Section III.

---

[18]In a replication of this experiment with different subjects we obtained similar results.

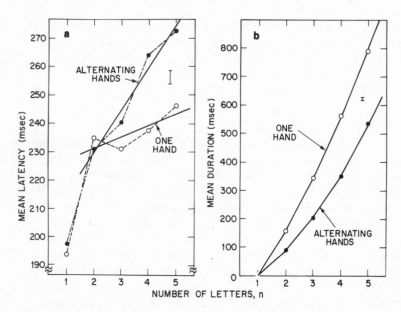

FIG. 15.5. Typewriting of lists of letters typed by fingers on alternating hands and by fingers on one hand only: The results are averaged over four subjects; about 200 observations per point. a. Mean latencies, estimate of $\pm SE$, and linear functions fitted to data for $n \geq 2$ (Table 15.1). b. Mean durations, estimate of $\pm SE$, and fitted quadratic functions (Table 15.1).

Response Durations and Interstroke Intervals

Both duration functions, shown in Fig. 15.5b, are significantly nonlinear but are well described by the fitted quadratic functions, in remarkable agreement with the speech data. Our subjects responded well to the exhortation that they complete their responses quickly: In the alternating-hands condition they produced about 9.3 strokes per second—a higher rate for these meaningless letter strings than they averaged in continuous prose. As expected, the one-hand condition produced substantially longer durations, but as in speech, element duration appears not to affect the quadratic coefficients. The rate functions in Fig. 15.6b again make the simplicity of the duration data more apparent and facilitate comparison to the speech data in Fig. 15.6a. The fitted linear functions that describe both sets of typing data so well are separated by about 70 msec and are almost perfectly parallel, with a mean slope difference of only 1.0 ± 2.5 msec/ letter. Thus, the effects on the mean time between successive strokes of the number of strokes and of the nature of the transition from one stroke to the next are almost perfectly additive. More experiments are needed before we can interpret the similarity of rate-function slopes in milliseconds per keystroke for typing and milliseconds per stress group for speech.

For the alternating-hands condition we observed still another property of the speech data that also characterizes typing: The sizes of the latency and rate effects, measured by the parameters θ and γ, respectively, are very similar, with $\hat{\gamma} - \hat{\theta} = 0.3 \pm 5.1$ msec/keystroke. However the conjecture that the two effects are in general mediated by the same mechanism, supported by these data as well as by the results from the speech experiments, is called into question by the one-hand data, where we observe a significant difference of $\hat{\gamma} - \hat{\theta} = 10.1 \pm 3.0$ msec/keystroke between these measures of the rate and latency effects. More work is needed to decide

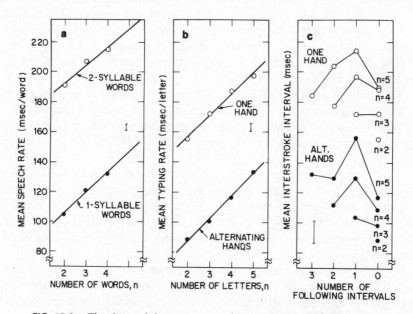

FIG. 15.6. Time intervals between successive response elements in speech and typing. a. Rate functions (mean interval versus response length) for speech and estimate of $\pm SE$. Fitted lines: $91.9 + 13.6(n - 1)$ for one-syllable words and $180.4 + 12.0(n - 1)$ for two-syllable words. The data are from Fig. 15.3b. b. Rate functions for typing and estimate of $\pm SE$. Fitted lines: $71.9 + 15.2(n - 1)$ for letter lists typed with alternating hands and $142.9 \pm 14.1(n - 1)$ for letter lists typed with one hand only. Data are from Fig. 15.5b. c. Mean interstroke interval for each serial position in letter lists of lengths $n = 2, 3, 4$, and 5 typed with alternating hands and with one hand only, and estimate of $\pm SE$. The results are averaged over four subjects; about 200 observations per point. Intervals early in a list have more intervals following them and appear toward the left of the plot. The SE estimate is based on the *serial-positions* $\times$ *subjects* interaction. The points in b represent means of the functions in c.

whether to give up the conjecture and explain the similarity of γ and θ values in some other way or to seek a special explanation for the dissociation of effects found only in one typing condition.

Figure 15.6c shows, for responses of length $n = 2, 3, 4$, and 5 in each condition, the individual intervals, $R_{kn} = T_{kn} - T_{k-1,n}$, between successive keystrokes that contribute to the means, $R_{.n}$, of Fig. 15.6b. The means of each of the $n - 1$ successive interstroke intervals contained in responses of length n are shown as functions of the number of *following* intervals—a number that appears to be a more powerful determinant of the forms of these functions than the number of preceding intervals.[19]

In every case, intervals followed by the same number (0, 1, or 2) of other intervals are longer when they are contained in longer responses, demonstrating the strength of the effect of sequence length on stroke rate. Note that even the time from the first stroke to the second (not lined up in Fig. 15.6c) is systematically greater for longer sequences. For sequences of four and five letters, the stroke rate is slower toward the middle of the sequence than at either end.

The patterns of interstroke intervals are very similar in the two conditions. To a first approximation, then, the two sets of R_{kn} functions differ by just a constant: The effect on interstroke interval of whether interstroke transition is within or between hands is roughly additive with the effect of serial position, at the same time as the effect on *mean* interstroke interval of transition type is almost perfectly additive with the effect of length. One way to explain such instances of additivity is to assume that the effects on interstroke interval of length and serial position, in the first place, and of transition type, in the second, are mediated by different *stages* of processing—separate operations that occur sequentially (Sternberg, 1969a).

An important challenge for any theoretical account of these duration data is to explain jointly the simplicity of performance at the macroscopic level (linearity with length at the level of the means) and the greater complexity at a microscopic level (nonlinearity with serial position).

VII. SUMMARY OF FINDINGS AND A TENTATIVE MODEL FOR THE LATENCY AND DURATION OF RAPID MOVEMENT SEQUENCES

Summary of Method and Findings

We begin this section by summarizing the main facts about rapid speech and typewriting that our experiments thus far have revealed. Subjects

---

[19]This might be taken as further evidence of the influence of advance planning.

made *responses* composed of short sequences of equivalent *response elements,* either spoken words or keystrokes. They were rewarded for completing these responses as quickly as possible after a reaction signal. We varied the *response length* (number of elements) over a range from $n = 1$ to $n = 5$. We also manipulated *element size* (or duration) by varying either the number of *constituents* (syllables per word) or the nature of the required movements (successive keystrokes by same versus alternating hands). The two main measures were *response latency,* L_n, from the reaction signal, and *response duration,* D_n, from the first element to the last. We found that a useful representation of duration data is provided by a *rate function,* $R_{.n}$, that describes the mean time interval between one element and the next, averaged over the $n - 1$ intervals in a response. In typing we also measured the individual time intervals, R_{kn}, between successive elements as a function of serial position, k, within the response.

We shall tentatively assume the correctness of our conclusion that in speech the *stress group* (a segment of speech associated with one primary stress) is the theoretically relevant response *unit,* based on the observation that it is in terms of this unit that our effects on both latencies and durations are most simply described.[20] In typing we shall identify the single keystroke as the response unit. For purposes of this summary, we shall also treat two of our findings as anomalies that, for the present, we shall not seek to explain. One is the shape of the latency function for one-handed typing, which is nonlinear over the $1 \leq n \leq 5$ range, and shallow over the $2 \leq n \leq 5$ range. The other is the downward concavity of the latency functions in the third speech experiment. Given that we set these exceptions aside, the main facts that we need to explain (for lists of up to at least five units) are as follows:

1. L_n (mean latency) increases with n (response length).
2. The increase is approximately linear.
3. L_n increases with number of constituents per unit.
4. Effects on L_n of number of units and number of constituents per unit are additive (do not interact).
5. $R_{.n}$ (mean time interval from one unit to the next) increases with n.
6. The increase is approximately linear.
7. Effects on $R_{.n}$ of number of units and unit size are additive.

---

[20]Note that for speech we happened to define an *element* (a response segment of arbitrary size) in such a way that it corresponded to what our results later suggested was a *unit* (a theoretically relevant response segment). Thus, in the speech experiments of Section II, our element was a *word* (rather than, for example, a syllable or a segment of specified duration), which was equivalent to a *stress group* in our materials. The convenient result is that response length, n, denotes the number of units as well as the number of elements, and unit size (in number of constituents or duration) is equivalent to element size.

8. Rates at which L_n and $R._n$ increase with n are similar.
9. R_{kn} (mean time interval from unit $k - 1$ to unit k in a response of length n) changes nonmonotonically with serial position, k.
10. Effects on R_{kn} of serial position and unit size are approximately additive.

A Tentative Model

Based on qualitative aspects of our data, we found the sequence-preparation hypothesis (Sec. III) to be the only survivor among the mechanisms we considered for the latency effect. This observation is the starting point for our tentative model. Next, because we are taking the similarity of the slopes of L_n and $R._n$ to be more than a coincidence, we prefer that the model account for both latencies and rates by means of the same mechanism. (If a dissociation between these slope parameters were discovered in later experiments, our preference might change, of course.) This decision, in turn, favors the second version of the preparation hypothesis (subprogram retrieval) over the first (program construction or activation) because Version 1 would require that the entire program be reconstructed or reactivated before the execution of each unit—a requirement that appears implausible to us. Our choice of model for the latency effect therefore depends on our findings about durations.

The particular retrieval mechanism suggested by our results is *self-terminating* sequential *search* through a *nonshrinking* buffer, rather than, for example, a process of direct access whose speed is limited by a capacity that must be shared among all the subprograms. *Search* seems to lead more naturally to linearity of time versus length, given the direct-access models of which we are currently aware. The buffer should be *nonshrinking* because otherwise $R._n$ would have half the slope of L_n, rather than approximately the same slope. The search is presumably necessary because subprograms are not arranged in the buffer in the order in which they must be executed. By assuming a *self-terminating* search rather than an exhaustive one (e.g., see Sternberg, 1969b), we are able to accommodate a wide variety of effects of serial position on R_{kn} (together with the approximate linearity and slope equality of L_n and $R._n$) by suitable assumptions about search order.

One aspect of search order is its variation from one trial to the next, which might depend, for example, on the order in which subprograms are stored in the buffer. Another aspect is its variation from the search for one subprogram to the next within a response: The search might start at the same location for each subprogram or at the location of the last subprogram retrieved, for example. In any case, it is the mean position of a subprogram in the search order when that subprogram is the one to be executed that determines serial-position effects. If the order is random, then all subprograms have the same mean position, and R_{kn} functions should be flat: The R_{kn} range, $\max\{R_{kn}\} - \min\{R_{kn}\}$, should be approximately zero. At the other extreme, if the order is fixed so that a subprogram in some one serial position is always found first and a subprogram in some other serial position is always found last, position effects are maximized and, ignoring sampling error, the R_{kn} range can be shown to be $2(n - 1)\gamma$. The ratio of the observed range to its estimated maximum provides a measure of the magnitude of position effects. For the typing data shown in Fig. 15.6c, we find the average value of this ratio for $n = 3$, 4, and 5 to be 0.04, 0.23, and 0.27, respectively, indicating that position effects were relatively small and implying that the order of the hypothesized search is closer to being random than fixed.[21] This finding is consistent with the approximate equality of L_n and $R_{.n}$ slopes, which requires us to assume that the mean search position of the first subprogram is approximately equal to the mean search position of the others.[22]

The structure of our model is governed, in part, by application of the additive-factor method (Sternberg, 1969a) and is to some extent independent of details of the retrieval and unpacking processes. For the latency, the additivity of effects of length and number of constituents per unit suggests the existence of separate processing stages whose durations are additive components of the latency and which are influenced selectively by these factors. This leads us to propose a *retrieval stage* (influenced by the number of units, but not their sizes) followed by an *unpacking stage* (influenced by the number of constituents in a unit, but not by the number of units; see Section IV). Both of these stages follow operations that mediate detection of the reaction signal and the decision to respond.

Our assumption that execution of later units involves the same mechanisms as execution of the first unit leads us to propose that durations of the same retrieval and unpacking stages are included in R_{kn} and hence in $R_{.n}$. That the effect of unit size on $R_{.n}$ (which again is additive with the effect of number of units) is so much larger than its effect on latency is explained by the existence of a *command stage* (again not influenced by the number of units) during which the sequence of commands is issued that cause execution of the constituents of the response unit.

---

[21]At present we can offer no convincing explanation for the shapes of the serial-position functions. We can assert, however, that the observed shapes are not incompatible with a self-terminating search. Indeed, ignoring sampling error, it can be shown that if the R_{kn} range is no greater than $n\gamma$, then *any* serial-position function can be accommodated by a suitable self-terminating search order.

[22]One-hand typing might be an exception in this respect, where the subprogram for the first unit had a privileged position in the buffer, thereby producing a flatter latency function.

Exactly what the commands specify about the ensuing movements—whether muscle contractions or target positions, for example (MacNeilage & MacNeilage, 1973)—is not critical for the model. But we have to place constraints on the time relations between the command stage for a response unit, which we do not measure directly, and the execution of that unit. According to our model, successive command stages are not only sequential, but are temporally discrete, being separated by search and unpacking operations—operations whose average duration is estimated to be about 40 msec longer in five-unit responses than in two-unit responses. Yet the movements produced (and the resulting sounds, in speech) often appear to be smooth, continuous, and even overlapping (Kent & Minifie, 1977). To reconcile our stage model with this observation, let us assume that execution of unit k can be prolonged so as to continue in parallel with the search and unpacking stages associated with unit $k + 1$. We assume further that if it is prolonged, it is nonetheless interrupted or modified by the execution of unit $k + 1$, in such a way that it does not delay the completion of that unit. The execution of the final unit in the response may also outlast its command stage, but the amount by which it is prolonged is independent of response length, n. From these assumptions, it follows that the measured duration of a response differs from the time between the beginning of the first command stage and the end of the last by at most a constant that is independent of n.

The model, then, introduces three types of processing stage. Let S_k denote the time to locate the subprogram for response unit k by means of a self-terminating search (or an alternative process, such as one involving direct access, that might later prove more appropriate). S_k depends on the number of units and on the serial position of unit k in the search order, but not on unit size. Let U_k denote the time between locating the subprogram and beginning the command sequence for unit k—the time to unpack the constituents—which depends only on the number of constituents per unit (length of the subprogram). Finally, let C_k denote the time to issue the sequence of commands that control unit k, which depends only on the size of the unit and not on either its serial position or the number of units.[23]

For the speech experiments, where the latency, L_n, is regarded as marking the *start* of the execution of the first response unit, we have

---

[23]An elaboration of these assumptions about C_k and/or U_k, for $k \geq 2$, is suggested by the weekdays experiment (Sec. II). There we found that responses consisting of repetitions of the same word differed only in duration from responses containing n different words, and that this "fatigue" effect was limited to an increased value of the parameter β. Given our model, this finding would require that repetition have an effect on only the duration $U_k + C_k$ of unpacking and command stages of units after the first, and that the increase in $U_k + C_k$ be as large on the first repetition as on later repetitions.

$$L_n = T_{1n}^* = T_b + S_1 + U_1 \tag{15.5}$$

where T_b denotes a "base time" during which the subject detects the signal and decides to respond. (Symbols are written in the same order as the corresponding stages are assumed to occur; see Sec. V for definitions of T_{kn} and T_{kn}^*.) For the typing experiment, where the latency is regarded as marking the *end* of the execution of the first response unit, we have[24]

$$L_n = T_{1n} = T_b + S_1 + U_1 + C_1 \tag{15.6}$$

For both kinds of experiment the interelement time is

$$R_{kn} = T_{kn} - T_{k-1,n} = S_k + U_k + C_k \quad (2 \le k \le n). \tag{15.7}$$

This tentative model is consistent with all ten of the facts listed earlier that our studies have revealed.

ACKNOWLEDGMENTS

The research reported here could not have been done without the expert hardware and systems-software support provided by A. S. Coriell and W. J. Kropfl. We are also indebted to M. Y. Liberman for advice on phonetics, to J. B. Kruskal and D. E. Meyer for comments on the manuscript, and to the skilled typists from the Word-Processing Center and Secretarial Service at Bell Laboratories, Murray Hill, who served as subjects.

REFERENCES

Adams, J. A. Issues for a closed-loop theory of motor learning. In G. E. Stelmach (Ed.), *Motor control: Issues and trends.* New York: Academic Press, 1976.

Anzola, G. P., Bertolini, G., Buchtel, H. A., & Rizzolatti, G. Spatial compatibility and anatomical factors in simple and choice reaction time. *Neuropsychologia*, 1977, *15*, 295–302.

Atkinson, R. C., & Shiffrin, R. M. Human memory: A proposed system and its control processes. In K. W. Spence & J. T. Spence (Eds.), *The psychology of learning and motivation: Advances in research and theory* (Vol. 2). New York: Academic Press, 1968.

Baddeley, A. D., Thomson, N., & Buchanan, M. Word length and the structure of short-term memory. *Journal of Verbal Learning and Verbal Behavior*, 1975, *14*, 575–589.

Berlyne, D. E. Conflict and choice time. *British Journal of Psychology*, 1957, *48*, 106–118.

---

[24]The fact that latencies for the one-hand and alternating-hand conditions are ever similar (as they are for $n = 1$ and $n = 2$) may indicate that values of $U_1 + C_1$ are approximately equal in the two kinds of sequence. But the difference between the rate functions for the two conditions shows that even if this is the case, the values of $U_k + C_k$ $(k > 1)$ must differ.

Brainard, R. W., Irby, T. S., Fitts, P. M., & Alluisi, E. A. Some variables influencing the rate of gain of information. *Journal of Experimental Psychology*, 1962, *63*, 105–110.

Butsch, R. L. C. Eye movements and the eye-hand span in typewriting. *Journal of Educational Psychology*, 1932, *23*, 104–121.

Callan, J., Klisz, D., & Parsons, O. A. Strength of auditory stimulus–response compatibility as a function of task complexity. *Journal of Experimental Psychology*, 1974, *102*, 1039–1045.

Coover, J. E. A method of teaching typewriting based on a psychological analysis of expert typing. *National Education Association Addresses and Proceedings*, 1923, *61,* 561–567.

Craik, F. I. M., & Levy, B. A. The concept of primary memory. In W. K. Estes (Ed.), *Handbook of learning and cognitive processes* (Vol. 4). *Attention and memory*. Hillsdale, N.J.: Lawrence Erlbaum Associates, 1976.

Crowder, R. G. *Principles of learning and memory*. Hillsdale, N.J.: Lawrence Erlbaum Associates, 1976.

Duncan, J. Response selection rules in spatial choice reaction tasks. In S. Dornič (Ed.), *Attention and performance VI*. Hillsdale, N.J.: Lawrence Erlbaum Associates, 1977.

Eccles, J. C. The coordination of information by the cerebellar cortex. In S. Locke (Ed.), *Modern neurology*. Boston: Little Brown, 1969.

Eriksen, C. W., Pollack, M. D., & Montague, W. E. Implicit speech: Mechanism in perceptual encoding? *Journal of Experimental Psychology*, 1970, *84*, 502–507.

Garner, W. R. *Uncertainty and structure as psychological concepts*. New York: Wiley, 1962.

Greenwald, A. G. Sensory feedback mechanisms in performance control: With special reference to the ideo-motor mechanism. *Psychological Review*, 1970, *77*, 73–99.

Hayes, K. C., & Marteniuk, R. G. Dimensions of motor task complexity. In G. E. Stelmach (Ed.), *Motor control: Issues and trends*. New York: Academic Press, 1976.

Henry, F. M., & Rogers, E. E. Increased response latency for complicated movements and a "memory drum" theory of neuromotor reaction. *Research Quarterly of the American Association for Health, Physical Education and Recreation*, 1960, *31*, 448–458.

Hudgins, C. V., & Stetson, R. H. Relative speed of articulatory movements. *Archives Néerlandaises de Phonétique Expérimentale*, 1937, *13*, 85–94.

Kallage, R. Electronic keyboard design with *N*-key rollover. *Computer Design*, February 1972, 57–61.

Keele, S. W. Movement control in skilled motor performance. *Psychological Bulletin*, 1968, *70*, 387–403.

Kent, R. D., & Minifie, F. D. Coarticulation in recent speech production models. *Journal of Phonetics*, 1977, *5*, 115–133.

Kent, R. D., & Moll, K. L. Articulatory timing in selected consonant sequences. *Brain and Language*, 1975, *2*, 304–323.

Kerr, B. Task factors that influence selection and preparation for voluntary movements. In G. E. Stelmach (Ed.), *Information processing in motor control and learning*. New York: Academic Press, 1978.

Klapp, S. T. Implicit speech inferred from response latencies in same-different decisions. *Journal of Experimental Psychology*, 1971, *91*, 262–267.

Klapp, S. T. Short-term memory as a response preparation state. *Memory & Cognition*, 1976, *4*, 721–729.

Kornblum, S. Response competition and/or inhibition in two-choice reaction time. *Psychonomic Science*, 1965, *2*, 55–56.

Kornhuber, H. H. Cerebral cortex, cerebellum and basal ganglia: An introduction to their motor functions. In F. O. Schmitt and F. G. Worden (Eds.), *The neurosciences: Third study program*. Cambridge: MIT Press, 1974.

Lahy, J. M. Motion study in typewriting. In *Studies and Reports,* Series J (Educational) No. 3. Geneva: International Labour Office, 1924.

Landauer, T. K. Rate of implicit speech. *Perceptual and Motor Skills,* 1962, *15,* 646.

Lashley, K. S. The problem of serial order in behavior. In L. A. Jeffress (Ed.), *Cerebral mechanisms in behavior.* New York: Wiley, 1951.

MacNeilage, P., & Ladefoged, P. The production of speech and language. In C. Carterette and M. P. Friedman (Eds.), *Handbook of perception (Vol. 7). Language and speech.* New York: Academic Press, 1976.

MacNeilage, P. F., & MacNeilage, L. A. Central processes controlling speech production during sleep and waking. In F. J. McGuigan (Ed.), *The psychophysiology of thinking.* New York: Academic Press, 1973.

Megaw, E. D. Direction and extent uncertainty in step tracking. *Journal of Motor Behavior,* 1972, *4,* 171–186.

Miles, F. A., & Evarts, E. V. Concepts of motor organization. *Annual Review of Psychology,* 1979, *30,* 327–362.

Monsell, S., & Sternberg, S. *The latency of short and rapid utterances: Evidence for response preprogramming.* Paper presented at the Seventh International Symposium on Attention and Performance, Sénanque, France, August, 1976.

Rosenbaum, D. A. Human movement initiation: Specification of arm, direction, and extent. *Journal of Experimental Psychology: General,* In press.

Russell, D. G. Spatial location cues and movement production. In G. E. Stelmach (Ed.), *Motor control: Issues and trends.* New York: Academic Press, 1976.

Sanders, A. F. Some variables affecting the relation between relative stimulus frequency and choice reaction time. *Acta Psychologica,* 1970, *33,* 45–55.

Schmidt, R. A. The index of preprogramming (IP): A statistical method for evaluating the role of feedback in simple movements. *Psychonomic Science,* 1972, *27,* 83–85.

Seibel, R. Data entry devices and procedures. In H. P. Van Cott and R. G. Kinkade (Eds.), *Human engineering guide to equipment design.* Washington, D.C.: American Institute for Research, 1972.

Shaffer, L. H. Intention and performance. *Psychological Review,* 1976, *83,* 375–393.

Shaffer, L. H., & Hardwick, J. Errors and error detection in typing. *Quarterly Journal of Experimental Psychology,* 1969, *21,* 209–213.

Sternberg, S. The discovery of processing stages: Extensions of Donders' method. In W. G. Koster (Ed.), *Attention and performance II. Acta Psychologica,* 1969, *30,* 276–315. (a)

Sternberg, S. Memory-scanning: Mental processes revealed by reaction-time experiments. *American Scientist,* 1969, *57,* 421–457. (b)

Van Nes, F. L. Analysis of keying errors. *Ergonomics,* 1976, *19,* 165–174.

Welford, A. T. On the sequencing of action. *Brain Research,* 1974, *71,* 381–392.

Wickelgren, W. A. Context-sensitive coding, associative memory, and serial order in (speech) behavior. *Psychological Review,* 1969, *76,* 1–15.

Wing, A. M. Response timing in handwriting. In G. E. Stelmach (Ed.), *Information processing in motor control and learning.* New York: Academic Press, 1978.

16

Motor Programs in Rapid Speech: Additional Evidence

Saul Sternberg

Charles E. Wright

Ronald L. Knoll
Bell Laboratories, Murray Hill, New Jersey

Stephen Monsell
University of Chicago

I. INTRODUCTION

In a previous article we reported a series of studies of the timing of rapid prespecified action sequences in speech and typewriting (Sternberg, Monsell, Knoll, & Wright, 1978; reprinted as Chap. 15 in the present volume). Under pressure to finish quickly, subjects responded to a signal by typing lists of letters or speaking lists of words that had been specified before the signal. Increments in sequence length increased the time to initiate the first response element (latency effect) and also increased the average time from one element to the next (duration effect). Our experiments permitted us to reject several interesting explanations of the latency effect, and the generality, robustness, and quantitative simplicity of the two effects encouraged us to develop a model for the latency and duration of rapid movement sequences that explained both phenomena in terms of retrieval of "subprograms" from a "motor program" for the whole sequence that had been compiled in advance. Our results also permitted us tentatively to identify a response *unit* in speech—the *stress group*—in terms of which the observed effects can be most simply described.

507

In this chapter we provide informal accounts of several studies of speech production that generalize and extend the earlier work and permit us to elaborate our model, defend it against a new contender, and test it further. In providing these accounts we depend heavily on Chapter 15, especially its Sections II, III, and VII, and refer to it extensively (as "LD," usually followed by a section number).

We first demonstrate the generality of the latency and duration phenomena over longer lists than previously reported, different sets of words, and conditions that produce high time uncertainty for the reaction signal (Sec. II). We then summarize findings about the effects of time uncertainty on parameters of latency and duration functions and thereby provide evidence against one class of explanations of the latency effect (Sec. III).

In Section IV we examine the effects of utterance length on the entire latency distribution, rather than just its mean, to provide assurance that the latency effect is not a consequence of a small proportion of long response delays. We then (Sec. V) report measurements of the effects of utterance length on initial values of two acoustic characteristics— fundamental frequency (F_0) and amplitude. The F_0 measurements permit us to reject an alternative explanation of the latency effect—based on peripheral biomechanics rather than central information processing—that was advanced by K. N. Stevens.

One pervasive property of "natural" speech is the decline in F_0 from beginning to end of an utterance; the effect of utterance length on the rate of declination has been taken to indicate advance planning of entire utterances. In Section VI we ask whether the unstructured rapidly spoken lists in our experiments reveal a similar declination effect.

In Section VII we report measurements that permit us to segment rapid utterances into their component words, and thereby to specify how the time interval from one word to the next depends on the serial position of the word pair within an utterance, as well as on utterance length. Although differing in detail, the resulting serial-position functions are similar in important respects to those we obtained in typewriting, and provide further evidence for the dependence of local features throughout the utterance on a representation ("motor program") of the entire utterance.

In Section VIII we report a first attempt to localize, *within* the time interval from the start of one response unit to the start of the next, the effects of utterance length and serial position; these measurements then permit relatively clean tests of two implications drawn from our model.

We turn finally (Sec. IX) to the role of lexical memory in the control of rapid speech, which we investigate by searching for qualitative and quantitative alterations in the latency and duration functions that arise when speakers are asked to produce utterances containing nonwords rather than words.[1]

II. RECITING OF LETTER AND DIGIT LISTS FOLLOWING A RANDOMLY VARIED FOREPERIOD

In the experiments reported in LD we attempted to minimize subjects' time uncertainty by using warning signals and a fixed foreperiod before the reaction signal; we tried to deal with the problem of "anticipation" of the reaction signal by introducing occasional "catch" trials, on which the reaction signal was omitted. In an earlier experiment we had incorporated neither warnings nor catch trials, had varied the foreperiod randomly over 15 equally spaced values ranging from 2.6 to 5.4 sec, and had used lists of letters or digits containing one to six different randomly ordered items; otherwise the procedure was as described in LD, II. Subjects were the same four who served in the speech experiments reported in LD, but before they had had such extensive practice in the task. We include the results here to demonstrate the generality of the latency and duration phenomena to longer lists, different sets of words, and conditions of high time uncertainty.[2] (In Section III we explicitly compare these findings to corresponding data collected under our more typical conditions of low time uncertainty.)

Mean results from the second and third day of the experiment are represented by the open circles in Fig. 16.1. Data shown are for correct responses only; error rates were negligible for $n \leq 5$, but for $n = 6$ the error rate was 9.6%.

Mean latency (Fig. 16.1a) again increased approximately linearly with list length; the slope is 7.3 ± 0.7 msec/word. The linear function accounts for 97.4% of the variance, and no higher order regression coefficients are significant.

Mean duration (Fig. 16.1b) is significantly nonlinear, but is well described by the fitted quadratic function, with 99.96% of the variance accounted for and no significant regression coefficients of order higher than

---

[1]The work described in Sections II–IV of the present chapter will be reported in detail elsewhere by Monsell and Sternberg; the work described in Sections V–IX will be reported in detail elsewhere by Sternberg, Knoll, and Wright.

[2]Let the range of list lengths be $1 \leq n \leq m$. Because the fitting of linear (quadratic) functions to speech latency (duration) data requires estimation of two (three) parameters, only $m - 2$ ($m - 3$) degrees of freedom remain for evaluating goodness of fit. Increasing m from $m = 4$ and 5 (as in LD) to $m = 6$ therefore substantially increases the sensitivity of such evaluations.

quadratic. Given the larger range of list lengths relative to those of the experiments in LD, this finding strengthens our claim that the duration function is quadratic.

Again, the slope of the latency function (7.3 msec/word) and the quadratic coefficient of the duration function (7.7 msec/word^2) are close in value. However, both parameters are smaller than the corresponding values in other, later speech experiments with the same subjects (see LD, Table 15.1). Another notable difference is the one-intercept of the latency function; its value of 284.9 msec is about 20 msec greater than in the later experiments (see LD, Table 15.1).[3] We show in the next section that only the last of these differences between experiments can be ascribed to time uncertainty.

III. EFFECTS OF TIME UNCERTAINTY ON LATENCY AND DURATION FUNCTIONS

To evaluate performance when time uncertainty was decreased, we also studied the same subjects with the same kinds and lengths of lists as described above, but in a procedure with a fixed foreperiod, countdown signals, and catch trials, like that of our later experiments. (See LD, II.) The procedures with fixed and varied foreperiod were run on different days in a balanced order, but data were collected in the former on only one day. Furthermore, with fixed foreperiods, error rates for lists of lengths 5 and 6 were unpleasantly high (8.0% and 14.8%, respectively), making the latency and duration data somewhat suspect. Data for correct responses are represented by the filled circles in Fig. 16.1.

The slope of the fitted linear latency function is 6.2 ± 0.8 msec/word; the difference of 1.1 ± 0.7 msec/word between slopes for fixed and varied foreperiods in this experiment is neither large nor statistically significant. The difference in latency-function slopes between this and later experiments is not, therefore, a consequence of time uncertainty. (Its source remains an open question.) As one might expect, however, introducing time uncertainty produced a large and statistically significant increase in mean latency (29.0 ± 3.4 msec, averaged over list lengths). Time uncertainty and list length therefore appear to have additive effects on mean latency. Evidence for such additivity supports models in which the two factors influence different processing "stages" (Sternberg, 1969). Additivity also argues against hypotheses about the latency effect such as

---

[3]The one-intercept, a convenient measure of the height of the latency function, reflects the time to start producing a single word, and is estimated by the parameter η in the latency functions of LD, Table 15.1.

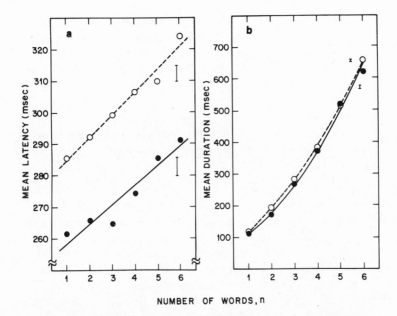

FIG. 16.1.   Fixed- and random-foreperiod experiments. Open circles and broken lines show results from the random-foreperiod experiment averaged over four subjects, two vocabularies (letters, digits), 15 foreperiods, and days 2 and 3; about 240 observations per point. Filled circles and unbroken lines show results from the fixed-foreperiod experiment averaged over four subjects and two vocabularies; about 80 observations per point. a. Mean latencies, estimates of standard error ($\pm SE$), and fitted linear functions (random foreperiod, $284.9 + 7.3(n - 1)$ msec; fixed foreperiod, $258.4 + 6.2(n - 1)$ msec). b. Mean durations, estimates of $\pm SE$, and fitted quadratic functions [random foreperiod, $117.1 + 67.9(n - 1) + 7.7(n - 1)^2$; fixed foreperiod, $110.9 + 53.7(n - 1) + 10.6(n - 1)^2$ msec]. See LD, Table 15.1, for fitting procedure.

"time-sharing" (LD, III), in which the effect of list length results from the subject's being unprepared for the reaction signal, and therefore being in a "rehearsal" state rather than a "readiness" state when the signal is presented. (If the effect of list length on latency resulted from such lack of preparation, we would expect any factor that increased time uncertainty also to increase the length effect.)

Mean duration in the fixed-foreperiod procedure (Fig. 16.1b) is again significantly nonlinear, and with no significant regression coefficients of order higher than quadratic. The fitted quadratic function accounts for 99.94% of the variance; deviations for $n \geqslant 5$, which are larger than usual, may be related to the high error rates. Because of these deviations, our estimate of the quadratic coefficient—10.6 ± 1.6 msec/word²—is more dependent than usual on the choice of estimation method.[4] Hence, although its value is closer than the varied-foreperiod experiment to those found in other experiments, the difference between coefficients cannot be taken seriously. The mean duration difference (averaged over list lengths) of 16.7 ± 12.5 msec is not statistically significant.

IV. EFFECTS OF LIST LENGTH ON THE DISTRIBUTION OF UTTERANCE LATENCIES

Especially because the effect of list length on mean utterance latency is small, with estimated slope values never exceeding about 15 msec/word, we felt it was important to examine its effect on other characteristics of the latency distribution in addition to its mean. One question this would enable us to answer is whether the small effect on the mean is a consequence of mixing a large effect on a few trials with no effect on most trials. (For example, if subjects were occasionally delayed by having to inhale after the reaction signal, despite our instructions to breathe either between trials or before the reaction signal, this would add a large increment to the latency.[5] If for longer lists they either breathed more deeply and hence for more time, or breathed with higher probability, this could have caused the increase in mean latency with list length.)

We used latency data from the experiment with lists of weekdays in normal, random, and repeating sequence (LD, II). For each subject and list length, we pooled the latencies of all correct responses over the three types of sequence, seven starting words, and three replications, to provide about 60 observations per distribution. We then obtained the maximum, mean, and minimum of each distribution, as well as estimates of a set of quantiles, $\{t_p\}$, where the proportion, p, ranged from $p = .05$ to $p = .95$. (If L is a random variable representing the latency, then the p-quantile of its distribution is defined as the latency value, t_p, for which

---

[4]The procedure for estimating the fitted duration functions whose equations are given in the caption of Fig. 16.1b (LD, Note to Table 15.1) uses the empirical *rate* function to estimate β and γ. When instead, the empirical *duration* functions were fitted directly, parameter estimates from the random-foreperiod data remained approximately invariant [$119.3 + 63.6(n - 1) + 8.6(n - 1)^2$], but estimates from the fixed-foreperiod data were altered [$103.9 + 62.5(n - 1) + 7.2(n - 1)^2$]. (The two estimation procedures can be regarded as differing in the relative weights placed on data from different list lengths.)

[5]We believe (but have not determined experimentally) that the time increment associated with even a shallow inhalation would be large relative to the spread of the latency distributions ($SD \simeq 30$ msec). See Conrad & Schönle (1979) for supporting evidence.

$\Pr\{L \leq t_p\} = p.$) Means of these statistics over subjects are displayed in Fig. 16.2 as a function of list length.

If the effect of list length on mean latency were the consequence of a few outliers, then the high quantiles should increase steeply and the low quantiles very little. Instead, all the statistics increase at respectable rates; slopes of fitted linear functions are provided in the figure caption. Even the minimum, often an unstable statistic, increases reliably with list length, at a rate of 8.4 ± 2.8 msec/word ($p < .05$). Slopes of the fitted functions do change systematically with p-value, indicating that the effect of list length on latency cannot be described merely as translation of its distribution with no change in shape. Instead, the increasing separation among quantiles with increasing list length reflects the existence of a modest increase in latency variability as well. (The mean standard deviation of the latency distribution increases from about 22 msec for $n = 1$ to 28 msec for $n = 5$, in the present experiment.)

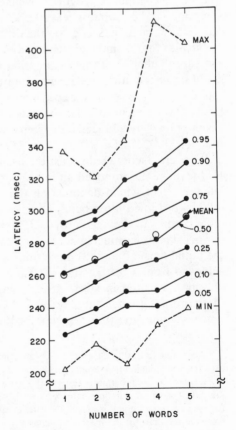

FIG. 16.2. Mean latency quantiles, mean latency extremes, and mean latency for lists of one to five words in the weekdays experiment. Each statistic was determined or estimated from a distribution of about 60 observations from each subject; values were then averaged over the four subjects. Quantiles (with p-value indicated) are shown by filled circles, minima and maxima are shown by triangles, and mean latencies are indicated by open circles. Slopes of linear functions fitted to each of these statistics, in msec/word, are: minimum, 8.4; mean, 8.7; maximum, 22.9; quantiles, from lowest to highest, 5.7, 6.7, 7.6, 8.1, 8.5, 10.6, 12.8.

V. TEST OF A PHYSIOLOGICAL HYPOTHESIS ABOUT THE LATENCY EFFECT BY MEASUREMENT OF INITIAL FUNDAMENTAL FREQUENCY

Our favored explanation of the effects of the length of an utterance on its latency and duration is the subprogram-retrieval version of the sequence-preparation hypothesis (LD, III).[6] This account, as well as the alternatives we presented in LD and rejected in its favor, attributes the effects to mental processes (e.g., subprogram retrieval) rather than to physiological or mechanical constraints on the articulators. One basis for our not having considered this latter class of peripheral physiological explanations was our assumption of *element invariance* (LD, I).

As it applies to the initial element (word) in an utterance, the strongest form of the element-invariance assumption asserts that no characteristics of this first element (other than when it is produced) are systematically influenced by sequence length. A weaker but sufficient version of the assumption (and one that is less likely to fail) asserts that sequence length has no systematic influence on the delay between the hypothetical motor commands for the initial element and the acoustic events that determine its measured latency. (If this assumption were to fail, then sequence length could influence utterance latency indirectly, through its direct effects on this delay.) In our early experiments, however, we included no direct tests of the element-invariance assumption; arguments for and against the assumption were adduced only from the degree of regularity of the latency function (LD, I; LD, VI).

We were encouraged to test the assumption more directly by Kenneth N. Stevens. He proposed an interesting physiological explanation of the latency effect which depends on the assumption being violated by the initial word in an utterance.[7]

According to Stevens' proposal, (1) before an utterance is initiated the laryngeal muscles must be tensed; (2) the longer the utterance, the greater the initial tension; and (3) more time is required for greater tension to be achieved from a resting state. (Utterance "length" here would presumably be measured in stress-group units, as discussed in LD, IV). Furthermore, (4) greater initial tension should produce a higher fundamental voice frequency (F_o) at the start of the utterance. It is this last part of

---

[6]According to this hypothesis, a program consisting of a set of n subprograms, one for each response unit in the utterance, is constructed prior to the signal. Then, before each unit is executed, its subprogram is retrieved. The retrieval process is one (such as sequential search) whose mean duration increases linearly with n. The effect of n on retrieval duration for the first subprogram produces the latency effect, and the sum of the effects of n on retrieval durations for the $n - 1$ remaining subprograms produces the duration effect.

[7]Stevens' proposal was made as a personal communication at the present Symposium.

Stevens' proposal that permits it to be tested in a straightforward way: In contrast to our element-invariance assumption, the proposal implies that the F_0 contour of the initial word of a longer utterance should be higher, or at least start higher.[8]

Sorenson and Cooper (Chap. 13, Table 13.5) give us some reason for expecting an increase in initial F_0 with utterance length. Under their perhaps more "natural" conditions for speech production, peak F_0 in the first stressed syllable in long sentences (13.8 words) was about 13.5 Hz (or 6%) higher than in short sentences (7.5 words). But there are at least three reasons why this finding may not apply to our situation: We used random words, not sentences; our range of list lengths is below their range of sentence lengths; and our subjects were encouraged to complete their utterances as rapidly as possible, unlike theirs. Furthermore, the first stressed syllable in Sorenson and Cooper's sentences was preceded by an unstressed syllable: Suppose that pitch contours (or, alternatively, F_0 targets for potential stressed syllables) were at equal heights at the initiation of sentences of different lengths, and declined more rapidly for shorter sentences (which they have been found to do; see references in Section VI.) Then the initial F_0 measure reported by Sorenson and Cooper would vary with utterance length, even though the actual F_0 associated with the initial unstressed syllable (or, alternatively, the F_0 target associated with an initial stressed syllable if one had existed) remained constant.

Given Stevens' proposal together with our observed effect of about 10 msec per stress group on utterance latency, how large an effect of utterance length on initial F_0 would we expect? One rough indication of the time difference needed to achieve different degrees of tension of the laryngeal muscles *prior* to voicing is perhaps provided by data on the relation between the size of an increase in F_0 *during* actual voicing and the minimum time to achieve that increase. (Such evidence can provide only an indication, however, since maximum rates of tension change may not be equal under voiced and silent conditions.) Sundberg (1979) and Ohala and Ewan (1973; data reported in Sundberg, 1979) have shown that the additional time needed for an F_0 increase of 12 semitones relative to 4 semitones is no more than about 25 msec, or about 3 msec per semitone.[9] (One semitone corresponds to an increase of 6% in frequency.) For a

---

[8]See Sorenson and Cooper (Chap. 13) for a discussion of F_0 and its measurement.

[9]One possible objection to regarding this kind of measurement as relevant to our problem is that insofar as F_0 changes are similar to aimed arm displacements, the time to make a change will depend on the required endpoint precision (which appears not to have been examined in detail in Sundberg's study, 1979) as well as the size of the required change (Fitts & Peterson, 1964).

latency increment of 40 msec (approximately the difference between utterances of $n = 1$ and $n = 5$ words) to be attributable to the time required to achieve a higher initial F_0, the difference between initial F_0 values would therefore have to be at least 13 semitones, or about an octave.

Lists in the experiment we used to test Stevens' proposal contained from $n = 1$ to $n = 5$ elements drawn from a vocabulary of five monosyllabic words: *bee, cow, day, pie,* and *toe.* We chose these words (all starting with stop consonants) so that word boundaries would be clearly indicated by minima in the amplitude envelope; the primary aim of the experiment was to permit us to measure the interword time intervals as a function of serial position (discussed in Sec. VII). We used two types of list, *homogeneous* lists, containing repetitions of the same word, and *heterogeneous* lists, containing n distinct words. For both types and for each length, each of the five words appeared equally often in each serial position. We used a new group of four female speakers. Each list appeared on three successive trials; the utterances subjected to the F_0 analysis include one list of each type with each starting word, drawn from one of the last two of these trials, (i.e., 10 utterances for each list length and each of the four subjects).

The procedure on each trial of the present experiment, as well as of the experiments to be described in Sections VIII and IX, was different from the procedure described in LD, II: After an auditory warning sounded and a visual fixation pattern appeared, the list of words was presented in a column. It remained visible until the end of the response. Except on "catch" trials, the reaction signal (a tone-burst) occurred $4.4 + 0.6n$ sec after display onset (where $1 \leq n \leq 5$ is the list length). The reaction signal was preceded at 0.7-sec intervals by two noise bursts that functioned as "countdown" signals. Subjects were instructed to complete each utterance as soon as possible after the reaction signal, consistent with high accuracy.

In conjunction with an LPC (linear predictive coding) analysis of each utterance, we computed an amplitude value for each 10 msec segment, as well as an F_0 value for each segment in which voicing had occurred.[10] Word boundaries were defined by minima in the resulting amplitude functions.

The experiment produced qualitatively typical latency effects for both homogeneous and heterogeneous lists; the slopes of a line fitted by least squares to the mean data are 14.0 ± 3.1 msec/word and 16.1 ± 2.8 msec/

---

[10]See Rabiner, Cheng, Rosenberg, & McGonegal (1976), Section II F, for a description of the pitch-detection algorithm, due to B. S. Atal; see Atal & Hanauer (1971) for a comprehensive discussion of LPC analysis of speech.

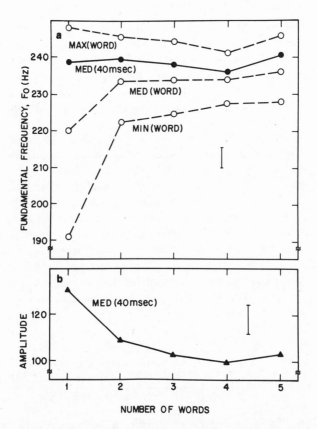

FIG. 16.3. Acoustic measures of the initial word in utterances of one to five monosyllabic words. Values are means of the indicated statistics over homogeneous and heterogeneous lists, five different initial words, and four subjects; 40 observations per point. Also shown are estimates of $\pm SE$ of these means, based on *subjects* × *list length* interactions. a. Fundamental frequency (F_0) in Hz is shown by circles: Open circles show maxima, medians, and minima over all 10-msec segments in voiced portion of first word; filled circles show medians over first four such segments (40 msec). b. Median amplitude over first four voiced segments, in arbitrary units.

word, respectively, somewhat larger values than we had obtained in earlier experiments with different subjects.

Acoustic measures of the first word are shown as a function of utterance length in Fig. 16.3. The measure that is most appropriate for testing Stevens' proposal is the fundamental frequency at the start of the first word; we have used the median of the four F_0 values obtained from the first four segments in each utterance where F_0 was defined (i.e., where voicing had occurred). As can be seen from the figure (filled circles), rather than increasing with list length this statistic is essentially invariant; the slope of a line fitted to the five points is 0.02 ± 1.85 Hz/word. The maximum F_0 over all voiced segments in the word (whose mean is within 1 Hz of the maximum over the first four such segments) can also be seen to be essentially invariant; the slope of a fitted line is -0.87 ± 1.65 Hz/word. These findings support the element-invariance assumption and require us to reject Stevens' proposal.

The other statistics do show effects of list length, however. Minimum F_0 and median F_0 during the voiced portion of the initial word are both significantly lower ($p < .01$) when $n = 1$ than when $n \geq 2$; differences among lengths $n \geq 2$ are not statistically significant. This observation is probably best thought of in relation to the fact that for $n = 1$ the first word is also the last, and therefore participates in a terminal fall in F_0. (See Sec. VI.) Similarly, the initial amplitude of the utterance is significantly higher ($p < .05$) when $n = 1$ than when $n \geq 2$; again, differences among lengths $n \geq 2$ are not statistically significant. The existence of distinctive frequency and amplitude characteristics for isolated words reinforces the reservation we expressed in LD, I as to whether single elements would satisfy the invariance assumption.

VI. EFFECTS OF UTTERANCE LENGTH AND SERIAL POSITION ON FUNDAMENTAL FREQUENCY: THE DECLINATION EFFECT IN RAPID SPEECH

The tendency for F_0 to drift downward from the beginning to the end of a natural speech utterance (or "intonation group" within an utterance) appears to characterize most languages (Bolinger, 1978; Ohala, 1978; Pierrehumbert, 1979). Measurements of isolated sentences in American English show the amount of declination to be 20–40 Hz and to be relatively independent of utterance length (e.g., Maeda, 1976; Sorenson & Cooper, Chap. 13). The approximate invariance of declination with length implies that the *rate* of declination varies inversely with length. Thus, a characteristic of the whole utterance (its length) is reflected in a local feature (rate of F_0 declination). This observation has been taken as evidence for the advance planning of the entire utterance, just as has our observation that, under conditions of time pressure, sequence length influences interelement time. (See Sec. VII.)

The similarity of these arguments encouraged our interest in whether the declination effect would appear under the conditions of our experiments. Here utterances were of unstructured lists (rather than phrases or sentences) which subjects were instructed and trained to complete as rapidly as possible; subjects were also asked to avoid phrasing, to stress each word equally, and to speak "in a monotone." The presence of F_0 declination might add to the evidence for advance planning, and would encourage us to feel that our subjects' utterances were not as "unnatural" as our experimental conditions might lead one to expect. Systematic differences in F_0 as a function of serial position and length would also bear on the validity of the element-invariance assumption.

The experiment and measurement procedure as well as the set of data used in the analysis were described in Section V. For the present analysis we determined, for each word, the median F_0 value over all its 10-msec voiced segments. Results, averaged over subjects and over all lists of each length, are shown in Fig. 16.4, together with the MED(40 msec) measure of initial F_0 from Fig. 16.3.

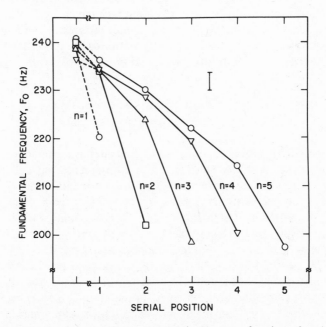

FIG. 16.4 Fundamental frequency (F_0) in Hz as a function of serial position in lists of lengths $n = 1$ to $n = 5$. For the leftmost points (no serial position indicated), median values of F_0 were taken over the first four 10-msec segments in the voiced portion of each initial word; points represent the means of these medians for each length. For other points, median values of F_0 were taken over *all* voiced segments in each word; points represent the means of these medians for each length and serial position. Also shown is an estimate of $\pm SE$ of the displayed means, based on the *subjects* × *serial-position* interaction. Means were taken over two types of list, five words, and four subjects; 40 observations per point. The mean time interval corresponding to a separation of one serial position was 143 msec.

Averaged over lengths $n \geq 2$, the mean declination, measured from initial F_0 (leftmost points in the figure), is large and significant: 39.5 ± 6.7 Hz. As has been reported for "natural" speech, the total drop in F_0 appears not to depend systematically on length; for $n = 2, 3, 4$, and 5, the mean declination values are 38.0, 40.1, 36.3, and 43.5 Hz, respectively. Excluding the final word at each length (whose median F_0 is affected by the terminal fall) and averaging over lengths $n \geq 3$, the effect is smaller but still highly significant: 19.4 ± 2.7 Hz. If the effect is measured over all serial positions (for $n \geq 2$) the *rate* of declination (F_0 change per serial position) declines significantly as n increases; if the final word is excluded, although the rate decreases with n, this decrease cannot be shown to be statistically significant with tests based on between-subject variability. However, taken together, these results suggest that the main features of the pitch declination phenomenon can be found in rapidly spoken lists. This finding adds to the evidence for advance planning, and indicates that even under the special conditions of our experiments, utterances display an important organizational property of natural speech.

VII. THE EFFECT OF SERIAL POSITION ON THE INTERWORD INTERVAL

One aspect of the findings reported in LD that we consider relatively important is the similarity of the duration functions for speech and typewriting.[11] Both are well approximated by quadratic functions, which indicates that the mean interval between successive elements increases linearly with number of elements. (See LD, Fig. 15.6a, b.)

In typewriting, because individual interstroke intervals are easily measured, we were also able to determine the mean interstroke interval for each serial position (LD, Fig. 15.6c). We found a dominance relation among serial-position functions: For each serial position (counting backward from the last interstroke interval in the series, or forward from the first), the duration of the mean interstroke interval increased with n. Furthermore, the serial-position functions were found to be concave downward, and indicated that for the longer sequences the stroke rate is slower toward the middle of the sequence than at either end. We felt it was important to examine further the generality of these findings by determining analogous serial-position functions for rapid speech.

---

[11]Sequence length also produces increases in typing latency. The duration and latency effects are therefore both found in motor performances that differ radically in training history, muscular complexity, measurement method, and the amount of time pressure and relative speed outside the laboratory. Given such generality, potential measurement artifacts are of less concern, and the underlying process is more likely to be fundamental.

The experiment described in Section V was designed to permit using the amplitude envelope of each utterance to determine the mean intervals between successive response units: We used words beginning with stop consonants and we balanced word identities across serial positions. However, identification of the "beginning" of the execution of a response unit embedded in continuous speech presents difficulties of definition as well as measurement, and such an effort depends on relatively arbitrary decisions. Furthermore, since in terms of our model (LD, VII) our aim is to measure events that indicate the time intervals between the beginnings of the *command stages* for successive units, these difficulties are compounded by our assumption that the execution of a unit can be prolonged beyond the termination of its command stage (to continue in parallel with the *retrieval* and *unpacking* stages for the next unit). In attempting to deal with these difficulties we made two assumptions. First, we assumed that each monosyllabic word is a response unit; second, we assumed that the occurrence time of an event relatively early in the word (the transition between the stop consonant and the vowel, which was associated with an abrupt rise in the amplitude envelope) would adequately measure (on the average, and to within an additive constant) the starting time of the command stage for the unit in that serial position.

We digitized subjects' speech at 10kHz and determined the mean absolute sample value (an amplitude measure) in adjacent 10-msec intervals. Linear interpolation between successive means then defined an amplitude envelope that usually showed a single peak for each word in the utterance and a single trough between each word and the next. On 86% of the correct trials we were able to choose a criterion amplitude value that intersected the ascending flanks of exactly n amplitude peaks. We chose an algorithm to do this that produced mean amplitude criteria that depended relatively little on n. The time differences between successive intersections then defined a series of $n - 1$ intervals between the "beginnings" of successive words. (We also established that these interword intervals were relatively independent of the value of the amplitude criterion—an important check, given the crudeness of the segmentation procedure.)

Results are shown separately in Fig. 16.5 for homogeneous and heterogeneous lists, in the same format as the typing data (LD, Fig. 15.6c) to facilitate comparison. The same dominance relation found in typing also appears in the speech data: At each serial position the mean interword interval increases with n, and with the exception of one value (homogeneous lists of length $n = 2$), the duration of the first interword interval increases with n. As in typing, therefore, a characteristic of the entire sequence—its length—influences the initiation delay of each of its constituents. The existence of such an effect supports the idea that execu-

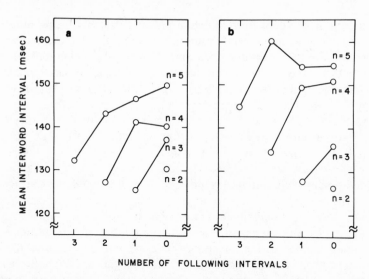

FIG. 16.5.   Mean interword interval for each serial position in lists of monosyllabic words of lengths $n = 2, 3, 4$, and 5. Results are averaged over four subjects; about 50 observations per point. a. Homogeneous lists. b. Heterogeneous lists. Intervals early in a list have more intervals following them and appear toward the left of the plots.

tion of the constituents is based on a representation of the entire sequence, and that at a level relevant to the control of timing, the entire sequence is represented during execution of each of its elements.

However, the average rate at which the interelement interval increases with serial position in speech is greater than in typing: Rapid utterances tend to slow down, and the final acceleration found in typed sequences is absent or much attenuated in the speech data. In terms of our subprogram-retrieval model (LD, VII), these differences in the effect of serial position on the interval between elements in speech and typing, in combination with the same (linear) effect of length on the *mean* interval, could be attributed to different average search *orders* in the context of the same mechanism of self-terminating search.

The separation between serial-position curves is smaller for homogeneous than heterogeneous lists, reflecting the fact that the slope of the mean rate function (or the quadratic coefficient of the duration function) is significantly smaller: Estimated coefficients are 4.7 and 14.3 msec/word^2 for homogeneous and heterogeneous lists, respectively.[12]

---

[12]Taken together with the substantial difference between *rate-function* slopes for homogeneous and heterogeneous lists, the similarity of the shapes of their *serial-position functions* challenges the assumption embodied in our model (LD, VII) that the same retrieval mechanism underlies both functions. Further evidence against the assumption appears in Section VIII. A second dissociation of effects that challenges our present model is suggested by the finding in this experiment that rate-function slopes can differ between two kinds of lists, without a corresponding difference in latency-function slopes (values in Sec. V).

This feature of the data from repeated monsyllabic words contrasts with our findings in the weekdays experiment (LD, II); there we found that neither the latency nor duration functions for lists composed of repetitions of the same weekday name were especially unusual. We have not yet identified the conditions under which homogeneous and heterogeneous lists are associated with parametrically distinct latency or duration functions.

VIII. LOCALIZATION WITHIN WORDS OF THE EFFECTS OF UTTERANCE LENGTH AND SERIAL POSITION

We have seen that under the conditions of our experiments the time per word increases with the length of an utterance and also tends to increase with serial position within an utterance. Since the utterance can be regarded as a stream of articulatory gestures partitioned into subsequences, each associated with a response unit, it is tempting to try to determine the loci within these subsequences of the length and serial-position effects: To what extent are these effects concentrated in specific parts of each response unit?

One possible answer is that the effects are not localized, but instead result from relatively global differences in the rates at which articulatory gestures occur. In its simplest form, however, our model (LD, VII) provides a very different answer. According to the model, utterances depend on a series of *command* stages, one for each response unit, which are interleaved with *retrieval* and *unpacking* stages. Utterance length influences the duration of only the retrieval stage, and does this by influencing the mean duration of a search process. Furthermore, the serial-position effects are produced by variation across serial positions in the duration of this same search process. Effects of both length and serial position are therefore restricted to the time intervals between the end of one command stage and the beginning of the next, and timing *within* command stages should not be affected. If the *execution* of a response unit coincided with its command stage, the consequence of this argument would be straightforward: There would be silent intervals between one unit and the next, and any effects of length or serial position would be localized exclusively within these intervals.

We have had to elaborate our model, however (LD, VII): To reconcile the continuity of speech with the temporal discreteness of the hypothesized sequence of command stages we assumed that the execution of a unit could be prolonged beyond the termination of its command stage, so as to continue in parallel with the search and unpacking stages associated with the next unit. To force utterance duration to be suitably sensitive to the durations of retrieval stages, we also had to assume that the portion of the response unit that was prolonged in this way could be adjusted or truncated so as not to delay the next unit. The elaborated model suggests that although the duration of an entire response unit may depend on utterance length and serial position, this may not be true for the timing of within-unit features that occur relatively early in the unit, because they depend on direct rather than delayed control from the command sequence and may not be subject to adjustment or truncation.[13]

We felt that a plausible initial test of the elaborated model would be provided by measuring utterances whose response units were two-syllable words. As a starting assumption, we conjectured that for each such response unit the command sequence would be in direct control until at least the beginning of the second syllable. Our model then implies that the time intervals between the beginnings of successive syllables in an utterance consisting of a sequence of such disyllables should not be equally sensitive to the effects of utterance length and serial position. Instead, these effects should be restricted to those intervals that include speech events from the beginning of the second syllable of one word to the beginning of the first syllable of the next. We shall call these "across-word" intervals, and the others "within-word" intervals.

To perform the test we constructed lists from a vocabulary of disyllables with primary stress on the first syllable. (Examples of the words we used are *copper, dagger, pebble,* and *token.*) Each word contained two stop consonants, one at the beginning of each syllable; all of the other constituent sounds were vowels or sonorants. The articulatory pattern of each word was therefore *closed* (C_1), *open* (V_1), *closed* (C_2), *open* (V_2). A transition between stop consonant and vowel or sonorant involves the release of the stop and the onset of voicing and is marked by an abrupt rise in the amplitude envelope. For each word, therefore, the amplitude envelope usually contained two distinct peaks, and the time between any two successive rises in amplitude provided a measure of an intersyllabic interval. The resulting decomposition of a three-word utterance is shown schematically in Fig. 16.6.[14] Word identities were balanced over lengths

---

[13]An alternative elaboration of the model, with different consequences, would postulate advance knowledge, as early as the beginning of the execution of unit k, of the duration of the unpacking and retrieval stages for unit $k + 1$. This information would be used to adjust the rate at which the articulatory gestures were executed throughout unit k, so as to allow them to fill the available time from one command stage to the next. This alternative seems less appealing, however, not only because of its greater complexity, but because it reduces the plausibility of a retrieval process being required to determine unit $k + 1$ after execution of unit k has begun.

[14]For expository clarity we have assumed that in the words used in our experiment, the second consonant, C_2 is included within the second syllable rather than the first. Syllabication of such words is a matter of controversy, however. Fortunately for our purposes, the transition between the stop and the following vowel or sonorant is near the beginning of the syllable, under any of the accepted definitions.

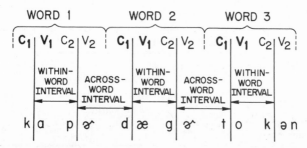

FIG. 16.6. Schematic representation of the decomposition of a three-word utterance. Each word can be regarded as a stressed syllable (designated $(C_1 V_1)$ followed by an unstressed syllable (designated $C_2 V_2$), where each syllable consists of a single stop-consonant (C_i) followed by a vowel and/or sonorant (V_i). Each vertical line represents an abrupt rise in the amplitude envelope at the transition from C_i to V_i, which intersects an amplitude criterion that is fixed for the entire utterance. Time intervals between successive intersection points correspond to within-word and across-word intervals, as shown. The decomposition of *copper, dagger, token* is shown as an example.

and serial positions. Lists were either heterogeneous ($1 \leqslant n \leqslant 4$) or homogeneous ($1 \leqslant n \leqslant 5$). Four subjects were run for two days, providing a total of about 200 trials per list length for each type of list. Our experimental procedure is described in Section V; our measurement methods were as in Section VII, with one exception: given an utterance of n words, we searched for a criterion amplitude value that intersected the ascending flanks of exactly $2n$ amplitude peaks, so as to define a series of time intervals between successive syllables.

It has to be recognized that this method of segmenting an utterance is relatively crude and may provide measures that distort the time intervals between the significant underlying articulatory events. We are particularly concerned about the potential distorting effects of amplitude variations, either between or within utterances. However, interpreted with proper caution, the method seemed suitable for an initial attempt to localize the effects of length and serial position, and clearcut results would help to justify it.

Results, averaged over the four subjects, are shown in Tables 16.1 and 16.2, with estimates of $\pm SE$ based on between-subject variability. In Table 16.1, under "within words" are shown measures of the effect of list length on the mean time interval from the amplitude rise of the first syllable in each word to the amplitude rise of the second. Durations of these intervals were averaged over serial positions; the resulting means were then regarded as a function of length and fitted by a straight line. Tabulated values are the slopes of such lines, averaged over subjects. Under "across words" is shown a corresponding measure derived from the time interval from the amplitude rise of the second syllable in each

TABLE 16.1
Rate of Increase with List Length, n, of Mean Time Interval between
Successive Syllables (msec/word)

	Within Words ($n \geqslant 1$)	Across Words ($n \geqslant 2$)	Difference
Homogeneous lists ($n \leqslant 5$)	0.9±1.6	4.6±0.9**	3.7±2.3
Heterogeneous lists ($n \leqslant 4$)	2.7±1.8	12.6±2.7**	9.9±3.8*

$*p < .05, **p < .01.$

word (excluding the last) to the amplitude rise of the first syllable of the next word. (The sum of the two measures estimates the rate at which the total time per word increases with utterance length—the slope of the rate function. The effect of type of list on this sum—15.3 msec/word versus 5.5 msec/word for heterogeneous and homogeneous lists, respectively—is similar to the effect found for lists of monosyllables, which we discussed in Sec. VII.)

Table 16.1 shows that for both kinds of list less than 20% of the overall effect of utterance length on production rate is reflected in our measure of within-word events. This is so despite the fact that the mean within-word interval (132.1 msec) was longer than the mean across-word interval (106.7 msec). That the length effect is almost entirely restricted to the later parts of each response unit supports the elaborated subprogram-retrieval model (and argues against any alternative model that would produce a global effect of length on articulation rate).

The effects of serial position on the within-word and across-word intervals are shown in Table 16.2. For each length, the duration of the relevant interval was regarded as a function of serial position and fitted by a straight line. (A linear function was not an unreasonable representation.) The slopes of these lines were then averaged over lengths to obtain the tabulated values. (The sum of the within-word and across-word measures estimates the rate at which the total time per word increases with serial position. The difference between these sums for the two kinds of list—11.8 msec/position versus 10.9 msec/position for heterogeneous and homogeneous lists, respectively—is very small, indicating similarity among serial-position functions, just as we found for lists of monosyllables.[15])

Table 16.2 shows that for both kinds of list almost all of the effect of serial position on the total time per word is reflected in our measure of within-word events—a result that clearly violates expectations based on our model. Thus, although the within-word interval is essentially inde-

---

[15]See footnote 12 on p. 522.

TABLE 16.2
Rate of Increase with Serial Position of Mean Time Interval between
Successive Syllables, Averaged over List Lengths, n (msec/position)

	Within Words	Across Words	Difference
Homogeneous lists ($2 \leq n \leq 5$)	8.7±1.8**	2.2±1.1	−6.5±2.8
Heterogeneous lists ($2 \leq n \leq 4$)	13.2±1.8**	−1.4±2.7	−14.6±3.3**

**$p < .01$

pendent of utterance length when *averaged* over serial positions (Table 16.1), it does depend strongly on serial position (Table 16.2). In contrast, the across-word interval is virtually independent of serial position (Table 16.2) but increases with length (Table 16.1). Thus the effects of length and serial position appear to have different loci in the stream of articulatory gestures. This double dissociation puts into further question the idea, embodied in our model, that the two effects are manifestations of the same retrieval process. If these findings can be confirmed with more refined measurements, we shall have to modify our model so as to provide an alternative account of the effect of serial position.

In one possible modification of the model, the serial-position effect is caused by planned variation of rates specified by *command* stages (represented in the corresponding subprograms) rather than with variation from unit to unit in *retrieval*-stage durations. Suppose that at the command level such variation influenced the representations of articulatory gestures *throughout* the response unit, rather than being arbitrarily restricted. Now consider the hypothesized influence (described earlier) of the start of the next command stage on termination time for the ongoing execution process. This influence (which mediates the length effect) would mask or dominate any effects of the proposed command-level variation on *later* parts of each execution process. Serial-position effects would then be restricted to early parts of each execution process, as observed, and the double dissociation would follow.[16]

---

[16].Any mechanism that generates the effect of serial position on the interword interval must be made consistent with the form of the length effect—i.e. with the observed linearity with length of the *mean* interword interval. Such consistency can follow naturally if both length and position effects are generated by the same self-terminating search process, as initially proposed. But for the modified serial-position mechanism, consistency requires a separate property: The mean (over positions) of the amount of lengthening it produces must be approximately independent of (or linear with) utterance length.

Consideration of these alternative serial-position mechanisms points up an important issue that bears on any programming model: the locus of effects that extend across units (also exemplified by coarticulation and pitch declination). Such effects may be embodied directly in the series of subprograms or, alternatively, may be regarded as emerging at "run" time as consequences, e.g., of interactions among successive execution processes.

IX. THE TIMING OF UTTERANCES COMPOSED OF WORDS VERSUS NONWORDS, AND THE ROLE OF LEXICAL MEMORY IN RAPID SPEECH

There has been much study of the overall process of transforming print into speech in naming tasks, and of the effects of prior experience with the words or letter strings named (e.g., Smith & Spoehr, 1974; Theios & Muise, 1977). But attempts to investigate separately the response-production mechanism in the naming of individual words have thus far yielded little information about how speech production itself interacts with and makes use of the stored information about words in long-term lexical memory. In this section we consider the role of lexical memory in the production of sequences of one or more words.

According to our model for the production of rapid prespecified utterances (LD, VII), the subject generates a motor program that contains one subprogram for each response *unit* in the utterance, where the unit is the *stress group* (LD, IV). Furthermore, the retrieval process responsible for the effects of utterance length on latency and duration operates at the level of these subprograms. The hypothesized process consists of a search through a buffer containing the set of subprograms that were assembled and loaded in advance of the reaction signal. For the experiments reported in the present chapter, each *word* is a stress-group unit; for utterances composed of lists of monosyllabic *nonwords* produced with the same stress pattern as word lists, each nonword is a unit.

Our aim in comparing words with nonwords was to contrast two kinds of units. For words, preexisting articulatory routines (which have perhaps evolved to be particularly efficient) may be stored in lexical memory. Nonwords, however, cannot have preexisting representations. Suppose such stored articulatory routines exist for words.[17] One possible role of lexical memory in speech production would then be to serve as a library of detailed word-production information that would be retrieved at execution time. In terms of our model, when the subprogram for a unit was executed, it would fetch the word routines required for its stress group from lexical memory. Information in the buffer would therefore control the sequence of lexical memory retrievals, but the buffer would not itself

---

[17]In another linguistic domain, Terzuolo and Viviani (1979) have argued from regularities in the timing of keystrokes that professional typists make use of stored routines ("motor engrams") for the typing of common words. On the other hand, studies of word and nonword naming suggest that phonological representations of words may often be "computed," rather than directly retrieved from memory. (See, e.g., Glushko, in press.) While this would not preclude the use of whole-word articulatory routines (accessed by the word's phonological representation rather than its "identity"), it would make such use less plausible.

contain all the information needed to produce the utterance. Production of an utterance containing a list of nonwords, for which lexical memory contained no routines, would require a qualitatively different mechanism; for word and nonword lists we would expect qualitatively different patterns of latencies and durations.

A second possible role of lexical memory would again be to furnish preexisting word routines, but here they would be retrieved and incorporated prior to program execution in the subprograms stored in the buffer. Although it might take more time to *assemble* the program for a list of nonwords, the same process of program *execution* would be used for nonword lists as for word lists, and we would expect a qualitatively similar pattern of latencies and durations. However, because the newly produced routines for nonwords might be less efficient than the preexisting routines for words, execution of the program might be slower, with consequent effects on parameters of the duration and/or latency functions. A third possibility is that lexical memory plays a minimal role in speech production. Even though an articulatory unit (the stress group) appears to control utterance timing, preexisting articulatory routines at the word level would be used in neither assembling nor executing the motor program. Instead, phonological representations of the words (or nonwords) in the utterance would first be obtained, by retrieval from lexical memory or by application of grapheme-phoneme rules, for example. These phonological representations would then be converted into articulatory routines for stress-group units either when the program was assembled or when it was executed. The conversion (which might use preexisting stored articulatory routines for lower-level phonic *subunits*) would be carried out afresh for each new utterance, whether it was composed of words or nonwords: we would expect to find no production-timing differences between the two kinds of utterance.

To compare the production of words and nonwords, while avoiding effects that might be due to accidental or systematic differences among their constituents, it seemed critical to use words and nonwords that were phonologically matched. The existence of coarticulation effects implied that not only should the sets of constituent phonemes be the same for words and nonwords, but also at least the set of pairs of adjacent phonemes, both within items and across item boundaries. We achieved this matching requirement by searching a phonetic dictionary for sets of phoneme triples containing four words and four nonwords related as shown in Table 16.3.

We used four such matched sets in the experiment, arranging them in either word lists or nonword lists that contained one to four different items. Subjects were instructed to pronounce the two kinds of list with the same stress pattern, attempting to stress each item equally. Different

TABLE 16.3
Phonologically-Matched Words and Nonwords

Examples		Symbolic Description[a]	
Words	Nonwords	Words	Nonwords
vote	vate	(1, 1, 1)	(1, 2, 1)
hone	hane	(2, 1, 2)	(2, 2, 2)
vain	vone	(1, 2, 2)	(1, 1, 2)
hate	hote	(2, 2, 1)	(2, 1, 1)

[a] The three ordered digits in the symbolic representation correspond respectively to the first, second, and third phoneme, each being drawn from a (different) pair of alternatives. For example, if F_1 and F_2 are alternative first phonemes, S_1 and S_2, second, and T_1 and T_2, third, then (2, 1, 2), which is *hone* in our example, corresponds to $F_2 S_1 T_2$.

lists were used on successive trials. For the data to be reported, we used the experimental procedure described in Section V.[18]

Latency and duration data are shown in Fig. 16.7. The latency functions are almost identical and are approximately linear, with the fitted lines accounting for 98.0% and 97.1% of the variance for words and nonwords, respectively; deviations from linearity were not statistically significant. Averaged over lengths, the latency difference is well within the experimental error: Mean latency for nonwords is 0.2 ± 2.5 msec greater than for words.

The mean duration data are fitted remarkably well by quadratic functions (even considering that only one degree of freedom remains after fitting): The fitted functions account for more than 99.9999% of the variance for both words and nonwords. However, the fitted quadratic functions differ by about 2 msec in both constant and linear coefficients; averaging over lengths, the duration per item for nonwords is 2.4 ± 1.0 msec greater than for words, a very small but statistically significant difference. (Given the mean duration per word of 142.5 msec, this difference represents only 1.7%.) Averaging over word and nonword lists, the mean slope of the latency function (15.0 ± 4.7 msec/word) and the mean quadratic coefficient of the duration function (17.3 ± 2.0 msec/word^2) differ little, as usual, but are somewhat larger than in other exper-

---

[18]For the present analysis we classified one of our eight subjects as an outlier, based on her performance with word lists. Even with these lists she was both unusually slow and unusually variable: Her duration mean and standard deviation were greater than the means of these statistics over the remaining seven subjects by 4.7 and 7.4 *SD*s, respectively.

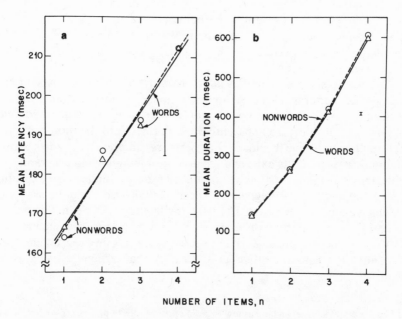

FIG. 16.7. Experiment comparing words and nonwords: Results are averaged over seven subjects; about 140 observations per point. Triangles and circles show results with words and nonwords, respectively. a. Mean latencies, estimate of $\pm SE$, and fitted linear functions [words, $166.8 + 14.6(n - 1)$ msec; nonwords, $166.1 + 15.3(n; - 1)$ msec]. b. Mean durations, estimate of $\pm SE$, and fitted quadratic functions [words, $144.3 + 99.5(n - 1) + 17.1(n - 1)^2$; nonwords $146.3 + 101.4(n - 1) + 17.4(n - 1)^2$]. See LD, Table 15.1 for fitting procedure. SE estimates in this figure were chosen to be appropriate for evaluating word–nonword differences. They are based on the *item-type* $\times$ *length* $\times$ *subjects* interactions in analyses of variance.

iments, probably because of sampling differences between groups of subjects.[19]

Spoken under time pressure, then, prespecified utterances composed of nonwords have latency and rate characteristics that are qualitatively the same and quantitatively almost the same as utterances composed of words. Since our method of phonological matching extended only to pairs

---

[19]In this experiment each set of words and nonwords was used to construct lists presented to subjects over a series of trials. Thus, on the average test trial on which the data displayed in Fig. 16.7 are based, subjects had had about 23 previous opportunities to pronounce each item. (Indeed, the trials that provided approximately the first eight opportunities per item were excluded from the displayed data.) Although unlikely, it seemed possible that even these few minutes of experience might invest nonwords with the properties of words.

In one evaluation of this possibility we analyzed sets of *initial* trials on which subjects

of adjacent phonemes whereas coarticulation effects are known to have a greater range (see, e.g., Kent & Minifie, 1977), it is even possible that the small duration difference we did find is a consequence of imperfect phonological matching.

Our results indicate that during the latent interval and the execution of prespecified utterances no reference is made to information stored in lexical memory; if any previously stored word-level articulatory routines are used at all, they are apparently incorporated into the motor program before the utterance begins.[20] Furthermore, if preexisting articulatory routines for word units exist and are used in assembling the program, their efficiency advantage over newly produced routines, in terms of execution speed, appears to be negligible. These results also support two other claims we have made: First (LD, III), the latency effect is not caused by variations in the load on ordinary short-term memory. And second (LD, IV), the response unit underlying performance in our experiments is articulatory (such as the stress group) rather than semantic (such as the word).[21]

---

had had an average of seven (and as few as zero) opportunities to pronounce each item. For these trials, the mean latency difference between words and nonwords is as small as in the main body of data, and not statistically significant; the mean duration difference per item, although not significantly different from zero, is twice as large for these trials as in the main data (4.8 ± 5.1 msec rather than 2.4 ± 1.0 msec).

In a second test of word-nonword equivalence we compared error rates for lists of words versus nonwords in the main body of data. The overall error rate was low (2.50% of trials, composed of 1.70% "pronunciation errors" and 0.80% "memory errors"). If stored articulatory routines were used during production of words, and such routines could be constructed for nonwords after a few trials, then we would expect pronunciation errors to be equally frequent for words and nonwords. Instead, most (68%) of the trials with pronunciation errors were nonword trials. When the lists were displayed only briefly, after comparable familiarization, the percentage of trials with pronunciation errors increased from 1.70% to 4.30%. Because this increase was restricted to nonwords, even more (83%) of these errors were now associated with the nonwords.

These subsidiary findings suggest that the remarkable similarity of the latency and duration functions for words and nonwords is not due to the existence of stored articulatory routines for the nonwords that developed during the experiment.

[20]Further support for this conclusion is provided by comparisons of articulation rates and latencies for lists of nouns drawn either from distinct semantic categories (*n*-category lists) or from one category. It is well known that both recognition and naming of printed words are facilitated by the existence of a semantic relation between successive words; the effect is as large as 50–100 msec per word. (See, e.g., Meyer & Schvaneveldt, 1976.) Furthermore, such effects have been explained in terms of the spread of excitation through a semantic network stored in long-term memory, which lowers word-detector thresholds. If production of prespecified utterances involved access to information stored in lexical memory, one might expect semantic relatedness to produce facilitation of production as well. (One argument against the facilitation of pronunciation per se when the utterance is *not* specified well in advance is that the facilitation of word naming—which does require overt pronunciation—is

ACKNOWLEDGMENTS

We are indebted to O. Fujimura, M. Y. Liberman, N. H. Macdonald, D. L. Scarborough, and K. N. Stevens for helpful discussions and advice, to A. S. Coriell, W. J. Kropfl, and M. J. Melchner for technical support, and to J. C. Johnston, D. L. Noreen, and J. S. Perkell for comments on the manuscript.

REFERENCES

Atal, B. S., & Hanauer, S. L. Speech analysis and synthesis by linear prediction of the speech wave. *Journal of the Acoustical Society of America*, 1971, *50*, 637–655.
Bolinger, D. Intonation across languages. In J. H. Greenberg, (Ed.), *Universals of human language: Volume 2, Phonology*. Stanford, Calif.: Stanford University Press, 1978.
Conrad, B., & Schönle, P. Speech and respiration. *Archiv für Psychiatrie und Nerven-krankheiten*, 1979, *226*, 251–268.
Fitts, P. M., & Peterson, J. R. Information capacity of discrete motor responses. *Journal of Experimental Psychology*, 1964, *67*, 103–112.
Glushko, R. J. The organization and activation of orthographic knowledge in reading aloud. *Journal of Experimental Psychology: Human Perception and Performance*, In Press.
Kent, R. D., & Minifie, F. D. Coarticulation in recent speech production models. *Journal of Phonetics*, 1977, *5*, 115–133.
Maeda, S. *A characterization of American English intonation*. Unpublished doctoral dissertation, Massachusetts Institute of Technology, Cambridge, Mass., 1976.
Meyer, D. E., & Schvaneveldt, R. W. Meaning, memory structure, and mental processes. *Science*, 1976, *192*, 27–33.

---

not significantly greater than the facilitation of word recognition—which does not; see Meyer & Schvaneveldt, 1976.) One-category lists should then be articulated substantially more rapidly than n-category lists. This appears not to be the case: In a pilot experiment with five subjects we constructed lists of the two kinds, of length $1 \leq n \leq 5$, from sets of five monosyllabic nouns drawn from the categories of animals, fruits, drinks, body parts, and house parts. Differences in latencies and rates were negligible and not significant. Averaged over lengths, mean latency for n-category lists was only 1.2 ± 5.3 msec greater than for 1-category lists; mean duration per word was 3.7 ± 3.7 msec greater, a difference of only 1.8%.

[21]The word-nonword experiment can be regarded as a demonstration that sequence familiarity at the level of phonemes or articulatory gestures has no effect on utterance timing. Evidence favoring an effect of sequence familiarity at the level of words (or stress groups), which complicates matters, is found in the experiment using lists of weekday names (LD, II). For lists of length $2 \leq n \leq 5$ the mean duration per word was 190.9 msec and 208.1 msec, for "normal" and random sequences, respectively; the difference of 17.2 ± 4.2 msec, or 9.0%, is highly significant. Furthermore, the effect seems to be associated with retrieval rather than command stages in our model, since it is localized in the quadratic rather than the linear coefficient of the duration function. (See caption of LD, Fig. 15.2.) One explanation (not yet tested) that is consistent with such specificity and that would avoid the need to modify our model is that familiar word sequences occasionally combine to form higher-order response units such that a stress group incorporates more than one word; this should be revealed through stress-pattern alterations.

Ohala, J. J. Production of tone. In V. A. Fromkin (Ed.), *Tone: A linguistic survey*. New York: Academic Press, 1978.

Ohala, J., & Ewan, W. G., Speed of pitch change. *Journal of the Acoustical Society of America*, 1973, *53*, 345.

Pierrehumbert, J. The perception of fundamental frequency declination. *Journal of the Acoustical Society of America*, 1979, *66*, 363–369.

Rabiner, L. R., Cheng, M. J., Rosenberg, A. E., & McGonegal, C. A. A comparative performance study of several pitch detection algorithms. *IEEE Transactions on Acoustics, Speech, and Signal Processing*, 1976, *ASSP-24*, 399–418.

Smith, E. E., & Spoehr, K. T. The perception of printed English: A theoretical perspective. In B. H. Kantowitz (Ed.), *Human information processing: Tutorials in performance and cognition*. Hillsdale, N.J.: Lawrence Erlbaum Associates, 1974.

Sternberg, S. The discovery of processing stages: Extensions of Donders' method. In W. G. Koster (Ed.), *Attention and performance II. Acta Psychologica*, 1969, *30*, 276–315.

Sternberg, S., Monsell, S., Knoll, R. L., & Wright, C. E. The latency and duration of rapid movement sequences: Comparisons of speech and typewriting. In G. E. Stelmach (Ed.), *Information processing in motor control and learning*. New York: Academic Press, 1978.

Sundberg, J. Maximum speed of pitch change in singers and untrained subjects. *Journal of Phonetics*, 1979, *7*, 71–79.

Terzuolo, C. A., & Viviani, P. About the central representation of learned motor patterns. In R. Talbot & D. R. Humphrey (Eds.), *Posture and movement: Perspectives for integrating neurophysiological research in sensory-motor systems*. New York: Raven Press, 1979.

Theios, J., & Muise, J. G. The word identification process in reading. In H. J. Castellan, Jr., D. B. Pisoni, & G. R. Potts (Eds.), *Cognitive theory* (Vol. 2). Hillsdale, N.J.: Lawrence Erlbaum Associates, 1977.

17
How to Win at Twenty Questions with Nature

Herbert A. Simon
Carnegie-Mellon University

Several of the chapters in this book have referred to the remarks that Allen Newell (1973) made at our cognitive symposium six years ago, which he titled, "You Can't Play Twenty Questions with Nature and Win." These remarks came to my mind also while I was reading the drafts of the preceding chapters by Sorenson and Cooper, Fay, and Sternberg, Monsell, Knoll and Wright. What I think these papers show, and what I want to demonstrate, is that there *is* a way to win that Twenty Questions game.

ON FACTS AND MODELS

If you have read Newell's paper, you will recall that it was composed of two black clouds of pessimism with one intermittent ray of hope peeking through them. But you will recall also that Newell said that his comments only spoke for one half of himself—a distressed and confused half. I hope, therefore, that you will interpret me as not so much disagreeing with Newell as speaking for his other half—the half he said was "content and clear on where we are going."

In the Twenty Questions paper, Newell undertook to characterize the prevailing style of research in experimental psychology. He then made an assessment of the future prospects of a scientific endeavor carried on in that style. Finally—the ray of hope—he prescribed what should be done to make the prognosis more favorable.

A Diagnosis

The characterization of psychological research was summed up in Newell's assertion that "the two constructions that drive our current experimental style are (1) at a low level, the discovery and empirical exploration of phenomena . . . ; and (2) . . . the formulation of questions to be put to nature that center on the resolution of binary oppositions [p. 287]." The notion of "phenomena" discovered and explored through experiment was explicated in his paper by a list (pp. 285–6) of 59 examples from the psychological literature; the notion of "binary oppositions in psychology" by a second list (p. 288) of 24 items. The phenomena included, for instance, Shepard's continuous rotation effect, Miller's chunks in short-term memory, and Sternberg's linear search in sets in short-term memory. The binary oppositions included, for instance, analog versus digital processing, continuous versus all-or-none learning, and existence versus nonexistence of latent learning.

The prognosis was gloomy, according to Newell, because (p. 291) the phenomena appeared merely to proliferate, not to cumulate, and because the binary oppositions never seemed to be resolved. In his words, "matters simply become muddier and muddier as we go down through time [pp. 288–9]."

Some Prescriptions

To avoid this bleak and murky future, Newell offered some quite specific advice, which—if interpreted as advice to theorists rather than experimenters—is quite sound. We were advised to eschew the isolated phenomenon and isolated pairs of opposing microhypotheses, and aim toward three unities:

1. We should seek to construct *complete* processing models of the whole cognitive man, instead of ad hoc models for each phenomenon.

2. We should select a single complex cognitive task and explore it exhaustively (instead of simply varying it in terms of binary oppositions we can define for it).

3. If we insist on studying a diverse collection of isolated experimental tasks, we should seek to construct a *single* model to account for behavior in all the tasks, instead of developing separate models for each.

To this prescription, I should like to add three additional pieces of advice, which I think are in the same spirit, although the third is addressed to experimenters more than to theorists.

4. Our models should give prominence to the *quantitative* invariants of the human information processing system, as well as to the qualitative features of its structure.

5. If we find it difficult to construct a single system that will operate over a whole range of experimental tasks, we should at least identify a small set of basic mechanisms, and then insist that all of the task-specific models we build be constructed out of members of this set. Following this advice will protect us against the more egregious forms of ad-hokery, and will provide the data base and underlying mechanisms for more comprehensive models.

6. We should continue, energetically and industriously, producing interesting experimental phenomena, exploring them, seeking earnestly to relate them to our models, and seeking to use those models in designing new experiments to resolve the binary oppositions that emerge. Curiosity-driven and theory-driven experiments both have their place in our science.

Is the Diagnosis Accurate?

I should like to examine the last three chapters in the light of the methodological canons implied by all of this advice. Is there a cumulative value to experimental research in psychology? I think it is important to address this question, because the papers under review are of the same genre as the ones Newell commented on six years ago, and if his pessimism was justified, the present papers are legitimate targets for the same criticism.

It is true that in psychology, as in most other sciences I know, phenomena come into the world as isolated sets of facts, each encapsulated in its own published paper with, at best, a few references to other appearances of the same phenomenon. Isolated facts do not make a science any more than isolated bricks make a cathedral. But cathedrals *are* made of brick (some of them), and sciences of fact. It is the mortar and the arrangement that make the difference. Fifty-nine facts, or even 5,900, are not too many to make a science when mortar and order are provided. The place to look for that mortar and order is not primarily in experimental papers, but in theoretical works that undertake to assemble the structure of a science from its bricks.

Is Psychology Fact-Happy?

Has psychology simply been stockpiling its facts, awaiting some future architect and masons? Such a claim could be countered by citing the long list of theoretical works that psychology has produced in the past fifty years. Instead of providing such a list, I will be more specific and focus on just one example—the EPAM theory postulated by Feigenbaum and myself (Feigenbaum, 1963). What makes this particular theory interesting in this context is that it has been tested extensively against data in the psychological literature that were produced by laboratory experiments designed with no thought or knowledge of EPAM, and often with little or no explicit theory-testing intent. The ultimate usefulness of these data for psychological theory went far beyond the immediate conceptual or phenomenological concerns that caused them to be gathered in the first place.

EPAM undertakes to explain some of the principal phenomena of rote verbal learning. In this domain, the fact-gathering and phenomenon-noticing go back at least a century, to Ebbinghaus (1885/1964). A major and massive effort was made in the 1930s, by Hull and his associates (1940), to build these facts into a coherent theory. Most of us would not consider that attempt to have been very successful, but that is a different issue from the mindless piling up of bricks. EPAM differs from Hull's effort, in that the facts have been reassembled in an arrangement more compatible with information-processing notions. EPAM is a formal model which makes quite specific qualitative and quantitative predictions about an extensive range of matters. It has a good deal to say about at least eight of the phenomena in the 59-item list in the Twenty Questions paper.

Specifically, EPAM provides an explanation for the weakness of backward associations (item 27), the von Restorff effect (33), constant time learning (43), induced chunking (54), rehearsal (55), and for important aspects of chess position perception (4), chunks in short-term memory (STM) (5), rapid STM loss with interpolated tasks (13), and perhaps other items on the Twenty Questions list.[1] No claim is made that EPAM provides a wholly correct or final explanation of all these phenomena, but the example does show that psychology has been as attentive to the cumulation as to the accumulation of facts. Organizing principles for other subsets of the 59 phenomena can be found in modern models of semantic node-link memory, in contemporary theories of linguistic processing, in theories of concept attainment, and so on. It would seem, then, that the six points of advice offered above—with the possible exception of the first item—describe pretty closely what has actually been going on in these domains of cognitive psychology.

---

[1]The principal references that describe empirical tests of EPAM against data drawn from the psychological literature are Feigenbaum & Simon (1962), Simon & Feigenbaum (1964), and Gregg & Simon (1967). The application of EPAM-like mechanisms to chess perception is described in Simon & Gilmartin (1973). EPAM-based memory models are extended further, and their empirical validity discussed, in Simon (1974) and Simon (1976). These papers have all now been collected in Simon (1979).

The optimistic half does not want to deny that fact-gathering is a very large part of the enterprise of experimental psychology. Nor does this half deny that some of the fact-gatherers may be relatively indifferent to the theoretical implications of their facts. And that even if they are not indifferent, they may fail to make much mention of them in publishing their reports of interesting phenomena.

The optimistic half does want to point out that the theory-building activity does also go on—vigorously, successfully, and cumulatively—and has gone on for a long time as an integral part of the total enterprise of psychology, and in effective symbiosis with the experimental part. Nor have fact-gathering and theory-building proceeded in isolation, as might be implied by the gloomy diagnosis. On the contrary, the theory-building efforts have had considerable success in organizing and reconciling rather large sets of phenomena reported in the experimental literature.

Are the Oppositions Unresolved?

But what of the other half of the charge: that psychological inquiry is guided by the construction of binary questions that are never answered? Here, too, the pessimistic half has been led astray by failing to look at the whole picture. To understand the binary oppositions, we must recognize that most of them emerge directly from theory-building activity. To build psychological models and theories, as the advice requires, we must make design decisions. Shall we design the system so that it will learn incrementally, or in an all-or-none fashion? Shall it be a serial system, or will many things go on at once? Will all of its learning be motivated, or will some occur "latently"—i.e., without explicit motivation?

To design is to synthesize, and synthesizing requires generating alternatives (they need not be binary), and choosing among them. This is a general characteristic of theory-building in science. There is nothing unique about the "oppositions" that we find in psychology. Is light made up of waves or particles? Does combustion release phlogiston or take up oxygen? Does evolution operate by natural selection or by inheritance of acquired characteristics?

We cannot have theory-building without binary (or n-ary) oppositions, and most of the specific oppositions listed in the Twenty Questions paper are central to the building of comprehensive theories of cognitive phenomena. Moreover, I do not see the historical evidence of retrogress, on each dichotomy, from initial clarity to terminal muddiness. In fact, several of the binary oppositions listed in the Twenty Questions paper had already been resolved successfully when that paper was published. Again, by way of specific example, EPAM resolves at least two of them. First, the conditions under which learning is incremental, and the conditions under which is sudden (item 3 on the binary oppositions list) are now quite clear, and are correctly and specifically predicted by EPAM (Gregg & Simon, 1967). Briefly, the theory asserts (and the facts show) that learning is all-or-none whenever the unit of learning (measured in numbers of familiar chunks) is small relative to the time per trial; and learning is incremental otherwise.

Second, an EPAM-like model also makes a resolution of the latent learning issue (item 16 on the list), consistent with what we know of attention management in a system where learning requires use of the limited short-term memory. Latent learning of unrewarded features of the environment will occur when the organism is not highly motivated to attend to other features, hence when it is relatively easily distracted (Simon, 1976). Nor is EPAM an isolated example. A number of the other binary oppositions on the list appear also to have been resolved or to be progressing steadily toward resolution. If the movement of psychology toward truth in these matters is sometimes helical, it is not circular.

Perhaps I have said enough about why I cannot accept the pessimistic message of the Twenty Questions paper, and how I propose to approach my review of the papers before us, which are put forward by their authors primarily as experimental contributions. I do not intend to look at each one as an isolated piece of science, but will ask instead where the solid bricks that they represent fit into the larger structure.

SPEECH PRODUCTION

When the papers on which one is asked to comment are of uniformly high quality, as these are, the task of the commentator becomes both harder and easier. It is harder because the authors present no easy targets for cheap shots; it is easier because the authors have defined some good issues that the comments can address.

The three papers reviewed here are all addressed to the phenomena of speech production, in contrast to other papers in this book, which deal with speech perception. Speech production has been much less studied by psychologists than speech perception. For that very reason, we should not expect the speech production area to *look* very much like a cathedral. We are still in the early stages of assembling the bricks—of identifying the critical phenomena.

As Sorensen and Cooper (Chap. 13) point out, there is an important connection between speech production and speech perception, that can be exploited in research in either area. The two processes are part of a single act of communication. The features that are detected by the recipient of the message during speech perception must be the features that were encoded into it by the producer during production. Hence, any knowledge we gain by studying one end of the total process becomes available to us in helping understand the other end. In particular, we may expect the substantial progress already made toward understanding speech perception to accelerate our rate of learning about speech production. Although the chapters here do not stress this reciprocity, I will later point out some instances where it is present implicitly.

In most of the papers in this book (Newell's and Sternberg's being exceptions), speech is dealt with sui generis, as a possibly unique set of processes, and without explicit reference to other human cognitive activities. Thus, the authors have chosen to employ mainly the second strategy of those listed above, "Select a single complex cognitive task and do all of it," instead of the possibly competing strategy, "Build a complete processing model or sysem that handles all of several experimental tasks." Sternberg and his co-authors, however, seeks to discover whether a single mechanism can account for both speech production and typing, while Newell, in fitting a speech recognition theory, Harpy, to the (possibly Procrustean) bed of his production system model, tries to satisfy simultaneously both injunctions.

Apart from their mutual concern with speech production, the three papers before us have relatively little in common. Sorensen and Cooper seek to identify prosodic features of speech production that might help the listener decode the communication. Fay is concerned with the control of speech by syntax—also an important component of the coding system shared between the producer of speech and the listener. But he is not satisfied, as linguists sometimes are, to characterize the grammar formally. He wants to describe it in such a way as to mirror the psychological processes involved in the production of the language stream.

Sternberg, Monsell, Knoll and Wright burrow down a level deeper toward the immediate processor in order to learn something about the memories that are involved in speech production and the way in which those memories are searched. The basic strategy used is one with which we are familiar from Sternberg's (1969) previous work on rapid memory scans, and their paper has some interesting implications for the first strategic canon: "Construct complete processing models."

At this point, the pessimistic half, if we had not silenced it, might complain again: "Three more isolated sets of phenomena. Will there never be an end to it?" The optimistic half will try to anticipate this plaint by indicating, as he goes along, where he believes the bricks fit in.

The Pitch of Speech

Sorensen and Cooper are trying to identify features of the speech signal that might provide invariants that would help the listener to decode it. Choosing the fundamental frequency as an interesting and possibly significant feature, they first of all do a fine, workmanlike job of defining an objective, reproducible measure of that feature. Second—and this is crucial for the cathedral-building aspects of the work—they construct the hypothesis: that the profile of intonation in the course of producing speech will be related to grammatical structure.

Because we already know that accurate analysis of grammatical structure is an essential part of speech understanding, prosodic features of speech production that correlate with syntax are excellent candidates for inclusion among the signaling cues. Because we know very little, however, about the basic prosodic structure of the English sentence, our ignorance makes it difficult to design appropriate stimuli for experiments on speech perception. Sorensen and Cooper decided, therefore, to search for prosodic cues by studying the speaker rather than the listener. Hypothesizing that the listener may use the fall and rise of pitch to detect the ends of clauses, they then proceeded, by manipulation of sentence structure, to determine what relations between adjoining clauses affect the intonation pattern, and in what ways. Here again, the interaction between phonetic and syntactic considerations is instructive.

It is a basic tenet of information-processing psychology that, in order to explain a phenomenon, you must describe the process that produces it. Sorensen and Cooper undertake to meet this demand by discovering invariant properties of the intonation pattern and then specifying a process that would account for the invariants. Although I applaud their concern with process, I have some difficulty in accepting the psychological reality of the specific mechanism they propose.

To oversimply, essentially what they found was that clauses tend to end on a relatively fixed fundamental frequency, dropping about half the distance from initial to final pitch in about one quarter of the total duration of the clause. Such a pattern seems to imply that the speaker, before he pronounces the entire clause, must be able to predict how long his utterance is going to be, and must be able to compute, at least implicitly, at what frequency level he should emit each part of it. This process requires that a speaker perform a rather sophisticated computation, and my Bayesian priors attach a very low probability to hypotheses about human processes that involve large amounts of human foresight, computing, and planning.

If it could be shown that the observed invariants could only be produced by a process like the one postulated by the authors, then we would have to live with that fact. But until such a proof is forthcoming, I think we should look very hard for alternatives. Let me give a crude example of the kind of possibility I have in mind, without making any claim that this particular solution is close to the truth. It would be nice if we could show that the invariant was a by-product of a simple physiological process—for example, a relation between the physiological mechanics for producing speech and the expected duration of that speech. The coordination of breathing with the articulation of clauses would be the sort of thing I have in mind, though I have no shred of evidence that the explanation lies in this particular direction. At any rate, to explain the mystery, I would look initially toward gross mechanisms of this general sort, which make the invariants by-products of the physiological processes of speech production rather than explicitly calculated signals.

Regardless of whether the paper provides a correct process explanation for the phenomenon it describes, it is interesting and noteworthy that the thrust of this research seeks to answer two kinds of questions: First, what is the invariant prosodic structure of an utterance, and how can a listener use this information to detect its syntactic structure? Second, what kind of process could produce this invariant structure? It is easy to see where research using this strategy will fit into theories of speech production and broader theories of communication by language.

But I think mostly the paper should be evaluated as just a very fine craftsmanlike, curiosity-driven effort to detect and measure quantitative invariants (viz., the fourth piece of advice, above) in complex behavior, with good awareness of their relevance to syntactic issues and with a concern for the processes that produce the invariance. And both of these criteria are essential, it seems to me, if the bricks produced by such research are to fit into any future cathedral.

Psychologically Relevant Grammars

Fay's paper is very much and very explicitly concerned with process—with the kind of mechanism the speaker could use to produce grammatically correct speech. We have recognized, almost from the beginnings of modern formal linguistics, that if linguistics is to be of any use to psychology, it must graduate from competence theories to performance theories, from theories that simply distinguish between grammatical and ungrammatical sentences to theories that tell us how a speaker actually produces a grammatical sentence.

Fay's paper uses data on errors that people make during speech production to test performance theories of syntax. The paper does not give us details of how the data were obtained; this is reported in another paper that the author references. Fay has mentioned to me that one of the difficulties in his approach is that in the 4,000 or 5,000 examples of errors he has collected, only a few bear on syntactic issues. Hence there is a problem, if this approach is to be fruitful in the future, of securing a corpus of data that is truly adequate to test conclusions decisively.

Clearly, the ultimate solution for this difficulty must be to automate the processing of long streams of speech, so as to detect ungrammaticality automatically, and thereby enlarge the sample of syntactic-errors to hundreds or thousands of examples instead of a handful. Perhaps this is a task for the next generation of Harpy-like systems. The syntatic analysis would not have to be exact—it must simply beneficiate the raw ore so that human experts could afford to search through the enriched samples.

Achieving this automation at a practical level is still some distance away. We'll have to have powerful analytic grammars to parse speech, and systems for understanding speech. When we have this technology in hand, we can look automatically at very large samples of speech. This may sound a little bit Buck Rogers today, but this kind of technological advance has already been made in other branches of science. Astronomers think nothing of scanning tens of thousands of photographic plates to find one new interesting object—or physicists of scanning tens of thousands of bubble-chamber pictures to identify one new particle event.

Fay's paper provides a few specific examples of how the error-analysis technique can be used to test a performance theory of syntax. In one of these examples, a transformational grammar accounts for the phenomena better than a case grammar. Since the latter seems to me inherently more plausible as a candidate for a human performance grammar than the former, I was a little unhappy with the outcome. Although I'm no linguist, as my friends and acquaintances are well aware, let me venture out on thin ice to suggest a taxonomic issue that might be examined before we choose between candidate grammars.

In some sense it seems odd to compare a case grammar with a transformational grammar, because the terms "case" and "transformation" refer to different dimensions. A *case* grammar is one that uses as its basic categories the semantic functions that words perform. Noncase grammars, then, are presumably grammars that classify words by syntactic functions. That's one dimension: taxonomy based on semantic or syntactic criteria, respectively.

When we talk about a productive *transformational* grammar, we're indicating the particular way in which the surface structure is generated from the deep structure, and asserting, in particular, that the procedure includes reorderings of the components. Such reorderings might be motivated by either syntax or semantics. Hence, I don't see why we can't have a hybrid animal like a transformational–case grammar or a nontransformational syntactic grammar. And it would be interesting to test whether we could construct a case grammar with transformations that could account for the particular example that was presented.

The reason for my hunch that this might be possible is that the production of sentences must somehow start with the meanings rather than the syntax. And that brings me to my final comment on Fay's paper. The assumption underlying the performance model is that speakers go from deep structure, as linguists understand that term, to the surface structure and then to the actual stream of sounds that is uttered. I wonder what hypotheses are either implied or intended by the model proposed in the paper as to how the deep structure is created at the moment when a person has the intention to communicate something.

When I tried to think of an example to illustrate the process to which I am alluding, the first sentence (surely random) that came to mind was: "It's time for lunch." To account for the example, a theory of speech production, it seems to me, has to talk about the representation in memory of some kind of nonlinguistic idea that it was "time to go to lunch," a representation which was transformed into a linguistic deep structure, and transformed again into the sound stream that you heard. Somewhere deep inside, my autonomic nervous system produced the sensation I've learned to call "hunger." What is the path that led from that sensation to the production of the sentence, "It's time for lunch"? And why that sentence, instead of "I'm hungry" or "Let's quit so we can eat"? At what point is the internal representation of a sensation converted into a representation of a linguistic entity?

One of the big issues not addressed in any of the papers is: What is the relation between the kinds of semantic structures that artificial intelligence researchers and cognitive psychologists postulate in long-term memory and the structures linguists refer to as deep structure? We have learned something from Fay and Sorensen and Cooper about what might be going on in syntactic processes, but we have not learned very much about the relation of these processes to nonlinguistic representations of meanings.

Latencies in Speech Production

The chapters by Sternberg, Monsell, Knoll, and Wright, unlike most of the other chapters in this volume, are not limited to speech, but rather view speech production as a motor skill to be compared with other motor skills—e.g., typing. Moreover, they differ from the other chapters in this book in attempting a complete model of the memory and control process involved, instead of restricting their focus to identifying one or more of these processes. Finally, they make use of the method, introduced by Sternberg (1969) some years ago, of recording latencies in a task where identical processes (searches through a memory set) are repeated a varying, but known, number of times.

The data are all remarkably clean and consistent—except for the anomalous four-second latency increment associated with one-handed typing. Since the authors have already carefully pointed out that anomaly to us, I cannot belabor them with it in this discussion. However, there is a brief, one-minute sermon I'd like to preach on it.

Here we have a fine body of quantitative data that ought to please all of us. Particularly striking is the near-equality of the second coefficient in the latency function with the third coefficient in the duration function over six of the seven tasks, together with the fact that none of these coefficients strays far from 12 msec. We ought to take such constancy very seriously, and assume, in building models of the process, that constancy of parameters implies common mechanism.

But then there's the anomalous value in the last row (too bad they thought of that final experimental condition). If we adopted a crude Popperian disconfirmation view, we would have to throw the whole hypothesis out. But I'm confident that we will not do that. In our house, we don't say, "Well, there's one fly in this ointment, and therefore we're going to throw out the ointment." We take a spoon, and very carefully scoop the fly out of the ointment.

We are never going to progress in psychology (or any other science) if we allow single flies to deprive us of all of our ointment, or if we try to choose between binary oppositions on the basis of isolated facts, no matter how well established those facts may be. Sometimes, we treat single anomalies so seriously that we regard them as refuting theories. We've got to be (and often we are) more sophisticated than that. We must be able to say, "Yes, we have a first-approximation theory that accounts for a large amount of data; but we still have one unpleasant anomaly in the data. That means we must find some way of improving our theory; it doesn't mean that the mechanisms we have postulated make no sense at all."

Sternberg and his co-authors have disclosed a remarkable pattern of nearly identical coefficients. Assertions of numerical invariance make for strong theories, hence theories that are easily disconfirmed in the Popperian sense. But it makes little sense to deny a striking regularity in nature simply because it is not a regularity *everywhere*. The proper treatment of anomalies is to find the conditions under which the observed regularities are violated, not to deny their existence because of individual observations that are discrepant. If we carry on our theory-building in this more sophisticated way, we won't feel quite so often that we've made no progress or that we're simply oscillating interminably between the poles of our binary oppositions.

However, there's a more substantive lesson to be learned from the quantitative invariants that emerged from these particular experiments. In this motor task, the most prominent invariant is in the neighborhood of 12 msec. In most of Sternberg's earlier studies of scanning in short-term memory, the constants that emerged were more nearly of the order of 50 msec (Sternberg, 1969). If we take near equality of parameters as a sign of identity of mechanism, then we must interpret large differences between estimated parameters as signs that different mechanisms are at work. In our desire to arrive at a unified picture of the human information-processing system, we must not overlook the very real possibility (I would even say probability) that many components of that system are specialized to motor or sensory subsystems.

This suggestion of particularity and plurality in cognitive mechanisms contrasts sharply with the hypothesis of generality and homogeneity that permeates the speech-recognition models of the papers by Raj Reddy, Dennis Klatt, and Allen Newell, on which Don Norman comments. Here we have a fine set of examples of contrasting research styles and binary oppositions—top-down theory construction from a hypothesis about the control system (Newell), versus bottom-up construction from careful quantitative observation of phenomena (Klatt and Reddy); a theory of a highly homogeneous cognitive mechanism, versus a theory of a specialized component for performing a particular range of tasks. I can agree with that old pessimistic half that these oppositions are not likely to be resolved soon, and even that the sharp lines between them may become a good deal muddied. But the optimistic half assures me that it is just through such a plurality of approaches and confrontation of design alternatives that we will grope our way to a deeper understanding of the human cognitive system, and of speech production and perception as parts of it.

CONCLUSION

Let me conclude, then, with just the general comment that these papers are three fine examples of bricklaying for a cathedral that is beginning to take shape. We have learned some new facts about the prosody of speech, which may help us understand how the speaker cues the listener to its structure. We have heard a description of a naturalistic technique, the collection and analysis of speakers' errors, that is helping us to choose between alternative performance models of grammar. And we have been told about some striking regularities in the timing of speech (and typing) acts. In all three cases, the speakers have chosen to move cautiously from their empirical data toward hypotheses about the structures and processes that might have produced them. All of this is in the very best tradition of empirical science, and I can only hope that we will have much more of it.

ACKNOWLEDGMENT

This research was supported by Research Grant MH-07722 from the National Institute of Mental Health. I am grateful to Allen Newell for comments on an earlier draft of this paper—which in no way implies that he agrees with its conclusions.

REFERENCES

Ebbinghaus, H. *Über das Gedachtnis*. Leipzig: Duncker & Humbolt, 1885. Translated by H. A. Ruger & C. E. Bussenius as *Memory: A contribution to experimental psychology*. New York: Dover, 1964.

Feigenbaum, E. A. The simulation of verbal learning behavior. In E. A. Feigenbaum & J. Feldman (Eds.), *Computers and thought*. New York: McGraw-Hill, 1963.

Feigenbaum, E. A., & Simon, H. A. Theory of the serial position effect. *British Journal of Psychology*, 1962, *53*, 307–323.

Gregg, L. W., & Simon, H. A. An information-processing explanation of one-trial and incremental learning. *Journal of Verbal Learning and Verbal Behavior*, 1967, *6*, 780–787.

Hull, C. L., Hovland, C. I., Ross, R. T., Hall, M., Perkins, D. T., & Fitch, F. B. *Mathematico-deductive theory of rote learning*. New Haven: Yale University Press, 1940.

Newell, A. You can't play 20 questions with nature and win. In W. G. Chase (Ed.), *Visual information processing*. New York: Academic Press, 1973.

Simon, H. A. How big is a chunk? *Science*, 1974, *183*, 482–488.

Simon, H. A. The information-storage system called "Human Memory." In M. R. Rosenzweig & E. L. Bennett (Eds.), *Neural mechanisms of learning and memory*. Cambridge, Mass: MIT Press, 1976.

Simon, H. A. *Models of thought*. New Haven: Yale University Press, 1979.

Simon, H. A., & Feigenbaum, E. A. An information-processing theory of some effects of similarity, familiarization, and meaningfulness in verbal learning. *Journal of Verbal Learning and Verbal Behavior*, 1964, *3*, 385–396.

Simon, H. A., & Gilmartin, K. A simulation of memory for chess positions. *Cognitive Psychology*, 1973, *5*, 29–46.

Sternberg, S. Memory-scanning: Mental processes revealed by reaction-time experiments. *American Scientist*, 1969, *57*, 421–457.

Author Index

Subject Index